1 MONTH OF
FREE
READING

at

www.ForgottenBooks.com

By purchasing this book you are eligible for one month membership to ForgottenBooks.com, giving you unlimited access to our entire collection of over 1,000,000 titles via our web site and mobile apps.

To claim your free month visit:

www.forgottenbooks.com/free217574

* Offer is valid for 45 days from date of purchase. Terms and conditions apply.

ISBN 978-0-266-21111-2
PIBN 10217574

This book is a reproduction of an important historical work. Forgotten Books uses state-of-the-art technology to digitally reconstruct the work, preserving the original format whilst repairing imperfections present in the aged copy. In rare cases, an imperfection in the original, such as a blemish or missing page, may be replicated in our edition. We do, however, repair the vast majority of imperfections successfully; any imperfections that remain are intentionally left to preserve the state of such historical works.

Forgotten Books is a registered trademark of FB &c Ltd.
Copyright © 2018 FB &c Ltd.
FB &c Ltd, Dalton House, 60 Windsor Avenue, London, SW19 2RR.
Company number 08720141. Registered in England and Wales.

For support please visit www.forgottenbooks.com

THE

YALE LITERARY MAGAZINE:

CONDUCTED

BY THE

STUDENTS OF YALE COLLEGE.

1737

"Dum mens grata manet, nomen laudesque YALENSES
Cantabunt SOBOLES, unanimque PATRES."

VOLUME NINTH.

NEW HAVEN:

PUBLISHED BY A. H. MALTBY.

HITCHCOCK & STAFFORD, PRINTERS.

MDCCCXLIV.

CONTENTS OF VOL. IX.

PROSE.

POETRY.

THE

YALE LITERARY MAGAZINE.

Vol. IX. NOVEMBER, 1843. No. 1.

THE PAST AND THE PRESENT, BY CARLYLE.

"Who is this Thomas Carlyle?" recently asked a friend of ours, taking his Past and Present from the table, and carelessly glancing over its pages. An important question, truly, at this epoch, and one which we confess we can but imperfectly answer. We have heard it said that he is one "who lives in quite an humble way in the suburbs of London. He was not born to titles, men have conferred on him no patent of nobility, nor is he rich in houses or lands or gold. His sole wealth and honor lie in possessions of quite another kind—those of the mind!" For ourselves, we have known him only—in earlier times, that is to say, some ten or fifteen years since—as the contributor of sundry powerful articles to Fraser's, the Edinburgh, and Blackwood's Magazine, among which, in passing, we especially notice the article on Burns, the noblest tribute which has yet been paid to the genius of the unfortunate, but gifted poet. In these earlier essays of our author, characterized by a manly, vigorous style, and fine critical acumen, we observe nothing otherwise specially remarkable; but in good old Saxon phrase, he was content to utter the truthful thoughts of an earnest heart, in such manner as none could gainsay or mistake.

But of late, "Cesar has grown ambitious." The stout and well-tried armor with which nature and the English language had arrayed him, does not satisfy his aspiring genius, but with the march of fame he must needs assume a more striking—shall we say more *chaste* and effective panoply? Being an original thinker, he must of course adopt an original style in which to convey his ideas, one which should clearly distinguish him from the *ignobile vulgus*, and most indubitably establish his claims to be considered "the lion" of English Literature. Accordingly we have known Thomas Carlyle in later times as the author of certain mysterious "voices," "utterances," and "Prophetic Articulations," the exact purport of which has not in all cases been clear to our comprehension. It is with no little mortification, however, that we feel constrained to make this admission, since, by all the admirers of Carlyle, who possess the "Inner Consciousness"—"the vision and the faculty divine"—we are liable to be considered and termed "consummate blockheads," shallow-brained ninnies, with other appellations of a like nature, which, however clear the evidence to one's own mind, or to others, of their being correctly applied, are, notwithstanding, to the truly modest man, (like ourselves,) not less painful, than man of genius, clear and logical reasoner, &c.

The first manifest indications of idiosyncracy in our author's genius, we observed some seven or eight years since in his Sartor Resartus. We well remember with what boyish curiosity (we were younger then than we are now) we first followed the worthy Herr Teufelsdrockle in his subtle disquisitions on the philosophy of Clothes; wondering, meanwhile, whether he of Weissnichto was in fact a veritable personage, as he professed himself to be, or only one of our author's Phantasms, or "Outward Appearances," which, in his later works, he is so fond of introducing to the notice of the reader. Be this as it may, however, we most cordially recommend Sartor Resartus to the candid attention of the student and man of letters, as the most analytical and learned investigation of the Philosophy of Clothes now extant. In this deeply important science, the learned Professor is perfectly at home. In a most masterly manner does he discuss the nature and use of Clothes, clearly pointing out their importance and necessity to mankind, as at present organized; nay, he has even gone deeper than this, and stripping man of his "three ply" of broadcloth, has subjected him to the rigid examination of a critical analysis, or, in his own chaste and elegant language, has shown him "the forked, straddling animal he actually is."

Next came his History (?) of the French Revolution, a truly noteworthy book, and one of which many things might be said, but of which, for the present, we are silent. Some three years later appeared sundry lectures on Heroes, Hero-Worship, and the Heroic in history—also, in many respects, a book of much note, and developing to the world more fully than had before been done, certain views of the editor on important subjects. Herein are we clearly informed of the estimation in which our author holds certain men who have acted distinguished parts in the great drama of life—no unimportant circumstance; and what is still more important, from some obscure hints and incidental remarks dropped at random throughout these pages, are we enabled to form some definite opinion of the religion of the man; *definite*, we say, though, perhaps, a mistaken one. If so, we think our author himself is justly accountable, for that one who professedly writes on morals and faith, who believes "that a man's religion is the chief fact concerning him," should state his own belief in terms so indefinite and unintelligible as to be misunderstood—such an one is, of all others, most inexcusable. The Past and the Present is the latest production from our author's prolific intellectual warehouse—in style and spirit resembling the last three named works; but of this more anon. It is in such capacity that we have known Thomas Carlyle in late years as an author—an author of rare industry, ingenuity, and power. Ingenuity, forsooth! let not that man be accused of lacking ingenuity, who can twist and torture language into as many Protean shapes as we find in Carlyle's later writings. Such words, too, as he has invented—shade of the departed Webster! From thy Olympian heights look down in pity on us poor benighted mortals, and issue some celestial supplement to thy ponderous quartos, that we may, by any means, obtain some dim insight into this distracted, cloudy "imbroglio" of Carlylism.

A powerful writer, too, is our author, as we easily gather fromt he effects which he produces. Perhaps the writings of no other man, of the present time, have been more read and studied by the intellectual and thinking part of community, or received with more universal favor. Nay, has he not here among ourselves his Dials, his Emersons, his Alcotts, in some sort, too, his Brownsons, who are treading carefully in his steps, and teaching his doctrine, even in the very style and language of their illustrious predecessor? Decidedly the richest and most irresistibly ludicrous specimens of literature we have met with in these degenerate times, are the efforts of certain youthful tyros, who possess not a tithe of the intellectual power of Carlyle, endeavoring to imitate him in his style and subject matter. A more felicitous illustration of the fable of the frog and the ox, related by Horace, we have seldom seen.

To endeavor to criticise the style of Carlyle, would be a most absurd and fruitless waste of time. It has been remarked, with justness, perhaps, that he is above all criticism. By what method will you proceed to criticise the style of a man who sets completely at defiance all the rules of grammar, logic, or rhetoric; who, regardless of all usage, ancient or modern, adopts a style *sui generis*, both unnatural and inimitable? Unnatural, we say, for we think none will contend that the original and fantastic style in which he has chosen to convey his ideas the past few years, can be the natural outflowing of his thoughts. Possessing an almost boundless command of language, he has left its legitimate use, to play upon words, to dazzle by flights of his genius, or astonish by his curious and inimitable arrangement of words and sentences. Whether this style be best adapted to gain the ends the author has in view, remains to be seen.

We have carefully read several times the later works of Carlyle, and cannot say, as of some other authors, that each re-perusal has been attended with increased pleasure. We attribute this, is great part at least, to the nature of the subjects on which he generally treats, and the spirit and style in which his ideas are uttered. The successful writer, who arrests the attention of his readers, to a greater or less extent carries their sympathies along with him. If a complaining or fault-finding spirit breathes through his pages, a corresponding influence will be felt on the mind of the reader. Such a spirit we think more peculiarly characterizes Carlyle than any other modern writer. His last work, especially, breathes an everlasting *Plorare* and *Miserere;* indicating a mind ill at ease with itself or others. True, indeed, we should not wish or expect to find an earnest heart speaking of such momentous subjects in a playful mood. But after all, to use our author's own language, "when a man is miserable, what does it most become him to do? To complain of this man or that, of this thing or that? To fill the world and street with lamentation, objurgation? Not so at all: the reverse of so."

In the comparisons which in almost every chapter he draws between past ages in English history and the present, it is always greatly to the disadvantage of the latter. To say nothing of the truth or error of this, we think its effect is anything but salutary on the reader. We agree with the sentiment of Channing, as expressed in one of his finest poems, that

"To call past ages better than what now
Man is enacting on life's crowded stage,
Cannot improve our worth."

And then, too, one does at length grow weary of hearing perpetual changes rung on Dilettantisms, Fanaticisms, Inner Consciousness, The Great Fact of Existence, with a long list of etceteras, some of which, we should judge from the connection in which they are used, have no very definite signification, even in the author's own mind. Nor does the peculiar style of Carlyle's writings especially increase the pleasure of a re-perusal. A style evidently forced, affected, and unnatural, although it may at first secure the attention by its novelty, must finally disgust, or at least displease the reader of refined taste.

For a single perusal of a single volume, it affords a pleasant and exciting amusement to be borne along in the chariot of this modern Aminidab, with Phaeton whip. The attention of the most listless reader cannot but be arrested with the numberless elisions, semibreves, crotchets, interrogations, and exclamations which crowd every page; but he at length begins to feel his patience weary in attempting to keep pace with the author. In our western country we have sometimes traveled in good old-fashioned wagons without springs, over bridges made of logs, placed near each other and projecting some inches above the general surface. Some of these, in swampy tracts, are a mile or so in extent, and are excellent for awakening the attention of the traveler to the beauties of the surrounding scenery, but ——!

Many of Carlyle's admirers, however, strenuously defend the characteristics which we censure, as being a powerful stimulus to thought—the true object of reading. It may be that this will be its natural effect, but the argument to our minds, at least, is a novel one. We have here a new theory of writing, one which is to produce an effect, not less surprising than the invention of printing itself. The means of attaining the great end of writing has hitherto been misunderstood. Campbell, Blair, and Whately, who have given us instruction and rules in the art of writing, were but ignorant, silly dupes, who knew nothing of the philosophy of mind, or the true province of the science which they taught. Clearness, simplicity, and precision are utterly eschewed by the Carlyle school, and considered only as vulgar and unimportant qualifications, entirely beneath the consideration of the true genius, who aspires to reach the spiritual and infinite, the Divine Idea in the nature of man.

Here, too, we see that Shakspeare, Milton, Addison, and the old English classic writers, knew nothing of the nature of mind, or the most effective method of employing language. Their style of writing was not calculated to waken thought in the mind, and consequently they have failed of attaining the true end of writing, and can by no means be considered men of genius, or worthy the gratitude of mankind. Indeed, it is wonderful by what obliquity of mental vision mankind have so long continued to admire such plain common sense writers. They were content to use language adapted to the comprehension of all capacities, terms whose signification was easily understood, with a clear, simple, straight-forward style, which, while not unworthy the attention of the most powerful intellects, was even such "that the wayfaring man, though a fool, need not err therein." Mistaken souls!

But to return—for in our discursive remarks we had well nigh forgotten the purpose for which we sat down to pen this article—a brief notice of the Past and Present. We observe the work appears under the auspices of Mr. Emerson, one of the 'Transcendal friends' of whom Mr. Carlyle speaks in the course of his work, his most ardent admirer, and who has re-echoed his sentiments on this side of the Atlantic, if with less power and effect, certainly with not less zeal and diligence. A similar favor for Emerson was performed by Mr. Carlyle, in England, not long since, who stood god-father to an edition of Emerson's works there issued. A peculiar sympathy and brotherly affinity seems to exist between these two minds, very pleasing to witness. If our 'Transcendal friend' has been zealously active in disseminating the opinions of the most 'profound original thinker in the old world,' he has the satisfaction of knowing that his labors have been highly appreciated and fully reciprocated by his Transatlantic brother. We remember having seen an article in one of the English Quarterlies, from the pen of Mr. Carlyle, in which he takes occasion to congratulate his readers that even in this Money-God-worshiping nation, there is yet *one* redeeming spirit, not entirely the slave of Mammon, Cant, Atheism, &c., but with far-seeing vision and trusting faith, is struggling, with manful earnestness, to bring back the soul to this soulless nation. "Tickle me Toby and I'll tickle thee." The object of the editor in the present work seems to have been to contrast the past state of England with the present, to paint in glowing colors, with a master hand, the wretched condition into which distracted England has fallen, and soundly belabor both rulers and ruled for being found and continuing in this condition.

The first thought which naturally strikes the reader as he lays down the work, is the unfair contrast which he has presented between the Past and Present, and the limited extent to which the parallel he has drawn between them holds true. Drawing aside the curtains which hide from our view the dim shadows of our ancestors' deeds, he looks far back—some six hundred years—into antiquity, and finds there certain "confused papers printed and other," written by one Jocelin of Brakelond, giving some account of a certain convent of St. Edmundsbury, in which monks once lived, prayed, and quarreled, even as in other convents they have been known to do. These Jocelina Chronica go on to tell us that in those days their abbott Hugo was grown old, and *aliquantulum caligarerunt oculi ejus*, how, in fine, he at last died, how they proceeded to an election, and made choice of one Samson subsacrista for abbott. This abbott Samson and his election forms a conspicuous figure in the Past and Present. It is by this 'rather circuitous way,' that the Editor attempts to 'illustrate our own poor country' in such way as he best can.

What connection there can be between a secluded monastery six hundred years ago, and the present condition of the English people, or how the condition of the one can be correctly illustrated by the election of an abbott, or the government of the other, after a careful perusal of the whole subject, we are at a loss to perceive.

The unbounded admiration of Carlye for every thing bearing the impress of antiquity, unfits him for a candid comparison of the past with the present, and leads him to take altogether a prejudiced and one-sided view of the subject. The same fault we observe in his Heroes in History. The dolorous wail is ever on his lips, *O Tempores! O Mores!* One would suppose from the present work, that England was in a far worse situation in every respect, than in the time of the good old abbott Samson. We cannot by any means arrive at such a conclusion, at least not from any facts presented in this work. We doubt not but that the condition of England is pitiable enough, even at this present, with her "Game-preserving Aristocratic Dilettantism, 'Dead sea Apism,' oppressions, and two million shirtless or ill shirted workers, who sit enchanted in Workhouse Bastiles;" still we believe no reasonable, unprejudiced man, would say she is in a worse condition, either physically, intellectually, or morally, than in the days of John Lackland. Our transcendental philosopher thinks those were 'comparatively blessed times, in which violence, war, disorder reigned,' to this perpetual 'cry of peace, peace, when there is no peace.' As an instance of their superior 'blessedness,' he mentions the fact, that a child might safely carry a bag of gold from one end of the kingdom to the other, in the reign of William the Conqueror, or 'Willelmus Conquestor,' as he must needs call him. We have read that the same might be done in the dominions of the Sultan, but never from that fact inferred the peculiar 'blessedness' of the people living under his government. There are many other points in the contrast which he has drawn between the Past and Present, we would fain notice, did our limits permit. Although we think he has by no means drawn a true parallel, yet we honor the feelings which have led him to err. Sympathy with his suffering, down-trodden brethren, natural unextinguishable hatred of the Idle, much-consuming Aristocracy, breathe through every page of this work, and bespeak a heart which does honor to humanity.

With regard to the much-boasted originality of Carlyle, we have a word to say. We have heard it asserted by his admirers, that he is the only original thinker and writer, which the present century has produced. Verily a modest claim! and one which we think their hero would hardly thank his friends for making in his behalf. That we frequently meet with original and striking thoughts in Carlyle, is true. But that his originality consists more in style and expression, than of thought, we think every careful and candid reader of his works will admit. The present work, especially, we think more lacking in this respect than some of his preceding. Many of his propositions and 'utterances' are but truisms, which have been harped upon from the time of the Grecian and Roman philosophers to the present day. For instance, he devotes several chapters in illustrating and enforcing the propositions that the Just only are the good, that this only is the lasting and true; and that not by 'oceans of horse hair, continents of parchment and learned sergeant eloquence,' can the unjust be made just. In the dialogue of Socrates with the sophists, as related in the Gorgeas of Plato, we have some dim recollection of having seen the same ideas expressed in nearly the same language. A striking similarity of ideas may be observed in certain other parts of the same work, with those expressed by our modern philosopher, of a more exceptionable nature, than those referred to, as the argument of Callicles, where he says, "ἡ δέ γε, οἶμαι, φύσις αὐτὴ ἀποφαίνει αὐτὸ, ὅτι δίκαιόν ἐστι τὸν ἀμείνω τοῦ χείρονος πλέον ἔχειν καὶ τὸν δυνατώτερον τοῦ ἀδυνατωτέρου," &c., *et sequens*, in which he endeavors to prove that the more powerful should have more than the less, and that might makes right.

This seems to be fully endorsed by Carlyle, where he says, "The bravest men who it is ever to be repeated and remembered are also on the whole, the wisest, strongest, every way best, had here with a respectable degree of accuracy been got selected, &c. The fighting too was indispensable for ascertaining who had the might over whom—the right over whom. By much hard fighting, as we once said, 'the unrealities beaten into dust flew gradually off,' and left the plain reality and fact, 'thou stronger than I, thou wiser than I, thou king, and subject I,' in a somewhat clearer condition." Again, where he inveighs against the folly of Mammon-worship, and insists that the "pursuit of wealth is not the true object of our existence—that he who makes it so has lost his soul,"—he seems to be indulging in the same train of ideas as Horace in one of his satires, where he says—

"——— quisquis
Ambitione malâ, aut argenti pallet amore;
Quisquis luxuriâ, tristive superstitione,
Aut alio mentis morbo calet; huc proprius me,
Dum doceo insanire omnes, vos ordine adite."

Speaking on the same subject in another place, to what a sage conclusion does our philosopher arrive in these words: "For in short, Mammon is not a god at all; but a devil, and even a very despicable devil. Follow the Devil faithfully, you are sure enough to *go* to the Devil: whither else *can* you go?" True, O veritable Diogenes, *where* the devil *can* you *go*, but to the Devil? Strange that no one had ever discovered this important truth before! But seriously—we do not offer it as an argument against the power or genius of Carlyle as a writer, that he abounds in oft-repeated truisms. That he can bring these home to the heart, make men listen to them and feel them, may indeed be an evidence of the highest genius. It has been truly remarked by Coleridge, that "genius produces impressions of novelty, while it rescues the most admitted truths from the impotence caused by the very circumstance of their universal admission." We only refer to this subject here, to remark the difference between originality of *thought* and that of style, or the manner of expressing thought, as indicating minds of very different order, though by some they seem to be considered as synonymous. Although, perhaps, Mr. Carlyle excels every English writer of the present day in command of language and power of expression, yet in true originality of thought, we believe him inferior to many.

But the most important feature in the later writings of Carlyle, is their moral and religious influence.

His literary character, the calibre of his mind, his style, are now to a good degree settled in the public mind, and the attention of all is now turned with a painful anxiety, to mark the influence which he is now exerting, and shall still exert, on the public mind, in a religious point of view. Mr. Carlyle is essentially a religious writer—*religious* in the sense in which he uses the term. Believing as he does that a man's religion is the chief fact concerning him, and writing chiefly of men, it would be strange if he did not make this a conspicuous subject in his essays. Accordingly, by no writer not professedly treating on religious topics, do we find more frequent allusions to this subject, than in the later works of our author, and especially in the "Past and Present." And yet of no writer is it more difficult to state what is his religious creed, or whether he has any definite religious belief at all. Whatever his belief may be, we hesitate not to say, that the influence of his opinions on this subject, especially on the young, is anything but beneficial. That he believes in a God, appears evident from the numerous allusions to such a being in his writings. Whether it is such a God as is spoken of in the Scriptures, there is good reason to doubt. He speaks of him, like Pythagoras, as synonymous with the "great soul of the Universe, just and not unjust. Look thou, if thou have eyes or soul left, into this great shoreless, Incomprehensible; in the heart of its Tumultuous Appearances, Embroilments, and mad Time-vortexes, is there not, silent, eternal, an All-just, an All-beautiful sole Reality, an ultimate controlling Power of the whole!" Well spoken, O disciple of Grecian philosophy. And how dost thou then regard the Saviour of men? "A Hero, greater perhaps than Odin, than Mahomet, than Dante even, the greatest of all Heroes is one whom we do not name here." In this character Carlyle sees something God-*like*, but no God—one who only deserves to be ranked among the noblest of men.

We can well believe Carlyle, when he says that "superstition is far from him; that Fanaticism, for any *Fanum* likely soon to arise on this earth, is far"! With a hearty good will, does he manfully assault any and every form of superstition—that which *he* considers such, whether it be Paganism, Catholicism, "The Thirty-nine Articles," or Methodism. Hear him on this latter:

"Methodism, with its eye turned forever on its own navel; asking itself with torturing anxiety of Hope and Fear, 'Am I right, am I wrong? Shall I be saved, shall I not be damned?' What is this at bottom but a new phasis of *Egoism* stretched out into the Infinite; not always the heavenlier for its infinitude! Brother, so soon as possible endeavor to rise above all that. 'Thou art wrong, thou art like to be damned;' consider that as the fact, reconcile thyself even to that, if thou be a man;—then first is the devouring Universe subdued under thee, and from the black murk of midnight and noise of greedy Acheron, dawn, as of an everlasting morning, how far above all Hope, all Fear, springs for thee, enlightening thy steep path, awakening in thy heart celestial Memnon's music."

Good! In this non-committal, conservative, time-serving age, it is refreshing to find here and there a man who has the moral courage to come out and take a decided stand in the cause of truth and religion. This modern divine here lays down a short and comprehensive system of theology, original it is true—essentially different from any other extant, but yet clear and explicit. You have only, kind reader, firmly to convince yourself there is a real eternal hell, to imagine that you already hear the raging of the quenchless fires, and the wail of anguish from the lost, to which add the satisfactory assurance, that in these pastimes you will yourself soon be a participant, and it shall cause the blessed light of eternity to dawn on thy poor benighted mind, and melodies celestial shall thrill thy enraptured soul! What inconceivable bliss must now be the portion of devils and the damned, who have long been the blessed partakers in these enjoyments! Of Puseyism too:

"O Heavens! what shall we say of Puseyism in comparison with twelfth-century Catholicism? Little or nothing; for indeed it is a matter to strike one dumb. That certain human souls living on this practical earth, should think to save themselves and a ruined world by noisy, theoretic demonstrations and laudations of *the* Church, instead of some unnoisy, unconscious, but *practical*, total heart-and-soul demonstrations of *a* Church; this, in the circle of revolving ages, this also was a thing we were to see," &c.

But to take his own definition of religion:

"Hast thou ever reflected, O serious reader, Advanced liberal, or other, that the one end, essence, use, of all religion, past, present, and to come, was this only; to keep that same moral conscience or Inner Light of ours alive and shining; which certainly the Phantasms, and 'turbid media' were not essential for! All revelation was here to remind us, better or worse, of what we already know better or worse, of the quite *infinite* difference there is between a good man and a Bad, to bid us love infinitely the one, and abhor infinitely the other—strive infinitely to *be* the one and not to be the other! All religion is due Practical Hero-Worship. He that has a soul unasphyxied will never want a religion; he that has a soul asphyxied, reduced to a succedaneum for salt, will never find any religion, though one rose from the dead to preach him one."

Now what do we find in this, more than would have been said by Hume, Voltaire, or Paine? No respectable infidel, who valued his own character, would hesitate to advise us to be moral and *Good*, in the sense in which Carlyle uses the term, rather than vicious and Bad. We search the writings of Carlyle in vain for any admission of the inspiration of the Scriptures, or of their indispensable necessity as a rule of faith and action. "The Bible of Universal History is the Eternal Bible and God's Book, and to discredit this, is Infidelity like no other." Such is the only Bible whose authority Mr. Carlyle acknowledges. He does indeed speak in the highest terms of eulogy of certain parts, as the book of Job, and some of the Prophecies, as the most sublime specimens of human eloquence and power of the imagination which he has ever read. But other than as a mere intellectual performance, he seems never to have read or thought of the Bible. He seems never to have dreamed of it as a revelation of the Divine will to man, through which alone we obtain a knowledge of our relation to God and each other, of our Duty and future Destiny. This 'Inner Light' or 'inner consciousness' which he speaks of so frequently, 'high as Heaven's splendor,' deep as 'Hell's darkness,' is the Great Law of Duty, all-sufficient for the guidance of man in this pilgrimage world. The doctrine, in plain language, is no other than this: Let a man follow implicitly the dictates of his own heart, and he is safe. We think Mr. Carlyle must be an advocate for the doctrine of 'irresponsibility of belief,' one of the most dangerous errors of the present day. This doctrine, that our Inner Consciousness is our sufficient Rule of Duty, is too much on the system of the Epicurean philosophy, which taught that man's supreme happiness consisted in pleasure.

Mr. Carlyle's 'Inner Consciousness' may, for aught we know, teach him at all times to do what is right; while another man's inner consciousness may lead him to do directly the opposite, yet which he may consider to be right. Lay aside the Bible as the standard of right and wrong, and we rush headlong, blindfold, into what awful 'Laissez-faire-*isms*, Dillettantisms, Sansculotteisms, Mamnonisms'! The unbounded admiration of Carlyle for the Actual and Practical, entirely absorbs his sympathy for the Virtual.

The only religion which he recognizes, is that of Hero-Worship—paying homage to those the world calls Heroes. He who has played his part well in life, who has gained a fame world-wide and time-enduring, whether as Odin, in old Norse battles, as Mahomet propagating the faith of Islam by fire and sword, an Abbott Samson bravely laboring for Twelfth-Century Catholicism, a Luther, sternly opposing the same Catholic faith, or a Napoleon, in awful Moscow conflagrations or Waterloo battle-fields, filling Europe with bloodshed and misery; such an one is the Hero of Carlyle—the religious man, the one worthy of our worship; 'for all religion issues in due Practical Hero-Worship.' Were that question of the old catechism, so often *inflicted* on our juvenile minds, proposed to our author, "What is the chief end of man?" he would have answered, Work—Labor—Toil. "The latest Gospel," says he, (and which he also considers the best,) "the latest Gospel preached on earth, is, that a man know his work and do it." We know many individuals upon whom the effect of the practical application of this Gospel would be most beneficial; but to lay it down as an axiom of universal application, we can hardly think safe, notwithstanding the wide latitude of meaning it may have. We can well believe, as our author observes, "that salvation lies not in tight lacing in these times," but yet can hardly think it lies in such loose lacing as he would recommend. Were there no other Gospel than this for the "two millions who sit enchanted in Workhouse Bastiles, and the five millions more in Ugolino Hunger-cellars," then were the condition of soulless brutes rather to be chosen. If this be indeed the only true Gospel, no nation on earth is so near salvation as our own, especially the Yankee part of it, since they surpass every other as inveterate workers.

Speaking of our own country—we should like above all things to have Mr. Carlyle spend a time with us, and give us a volume on the condition and prospects of our nation. We have some characteristics which would peculiarly strike his fancy, and others, doubtless, which he would as severely condemn. With all his sympathy for the poor and oppressed, it is evident he has none for American Democracy. There is no Hero-Worship in it. "All this," he observes in his Heroes in History, "All this of Liberty, Equality, Electoral Suffrage, Independence, and so forth, we will take therefore to be a temporary phenomenon, and not a final one. Though likely to last a long time, with sad enough embroilments for us all, we must welcome it as the penalty of sins that are past, the pledge of inestimable benefits that are coming." That men are capable of governing themselves, as we simple hearted republicans believe, is an idea which he regards with the most supreme contempt. "But oppression by your Mock-Superiors well shaken off, the grand problem yet remains to be solved, that of finding government by your Real-Superiors! Alas, how shall we ever learn the solution of that, benighted, bewildered, sniffing, sneering, god-forgetting unfortunates as we are?" We fear from some remarks which he drops in the last chapter of the Past and Present, that our author is indulging in some visionary speculations and unwarrantable hopes in regard to our promising country. He says—

"But truly it is beautiful to see the brutish empire of Mammon cracking everywhere, giving some promise of dying or of being changed. A strange, chill, almost ghastly dayspring, strikes up in Yankeeland itself; my Transcendal friends announce there, in a distinct, though somewhat lankhaired, ungainly manner, that the Demiurgus Dollar is dethroned; that new unheard-of Demiurgusships, Priesthoods, Aristocracies, Growths, and Destructions, are already visible in the grey of coming time. Chronos is dethroned by Jove; Odin by St. Olaf; the Dollar cannot rule in Heaven forever. No; I reckon not. Socinian preachers quit their pulpits in Yankeeland, saying, 'Friends, this is all gone to a colored cobweb, we regret to say!' and retire into fields to cultivate onion-beds, and live frugally on cabbages. It is very notable. Old godlike Calvinism declares that its old body is now fallen to tatters and done; and its mournful ghost, disembodied, seeking new embodiment, pipes again in the winds;—a ghost and spirit as yet, but heralding new Spirit-worlds, and better Dynasties than the Dollar one."

Decidedly rich! Yet be not too severe on thy "Transcendal friends," O Magnus Apollo, even if they do announce in a somewhat "lankhaired, ungainly manner," the progress of Transcendal principles in this land, which, to use their own language, is the "most favored of all lands that possess no government." It is true, thy Transatlantic Transcendal friends have not yet reached the "Ultimum Thule," the true scientific touch of the Carlyle school, yet they have shown themselves apt scholars, and deserve great credit for the rapid progress they have made. Some of them have already attained a style as uncouth and obscure as the most genuine Transcendentalist could desire, and give good promise of yet equaling, in this respect, their illustrious cotemporaries of the old world. Yet let not thy trusting heart, which beats for the interests of suffering humanity, too eagerly swallow all the accounts of thy Democratic friends in this new field of philanthropy.

Though they have labored with a most commendable diligence and perseverance, yet we fear their success has not been at all times commensurate with their zeal, and that not unfrequently they have mistaken their own ardent wishes, for the reality and assurance of success.

We have even heard it hinted, by those most familiar with him, that the great High-Priest of Transcendentalism among us—"the knight of the Socinian pulpit, who has retired into the fields, to cultivate onion-beds, and live on cabbages," is somewhat affected with *Egoism*, the peculiar abhorrence of the Hero-Worshiper, which might lead him to estimate the effect and importance of his labors, as far more considerable than would an ungrateful and prejudiced public Sorry are we to say, at least, that the Demiurgus Dollar seems by no means yet dethroned, and that whatever other "Demiurgusships, Priesthoods," &c. may be visible in the "grey of coming time," this seems likely long to hold its sway. "Old godlike Calvinism," too, whose body they think "fallen to tatters and done"—even this, we judge from present appearances, will not give up the ghost without some manful struggles!

We had intended to notice some of the excellencies of the Past and Present—excellencies, neither few in number nor of small merit—but the limits of this article forbid. We have spoken more particularly of the faults which characterize this and other works of Carlyle, both because they seem little noticed, almost every review coming to us loaded with indiscriminate praise, and because these faults, though some of them of the most dangerous tendency, are yet in a great manner concealed to the unsuspecting reader, by the excellencies to which we have referred, such indeed as are found in no other writer of the present day. Yet we can almost excuse all that we consider blameworthy, for the noble, manly spirit which breathes through every page. His heart is far above all low, sordid considerations of wealth and human applause. Who would not admire and love the soul which *feels*, and bravely defends sentiments like these? "The wealth of a man is the number of things which he loves and blesses, which he is loved and blessed by." "For there is a perennial nobleness, and even sacredness in work. Were he ever so benighted, forgetful of his high calling, there is always hope in a man that actually and earnestly works: in Idleness alone there is perpetual despair." It is delightful to see in what merciless style he handles the purse-proud English Aristocracy, with the most bitter sarcasm, showing them up as objects worthy our supreme contempt. His description of a Dandy, and the Pope too—capital! Get the book and read it!

AN OLD MAN'S RETROSPECT.

Oh! swiftly they fled—my boyhood's bright years—
Ere sorrow had darkened these eyes with tears;
While the Meteor hope before me gleam'd,
And life but a fountain of gladness seem'd.
The blue sky above and the earth below,
Young fancy arrayed in its own warm glow.
Too pure was that happiness long to last,
And Memory whispers, 'tis past, 'tis past.

Old Time hurried on in his ceaseless flight,
But strong were my limbs, and my eye was bright,
And love threw a halo around me then,
A glory this earth cannot give—again.
How lovely the morn when with transport and pride,
I clasp'd to my bosom my own chosen bride!
Those transports I never again shall taste,
For Memory whispers, they're past, they're past.

But Manhood usurp'd the station of youth,
And my heart forgot its earlier truth.
Disease and affliction hung o'er my head,
While swiftly the hopes of my boyhood fled.
Yet moments of happiness often I found,
The joys of the fireside on home's hallow'd ground.
But sorrows and pleasures have sped full fast,
And Memory whispers, they're past, they're past.

I know that my locks are now silver'd o'er,
And the strength that was mine, is mine no more!
That my form is bow'd with the weight of years,
And my eyes are dim with fast-flowing tears.
Acquaintance, and friends, and belov'd ones have fled—
The sods of the valley lie cold o'er the dead!
And I long, O! I long away to haste
To the land where sorrows are past, are past.

THE WITCH.

A TALE OF THE LAST CENTURY.

BY CUJUS.

"The earth has bubbles, as the water hath."—MACBETH.

CHAPTER I.

THERE is a rough district in the southern part of New England, which we believe has been little celebrated in song or story, though there are places there which might afford inspiration to the poet, or well be chosen as scenes of wild adventure. Dark passes winding between pine-covered cliffs, gently undulating hills, retired valleys, watered by the sparkling brook or slow-moving river, and little lakes high up among the mountains or embosomed in the woods, are certainly romantic objects and agreeable to the sight, and *as* certainly may be found in the section of country to which we have alluded. Some seventy or eighty years ago there existed another feature of the landscape, which has now entirely disappeared—portions of the huge primeval forest, as yet untouched by the axe of the settler. Several rocky ranges of hills, which diversified the region in question, were thus protected, their sides and summits being covered with hemlocks, pines, and oaks which might have stood there a thousand years, and among whose branches the bald eagle still built her nest, while the bear and the wolf couched beneath. At the foot of one of these ridges, or rather in a wide valley which lies between two of them, stands the town of D———, at the time when our story commences, a gossiping little Yankee village, whose inhabitants then, as now, were distinguished by their fondness for scandal and a certain garden vegetable—and indeed, their skill in the cultivation of this latter article has gained for the place a *soubriquet* neither very classical or euphonious. Villages of this description were once numerous in New England, the dwellers in which busied themselves with the thousand occupations characteristic of the Yankee, adhered closely to the Puritanic manner of dress and thought, and went down to their graves, leaving behind them a numerous posterity, whose children might be destined to carry their fathers' names to the remotest corners of this favored land. But, alas! the people of the present day are not the people of the past; and though the sons of New England still retain much of their wonted enterprise, in other respects they have sadly deviated from the good customs of their ancestors. The male portion of the latter were satisfied to be *men*, they cared not whether others called them gentlemen or not; the girls were girls, and the women, women; they were *old-fashioned* in every sense of the word; they aped neither Paris, London, or New York; they wore no inexpressibles, which, should the wearer chance to stoop, would burst in sunder; and touranours and flounces were things unheard of. Now—mark the change—but we will say no more, perhaps the world is improving; *perhaps not.*

About the year 1768, a considerable excitement was created in the village of D——, by the arrival of an old woman and a little girl, who took lodgings in a remote part of the town, visited nobody, attended solely to their own business, and defied all attempts of their neighbors to learn their genealogy, former or future occupation, with the score of other inquiries propagated by New England curiosity. The old lady called herself Mrs. Stanfield, and was ugly in the extreme, while the girl, though she addressed her companion as grandmother, was pronounced by all a perfect specimen of childish beauty. She could not have been more than eight or nine years of age, yet she evaded all the questions put to her by the inquisitive townsfolk, as effectually as Mrs. Stanfield herself. There was also a huge black cat, which followed the strangers wherever they went, and after a few combats, gained a decided superiority over all the village curs. All this was very mysterious, and, therefore, very provoking, and when it was understood that the new comers had purchased a piece of *cleared* land somewhere off among the mountains, and were proceeding to build a dwelling there, the wonder and indignation were proportionately increased. Still the house or hut was begun and finished, in spite of the clamor of the villagers, and one bright May morning, Mrs. Stanfield, her granddaughter, and the cat removed to their new residence. In the afternoon of the same day, Mrs. Wilkins, a matron of forty-five, and Miss Lappet, a maiden lady of a somewhat questionable age, made a friendly call upon Mrs. Deborah Brown, in whose house the strangers had resided during their stay in the village.

"Wal!" said Mrs. Wilkins, when the hostess had put away their 'things,' "wal! your folks have gone, have they, finally?"

"Yis, and what on airth they should go to live off there in the woods for, I don't see!"

"Nor I neither," exclaimed Miss Lappet, "and sich a nice place as they had to live in here, too."

"Wal!" replied Mrs. B., evidently pleased with the compliment, "I don't say nothin' about that; but what do you think my husband said, when he got back from there this mornin'?—for you know he wanted to help 'em along a little and to see how they'd manage to live up there—wal, when he got back, he told me that for all the house looked rather rough on the outside, they'd got it finished off as nice—as nice as *this* is inside; a kitchen and two bed-rooms—now what could they want of two bed-rooms, *I* should like to know."

"*Two* bed-rooms!" ejaculated Mrs. Wilkins, "why law! now do tell! two bed-rooms! why of course they'd sleep together, and what *could* they want to do with *two* bed-rooms?"

"And *sich* a nice cubbard (Anglice cupboard) as they'd got!"

"A cubbard!" exclaimed both the visitors.

"And chairs, and crockery, and cookin' things, and books, and two rifles"—

"Two RIFLES!" screamed Mrs. Wilkins and Miss Lappet; "Lord ha' massy on us! two rifles! wal! I never heerd the like in all my born days!"

"Yis, and three great oak chists; now what do you 'spose them chists has got in 'em?"

"Wal, now raally, I can't think; what was it, bedclothes?"

"Bedclothes!" said Mrs. Brown, contemptuously, "I wish they *was* bedclothes. Wal, now what do you think—Mr. Brown said that when the old woman and the gal was out doors, he jest took hold of one of them chists and shook it, and that great black cat—you know that cat"—

"Yis, yis," exclaimed the listeners, breathlessly.

"Wal! that cat jumped right at him as savage as an Injun, and he said," and here she lowered her voice and looked around, "he said that *he* believed there was bones in that 'ere chist!"

"Bones! why, massy on us! Bones! what kind of bones?"

"Human bein's bones, of course!"

"Massy on us!" screamed the visitors again, "an' couldn't he open it?"

"No, they was all locked, all three on 'em; and before he could shake the other two, the old woman came in, and *sich* a scoldin' as she gave him."

"Wal, I should like to know how they git their livin'."

"Nobody knows. Mrs. Babs—they bought the land of her husband, you know—says they paid for it in raal goold guineas, and they paid Mr. Brown jest so for their rent."

"But how did they git all them things up there?" inquired Miss L.

"Wal now, that's jest the queerest on't. Mr. Brown and I was both wonderin' about it; he says she didn't buy 'em in D——, and he don't believe any of our folks carried 'em there. Now if you won't mention it to nobody, I'll jest tell you what my husband says about it. Now you won't say anything about it, will you?"

"Oh! no, no, certainly not," said the visitors.

"Wal, my husband, when he'd been tellin' me all this, 'Debby,' says he, 'Debby, I don't hardly know what to think of that old woman; and,' says he, 'I jest took up one of them 'ere books, and opened it, and it was all sich jabberish, I couldn't read it, no more'n if it had been Injun, and it was all full of the strangest picturs, men and women with wings, and all sich; and all the time I was lookin' at it, that great black cat kept starin' right in my face; and,' says he, 'I rather calculate Mrs. Stanfield aint no better than she should be, and when *I* was a boy, folks would ha' called her a WITCH.'"

"A witch!" exclaimed Mrs. Wilkins, "O! massy on us! what *shall* we do?"

"But you know," said Miss Lappet, "that there ain't no such things as witches now-a-days."

"No such things!" replied Mrs. Wilkins; "I wish they wasn't, but you see, I know there is. Why it was only year afore last, that my cousin Mary—you know Mary, she married John Spalding down in

R——; wal, she said—let me see—yis, 'twas year afore last, 'cause that fall my husband and I went down there to Thanksgivin', and we expected 'em up here last fall, but they didn't come, and I know I shan't go there agin till they come up here; she needn't think 'cause her husband keeps a store, that they're above common folks; why, what do you think they had for Thanksgivin' supper? nothin' but chickens, not a single turkey, or so much as a goose;—wal, what I was sayin'—O! wal, cousin Mary told me that Deacon James' wife told her—you know Deacon James' wife, proud cretur—Deacon James' wife told her that she heerd—you see they got to talkin' about witches—that she heerd that a few years afore, there was an old woman came to live in them parts that had a great big gray cat, and she lived all alone with that cat. Nobody know'd who she was or where she come from; but the folks didn't think much about it, till one day there was a boy there that used to set squirrel traps. Wal, one fine mornin' he went to his traps and found he'd ketched a raal nice gray squirrel, and he took it out and was lookin' at it, and he saw somethin', a bunch like, on its under jaw, and just as he was lookin' at it the squirrel laughed right out"—

"Laughed!"

"Yis, laughed jest like a human bein', and jumped right out of his hand, and went up into the air, and he didn't see any more on him. Wal, the boy was awfully scared, and he came over to Deacon James' store, and was tellin' on't, when some of the men folks said that this 'ere old woman had jest sich a bunch on *her* chin; and then some of 'em went over to see her, jest as if nothin' had happened, and they'd come to see how she got along; and there she sat right by the fire, and that great gray cat too, and the old woman looked up when they come in, and sure enough there was a wart right on her chin, a great hairy wart!"

"Why, do tell now!" said Miss L.; "and what did they do with her?"

"Oh! nothin'; it got around that she was a witch, and nobody would have anything to do with her, and the boys hollered at her when she came into the streets, and so finally she moved off somewhere else."

"Why deary me!" exclaimed Mrs. Wilkins, "how late 'tis gittin', and I promised Mrs. Babs that I'd come up and take tea with her this a'ternoon; wal! I declare I must go."

"And so must I," said Miss Lappet; "so we'll take our things, if you please, Mrs. Brown."

"Why now do stay to tea, won't you? Wal, if you must go I'll git your things. Good a'ternoon, ladies," continued Mrs. Brown, as the visitors departed; "now do call agin, won't you? I shall be awful lonesome now." "A couple of lazy, pryin' creturs," said she, as she closed the door, "comin' down here as soon as Mrs. Stanfield 's got away, to find out all about her, so 's to tattle it all over town; I'm e'ena'most sorry I told them what I did, for I know they'll go and tell on't; wal, I asked 'em not to!" and with this comforting reflection she hastened to prepare for supper.

By the laudable activity of Mrs. Wilkins and Miss Lappet, not a week elapsed before the majority of the good people of D—— were convinced that Mrs. Stanfield was endued with supernatural powers—in short, that she was a—witch. Yet she seemed to live very composedly through the whole, and to take but little notice of the distrust and terror which she excited. She very rarely came into the village, her little business there being mainly conducted by an Indian who for several years had been hanging about the place. Two or three years passed away in this manner, and the fears of the villagers with respect to the old woman had been mostly forgotten, till suddenly an epidemic broke out among the cattle of D——, by which their numbers were terribly thinned. The disease appeared incurable; and after much speculation and inquiry, suspicion of witchcraft began to prevail among the townsfolk. Mrs. Stanfield a few weeks before had been into the village, an occurrence by no means common, and several idle boys had wantonly insulted her; the old lady was highly incensed, and as she passed through the street on her return, was observed to mutter much to herself, though not sufficiently loud to be understood. At length several of the young men of the place made a visit to the residence of the supposed sorceress, more for the sake of adventure than from any definite purpose. The company found Mrs. Stanfield and her granddaughter sitting on a rude bench before the door of the house—which house and its environs we shall hereafter describe—the latter conning over a self-given lesson, the former apparently watching the changing shapes of the summer clouds. One of the new comers, a wild, reckless young man, advanced, and, seizing the old woman by the arm, exclaimed,

"Wal, old lady, we've got somethin' to say to you about this murrain down in D——. Some folks rather calculate that you know about as much about it as anybody else."

Mrs. Stanfield arose from her seat, looked at the speaker steadfastly for a moment, and then taking the hand of the girl, said in a low tone, "Come, Orra, let us go in."

"Not so easily," said the young man, "we don't let you off quite yet. Now jest to tell the truth, our folks begin to think that witchcraft ain't quite so much of a humbug as it might be; so, old woman, if you've had any dealings with the devil, own up, kill that 'ere cat, and let *us* alone, and we won't do you any harm. Look there," continued he, pointing to a sheet of water a few rods distant, "if you'd get rid of bein' better acquainted with that pond, you might as well confess at once."

The person whom he addressed, hastily shook off his hand, and exclaimed bitterly, "A worthy expedition is this of yours, young men, to terrify old age and insult its gray hairs. Fools that ye are, to own yourselves silly enough to believe the mad tales of dotards and villains. Did ye think that if my power were what you would fain think it, you could have come thus far in safety? And for you, John Martin," said she, turning to the self-constituted spokesman of the party, "the curse of age and poverty be upon you; may you meet with an early and bloody grave"—

"Duck the old hag," interrupted several voices, "throw her into the pond."

"Oh! gentlemen," exclaimed the little girl, clinging to her grandmother's dress with one hand, and extending the other imploringly, "do go away, do; we have never harmed you, indeed we have not."

At this moment, a youth of some seventeen or eighteen years stepped from among the rest, saying, "Come, friends, we've carried the matter too far already; there is evidently no witchcraft here; let the old woman alone, and let's go back again."

"No witchcraft!" said John Martin, "how the devil did she know my name then? No, no, I'm for giving her a taste of the pond; what do you say, fellows?"

"Yes, yes, in with her," said a few voices, but many were silent. Martin again seized Mrs. Stanfield by the arm, and was dragging her away from the house, when the youth who had first opposed him sprang to his side, exclaiming, "And I say no! It is a shame to treat a female thus, even if she be old and fools are frightened at her. Let her go, let her go."

"Hugh Warden," exclaimed Martin, "don't get in my way now; I am not so much your friend as to be bullied by you;" and pushing the young man back, he dragged the old woman forward several paces. The next moment a blow from Warden prostrated him to the earth.

"Now, Mrs. Stanfield," said the latter, "go into your house, quick." The accused had not said a word for some time, and now in silence taking Orra by the hand, she hastily entered the hut.

When Martin arose, somewhat stunned by the violence of the blow, he found most of the party siding with Hugh, and already turning their steps towards D——; and muttering something between his teeth, he hurried homeward by a different route from that which they had taken.

CHAPTER II.

About two or three miles in a southwesterly direction from the town of D——, and situated on the very summit of a range of hills, is a little sheet of water, known at the time to which our story refers, by the name of Rapaug Pond. The woody ridge which overlooks the village from the west, in this place widens upon the top, without diminishing in height, so as to form a considerable area, in the very centre of which lies the miniature lake. Some fifty or sixty years ago, there was a kind of sublimity in its calm appearance, as it lay dark and deep, and surrounded by the majestic primeval forest. The whole eastern and southern portion, with the exception of one narrow strip of land, of which we shall hereafter speak, was skirted by hemlock trees, that came nearly to the water's edge, and might have been the growth of centuries. Oaks and birches, of equal or greater antiquity, screened the northern and western sides. The pond itself was about twelve furlongs in circumference, and in figure nearly circular. It had but one small outlet, that was hardly distinguishable among the woods on the eastern side. The narrow strip of land to which we have alluded, had been partially cleared many years before, and now extended in a gentle ascent from the verge of the waters some three or four hundred yards back into the hemlock forest. Its width might have been fifty feet, and it was covered with a beautiful verdure. At the farther extremity, and shaded by the dark branches of the evergreens, stood a small, rude dwelling, the lower part of which was built of logs, the upper portion and roof of rough boards laid over each other, after the prevailing fashion of the present day. It had but one story, and was, perhaps, thirty feet in length to twenty in width In the middle of the side which looked toward the pond, and which might, by distinction, be called the front, was the only door that the building contained. There were but four windows, two of which were placed in front, on the right and left of the entrance, and two on the western side of the house. The top of a rough stone chimney rose some two or three feet over the eastern extremity of the hut, giving to it an appearance of much greater antiquity than it really possessed. There was a path from the door down to the verge of the pond, and two others which led in opposite directions into the forest. There appeared to be no garden attached to the house, but there was a profusion of wild roses and other flowers of native growth about it, which bore manifest marks of careful cultivation.

It was autumn, and the bluish haze which overspread the landscape, mellowing into still finer tints the changing hues of the forest leaves, proclaimed that it was that peculiarly American season which has been called Indian summer. It wanted, perhaps, an hour of sunset, and lovely indeed was the little scene which we have been endeavoring to describe. As visible from the house, it was a world within itself. The pond lay in quiet beauty; not a breath of wind was stirring, to ripple its smooth surface, and the old forest that surrounded it and hid all beyond from sight, was silent as the grave. The departing sun kindled the hazy atmosphere into a golden lustre, through which the party-colored foliage glistened like the confines of fairy-land. Now and then, scattered flocks of wild pigeons would fly noiselessly across, appearing and disappearing in a moment, and a party of ducks, which, twenty-four hours before, might have been feeding upon the shores of Labrador, were now quietly collected together at the opening of the little outlet that we have mentioned. But other objects claim our more particular attention. On a rude bench, which stood immediately in front of the house, were seated two females. The elder might have passed the age of threescore and ten, but the weight of years seemed to have rested lightly upon her, for her tall form was still unbent, and her sharp gray eyes glittered as brightly as they might have done half a century before. Yet time had covered her face with wrinkles, and her hawk nose, her thin lips, and the long gray locks that fell loosely upon her shoulders,—for she wore no cap or other covering for the head,—rendered her whole figure extremely unpleasing. A huge black cat, in those days an object of suspicion and terror to the vulgar, sat by her side, now and then staring up into his mistress' face with a look—so those who had seen it affirmed—almost human. The appearance of the other female was in strange contrast with that of her companion. She could not have seen more than seventeen summers, and she was of that exceeding loveliness which makes the gazer loth to turn away his eyes. Dark locks, shading a brow of exquisite purity, eyes of the hue of the sky of May, features just sufficiently removed from regular, to overthrow the charge of tameness, and a graceful figure, already rounding into womanhood, formed a combination of charms that might have been dangerous even in a London assembly-room. Both had been sitting for some time in perfect silence, the elder gazing steadfastly in one direction, without changing her position in the least, the younger glancing anxiously from time to time toward one of the paths which led into the surrounding woods.

"Grandmother," said the latter, suddenly, "you know that the last time Hugh was here, he told us of a Declaration of Independence that the Congress had made."

"Well, child," replied her companion, "and what of that?"

"Why, he said, too, that this is now a free people,—that the war is between nation and nation, and he feared it would be a long time before it ended,—and, grandmother, *he* belongs to the American army, and—and"—

"And what?" interrupted the other, impatiently.

"Oh! grandmother," said the maiden, laying her hand on the old woman's arm, "if any thing should happen to Hugh!"

"Well, no great harm would be done."

"Indeed, indeed, there would," exclaimed the girl, the tears starting into her eyes, "for who could protect us then? It was Hugh that stood between us and insult, when, five years ago, they called you witch; and has he not been our only friend ever since? Oh! grandmother, how *can* you say there would be no harm done?"

"Yes, they did call me witch,—curse them for it!—and a part the pestilence* hath cursed: may the remainder perish in the blaze of their own dwellings!" and she arose and hastily entered the house. The girl looked sorrowfully after her for a moment, and was rising to follow, when a young man, dressed in the uniform of an American officer, with a rifle in his hand, stepped out from under the hemlocks on the left, with a noise that caught her ear. She turned and eagerly sprang toward him, exclaiming, "Oh! Hugh, I am so glad you have come!"

"Orra, dear Orra," said the young man, passing his arm around her and kissing her cheek; "what! tears in your eyes? more harshness from the old hag"—

* "In the year 1775, an epidemic disorder, extremely fatal, prevailed throughout the town of D——. The number of deaths during the year was 130, though the place was at that time very small."—*Historical Collections.*

"Don't speak thus of her, Hugh," said the girl, gently extricating herself from his embrace, "she is my own grandmother, and although"—

"Well, and what if she is? that gives her no right to abuse you; but I'll say no more of her. I met with something of an adventure in coming through the woods."

"Sit down, then, and relate it," said the maiden, pointing to the bench; "mountain accommodations, Hugh, but befitting a soldier."

"Well," said Hugh, seating himself, and drawing her to his side, "as I was coming through the oaks, near the foot of the hill, a noise, at a little distance on my right, attracted my attention, and as I turned my head, crack! went a rifle, the ball whizzing within an inch of my cheek. Of course I sprang toward the shooter, when, behold! out stepped, from behind a huge tree, the same Indian that acted as purveyor to you long since, and deserted you so suddenly some four or five years ago."

"Grahtimut!" exclaimed the girl, in astonishment.

"The very same. I knew him the minute I saw him, and pointing my rifle at his head, I asked what he meant. The rascal very coolly answered, that he mistook me for a wolf, in the forest. Do I look wolfish, Orra? do, eh? Well, the red scoundrel trotted off; but I believe I caught a glimpse of him once or twice afterward: still, I can't imagine that he had any intention of harming me."

"But it is singular," said his companion, "that he should be back here and we not know it. I never discovered any thing malignant in his disposition, however, and perhaps he really did mistake you for a wolf," continued she, laughing.

"Ay! well, that is all my adventure."

"And like a true knight-errant, you have come to tell it to"—she stopped, hesitatingly.

"My ladye-love, Orra! and now I must tell you my real object in coming here. To-morrow I leave to join my regiment, and I know not when I shall see Rapaug again, if I ever do. You have become very dear to me, Orra,—more than I was aware of, till it became necessary for me to think of parting with you; but I know now that I do love you as I never can love another, and this is what I have come hither to say to you, and sometimes I have hoped that I was not altogether indifferent in *your* eyes; and I have feared, too,—for we have been to each other as brother and sister,—that thus, perhaps, you have loved me, and thus only. Orra! is it so?"

The maiden did not at once reply, and when at length she spoke, her tones were low and tremulous. "You know, Hugh," said she, "that I have seen but little of the world. I was young when my grandmother brought me to this place, and since then I have had but little opportunity of learning the doings of men, except from what you have yourself told me, and from the books that you have from time to time brought hither. You have been very, *very* kind to me and mine, and I feel that I am unworthy of you;"—a deep blush overspread her face, but her bright eyes looked steadily into his, as she continued, "yet the love that I have is yours, dear Hugh, all yours."

"My own Orra!" exclaimed the delighted young man, as he clasped his arm around her slender waist, and pressed the first kiss of acknowledged love upon her lips, "and when this gloomy war is ended, you will become"—

"Ho, ho!" interrupted a shrill voice from the hut, "courting and kissing, when the old witch is out o' sight." The door opened, and the woman walked out and stopped immediately in front of them. "This is well, Hugh Warden," she proceeded, "entice her away to the wars with ye, and leave the parent that hath nourished her to rot in the woods! A goodly leman will she be for a soldier's camp! And you, girl, can believe his lying words, for ye know not that the world is full of man's treachery, and that a fair maiden is ever the lawful prey of falsehood. No doubt, ye're agreed to leave the old hag to die, forgetting that the remembrance of her may one day be sharper to your bosoms than a two-edged sword!"

"Mrs. Stanfield," said Hugh, rising, "I have loved your granddaughter NOT falsely, and it is my heart's best desire that she may one day become my wedded wife."

"Fine words, fine words, truly," replied the crone, "but think not ye deceive me. And were ye e'en in earnest, Hugh Warden, ye're not the man for Orra Stanfield's husband, and were ye standing before the holy altar, as sure as yonder sun's now setting, my curse should come between ye, to part ye!" She turned and re-entered the hut.

"Confound the old witch," muttered Hugh between his teeth. The next moment, the hand of Orra was laid gently upon his arm, and she exclaimed, earnestly—

"Oh, Hugh! you must go now, indeed, for night is fast coming, and I fear *her*."

"A strange way you have," said Warden, smiling, "of showing your affection for your accepted lover, to drive him away five minutes after"—

"It is no time for jesting now, Hugh," replied the girl, sadly: "I have told you my feelings perhaps too frankly for maidenly modesty; but my life among the mountains hath taught me to speak the truth without reserve, and I could not doubt *you*. But the sun has already been behind the woods a full half hour, and your delay, I fear, only irritates my grandmother."

"You are right, dear Orra, quite right. I have no love-token for you, but sure I am that you will not forget me, and so—good bye!" One embrace, one kiss, and Hugh snatched up his rifle and disappeared in the forest. The maiden looked after him for a moment, and then entered the house.

The path which Warden had taken led around toward the west side of the pond, and in one place passed over a bare rock by the very edge of the water. He had hardly entered the woods, before he thought he heard the sound of receding feet; but when he listened, all was still, and though the noise caught his ear once or twice afterward, he conjectured that it proceeded from some of the smaller wild animals, and gave it no attention. He came at length to the rock, and there stopped a moment to look back toward the clearing. His thoughts were sad, for he had often sat on this very rock, with Orra by his side, and watched the tiny waves as they broke against it. The water was very deep below him, and this had been for years his favorite fishing spot. As he gazed toward the house of Mrs. Stanfield, which was hidden from his sight by the intervening forest, and saw a thin smoke curling over the tops of the trees, he thought how long it might be before he should again behold that scene; and then the war came to his recollection, with all its gloom, and he turned sadly to depart, but before he had moved a single step, with a sharp cry he clapped his hand to his forehead—the report of a rifle sounded through the wood—he staggered, and the next moment fell headlong into the pond.

[TO BE CONTINUED.]

LAST HOURS OF JOAN D'ARC.

I.

Upon thy dungeon walls, Rouen,
Midnight in gloomy silence hung,
And o'er the thoughts of weary men
The mantle of oblivion flung,
Those dungeons where the livelong day,
Traitors were on their dark thoughts feeding,
Chained to whose loathsome sides there lay
Brave martyrs for their country bleeding;
On all, from knight of lordly name,
To slaves of guilt and wretchedness,
Sleep, like a blessed angel, came
With balm of sweet forgetfulness—
All, save one form of queenly grace,
Of youthful brow, yet worn with care;
Whose sad, fixed countenance bore trace
Of the deep workings of despair.
Still in her warrior garb arrayed,
Joan was on the cold ground kneeling,
And to the Virgin Mother prayed
With all a saint's deep, holy feeling—
How could she close in sleep her eyes,
Which she shall close in death to-morrow?
How should she check those rising sighs,
The first wild burst of maiden sorrow?
A captive to her haughty foes,
Who strove with bitter taunt and jeer,
And hellish threats, and coward blows,
To bend her maiden soul in fear;
Strove, in that hour of deep distress,
E'en though themselves could not believe her,
To make her woman's heart confess
She had been but a base deceiver;
Yet still, though life was fading fast,
With death of deep disgrace in view,
Confession from her lips ne'er passed,
That she had spoken aught untrue.

II.

I said she could not sleep; but still,
When her grief-wearied spirit felt
The calm of holy thoughts which fill
The soul in prayer, e'en as she knelt
On that cold earth-damp dungeon floor,
An angel vision, softly stealing,
O'er her hushed spirit came once more,
To her enraptured mind revealing
The scenes and glorious deeds of yore.
Again Domremy's hamlet wild,
With free and lightsome step she trod;
Again a gay, light-hearted child,

Played on the verdant, flowery sod;
Again a simple peasant maid,
She drove her father's herds afield,
Where intermingling sun and shade,
And streams, did richest herbage yield;
Then danced around the fairy tree,
The fairy tree of Bois Chesnu,
While through the branches light and free
The easy pinioned breezes flew;
Where first to her astonished sight
Rose that mysterious cloud of flame;
Where first from saints in robes of light,
The word of inspiration came;
Came sainted spirits down to earth,
And holy angels came with them,
As at the humble Saviour's birth—
The blessed babe of Bethlehem.
And as the heavenly music then
Rang through the arches of the sky,
"On earth peace and good will to men,
Glory and praise to God on high;"
Thus now the angel of Provénce—*
"Hail, favored maid! chosen to be
The Saviour of down-trodden France,
To set her groaning millions free."
Then in her dream she stood before
The haughty Baudricourt, and spake
The high commission which she bore,
The hated Briton's yoke to break.
She meekly prayed that he would grant
Before the king to speak her name—
'Twas but to meet with bitter taunt,
Insulting jeer, and words of shame:
"And does the simple maiden deem
Her monarch's ear will open be
To every passing, idle dream,
Of wandering vagrants such as she?
Bid her go tell the silly tale
To some light-hearted rustic swain;
Her story, doubtless, will not fail
His simple, trusting heart to gain."

* * * * * *

III.

And then the vision changed, and she heard the tramp of men,
The foot were twenty thousand, and the horse were thousands ten;
She saw their glittering armor, and their banners floating free,
And knew the angel prophecy should then accomplished be.

Herself in knightly armor clad, rode at the army's head,
And towards ill-fated Orleans' walls her mail-clad warriors led,
With sacred vivats long and loud—she knew the signal well—
"God save his chosen country, France, and God save La Pucelle."

As onward still that fearful cry before them cleared the way;
Victorious marching through the gates, it held their foes at bay;
And ever to their quaking hearts it sounded like a knell—
"God save his chosen country, France, and God save La Pucelle."

The flower of England's chivalry, which never knew defeat,
Before the terror of that name in foul disgrace retreat;
Back, back from Orleans' crumbling walls, in headlong haste they go,
As melts before the noonday sun, the April morning snow.

Right on to Rheims the godlike maid holds her victorious way,
Nor high walled towns nor hostile troops her conquering march can stay;
There crowns the rightful king of France, and thus the prophecy
Fulfills, mid streets which swim with gore, and shouts of victory.

* St. Margaret was considered the guardian angel of this part of France.

IV.

Hark! gates on rusted hinges swinging,
  The maid from that bright vision woke,
With axes in the court yard ringing,
  Ere the first gray of morning broke.
Would that the dream had lasted ever—
  Dream of such sweet forgetfulness!
Would that the fancy life had never
  Changed to its real wretchedness.
Before her, in that noisome cell,
  Stood priest with downcast eye and air,
With cowl and candle, book and bell,
  To save or damn her soul by prayer.
Then thus her foe, Joan addressing,
  The haughty prelate of Beauvais,
"Seek soon, fair maid, thy Maker's bless-
    ing,
  Thy flesh shall feed the flames to-day."
Sudden she starts, in anguish sighing,
  And all her woman's heart comes back,
With quivering flesh as she were dying
  A thousand deaths upon the rack;
"O Jesus!" thus in agony
  She called upon her Saviour's name—
"Jesus save, O, Father save me
  From death by the devouring flame.
Must like a wretched outcast, I,
  Shamed and disgraced by friend and foe,
In ignominious torments die,
  Nor rite of Christian burial know?"
'Twas but a moment, and the cloud
  Of grief and anguish flitted by,
As morning mists which sometimes shroud
  The sun of an unclouded sky.
Calmly she met her foes, and now
  A blessed spirit seemed to them
The light of thought upon her brow
  Was like an angel's diadem;
And from her flashing eye once more
  The fire of inspiration shone,
Clearly as when, in days of yore,
  Freedom's insulted flag alone
To glorious victory she bore.
One withering glance of scorn she cast
  On England's chivalry, who came
To see the sorceress fettered fast
  In ignominious torturing flame;
One prayerful look to heaven she turned;
  Turned once to earth her longing eye;
Then to her haughty foes, who burned
  For vengeance, gave this proud reply:

V.

Ha! gather round your noblest,
  Your bravest here draw nigh,
'Twill be a glorious sight to see
  A helpless maiden die!
Ho! sound a peal of trumpets,
  A strain of victory,
From your long night of craven fear
  This day shall set you free.
Thanks for your cruel kindness,
  Thanks for your deed of shame,
The honor of a martyr's death,
  The chariot of flame.
And if a woman's weakness
  Ye see me there betray—
If tortures from my lips force words
  My soul would never say—
O deem not ye have broken
  This heart in childish fear,
Nor brand with cowardice the name
  Which cowards dread to hear.
How well I dared your bravest,
  Proud Orleans' field shall tell,
Where that great bulwark of your troops,
  Lord Salisbury, fell;
Where sank mid the red slaughter,
  Your boasted strength, Glasdale,
And three score mail-clad knights before
  This single arm turned pale.
Talbot will long remember
  Jargeau and red Patay,
Where he, with thrice three thousand men,
  Fell prisoners in the fray.
Ay, torture, rack, or burn me,
  Do with me as you will,
I have defied your bravest oft,
  I do defy them still.
But think not ye shall ever
  Returning fortune see,
Nor that my death shall backward roll
  The tide of victory.

In vengeance for this deed, our knights
  Shall pay the debt they owe;
And English blood shall curdle thick
  Our rivers as they flow.
But worse than flight or gory fields,
  This coward act of shame,
Which gives the name Joan d'Arc
  To everlasting fame;
On England's proud escutcheon, this,
  The deepest, darkest stain,
Which ages of brave deeds shall seek
  To wash away in vain.

And now why do ye linger?
  Why trembling stand aside?
Why does the destined altar wait,
  While waiting stands the bride?
My country! O my country! take
  The sacrifice I bring;
And, for an humble maiden's life,
  Accept your lawful king.
My race of glory now is run;
  My country now is free;
And, like an angel messenger,
  Death welcome comes to me.

WOMAN.

"A fearful gift upon thy heart is laid,
Woman! a power to suffer and to love."

It is hardly to be supposed that so rich and interesting a subject needs to be specially commended to the attention of 'young men seeking an education,' who form a large majority of the readers of this Magazine; and in view of the fact that so much space has been devoted to her by the writers of every age, some may think that time but little better than wasted, which we shall occupy in setting forth our few thoughts on the true character and social position of Woman. Such can easily *pass on*.

Let it be premised in the outset, that it is no part of the writer's design to add one to the list, happily not *very* great, of rabid declaimers for "Woman's Rights"—a sect of *philogunists* somewhat peculiar to our day, and which, it is most ardently to be hoped, will pass away with it. We do not care to stand forth as a champion of the sex, to contend for 'rights' no sensible woman ever claimed to possess. We have no desire to arrogate again the factitious place awarded her by the enthusiasm of the age of chivalry; nor, on the other hand, can we willingly see, in the minds of any, a tendency, however slight, towards assigning her to the wretched degradation of heathenish orientalism.

Were we first to settle in our minds what is woman's true character, we might thence legitimately infer the position in society which Providence designed for her. This, however, is not the easiest of all possible tasks; since there are few subjects on which the opinions of mankind have been, and continue to be, so utterly at variance.

In looking at the record of her condition, we are at once struck with the great disparity of estimation in which she has been held in various times and countries. In one age she is degraded and despised; in the next, it may be, almost worshiped. With this people, even the thought of labor is too much for her to bear, and she is closely locked up in the harem, to pass the hours in decorating herself with tinsel finery, and in the practice of various feminine arts of enticement—the merest toy of her master. With another tribe, separated from the former but by a narrow river or a range of hills, she is doomed to perform all the out-door drudgery—to draw water, to plant, to reap, and thresh—the slave of her husband and owner. Occasionally these two are blended; as when we read of 'the beloved Andromache' now engaged at her embroidery, and, a little farther on, officiating as groom and taking care of her Hector's horses.

Not less noticeable is the tendency among writers on this subject to extremes either of praise or invective; both of which—being equally distant from truth—have served to mislead the unreflecting and to disgust the judicious, of 'the sex.' Now, some love-sick poet is taking cold under the window of his fair one, while striving to take her heart; and in touching strains swears she is neither more nor less than a genuine angel. Anon, some satiric Swift gravely pronounces her the connecting link between man and the monkey! Sage philosophers, both—'par nobile fratrum!' Is it presumption to surmise that these discrepant worthies may have taken their cue from the Son of Sirach? who wrote of old, "From garments cometh a moth, and from women wickedness." "All wickedness is but little to the wickedness of a woman." And again, in quite a different strain, "Blessed is the man that hath a virtuous wife, for the number of his days shall be doubled."

If we attempt, by a recurrence to history, to settle the question of woman's character and position, we find that during the lapse of ages, in the rise and fall of nations, there is no position she has not held, no character she has not exhibited. Indeed, if we look over the world at this hour, we may find examples still extant of every variety of condition which we read of in 'the chronicles of eld.'

The women of Turkey and Persia are still the ignorant and imprisoned slaves of their masters' caprice and passion: to-day petted and loaded with costly presents, to-morrow, perchance, murdered to gratify the whim of some newer favorite. The Chinese *lady* is still bought and sold in marriage, and hobbles about on tortured feet from day to day, learning 'manners' or tending silk-worms; and the Chinese *woman* still drags the plough through the hot rice-fields, with her infant at her back, while the lordly husband walks behind, and performs the laborious office of driver; reflecting, it may be, on the limitation the law has set to his precious rights, since he cannot divorce her but for "some dislike, incompatibility of temper, or too great loquacity."

Those admirers of antiquity who would have us go back to patriarchal times, and assume that woman must have had her appropriate place in those ages of barbarism, because, forsooth, she lived under a Theocracy, are invited to answer this question: If we must learn from the Jews to consider females as property, and employ them in the grinding of corn, tending flocks, and drawing water; shall we not also, with equal propriety, adopt from them our code of politeness, and imitate the shepherds of Midian, who drove away the seven princess-daughters of Jethro from the well at which they were watering the flocks of their father? It is to be feared that in the process of less than five centuries of such primitive simplicity, the rulers of the land, if emulous at all of the fame of the wisest of kings, would imitate him rather in the number of his wives, than in the acquisition of 'all the wisdom of Solomon.' To supply the increased demand, the old Babylonian practice might perhaps be revived, of selling young women in marriage at auction to the highest bidder; but it is to be doubted whether a genuine, calculating Yankee, however antiquated his notions, would so far forget his nature as to restore that part of the custom which distributed the price of the beautiful in dowries for the ugly.

We will cite a few of the instances, in which no period has been deficient, where woman has left the sphere that nature and reason alike assign to her, and exercised the prerogatives of the sterner sex.

In the earliest ages, Greek women for a time voted in the public assemblies of the nation.

Heliogabalus made his mother and grandmother colleagues on the throne, and placed them at the head of a female senate, which is said to have legislated extensively on the 'feminine mysteries of dress and fashion.'

To say nothing of the warring Amazons, so famous in story, but of so doubtful existence; or of the fair and frail queen of France, who commanded, in the wars of the holy land, the "regiment of the boots of gold;" the world has seen more than one counterpart to Semiramis and Zenobia, to Artemisia and Joan of Arc; and many a battle has numbered in its ranks female soldiers, not a few of whom have been distinguished for deeds of manly bravery, both by sea and land.

Even in England, it has been decided by law that an unmarried woman having a freehold might vote for members of Parliament; and one lady, at least, is recorded as having returned two members. English ladies, too, have been keepers of prisons and governors of houses of correction, and have repeatedly held the offices of champion, grand-chamberlain, and clerk of the Court of King's Bench. The Countess of Pembroke was sheriff of Westmoreland, and exercised her office in person, sitting on the bench of judges. The Duchesses of Gordon and Devonshire took active and conspicuous parts in the Pitt and Fox controversy, and kissed, bribed, and harrangued the voters in public. Of female sovereigns, the world has seen an abundance, and of course will continue to see them, so long as hereditary governments exist.

Now to form an opinion of woman from such specimens as these, would be about as sound philosophy as to judge of the general female character near the court of Charles the Second, from that of the intelligent and virtuous Lady Russell.

It is the uniform lesson of the past, that the character and condition of woman have always closely corresponded to those of the other sex. Where mankind has been most savage, ignorant, and vicious, woman has been treated with most dishonor and contempt; and in proportion to the advance of civilization, enlightenment, and virtue, has been her elevation in the scale of being and in the estimation of man. It is not to be laid to the charge of the sex, if we do not find woman exhibiting the holiest and purest affections in those eastern climes, where her first acquaintance with the partner of her life is formed after having been purchased without her consent, and is in name a wife, but in reality a slave. We are not to wonder, if we see no brilliant displays of female intellect in those lands where all mental culture is discouraged, esteemed disgraceful, and confined to the vilest of her sex. We are not to look for eminent virtue, during the reign of a licentious monarch, and within the corrupting influence of his profligate court: and the few exceptions there will always be, in either sex, to the general character of such an age, shine brighter from the surrounding gloom. They falsely judge, too, who look to find the perfection of female character in the ranks of the most wealthy. They forget that a superficial and showy education commonly keeps pace with luxurious habits, and that while no course of training is so poorly adapted to bring out the real character, none is more sure to crush and destroy all those qualities which make woman lovely, than the so called *accomplishments* of the gay and frivolous circles of fashion.

But to obtain a correct view of the female character, we should study it as developed where the Christian religion exerts its appropriate influence on her mind and heart, and on society at large. It would be easy to show, what few now deny, that the sex owes more of its present elevation to this cause, than to all others combined. The luxurious character of the Roman women at the introduction of Christianity into that city, is matter of history. They were so given up to pleasure, as openly to worship, in a temple built to her honor, the image of Voluptas, treading Virtue under her feet. It is also a matter of history, that, as the leaven of Christianity penetrated this mass of sensuality, the native gentleness and love of the sex began to show itself, and her character was soon transformed. Now she was seen, with true female benevolence and sympathy, seeking the miserable and suffering in their huts of poverty, and, as a kind and gentle nurse, entering the cells of disease and wretchedness. That spirit has been in continual progress to this day. The general impulse given by Christianity to mind at large, has brought her intellect into active exercise, and shown that she *has* a mind, Mahomet to the contrary notwithstanding. We will not stop to discuss the question whether her intellect is equal to that of the other sex. Suffice it to say, it has not precisely the *same* characteristics; and though women in general may be averse to profound speculation, yet the influence of a De Stael's vigorous understanding still remains to show that she, at least, was capable of appreciating the great principles of political science. The numerous volumes of 'the inventive de Genlis,' the pathetic tales of Madame Cottin, and the letters of 'the lively and graceful Montagu,' still find readers in their own and other lands. Who has not dwelt, with thrilling interest, on the pages of Mrs. Hemans—and may we not couple with her name our own Mrs. Sigourney?—both poets of the heart! Indeed, it is as a poet that woman must ever excel in literature. Her natural delicacy, ingenuity, imagination, and taste; her habits of close observation; her keen susceptibility, originally highly refined, and made more so by freedom from that rude contact with the out-door world which so dulls the finer qualities of man's mind; all these combine with woman's intense and undying affections to constitute her a poet. While qualities like these go to form such a character as Gertrude Van der Wart, they also enable such an one as Mrs. Hemans to set forth that character, in strains that reach the coldest heart. Were not a woman the writer of that touching poem of 'Gertrude,' it had not contained these lines:

> "Hath the world aught for me to fear,
> When death is on thy brow?
> The world! what means it?—*mine is here;*
> I will not leave thee now!"

But, after all, it is not as a *writer* alone, of whatever order, that woman best fulfills her mission. We believe that Nature, Reason, and Revelation, all unite in declaring her true station to be the one she now occupies in the hearts of the intelligent portion of the American people—that of the pure, honored, intellectual companion and confidential friend of man. Dependent on him she must, from her inferior strength, necessarily be; but it is only so far as every virtuous female loves to lean, for kind and cheerful protection and support: and they unite in that true and perfect companionship which gives to each a "complete freedom in their places, without a restless desire to go out of them." De Tocqueville has said, "There is no country where woman has so much freedom and so much influence as the wives, sisters, and daughters of America; no country where they have so perfectly the respect, esteem, and confidence of the other sex." May it ever be said of them!

> "Blest with such sweet and loved companionship,
> Man wanders not to seek for happiness."

It is this delightful interchange of confidence and affection, which renders life desirable. It is this which blunts the edge of sorrow, and adds a double charm to every joy.

Themistocles was wont to say, "My little boy governs Athens, for he rules his mother, and she rules me." What share the wives, sisters, and daughters of our great men have in the government of our country, is not for the uninitiated to know. We would ask for no Aspasia at the capitol; but may the time never come, when woman's silent and unobtrusive influence shall cease to be felt there!

Let them show their love for that religion to which they owe so much, by obeying its blessed precepts; and, careless of the abuse of some few misguided zealots, let them abide in the sphere of duty the Scriptures so clearly mark out for them: and where shall we find a lovelier picture of woman in her various stations, than that presented in the Bible? Let them still preside over the household; cheer, with their happy smiles and voices, the domestic fireside, and train to purity, patriotism, and religion, the youthful sons and daughters of the republic. Let the world continue to witness the depth of woman's affection, and the strength of her virtue, in the faithful discharge of her duties as a sister, a daughter, a wife, or mother. Let them still be man's solace in hours of sorrow and trial, and minister consolation at the bedside of the sick and dying. May the poor and suffering continue to welcome their visits of active benevolence, and the tear of gratitude still fall at the remembrance of their deeds of heavenly charity.

The names of our great *men* are wafted on every gale over the earth. Let them be known in all the world, to the end of time! Yet it will be long ere one of them shall gain a richer tribute of respect, than was bestowed upon a *woman's* memory, when a grateful nation inscribed on her simple, but priceless monument, "MARY, THE MOTHER OF WASHINGTON!"

CL.

LOOSE LEAVES FROM AN OLD PORT-FOLIO.

BY A QUIET MAN.

NO. I.

READER: I bespeak your kind indulgence. Being a modest personage and fond of retirement, I seldom appear before the world, though not unfrequently have I been extremely curious to know what others would think of my crude conceits and ill-digested vagaries. With but a moderate capacity for writing, I have, nevertheless, often been affected with the *cacoethes scribendi*, and in an old port-folio have accumulated a huge mass of papers, which I have never ventured to exhibit. The truth is, I fear the critic, that hideous green-eyed monster, and, mimosa-like, have ever shrunk away from his rude touch. If there are such things as evil spirits in the world, the critic certainly must be one of them; a kind of horrible ogre, tainting with his poisonous breath all that is good and beautiful. The 'untoward fate' of poor Keats, has caused many a weak authorling like myself to prefer obscurity and insignificance, to all the pleasures which fame and notoriety could bring, attended as they might be with the cruel shafts of the malicious critic. Still, I have always been anxious to see how my little weaknesses would look in print, and now with a fluttering heart I suffer a few loose leaves to be presented to the public eye. Like all the rest of the world, I have wished to build up for myself a reputation, and to inscribe my name on the records of the great, not caring to have on my tombstone the expressive epitaph, "*here lies one, whose name was writ in water.*"

In my room, while the hoarse wind is howling round my casement, and the big drops pattering against the window, with a blazing fire of anthracite before me, here I sit, reader, endeavoring to catch a few fleeting, misty conceptions and idealities—brain-children of mine, that are hovering somewhere in the region of fancy—and to give them shape and embodiment for thine own particular edification. It is no easy matter to do this. Unwritten ideas are airy things, wonderfully apt to evaporate. And then the dress in which we were to clothe them, is seldom so gaudy and rich as our imagination had pictured it. Very few can give their reveries and fancies the elegant array that they had intended. The expressions, that before glowed with feeling and thought, often lose their force; the fine arrangement of the words, and the sweet cadence of the sentences, are changed into a senseless jargon; and the figures and images with which the brain was filled, appear on paper but tawdry embellishments, without beauty or grace.

In regard to style, the notions that are prevalent in college, are, for the most part, false and ridiculous. They are not such, I apprehend, as would pass current with the world at large. We seem to have a higher admiration of sound than sense. The thought and the sentiment are less regarded than the jingle of the words. To introduce an apt quotation, to lug in strange words and phrases, to express a flowing period and a high-sounding sentence, seem to form among us the acme of good composition. The student too often leaves the practical for the fanciful, and wraps himself up in mist and moonshine. To my mind there is nothing more disagreeable than to see a writer affect a brilliant imagination and great depth of thought, when he has no genius to aid him in the effort. His metaphors and tinseled language may dazzle, but will not convince; his fustian style will be stiff, unnatural, and ineffective, and expose him to ridicule and contempt. These faults are conspicuous in college literature, and call loudly for attention and reform.

Speaking of literature, upon what subject in the wide world is there more rant and insipidity displayed, than upon this? It is a kind of universal theme, to which, in case of necessity, all can resort. The youth and prospects of our own literature—the noble materials we have for its ground-work—the awful necessity of preserving its nationality—the encouragement of native authors and the attacks and dreadful inroads made by foreigners, the Fidlers, the Halls, the Trollopes, *et id omne genus*—these are topics upon which every tyro, as soon as he can handle the pen, is ready to give us his views and instructions. He loads himself with a heavy charge, and takes deadly aim at the heart of those savages, the Foreign Reviewers. Like a valiant Don Quixote, he fights against this foul oppression, and denies the want of originality and fertility of invention among our men of letters; he can prate, too, of poets and poetry—muses and inspirations, lyres and lutes. Pegasus, Parnassus, and Hippocrene are as familiar as household words. Indeed, he harps upon every idea connected with literature, until the whole subject has become stale and threadbare.

What a multitude at the present day are devoting their attention to literature? The market is glutted. Every one who can make any pretension to literary attainment, from the proud virtuoso to the poor and humble student, is wielding his pen with unwonted assiduity, and spreading the result before the public. The great question seems tc be, not how well, but how much. The press is kept in operatior night and day; every ship that arrives is loaded down with Novels and Romances, Sketches and Poems, Histories and Biographies, and with all the froth and trash of foreign countries. Writers, that are remarkable only for great intellectual inanity and stolidity, are incessantly engaged in endeavoring to satisfy the demand of the public which, like the horse-leech, is crying, Give, give. But how few of al these writers—and their name is legion—will ever acquire a lasting reputation! How few, indeed, ever exhibit any real excellence! Even were they capable of producing works that would endure, they write with too much haste and carelessness to be successful. Book-making has degenerated into a mere profession. Selfish and sordid men, without talent or genius, now turn their attention to literature, and senc forth their productions, influenced solely by cupidity or avarice. Bu their works are ephemeral; the foam of the sea will endure as long They do not write for posterity, and it will be by the merest chance that their names will be known to a future age.

Aside from the want of encouragement and patronage, there are some reasons which might well discourage the student from devoting his life to the pursuit of letters. The harpies of criticism are always ready to destroy the reputation of the author. Whenever he presents a work to the public, they spring up from all the highways and byways of life,

> "et magnis quatiunt clangoribus alas:
> Diripiuntque dapis, contactuque omnia fœdant
> Immundo."

Even if the work possesses merit, it does not receive the credit i deserves, while its faults are detected and magnified with a louc flourish of trumpets. As some one has truly remarked, "the pen is a weapon that may wound to distant ages: both policy and humanity require it to be wielded with caution." It is indeed a weapon too dangerous for foolish and weak-minded men to play with; yet the little critikin exalts himself, and puffed with pride and arrogance, he slashes about to the right and left with great indifference, transmuting silly rhymes into the outpourings of a poetic soul, and converting the man of genius into a stupid plodder. The sensitive mind is chilled and discouraged by his coarse and unfeeling mockery, and the soul that possesses energies and sympathies too deep for immediate development, is crushed ere it can arrive at full maturity. Like the worm in the bud, the critic oftentimes destroys those silken folds, that else would have formed a flower of rich luxuriance and beauty. His legitimate business is to direct public taste; to act the part of an interpreter between the inspired and uninspired; to expose the faults and defects of an author, and to bring out his merits and beauties in brighter relief yet of those who profess to be critics, so few understand their duties that in general far more injury than benefit is done to the interests of literature.

Still there are few, I imagine, who have been frightened by the critic from making literature their profession. The man of true ambition will not be deterred by the mere detractor; he is willing to await the verdict of posterity.* In all ages, even in the wildest times, authors have found sufficient reasons for devoting their lives and energies to the cultivation of letters, and have shown that they have regarded it as a noble pursuit. When poverty frowned, and darkness enveloped them, when they saw in the future,

"Neglect and grinning Scorn and Want combined,"

they have clung to their profession, unaided by the kind offices of friends, uncheered by the sympathies and encouragements of the multitude. The toil and suffering, the drudgery and privation that they have endured, the prison, the rack, and the poisoned chalice, with which the world has rewarded them, furnish a revolting chapter in the history of the human race. "Cherishing, it may be, the loftiest thoughts, and clogged with the meanest wants; of pure and holy purposes, yet ever driven from the straight path by the pressure of necessity or the impulse of passion, thirsting for glory, and frequently in want of daily bread; cramped and foiled in his most strenuous exertions; dissatisfied with his best performances, disgusted with his fortune, this Man of Letters too often spends his weary days in conflict with obscure misery; the victim at once of tyranny or farce; the last forlorn outpost in the war of Mind against Matter." Literary men do not partake of nectar and ambrosia, nor tread upon a carpet of roses. Some are consumed by the ardor of their own genius, before their tasks are finished, and when their minds are expanding with strength and beauty. Tasso languished in a madman's cell, a victim to the terrors of his imagination; Cowper was crazed and stricken down by grim melancholy; Byron, with his brain tortured into a state of feverish excitement by the slanders of the reviewers, lived estranged from his country, his passions changed into a fountain of bitterness, and all the nobler feelings of his nature converted into misanthropy and hate. Chatterton, too, 'the marvelous boy,' chilled by neglect, bade adieu to toil, penury, and want, and turning away from the world, sought repose in death; and, as Coleridge says:

"Spenser, gentlest bard divine,
Beneath chill Disappointment's shade,
His weary limbs in lonely anguish laid.

* *Tickler.* I care not a single curse for all the criticism that was ever canted or decanted or recanted. Neither does the world. The world takes a poet as it finds him, and seats him accordingly above or below the salt. The world is as obstinate as a million of mules, and will not turn its head on one side or another for all the shouting of the critical population that was ever shouted. Well then—appeal to posterity and be hanged to you—and posterity will affirm the judgment with costs.—*Noctes Ambrosianae.*

> And o'er her darling dead,
> Pity, hopeless, hung her head,
> While, "'mid the pelting of that merciless storm,'
> Sunk to the cold earth, Otway's famished form."

Milton was harassed by a miserable life. Sick, blind, and persecuted, among dangers and troubles, and cheered only by the music of his thoughts, the old man struggled on, and sung his immortal song. Did Homer live in luxury? Poor and a wanderer, with clouds and darkness around him, he contended in wild warfare for the "Amreeta-cup of immortality." Like a stray leaf from some distant clime, his name has floated down to our day, while multitudes of the great and noble are forgotten. This was his exceeding great reward. And for this it is, that authors have made literature their profession, exchanging the palace for the dungeon, ease and enjoyment for the stake and the torture, luxury and pleasure for hunger and nakedness. They labored from no sordid motive. They wrote not merely for their own age, but for posterity. Their words were to go forth and find a resting place in the hearts of men of all time. They were to speak, and a mighty audience would listen. Their voices were to have a wider and deeper influence than that of the greatest orator that ever woke the drowsy echoes of a legislative hall by his eloquence.

Such thoughts ever have been and ever will be sufficient to induce the man of genius to embrace the uncertain fortunes of an author's life, even when scarcely able to wring from his hoarded means the pittance necessary to give him life and strength. We often hear it said, that genius will remain unknown to fame, 'mute and inglorious,' unless some favorable opportunity shall offer for its development. But there is reason to doubt the truth of this observation. Its restless powers are not so easily kept in obscurity. They often flash out in spite of all opposition. Burns was a mere farmer's boy, and dwelt amid the rugged hills of Scotland, yet he has sent forth his little snatches of song, "dew-drops of celestial melody," and shown that he possessed a high order of poetic genius. This remark to be sure does not agree with the beautiful lines of Wordsworth's, often quoted, and which, in conclusion, I will quote again:

> "O, many are the noble souls that are sown
> By Nature; men endowed with highest gifts,
> The vision sent, the faculty divine,
> Yet wanting the accomplishment of verse.
> Not having e'er, as life advanced, been led
> By circumstance to take unto the height
> The measure of themselves, these favored beings,
> All but a scattered few, live out their time,
> Husbanding that which they possess within,
> And go to the grave unthought of. Strongest minds
> Are often those of whom the noisy world
> Hears least."

THAT GOLDEN TIME—IT COMETH NOT AGAIN.

"Think oft, ye brethren,
Think of the gladness of our youthful prime,
It cometh not again—that golden time." COMMER'S BOOK.

THAT golden time! When childhood's happy dream
Of life's existence bathing every part
In rainbow hues, burst like a joyous gleam
Of April sunshine on the enraptur'd heart;
When golden clouds, gay birds, and blooming flowers,
All earth below, the bright blue sky above,
A magic charm lent to the passing hours,
And filled the soul with melody of love.
Oft think, ye brethren, that glad season o'er,
It cometh to the care-worn heart no more.

But brighter far, days of our youthful prime!
In glorious visions speaking to the eye;
The spirit-dream of early love, the time
Of glowing hopes, and aspirations high.
O how the bounding spirit long'd to break
The galling chains which fettered it to earth,
In upward flight its eagle pinions shake,
And solve the mystery of its heavenly birth!
These visions come not now. Yet, brethren, still
Their mem'ries in our 'heart of hearts' shall be
Enshrined forever, and shall often thrill
The soul with pure and holy ecstasy.
Think of the gladness of our youthful prime,
It cometh not again—that golden time.

MNEMEANA.

MESSRS. EDITORS:—A few evenings ago, I sat by my window, and read 'The Pleasures of Memory' till the daylight faded so that I could no longer discern the words. I closed the book with a sigh, laid it on the table, and returned to my seat, to meditate upon what I had been perusing; and from thinking of the poetry, I very naturally fell to dreaming over my own recollections and observations. As the smoke from my pipe curled around my head, old familiar faces peered at me through it, and almost forgotten scenes and adventures came back again, even as I had once known them. I could see a little village with its white houses, the brook that watered its meadows, the green hills and the forests, and then forms well-known, aye, and well-beloved too, appeared, and then—my pipe went out. My reverie was ended, but I sat still and planned a scheme. I determined to write an article for the Yale Literary Magazine! I had never dreamed of such a thing before, and some difficulty might have been apprehended in the collecting of materials; but I found in the reveries, in which I am wont to indulge, an inexhaustible mine of—nonsense, perhaps. It was necessary to choose a title, and after alternately selecting and rejecting some hundreds, I pitched upon MNEMEANA, as best conveying the idea of my intentions to the mind of the reader.*

I have been, and now am, both by inclination and practice, a man of sloth—one of that class of individuals, who prefer sitting still and gazing desperately at nothing, to any other earthly enjoyment. My teachers used to tell me that I should always be a "mere blot upon the surface of creation." Books in general are to me a bore; I read the Pleasures of Memory, because a dear friend gave it to me, and I feel a sort of obligation to do so; but as for the empire of letters, I would not give a farthing to be monarch of the whole; your book-learned men are often terrible pedants. True, I have read a little here and there, but it has been at random, as the whim of the moment prompted me to open a volume, hurry through a dozen lines, and throw it down again. Anything connected in the way of reading, irks me. I could never have the patience to peruse five pages of the most interesting novel under the sun; and as for poetry or history, I know as little of them as of the climate of the moon. Short extracts please me; passages of Jean Paul afford some amusement; the beauties of Shakspeare are agreeable; but dictionaries are my favorite works, and I consider Johnson and Webster my greatest benefactors.

You ask me—How then can you sit down before a foolscap sheet, with the faintest expectations of ever writing a page of it? Why, my good Editors, I *have no* such expectation; but I am becoming ashamed of sheer do-nothingness, and shall hereafter note down some of the more remarkable ideas which cross my mind, during my fits of reverie; and if I ever get enough, ask some kind friend to copy them out, and send the sheets to your Magazine. Perhaps you consider this rather hazardous business, as there may be some doubt of their gaining admission to your pages. Well, I don't care a straw whether they gain admission or not: *I* shall not suffer by it; your readers may. You think me egotistical: No! I am only an ignoramus. Everybody has his own portion of egotism, and takes more interest in himself than in any other being. Just so with me; γνωθι σέαυτον.

Shooting is rare sport, and, as somebody says, 'I think myself considerable shakes of a shot.' I remember distinctly the first all-day's excursion that I ever took. I was a mere boy, my gun, an old single-barreled fowling-piece, my dog a favorite Newfoundland, that was about as well acquainted with the science of sporting as with logic, and

* μνημη, memory.

might have mistaken a partridge for a peacock. I arose at daylight, and started for the distant pine woods. The frost was white upon the grass and the fences, and, at every step I took, crackled like dry leaves under my feet. Triton, my dog, leaped and whined, and tossed every loose object into the air, in very intensity of mirthfulness. In somewhat less than an hour, I had reached the summit of a high hill, some miles to the west of my home, and there I stopped for a few moments to rest and to look back. Heavens and earth, what a prospect! Immediately below me, and far, far on to the eastward, the valleys are filled with the thick night-mists, which, in the distance, resemble a mighty lake. But the tops of the hills, rocky, woody, or covered with green verdure, rise above the surface of the seeming waters, and the wide expanse appears studded with innumerable fairy islands. And yonder, see, the square tower of the church and the tapering spire of the meeting-house are also visible, and the golden dawn bathes the whole in a splendor more than earthly! The glorious lustre of that eastern sky tells us that Phœbus himself is coming to view the scene; and already the mountain on our right has its summit gilded with his earliest rays. But why this commotion in the vapory sea below us? It heaves and rolls as if a mighty wind were stirring its very depths, and yet not a breath rustles the forest leaf by our side. Again, vast chasms seem opening; and now, as the sun rises in full glory over the horizon, behold! how the huge wreaths twist, and roll, and writhe upward toward the hill-tops; the valleys are empty; we can see no more, for the mists are upon us and around us, yet but for a moment; they are gone, and lo! yonder is the smiling village; the meadows, the corn-fields, the swamps, the brooks—all visible in the sunlight, and there, slowly disappearing, are a few fleecy clouds! Has not the scene its moral?

I turned and resumed my journey. Over hills, through woods and valleys, and across many a purling brook, I went; but not a bird was to be found. The sun rose higher and higher, and its heat grew almost intense, as, weary and perspiring at every pore, I pursued my unprofitable course. I reached, at length, a grove of pine-trees, and, penetrating the cool retreat, threw myself upon the ground. A slight breeze had sprung up, and it played across my forehead, soft as the breath of affection. And how strangely it sounded through the dark branches above! Low and mournfully—no, not mournfully, but with a kind of sweet, melancholy, gentle noise—the pine forest sighed to that autumn wind. As I laid my head almost to the earth, and looked out upon the thick shade, I could see the yellow leaves of the oak, the chesnut, and the elm, falling incessantly, and I thought that the evergreens were grieving because a few more frosts and storms would leave them alone in their dark foliage. Hark! how they blend together—the airy monotones, the murmur of a rivulet in the woods, the tapping of a solitary woodpecker in the distance, and the far, far-off cooing of the wild-dove. And then, forms wildly beautiful seemed to flit before me—the scenery around faded from my sight—there was a noise like the rustling of spirits' pinions, and—I slept.

* * * * * * *

—— I had wings. Up, up, toward the blue sky I flew, and away through the boundless realms of air. I felt an indefinable sensation of liberty—of perfect freedom. I looked down : how contemptible the earth !—a great, clumsy, rough lump of dirt, with here and there a shining spot upon it, which served to heighten the ugliness of the rest. I lowered my flight, and drew nearer. Now, mountains and cities began to appear, and I could distinguish the roar of the ocean ; still lower, and the forms of men were visible. Ho ! yonder is a battle-field, and upon it, little, tiny specks are rushing to and fro, and a faint vapor overshadows the whole—the smoke of gunpowder, no doubt—and cannons are roaring there, and soldiers shouting, shrieking, and moaning ; but hither the sounds come not, and you only discern a strip of earth, a mist, and a dark spot, which is——armies. Is it Arbela, Pharsalia, or Waterloo ? Bah ! it may be either or all, we care not. Back again, ad astra. Zounds ! rather cool up here—absolutely freezing. The middle of an iceberg would be a luxury just now ; really, I am getting faintish ; my wings refuse to move ; horror ! I am falling—down—down—right into the Arctic ocean.

* * * * * * *

What a sneeze ! Well, thank Heaven, I am awake and alive, instead of being drowned under the Polar circle. Blow—howl—roar—a regular autumnal storm is rising. Half the sky already is covered with the wintry-looking clouds, and the air seems alive with yellow leaves which the wind has detached from their frail stems, and is scattering abroad in all directions. But hark ! these old pines ; the gentle sighing has ceased, and the dark branches are tossing and creaking and groaning in anticipation of the coming tempest. A pause—then a low murmur, growing louder and louder, till it becomes a perfect roar. I feel the spirit of mad, old Lear :—

> " Blow, winds, and crack your cheeks ! rage ! blow !"

Out from the shelter into the open air: yonder, fly a number of cawing crows. How the storm carries them up, down, and away, shrieking and calling to each other ; the tempest-demons !

Plash ! a huge drop of rain, cold as ice, on my forehead—three miles from home—catch me falling asleep again in the woods ! Triton, you have a most disconsolate look ; but cheer up, dog ! And now for the seven-league boots, and we'll soon be safe at the supper-table. I got home, wet to the skin, and with an incipient cold, that tormented me for a month.

I remember her when she was but twelve years old. At that early age she was very beautiful, and as gentle and affectionate as her own pet dove. She seemed to live in an atmosphere of kindly feeling ; her sympathies extended to every thing around ; she loved her parents and her friends with an intensity and depth which few could penetrate ; but she loved the brute creation about her also, and the birds, the trees, and the flowers, and she would talk to them as if she thought they could understand her. She used sometimes to sit on a greensward bank, by the side of her father's house, with a heap of spring-flowers in her lap, and look them over and arrange them, all the while singing in a low, sweet tone, which made the listener stop and think of other worlds than this. When I saw her thus, I could have fallen down and worshiped her, for she appeared to me no less than an angel from heaven. And wonderful, indeed, for one so young, was her knowledge of books. No one could tell what it was that first excited in her mind the love of reading; but so it was, and often would she sit apart from her play-mates, with no other companion than a volume of poems, or perchance some well-known history of ancient or feudal times. Yet she was never morose or ill-tempered, and when engaged in childish sports with those of her own age, she was the gayest of the gay. Neither did she neglect her household duties, for her parents were poor; but her mother blessed her, because she was ever ready to leave her flowers, her companions, and even her books, to assist in domestic occupations.

Years rolled on, and her nineteenth summer came. She was betrothed to a young man of her own village—one apparently every way worthy of her, with a noble face and figure, and a naturally powerful mind, cultivated by a liberal education. And she loved him. Oh! none can guess the full intensity of that love; it was her all in all, her life, her very being. They were married. A twelve-month past away, and the young lover had become a cold and careless husband. Yet she bore it well, not a murmur escaped her lips, and none but those who marked her sunken cheek and swollen eyes, dreamed of any thing wrong. Afterward came vice and open ill-treatment—still the young wife complained not, and to *him* her face ever wore the same sweet smile, though she knew but too well that her heart was breaking.

At last he came home, half intoxicated, and brought into HER presence a strange woman, his companion in sin. It was too much for human nature to bear. The injured, slighted wife, arose and with tearless eye, but a face white as death, and quivering lips, slowly prepared to depart from the mansion. "Where are you going?" said he, roughly. "Home!" was the faint, but firm reply. "No, by ——!" he exclaimed, seizing her arm. She shrunk back instinctively, a low moan escaped her lips, and she fell dead at his feet!

Reader! compare not this fragment with the tales of fiction somewhat similar, perhaps, that you may have seen, for THIS IS TRUE.

A scene from my window, taken as exactly as my descriptive powers will permit. Immediately opposite, a store; no sign out, but a tub of quinces, a pile of grindstones, and a fat man with a red nose standing before. That man is a perfect torment to me. I spring from my bed in the morning, rush to the window, and there he stands, his nose all a-glow, his hands in his pockets, and himself gazing around with an air of self-complacent abstraction, which tells as plain as daylight, of bank stock and real estate. After dinner he is there again, a cigar in his mouth, but otherwise just as before, and now and then nodding familiarly to some passing acquaintance. Now of all things I detest a cigar. I try to smoke one, but it excoriates my lips, burns my tongue, sets my eyes a-running and my nose a-tingling, and ends in making me sick. Why cannot people use pipes? Clay isn't juicy—the fragrant vapory cools, and when puffed from the mouth curls about the head in such magnificent snowy and violet wreaths. But to my description. I live on a corner, and as I look out, I see three different roads branching off into the country. Afar in the distance are the blue mountains, no, not blue, for the autumnal frosts have fallen upon them, and they are as many-hued as the rainbow. Nearer, white houses, trees, a liberty pole, and immediately before me, in the widening street, horses, oxen, coal carts, lumber wagons, merchants, farmers, mechanics, dogs. But softly, who is this coming along the opposite sidewalk? A FRESHMAN. Mark him well, that dress, it was the chef d'œuvre of the village tailor, and his fond father intended it only for Sunday wear, but the student hath got into a new world now, and already doth that coat exhibit marks of every-day use. Four years of college life before him, and O! how long, how insupportably long do they seem in the prospect. But there are high thoughts in that young breast; though perhaps the bashful tyro would hardly acknowledge them even to his own soul. A long life, health, a happy family circle, reputation, fame! all these gleam before him, sometimes in the daily walk, but most often in the silent, solitary hours of night. May his most ardent wishes be gratified! yet let him not forget that the brightest day hath its clouds, the clearest fountain is sometimes turbid, the fairest blossom sometimes blasted. Let him not trust to the voice that tells him hard study is foolishness, for IT IS NOT; let him not think he can select a better path to the temple of knowledge than that which gray-haired experience has pointed out, for HE CANNOT; let him not hope that he will enter upon the duties of life as readily or as easily, even though he spend these four years in the pursuit of the gratifications and pleasures of the passing hour, for HE WILL NOT. Though we mourn over it never so bitterly in after years, the spring-time of youth once gone, is gone forever.

LITERARY NOTICES.

WARREN'S GEOGRAPHY. A systematic view of Geography; by William Warren. Portland, Me., William Hyde.

THE third edition of this work is upon our table. The author appears to be a man desirous of extending the sphere of useful knowledge as much as possible, by rendering access to it so easy that all may enter. Himself a teacher, and of established reputation, we might expect that he would be especially qualified for the task he has undertaken. The manner in which he has accomplished this work, proves that he is so. The first thing that arrested our attention upon opening the book, was its simplicity and clearness. The whole is arranged according to a uniform system, which renders it plain to the comprehension of the learner, and fixes the lessons in his memory. The superfluous matter with which the old books of geography were loaded, is cast off entirely in Mr. Warren's work, and the definite facts that are really important, are given with accuracy and fidelity. The Atlas contains the latest discoveries, and is arranged on a plan, we believe, altogether new.

It cannot be expected that in our limited space that we can give even a synopsis of Mr. Warner's book; but after having carefully examined it, we would cheerfully recommend it to all, to parents, schoolmasters, and children alike.

THE RELIGIOUS AND LITERARY GEM.—The September No. of this Magazine has been for some time on our table. It is a union of the "Gem" and "Lady's Pearl," and appears to be ably conducted. Several of the articles are selected from other periodicals, and in the selection the author has evinced much discrimination. It contains a beautiful engraving of the "Sisters of Bethany." The work deserves support, and we presume it will obtain it, since it numbers among its contributors such writers as Mrs. Sigourney, Mrs. Orne, J. G. Whittier, William B. Tappan, and others of well known literary reputation. Its typographical execution is creditable to the publisher. It is edited by Rev. C. W. Dennison. (Boston: Joseph H. Sears, 32 Cornhill.)

The Dartmouth for September, though late, was received with pleasure. It has entered upon its fifth volume in a new dress, with new type, and containing, as they assure us, one fifth more matter than any preceding number. We congratulate them on its improved appearance. We are unable to learn their terms; but surely, whatever it may cost, when such exertions are made to elevate the character of this organ of their literary taste and attainments, there can be no one of their number so pitifully mean, as to refuse to give it his earnest and hearty support.

The Nassau Monthly for September is welcomed. Its character for spirit, originality, and variety, is fully sustained. Since the appearance of the August Number, we have regarded it with great affection, and always press it to our editorial heart with peculiarly pleasing emotions. *Macte virtute!*

*** The Ladies' Companion, Eclectic, and other periodicals, lie on our table, but we have no room to notice them in this number.

EDITORS' TABLE.

READER, didst ever spend a vacation in the City of Elms? No? Then we do assure thee, whether graduate or other, thou art far from having completed thy College education. We care not whether he can demonstrate a single proposition of his Euclid, or retains a mathematical principle in his memory—whether he can render a sentence of Latin or Greek—yet that student has not studied in vain, who can *live* those six mortal weeks in this goodly city.

He has the pleasing consciousness in his bosom that he has fulfilled that important command of the Apostle, "Let patience have her perfect work!" He has moreover the satisfactory assurance that he can never die of *ennui*.

To one who has witnessed the bustle and activity of the city during term time, it is almost impossible to convey an adequate idea of its appearance during vacation. Indeed, one can hardly persuade himself it is the same place—it seems rather like a city of the Tombs.

The sun does indeed rise in the morning, but by no means at the time at which we are wont to expect him at that season of the year. Very seldom did we see him up before seven or eight, and sometimes it was even ten o'clock in the morning before we saw any indications of his appearance. And then, too, in such a dull, plodding manner does he pursue his journey through the heavens, dispensing his light in a lifeless, mechanical sort of way, as if grudging you its enjoyment, that you really feel it a relief to have him again out of the way, and be left to your own uninterrupted *knightly* pursuits. The moon, too, it must be confessed, did sometimes shine; not, however, as "gentle Cynthia with radiance serene"—rather with a pale and sickly light, such as we might suppose would emanate from a monstrous green cheese revolving around our earth.

And then the magnificent forest trees, which make our city the pride of New England, the Queen of the Union, seem to have caught the general infection, and wave not their branches nor rustle their leaves at the touch of the summer breezes which play listlessly around them, but stand in mournful silence, as if they felt and sympathized in the general gloom which pervades the face of nature.

The streets, too—how deserted! how lifeless! The hum of business is hushed—the rattle of carriages is heard no more, save now and then some empty hack or dray moving lazily along in search of employment. Occasionally, perchance, you will see some honest country Jonathan, with his wagon full of 'Yankee notions,' which he has brought in to 'peddle,' driving through the streets with a vacant, wondering stare, as if he had missed the place of his destination, and at night, with downcast, puzzled look, plodding homeward with his unsaleable merchandise, his Yankee tact and shrewdness for once completely nonplussed.

We walk down Chapel—"what a change comes over the spirit of our dream!" Through no crowded thoroughfare are we now compelled to thread our way—no familiar faces meet our gaze. Rich silks and broadcloths, gaudy prints, glittering jewelry, imposing placards of new books, line the streets as usual, crying, "come and buy me," but in vain—no purchaser appears. Idle shopmen may be seen peering out from behind their counters with curious gaze at the solitary passer-by, or another more bold perchance standing in the door, whose earnest, entreating countenance seems to ask, "Shall I have the pleasure of showing you some goods to-day, sir?" The ladies, too, whose attractions give such life and animation to our splendid promenades during fine weather in term time, and make our city almost an earthly paradise, are seen no more after commencement until the beginning of another term. The Springs, Niagara, Nahant, or Rockaway, are enlivened by their smiles and their wit—a far more rational and sensible manner of spending their time, than by remaining in the city,

> ——— "to blush unseen,
> And waste their sweetness on the desert air."

But we forget the lonely, weary hours of the 'long vacation,' amid the joyous, hearty greetings of returning friends. Every countenance beams with pleasure—every pulse beats high with joy. Even the mighty elms awake from their long slumbers, tossing their giant arms to the Autumn winds, as they would welcome with a glorious "live thou Hoch!" familiar friends. But hush! even as we speak, a note of sorrow strikes upon the ear, a chill of sadness comes stealing o'er the heart. Instead of the accustomed tones of our College bell, to-day a knell calls us to the house of God; and amid the hushed silence of the thronging crowd, a coffin is borne up the Chapel aisle. One who but three years since left these honored halls with the most distinguished honors of his Alma Mater, who was yesterday discharging the duties of an officer of the Institution, lies there to-day in the cold embrace of death. No questions here do we ask, no praises add, while the 'heart is throbbing with its untold anguish,' for at such an hour would Eulogy herself be silent, as she reads upon the coffin lid the name of John B. Dwight.

> "Leaves have their time to fall,
> And flowers to wither at the north wind's breath,
> And stars to set—but all,
> Thou hast all seasons for thine own, oh! Death."

But to return—for we fear, kind reader, lest we should weary your patience in these discursive wanderings; 'therefore (as saith the limb of the law) we will come to the point at once, and immediately we will come to the point.'

We sat down for a few moments' gossip with our *patrons* respecting our—perhaps we should say *their* Magazine—the subject ever uppermost in our thoughts. We greet you to-day with the first number of our ninth volume, a new era in our history. We confess we feel an honest pride, when we look back upon the past and mark what has already been accomplished—when we look forward to the future and realize in fancy what we have good hopes shall yet be effected. Eight years through 'sunshine and through shade,' has 'Maga' nobly battled against the waves of contending fortune. Sometimes it has for a moment seemed she must strike her colors and go down, but again she has risen above all opposing obstacles, and to-day she stands on a firmer foundation than at any preceding time. She is fast laying aside the dress and appearance of childhood and youth, and already assuming an air of matronly grace and dignity. Even since the last appeared before you she has added one sixth to her fair proportions, whether with a corresponding increase in excellence and variety of matter, beauty and finish of execution, she will speak for herself. She is now the pioneer in College literature, in age and size far in advance of her competitors in sister institutions. How she compares with them in literary merit, it becomes not us to judge. While we would not speak of these accidental advantages in a boasting spirit, and realize it must be to the possession of other qualities that our Magazine derives its claim to be considered first in the field of College literature, we yet feel the responsibilities these advantages impose on us, to be faithful to our trust. We are aware that the Magazine has not at all times, during the last two or three years, especially fulfilled the expectations of its patrons. According to the old proverb, the best of men (and we would also add of Magazines) have their failings:

—— "quandoque bonus dormitat Homerus."

Availing ourselves of the experience of the past, we confidently hope to remedy some faults in the management and character of the Magazine during the past two or three years. At the same time, we confess we do not expect, nor shall we attempt, to please all. While we receive with kindness, and weigh with consideration, the suggestions of our friends, for the improvement of the Magazine, we shall by no means feel ourselves bound to follow their advice, but shall pursue the 'even tenor of our way,' in such manner as we think most conducive to its best interests.

And now, Juniors especially, and all whom it may concern, a word in your ear! As you will doubtless from time to time appear before your class, as competitors for its honors, in the pages of the Magazine, permit us to give you a few hints, which may save you a needless waste of time. A solemn conclave of the 'corps Editorial' was recently held in our sanctum, (to which, by the way, kind reader, we on another occasion may introduce thee,) at which business of vital importance to the interests of humanity, and our Magazine in particular, was discussed. Several members of the 'corps' became highly excited. The most serious consequences seemed about to ensue. At length, however, by the most strenuous exertions of the Moderator, order was restored, and the following resolutions unanimously passed, and ordered to be published, for the benefit of our contributors:

Whereas, we have learned with unfeigned regret, from various authentic sources the decease of John Milton, Edwin Spenser, Ben Johnson, (otherwise known as 'honest Ben,') and a host of other English worthies, whose names are distinguished in the annals of Literature; and whereas, the young and tender minds of our correspondents have been so deeply affected with this painful dispensation of Providence that they have been able to write of little else during the past few months, thus throwing a *gloom* and *seriousness* over the pages of our Magazine, entirely inconsistent with its original design—

Therefore Resolved, That for any person to bring the remains, character, history or writings of these individuals before the public in the columns of the Yale Literary Magazine, thus *lacerating* the feelings of a wide circle of friends, be considered an act of heinous sacrilege, and meet our decided disapprobation.

Furthermore Resolved, That as the most effectual method of diverting their minds from these *painfully* absorbing subjects, our correspondents be earnestly recommended to employ their talents on lighter and more amusing articles, or at least those of a more practical nature, thus *enlivening* and rendering more acceptable to our readers the pages of the Magazine, and deriving more real benefit to themselves.

Gentlemen, do you take? Such are the decisions of the Fates, by which we intend to abide, so you have fair warning. Occasionally a spirited review on some late and interesting work, may meet with acceptance, or perchance an essay on some distinguished living individual, provided it be characterized by the power and genius of Macaulay, Carlyle, or North—none other need apply. In accordance with the above resolutions, we return to the authors, without further comment, the essays on "Burke,

"Shakspeare," (ye gods! only think of a *criticism* on Shakspeare,) and "Shelley;" some of which, we are happy to remark, indicate talents, which, had they been employed on other subjects, would have at once obtained them a place in our Magazine. One word about poetry. We judge from communications we have received, that some persons supposed an hour's leisure in throwing together rhymes at random, would gain them a hearing in our columns. We beg leave to suggest to these aspiring geniuses, the propriety of selecting some more suitable channel through which to acquire an 'immortality of fame,' than the pages of our humble periodical. The Democratic Review, New Englander, or Knickerbocker, will bring them at once more fully into the notice of the public, at whose discriminating tribunal they will doubtless receive the reward due their merit. Some of our poetic communications, which bear the impress of genius and labor, we receive with pleasure; with others of a contrary description, we sometimes lose all patience. But more of this anon, while we have a word with

OUR CORRESPONDENTS.

The author of the lines to "M. A. R." is informed, that, according to his request, we shall not notice his communication.

The "Dithyrambic from Schiller" is respectfully declined.

We have received a poetical communication of some three pages of foolscap, with notes, entitled,

"OLD BOL,
'A steed right valiant he.'
Obiit Kalendis Aprilis MDCCCXLI, Æ. IX."

This is one of the most remarkable poetical productions we have perused in a long time. Combining the highest flights of the imagination, and the most pathetic appeals to the tender feelings, with beauty of expression, and justness of sentiment, it possesses all the elements of true poetry. As an instance, we select at random a single stanza, in the first line of which is forcibly portrayed the author's just taste and nice observation of the *works* of nature; in the next, he settles an important point in moral philosophy, which Paley has not treated of; and finally, in the remainder, displays a heart keenly alive to the interests of the brute creation and suffering humanity.

"A long tail to a horse is a beautiful item—
Tis a sin to dock a nag's tail off short like a rabbit;
For this is his only defense when flies bite him,
And without it in dogdays he runs the risk of going rabbid"

One more stanza, showing his unrivaled powers of description:

"In taking his meals Bob was not over nice—
With few prolegomena he into them dives,
Corn, hay, and oats, disappeared in a trice,
In a way that would quite have astonished the natives."

Accent on the last syllable, if you please! There's poetry for you with a vengeance.

The author of "The Maniac's Monody" fairly out-Russells Russell, the king of mad poetry. A regard to the dangerous consequences that might ensue to some of our readers, of sensitive nerves, alone prevents us from giving the poem entire. venture to present one or two *exquisitely touching* stanzas.

> "My hopes all fled like spectres wan,
> And oft there heaved the deep drawn sigh,
> And then a bright glance in this eye
> Did *scorch* whate'er it looked upon;
> And strangers oft, with visage sad,
> Enquired, and heard *Poor Kate is mad!*"

Once more:

> ——"See there stands
> The traitor that with serpent art
> Beguiled me of my spotless heart,
> And crushed it in his ruthless hands."

This reminds us of a striking couplet by a young tradesman, alluded to by ridge, in his Biographia Literaria:

> "No more will I endure love's pleasing pain,
> Or round my *heart's leg* bind his galling chain."

To which some one has added, in pencil marks, "Go it"! So mote it be.

*** We observe a donation of one thousand dollars has been made to Yale College, by Isaac H. Townsend, the interests and profits of which are to be paid in premiums for English composition. A more noble object for such a munificent present could not have been devised, and we anticipate the most beneficial results from the measure. One condition on which this sum is presented, is the following:

"The said Corporation [The President and Fellows of Yale College in New Haven] shall annually pay out the interests and profits of the loans aforesaid in five (5) premiums of twelve dollars ($12) each, to the authors in the Senior Class of the best original compositions in the English language. The subjects for said compositions shall be proposed from time to time soon after the beginning of each academical year; and all the members of the Senior Class in said College for the time being shall have liberty to write for the premiums. The subjects shall be selected by the Faculty of the College; unless in any year or years the Faculty shall consider it expedient to refer to each student the selection of his own subject. The premiums shall be awarded by the Faculty, or by a committee designated by the Faculty for the purpose. No discrimination shall be made among the compositions to which premiums shall be awarded. All compositions receiving premiums shall be read in public at a meeting of the members of the College, and as far as practicable by their respective authors; and shall then be preserved among the papers of the College."

Several volumes of back numbers of the Yale Literary on hand, which will be disposed of on the most reasonable terms.

Communications for the next number must be handed in immediately.

THE

YALE LITERARY MAGAZINE.

Vol. IX. DECEMBER, 1843. No. 2.

THE POET'S MISSION.

Oh, that Charles Lamb were here to write 'a complaint on the decay of' poets in the republic—yea, and in the world! It is now many years since Sir Philip Sidney made his famous "Defense of Poesie"—a defense which will go down to the latest age as embracing, in its comprehensive generalization, all that need be—not to say can be—said upon the subject; and, though by no means forgotten, it would seem to be read to little purpose in these latter days. Could that 'gentle scholar' at this hour look out from his honored resting place beneath Saint Paul's, on the poetic world, might he not at first suppose his eyes had opened upon Plato's commonwealth, whence the whole race of rhymers was ignobly banished; or rather upon the dominions of that Sultan who threatened to 'cut off the head of the first man that made a reflection?'

Surely he might be pardoned for such a supposition, in view of the wide difference between his idea of the poet and that which prevails quite extensively at present. There is no end to the numbers who lay claim to this title, and who actually do send forth to the world whole reams of rhymed lines, regularly divided into stanzas, and copiously interlarded with those hackneyed phrases of prettiness, which, for aught that appears to the contrary, were in vogue before the confusion of tongues, and were carried by the scattered colonists from the plain of Shinar to every corner of the talking world. In one respect, it is saddening to know that such productions do not give an honest title to this high dignity; for, in our greener days, even we have been found guilty of sundry melodious numbers, which it is to be feared future ages will 'willingly let die.' A malicious posterity may take courage from the fact that no disposition to the contrary has as yet been manifested by a discerning public!

But though it is the death blow to our own fond hopes, we yield an unqualified assent to the assertion of Sir Philip, that "Not rhyming and versing make a poet, for one may be a poet without versing, and a versifier without poetry." And again, "A poet no industry can make, if his own genius be not carried into it."

Yet we believe he may know what constitutes a poet, who is not one himself, and may have some idea of the duties implied in that name, even though their performance may far surpass his own ability. It is this assurance which has emboldened us to enter on the theme we have chosen.

The true poet is not an every-day character, and his mission to this earth is no ordinary mission;—a truth which has been felt, and in various ways acknowledged, by all nations and from the remotest antiquity. The Romans, when they gave him the title of "Seer," and the Greeks, when they called him "the Creator," evinced the same feeling of reverence which more barbarous nations had ever shown the bard; and moreover, that they had some worthy notions of the ground of his claim to superiority.

No one, whatever may be his skill in metrical composition, can justly be called a poet, who is not gifted by nature with a high degree of imagination; an extraordinary sensibility or capacity for receiving impressions from the external world through the medium of the senses, and from the workings of the soul itself by reflection; and superadded to these, an exquisite taste, to guide him in the selection of subjects, the manner of treating them, and in the choice of language.

It is by no means uncommon for those possessed of one of these characteristics, to the exclusion of the others, conscious that they are not in all respects like the rest of the world around them, to suppose that theirs is the true 'diviner mind,' and to wreak upon rythmical expressions their half formed or half clothed fancies. Accordingly, the imaginative youth in vain strives to gain the public ear, and to procure for his "airy nothings a local habitation and a name;" the too sensitive swain wonders that the world has no sympathy with his tears, and cannot realize the depth of his poetic sorrows; while he of taste alone, comes on with cold and stately air, and sits to Cowper for his portrait:

> "*Manner* is all in all—whate'er is writ;—
> The substitute for genius, sense, and wit."

But the fortunate being who finds in himself the felicitous combination of qualities we have enumerated, may safely feel warranted in entering on a course of study for the poetical profession. Not that he may not deserve the name without severe, methodical, and protracted study—for many examples of success in uneducated poets will occur to every memory—but it is an art of sufficient dignity and utility to deserve the study of a life, and without it, one can never climb the highest summits of 'the Aonian mount.'

Nothing has more to do with the complete success of a candidate for poetic honors, than the motive with which he enters on his course; for a motive he must have, and that a powerful one, or he will soon tire in that pathway which, though strown with flowers, is rugged still. The experience of the muses' votaries through all time would seem enough to deter every one from writing for pecuniary reward. Should one be bold enough yet to indulge thoughts of cultivating poetry for the profit of the thing, let him not commence the execution of his plans till he has pondered well these words of the gifted Hillhouse, than whom none ever wrote with purer motives:—"A tissue wrought and unwrought like Penelope's, flowered over with the hues of life, glittering and massive with costly materials and patient toil, cannot be manufactured in modern times as a gainful article:—the daughter of Icarus cannot weave with the handmaids of Arkwright!"

Nor should the love of fame—that universal stimulus to action and peculiar curse of literary men—be suffered to lead the mind astray; for the breath of popular applause is almost sure to sway us from the line of true success and permanent honor. Even the approval of the wisest and best of men should not be set up as the leading incentive to a life's employment, or the highest reward of literary excellence. There is a stronger motive than the love of money or of fame; and a nobler reward than the praise of men awaits him who, yielding his whole soul to the influence of that motive, adopts poetry as his vocation.

Consciousness of power, a just sense of the grandeur and utility of his art, and a real desire to use it for the greatest good of his fellow-men, should influence the poet in his outset, and should accompany him in every step of his progress. If he distrusts his own ability, or doubts the interest of others in his employment; if he knows not fully the nature of the instrument he wields, or has little confidence in its power; if conscience reproaches him for selfish or ignoble ends, his heart will falter, his arm be paralyzed, and the puny execution will reveal, too late, the fatal deficiency. But of all men in the world, the poet should be the last to feel any distrust of his art. True, it has been often abused, and thoughtless men have thence argued against poetry itself, instead of its abuser; but the coldest heart among them rises up in condemnation of so unjust a sentence, when the eye falls by chance upon some thrilling page, and fills with tears of joy or sorrow, as the weird enchanter summons up the memory of some past hour and scene—it may be of childhood—pleasant or mournful to the soul.

The poet should be aware of the universality of those principles of the mind on which his art is founded; universal, inasmuch as all are endowed in some degree with the capacity to recognize and love what is truly beautiful in the physical, intellectual, and moral world: and this is the groundwork of poetry. While man exists, susceptible to intellectual pleasure and to powerful appeals to his passions, imaginations, and sympathies; while nature is full of beauty, and the mind has power to compare, select, and arrange what is ennobling and refined in her myriad associations; while the world affords its "strong contrast of station, character, and scene;" while the soul is filled with its restless aspirations for some better world and some higher life than this; true poetry will meet with a ready response in the human heart, and the lyre will never be unstrung, nor attuned in vain to its varied harmonies.

Let not any believe the oft-repeated assertion, that the poet's labor has been all anticipated. True, it has been a favorite occupation with man, and almost every conceivable thing has, at one time or another, been a theme for poetic inspiration. Even if it is difficult to find new topics, one may at least give the peculiar coloring and drapery of his own genius to the old. But "much yet remains unsung;" and we should remember that each of the great masters who has gone before us, was but "one successful diver in that sea whose floor of pearls is all our own." Let not the poet complain of a dearth of subjects fitted to bring his powers into the fullest exercise, while nature continues to make her mute but touching appeals to the heart of humanity. Is not the same calm, blue sky spread out above our heads, that hung over the primeval dwellers in paradise? The same sun and moon which lighted their pathway, do they not shine on ours? And the pure stars that bend down to us their meek and quiet eyes, are they not the same bright constellations that moved the harp of David to heavenly music? Here and there, the same rocky mountain lifts up its huge, dark form, now, to receive a glowing crown, radiant with a thousand sweetest tints, and anon, to stay the storm-cloud in its fierce career, and to roll off from its bald, scathed front, the bolt which would else have sent desolation and ruin into the plain below. The ancient forest still stands in its solitude, unbroken since the world began, save by the tread of the wild beast seeking for others weaker than he; or by the songs of birds, whose life is all one flow of melody, unchilled by fear, untamed by slavery. The meadow still knows its quiet stream, and the mountain crag its rushing torrent. Old ocean still "pours round all his gray and melancholy waste;" still sends its murmuring ripple to the beach, or blends its hoarse roar with the thunder that rolls along its mountain-surges, crested with the lightning's glare. The glories of the rising and the setting sun, the gentle twilight hour, and night, spreading her robe of silence and of darkness round the earth, still crowd their thoughts upon the poet, and teach him the lessons of beauty and of love. The seasons still keep on their annual round, decking the earth with flowers, warming it into full life and verdure, crowning it with golden harvests, and throwing over it the white veil of sorrow for happy days gone by. Oh, Nature is ever young! To him who has ears to hear, she speaks the same voice she has spoken to the countless generations she has seen grow old and die; and the same truths she will utter to the end of time.

Here, too, is man, with all that is sublime or contemptible connected with his wondrous powers, his passions, his memories, his hopes, and fears—man, with all his relations to his race and to his God—the noblest theme that can occupy the poet's mind or guide his pen! Here is woman, filling with honor her lovely sphere; shedding on the darkest hour the light of her undying hope and faith ; cheering and upholding man, through all his way, with her disinterested self-sacrifice, her sympathy, her constancy, her patient suffering ; and, above all, with her unfailing love, that eases "the anguish of many a torturing hour ;" her love

"That alters not with Time's brief hours and weeks,
But bears it out even to the verge of doom."

If it be true that "the aim of poetry is to teach and delight mankind, making use of verse only as a dress best suited to the dignity of the work," how can the poet ever want for subjects ? Can he not be ever enriching his mind, by adding to its stores of wit, and knowledge, and judgment ; and ever bringing these to subserve his great object,—to teach men what goodness is, and to delight them to the love of it ? If virtue is the end of wisdom, how can the poet's labors ever fail, while imagination enables him to set forth characters of greatness and of goodness, arrayed in robes of grace and dignity that shall win the homage of the heart and the consent of a conquered will ? All thoughts and deeds of all men are his ; the riches of the past and the present ; history, science, and art ; external nature and intellectual and moral life are his ; and then Imagination wandering at her own sweet will, "bodies forth the forms of things unknown," and pours her treasures at his feet. All these, "in the quick forge and working-house of thought," the poet moulds to his own chosen ends.

The historian busies himself with the musty records of the past, and brings to light a thousand examples of the good and bad, in individuals or nations, and sets them in order before us for our encouragement or warning. The man of science produces his theories, accounts for things before unknown, and excites our wonder at the vast reach of the human intellect. The moral philosopher comes forward with his volumes of abstract truths and precepts, in the hope that thus he is to reform the world. But the poet makes the past live before us, and merges all time in the glowing present. We stand in the presence of the men of other days ; we listen to their words ; we are with them in public and in private, in the council and on the battle-field ; and we ourselves witness their deeds of glory or of shame. He twines with his green wreath of "ivy never sere," the rough and forbidding trunk of the tree of knowledge ; and they who sow with him for a companion, not only bring home in season their full sheaves and glowing clusters, but their harvest-song goes up laden with the sweet breath of perennial flowers, that garland and bedeck the fruits of autumn. He may not lay down for the regulation of our conduct any formal system of morals, but in his pictures of actual life, we see virtue as she is, and our natures are delighted, exalted, and purified, by the contemplation. Vice, too, comes before us unwashed, works out with terrific energy its fatal consequences, and the contrast stands out so boldly, that we must not only recognize, but feel its power.

It is by no means implied that the poet should confine himself to topics which have in view the direct inculcation of moral or even of intellectual truth. He may concern himself with aught that in any way interests humanity. Still may the pastoral pipe praise the delights of humble, rural life, far removed from the envious strifes and contentions of the world; the elegiac strain may sigh at every note of grief, from sadness to despair; the satiric may still laugh at the changing shades of human folly; the bitter iambic cause meanness and villainy to hide their heads for shame; and the heroic may hand down to lasting fame the honored deeds of patriotism and valor. The dramatic poet may yet find materiel enough for his highest efforts in the varied conduct of man under all the chances and changes of life. He finds it in all the workings of wrath, envy, revenge, and jealousy; in love and hatred; in poverty and wealth; in joy and sorrow; in all the ties of blood and friendship; in the sad or joyous sighings of hope and memory; in all that is beautiful, tender or sublime in life; in all that is touching or awful in death and the grave. The lyrist may find ample subjects for his song in celebrating the praises of good men and virtuous deeds, and, more than all, in chanting the praises of God.

But here we are met with the assertion that religion is no theme for poetry, and are pointed to the example of bards of every age and clime, who have preferred any subjects to those which the Scriptures offer. It is freely admitted that the old mythologies of the heathen have been far more frequently resorted to, by the sons of song, than the Christian system, and doubtless to the end of time they will be made use of for illustration and ornament. But he who would produce a great work, that shall defy the eating rust of time, must not only call in religion for a theme, but he must feel its influence upon his heart and life. It has too much to do with intellectual growth and vigor, to be slighted by any scholar; it has too much to do with the thoughts and feelings of man; it is too closely interwoven with their temporal interests and their eternal destiny, to be passed over in silence by that poet who would enshrine himself in the memory of his race.

But in what respect is religion second in adaptedness to poetic uses, to the mythologies of Greece or Rome? Is there not intellectual pleasure in the bare contemplation of such a system,—one which elevates man so far above the influence of sordid affections, of sensuality and selfishness? Does religion detract from our sensibility or deep love of the beautiful? Does it take away any one of those influences by which imagination is excited to the creation of its "passion-colored images of life?" Does the pure lesson which nature teaches every poet, appeal with less vividness to him who gazes on all her works with adoration mingled with his wonder, and says, "My Father made them all"? Since the revelation of an omnipotent Author of nature presiding over all her mild or sterner moods, is there less of the poetic in those great convulsions which shake the globe itself, than when the bard of old saw in them some token of the wrath of Jove, whom perchance he might meet to-morrow on a gay errand of dalliance with some of the fair but loosely-cinctured daughters of men? It was not till the great Christian revelation, that to man

"The common air, the earth, the skies,
Become an opening paradise."

The modest flower that lifts its eye to heaven, grew at the feet of the bard of mythological times, but if he stooped to notice, he saw in it only beauty. The Christian poet knows who placed that flower there, and why He clothed it in its rainbow garment, and shed into its bosom a delightful fragrance; and its beauty elevates his affections to the Giver of all. It is thus that

"To him the meanest flower that blows can give
Thoughts that do often lie too deep for tears."

How narrow and low were their ideas of man and his relations—and that of necessity—knowing so little as they did of his nature and destiny! Their man was but the outward manifestation. The private and retired walks of life they passed by unnoticed, and were attracted mostly by man as the hero! It is Christianity which has given to the poet all those stern conflicts of the soul with its passions and propensities, and thus wrought out that lofty example of the moral sublime—the independence of the human will! Christianity has given its charm to domestic life; it has rescued woman from the degradation of heathenism, and love from the depths of sensuality, and has given them in all their purity to the poet of modern times. In fine, it is this which has 'joined mute nature to ethereal mind, and made that link a melody.'

Cowley has ably demonstrated the richness of the Bible in poetic themes, by collecting many of those it offers and contrasting them with such as have been favorites with the poets of former ages. Our own poet, WILLIS, has availed himself of some few of these themes, and in his sacred pieces has produced decidedly the finest specimens we have to show of American poetry. If Bible themes are not poetical, why have the first artists of the world so often taken from it subjects for the canvas? Whence are the psalms of David and the poetry of Job? Whence come those sublime passages which glow on every page, from the song of Moses and Miriam—'the first to liberty that e'er was sung'—to the seraphic visions of the seer of Patmos?

Does religion lack any of the outward essentials, or machinery of poetry? It reveals to us an universe, with the Creator at its head, infinite in every glorious and powerful attribute; and in his Son the mysterious union of the human and divine. It has its angels in multitudes which no man can number; from the archangel by the throne to the infant spirits that go unseen on their errands of love 'to the heirs of salvation.' It has its malicious spirits, at whose head stands Lucifer, 'not less than archangel ruined.' It has removed the pall which hid eternity from the wisest of ancient philosophers, and reveals its heaven of life and blessedness, and its hell of unending despair. What sublimity, tenderness, and pathos does it place within the poet's reach! How full is it of every higher and nobler quality of poetry; and how trifling appears the machinery of mythology—splendid as it seemed by itself—when brought up in the comparison! How strongly it reminds one of the pasteboard and tinsel ornaments, of the cannon-ball and sheet-iron thunder of the playhouse!

But with all its glorious revelations of truth, has religion left no room for the expansion of the imagination? Attempt to fathom the mysteries of redemption, of the resurrection, and the worlds beyond the grave! Tell us of the New Jerusalem, and describe the 'Lamb who is the light thereof!' Vie with the cherubim and seraphim, or the sweet singer of Israel, and you will find that religion is full of poetry; that 'the world is not dark or nature unlovely, when gazed upon by the seraph eye of the Christian;' and you will no longer wonder that he is not content with soaring where any eye can follow, 'who knows of worlds beyond Olympus, and of a life that begins when mortals years have vanished.'

If such as we have seen be the lofty mission of the poet, who shall dare to undertake it? None but he to whom it is given; he in whose soul are ever rising

"Thoughts that *voluntary* move harmonious numbers."

Let such an one be cheered by the reflection, that though his labor be arduous, it is sublime; and even in this life brings a noble recompense. Coleridge said, in looking back on his career, "Poetry has been to me its own exceeding great reward. It has soothed my afflictions; it has multiplied and refined my enjoyments; it has endeared solitude; and it has given me the habit of wishing to discover the beautiful and the good in all that meets and surrounds me."

Let him who feels that he is gifted with 'the vision and the faculty divine,' fix his eye upon that ideal standard of excellence, which can never be attained till one shall arise in whom are blended the universal genius of Shakspeare and his minute interest in all the affairs of men, with the lofty imagination, the profound and varied learning, and the simple piety of him who sung 'the dirge of a lost Paradise.' And what more sublime character than this can we conceive, and yet clothe it with the vesture of humanity?

And how glorious a destiny must await such a being, when—having well fulfilled his mission—he enters on his reward, and expatiates upon those heavenly plains whose beauty and love even here had begun to flow into the inner depths of his being; and, by the still waters of Life's river, attunes his golden harp to sublimer strains than ever ravished the ear of mortal;—strains which shall know no end but with the life of the ETERNAL ONE!

CL.

MUSIC AND MEMORY.

The world is full of music. When the ear
Is first attuned to harmony there come
Borne on the gently passing breeze, sweet sounds
Of rapturous melody; as if the world
Were one vast lyre Æolienne, which God
Had formed for his good pleasure, with its huge
And deeply-sounding strings from pole to pole
With wondrous skill outstretched, that not a breath
Might idly fly away, but wake a strain
Of passing sweetness, soothing with its tones
The heart of man oppressed with grief and care,—
Give joy where joy was never known before,—
And where man's lot was happy, add still more
Unto his cup of bliss.

Ah! memory now
Is bringing back the scenes of other years.
I feel as though I were a child again,
When all the world seemed pure, and bright, and fair.
Oh that it were so,—that the beautiful dream
Of life's unchanging peace, and love, and bliss,
Had ne'er been broken,—that I had not lived
To know that love could languish, and that man
Could hate. Then had I thought the world indeed
A place of sunshine and of flowers, nor dreamed
That clouds could dim the brightness of the one,
Or death deprive the others of their beauty.

Yet such a wish were impious. No! 'Tis well
To live and learn that only One is true,
So that our love may not be satisfied
With what the earth can give, but seek in heaven
A constant friend, and never-failing joys.

In life's young days how sweet each Sabbath morn
Was ushered in, when on the silent air
The bell poured from its lofty tower such strains
As might enchant an angel. Beautiful rose
That tapering tower, in its spotless grace
Pointing to heaven. And when the rising moon
Shone on its fair proportions, to the eye
Of careless youth it seemed a pyramid
Of purest silver painted on the sky.

The spire is gone. The bell is silent now.
Nor doth it grieve me much, for it is well
That life's first years should with such memories
Of pure delight be linked.

* * * * * *

'Tis morning now.
See with what beauty lingering on their way
The sun's last rays are painting in the west
The fleecy clouds. How soft! How bright! How fair!

I.

Hark! the bell is ringing
In the ivied tower,
Angel-voices singing
Charm the evening hour.

II.

How the sounds are swelling
In the air of even,
Like the life-springs welling
In the courts of heaven.

III.

Now they come increasing,
On the zephyr flying—
List! for almost ceasing,
They are gently dying.

IV.

Now again advancing,
Sweetly are they sounding,
On the hill-top dancing,
Through the vale rebounding.

V.

Far away retreating,
Ah! how swift ye leave me.
Kindly was your greeting,
Why did ye deceive me?

VI.

Why, ah! why so fleetly
Seek the wild-wood flower,
While your notes so sweetly
Charmed the evening hour?

VII.

Now the bell is tolling, tolling,
In the ivied tower;
So life's tide is rolling, rolling,
During life's short hour.

VIII.

Time away is stealing, stealing,
Swift the sands are flowing:
'Tis the hour for acting, feeling,
While life's fire is glowing.

IX.

May our lamps be burning, burning,
Bright the flame shine ever:
Soon we'll pass away, returning
Never more,—oh, never!

C.

HORÆ COLLEGIANÆ.

Reader, hast thou a clock—an honest, square-faced clock—a genuine son of the true Yankee breed? Thou hast; and, often as thou gazest on its expressive lineaments and truth-telling figures, thy heart warms towards it. Compared with it, thy stove, though it shine warmly on thee with its red Cyclops eye, and soothe thee to sleep perchance, with its soft, low song, is but a dull companion, uttering no voice to thee. Thy secretary—but mayhap thou art not one that loves to burn the midnight oil, and owest to it, the scene of the labors of thy surcharged brain, some latent grudge. Thy mirror, though a faithful and truth-telling friend, is but a profitless companion, that shows thee naught but what it may read in thy own face. In short, it is to thy old clock alone, that thy heart goes forth in hearty fellowship. Then, reader, there exists a bond of sympathy that links my heart to thine.

For me the gay assemblies of society, with their vain projects, their rankling jealousies, only half hid beneath the flattering velvet of conventional benignity, their endless repetitions of worn-out inanities, have no charms. The dreamy stillness of my room, broken only by the ticking of my old friend upon the shelf—the sweet consciousness of loneliness, uninterrupted by courteous laughter at forced wit, leave me free to stray in reveries more congenial far than the mirth that answers to the call of each gay circle. Mayhap this is not all; feelings less pure within me, may nourish this secret discontent. Unfitted by nature to dazzle amid the glare of lights, or successfully engage in rivalry for admiration and applause, not gifted with the ready wit that alone can give one ease in social intercourse, diffidence leads me to walk in less frequented paths. Not that I would not rejoice to hear the voice and catch the approving smile of female loveliness. Cold is the heart that beats not high at the thought. Colder than mine, selfish though it be. I must confess, that with all my stoicism, (and what cynic, did he tell the truth, would not confess the same?) gladly would I catch at the love of some bright being now imaged in my fancy. But condescending pity—that I cannot endure. No! rather let me wear for life the weeds of single blessedness. How many shrink from the rude contact of the world around them, and hoard within their breasts feelings fond and deep, that might steep in happiness many an unmated soul. They care not in these crowded lists to run a tilt for ladies' smiles, but bury in their bosoms the budding affections which should bear roses, but yield only thorns to pierce the aching heart. Would that all such might taste the true fruits of social intercourse. But it may not be. Nature and cherished morbidness alike forbid the hope.

Hail then Solitude! and thou, too, my Clock! be ye my mistresses—to you let me fill, in imagination, the brimming cup—to you pay my *devoirs*, and seek with you to sport the glad companionship I may not claim with love and beauty.

Horæ Collegianæ! College hours! hours? nay, days—weeks—years—how swift their flight! They come and go with a speed that scarce leaves room for thought or consciousness. We but catch the first glimpse of their approaching steps, ere they are past—past forever! We may strive to recall them, but they come not again at our bidding. Their receding forms flit by us, and glide down the stream, to return no more.

> "The gladness of our youthful prime,
> It cometh not again—that golden time."

'Tis sad to think that this joyous season of youth is so rapidly fleeting,—that the last of our college days will so soon be spent. Though we may but have entered on its term, yet is its close at hand. And when it shall have come, dear reader, and thou art about to launch out thy bark upon the waters of the wide world, will its hours have passed over thy head as waves pass over the pebble, rounding and polishing thy form, but leaving no lasting impression on the soul within? Will thy college course have been to thee but so many revolutions of the hands upon thy clock face, so many rising and setting suns; or, as thou callest the roll of its hours, shall each show to thee its talent, well increased by usury? Believe me, if thou dost not use them aright, sooner or later they will confront thee with a heavy reckoning—spirits that will not down at thy command. I would not accuse *thee*, but have we not those within our college walls, upon whom the events of life make as little impression as breezes on the solid rock, or blarney on a bull-dog,—men to whom time is a blank, and thought a thing unknown? Mere "numerus," as Horace hath it,—

> "Sponsi Penelopæ, nebulones, Alcinoique
> In cute curanda plus æquo operata juventus;
> Cui pulchrum fuit in medios dormire dies."

They seem to exist for no purpose under Heaven save to digest the food that instinct leads them to deposit within their œsophagi—walking, or rather creeping, through life, without aim or effort—bestowing the least possible labor on this irksome task of existence, that must be gone through with. Yet, though these votaries of Vacuna seem ever aiming (striving is too strong a word for these vegetable soups) to make the current of life flow smooth and swift,—they seem not to wish it ended. Singular perversity, to wish so great a bore as life protracted!

Doubtless you, my reader, have seen such. It has been my lot to light upon one, and that a perfect specimen of these "ostrea viventia," that do nought but gape from year to year, and seem quite out of their element when taken from their native bed.

Fullman was in truth the very prince of sluggards. Were I a believer in the doctrines of transmigration, I would say with certainty, that he was inhabited by a soul fresh from the body of a sloth, not yet aware of its liberation. With half an eye you could see that he was born with his eyes shut, and at twenty he had scarce got them open. Nothing could disturb his deep tranquillity. The same placid vacuity of expression ever beamed in his full blown face, which seemed the favored resting place of sleep. One glance at him was enough to engender an uncontrollable yawn. To gaze on him for one minute was certain oblivion. Laudanum would be exciting beside him—the soothing strains of Mercury a merry jig, compared with his deep-drawn breath. Often has the recitation room been all agape with the influence that flowed from him in a steady stream; nay, once, *horresco referens*, when called upon to recite he turned upon the tutor, as he rose, a look so piteous, that, though vigilant as Cerberus, he yielded to his blandishments, and oping wide the portals of his jaws, he yawned aloud. That day poor Fullman was *flunked*, and was never again reinstated in the good graces of our officer. From that time his spirits failed him—he became melancholy and languid—his vivacity was gone. He felt that he was not appreciated, and determined to seek some spot in which the wings of his genius would not feel the fetters that here cramped their flight.

His departure left a sad vacancy—we feel it yet, though he deserted college full a year ago. We miss his slow and steady step ascending the chapel aisle, after all others are seated, and the solid sound with which he dropped his broad proportions on the bench. We meet him no more taking his noon-day walk, full three hundred yards, from his room to his boarding house. We feel that something is wanting to fill the measure of our daily observations, and know not what it is, till we look round and see that Fullman's seat is vacant. But stop, I recollect an incident that will throw his character into much more prominent relief than any description I can give.

Walking one day, at noon, with Dandie Blake, (Dandie, be it known, is a corruption of Andrew,) we happened on Fullman, who had got through a good part of his daily journey to dinner. Dandie, who by the way is a jovial dog, and an especial friend of mine, broke out with, "What will you bet me, Harry," (my name, when it has Jackson after it,) "I can't start old Hasty from a walk?" (He is called Hasty on account of his fondness for the dish vulgarly known as hasty pudding, which, with pork and molasses, is esteemed a great delicacy in our parts, and not on account of any speediness of gait beyond other men.)

"Bet you!" I answered, "I wont let you take such fearful odds, but if you move him from his gait, hold me indebted for a treat. Of course you don't expect to succeed, but you can try."

I dropped astern, and Dandie soon overhauled the chase, no great sailer at best, and now without all sail set, port being near, and time plenty. Whilst he hailed him, I followed, slowly as I could, yet not so slowly but that I made on them, and listened to the parley.

" A fine day, Hasty, a very fine day, cold and lively," said Dandie, as he reached him, giving him a slap on the back at the same time.

" Yes,—but you need n't do that again," was the laconic reply, in a tone of so greasy a profundity that it seemed to well up from the bottom of an oil cask. (For the thousandth time I shook with laughter as I heard it)

" Why, Hasty, my fine fellow," resumed his assailant, " keep cool; you are getting to be so fiery I am almost afraid to come near you Do curb your spirits."

" I'm rather hungry," put in Fullman parenthetically, " aint you ?"

" Yes ! yes ! but would n't you like to walk to East Rock, after dinner ? It will be a grand excursion this keen day."

" I think not," answered our oil can.

" Come ! come ! you will, I know you will !"

" I tell you I wont," said Fullman, with a positive air, evidently becoming excited, for his visual orbs rolled lusciously in their saucer-like sockets.

" You must ! you shall ! or by Heavens your day is at hand !" shouted Dandie, threatningly brandishing a penknife in one hand, whilst with the other he plunged a pin up to its head in his broadest part. Poor Hasty actually roared as he felt the iron enter his soul, and turning on his tormentor with unexpected energy, and

" With eyes as red as new enkindled fire,"

seized him by the neck and heels and tossed him into the middle of the street, then rushed furiously through his club room door, which was at hand, and appeared again at evening recitation, calm and unruffled as the dying swan, that pipes its last sweet quaver to attentive ducks, ere it seeks some happier bower, " In the land to which other swans go."

Harry, thanks to a small hillock of rubbish, no unfrequent ornament of the unpaved and unswept streets of our goodly City of Elms, escaped without any broken bones. He came limping towards me with a most doleful countenance, brushing the dirt from his coat and muttering in an under tone, " brute—bear—call him out—the biter bit, that 's a fact—still streams deep—insulted me—thrash him sometime."

" What ! did the bear hug too tight, Dandie ? Who has won now ! Shall we leave it to the Club ?"

" No ! no ! no more of that, an thou lovest me, Hal."

Singular to relate, the story *was* told, and Dandie was laughed at. But as to whether he or I treated—the deponent farther saith not.

Beshrew the man, I say, that will not laugh. Within our college walls none such are harbored. Kind nature hath granted us, in exchange for the large modicum of exercise bestowed on other men, an increased proportion of laughter, that notorious promoter of digestion.

"Laughter, holding both his sides," wraps not long, bony arms about a lank, loose-skinned, shriveled frame! No! goodly proportions and jollity are synonymous. Summon the merry elf. Comes he before the mind's eye lean and ill-favored! A lean Falstaff were not more preposterous. Indeed, the sturdy Stuyvesant was not more undone without his pipe, than we would be if laughter were banished. We can safely boast that in this one thing, at least, the student excels all other classes—in his tendency to mirth. We have a morbid predisposition to put a ludicrous construction on every thing, and then to laugh at it. It is, in all probability, owing rather to the necessity of recruiting the strength of our risibles, than to any disinclination on our part, that the muscles of our mouths are ever drawn down instead of up. Nothing which by any possible torturing of construction can be twisted into food for mirth, escapes our notice. All that may beget a smile, is seized and swallowed with shark-like avidity; and, after passing through some dozen hands and mouths, it is generally, permit me to notify thee, kind reader, much better digested than the watches, tin cases, jack knives, and anchors, reputed to be specially appetized by those snappish gentlemen of the deep.

Need we wonder at this? How can it but be, that so much hot and mettlesome young blood, shut up within close rooms, and made to gain by mensuration, access to inaccessible towers,—to weigh the sun,—measure the moon's shadow, and count the stars,—to analyze the choking gas that clogs the lungs, till the aching head, faithful servant though it be, refuse obedience to the sovereign will,—how can it but be, that when set free from thought and care, we run, mayhap extravagantly, into the opposite extreme? Numbers and age both make us prone to smiles.

Be the cause what it may, the truth is most apparent, that we are ever on the watch for jest and joke, ever ready to enter into the spirit of any mad prank. And most surprising it is to see how easily our jaws are set a-wagging. The tail of the little dog Apollo is not more ready to perform. How vast a fund of amusement have we in the witty tricks of our classmates? A pocket neatly picked,—a paper bearing perhaps some significant inscription, slily thrust beneath your neighbor's coat collar! What could be more humorous! And, when we have a hundred scenes equally amusing, what wonder is it that we are ever on the giggle. But how shall I do justice to the peals of laughter that follow the mysterious renderings of the venerable classics, by some luckless wight! If it were not that it would seem invidious to particularize, I would quote some of our modern translators. Truly, the race of giants is not extinct. "I have eaten a monument more lasting than brass," is a small calf—a mere baby compared with the full grown bulls, that greet our ears from time to time.

These little episodes are like bright oases in our ramblings through the barren groves of Academus, and such other wildernesses as we are called to cross. Both mind and body are refreshed by this titillation of the nerves, so that often hours pass swiftly and pleasantly, amid the smoky atmosphere that rings a halo round the tutor's brow, even to those whose dreams have been disturbed, and whose presence torn from "some sweet bower to hum." Yet is all this as nothing, beside the applause with which we hail the joke that falls from the Professor's lips—the perennial witticisms that distill from out the "Chair." By nature we are all prone to flattery, but this is far from flattery. It is the free expression of that heart-felt joy, with which we see those who to us at least are great, unbend, and feel that those whom we revere, can lay aside their dignity and join with us in mirth. Is our pleasure great, then is the measure of its manifestation proportionably great. Here laughter gains its climax. Most learned reader,—embryo professor, (how soon thou wilt arrive at perfection I dare not say,) when thou hast attained the mark at which thy wishes aim, forget not thy experience. Why have we youth granted us, why are we not born clad in the full panoply of manhood, if we are not to learn from the past to look with gentle eyes on lightsome spirits, and know that it is good at times to laugh? Remember, then, yet unfledged aspirant, when cased in honors, the buoyancy of early years, their feelings and their sympathies—deign, as thou restest thy right worshipful body in thy capacious chair, (that is to be,) to throw dignity to the dogs, cast off all sternness, and yield to the relaxation of an occasional jest. If thy dignity be of the true stamp, then will it not suffer by this condescension.

The love of fun has become so thoroughly incorporated into this our body collegiate, that laughter is to us almost one of the necessaries of life. We could as well dispense with food as fun. Far be it from me to wish it otherwise, for it is in truth most fortunate, that we ever have within our reach so unfailing a source of pleasure—pleasure, too, which gives health to both mind and body, for—

> "'Tis mirth that fills the veins with blood,
> More than wine, or sleep, or food."

We ask not here for flashing wit, or the too keen edge of irony, to keep far off the "azure imps." Happily, our palates, subtilely sensible to the ludicrous, require not to be stimulated by these hot condiments.

True mirth cannot exist apart from innocence—a mind at ease begets the ready laugh. At least 'twas so with Bob S——. He was innocence and jollity from top to toe. Even the pewter buttons on his mixed gray coat, and the blue patches at his knees, wore a comic look that matched well his merry phiz. To him, every thing, to use his favorite word, was inexpressibly "funny." From morning till evening he was one unbroken smile, always excepting three occasions each day on which his mouth was otherwise employed. At these seasons his motto was, "business first, pleasure afterwards." Tradition says, that he was born smiling, and when two days and three hours old was heard to laugh audibly. This, however, I cannot with certainty affirm, although he has often told me that the guardian angel of his infantine days assured him, with hands upraised as two fat notes of admiration, that "he was the darlingest, sweetest, smilingest little creetur she ever did have in her arms,"—(and that was no small number.) I can well believe the old lady, judging from his imperturbable good humor at the time I knew him. Nothing could put him *hors du combat,* so far as laughter was concerned.

This habit brought him into a thousand scrapes, all of which, however, he found vastly amusing, when he was well rid of the consequences. The day of his assumption of the virile toga, (that is, of his first induction into breeches,) which he will ever remember as the day on which he was introduced to the school of Mr. Menelaus Switchem, saw him well castigated for tittering at the most pathetic part of an initiatory oration delivered by said M. Switchem, Esq., on the nature and evidence of obedience. This, he observed, with tears in his eyes, was "very funny." Whether it was the whole affair or merely the thrashing, that was so highly amusing, has never been definitely decided. At church he was regularly reprimanded for laughing every time his father (bless your soul, *he* never nodded) wished to rest his eyes. At his sister's wedding, though playing the important part of groomsman, instead of handing salts, he roared in the bride's face at the very crisis of the ceremony. In short, as a last resort, he was sent to college, because his good humor was perfectly intolerable at home. Happy S———!

> "No condition of this changeful life,
> So manifold in cares, whose every day
> Brings its own evil with it,"

could make thy laughter less. Even when a Freshman, he maintained that this was one of his inalienable rights. Truly it was his by possession—nine points of the law, at least. How he was able to pass through examination without any breach of decorum, has been a subject of much unsatisfactory speculation, though it has been hinted that terror kept his mouth shut, till all was over. If so, he has since well made up for the time he lost. Sleep brings not to him idleness: even then his waking thoughts dance in their wonted fantastic style before his mind, recalling to their well known post the smile or laugh. In fact, he is rather a noisy bed-fellow. Bob was an invaluable member of our Club; his hearty good humor was irresistibly contagious, effectually preventing all ill-feeling, for how could any one be angry, with Bob S——— in the room!—the idea is absurd. Although he often began stories, he is not known, so far as I can learn, ever to have finished one; long before he reached the apex, himself and all present were sure to be convulsed with sympathetic laughter. Though no one ever asked why it was, or could tell what under the sun the story was about, yet, by some mysterious induction, the result was sure to be a general burst. Bob passed for a wit.

Poor Bob, however, unfortunately laughed once too often. One morning, his tutor preceding him a few steps to the recitation roo drew from his pocket, in place of a handkerchief, a lady's cape, whic by some unaccountable mischance, had found its way thither. (course Bob was in ecstacies. "It was the funniest thing he had ev seen." His merriment by no means tended to allay the blushes of o officer, who was really a fine fellow, and respected by us all, but h a perfect horror of being supposed guilty of visiting any of the fair se To be laughed at under any circumstances would have been provoki enough, but before students, and with so good cause—even the mi Mr. C—— was ruffled at the thought. During the recitation, Bob most suffocated himself by his efforts to suppress his laughter. T bench on which he sat creaked nervously, his face grew now red, no purple, his hands were clapped first to his side, then to his mouth, gi ing, as tears of joy streamed down his cheeks, and his foot stamp furiously on the floor, unmistakable evidence of a state of most e quisite enjoyment. He contended nobly, but it was of no avail, a desperately covering his face with his handkerchief, he rushed f the door. His exit, for the struggle had not passed unnoticed, was fo lowed by an universal shout. That evening he was privately rep manded by Tutor C———, being able to make no defense, save, th "it was tremendous funny."

About a week after this poor Bob was summoned to appear befo the Faculty for some slight misdeeds, and at the appointed time pr pared to meet that most respectable body, in the expectation of recei ing a wholesome admonition. I accompanied him to the dread thres hold, striving to impress him with the necessity of decorous behavior his superiors, charging him above all to beware of laughter. Notwi standing a most smiling promise to be stern as Brutus and sober as judge, I doubted his strength, and, as the event proved, not without go reason. The next morning, repairing to his room, I found him in t midst of a confused assemblage of books, boots, hair-brushes and coa filling a trunk which might have been made from the skin of the hor for which King Richard called, or mayhap from one of those that No drove into the ark, judging from its rustiness. "Where are you goi Bob?" said I.

"Going home—funny, aint it?"

"Why—what is the matter now?"

"Sent off—the Faculty—funny fellows, aint they?"

"What have you been doing?"

"Laughing,"—and that was all I could ever get from him on t subject—"that the Faculty were funny fellows, very—had sent him for laughing." He fairly laughed his way through college, and at l laughed himself out of it. A troop of us escorted him to the wharf, a heard his valedictory laugh as the boat left the shore. I have not hea from him since, but doubtless he is at his old trade still, and if there the least truth in the proverb "laugh and grow fat," has well nigh tained the fair proportions of a Lambert.

Most assuredly Cicero must have had his eye on Bob S——, when he said, "Ore, vultu, voce, denique ipso corpore ridetur."

Reader, art thou a sluggard? Dost love thy morning's nap? Summer and winter, dost hug thy couch, and when the bell rings forth its song, dost turn and cry "yet a little sleep, a little slumber, a little folding of the hands to sleep?" Dost till "the field of the slothful?" Then have I no sympathy with thee. If thou hast not a soul to quit the embraces of sleep, which take from thee thy life and reason, to look upon the young beauty of the breaking day, to breathe its keen wintry freshness, or its summer fragrance, then hath Nature given thee in vain the capacity to enjoy her noblest pleasures, and to no purpose are spread before thee the choicest bounties of an all-bountiful Creator. But no, it cannot be that thou despisest these enjoyments; thou hast never tasted them, and knowest not their piquancy. I must confess that but one glimpse of the rising sun, makes me to feel a conscious superiority to him who lies steeped in stupid slumbers, inhaling the bed-room's noxious gases.

'Tis now early morning, and the waning light of the single star that pales beside the setting moon, give token that the king of day resumes his throne; and now, his first rays tint with blushing hues the hills that rise before my window—and now they are bathed in the full sunlight. Let me throw up the casement. The mild breath of May has strayed from southern climes, and coaxed old Boreas from his rugged mood. Though winter, yet it is such a spring morning as at times, in revery, seems to float over us, bearing the fragrance of flowers and groves. Whilst I enjoy its loveliness, how can I but lament that any should degrade these hours with sleep. Bah! they are fools! To give them eyes, and ears, and nerves, is a very casting pearls before swine—gilding oats for asses.

But let me forget, since I cannot forgive them.

Hah! there is my feathered friend in yonder garden, preparing to send me his morning salutation. Mark the aristocratic air with which he struts, seeming "monarch of all he surveys." He bends his head, turns towards me his glistening eye—and now he is on the fence, to bid me a very good morning;—his greeting comes *ab imo pectore*—he listens to hear it answered. There, the alarm is spreading, now it comes from the yard over the way; and, from the next and next, till it dies away in the distance, and the circuit is commenced again. At last he is done, and leaves the rostrum. Look at the fellow! (he is a great favorite of mine.) Observe his proud dignity,—his consciousness of grace! See with how lordly an air he steps amid his obedient harem—with how much deference they treat their acknowledged lord and master! Truly it is the model of a well-regulated family. He has lit upon some hidden treasure—how gallant, how patronizing are his actions! This, without his spurs, would show his knightly breeding. Desperate in courage—his motto 'victory or death,' an early riser and the very model of politeness, the cock is in fact your true gentleman.

His name declares it, for, does he not rejoice in the same appellative with that most *gallant* of all men, *Gallus*, the Frenchman?

Speaking of Frenchmen and politeness, brings to my mind the almost forgotten form of a little German, who in the latter respect was truly the first of men. From often meeting him in my morning walks, I had struck up a slight acquaintance with him, which after a while ripened into intimacy. He rises before me now, as he appeared when first I met him, some years since. I see him as then, small in stature, but making up in dignity what he lacked in size—thin and erect as the most genuine Johnny Crepaud that ever breakfasted on frogs—seeming determined to offer some resistance to the wind that passed him with as little noise as though he were the keen edge of a knife and as little respect as though he were some ill-dressed vagabond not worthy of its notice. His dapper, russet pantaloons were half hidden by a huge red waistcoat, and his face by a nose to match. As the poet beautifully observes,

"They both were red, and one was wonderful."

Yes! his nose was wonderful! Surely it should not be lightly spoken of. It was one of those features which a painter loves to sketch which it would have rejoiced the heart of Vandyke to behold, and to which he alone could have done justice. Had my little German but lived in the days of that great painter, a Vandyke nose would be as well understood, as is now a Vandyke collar. Could the great limner have seen with prophetic eye the day on which such a nose would have been born into the world, he would have cried, unlike the poet "*I* have lived two centuries *too soon* to paint a portrait."

If, as Tom Tweer says, "we may take a handle from the size of his nose, to judge of the size of his intellects," then was Meinherr Grossennase a mental giant. Think not it was one of your turn up, *retroussés*,—it was not; nor an aquiline, nor a Grecian—but a regular up and down cut and thrust, pass-me-if-you-dare nose. But why should I enlarge on that which was large enough without any help of mine. It was one misty morning, that my little man, coming in an opposite direction, as turned the corner, ran (that is, his advanced guard did) plump against my breast. I caught my breath, he his proboscis, each of us a thump. He wiped the tears from his eyes, then turning to me, he inquired with more than continental politeness, if I were hurt.

Now, though the proposition of philosophy be true, which asserts that action and reaction are in opposite directions and equal, yet, in this case, the parts brought into contact differed so widely in sensibility that most certainly he was the injured party. This, however, did not seem to diminish his regret and self-condemnation. I assured him that I was not hurt, and inquired in turn after his state of preservation. Without regarding my question, he rushed on in a train of apologies, at the close of each, exclaiming with sincere fervor, that he "was unco sally displeased, ant peged my pardon a hundert tousend times." After he had pretty well unburthened his conscience of self-reproaches, he gradually fell into conversation, and I found that there was in his nature, mixed with a good deal of pleasantry, and not a little *naiveté*, as the Frenchmen say, (*we* call it greenness,) much that was interesting and even instructive. I learnt from him the thoughts and feelings of the middling classes of Europe on aristocracy, and many influences of which we know nothing. I learnt, too, the cause of his desertion of the *Fatherland*. The dense population of the old country, "dough it was a goot Faterlant," suited him not; in its crowded thoroughfares "men did allwise run into one anodder, ant hit dere noses; it woot not do, de press was too oonlicensed." In our freer air he had found some alleviation, but not a perfect riddance of his troubles. Here, too, from time to time his feelings were shocked by the rude jostlings of the multitude. For some time, however, he got along very well, by keeping himself secluded on election days and the fourth of July, from all contact with the vulgar.

The overstrained politeness which was his most distinguishing characteristic, would occasionally exhibit itself rather ludicrously. No matter how much aggrieved, he was "unoosally displeased ant peged pardon." I remember, on one occasion, (he was walking with me at the time,) a generous serving-maid threw a bucket of water completely over him; he immediately turned and touched his hat with a low salaam, "hoped de yung-frau woot excuse him, for he did not unterstant she vas to trow de vasser, or he woot haf stopt." "Lauk, Sir!" exclaimed the astonished Abigail, "you need n't mind it, the water was dirty, and I did n't want it." He took every thing in good part.

Poor fellow! one morning, having been caught at a mass meeting the preceding day, he seemed much depressed, and said he must go to the West; he should like to see the prairies, he had heard that there were not rees there. Since then I have looked for him in vain. He is doubtless rubbing through life nearer the setting sun, and if he has not stopped, may ere this have overtaken old Leather Stocking, in the pursuit of unrestricted liberty. Ah! Herr Grossennase, freely would I give twenty-five cents to see thy nose once more, once more to feast my eyes upon its fair proportions, for well I know that, take it all in all, I ne'er shall see its like again. Farewell! my friend! and mayest thou find a land in which thy form may grow uncramped.

MORNING.

FROM THE GERMAN OF GESSNER.

WELCOME! early morning light,
  Welcome! youthful day;
Yonder from the woody mount
  Flashes now its golden ray.

In the waterfall it glitters,
  From the dewy leaf it gleams,
Joy, and life, and hope are springing
Wheresoe'er the morning beams.

Now the host of rosy dreams
  Flieth forth from every breast,
Still like love-gods sporting round
  The cheeks of Chloe in her rest.

The zephyr leaves its perfumed bed
  Upon the bosom of the flower,
And fluttering through the moistened leaves,
  Awakes the blossoms in the bower.

Fly! zephyr, fly! and steal for me
  The choicest sweets the morning brings;
Then bear them to my Chloe hence,
  Wafted upon thy dewy wings.

Awake for me the beauteous child,
  Fluttering above her snow-white bed;
Play softly o'er her maiden breast,
  And lips so rosy red.

When she awakes, then whisper her
  That since the morning sun,
I tarry at the water-fall,
  And wait her there, alone.

J. A. P.

THE WITCH.

A TALE OF THE LAST CENTURY.

BY CUJUS.

"The earth has bubbles, as the water hath."—MACBETH.

CHAPTER III.

ABOUT half a mile to the southwest of Rapaug Pond, there is a wild spot, little known at present, and visited only at long intervals by some solitary sportsman. It appears as if, at some remote time, an attempt had been made to cut through the ridge, down to its very base, but that the work, after progressing a little distance, had been given over in despair. A narrow hollow, or dell, not more than thirty feet in width, extends eastward nearly a hundred yards directly into the mountain. Its sides, at the entrance, are of course but little elevated, but they grow higher and more precipitous as it penetrates farther, till, at its inmost extremity, it is stopped abruptly by a cracked and ragged cliff, which rises some forty or fifty feet above the rough ground of the bottom. The soil of the dell is rich,—though fragments of rock are scattered here and there along its whole extent,—and the stout old trees that spring from it, rear their green crests high above its craggy wall. It is a pleasant place for the weary pedestrian to rest himself during the heat of the day; for the summer rays scarcely penetrate there, the wild flowers grow profusely around, a little sparkling fountain, gushing from the rock, trickles through, and the winds sigh softly among the branches of the hemlocks which darken the mountain above.

We return now to the time of the events detailed in the preceding chapter. The sun was yet at some distance above the western horizon, when a man, armed with a rifle, advanced cautiously from the interior of the dell we have described, listening and looking anxiously through the forest, as if expecting some companion. After standing a few minutes, he turned, as if to retrace his steps, hesitated, and finally sat down on a fragment of rock. His person was tall and powerfully made, and his features regular; but there was an angry curl of the lip, a dilation of the nostril, a gleam of the dark eyes and a settled scowl upon his forehead, which gave him an extremely repulsive look. He was clothed in a hunting-shirt, deer skin leggins and moccassins, and wore upon his head a shaggy fur cap. A powder horn and bullet pouch were suspended from his shoulders, and, in the belt which was drawn tight around his waist, was thrust a long, glittering knife, without any sheath, or other covering. His meditations seemed to be any thing but pleasant, for he muttered angrily to himself, and every now and then, as some decayed bough, or rustling leaf, or squirrel-eaten nut fell to the ground, he would start up, glance into the woods, listen a moment, and finally resume his old attitude. At length a stick broke close by his side; he turned, sprang up and beheld the object of his expectation: an Indian, a remnant of one of the perished or fast perishing tribes of that portion of the country. The savage stood as silent and apparently as unmoved as any of the old trees around, till his white companion exclaimed,

"Grahtimut! where have you dropped from?"

"Grahtimut is the wild cat," was the reply, "his step no make sound when he wish."

"Did you see him?"

"Ugh! shoot at him, could n't see plain, no hit."

"No hit! well, where the devil is he now?"

"Grahtimut old, he no longer young panther—but—*he no miss twice.* Soldier up to Rapaug with young squaw."

For a time both were silent; the Indian was a good specimen of his race, but, as he said, old, for he must have seen three score winters, yet his countenance retained much of its native ferocity, though long intercourse with the whites had given it an expression at once of submission and cunning. He was accoutred mainly in the same manner as the other, but he wore no cap, and his hair was entirely removed, with the exception of one coarse tuft, or scalp lock, on the top of his head.

"Damn him!" exclaimed the white, at last, "I hate him. He struck me, Grahtimut, felled me to the earth, to save an old woman from a ducking."

"Cap'n Martin want him scalp?"

"Yes, I want his scalp,—and when I refused to join the rebels he threatened to denounce me as a tory unless I left the State, and I *did* leave it. Ha! ha! he little thinks how near I am. Grahtimut, as you say, I must have his scalp."

"Ugh!"

"He 'll be off for his regiment before long; and we may not have another opportunity like the present; he is a rebel, too; it is but doing our duty to the king to destroy him."

"Ugh!"

"It will not do for me to attempt it,—they know me in these parts, and should I be seen by any of the rascally rebels I 'll be strung up in less than a week. Grahtimut," he continued, holding up a well-filled purse, "it is yours if you do the job—here, take my rifle—it 's a better one than that"—his brow grew black as night—"don't miss him again."

"Grahtimut never miss twice," said the Indian, taking the weapon and giving his own in exchange.

"By the way," said Martin, "is the girl handsome?"

"The young squaw is Manokee—the spring flower!"

"Good! we 'll take care of her, by and by;" he turned and retired into the recesses of the dell, while the savage, with the peculiar gait of his race, hastened into the forest.

For a short time all was quiet, till suddenly a tall, gaunt figure stepped out from behind a large rock, which lay a little to the right of the entrance to the hollow, and hurried away, with a noiseless tread, in the direction which Grahtimut had taken, exclaiming, in a suppressed tone,

"Pos-si-bil-i-ty! Wal! we 'll see 'bout that 'ere!"

The dress of this individual was peculiar; he wore moccasins and leggins, but instead of a hunting shirt he had on a coarse, home-spun coat, made somewhat after the fashion of those worn by the Quakers of the present day. A cotton handkerchief was tied tightly around his neck, and his head was protected by a low-crowned black hat, in the band of which was stuck the stump of a red feather. His hands were large and bony, and his face was browned by long exposure, but it wore an expression as honest as the sunlight. The short knife which was thrust into a belt that passed around his waist, under his coat, and the clumsy rifle in his hand, showed that he was on a hunting excursion.

For some time he continued his course in silence, now and then pausing to examine more closely the crushed leaves of the trail. It took him but a little while to gain a sight of the object of pursuit, and at first, as he did so, he raised his gun to his shoulder, but shook his head and dropped it again, muttering,

"No, no, it 's no use to shed the blood of a fellow-cretur when you can help it, even if the cretur be a tarnal Injun: it 's kinder cowardly, too, and p'raps, arter all, Mister Hugh ain't there, and then the red rascal may sneak back agin. Darn it! who 'd ha' thought that *infarnal* Tory, John Martin, was off here in Rapaug woods! Wal! he was right about it, arter all; rather guess he *will* get strung up, he! he! he! Won 't it make Mister Hugh all-fired mad though, when he hears on 't. And John thinks 'he 'll take care of the gal by and by,' does he, ho! ho! he! he! pos-si-bil-i-ty! Wal! we 'll see about that 'ere, too!"

Both the Indian and his pursuer advanced, rapidly and noiselessly, over the mountain toward the Pond, and when at length the former reached the edge of the clearing, he stopped short, as if to reconnoitre. The hunter immediately sprang behind one of the huge trees, and in good time, for he had scarcely done so, when the savage turned, and hastily coming back directly toward him, passed by almost within arm's length. The sun was now set, and the woods were fast becoming dark, so that the tall forester stepped from behind his retreat, having allowed Grahtimut to gain a distance from him somewhat less than he had kept before. Their course now lay toward the west side of the Pond, and the huntsman was beginning to conjecture that Hugh had returned home, when suddenly the Indian stopped, and brought his rifle to his shoulder.

"What in thunder 's the cretur shootin' at? Hallo! there 's Mister Hugh on the rock!" He raised his gun,—it was too late, the crack of Grahtimut's piece sounded through the woods, and the Indian sprang forward just in time to save his own life, for the bullet of the hunter whistled close past his ear, and with a yell of surprise he leaped away, and disappeared in the forest.

It was but the work of a moment with our gaunt friend to bound through the trees, spring into the Pond, and drag Hugh Warden, apparently lifeless, out upon the rock.

"Pos-si-bil-i-ty," exclaimed he, the tears mingling with the water-drops upon his cheek, "the critur 's killed him; no he han't neither," he shouted, as Hugh opened his eyes faintly and closed them again, while his frame was convulsed with a strong shudder. "O, Mister Hugh, I might have shot the infarnal Injun in the woods, cuss him!"

Again the sufferer opened his eyes, and the water poured profusely from his mouth, while his preserver caught him up in his arms, as if he had been a child, and bore him away toward the clearing. As he reached the green sward before the hut he paused, and the wounded man, raising himself by a strong effort, inquired in a feeble voice,

"Why, Richard, what is the matter?"

"Matter enough, Mister Hugh, but do n't speak any more just now," answered the hunter, while he carried him to the door of the hut. Without waiting to knock, he raised the latch and entered.

The apartment into which they so abruptly intruded, was of a description common in those days, and wore an air of cheerfulness and comfort which the exterior of the building would hardly promise. In shape it was nearly square; the walls were neatly plastered and white-washed, and decorated here and there with sprigs of evergreen. One side of the room, the eastern, was half occupied by the huge fire place, in which, on old-fashioned andirons, a pile of oaken sticks was blazing brightly. On the wide mantel-piece above, were placed two or three vases, filled with the last flowers of the year, a few sea-shells, and some half dozen books. A small square stand, or table, stood in the centre of the apartment, on which was a pair of lighted lamps. A tall old clock ticking in one corner, a table placed against the wall, over which hung a mirror, with a grotesquely carved mahogany frame, and several chairs arranged about the room, completed the ordinary furniture. On the western side, immediately opposite the fire place, two doors, standing slightly ajar, opened into the sleeping apartments, which were completely separated from each other by a white-washed wooden partition.

As the huntsman entered, still supporting the wounded man, Orra started from her seat near the stand, glanced at them fearfully a moment, and then springing forward, exclaimed,

"Hugh! Richard! what is it?"

"Nothing serious, Orra," answered Warden, "I had the bad luck to fall into the Pond, and might have been drowned but for the timely aid of our faithful friend here."

"Better tell the truth at once, Mister Hugh," said the hunter; "he fell into the Pond, Miss Orra, 'cause the tarnal Injun shot him, and if he had n't been wounded he 'd got out himself easy enough."

"Wounded, Hugh!" said the girl faintly, turning pale as death, and catching at a chair for support.

"A mere scratch," replied Warden, "but I fear enough to make me intrude on your hospitality for the night."

Perhaps our heroine should have fainted, but she did not, and recovering herself, though with a bloodless cheek and quivering lip, she advanced gently to the side of her lover, and exclaimed, "Here, Hugh, Richard, here," then taking a lamp from the table, she threw open the door of one of the sleeping rooms, while the forester hastily bore Warden forward and laid him on the couch.

"And now, Miss Orra," said he, "if you 'll git me some cloth I 'll fix his wound, and I rather calculate natur 'll do the rest."

Bandages were soon procured, when the hunter, taking the maiden gently by the hand, and leading her into the sitting room, said to her in a low tone, "God bless you, Miss Orra, but it is n't good for young and lovin' eyes to look at sufferin', and Mister Warden will soon be well of this, indeed he will."

The girl's eyes filled with tears as she sunk into a chair, by the table, and leaning down upon it, she hid her face with her hands, while the huntsman returned to the room of the wounded Hugh, and closed the door behind him.

During all this time Mrs. Stanfield, who was sitting in an old-fashioned arm-chair, by the side of the fire-place, with the cat at her feet, had not spoken, or even looked around; but now she glanced once or twice sharply at the maiden, and muttered,

"Fine doings! fine doings, indeed! who cares for the old hag? She lives in her granddaughter's home, and the girl 's got a stout soldier for a lover, and no need to ask the crone where to put him, or even whether he may enter the house; but in with him if he chances to be scratched; the gray-headed woman can sit by the fire-side till the morning, well enough."

"Oh! grandmother," said Orra, rising and walking to her side, "why do you speak thus? I have given my own little room to Hugh; there is yours; you can be alone there as well as if there were but us two in the house, for I shall not sleep to night—I shall not!"

"Yes, yes! and rise in the morning to find the door open and the soldier and grandchild fled together; away, away to the wars; it 's a merry thought, child, ho! ho! ho! is n't it? Yes, yes, a merry thought, ho! ho! ho!"

The girl made no reply, but returned to her seat, and resumed her former position, while her form trembled, and now and then shook convulsively, as if with repressed sobs.

In a few moments the door of the wounded man's apartment opened, and the huntsman came forth. Orra raised her head and looked at him inquiringly.

"Yis," said he, "you can see him now, it 's nothin' very serious arter all."

The maiden arose and went into the room. It was a small chamber, with but one window, which was covered with a curtain, fringed and worked by the hand of Orra. There was a little table in the farther corner, on which was placed a pile of needle-work and the lamp, and near it were two chairs, the only ones that the room contained. A small book-case hung against the wall opposite the bed, filled with neatly arranged volumes, on the blank leaves of most of which might have been read, by any one who should chance to open them, " From Hugh Warden." A bonnet and a shawl were hung on either side of this, and immediately beneath, on a large oaken chest, stood several flower-pots, mostly containing the common wild rose. On a shelf which was put up between the head of the couch and the window frame, lay the usual toilet apparatus and AN OPEN BIBLE. The bed itself was placed against the partition which separated the room from Mrs. Stanfield's; it was small and of simple materials, but the sheets and coverlid were white as the driven snow. In this couch lay the wounded soldier; his face was pale and wore an anxious look, but a flush overspread his cheek and his eye brightened, as the light step of the maidon crossed the threshhold.

"Hugh!" she exclaimed, sinking into a chair which the forester placed by the bed-side, " tell me how it is."

" A slight wound, Orra; I turned just as the shot was fired, and thus in all probability saved my life; the ball struck my shoulder, and glancing off from the bone passed through the fleshy part of my arm above the elbow; the shock caused my fall into the pond, where I might have drowned, indeed, but for the timely aid of Richard, who, by the way, has n't told me how he happened to be at hand at so seasonable a moment."

"Richard?" said the girl, looking at him inquiringly.

The hunter was sitting in a corner of the room busily inspecting his wet rifle, but upon being thus addressed, he answered,

" Why, you see, Miss Orra, I know'd that Mister Hugh was gone up into the mountains, 'cause he was calculatin' to go away to-morrow, you know; and I thought that if I should take the old piece here and come round this way, I might chance to kill somethin' and have *his* company home too. Wal, off I come, took a kind of round about track, and, as I was passin' by a kind of darned queer place down below here, I thought I heard somebody talkin', and then I heard Mister Hugh's name, and I got behind a rock and looked round it, and there I see'd that ere Injun of yourn, cuss his tarnal red skin—beg your pardon, Miss Orra, but I can't help it—conflabberin' away with a white man, never mind who that was; and I made out that the pale chap and he were gittin' up a plan to shoot you, Mister Warden, and the white feller showed a money-bag, and the Injun took his rifle and off he started. 'Pos-si-bil-i-ty!' says I, and off I started arter him. I got a chance to shoot him once or twice, but somehow or other I could n't make up my mind to, and when we got up there by the Pond, I see'd him raise his rifle, but I could n't see nothin' at first of any thing to shoot at. Pretty soon I saw you, however, on the rock, and I fired at the red-skin quicker than lightnin'; but he'd fired first and jumped, so I did n't hit him, and away he went into the woods like a deer, and I into the Pond like a duck. You know the rest, Mister Hugh."

"Well, but, Richard, who was the white man?"

"John Martin."

"John Martin!" exclaimed Hugh, starting up and immediately sinking back, with a slight exclamation of pain. The girl started too, and repeated the exclamation.

"Yis!" said the hunter, "John Martin, that infarnal tory."

"This must be looked to, Richard," said the young man thoughtfully, "indeed it must."

"But you cannot look to it to-night, Hugh," said the maiden, smiling sadly, "so think not of it. But I hear my grandmother calling—good night, talk no more," continued she, placing her hand upon his lips, "but rest, for you need it much," and she left the room, closing the door after her as she passed out.

"The gal's about right, Mister Hugh," said the hunter, throwing himself upon the floor, "so you need n't ask any more questions; I'm done with talkin' till to-morrow mornin'."

CHAPTER IV.

It wanted yet somewhat more than an hour of midnight. The moon rode high in the unclouded heavens, and the landscape lay stretched out beneath, still, quiet, and checkered with a thousand alternations of light and shadow. The forest was hushed, all except a deep, continual, faintly-murmuring sound like the noise of the distant ocean, and now and then the sharp cry of some wild beast, or the dismal shrieking of the night-owl. What a strange mystery hangs over the silent night! Day we become familiarized to, the sunlight comes, and comes, and comes again, but we cease to think of it, engaged in the continual round of business, and each succeeding hour is the same with that which shone on us yester-morn or noon, only that they pass away more swiftly as we grow older, till they all end in the peaceful grave. Not so with night; to *it*, we cannot familiarize ourselves; it is a fit emblem of death, of the time "when no man can work;" it is fearful, for under its dark shadow deeds of terrible iniquity are planned and committed; theft, lust, and murder stalk abroad during its silent hours, and the shriek of agony too often breaks its dread repose. It is the time, too, when superstition exults in her power, and the heart dies within us at her ghastly presence. Who is there that walks solitary at midnight and feels no quicker throbbings in his bosom, or has no oft-repeated inclination to look back, as if some phantom were pursuing him? But we are wandering from our narrative.

We return once more to the retreat of the tory. At the inmost extremity of the dell a kind of hut had been constructed, the walls of which were formed in part of the solid rock, and in part of a rude stone work, built up to the height of some eight or ten feet. It was covered with poles, the smaller ends of which were thrust into the fissures of the cliff, while the others rested upon the top of the stone-work, and upon these were piled large quantities of the dried leaves of the forest.

The entrance was low, and guarded by a rough door, made of sticks bound together by strips of bark.

In this hut, on a couch of skins, lay John Martin, asleep. His slumber was disturbed, for he tossed uneasily, and now and then muttered broken sentences. Suddenly a sharp whoop resounded through the hollow, and the tory, starting up hastily, pushed aside the door and sprang into the open air. The dell was almost perfectly dark, and it was impossible to see any object with distinctness.

"Grahtimut," shouted Martin, "is it you?"

"Ugh! Cap'n Martin," answered the Indian, stepping to his side.

"Have you seen him, Grahtimut?"

"Ugh."

"The scalp, the scalp."

"No got it."

"Missed him again, by ——!"

"Grahtimut never miss twice."

"Where the devil is he, then?"

"Bottom of Rapaug."

"What!"

"Mis'er Warden on rock. Grahtimut creep up like wild-cat,—fire—never miss twice,—pale-face throw up his arms, and fall dead into the Pond; more pale-faces come, shoot at me, feel here, Cap'n Martin."

The tory did as desired, and placing his hand to the side of the Indian's head, felt the blood clotted on the scratch made by the huntsman's bullet.

"A narrow escape, Grahtimut, but a great deal better than none; how many were there in the party that fired at you?"

"No count; heard 'em in the woods; see Mis'er Warden fall; *he dead*, Cap'n."

"Good; well, here is the purse; you say the girl is handsome, eh?"

"Young squaw is Manokee!"

"Well—stop, though; where did the pale-faces go?"

"No tell; down to D——, s'pose."

"The devil!" said Martin, thoughtfully, "they can't have stopped there; no, no, the old witch would n't allow it. Grahtimut," he continued, turning to the Indian, "go into the hut and sleep, I've got business of my own now."

The savage obeyed, and Martin, after drawing his belt somewhat tighter about his waist, feeling the handle of his knife, and examining with his finger the priming of his rifle, started into the forest. He bent his course toward the Pond, muttering as he went,

"It would n't have done for me to have shot Hugh Warden; the d—d rebels would then certainly have showed no mercy if they had ever caught me; and it 's cursed doubtful now; but I do n't think they 'll get hold of me right off; no, no. But this old hag they hate, and 't won't make any difference what I do there. Grahtimut seems to be half in love with the girl himself, ha! ha! Manokee,—the spring-flower, eh!

Hallo! what the devil 's that?" he exclaimed, as a wild animal bounded from his path; "confound the beast, how he scared me!"

He proceeded rapidly through the forest, muttering to himself at intervals, till he reached the clearing. Here he paused, and crept cautiously up to the house, and peered into one of the windows on the side fronting the Pond. The lamp was burning dimly upon the table, at which sat Orra, with an open book in her hand, though her eyes were often wandering from it; in the corner sat the old woman, in the position described in the preceding chapter.

The tory, as if convinced that no others were near, raised himself up boldly, and without knocking entered the hut. The girl started up with a half shriek, gazed for a moment full in his face, and then, as not recognizing him, walked back a little way, and stood as if awaiting the announcement of his errand. The cat sprang with one bound to the top of the old clock, and turning round, stared with her fierce gray eyes at the intruder, while the old woman, looking up, exclaimed in a sharp, angry tone, "John Martin?"

"Yes, John Martin," replied he, coolly seating himself in the chair which Orra had vacated, "and how are *you* and your friend, the devil? Both well, I suppose. Do n't be frightened, Miss," continued he, looking at Orra; "the Indian was right, by ——! Very comfortable here, very; I think of exchanging my residence; room for a lodger, eh? Do n't look so d—d savage, old woman; nobody means you any harm."

"John Martin," said Mrs. Stanfield, rising, "go back to your hiding place in the hollow. You 're a fool for coming abroad to-night; I know your intentions, but do n't anger me again, it is n't safe; I tell you, go; a few minutes more will be too late."

The tory quailed a moment before her impetuosity, but recovering himself, he exclaimed, "None of that, if you please; your hero of five years ago must be called from the bottom of Rapaug, if at all; so look to yourself rather than to me; seat yourself, my dear," he continued, starting up and advancing toward Orra, "a kiss first, though," and he threw his arm around her; the old woman clapped her hands suddenly, and the cat leaped from the clock with a fearful yell, full into his face, and fastening upon his head and shoulder, tore with teeth and claws, deep into the flesh. The intruder relinquished his hold of the maiden, and, half blinded with rage and pain, grasped at the handle of his knife; when the door of one of the sleeping apartments burst open and a heavy blow from the butt of a rifle prostrated him upon the floor.

"There, darn ye, take that," shouted the hunter, standing over him, "pos-si-bil-i-ty, though; is that the way the Britishers larnt ye to treat a gal, blast your infarnal pictur! I 've a darned good mind to cut your throat; but I 'll save ye for a more desarvin' eend, I will," and unloosing his belt, he tied the hands of the senseless tory tightly behind his back. This operation completed, he looked up at the cat, which had resumed its original position, and exclaimed, "Wal! you 're considerable of a critur now, you are, by thunder! you etarnal, great, green-eyed, black devil! Hallo! there; you 've come to agin, have you," said he, as

Martin opened his eyes and groaned heavily. In a few moments more the prisoner recovered his senses entirely, and glared fiercely around the room; suddenly he looked toward the open door of the bed-room; he started as if shot, bounded convulsively upward, and, with a horrible shriek, fell back senseless as before. The hunter turned, and behind him stood Warden, partly dressed, and with the white coverlid drawn around his shoulders.

"Mister Hugh," said the huntsman, "what on airth are you out here for? Pr'aps you calculate I could n't manage the infarnal scoundrel; did n't I tell ye not to stir? But I 'm eenamost glad you come, arter all. He thought you was a ghost, he! he! he! There, he 's comin' to agin."

The tory opened his eyes, and looking steadfastly at Warden, muttered something in an indistinct tone.

"Yis, yis, John Martin," said his captor, "it 's him, alive and kickin'. Guess it 'll take two or three Injuns and a half a dozen tories to kill him, when Richard Brownhead 's in the neighborhood, ho! ho! he!"

"Well, but, Richard," said Hugh, "what shall we do with the prisoner till the morning?"

"I 'll take care of that," replied the hunter; "this way, if you please, Mr. Martin;" and lifting the prisoner from the floor, he partly led, partly dragged him, still bound, into the chamber which we have before described. Here he laid him upon the floor, and having fastened his feet together, left him. When he came out Hugh and Orra were sitting together, conversing in a low tone, and the old woman was apparently dozing in her chair. After standing and looking at the lovers a moment he muttered softly,

"Pos-si-bil-i-ty, he! he! he!" and with a countenance contorted with intense delight, walked across the room, and seating himself, commenced an examination of the tory's rifle.

Nearly two hours passed away, to the lovers of course almost imperceptibly, but Richard had been for some time nodding over the side of his chair, when a stifled noise in the prisoner's chamber caught his ear and at once aroused him; he listened a moment, the sound was repeated, and something like a fall was distinctly audible. The hunter sprang up, burst open the door and entered the room; the belt and cord lay broken upon the floor, the window was raised, and Martin—gone. Without a word the huntsman leaped from the window, and by the faint light of the morning, now beginning to illuminate the eastern sky, searched for the trail; there was none to be found, no broken soil, no track or trace of the fugitive, and after a tedious inspection of the ground, he re-entered the house, and looking with a blank face at the astonished inmates, exclaimed,

"Wal! Mister Hugh, the blasted, infarnal, sneaking critur has been just a leetle too 'cute for us this time, and we might as well be gettin' back to D—— now, for it 's no use stayin' here, and the folks 'll wonder what on airth has become on us."

"Orra," said Hugh, rising, "I cannot leave you here to the mercy of this villain. The mountains are unsafe for two defenseless women; why not seek a refuge in the village?"

"Go home, Hugh Warden," said the old woman, rising, "defend yourself; Orra Stanfield and her grandmother can protect themselves; better trust to the beasts of the forest, or to the worse than beasts that hide their heads there, than to the rabble of a town; I can defend my child, and could have done it this night without your aid. She loves you, she does; I have seen love before and know its strength, but I tell you again she can NEVER become your bride. Depart!" She turned away and resumed her seat in silence. Hugh whispered a few words in the maiden's ear, to which she replied in a low, mournful voice, "No, Hugh, no, I cannot leave her, you would not love me if I could. Go, *dear* Hugh, go, I feel assured I shall not be harmed, for the God of the orphan will be my protector."

"You are perhaps right, Orra," said the young man sadly, but I cannot bear the thought of leaving you here; yet I *will* go; this wound will detain me at home, I foresee, for unless I join my regiment soon, which it will not permit, it will be a wiser course to remain here; the enemy is making demonstrations in this direction, too; and while I do remain, Richard and I can keep watch about you, and"—

"Come, come, Mister Hugh," interrupted the hunter, "if Miss Orra can't go, and the old woman won't, we must."

"Good bye, Orra, dear Orra," said Hugh, as he pressed his lips upon her pale forehead; the maiden murmured some low words; the door opened—closed again, and Mrs. Stanfield and her granddaughter were alone.

[TO BE CONTINUED.]

THE CHILD'S CONSOLATION.*

A MOTHER sat apart and wept,
And would no word of comfort hear;
Some grief lay heavy at her heart,
Which spake in many a bitter tear.

Her child, returning from its play,
Wonder'd to see its mother sad;
So little of the world she knew,
She thought the good were always glad.

Fain would she speak some gentle word
To comfort her, and yet she fears;
Her mother must have sinned, she thought,
For sin alone was cause for tears.

* The above is a simple narration of a real incident.

So gently stealing to her side,
And lifting up her eyes of blue,
"Mother," she said, "do so no more,
And God will pardon you."

Sweet child! thy Innocence is Truth;
Sorrow for sin alone is given,
And though it fall on guiltless heads,
If Sin were not, then Earth were Heaven.

J. A. P.

THE LAST LEAF FROM THE LIFE OF CHATTERTON.

"In winter's tedious nights, sit by the fire
With good old folks; and let them tell thee tales
Of woful ages, long ago betid:
And ere thou bid good night, to quit their grief,
Tell thou the lamentable fall of me,
And send the hearers weeping to their beds."

Shakspeare's Richard Second.

Whatever estimate may have been put upon the literary merits of the author of the 'Rowleian Antiquities' in his own age, little reflection is needed at this late day to convince us that he possessed a genius as brilliant and astonishing as ever burst upon the theatre of literary life. A mere youth, 'to fortune and to fame unknown,' he displayed a maturity and grasp of mind the wrestlers for the wreaths of intellectual might may well propose for their imitation.

Thomas Chatterton was born in Bristol, in the October of 1752, under circumstances that would forever forbid ordinary minds indulging the faintest speculations concerning distinction in life. At the age of five years he was bound to a charity school by his widowed mother, herself totally ignorant of any employment she might find for him hereafter. But, like many more on whom the world now doats with affectionate pride, he was considered by his instructors 'a boy too dull to learn,' and dismissed to his mother with this mortifying intelligence. A mind naturally inquisitive, united with the careful teachings of a troubled parent, soon, however, regained to him what he had lost by his dismissal, and he continued to make a progress in learning altogether surprising. At fifteen he was apprenticed, for want of a more convenient employment, to an attorney in Bristol, where he unfortunately remained the rest of his life, if we except only a few months in London. It was in this capacity that he sent forth to the world the result of his antiquarian researches, maintaining their authenticity with no ordinary ingenuity. But, if his success vanished before the sweeping investigations of the learned and inquisitive, we would, from mere charity, to say nothing of admiration, call it his misfortune, not his fault. The conduct of Horace Walpole, who through his passionate love for antiquated manuscripts and paintings had made him honorable professions of regard, and generous promises of assistance, on receiving a letter from our poet, hinting the possibility of their being forgeries, by informing him that these were the only means of his subsistence, has ever been a subject of general dissatisfaction, notwithstanding the repeated attempts of his biographer to gloss it with a fair explanation.

But Chatterton's success in Bristol was far short of his most moderate anticipations, and he longed to embark his fortunes in the metropolis of London, where the spirits of a Shakspeare, a Milton, a Jonson, and a Garrick, had successfully gone before him. To free himself, then, from the legal claims of his master, was his next object, and this, as we shall see, he effected with little difficulty. His plan was, partly, we believe, through a desire to inspire fear, and partly in obedience to the promptings of gloomy despair, to throw out repeated threats of self-destruction: which, however, at last were so often repeated as to pass unnoticed and uncared for. But the discovery, one morning, of a formal will lying on his table, gave the subject a more practical appearance, and procured for him what he had so long desired. Once fairly dismissed from his uncongenial employment, and made dependent solely on the fertility of his genius, his hypocondriacal temper deserted him, and he prosecuted those literary subjects, to which his taste originally directed him, with renewed ardor, and, for a time, with wonderful success. He appeared in most of the popular magazines, but it was chiefly in the 'Town and Country,' that he became an object of universal inquiry. In the columns of this periodical he exhibited many copies of papers in his possession, professing them to have belonged to an old monk, Rowley, in the fourteenth century, and discovered in an old chest, secreted in St. Mary, Edgeville church, by his own father, while sexton. Among these, the most striking were papers relating to 'William Canynge,' the tragical interlude entitled 'Alla,' 'Battle of Hastings,' the 'Elegy of Sir Charles Bawden,' and 'on the Fryars first passing over the Old Bridge.' In polemical writing on political topics, in composing songs for the public gardens, or in arranging tales for depicting the customs of his day, he everywhere displayed an astonishing versatility of talent. If we consider the amount alone of his labor, it staggers our utmost credulity: his pen was ever his constant companion,—his mind ever in pursuit of new objects. But it was chiefly under the character of 'Rowley,' that he wished to secrete himself, and acquire, like the modern 'Junius,' a reputation, rendered doubly valuable by the veil of secrecy thrown over it.

Thus had this 'boy bard,' as one of England's later poets styles him, passed three months in his new field of labor, when suspicions of his imposition gave his circumstances an entirely different aspect. His fortunes turned, and however much a little had before been to him, poverty would now thrust a farthing in his face, and grinningly tell him 'twas his last. Already for two long days he had tasted nothing; his expectations of gaining food by solicitation were overreached by his pride, and he resolved that earthly miseries should soon have an end with him. On the evening of August 24th, 1770, scarcely yet having attained his eighteenth year, he destroyed himself with poison. He was found on the following morning, stretched on his bed, an awful spectacle. A mere 'shell' received his distorted remains, and Chatterton slept with the dead. Such was the life and death of one upon whom the world will never cease to gaze in wonder,—" a *comet* in the hemisphere of genius, ordained sometime to illumine the world with its miraculous splendor, and which then retires for ages, whilst an admiring nation observes the irruption in the order of things, and is lost in the contemplation of its unknown laws."

In whatever aspect we behold him, he is sure to awaken feelings of mingled admiration and sorrow; admiration, at beholding an age so tender made the receptacle of Heaven's brightest gifts; sorrow, in knowing ourselves thus early bereft of a gem, that would have shed a lustre on the brightest page of the history of literature.

> " His life was gentle; and the elements
> So mixed in him, that Nature might stand up
> And say to all the world,—*This was a man!*"

* * * * * * *

Turn with me, reader, into this narrow, secluded lane of noisy London. Ascend this flight of steps, push onward through that long, half-lighted hall, mount another flight of rickety stairs, and at their head are the entire earthly dominions of the noblest literary monarch known. From his little window, curtained only by the fine woofs of the industrious spider, and repeated coatings of dust raised from occasionally disturbing his pile of manuscripts, can be seen in the distance the majestic front of the 'Tower,' and the heavenward pointing spire of St. Paul's. Solemn and sad were the tones of the old clock, as it sounded forth the knell of departing hours, bringing with them, to him, their full measure of sorrow and misery.

Here might we see him sometimes for whole nights together, bending a feeble and fast-sinking frame over labor that was to prove to him worse than useless. Sleep he could not, for with such a writhing spirit as his the calmness of sleep could have no possible sympathy. After exhaustion from his labor he would toss upon his bed, beat his temples with the palms of his hands, and in almost insupportable agony exclaim, in the language of the troubled Macbeth,

> " Out, out, brief candle!
> Life's but a walking shadow: a poor player,
> That struts and frets his hour upon the stage,
> And then is heard no more."—

Again he would start from his couch and speed his pen for hours, wholly engrossed in the subject before him. It was only after such repeated tortures of his mind, that he would sink back at last upon his bed, overcome with entire exhaustion, and bury his cares in sleep. The rays of the morning sun would long have found their way through the dusty film that enveloped his window, ere they penetrated *his* heavy lids.

He had returned to his humble tenement one evening in the latter part of August, at an hour so late that he started himself with surprise on counting the heavy strokes of the old clock. But from no scenes of festivity and mirth; his brow was clouded, and manifestly something hung heavily on his heart, whose weight he showed not the least desire to dissipate. Flinging aside his cap, he paced his little domain in a state of excitement almost amounting to frenzy. 'Relief must come soon,' cried he in anguish, 'or all will be over,' and he hastily threw himself on the chest, that stood by his window, and tried in vain to gaze on the cold face of the moon. 'Yes, all will be over,—the ordeal of fate must soon be gone through,' and he shed a flood of scalding tears, that seemed to trace, as they coursed down his emaciated cheeks, the furrows of torment. 'Yesterday's sun,' continued he, 'saw my last morsel, and, O, Heaven! must it be that in London humanity and learning will behold the unfortunate die, in the very act of laboring for sustenance! The life of the attorney was indeed a thankless one, and I could have expected from it nothing *less* than starvation. But friends, who are so no longer, advised me to desert that for the more agreeable profession of letters: and must I, beside the path of literature, erect my own solitary mound, and inscribe my own epitaph!'

As if to presage the melancholy gloom in which the future was shrouded, his candle glared with intense brightness, and sunk into its socket, leaving him entirely alone, for even in solitude one feels a companionship in any object around him, that requires the least share of his attention. 'Thus am I left alone,' said he, after a moment's pause and reflection, 'a wretched, *most* wretched item in this world's history. Well enough am I acquainted with it,—it is the wisdom of a fool that seeks to know more. But there is another, pictured by scenes of joy and knowledge, where I may roam unfettered through *all* science, and soon may it find me among its happiest occupants. Sainted Father! may it be mine to quench my thirst from the same fountain with thee!'

Again he paused, seemingly overpowered by the intensity of his feelings. A clammy sweat stood upon his throbbing temples, as if his proud soul were struggling to free itself from its exhausted tenement. He rolled his head, first upon one side, then upon the other, and seemed to court ease in the very motion. But though he sought rest for his bodily powers, already strained to their utmost, his soul was a stranger to any such desire. There was evidently some great commotion within, some fiery working of the feelings, that bespoke momentous results, as the sequel of our narrative will show. Twice he sprang in a frenzy to the floor, and as often sank back in silence on his uncushioned seat, muttering expressions, first of triumphant confidence, then of wavering doubt. The innocence and purity of the youth was engaged in a violent struggle with the passions of the man, and it was only a feeling of stout-hearted manliness within him, developed beneath the Ætna pressure of his cares, that nerved him calmly to witness so easy a vanquishment of the former.

With an energy, fired only by despair, he made a third attempt, and stood by his table in the middle of the floor. Clenching his fist in inconceivable agony, he struck it forcibly on his pile of papers, and turning his gaze through the windows up to the spangled vault of heaven, whence the moon seemed to look down in cold pity, exclaimed :—'God of the Universe! hear my last, solemn vow! thy benevolence in placing me here has strangely proved to me a blighting curse: the false-heartedness of man, his treacherous protection and disguised sympathy, could never have been designed by thee either for my happiness or interest. I must find relief, and that soon, or escape the pangs of a beggar's shame, and the lingering torments of starvation, by my own hand. Unless thou shalt raise me up some supporter in *this* world, to-morrow's moon shall behold me resting on thy arm, a support as lasting as eternity.'

He groped by the light of the moon for another candle, and placed it in the emptied socket: it was the last he had, but not so much as a sigh escaped him as he prepared to light it, for from this time he looked upon every thing as going. Then, with a firmness of spirit, lent him as it were prematurely from the other world, after conning the titles of his manuscripts and arranging them in order, he calmly penned a final letter to his widowed parent, nor suffered his pen to rest till his task was completed. As if a recapitulation of its miseries could alleviate in the least a spirit already *buried* beneath them, he spread out the scrawled sheet, and thus read aloud :—

LONDON, August 23rd, 1770.

DEAREST MOTHER,—

The unworthy affection I bear you bids me leave you at least *one* memorial of myself, which you will behold in these farewell words. What I am now penning is my last and only bequest: did I possess the touch of a Midas, haggard want should never know you, and the world would not thus scornfully trample on its most devoted son. My fate has been sealed:—I have sworn to rid myself of this fickle thing—life—in one day's lapse, if assistance does not meet me in the mean time. Since I left my uncongenial employment in Bristol, fortune, ever varying, has visited me with many sad reverses. To disappointments frequent experience has so far accustomed me, that I can bear them even without murmuring or much remorse. Indeed, I should feel out of my proper course, did not Heaven visit me with a *large* share of misery: but when poverty rolls over my soul like the ocean waves over a drowning wretch, and disappointment increases her festering torment to that of the good,—when my brightest hopes, on which, alas! hung all that is dear to me in this life, lie crushed at my feet, and I am compelled to behold them as a phantom, dispelled on approach,—*then* it is, mother, that courage deserts me, and I call on death.

I have been urged to press on,—to show no faltering distrust at the approach of poverty, and a 'shining mark' is mine. Ah! could the world but know the corroding canker that lies at my heart's vitals,—if men would exercise penetration enough to perceive the close relation of mind and body, of the essential and invisible, I should need but little stimulus to lead me on through paths the most intricate and arduous.

Of late I have held a limited correspondence with his Majesty's minister, the Hon. Horace Walpole, and if you, mother, from such a slight means could learn so thoroughly the glorious cheat of human nature,—the hypocrisy and treachery that clothes itself in the garb of honor and power, you could as easily as myself be disgusted with all the professions of this false world, and pray for a speedy removal to a better. May he yet discover his error, though it be too late, and the world yet know it has spurned its own beggared child, though its tears of affectionate regret be unavailing.

Of the Heavenly muse I have ever been an ardent worshiper: not one to traffic my noble nature for the mere tinselry of earthly gifts—and woo her only when arrayed with the wealth of the Queen of Sheba; in the calm seclusion of solitude I have ever been happy to hold nocturnal conferences with my Egeria, when I could not believe a sordid desire might have polluted my orisons. As I have courted the muse in life, so I believe she will soothe and charm me in death: my mind grows brighter as I approach it, and will shine forth unclouded at its consummation. It is the pressure of my circumstances alone that drives me to this step; think not I am mad, *I am starving*. Yet I *will* not beg: there are enough in wealth and power, before whom I have laid my condition,—my labors for an honorable subsistence have at no time been remitted, and the curse of my dark death may grate on their soul's happiness till we meet at the general reckoning. My few books and papers I have carefully arranged, and here they will remain for your disposal. Do not regard me when gone as a reckless suicide, but believe with me that I obey a merciful summons from above. May Heaven lighten your burthen in this world and satisfy you with undisturbed rest in another, where we hope to meet again. Farewell!

THOMAS.

Folding this with trembling hands, he sealed it, inscribed his mother's name upon the back and laid it with his manuscripts. Rising abruptly from his seat at the table, he re-commenced pacing his room, stopping ever and anon to catch the sound of footsteps in the dismal hall, or to gaze for a moment on the pale face of the moon, now fast sinking in the West. Suddenly he starts at the sound of approaching footsteps, and trembles for the very fear it may after all prove a delusion. 'Yes,' said he, 'an Angel of Mercy!" A low knock was heard at his door, and at his bidding a stranger entered and quietly seated himself by the window. After the usual salutations he commenced a conversation, in the course of which our young poet made such heart-rending disclosures of his condition, as to bring tears to his eyes. That he might not augment another's sufferings by the addition of his own grief, and believing he had, though accidentally, found an object worthy of immediate and generous relief, he left him again to the stings of reflection, intending to return at an early hour on the following day, and surprise him with assistance.

"What *can* this mean?" exclaimed Chatterton, ere yet his visitor's footsteps had ceased to echo in the hall. 'Has Heaven cruelly deluded me, that my straining spirit may relapse again into torments greater than before! O, that there were one in the wide world to call *friend*,' and he repeated it, as if the title sounded strangely to his ear: 'not one whose favors are bought with money or the detestable coin of flattery: no, I would know no more of these,—the world swarms with them, and their contact is to be avoided as the viper's. But come, Death; I have courage and fortitude at any time to meet thee.'

The exhaustion such an ebullition of his inmost feelings naturally produced, drove him at last to his pallet, where incessant weeping and sobbing induced a sleep so vigorous as to be prolonged to a late hour the next morning. His last farthing was long since gone, and he troubled himself with no farther expectations for good, but went on with his remaining duties with resignation and fortitude. He arranged his simple dress with more than usual care, separated and adjusted his various articles of clothing and furniture, and prepared himself for his last hours with the firmness of a Socrates. The morning hours lagged heavily, yet rapidly they flew by: noon came, still no relief,—afternoon, his hopes grew fainter and his feelings deeper,—the old clock tolled out successively the hours of four, five, and six; the shadows in the streets grew longer,—twilight came slowly creeping over nature, and it was evening. The seventh hour had come in its place and the eighth was at hand, when his heart should no longer throb with the impulses of agony and fear. At the foot of his bed he might *now* be seen sitting, in suspense for the next stroke, the veins on his neck and temples distended to an awful and alarming size. In the silence that prevailed, the rapid pulsations of his heart could be heard distinctly, occasionally only interrupted by a deep-fetched sigh.

Thus situated—his feelings poised between the two worlds—he might have forgotten himself in dreamy musings, had not the tones of St. Paul's fearfully sounded his death-knell. 'Ah, my poor mother!' he exclaimed, 'may you never know the sufferings of your son!' Rising calmly from his seat he walked to his window, extended his hand towards his chest, and opening it took therefrom a vial containing *poison*. His chest he slowly shut again, re-seated himself at the foot of his bed, and pouring its fatal contents into a tumbler that stood ready on his table, without so much as the quivering of a muscle, he drank it off at a draught. He replaced the glass upon the table, simply murmuring in a suppressed tone,—'Such is human existence.' Aware that the strength of his potion would almost immediately prostrate his bodily powers, he stretched himself at length upon his couch and awaited his final struggles with resignation. Nor were his expectations long delayed. The grim shadows of death stole slowly over him, and the powers of his vigorous mind almost imperceptibly relapsed into the torpor of forgetfulness. Now thick and fast danced unseen spirits round his bewildered brain: the demons of pain grappled fearfully with his benumbed body, wringing large drops of sweat from his brow. Once he threw out his arms and struggled with all his dying exertions,—raised his head and stared wildly around his room,—threw it back again upon his pillow, groaning faintly, 'What a world!' either in retrospect or in looking forward to that he was about entering,—closed his heavy lids and gasped his last. Thus ended the eventful existence of Thomas Chatterton, the history of whose sufferings is but the history of a thousand others in every age. E.

STANZAS.

FROM THE GERMAN OF WASSERMANN.

AHNUNG.

Ich höre Glockenlaute,
Sie dringen mir ins Herz,
So dumpf wie ihr Gesumme,
So dumpf ist auch mein Schmerz.

Ich höre Glockenlaute,
Sie ziehen in die Luft,
Es wohnt mir in dem Busen
Ein Sehnen nach der Gruft.

Ich höre Glockenlaute,
Die Thräne quillt herab,
Ich fühl 'es, meine Qualen
Verlöschen erst im Grab.

FOREBODING.

I hear the chime of bells,
Straight to my heart it goes,
Heavy as that deep music swells,
So heavy are my woes.

I hear the chime of bells
Ring out to wind and wave,
Ever within my bosom dwells
A longing for the grave.

I hear the chime of bells,
Faster the warm tear flows;
Where rest the dead in quiet cells,
There only cease my woes.

MORAL PRINCIPLE AND LAW,

AS CONSERVATORS OF GOOD ORDER.

A SINGLE glance will suffice to convince us that nothing is more variable than moral principle in different individuals. It rises up before one as an ever-present and smoking Sinai; whence he receives the "Tables of the Law" of his heart and life. To another individual, on the contrary, moral principle never presents itself; or, if so, not as a mount of authority, but as a rock of stumbling and offense. He is a child of passion, a devout worshiper of blind, contradictory chance; a vacillating, reeling creature of impulse, as changeful in action as Proteus in shape.

If now we search after the efficient cause of this diversity in the moral principles of men, we shall find it, not in any original difference in moral constitution and tendency, but in the different influences under which these principles have been formed. We always predict a vicious manhood of the child that is educated amid the polluting influences of of corrupt examples. And, on the other hand, we expect a virtuous life of the child of virtuous parents. So uniformly have our experience and observation shown it to be a fact, that the moral character of the chief source of authority ever assimilates its subjects to itself.

Law is to the man what the parent is to the child. The child is a member of a household; subject to its regulations; and an imitator of the moral character of its legally constituted head. The man is a member of society; amenable to its enactments and prescriptions; influenced in his thoughts, governed in his conduct by them. Are they not likely, then, materially to shape his character? What is law? What are these rules and regulations of society? these international laws, these civil enactments, these penal codes with their tremendous sanctions? What are these halls of legislation, these judgment seats, these officers of law, these dungeons, gibbets, and penitentiaries? Are they not a vast fabric—a sublime and spacious Temple, reared by the toil, the wisdom, the virtue of all ages, to hoary headed Justice? And shall the man who daily treads its solemn aisles; who beholds its impressive ceremonials; who listens to the language of its priests; who witnesses the sacrifices—the tears and groans of injustice and wrong:—who sees the victims—wicked men—reeking on its gore-stained altars;—shall the spectator of scenes like these, I say, turn away and be unjust still? Must not an abiding sense of the inflexible sternness and rigidity of justice sink deep into his heart? Will not moral principle grow strong beneath such congenial influences.

The proof of the position I have here maintained, in theory, might easily be confirmed by facts, were we to compare the moral principle of the same, or of different nations, when under a lax, and when under a rigid government. But I deem it already sufficiently substantiated. Very much of the influence, therefore, which moral principle exerts on society, is to be ascribed to law; inasmuch as law is the schoolmaster to educate and fit it to wield this influence. Indeed, this is one very important medium through which law secures the well-being of society. Like a skillful general, it does not essay to guard every inlet to harm by its own personal presence; but, training up others, it stations them as sentinels at the posts of danger.

But, for the sake of argument, I will consider moral principle *as it is;* without reference to the means of its development and growth. What, then, is the true amount of influence that moral principle has on American society?

Law is designed to prevent only the more capital crimes. There is a lower class of offenses; such as falsehood, cheating, sinful thoughts and purposes never bodied forth in action—each and all as offensive to the pure eye of Justice as any other—but of which human law takes no cognizance. This department of human waywardness and guilt has been confided to the guardianship of moral principle; and this, I might add, is its appropriate sphere of employment.

Look abroad now, over society, and see how great its efficiency proves to be in this its peculiar department of exertion. Some there are, attentive and obedient to its admonitions. No one, however, acquainted with society, will pretend that even here, in this favored land, these constitute a majority; much less then in other lands. The constant repetition of the misdeeds I have named, shows at once the impotency of moral principle and the depravity of humanity. The soil of the human heart is, indeed, prolific in crime. Moral principle labors nobly; but the rank weeds of vice are springing up at its feet; around its altars; yes, and ofttimes within the Church of the living God!

If, then, moral principle is insufficient security against these smaller offenses, what security can it afford against the higher? If it is incompetent to watch over a small department, what sort of guardianship can it exercise over the whole calendar of crimes? If it cannot cure the disease in its incipient stages, what impression can it make after it has assumed the incorrigible malignity of a settled hereditary disease. If it does not stifle the first oath that is trembling on the lips of the conscience stricken boy; if it does not prevent him from willfully disobeying his parents; how shall it quench the torch of the incendiary? how prevent the depredations of the hardened thief? what shield oppose to the dagger of the midnight assassin? what barrier raise against the tempestuous surges of popular fury?

But what is moral principle, from its very nature, fitted to effect? The mode of its operation is moral suasion. The motives which it presents to virtue are, a good or bad reputation—as the act may be—an approving conscience, inward peace. But what are these that they should essay ascendancy over the prejudice, passion, selfishness, and ambition of the human heart? Every day shows them scoffed at and trampled under foot, though aided and enforced by the most vigorous laws. What, then, could they accomplish alone? Under such a system the villain and murderer would roam unmolested; nay, commit their nefarious deeds in the broad light of day. Moral principle would stretch out no arm to arrest them; constitute no tribunal to judge; open no dungeon to receive them! It might, to be sure, jog them gently on the shoulder, and remind them that their conduct would, probably, prove destructive of inward peace; and moreover, might, possibly, be disorganizing to society. Excepting this, they would be unrestrained; their only check the natural limit of their ferocity; their only law a satiety of blood! Should crimes, therefore, under such a system, be no more frequent than now; and moral principle retain its present vigor—as they would *not*—we can easily see, that, in the absence of security to life and property, society must be resolved into its original elements.

We have, hitherto, considered only one thing which is requisite to the good order of society; and that is the prevention of crime. This, however, is but a very imperfect account of the matter. Society involves innumerable duties and relations; all of which must be distinctly defined and carefully arranged, in order that there be no jostling and clashing of parts. The rights of the citizens, the sources of power, the duties of the legislative, judicial and executive departments, the medium of currency, the modes of holding and transferring property, international relations,—all need to be judiciously balanced and systematically adjusted to their proper spheres. In a word, the intricate machinery of a comprehensive system of government is to be fabricated and kept in operation; every wheel of which shall be adapted to its proper place, and have that place assigned it, in order that all may move on in unbroken harmony. What, then, I ask, is competent to this arduous task—to this stupendous result? Nothing! nothing but the mighty energy of law!

Perhaps it will be said that law itself is the offspring of moral principle; and, therefore, whatever good order law secures to society, is to be attributed to moral principle.

It may seem a bold assertion, yet I presume to make it, that not one solitary enactment can be pointed out on our statute books, the origin of which can, with any truth, be assigned to the moral principle of the nation. Many of them do not at all involve moral considerations. Some of them do. But moral principle was not the point on which their adoption turned. Utility, expediency, are the watch-words that echo through our Congressional Halls! These, doubtless, always coincide, in fact, with moral principle. But sometimes they seem to conflict. Which, then, has the preference? Does moral principle propel these mail-laden cars, all over the United States, on the Christian's Sabbath? Besides, is moral principle one of the qualifications which we require of our candidates for public offices? If not, with what show of truth can we maintain that they are governed by moral principle in their official acts? I do not now say what was the primary origin of Government; but one thing seems evident; it has been perpetuated by the necessities, and for the advantages of the race. Moral principle can now, even in this age, be said to be the source, or foundation of law, in no sense whatever.

I say *even in this age;* for if we go back and contemplate the infancy of the race and the inception of society, no one will pretend that mankind were induced, by moral principle, to associate together under some form of government; and, that the laws by which they regulated themselves, as members of a civil compact, were the transcript of this internal principle of virtue; for this is to suppose that an uncivilized and barbarous people are more obedient to the dictates of virtue than our own experience, as has been already remarked, shows an enlightened people to be; nay, more, it is to suppose the existence of that, which, had it existed, would have precluded the need of law. The truth is, the first law of nature—a regard to security and self-preservation—small, at first, have induced men to assume and brook the restraints of government.

Society being once established, a new order of duties and wants, peculiar to itself, is at once created. The latent energies of the mind —always equal to any emergency—awakes to meet and satisfy this demand. Thus society progresses; augmenting in numbers, and increasing the variety and frequency of its applications to human ingenuity, prudence, and foresight. But, for a long period, both public and private attention are directed, almost exclusively, to physical well-being.

The impulsive energy of man's religious tendency then manifests itself. Invention is taxed and tortured to contrive objects of religious homage. Hill, vale, stream, and mountain and sea are peopled with thronging deities. Mighty gods ride thundering over land and sea, or assemble in solemn conclave on the heights of dread Olympus. Kings and chieftains too, go forth at the head of marshaled millions to do battle with heroes as powerful as themselves. Conquests succeed. Wealth flows in. The fine arts spring up. Orpheus tames the ferocity of savage beasts and leads the forests captive by the music-tones of his lyre! The inspired bard breaks forth in rude, impassioned song! But, what participator in all this gorgeous pageantry—what actor in this splendid drama ever stops to inquire, seriously and earnestly, what is right? Their heroes, statesmen, poets, and philosophers are here, enthusiastic, generous, warm-hearted, immoral. Their deities are complaisant or morose, stern or indulgent, cruel or lenient, as the humor of the moment chance; but always liberal, wanton, and lascivious. The highest virtues of the former are patriotism, courage, and natural affection; the chief aim of the latter power, mischief and enjoyment. Moral principle, an unbending adherence to right, scarce finds a resting-place in the thoughts of all the millions of antiquity. Their attention is ever directed *outwards*. Seldom does the eye turned inwards gaze down into the mysterious depths of their moral nature. In their passionate attachment to the eternal and physical, might is bowed down to as the highest attribute of humanity, and the only legitimate source of authority. Even the inalienable rights of men, first descried as through a glass, darkly, by the Reformers in England, were destined to have their first and final demonstration wrought out, in characters of blood, by the patriots of the American Revolution.

While such ignorance and utter disregard of the essential nature of man prevailed, it was impossible that moral principle should materially affect public government or individual conduct. In both, considerations of self-aggrandizement and emolument prevailed over all others. Temporary expediency ruled the world. It was the foundation of all law—the source of all action. And although, in the onward progress of society, under the salutary influence of law, moral principle has been greatly developed, yet it does not appear that it has ever yet been much regarded in acts of legislation. Never, we believe, till within the present century, have any genuine attempts been made to render it the basis of legislative enactments. The failure of these attempts in nearly every instance, is incontestible evidence that law still rests on its ancient foundation.

Now it must be admitted that quite as high a degree of good order prevailed among many of the nations of antiquity, as among any that at present exist; and there is nothing else to which we can attribute it, but to the supremacy of law. Who, then, will deny that the same effect which we witness is to be traced to the same cause, which still exists? Who can deny that, as good order was then secured to society through the agency of law, it is likewise secured now by the same agency?

We have thus examined the comparative influence which moral principle and human law exert towards preserving the good order of society. We have proved that moral principle owes, in a great measure, its development and vigor to law; that, even thus, it is inadequate to prevent the smaller offenses; how then the higher? Indeed, we have proved that, from its very nature, it is utterly unfitted to check those wild outbursts of passion and demoniac malignity, which, unchecked, would rend society in sunder, as by the energy of volcanic fires.

Law, on the other hand, springing up, not from moral principle, but from the deep necessities of the race, spreads out its ample and potent influence over the warring and shapeless elements of humanity; like that spirit which,

> "With mighty wings outspread,
> Dove-like sat'st brooding on the vast abyss,
> And mad'st it pregnant."

Forms of beauty and comeliness arise from the elemental disorder! Peace takes the place of war—love, of hatred—harmony, of discord. Nations are born. The smiling arts of peace appear. Commerce spreads her wings for a flight beyond the sea! Education reveals her inexhaustible mines!

Such are the effects of Law. Society is as truly built upon it, as the human body on bones and sinews! And never will it cease to be the foundation and security of society, till selfishness is banished from the human heart; till man becomes, by the ties of love, a brother of his fellow-man; and all are bound, by a sweet moral affinity, to the throne of Infinite Benevolence.

LITERARY NOTICE.

Poems on Man. By Cornelius Mathews, author of "the Motley Book," "Behemoth," "Puffer Hopkins," &c. &c. &c. New York, Wiley & Putnam, 1843.

We live in an age of poetry; "the faculty divine" is no longer doled out to a few scattered individuals, but is sown broadcast throughout the length and breadth of the civilized world. Every tree and bush has its warbler, though sometimes the only music produced is a hoarse, nerve-grating 'caw.'

Of course America has received her portion of the heaven-sent bounty, and we think we can verily boast that we now have a Poet. In fact, our genius in this line is no longer to be sneezed at; a star *has* appeared even among us, and the name of Cornelius Mathews will

> "Gather all kindreds of this boundless realm,"

together in mute admiration. "Cornelius Mathews!" we hear some one exclaim; "why, who is he?" The author of Puffer Hopkins, Behemoth, Wakondah, &c., and the whilom editor of 'Arcturus.' "Never heard of any of them before." Astounding ignorance! This 'argues yourself unknown.' But turn with us to the "Poems on Man," and learn something of this candidate for poetic laurels. It is said that the best method of criticising a work is to present passages and leave the reader to form his own judgment. As we have no time to waste on Mr. Mathews, we shall adopt this course. We open the book at the first "*Poem*," "the Child." We remind our readers in the first place that the infant is lying in his cradle, and Mr. Mathews is watching his 'development.' Hear the poet apostrophize:

"At every lifting of thine arms they [mankind] feel
The ribbed and rusty bulk of Empire shake,
And from the fashion of thy features take
The hope and image of the common-weal!"

Here is occupation for our statesmen; if they would attend to the 'commonweal,' let them become wet-nurses, and examine the 'fashion' of their charges' 'features' for the 'image of the' aforesaid 'commonweal.' But we quote farther:

"See! through the white skin beats the ruddy tide!
The pulses of thine heart, that come and go,
Like the great circles of the ocean, flow
And dash a CONTINENT *at either side.*" !!!

Open at another place, "the Citizen." Hear him!

"Feel well with the poised ballot in thy hand,
Thine unmatch'd sovereignty of right and wrong,
'Tis thine to bless, or blast the waiting land,
To shorten up its life or make it long."

We presume there is considerable difference between "*shortening*" a life and "*shortening it up*;" or perhaps Mr. Mathews put in the word *up* for the sake of metre; a good idea, certainly. But a little more of "the Citizen:"

"Nowhere within the great globe's skyey round,
Cans't thou escape thy duty grand and high,
A man unbadged, unbonnetted, unbound,
Walk to the Tropic, to the Desert fly."

Another improvement, and in orthography Mr. Mathews can doubtless tell us what letter originally intervened in the last syllable of 'cans't;' his apostrophe at least intimates it. One or two more extracts before we throw the book in the fire; both from "the Farmer." He is addressing the husbandman:

"When cities rising shake th' Atlantic shore,
THOU MIGHTY INLAND! calm with plenteous peace,
Oh temper and assuage the wild uproar,
And bring the sick, vexed masses balmy ease."

Here is a soubriquet for our farmers. "Thou mighty inland!" νεφεληγερέτα Ζεύς! what an epithet! Again:

"Better to watch the live-long day,
The clouds that come and go,
Wearying the heaven they idle through,
And fretting out its everlasting blue!"

Ohe! jam satis! enough! and this is the trash which the Democratic Review lauds to the skies for its depth (!) and originality. (!!) If Mr. Mathews ever should again feel the approach of the *cacoethes scribendi*, we would advise him to get some kind friend to tie his hands behind him and lock him up. "Arcturus" has set; "Puffer Hopkins" has blown his last breath; and we verily believe that "the Poems on Man" will prove still-born. After a careful perusal of the book, save us from another such infliction! We are forced to conclude that nothing in it is good which is not plagiarized, and nothing original which is not execrable.

EDITORS' TABLE.

Once more, kind reader, we are about to enter, nay even now are in thy presence, bearing our unpretending budget, hoping to please by the will if not by the power to entertain. If thou dost not like our dress, remove, we beseech thee, our outer cuticle, and pass sentence on our inner man. Here, we trust, thou wilt be satisfied. If not, then be assured that the fault lieth with thyself and not with us; thou art afflicted with the spleen, or thou art hungry and thy empty stomach vexeth thee with its unmannerly grumblings, so that thy better judgment ruleth not: wait till thy humor be amended—till thy spirits become more jovial. Then, when thou feelest at amity with all mankind, thou mayest read with some hope of being pleased—till then we warn thee to desist. But, if thou maintainest that our contents are too musty and too stupid, hail the first thou meetest who holds they are too flimsy, take him by the ears, and fight it out fairly, like a couple of discontented curs, thanking us that we give you so good a cause for quarrel. As the good woman observed when her husband and the bear engaged in mortal conflict, "it 's the first fight I ever saw when I did n't care which licked." What would the consequence be should all the flood of criticism vented on us be kept bottled up in the College bosom! 'Tis fearful to think of the explosions dire that would result. Assuredly we are the safety valves of our dear institution.

Thou doubtless hast ere this observed, that we have obtained for this number of our Magazine an engraving of the College Library Building. For this be thankful, since it hath been procured without trouble or expense on thy part. To praise it would be unnecessary,—its merits declare themselves. We will merely say, for the benefit of our ultra-collegian readers, that it is a most striking likeness, having been recognized by several persons as soon as seen,—and several more declared, when told what it was, that if we had not said a word they should have known it. To prevent all mistakes, however, its name is very judiciously appended to our engraving, after the fashion of the painters of the olden time, who were accustomed to inscribe upon the productions of their skill, "This is a horse,—this a house,—this a tree."

Reader, we had intended to tell thee, how that amid the crash of plates, on this Thanksgiving day, our editorial wants had not wholly been neglected—that we are not strangers to the kindly effects of the "unctious and palate-soothing flesh" of turkies slain and roast, and other rich staples of the day—we had intended to tell thee how that a benevolent widow, taking compassion on our friendless, lean and wobegone appearance, did summon us to her well-filled table, and caused our inner man to sing for joy—we had intended to tell thee how our leanness vanished, and how our once meager features filled out their folds and grimly smiled—how our condescension was equalled only by our hunger, our wit by our appetite. We had intended—but why tantalize thee farther by hinting what we might have done, had we not been on our last page? This true Procrustes' bed of ours cuts short with its stern iron walls the tale of all our mighty, wise, and noble deeds, at this most memorable of all Thanksgiving dinners.

Yet has every rose its thorn. We had but just composed our editorial form and caught a shadowy glimpse of mild Oblivion's wing, when the Apollyon of the press roused us with his doleful cry. Had we not been in the best mood imaginable, it had vexed our righteous soul. But we were calm, and smiling on him, begged him to present, kind Readers, one and all, our best respects to you.

THE

YALE LITERARY MAGAZINE.

Vol. IX. JANUARY, 1844. No. 3.

MODERN TENDENCIES TO DEMOCRACY.

"In this world of ours, which has both an indestructible hope in the future, and an indestructible tendency to persevere as in the past, must Innovation and conservation wage their perpetual conflict as they may and can."—Carlyle's French Revolution.

There is probably no word of such general use, concerning whose real meaning and extent there exists at the same time such general ignorance, as Democracy. With us, here in the United States, it acts like the spell of the magician, calming the waves of public feeling, or rousing them into tempestuous fury, according to the will of him who best understands the method of its application. All parties claim an exclusive right to be considered its advocates; the great statesman, the sleek-faced demagogue, the shrewd Yankee, and the ragged hod-carrier from green Erin, must profess equal readiness to obey and defend the supremacy of the people. A convention of one political sect assembles in this place; of another in that; resolutions are passed by both, and speeches made, diametrically opposed upon every great national question, but upon this one point they display the most remarkable unanimity, and Administration and Opposition each and all join with alacrity in the grand shout for the sovereign Democracy. Yet it is an indubitable fact, that hardly a dozen individuals out of these thousands could satisfactorily explain their own meaning. If the matter ended here, it would scarcely be worthy of serious notice; but it does not; there is introduced among us a morbid desire for some unknown, inconceivable good; an uneasy, restless looking-forward to a new and more glorious era; a confused hurry, a precipitate fickleness, which but too often disregards all the restraints of honor, good faith, and private and public duty.

Neither are these feelings confined to the western shores of the Atlantic; Europe has witnessed their terrific energy. We have seen the volcanic flame burst forth in France; we have seen the land strewn with human corses, the foundations of government shattered to atoms, and the shrines of religion prostrated—the effects of the tremendous eruption. True, the fire is no longer visible; the thunders have ceased from their roaring; the ground no more cleaves asunder; but the appearance of the soil tells of danger; the occasional rockings of the earth give warning that the embers are yet smouldering, the fuel yet unexhausted. In England too, strange as it may seem, Democracy has gained a footing. Thousands of excited, exasperated men, are there—exasperated perhaps by real grievances—who are looking for a redress of their wrongs, not to the constituted government, but to an entire overthrow of existing authorities, and the establishment of new laws, new rulers, new institutions. If what we have now said be true, the inquiries why is this, whither does it tend and what may be its effects, are surely worthy of consideration.

The origin of the liberal sentiments, which now prevail in this country and throughout a great portion of Europe, has been frequently and justly traced back to the period of the Reformation, and it would be superfluous in us to repeat what has already been so often domonstrated. That free opinions had been extensively developed and strenuously defended—that they had taken strong hold of the minds of men and were exercising a powerful influence before the middle of the last century, is a fact not to be disputed. Our object is to consider more especially the advance which they have made,—if they have made any,—since the treaty which concluded the war of the American Revolution, and inquire whether we have not reason to fear that they are degenerating into open and excessive Radicalism, the parent of anarchy and misrule. In so doing we shall confine our attention to France, England, and the United States, for the reason that these countries afford the most striking proofs of our positions, and are now exercising the greatest influence upon other nations.

At the death of Louis the Fifteenth tyranny in France had reached its zenith. Civil freedom had fled from the land, and there appeared little hope of a speedy return. Yet observers saw that some contest was fast approaching, though it was impossible to predict the issue. The priesthood, still powerful, but hypocritical, unbelieving—wolves in sheep's clothing—the infidel philosophers, swaying the public mind and disseminating on all sides and in the same breath, high aspirations for liberty and bold blasphemy against all religion,—the monarch, the state,—the court, a splendid brothel,—and twenty-five millions of starving men raging like wild beasts for their daily food,—these were the omens everywhere discernible. One year later came the news of the battle of Lexington, and the symptoms of the coming outbreak became more decisive. It would be apart from our purpose to detail the events which took place between this period and the first violent revolutionary outbreak, or to attempt a historical sketch of the Revolution itself. The weakness of the monarch, the vain confidence of his ministers, the utopian schemes and visionary hopes of the philosophers, the rejoicings of the people when they believed that the day of perfect liberty had dawned, and the dark and terrible eclipse which followed, are too fresh in our memories to need a recapitulation. The French people were not ready to become freemen; despotism had been to them a cage-prison; the bars broken, they burst out, beasts of prey. There is a portion of the allegory of Spenser, where Una falls into the hands of the "faytour knight" Sansloy, and in the hour of her utmost need is rescued by the Satyrs,

> "A rude, misshapen, monstrous rablement."

Struck with her wondrous beauty, they bow down before her in worship, and when attempting to point them to a higher divinity she restrains their blind adoration, they transfer their idolatry to the beast on which she rode:

> ——"her wit she plyes
> To teach them truth which worshipt her in vaine,
> And made her th' image of idolatryes;
> But when their bootlesse zeal she did restrayne
> From her own worship, they her asse would worship fayne."

So in France: truth, fallen into the hands of sneering, faithless philosophers, seemed about to be despoiled of all her beauty and innocence, when the *sans culottes*, the

> "rude, mis-shapen, monstrous rabblement,"

hurried to the rescue; but alas! their brute nature could not understand her high mission, and instead of obeying her holy precepts, they worshiped with sacrifice of blood and fire, dumb Reason—the beast on which she rode! But the years of the Revolution passed away; on the 14th of July, 1789, the Bastile was destroyed, on the 5th of October, 1795, NAPOLEON BUONAPARTE drove the Paris mob back into its den.

The gradual conversion of the *republic* into an empire, the mad career of ambition and conquest, and the sudden and final overthrow of the conqueror, are topics upon which we need not dwell. The French under the dominion of Napoleon were intoxicated by national vanity; they forgot every thing, right, liberty, and law, when they saw him victorious over Italy, Austria, and Prussia, and advancing with rapid steps to still more splendid conquests. When he fell, as a nation they were humbled; twenty-five years of continual war,—war not like other wars, but at first raging at home, fierce, relentless, covetous of blood, and afterwards completely exhausting the resources and energy of the state,—had filled the kingdom with mourning and left a place desolate by almost every fire-side. From the succession of Louis the Eighteenth to that of Charles Tenth, the people were comparatively quiet; they endured a king because they were too feeble to rebel, and because the sovereign suited his measures in some sort to the popular feeling. But when the latter monarch ascended the throne, forgetting that time enough had elapsed to re-invigorate the nation, with a folly almost incredible, he commenced a series of acts whose direct tendency was to establish anew the authority of the ancient regime. For six years they endured his dominion, though with many threats and much vociferous complaint, and then indignantly drove him from his throne and his country. Since that event, now some thirteen years, Louis the schoolmaster has been King of *the French*, for a King of France exists no longer even in name.

We are now to consider the condition of that nation as exhibited at the present time. Do peace and contentment dwell there? Are voluntary preservation of order and cheerful obedience to law its prevailing characteristics? Alas! we must answer, they are not. We have said that the days of the Revolution passed away; but the actors therein are not all gone; the Revolution itself is not fully accomplished. Gray-headed veterans are yet living, whose hands were red with blood in the September massacres; and men of ripe years may be found, who in their childish days shouted "Vive la Republique!" at the execution of Louis XVI. The sympathies of hundreds of thousands of Frenchmen are all republican; they abhor the very name of King; they are quiet because they dare not be otherwise. Their submission is forced, their numbers formidable. A still more powerful party there are clamoring for universal suffrage; they do not proscribe monarchical institutions openly, they claim only for every man the immediate liberty of depositing his vote. They overlook the twelve millions of their countrymen who can neither read nor write, whose only instruction has been, how to live; they ask for enfranchisement first and education afterward, a course which this world has never yet seen adopted with success. They appear to believe that the only object of the sovereign and his immediate coadjutors is to make the best use of the nation for their own private advantage. "I compare," says Faust—the book is not at hand and we must quote the idea from memory, "I compare the king and his ministers to shears, and the people to the paper,—the blades of the instrument (one of which is the king, the other the ministers) seem ever opposed, ever slashing each other; but each other they harm not—*they only cut the paper.*" This seems to be the sentiment of a large class in France, and for protection against such evils they call for *universal suffrage*.

Another distemper which it seems hard to remedy in the present condition of the country, is the scarcity of labor. Work cannot be provided in the ordinary way for thousands who desire it, and in consequence it must be provided at the expense of the government or of the monarch. This is the secret of the numerous great labor-requiring undertakings, in the capital and elsewhere; idleness is the root of all disorder; and Louis Philippe dare not leave his subjects in want of employment. Thus far he has succeeded, owing to his immense private wealth, but should a deficit in funds again occur, the fearful consequences may easily be foreseen. Should France suffer a season of distress like that which prevailed in this country in 1837. we might with confidence expect another revolution. Political writers also are continually disseminating the most pernicious principles throughout the kingdom; principles which tend to the subversion of law and religion, and which the ignorant or depraved are eager to seize and circulate still more widely. As described by one well acquainted with their conduct and influence, they are "a swarm of empty and hungry journalists and pamphleteers, creatures as ravenous as the beasts of the desert, and endowed with about as much reason as Heaven gives the ape. They seem the very impersonation of evil,—civil, social, and religious. Without principle, without faith, and without fear they deluge some places with their infamous publications, advocating a partition of goods, *universal suffrage*, a great social communion and all the kindred topics. Their tongues would set on fire the course of nature, and seem themselves set on fire of hell."

Such is in part the present condition of France; we have not space for a fuller delineation; we think we have shown enough to prove that much danger is still lurking there. In the strong language of Carlyle, "Democracy was BORN" in that kingdom, fifty years ago, and has by no means as yet expired. Couched under one form and another it is exercising a powerful influence in that sunny land. What it will accomplish cannot well be foreseen; we can only say with confidence, "the end is not yet."

England, at the end of the last century, was strongly agitated by the political revolutions across the channel. Men ready to arouse the public mind to folly or madness are never wanting in any country, and at this period they started up from every corner of the island, and echoed back the enthusiastic or fanatic aspirations of the French republicans. Their conduct called forth from Burke some of his noblest productions, in which satire and sound argument were brought to bear with irresistible force against them. From that time to the present moment there has been a large body of British radicals, more or less powerful, according to the disposition of the whole nation. At one time they seemed almost to have disappeared from the land;—it was when Buonaparte was threatening to invade England. It is hardly possible to conceive of the enthusiasm then existing; volunteers by thousands poured down to the sea-side, prepared for any thing rather than defeat. Every nerve, every sinew of Britain was braced for the conflict, and as has always been the case when the national spirit has been fully aroused, she was victorious. Napoleon exiled to St. Helena, Europe liberated and the world once more at peace, external appearances all indicated prosperity. But in reality this was the very hour of danger. The evils which, in the excitement of war, had been patiently borne, now seemed of ten fold intensity. An immense national debt had been incurred; commerce and manufactures had been fettered, and agriculture had of course suffered with them; the prices of every article the most necessary to existence were enormously high; taxes were immense; aristocratic privileges were extensive and odious; pauperism stood worn and haggard on every side. Radicalism at this crisis started from its lurking places and with vociferous clamor urged its complaint. To that complaint Tory ministers were little inclined to listen, they treated it rather with contemptuous neglect. Years rolled away and misery was borne because it seemed irremediable. Once, when the Whigs came into power, great hopes were entertained by the discontented class of some amelioration of their condition. In fact, however, matters seemed daily growing worse, and the Tories were restored. Of late we have heard other sounds there than those of petition or remonstrance. There has been a clanking of steel, a rattling of fire-arms. "*How happens it*," said the laborers of Manchester, "*that we who produce every thing*, HAVE NOTHING?" The Saxon blood of the English workingman is aroused; he sees clearly that something *must* be done or he must perish, and his voice is loud for Reform, though of the manner and means thereof he knows nothing. But these are not all the Reformers of England; an intelligent, enterprising, nay, often wealthy, rising generation are demanding the same; but they too know not how to obtain it. They are divided among themselves; the dearest object of some is to separate Church and State; of others to limit royal expenditures; of others still to abolish hereditary privileges; to extend suffrage; to establish free trade; *to make a republic*. But in truth these things cannot be done. A separation of the church and state might indeed benefit the former, but it would prove of irreparable injury to the latter. This may appear paradoxical, but it is nevertheless true. The constitution of the English government is interwoven with the established church; they have stood together for centuries, and endured the shocks of Papal power and the assaults of fanatic enthusiasm. They have together been the bulwark of Protestantism in Europe, and they cannot be disjoined without the most disastrous consequences. Should a separation be effected, the lovers of the church would cluster around her and sustain her as well, nay, better than she is sustained at present. Experience in our own country has shown this to be true. But just in proportion as their devotion to the religious institution would be increased by such an event, would their affection for the civil be diminished. And this is not all. The minds of the English people have become habituated to a union of church and state, and should the present system be removed, some other would almost necessarily be called to take its place. A great majority of the English themselves is undoubtedly attached to Episcopacy; they could not endure the change with patience; and a religious tumult, a sectarian discord, of all commotions the most violent, most unsparing, most odious to God and man, would ensue.

To attempt to abolish the British aristocracy would be equally inexpedient. No nation of Europe can boast of an order of nobility equal in any respect to that of England. There are, it is true, among them examples of folly, vanity, and vice, but the same may be said of any body of men under heaven. But as a whole, for the discharge of the important functions to which they are called, as leaders in war, as counsellors in the senate, as ministers in the cabinet, we very much doubt whether any form of popular election would make a better provision than the present. The English order of nobility cannot be destroyed till a majority of the English people have become completely changed in habit and sentiment. Like the established church, it is connected with every thing that is venerable in the mind of the British subject. The victories of olden time, the trophies of warlike honors, the ancient nonuments of illustrious men, forbid the undertaking. Scarce a pleaant valley, a rocky hill, a winding stream, or barge-freighted river, but ells of the achievements, the virtue, and the patriotism of the ancestors of the present aristocracy. In every thing which could conduce to the honor or the advantage of England, the nobility have been found in he foremost ranks. The order too is interwoven in its interests with he constitution of the kingdom, and we deem it not too much to say, that for the present, at least, one cannot stand without the other. In support of this assertion we may notice that all, or nearly all those statesmen, who in their youth were among the violent Whigs, aiming at the overthrow of these institutions, as they advance in age, and atain high political stations, recede from their old grounds and become in some sort conservatives.

Still there is in England a powerful minority, who cherish democratic principles as the only safeguard for the lower classes; demand equal privileges with all and for all, and the immediate tendency of whose sentiments is to the overthrow of the Monarchy and the Constitution. Existing grievances afford them a plausible ground for complaint, and the condition of our own country for argument. They point to the petty salaries of *our* chief officers, and contrast them with the enormous sums expended by *their* rulers. They hold up the high price of labor *here* as the immediate effects of our Republican form of government, and invite the ignorant *at home* to aspire to the same. These are at the bottom of many of the disgraceful riots lately perpetrated in the large manufacturing towns. Either wilfully or blindly they would have the nation rush upon sure destruction. They are the pests of community, the bane of social quiet and good order. Looking at them as we do, across the ocean, our visions blinded by our anti-monarchical principles, and hearing their often too just complaints, we are apt to sympathize with and even encourage them. In them and their influence there is much danger; and we repeat, England has little to fear from abroad; let her guard jealously her own subjects.

We have now arrived at that portion of our subject which most immediately interests ourselves; the present tendency of Democratic principles in the United States. We are aware that we are here approaching a delicate topic, and that we may incur the censure of political partisans: but we cannot hesitate to raise our feeble voice in opposition to such principles as we deem subversive of law and order, wherever they may be found, at home or abroad. If we have ultra feelings in this country upon the subject of government as well as upon every thing else, and if these feelings, unless checked in the outset, would lead to disastrous consequences, it is time that we should be well aware of the fact, and ready to provide for any contingency.

When this nation became independent and adopted a republican constitution, there existed throughout its whole extent a confirmed abhorrence of monarchical government. To set a new example in the New World, to realize in some sort, plans which many had considered as utopian visions, and to render oppression forever impracticable in his land, was the general desire. We imagine that these sentiments have lost none of their original energy,—that we have as little relish for kingly power at present as at any former period, but we also imagine that in avoiding one extremity we are rushing madly to the other—steering wide of Scylla to be swallowed in Charybdis. Frightened at the very shadow of Aristocracy, we precipitate ourselves rashly into the arms of Democracy; a power more potent for evil than for good, and which has ever been the fruitful parent of injustice to the individual, and commotion in the State. It may be true that we have little to fear in the next ten or twenty years, but should radical sentiments continue to gain ground as rapidly as they have done of late, we shall have reason to fear that our grand experiment in government will prove but a ruinous failure. We have a party among us, which has exerted, and is exerting all its strength to set the poor against the rich; to convince the former that their interests are opposed to those of the latter; and that their individual rights are in danger from wealthy aristocrats. Now we conceive that no political doctine ever has been, or ever can be more dangerous than this; it has been the source of the most frightful evils, both in ancient and modern times; it is false at bottom; it can produce no advantage except the ascendency of some one political sect. Yet it is gaining ground; no measure of state policy can be proposed but that this will be used on one side or the other; thousands have already been brought to believe it; other thousands are ready to be convinced. It is sewing discontent, for its direct tendency is to force men to conclude that poverty is itself an infringement of right; in a word, it leads at once to Agrarianism. Another principle, which, strange as it may appear, all parties seems to acknowledge, is, that "to the victors belong the spoils." To eject a man unceremoniously from office, merely for his private opinions, is now considered no disgrace to an Executive, but rather applauded as evincing his zeal for his party. Does this become a free nation? Is it not in fact the worst sort of oppression, the restriction of man's liberty of conscience? It exposes the ballot-box to bribery and corruption of every description; it renders the highest offices in the land subservient to any thing but the interests of the country, tools of party, and so far as the patronage extends, engines of despotic power.

A third doctrine, nearly on a par with those above mentioned, declares that all public officers are literally "*the servants of the people.*" The judge on the bench, the legislator in his seat, the executive in his high commission, must obey without discretion the will of the sovereign people. Why then, let us ask, have we laws? What use for a judge to decide thereupon, and why cannot *the people* revoke his decision? Because the doctrine is false. Why do our senators and representatives convene to discuss the interests of the nation, and to enact statutes for its governance? Why not ask the people their will, and vote accordingly, without debate or even convention? Why must this same people obey the injunctions of the statute-book, on penalty of life or death, instead of arising in their majesty and putting them down? Because the notion is absurd. Why are our executive officers called our rulers and our governors? Why have they often acted—why did Washington himself act in direct opposition to the clamorous demands of a majority of the nation? Because the principle is unsound—rotten to the core. Still it is a party doctrine, and its evil tendencies are manifold and obvious. It would bring into contempt the magistrates, and of course their decisions in like manner, and if there were any obedience, it must be the obedience of fear, not of rectitude.

Finally, the maxim, that in a government, as in all political questions or elections, the will of the majority should rule, is being carried to the most unjustifiable lengths. The constitution of these United States declares that a petition to Congress upon any subject whatever, *even to the dissolution of the Union*, shall be received, read, and voted upon. Now, in defiance of this wise provision, we have seen a faction in our national legislature declare that this shall not be done in all cases—and why? The only argument of any validity is that of brute force—the majority wills it. Again, a law is passed making certain regulations with respect to elections; several States disobey this law, set Congress in defiance, and because these States happen to be of a certain party, they are allowed not only to do this with impunity, but even encouraged to a repetition of the same lawless proceeding. For what reason? The majority wills it. Whither then will this principle carry us? It will make it a rule that whatever regulation, provision, or even statute, may be determined upon by the constituted authorities, whenever a *majority* may be in opposition, it shall be of no avail. It will render all law nugatory, all government ineffectual. It will introduce anarchy and confusion, and render this land the chosen residence of discord, the home of desolation. We have now exhibited some portion of our danger as a nation, from ultra democratic principles. We may be wrong, Heaven grant that we are; but while we imagine that we see these evils approaching, we would lift our hands to stay their progress.

THE OLD CHURCH BELL.

> "Say! how canst thou mourn?
> How canst thou rejoice?
> Art but metal dull!" LONGFELLOW.

HIGH up within yon gray old tower
  There hangs a massive bell;
It chimes with the wind, and each passing hour
  Its flight by its tones doth tell.
As they melt away on the air so clear,
How mournfully linger they on the ear.

And as I gaze on that tower so gray,
  Where the dove her circuit makes,
And the hooting owl at set of day
  His nightly vigil takes;
I think of the songs that bell hath sung,
Of the mellow peals from its swinging tongue:
Its thrill of joy on a bridal day,
And its mournful tones o'er the lifeless clay;
Still linger they on my list'ning ear,
In their silvery tones so faint and clear.

'Tis a faithful monitor, that bell,
To the heart that knoweth its sounds so well;
Each passing hour of the 'live-long day'
It calls to the mind ere it flies away:
The joys of Love—the pangs of Fear,
Though past, yet are not gone fore'er,—
At its mellow sound they hover near.
As it swings away by the pond'rous wheel
  And its tongue beats the sides worn bright,
While the day streams in or shadows steal
  Through the lattice that screens it from sight—
Thus sings it out its merry song,
The wild winds on their wings prolong,
While distant hills its echoes throng:—

  Day follows day,
  Years glide away,
Still onward marches Time;
  His scythe I hear,
  Its clang sounds near,
How solemn is the chime!

  From out my screen
  Life's busy scene
I reach with varied song:
  The haunts of men,—
  The fields,—the glen,
Its echoes clear prolong.

  And o'er the soul
  I have control,
Of feelings sad or gay;
  The sympathy
  Man holds with me,
Can ne'er be thrown away.

  The hurried strife
  Of mortal Life
My merry peals excite:
  But deep and long
  A funeral song
I sing o'er Death's sad blight:

Years roll away, yet its clear notes rise
Like incense to the arching skies;
While mortals live, then disappear,
Still rings it on so calm—so clear.

SAMUEL TAYLOR COLERIDGE.

Biography is of two kinds, one pertaining to the outer, the other to the inner man. The one describing the nature, diseases, and achievements of the body, the other of the soul. The former is valuable only as a fact or a number of facts in natural history. The latter is invaluable; it is the ground-work of mental philosophy. Within it lie, sometimes confused, sometimes beautifully arranged thoughts and germs of thoughts, which, when classified and combined, form those broad and deep principles which constitute the philosophy of mind. The biography of a great man is a grand discovery, or rather a series of them, in this department. It may be unwritten, or it may be badly written, yet it furnishes facts which are of more value than the discovery of stars to the astronomer. Such a biography we have in the life, partly written, partly unwritten, of Samuel Taylor Coleridge.

To many who admire Coleridge, and to others who do not, the very idea of an undergraduate writing about him will appear ridiculous. We are not writing his life, nor his eulogy, nor a commentary on his works. The child cannot write his father's epitaph, nor build a monument over his grave, yet he may plant a flower upon it, even though it be but a daisy, and that a rootless one. If we can do but this for the bard and sage of Nether Stowey we shall be satisfied. If, however, when the sun is up, and because it hath no depth—of earth, it wither away, be it so; roses and lillies have withered too.

Some great and good men admire Coleridge, others dislike, and others still despise him. There is but one other prominent scholar in modern times that has been more loved and laughed at—his own bosom friend, Wordsworth. Neither is it our object to speak of him as we would, as we feel. We simply design to show, that however much his philosophy or his manner of explaining it may be objected to, and reasoned against, he is not to be despised and ridiculed. That his errors, if errors they be, are the errors of a philosopher, not of a fool; and that it is unmanly and unscholarlike to treat the author of the "Aids to Reflection" as we would the author of a disquisition "On the Morning and Evening State of an Angel's Understanding."

Two hundred years hence the nineteenth century will be spoken of by the people of England and America as we are accustomed to speak of the seventeenth. What a crowd of scholars has it already sent forth; poets, statesmen, and historians! Rather are we inclined to believe, that it will be looked upon as the dawn of a new epoch in the progress of opinion; of the introduction of a system of Christian philosophy which has God for its ultimate end, and man as an immortal being for its object. In this light histories and poems are now written and read, the origin and constitution of government examined, and the Bible studied and more deeply and intelligently loved. Prominent if not foremost among the great minds of this period is Coleridge. Considered merely as an author, he deserves common respect. This may appear very much like a *simple* proposition. It is only stated, however, to place over against a still simpler one—its converse. It is a fact, and can be easily proved, that the very name of Coleridge to many minds, to the minds even of some scholars who are respected and admired, has been connected with such associations as to induce them to discard from thought and sight any thing directly or remotely allied to it. Now though it may not be true that we must first partake of poison before expressing an opinion upon its nature; nor that we should indulge in the revelings of a brothel, in order to know their polluting effects upon soul and body; it is not true that we should scorn, a priori, a man who was through life the bosom friend of Wordsworth, Southey, Lamb, and Hazlitt; who is admired by Talfourd and Lockhart, and who is now the idol of not a few distinguished sons of church and state in both hemispheres. It does not follow that we are sneeringly to dismiss with the epithets "dreamy," "transcendental," "blackness of darkness," opinions and principles that are entering into, and, to say the least, deeply coloring old established systems of mental and moral philosophy and theology. We know indeed that Byron sneered at him, but Byron hated man. To ridicule and to scoff would have answered very well three or four centuries ago. They were the arguments to which intellectual despots then resorted; just as the stake and the rack were the arguments of religious despots. But as it has come to pass in these last days that truth and reason are the powers that be, so must their arms be brought to bear upon opinions or systems before they can or will be successfully overthrown. A bad cause or system, when skilfully presented and sustained by ingenious reasoning, will gain more hearers and proselytes than a good one boldly asserted and stubbornly reiterated.

No scholar that has ever carefully read twenty pages of Coleridge's Works has despised him. If they have not been awed into admiration by his height and his depth, his nice perception of the moral and spiritual sublime, his analytic acuteness, his precision and power of language, they have at least been convinced that he was more than a dreamer. Critics whose hearts have palpitated to "damn him to everlasting fame," have unconsciously dropped sentences which, if their words could immortalize any man, would immortalize him. Dr. Johnson, speaking of Dr. Watts' Works, says, "the reader's attention is caught by indirect instruction, and he that sat down only to reason is on a sudden compelled to pray." Similar and almost as sudden, in many instances, has been the reflux of feeling toward our philosopher. Forewarned by their minister, teacher, or the town sage, of his heresy, pantheism, or infidelity, many young men brace themselves at once against the slightest influence from him. They shape to themselves a dark, gloomy, hideous monster, like the image we first form of him who "goeth about like a roaring lion," whose touch is pollution, and whose embrace is death. If, however, at some unguarded moment, the sinful propensities of our nature gain the supremacy, that curiosity that will pry into forbidden things is aroused. The "Biographia Literaria," the "Aids," or the "Table Talk" is opened. Curiosity gratified to the ll, gives place to interest. Examination succeeds and soon results in espect and admiration for the spirit that could penetrate so deeply into fe and truth, and the genius and power that could bring thence pearls o brilliant and so rare. There is not a work or thought, complete or nperfect, where we cannot discern the same master mind. In the riginality and exquisite beauty of his figures and illustrations, in the iajesty of his thoughts, in his perfect knowledge, we might almost say umiliarity with the "dead past," and with the arcana of the spirit of ian, and in his far-piercing glance into centuries and worlds in the fuire, he has but very few if any uninspired equals.

As a poet we might justly speak of him in high, almost the highest rms. If that had been the work which was given him to do, we ould use the superlative. Yet even fragments, as most of his pieces re, they are splendid fragments. They prove the presiding energy of transcendent mind, the effusions of a spirit touched "with celestial re." The marbles in the British Museum, which Lord Elgin brought om the Acropolis, are mostly fragments, yet in these pale, cold, old elics can be seen breathing forth, almost audibly, the spirit of that iighty genius that conceived and executed the Athenian Minerva and Ilympian Jove. The "Ancient Mariner," "Christabel," "The Æolian Harp," "Genevieve," and several fugitive pieces, might be cited as roof. There is in the thoughts as well as in the language a symphony nd an exalted tone, that bears us along almost insensibly "until," in ie charming lines of Wordsworth,

"the breath of this corporeal frame,
And even the motion of our human blood
Almost suspended, we are laid asleep
In body, and become a living soul."

To the "forms of things unknown" which "imagination bodies forth," e gives not only a habitation, but one adapted to their heavenly nature. His creatures are not naked and invisible essences, but living and lovng realities, richly "clothed, and in their right mind."

"No man," says he, "was ever yet a great poet, without being at ie same time a great philosopher." He himself, in his lectures before ie Surrey Institute, was the first* to exhibit this grand truth, as illusrated in Shakspeare. Milton, Wordsworth, and Cowper, furnish bundant evidence of the same fact; and we might include him in the st if, as we have already stated, this had been his mission. But it is as philosopher he came, as a philosopher he is beginning to be studied nd revered, and as a philosopher he will be known and appealed to, vhen the ashes of his detractors and of their works are manuring the arth.

* This honor, we notice, is claimed, by a writer in the last Foreign Quarterly, for A. V. Schlegel, and an attempt is made to prove his right to it; but we prefer to believe oleridge's own statement, especially when corroborated by the testimony of Sir Geo. eaumont, Sir Humphrey Davy, and Hazlitt.

As Coleridge belonged to no school or party as such, in poetry and politics, so he owned allegiance to none in philosophy. Not that he despised or envied either. No man could see worth sooner, appreciate it more fully, or be more forward in encouraging and commending it, whether possessed by a beggar or a prince. But he felt a power and an energy within him that could grapple with any subject, however deep or comprehensive, and educe an opinion for himself. In poetry, intimate as he was with the founder of the Lake School, he occupies several chapters of the "Biographia" with a profound inquiry into, and a complete refutation of some of their chief tenets. In politics, he was at one time considered a Jacobin, and closely watched by a government spy; at another we find him dealing equally heavy and effective blows at ultra democracy and unlimited monarchy. Alison, in his great history, has paid a noble tribute to his penetration, even in this department. After describing in his glowing style the brilliant characters that shed such a glory around the last years of the reign of George III, when the 'fiery surge' of the French Revolution had subsided, he adds, "But the genius of these men, great and immortal as it was, did not arrive at the bottom of things. They shared in the animation of passing events, and were roused by the storm which shook the world. But they did not reach the caves whence the whirlwind issued, nor perceive what spirit had let loose the tempest. In the bosom of retirement, in the recesses of solitary thought, the awful source was discovered, and Æolus stood forth revealed in the original antagonist power of wickedness. *The thought of Coleridge*, even during the whirl of passing events, discovered their hidden springs, and poured forth in an obscure style, and to an unheeding age, the great moral truths which were then proclaiming in characters of fire to mankind."

Upon his philosophy we said we intended to give no commentary. The attempt might prove what several such by older heads and more experienced pens have proved—a successful failure. In this the most numerous and most valuable class of his writings, he has been frequently and boldly charged with theft. Such a charge reflects far more disgrace on the accusers than the accused. It existed, or rather the feeling which prompted it existed, long before he became known as an author. His sympathy and communion with unpopular authors of that day brought it upon him; and now that he has won his laurels and his enemies have silently been vanquished, they would make one desperate effort to tear them from his tomb, by charging him with plagiarism. First, he could not originate a thought; secondly, those which he did originate were cloudy, mystical, and inane; and thirdly, all his brilliant, glowing, heart-swelling thoughts have been stolen from the Germans.

Now we cannot say how much Coleridge has or has not stolen from Leibnitz, Kant, Schelling, or any other author on the continent, because we do not know. We do say, however, that if the test of originality applied to him, be applied to any other of the laureled heroes of English literature, the garland that a grateful and an admiring posterity has wreathed for them will soon fade and wither. To cite a single instance:

n a recent biographical sketch of Milton, there are given the names of ifteen Italian, French, and English authors, from whom he is said to iave borrowed. To these we might add, with much more propriety ınd truth, Moses, David, Ezekiel, Habakkuk, Paul, and John the Evan-gelist, besides Homer and Virgil. Nor is he indebted to them for llusions and figures alone, but for thoughts and even words. Yet vhose ardor of affection is cooled, whose tribute of praise is diminished, vhose memory will not ever preserve engraven on its tablets the name ınd the honor of Milton? As well might we depreciate the merit of he astronomer, because he did not make the stars or the telescope, ashion the eye or originate eternal axioms.

Yet even allowing all the charges of his enemies to be true; allow-ng those thoughts and passages, of whose theft he has been accused, o belong to others; there still remains enough in his philosophy to ustify all the praise bestowed on him, and entitle him to the first lace among modern metaphysicians. What then, in brief, are some f those peculiar characteristics of Coleridge's philosophy, taken as a vhole?

Its very nature is to beget in the mind of the student a thoughtful ıctivity of mind.

The age has been styled superficial. Men and scholars too have ›een so eager to keep step with the progress of financial speculations ınd 'light literature,' that they have taken opinions upon the credit of ıames. Coleridge stops them at the very threshold, and sends the nind in to the oracle that is within, to ascertain whether these things ıre so. He compels it to enter, and reflect upon its hitherto unknown ıature and powers. It is called a vague, dreamy system. It may be lreamy. But it is not a nightmare philosophy, that scares and terrifies he soul while it holds it firm in its lank, skinless grasp. His dreams ıre like Jacob's. In them the soul encounters and boldly wrestles vith the angel of truth all night even to the breaking of the day, until t has received a blessing. It is a man-ennobling philosophy. From he refinements and reasonings of previous philosophers we had hardly ›een able to determine—certainly not to *know*—whether we stood much ıigher in the scale of being than the brutes; whether what was predi-cated of the bee or the beaver, *might* not be predicated of man; vhether our spiritual nature was mortal or immortal. The distinction vhich Coleridge has made between the reason and the understanding, ınd his definitions of nature, the will, and the imagination, have illu-nined "what was dark within us," and immovably established the nfinite superiority of man, not in degree, but in kind, to the brutes that lie and live no more.

There is but one other mind that we are acquainted with which esembles Coleridge's in this as well as in several other points. Had ıe lived in an age and a country illustrated by Protestantism, where pinion was unfettered and the Gospel free, he would undoubtedly have ›een a bold and distinguished disciple of this system. We mean Pascal. A single paragraph taken from his "Thoughts" may suffice;

for beauty of expression and grandeur of thought, comparat some of the English philosopher's :

"Man is so great that his greatness appears even in the ness of his misery. A tree does not know itself to be mise is true that it is misery indeed to know one's self to be mis then it is greatness also. In this way all man's miseries g his greatness. They are the miseries of a mighty potent dethroned monarch."

The last grand and distinguishing characteristic of it tha mention is, that it is Christian. One of the objects he info has in view in his system, is "to show the perfect rationality articles of faith that are rightly classed among the myst peculiar doctrines of Christianity." Other systems have wh rated intellectual from moral philosophy, reason from revel time from eternity. His unites all; makes time but a nan the image and offspring of God within us, "and (as far as m cerned) the source of living and actual truths." Intellectual moral and spiritual philosophy, all converging towards and ce the Cause of Causes. Reflecting and investigating by mea light, we are enabled to see the consistency, the harmony unity of Truth, the greatness of our nature, and the inexpress of Him who is the Fountain of Truth and of Life.

Let scholars then honestly and diligently study Coleridg shall not be afraid of the result. Let them scrutinize and we thought and every word. He himself requests and demand them not sneer at him: it is unmanly. Let them not sp "some have entertained angels unawares."

FROM ANACREON.

Nature had bulls endowed with horns,
To horses hoofs had given.
Had made the timid hare as fleet
As are the winds of Heaven.
Great teeth she gave to lions,
Fishes she taught to swim,
And gave to swift winged birds
Through liquid air to skim.
To man (the best of all her gifts)
She understanding gave,
And reason that might teach him how
Himself from ills to save.
Nature had freely now bestowed
Of all she had in store.

Defense unto both man and beast,
And there remained no more.
What gifts shall nature then impart,
Fair woman to protect?
This boon to woman hath been given,
With beauty to be decked.
And beauty yields more sure defense
Than warrior's shields afford.
For she that is a woman fair
Can conquer fire and sword. E.

THE WITCH.

A TALE OF THE LAST CENTURY.

BY CUJUS.

"The earth has bubbles, as the water hath."—MACBETH.

CHAPTER V.

HUGH WARDEN was an only child. His parents both died during his boyhood, leaving their son to the care of a bachelor uncle in D——. They had been in opulent circumstances, and dwelt with their family in New York till the period of their death. Immediately after that melancholy event the young Hugh was removed to the residence of his guardian, where he remained at the commencement of our story. This guardian, Mr. John Warden, was, as we have said, the uncle of our hero, and a fitter person to supply the place of a father to the orphan boy, could not have been found. In his youth he had been betrothed, but his affianced bride was stricken by disease, and on the very day which had been set apart for the nuptial ceremony, he saw her laid in the grave. This was a sore blow, and at first it seemed almost to prostrate all his energies; but time gradually healed the wound, and though it was long before his face recovered much of its wonted cheerfulness—for indeed he never became entirely the same man that he had been—yet at the age of forty-five, when he removed from New York to D——, having amassed a comfortable fortune, he was looked upon as a benevolent, contented, though somewhat eccentric old bachelor. About six or seven years after Mr. Warden had taken up his new residence, Hugh, then a boy of ten, was committed to his charge, and soon grew as dear to him as an own child could have been. The only other member of the family besides the uncle and his ward, was Mrs. Martha Barton, a widow woman whom Mr. Warden had engaged as a housekeeper when he first came to D——, and who had dwelt with him in that capacity ever since. We said the *only* other member—

though we perhaps should have mentioned Richard Brownhead, a kind of nondescript character, who lived entirely alone in an old house on the outskirts of the village, gaining a subsistence by assisting the farmers during some portions of the year, and at other times mainly by hunting. Between him and Hugh an intimacy was formed almost as soon as the latter entered the village; and as the boy grew older, Richard took him under his protection, taught him to shoot, and allowed him to become his companion in many of his long excursions into the mountains. He made himself useful to the uncle also in various ways, furnishing him often with game, for which he would receive no compensation; and as he had conceived a strong liking for the youth, which Hugh on his part cordially returned, he finally became in some sort domiciliated in the family.

It was during a College vacation that Hugh first saw Orra Stanfield; the circumstances of their meeting we have already narrated in our first chapter. Warden accompanied the young men on their witch-hunting excursion, without any definite knowledge of the party accused, though he had heard vague and exaggerated stories concerning the old woman from the superstitious villagers. His surprise at seeing Mrs. Stanfield, and still more at seeing her grandchild, may hence be easily imagined. He found Orra much better educated than was wont with those of her own age, and eager for opportunities of extending her information. Her kind and affectionate disposition, united with her singular beauty, endeared her to him, and he tacitly undertook the charge of continuing her instruction. Books were plenty at his uncle's house, and these he either gave or loaned to her, according to her own inclination. But there was a mystery about the maiden which Hugh was unable to penetrate. When he questioned her about her parents, she could make no reply; she remembered living in a handsome residence in the metropolis, and nothing more; and when the youth ventured to inquire of Mrs. Stanfield, his curiosity met with a cold repulse.

Thus some two or three years passed away; Hugh had finished his education, and had dwelt about a couple of twelvemonths in D——, when the battles of Lexington and Bunker's Hill took place, and the war of the Revolution burst forth in earnest. A company had been hastily formed in D——, and our hero was placed in command. With this little band he marched to Cambridge and joined the army under General Washington, during the autumn preceding the evacuation of Boston by the English. He continued with the American forces during the disastrous campaign which followed that event, until New York fell into the power of the British under Generals Howe and Clinton. Immediately after this, having received his captain's commission from Washington himself, he was called home by the serious illness of his uncle. The bachelor recovered, however, soon after his nephew's return, and the young soldier spent the greater part of his time in the vicinity of Rapaug, in company with Orra. His boyish attachment had long ere this ripened into love, and we have already witnessed the avowal of his affection on the very day before the expiration of his furlough.

It was on as pleasant a November morning as one often witnesses, that Mr. John Warden sat down to breakfast in the comfortable sitting-room of his snug residence in D——. The bachelor seemed in rather ill humor, for he looked moodily at the beef and hot cakes which the careful housekeeper had placed before him, and pushed aside the coffee with such vehemence that the cup was upset, and the scalding liquid poured over the edge of the table upon his leg.

"Martha! Martha! blast the coffee!" he shouted, springing up; "Martha! where the devil are you?"

"Oh dear! massy on us! he's spilt the hot coffee on his leg!" screamed the housekeeper, emerging hastily from the kitchen, with a basin of cold water, the contents of which she dashed profusely upon the burnt limb.

"What under heaven do you make your coffee so hot for, Mrs Barton?" said the bachelor, savagely.

"Oh dear, sir, why, sir, yesterday mornin' you said it was cold as pump-water, and now, sir, and now"—

"Well, never mind, Martha," said he, considerably mollified by the widow's anxiety, "I don't think it's burnt much—scared me, though," and he reseated himself at the opposite side of the table, while Mrs. Barton returned to the kitchen arranging her disordered cap.

Mr. Warden now cut off a piece of steak and deposited it on his plate, muttering, "it's strange, though, that the boy has not returned;—Martha! pour me another cup of coffee;—why, zounds! the woman's disappeared. Mrs. Barton!"

The housekeeper entered again, bringing with her a small coffee-pot: "there, Martha, set it down, and then sit down yourself; I feel lonely this morning; I wonder where Hugh is."

The widow seated herself at the table, and having poured out another cup of the beverage, handed it to the bachelor, at the same time remarking, "why, you know, he went off to Rapaug woods yisterday a'ternoon, and Richard went off too in a little while, and I s'pose they're huntin' together up there somewheres."

"Pshaw!" said the old gentleman, pushing his plate from him. "I can't eat this morning; hunting! and he was to leave us to-day; well, if he's been all this time prowling around the woods, instead of coming home to spend an hour or two with his old uncle—zounds! I'll disinherit him, I'll"—

"No you won't, either," interrupted Mrs. B., for her love of Hugh was stronger than her fear of her master, "you won't do any sich thing."

"I won't, hey! you—you—I won't? I'll be d——d if I don't, though. I won't do what I please, I suppose, and you'll stop me, hey? The young rascal—what does he go up to the mountain for every day; hunting? Where's his game? Tell me that; where's his game? I tell you what, Mrs. Barton, I'll turn him out of my house—he never shall come into it again, he shan't!"

"Ain't you ashamed, Mr. Warden, old as you are, to fly into sich a passion about nothin'?"

"I've a right to be in a passion; it's my duty to be in a passion! The boy han't been brought up right; and now he's conspiring with my housekeeper against me. Zounds! I *will* be in a passion!"

"Oh, Mi-ister W-warden!" said the widow, sobbing, "who'd ha' thought this o' you? S'pose the poor boy should be hurt—bu'st his rifle, or fallen into the pond, or—or"—

"Hurt!" said the bachelor, turning very red, and then very pale, "don't cry, Martha. You know I didn't mean what I said. I'm getting old—into my dotage, perhaps—hurt—let's go and see." He sprang from his chair. "Where's my boots—my hat?"

"Wait a minute, sir," said Mrs. Barton, clearing up her countenance, "he can't be hurt, because Richard is with him, you know."

"So he is: no, he can't be hurt; but where the devil is he, then?"

"Wal! I calculate he ain't a great way off," said a voice in the hall.

"There's Richard!" screamed the widow, and the next moment our two adventurers entered the room, Hugh looking somewhat pale, and leaning upon the arm of the hunter.

"Now, boy," said the bachelor, "give an account of yourself!"

"P'raps," exclaimed Richard, "you'll wait a little till he's got breath, and had his wound fixed."

"Wound! Richard," ejaculated the bachelor and the widow in the same breath, "is he wounded?" "Lord o' massy!" continued Mrs. Barton, "let me go to the medicine-chist. What shall I git, Mr. Brownhead?"

"Some stout linen for bandages, that's all." Hugh assured his uncle that the hurt was nothing serious, and gave an account of his adventure in full, with the exception of some *unimportant* passages concerning his doings at the hut, while Richard was removing the former bandages from his wounded shoulder, and applying new ones.

"John Martin up there, and that infernal red-skin," said the bachelor. "Well, but, Hugh, what on earth was you doing there? I don't see into it."

"This is not the proper opportunity to explain it, uncle. As my furlough must needs be extended for the present, there will be time enough for explanations."

The housekeeper, who had left the room for a few minutes, now entered with a look of joyful surprise, exclaiming, "Oh! Mr. Warden, the general's comin' here; I saw him openin' the gate."

"Hey, the general coming," said the bachelor, "what's in the wind now? I say, Hugh!—why, the boy's gone!" The young soldier had slipped from the room as Mrs. Barton entered. "Well, but, Richard," continued Mr. Warden, turning toward the place where the hunter had been sitting, but he too had disappeared. A loud knock was now heard at the door, and the widow left the apartment, and returning in a few moments, ushered in a dignified looking gentleman, dressed in the uniform of a military officer of rank.

"General Silliman,"* said the bachelor, bowing, and offering the

* Brigadier General Silliman, son of the Hon. Ebenezer Silliman, and father of the present distinguished Professor of Chemistry in Yale College.

visitor a seat, "I am happy to see you at my house. Any news from below ?

"Very little, sir, very little," replied the other, seating himself. "Captain Hugh Warden is, I believe, at home at present on furlough ?"

"Yes, sir, he has but this moment left the room, and as he is aware of your presence, I presume he will speedily return. Breakfasted, General ?" continued he, as Hugh, having changed his dress, entered the room.

"Thank you, sir, I have. Ah—here he is. Good morning, Captain Warden. What! you look ill."

"I received a slight wound in the shoulder yesterday, of just sufficient consequence to lengthen my furlough indefinitely."

"If the hurt is not serious," said the general, "nothing could be more pat to my purposes. I was considering by what means to detain you here this winter. I believe, sir," he continued, turning to the uncle, "that you are favorable to the American cause, and it will do no harm to mention our plan of operations in your presence. We need some place where we can gather a supply of stores, provisions, &c. As D—— is at some distance from the Sound, and somewhat of a central place, we have chosen it for this purpose. We shall immediately commence the work, and as I cannot remain here myself, there is need of some active and faithful officer to superintend. Knowing that Captain Warden was at home, I called to make arrangements to secure his services. His wound, I trust, will soon be healed, and I will to-day write to head-quarters to obtain permission for his stay: meanwhile he can remain by my authority. Stop, though—is there any enemy in these quarters ? How did you receive your wound, captain ?"

Hugh gave the outline of his story, and dwelt particularly upon the necessity of capturing the tory and his associates.

"You are right," said the general, thoughtfully, "you are right. What force have you in the place ?"

"Small, sir, very small," replied Hugh, "in fact none. Men enough, however, can be collected for this object. I will go myself, and with me Richard Brownhead, and two or three others that I think of."

"No, captain," interposed the senior officer, "no, you are not well enough to perform this service. I have heard of this Brownhead. Can you not obtain the others that you mention, and allow him to take the command ? If any one can catch the scoundrel, from his reputation I should think he might."

"If you insist upon it that I shall not go, general, I believe Richard can and will perform the service."

"Let it be attended to at once, then. Remember, Captain Warden, that you are to direct the collection and depositing of the stores. The defense of the place will be entrusted to Col. Cook, whom I shall send up with a detachment for that purpose. He will bring you further directions, for our arrangements are not yet completed. Meanwhile I shall return to F——, waiting, however, to see some persons sent out after this Martin."

"I will call in Richard immediately," said Hugh, "but there's necessity for that, for here he comes."

As he spoke, the hunter entered and doffed his hat to the genera

"Richard," continued Captain Warden, "we wish to seize, if possi John Martin and the Indian. As I cannot well undertake it myself, have concluded to put you in command of such persons as you can or may select, and send you after him."

"Pos-si-bil-i-ty! wal! Mister Hugh, he's as good as caught."

"Who can you find to accompany you?" said the general.

"Why, you see, gin'ral, I calculate I *could* do the job alone; but always best to make sure and—let me see—there's John Treadwa reg'lar 'cute un, and Tom Morris—and—and—that's it, Bill Armstr the nigger! Reckon we four can do it."

"Good morning, then," said the general, "I must hasten my retu and he left the room.

"Now, perhaps, we can eat some breakfast," said the bachelor, s ing himself at the table, while the others followed his example, " mustn't start on your expedition with an empty stomach."

"Wal! that's my calculation," replied the hunter, applying him to the provisions with a readiness and despatch which fully proved correctness of his reckoning.

CHAPTER VI.

About an hour after the events just detailed, a party of four n three whites and a negro, might have been seen collected togethe the entrance of a kind of lane (now a high road) leading from the t of D—— up into the Rapaug forest. One of them was our old fri Richard Brownhead, the others, the companions he had selected to sist in the capture of the tory. The forester was clothed in the man we have already described; the other whites wore the common h ing-dress; but the attire of the negro was somewhat unique. His was an old straw one, the brim of which had been half torn away, an the top of the crown was stuck a red feather. A hunting-frock of low and red striped cloth, a pair of calf-skin leggins, and ordinary m casins, and a clumsy musket, completed his equipments. He originally been a slave, for slavery then existed in New England well as elsewhere, but upon the death of his old master had gained liberty.

They were engaged in earnest conversation about the method of p cedure; Richard thinking it necessary to proceed first to the Pond, afterward to the Dell. Morris sided with him, while Treadway the negro, for they had all heard his story, were for hastening at o to the tory's hiding-place.

"Ki!" exclaimed the negro, "what you want for to go there Mis'er Brownhead, hey? Martin aint there, he run away, out window, hey!"

"Pos-si-bil-i-ty! you black rascal! who told you to speak? Rich

Brownhead's commander of this regiment; hang the mutineers." Thus saying, he trudged manfully along the lane, followed, though somewhat grumblingly, by the others.

On they went, into the forest, and over all kinds of obstructions, till they gained a sight of the Pond. Here the hunter commanded another halt, in order to determine their plans, and after much noiseless discussion, it was agreed that they should divide, two going round by the west and two by the east side of the Pond.

"Bill, you son of darkness," said the hunter, "you go with me, by the east; and step as light as a cricket, for the Injun may be within two rods of us now; you, Morris, go the other way, with John. We'll meet at the hut, and if we don't find him there, we'll go down to his burrow, blast him!"

There we leave the party for the present, to follow the course of another individual, who had been following and watching them, unobserved, almost since they entered the forest. This was Grahtimut, who, as they separated, started off in another direction, with great speed. A few moments brought him to the Dell, whither Martin had returned after his escape, and was now sleeping, being exhausted with the fatigues of the preceding day. As the Indian struck his rifle against the rude stone-work of the cabin, the tory came forth, with an angry countenance, and exclaimed,

"Well! where are they now?"

"Cap'in Warden gone home, s'pose."

"Damnation! did you see him?"

"No! when you come back, Grahtimut go straight to the hut, old squaw, young squaw there; young squaw crying; pale-faces gone. Follow trail till it go out of the forest; then wait for see more. One, two, three hours; then they come, so many," holding up four fingers, "hear 'em talk; after d—d tory, they say; too many to shoot; leave 'em at Rapaug; come down here like wild-cat, they comin' too."

"The devil they are! I must be off, then."

"Ugh!"

"Have you got another rifle?"

"Here yours; got it at the hut."

"Good! wait a minute till I get my ammunition."

He entered the cabin, and after remaining there a few moments, came forth with his bullet-pouch and powder-flask slung over his shoulders. They started toward the entrance of the hollow, but before they gained it Martin sprang back, exclaiming, in a suppressed voice, "God! here they come!"

"Back, back!" said the Indian, retreating hastily to the cabin.

"Grahtimut, we've got to fight for it!"

"Ugh! get behind tree, Cap'in Martin, when you see 'em, shoot straight; kill two and get away."

Scarcely had they placed themselves behind two contiguous trees, when Richard and his party appeared, carefully examining the fresh trail of the Indian.

"They're here," said the hunter, in a whisper, "keep behind the trees, and look sharp," at the same time protecting himself by the body of a huge oak, while the negro followed his example. Morris and Treadway were not so cautious; they stood, hesitating for a fatal moment as to the choice of a shelter; the next moment a simultaneous report of the rifles of the tory and the Indian sounded through the wood; Morris, giving a fearful shriek, leaped into the air, and fell dead, while Treadway, staggering back, dropped, mortally wounded.

"Upon them," said the hunter, fiercely springing from his covert, followed by the negro. No time to reload was allowed, and Martin exclaiming "we must meet them half way," darted out; Richard brought his rifle to his shoulder and snapped; it missed fire! and the next moment a blow from the butt end of the tory's piece sent him reeling against a tree. As the savage came forth the negro fired, and Grahtimut, stumbling headlong, fell, apparently dead, at his very feet.

"You've settled him, Bill," exclaimed the hunter, "now for Martin," and, with the negro at his side, he bounded off in pursuit of the tory. They stopped a moment at the bodies of their friends, and seizing the loaded rifles which lay near them, left their own and hastened away.

The track continued fresh for some distance, and they continually expected to come in sight of the object of pursuit. It went in a southerly direction from the Pond, but after proceeding about a mile it grew fainter and fainter, and finally disappeared altogether. Near where it was completely indiscernible was a small stream, and Richard, after pausing an instant, exclaimed, "He's taken to the brook; let's follow it." For nearly another mile they followed the course of the rivulet, till it came out into the open fields. Here they found the marks of Martin's feet again, where he had left the stream, and the trail quite fresh; they pursued it to an opening in the rude worm fence, where it ended, and the tracks of a horse were alone visible.

"He's stolen a horse, by ——!" shouted the hunter, fiercely excited, "and is safe. Only let him come in Richard Brownhead's way once more, blast the infarnal scoundrel! Bill, we must go back, it's no use.

"Golly! Mis'er Richard," exclaimed the negro, "what'll Cap'in Warden think?"

"He'll think I'm a cussed fool! no, he won't either—wal! it's no use now; we must go back."

They turned, and in silence, but with a rapid pace retraced their steps; when they arrived at the dell, the first thing that caught their attention was the bodies of their friends—both scalped. Richard, with an ejaculation, rushed into the hollow—the Indian was gone. He had evidently been wounded, for there was much blood where he had lain, but not mortally, or even very severely, for the track to the bodies of the men was steady, and the whole appearance of the matter betokened cool deliberation. No trail from the bodies was to be found; and after much search the pursuers gave it up in despair, and hastened toward the village, in order to procure assistance to remove the corpses.

STANZAS.

Now Zephyr gently breathes adown the lawn,
Lo! 'tis the grateful hour of closing day,
The torrid heat of noon-tide now is gone,
And burning Phœbus dims his brilliant ray,
And slowly sinks from human sight away.—
Twilight's soft shade comes down from all the sky,
Enrobing land and sea in sober gray—
The gaudy glare of day dies silently,
And leaves Heaven's deathless lamps unveil'd to every eye.

So breathes old age his last expiring breath,
So his sun languishes into the tomb—
Fast on his eyes spread forth the shades of death,
And gathers round his head contagious gloom;
But faith reveals a brighter world to come,
Where light undying gilds the blessed shore—
There every way-worn pilgrim finds a home,
And earth's vain pageant cheats the heart no more.

Thou too art laid to rest in thy last home,
And thy cold ear lists not the triumph of fame,
Nor break upon the quiet of thy tomb
The world-wide echoes of thine honored name.
Long shall thy monumental pile inflame
The youth of coming times with kindred fire—
Long as thy country holds one generous aim
Thy canvas shall the patriot heart inspire,
And Trumbull's name shall pass through lips of son and sire.

Lo! in the Senate, where in dead suspense
Discussion shapes a nation's woe or weal,
The storied walls rouse patriot eloquence,
And force the state into ancestral zeal.
O may thy art give latest times to feel
The mighty souls that fired the heroic age,
And Freedom's glorious battle-ground reveal
The warrior's prowess and his noble rage,
Till distant centuries in Freedom's war engage!

Oh! earthly immortality—a cheat thou art!
Hast filled full many a heart with maddening strife,
But happy thou did choose a better part,

And gain the blessed boon of endless life,
An immortality with glory rife,
That grows not dim when canvas fades away.
It is not worn by time, or care, or grief,
Earth's fairest thing shall sink to low decay,
But fame in Heaven shall brighten to eternal day.

THE CHARACTER OF TRUE GREATNESS.

What is greatness? As mankind in general view this question, a solution of it has already been found in the various parts which many of their number have acted. Some, whom public exigencies or political revolutions have called from the humbler spheres of life, have had their peculiar characters developed by the momentous scenes in which they engaged. The suddenness of their transition, and the brilliancy that attended it, and succeeding events, appeal to the wonder and astonishment of men. Energies, before latent, are brought into action; are concentrated with irresistible power upon a given object. But they do not go on unassisted—they command, nay, they compel the abject subsorviency of mind and matter. The world yields a ready obedience, for it is charmed and overpowered as it gazes upon the noon-day splendor of these newly risen orbs, and worships their talismanic presence. Again, there are others who slowly, silently, but surely wend their way from obscurity up to honor and eminence. Their fellow-men are not awe-struck at the *manner* and *celerity* by which they have attained that position, but at the *fact*. Under the influence of that feeling which pervades the soul whenever we look up to exaltation, however it may have obtained, we entitle it *greatness*. Yet in what does it consist but in a bare superiority, to the acquisition and importance of which, circumstances may have been chief contributors? But is this to be the test of a position to which we pay our homage, and of an individual who is to fix the eyes of his fellow-men upon himself? In either of the cases mentioned above, it is not impossible or improbable, that he who first appeared upon the horizon, and sooner or later gained the meridian, employed the means he found most suitable to reach his desired height. But we do not consider the character of these means he himself uses for his elevation. The mistake is in not inquiring who and what he is, but what is his station. How unreasonable and unworthy does this blind adoration appear, and such is it that the world manifests toward those who have been its tyrants and murderers, whose self was to them more than all beside, and who have lived but to be a scourge. It is evident then, that to answer this question agreeably with reason and justice, we must apply some other test, than this brilliancy which dazzles our eyes and perverts our judgment. And what it shall be, let reason and conscience dictate, in view of the defect of such a criterion. But where was the defect? In the heart, the originator and source of human conduct, in the inner man, which is seen only by its outward developments? then it is here we must look for our standard and guide, when we would judge of other men, and also when we would judge ourselves. It is the motives of an action which decide its character and make it worthy of being called great. When the lives of those who have been the prime movers of the world's affairs, who have incorporated themselves into its history, and thus have to their names this poor honor paid, are subjected to this trial, they are divested of the pomp and glory that conceal their nature. Before this all-seeing Argus, naught but naked truth is unblemished. It is an ordeal from whose refining fire there is no escape—and let him who cannot endure, perish—but whatever does, we may rest assured is pure. Therefore we infer, that all true greatness falls back upon principle as its ultimate source—that it is its immediate and necessary result.

Action and suffering are the two great theatres which display its triumph, and its infinite superiority to all subordinate motives—in both it shines forth like the sun with inherent light. Since then we have here such a cause, its effects cannot but partake of its high nature. And first as it develops itself in action. Conduct is the index of character—and whatever mystery at times envelops it, and presents to human observation strange inconsistencies which becloud our vision when we would look into the heart, there is no reason to doubt the application of it as a universal rule. The hypocrite cannot be one always—nature will manifest itself; if it were not so, this would be the most inexplicable of all anomalies. Yet one has but to observe, to see that what is here theoretical, is practical. It is not then an indefinite criterion by which we would judge of the character of an act—and this is all that is necessary to consider, in forming our estimate. The development of this principle living within, is just the reverse of an ambition whose boundaries are self—it is too mighty, too great to be confined by limits so restricted—its energies can act only on a broad, expanded field, upon objects worthy of itself—these compose all the interests of man as a moral being, and as a member of civil society. Its design is to build up, and not destroy—to bring with it happiness, the great end of all human concerns.

The action it prompts and governs does not, however, limit itself to any one channel—it is not the rivulet, nor yet the mighty river, but the *Ocean* encompassing in its vast expansion, the whole world. In all the political convulsions in which men have been involved, there have stood up some who seemed the ruling spirits of the storm, under whose guidance and by whose own creative energies, governments and nations have sprung into existence. At their bidding, the waste and desolation which always succeed a revolution of any kind, are recalled to life and prosperity. It is for them to collect the rude materials which are then spread about them, and fashion them with the hand of the skillful artist, till all coalesce into one symmetrical whole. Political fabrics thus erected, the world will admire for the character of their architects, and for their inherent beauty and utility. This is a field where human wisdom and rectitude of purpose are seen in the most exalted state, and must be inseparable in order to be successfu By this we mean, in establishing a government, the express design c which is to confer happiness upon its subjects—but to produce a di ferent one by acting from any sinister schemes, presupposes an entir ly different case from the present one, for only when the hero is d vested of these, does he become the patriot. They who thus contr the course of the world's affairs, attach to themselves a sublimity th justly places them in that truly elevated position which commands th admiration and profoundest regard of their fellow-men. But what wa it that so covered them with more than royal robes, that gave them th sway of these mental commotions, that inspired them, as it were, wit this attribute of omnipotence? Some indwelling motive, whose inhe ent power and greatness were commensurate with such an effect— which could bring light out of darkness, peace out of contention— which could harmonize these warring elements of society, and con bine them so as to produce the increased happiness of mankind. Bu it could be no selfish desire or incentive—for that would be inadequat to the result—but it must have been a principle in the soul, that th acted, commanded, created. They who in this way claim our highe honor, were but its instruments, the subjects of its will, which wa their law.

The moral reformer is also under the sway of a kindred spirit. B a reformer, we do not mean the wild and frenzied enthusiasts who hav always existed in the world. It is most emphatically true that refor has been the watchword of the past and present—but when reform b comes radicalism, it knows no bounds, and merely introduces extrav gant innovations which are not improvements. But we would give th appellation to him only, who where evils do actually exist, has wisdo to see them and scrutinize their nature, and judicious courage to guid him in their eradication. The former act under those impulsive fee ings and passions which carried but one step too far, never fail of b ing derogatory to the inborn dignity of human nature. The latter a buried up, and overpowered in the contest, by fixed principles of du and philanthropy. The warfare into which such an one enters, th causes of it, and the effects it is intended to produce, are all calculat of themselves to infuse into him an energy and efficacy of action, co respondent to their importance. It is a thought which history w substantiate, that every revolution worthy of the name of a reformatio has been guided by men who truly seemed to be nerved and ill mined with more than human strength and wisdom. The gigant powers which were slumbering within, needed but some momento occasion or subject to awaken them to their full vigor; but when the were called into action, the world trembled at their blows—well migl it be abashed in the presence of a soul so sublime in character. Whe even one thus enters into the battle, enemies and obstacles fall an vanish before him—opposition he will encounter, but that will as ce tainly be overcome. The arm that is raised against him is paralyzed— the deadly arrow falls by him harmless. Is it asked why this invin bility? Truth is his banner, God his leader and shield—he must prevail. Times and men like these have existed in the past history of the moral and political world. But especially is this true in the Reformation of the sixteenth century. What stronger incentives to the mightiest exertions could be presented to him, who could look over Europe then, comprehend its actual state, see its sleep of death, and feel himself called to be its reviver? If he could feel what his eye saw, his resolutions would but correspond to the emotions of his heart, and his life with his resolutions. Without entering upon a discussion of the causes and character of that Reformation, we merely wish to introduce the champion of it, as an eminent illustration of the opinions we have advanced, that acting in accordance with fixed principles, whenever and however they be exercised, is the basis of all true greatness. Who at the present day, as he transfers himself back to that period, would conjecture that from an humble ascetic of a convent, such overwhelming results should have gone forth? But if we could watch the gradual but decisive renovation that went on in the heart of Luther himself first, and the increasing strength of his new principles, ought he to wonder that under incentives like these, the hidden powers of his soul should prove capable of what they did perform? Yet with whatever degree of astonishment we are struck at the fact, we have here inscribed on the world's records, one of the sublimest examples it has ever witnessed, of what man *can* accomplish when truth and duty engage his zeal and action. Thus was *he* influenced—he felt their commanding authority, and from it there was no escape. He lighted the blaze which ere long kindled into a conflagration that spread over Europe in its wild fury, consuming and purifying with unquenchable energy. When he girded himself with his simple armor, and went out to meet the enemy, no Goliath stood forth to combat him single-handed, but the united hosts of the Philistines arrayed themselves against him. But neither their defiance nor threatening could intimidate or deter him from the faithful and successful prosecution of his cause. Such enthusiasm and power were not to be smothered and subdued by human endeavors, or the strenuous efforts which were made to effect this very object, would have attained their end. In none of his opponents was there this strength of the inner man, which as it unfolded itself was an engine irresistible in attack or defense. In his intellectual powers, considered by themselves, he probably was not superior to some of his cotemporaries—but it was the cause he advocated, which covered him with an impermeable panoply. All that we have seen him exhibit, however, we do not ascribe to the man; it was the truth and its higher Friend, that spoke and acted through him—he was but the instrument. Language would fail us to describe his victory—but the world will continue to bear testimony to it, until the fire that he then kindled, shall be absorbed in the greater conflagration of the universe. And equally feeble is it to portray the sublimity of his character and life—it is something more than mere greatness—it attaches to itself the attributes and likeness of infinite majesty.

Thus in each of these two fields of the greatest action, we have seen the display of a governing principle pure and untarnished in itself, and in its consequences, possessed of the highest dignity which can grace human nature. But although it be assimilated to such perfection and glory, it is not confined to these most impressive manifestations. It is a kindred spirit to that which leads the philanthropist in his more humble and unobserved walks. It here assumes a milder aspect. Its language is "peace, good will toward men." It enters with sympathizing interest into all the woes of humanity, to mitigate and soothe their intensity—in all its effects it bespeaks its high origin. It is the same in ultimate character with that upon which the dignity and glory of the two great moral and political reformations of the sixteenth and eighteenth centuries rests. Whether it ride upon the whirlwind in terrible majesty, or whisper with the still small voice of mercy, in the ear of sorrow, it changes not its nature, but its form.

Under these considerations, which we deem admissible in every respect, we would ask, are the selfish and contracted aims which govern most whom the world honors, worthy to be the competitors of such for the character of true greatness? It is true they might, if they were not diametrically opposed to the very constitution of human society, the first ingredient of which is, the mutual dependence of all its members, and their consequently reciprocal obligations. And moreover, if we are at a loss to decide upon the kind of motives which at any time overrule or influence an act, we have one sure criterion by which to judge of it—this is found in the consequence it does or is suited to produce. If this guide were always followed, a more just estimate would be formed of men who have rather astonished the world than benefitted it. An appeal to the mistaken judgments that have been formed upon other grounds, leaves us to determine at once their irrationality.

The magnanimity of soul which is displayed in suffering is also due to the same source. There is not so much room for deception here, as in the former. But very rarely or never do we witness that calm unmoveable fortitude, which murmurs not in adversity, successfully counterfeited. The reason is obvious—because it is not the gift of nature, nor the result of mere animal courage. It springs from something higher and nobler, and derived its own exalted qualities from those of its origin. We cannot find a sublimer spectacle in this world, than what is here presented us, and we instinctively acknowledge its inherent moral grandeur. The soul, which like the eagle soars up into a cloudless sky, and looks down upon the raging storm with tranquil serenity, exhibits a greatness of which we can form only an inadequate conception. It has incorporated into itself some principle of elevated excellence, which thus sustains it firm and unwavering. The history of our race furnishes us with some worthy exemplifications of this sentiment, and generally those individuals have been those in whose actions likewise, the same unconquerable power, no way passive, has displayed its energies. Hence the song of joyous triumph which has arisen amid the flames of the stake and all the tortures of malicious cruelty. When we consider the character and origin of those principles themselves, need we wonder that such are their results? Taking their rise far back of the human race, from their Creator, they were fixed before each individual soul, that it might see and feel their excellence. The honor they confer upon him through whom they thus live before the world, is not ephemeral—it abides but to become brighter and more transcendantly glorious—time and reflection, those touch stones of human conduct, will try in vain to find defects and mortality here. Oblivion will open no grave for such greatness, for how can immortality die? No more can that which bears the impress of eternity, perish with its possessor.

E. E.

THE HOAXED

READER, your kind attention is invited to a short story founded, as they say, on fact, and interspersed with certain moral reflections. The main incidents related came under my personal observation, while a rusticated student at M——, a country village remarkable for its healthful air and steady habits, situated within a day's ride of my alma mater —Harvard University. The moral reflections are, of course, the offspring of later and wiser years.

The village of M—— had long been reputed an excellent residence for those invalid undergraduates who need country air and regimen. This was in part owing to the fact that Rev. Mr. D—— dwelt there,—a learned and stern old gentleman, who, besides performing his parish duties, (revival and protracted meetings were unknown in those Arminian days,) found ample time to instruct several youthful aspirants to a college education, in their classical studies, and at the same time, keeping a fatherly watch over any transient collegians who might be recommended to his attention.

Abraham F. Smith, as his parents and friends called him, (he always wrote it A. Fitz-Henry Smythe,) was the only son of an old Wall street broker, who had for many years retired from business, and was laid up at home with the gout. Abraham, being designed for one of the learned professions, had been kept at school from his infancy. A literary course had been chosen for him, because, in the judgment of his wise father, he had hardly sense enough for mercantile business, or sufficient strength to live in any out-door occupation. By constant nursing and great medical care he had been raised to incipient manhood, when he was sent to M——, that Parson D—— might superintend the five or six last years of his preparatory course. Abraham was a spoilt youth. His common sense, if he ever had any, was obliterated by a false education. Time and money had always been to him quite unimportant trifles, worthy the consideration only of vulgar minds. Having promenaded Broadway, and been up the North River to the Springs, he professed an extensive knowledge of human nature, and the outward world generally. But, while he was entirely ignorant of other men, because he had spent his whole life in the contemplation of himself, he had less of real self-knowledge than any other sort. Abraham, in several of his circumstances and characteristics, represents quite a large class of young men, who enter college only to make themselves fools, and to become the minus quantities of society. They are generally the sons of rich men, who send them to college, as a matter of course, having nothing else for them to do, and without the least regard to their natural tastes and capabilities; thus teaching them to disdain all laborious and useful employments, and to consider all study an evil in itself, and necessary merely as an accomplishment. They go from the nursery to a boarding-school, and from the boarding-school to college, where they learn to spend money and waste time; acquire indolent habits; dissipate both body and mind; and graduate, as ignorant of the world they enter as children. The hard-earned family wealth generally departs with this generation.

But to return to Abraham. I saw him first in the bar-room of the village hotel, engaged in smoking a cigar, at the same time evidently exerting himself to look exceedingly knowing and independent. His collar was put on in the true carelessness of the Byronic style, and his glossy hair, according to the same design, flowed in fine dark ringlets to an unusual length. Neither nature nor art could do more for him, for his face was somewhat pale and freckled, his eyes very light blue, and his figure very lank: so that his *tout ensemble* was far from being truly poetic. I afterwards discovered, in a way which shall be related, that his natural hair was in keeping with his complexion, both sandy and straight. Having unfortunately lost it through the effects of a fever a year or two before, he had worn this admirable wig as a temporary substitute ever since, until he seemed, through an eccentricity of genius, to prefer it to the original. Abraham was a youth of an exceedingly chivalrous disposition. He talked very largely concerning his honor as a gentleman, and was inordinately fond of pretty damsels; though the secret of this last passion seemed to a close observer to be rather his own power of fascination than theirs. He had already, by means of his impudence, figured extensively in the society of M——. It was not an unusual custom with him to be present at all parties of note, without waiting for an invitation, relying upon his own peculiar merits for a welcome reception, and making the next day, if he saw fit, a long and excessively polite apology for his mistake, through the post office. He was moreover always (ready and waiting) in the meeting-house porch at evening lecture, and always affronting some honest country youth, by escorting home the best-looking young ladies; until he at last flattered all the sensible girls in the village into utter abhorrence of him.

It was on the evening of my arrival that I saw Abraham. Having surveyed me with a very wise and patronizing air, for a moment, he swaggered towards me, and introduced himself by hazarding several vague conclusions with regard to my object in coming to M——. After I had partially satisfied his curiosity, and proposed to him some incidental questions, he became quite affable, described my future guardian, Parson D——, as a great rascal; cursed the town of M——, and all its inhabitants; excepting, however, with a huge oath, several pretty girls, whose persons and character he began to describe very freely. Growing heartily tired of his conversation, I seized a candle, and bidding him a gruff good night, asked to be shown to my room, which office he immediately took upon himself, expressing the greatest delight at the very singular and lucky circumstance of our rooms being situated in the same story. I left him with a dismal foreboding of the future evils which would result from his near acquaintance.

Thanksgiving day was a very pleasant episode in my monotonous life at M——. I had been invited to dine with Squire Mason, the wealthiest and most influential man in the village. A merry group assembled around the dinner table, for the good-hearted old squire had gathered together all his nephews, nieces, and grandchildren to partake of his good cheer.

It was my good fortune to be seated by the side of Ellen Mason—a merry, fair-haired girl, with a very cunning look, and a very bewitching eye. Having heard Abraham often mention her as one of his especial favorites, and boast of gaining her simple heart, I incidentally mentioned his name in our conversation. I saw that it caused the fair girl pain. A flush of anger passed over her brow, and she frankly expressed her strong dislike of Mr. Smith. There was no lack of sympathy on my part, and little measuring of terms wherewith to prove my heartfelt contempt for that individual. Then followed the stories of Abraham's disgusting behavior towards her, and of the many petty annoyances she constantly suffered from him. As I listened to her earnest voice, and watched her flashing eye, lighting up those beautiful features with unaffected sincerity, a strange and unaccountable sympathy took possession of my heart. I have since found that it was something more than merely the sympathy which belonged to the occasion; for it has never stopt increasing from that day to this, and—but what I was about to say is quite irrelevant to the story.

There was to be a grand party at the 'squire's in the evening. It was already growing dusk, and the village began to be enlivened by the merry sound of sleigh-bells, while the 'squire's parlors shone every moment with a brighter array of beautiful country damsels, the fashion and beauty of M——. The festivities of the evening had commenced, for the varied group of young and old, gay and grave. the rosy-cheeked damsels, with here and there a languishing, sentimental city cousin, whose lily complexion formed a pleasing contrast in the bright bouquet, had nearly all assembled, and every face beamed with pleasure. It was a bright moonlight night without. Happening to stand by a window, my attention was drawn to the gaunt figure of Abraham striding up the Avenue, his ambrosial locks streaming in the wind. By his side was Charles Turner, my most intimate friend, a careless, noble-hearted, fun-loving fellow, who very heartily despised Abraham. Yet now they seemed extremely merry and amicable, as, like two old friends, they cozily ascended the steps, arm in arm. I was puzzling my wits to conjecture how Abraham could have the impudence to intrude himself upon our circle in such good company, when Ellen Mason's little brother pulled my sleeve, and said that Mr. Turner wished to see me in the hall. There he was, with a broad grin upon his merry round face. Rubbing his hands with glee, he exclaimed, with a quiet tone of complete satisfaction, "Smith's up stairs."

"Well," said I, "that seems to please you wonderfully. What's he up there for?"

"Why, fixing his wig, and getting ready for the party, of course; but somehow or other, he's blundered into the ladies' dressing-room. Let's go up and see what he's about there."

The door was ajar just enough to give us a fair view of Abraham, who was very carefully adjusting his curls for future effect. He seemed very much perplexed whether to have a few ringlets fall negligently over the left eye, or to display the full extent of his narrow forehead. He shook away the curls, stepped back with a tragic air to witness the effect, and immediately decided to adopt the former method. Having tied an outlandish, piratical looking knot in his cravat, and stuffed a white handkerchief into his bosom, he drew out a pair of white kid gloves, (articles seldom used in M——,) and at once commenced making several sorts of bows, at the same time remarking, with a bland smile, and in a tone exceedingly polite, "Shall I have the *very* extreme pleasure of a dance with you this evening, Miss Mason?" "No I thank you, sir," tittered out a half-smothered voice from behind a fire-screen in the corner; for two or three young ladies, whom Abraham had interrupted in their toilet, had been amused spectators of his practice.

"Please, sir," stammered out a maid-servant, who had been for some time summoning courage enough to speak audibly, "you have got the wrong room, sir. The gentlemen's room is right opposite, sir."

We stood back a little, while Abraham rushed desperately across the hall.

"Run down stairs, John," whispered Turner, "and prepare the way for Abraham's reception. He'll be there in a minute. Tell 'em he's coming."

I thought Abraham would make that fact known soon enough himself. Upon entering the drawing-room, I found that his presence was already known to the company, for the young ladies of the toilet scene had told their story. All seemed to be awaiting Abraham's appearance, and every one knew him to be an intruder.

"He's coming," whispered a little girl in the door-way.

"Hush, my dear," said a lady near her. This was obeyed as a general command, and the whole company was on the *qui vive* excepting Parson D——, and some other gray-headed old gentlemen, who were kept continually amused by a long story the 'squire was telling them in the chimney-corner.

Abraham entered the room with a fixed smile, which was the result of long practice, and altogether peculiar to himself. He bowed slightly and stiffly to the company, who opened for him to the right and left, his dignity evidently increasing with the astonishing deference shown to his person, until he reached Miss Ellen, the mistress of ceremonies. Then commenced the performance of his lowest and most polite bow. At that critical and interesting moment, Charles Turner, who had followed, imitating his main actions with mock gravity, very gently and dexterously twitched off his wig. No human being ever looked more ridiculous than Abraham just then. He instinctively grasped his yellow head, the stiff short hair bristling out in every direction, but it was too late—the wig was gone. His face grew redder and more red every instant, as the universal merriment became greater. Even old Parson D—— laughed till his little gray eyes watered. Abraham rushed for the door. He cursed Turner outright, and then cursed the hall door because it didn't open readily of its own accord. A young lady handed him his wig. He swore at the wig, and stuffed it into his coat pocket. Seizing his hat from a servant in a most furious rage, he crammed it upon his head, but owing to the absence of the wig, it entirely covered his eyes. Another burst of merriment resulted from his desperate efforts to take it off, which he finally succeeded in doing, at the expense of the lining. Abraham was now completely blind with rage. Having cursed his hat and stamped upon it, he rushed bare-headed down the Avenue.

The good natured 'squire immediately sent a servant after him with his cane, cloak, and torn hat—and poor Abraham was soon forgotten in the merry games and joyful dance which enlivened the rest of the evening.

Edward Sanford, a dashing young Southerner from Mobile, was my next door neighbor in the Mansion Hotel. He had graduated at the Virginia University, and was then studying law with Squire Mason. From his experience in fashionable life, he was considered a perfect oracle by the young sprigs of M—— in all matters pertaining to etiquette and the laws of honor. Now Abraham had a most exalted idea of Southern chivalry, and the code of honor. Whenever he walked the streets of M—— after sun-down, he wore a dirk, and was accustomed to make a great display of a brace of pocket pistols to the loungers of the hotel. He was especially annoyed and excited by the term Abolitionist—often working himself into such a rage on the subject as would lead a stranger to suppose that he owned a large plantation of negroes, all in danger of immediate emancipation.

Abraham allowed himself to be led by the nose in any direction which Sanford might choose. On all occasions he sought that gentleman's advice and invariably followed it with implicit obedience. Upon returning from Squire Mason's after the party, I heard Abraham's voice apparently engaged in low and serious conference with his usual adviser.

The next morning I often looked up and down the street with the expectation of seeing Abraham promenading it, armed with a large cowhide; for I felt assured that some desperate measure had been advised by Sanford, who would never let pass an opportunity for a row. But Abraham was nowhere visible.

Just after dinner, a rap announced visitors, and in walked Charles Turner and Edward Sanford. They seated themselves with a very wise and serio-comic demeanor, as if they had some thing of high importance to communicate.

"Well, gentlemen," said I, "what's the news?"

"News indeed," replied Sanford, "such as was never heard of in this old Puritan town since the Pilgrim Fathers came over, and its just this. A duel is going to come off and we have called to obtain your connivance and assistance in the bloody transaction."

"A duel! good heavens! You don't mean that Abraham is going to shoot anybody on account of that wig of his?"

"Well, that *is* his present design, I believe, and moreover you must be Turner's second. You see we have got the affair under considerable headway; but in order to give you a better understanding of the data upon which we proceed, you must know that Abraham came to my room last night in a highly excited state, and informed me concerning a deadly insult he had received. You know the circumstances better than I. Well, he asked my advice as to his future proceedings in the case. I saw that he considered it an extremely serious matter, and accordingly told him, that, as it was an affair of honor, it could be settled in no other way than by challenging the insulting party. He meditated upon it a long time, and finally concluded himself that it was the only possible way of managing the case. We both, of course, deeply regretted the necessity of such extreme measures, but I reckon he regretted it *rather* more than I did. Now, gentlemen, I am his second; wherefore, let's proceed in a business way to the arrangements. In the first place, nobody must be hurt,—nothing illegal must be done; and, secondly, no mortal must know of it excepting old Dr. White and Sheriff Jones. They are old heads, used to such gammon in their young days, and will help us carry this out in the regular style. As we are all on hand, there's no use in being ceremonious, writing notes, or any thing of that sort; but we'll have it all done up on the spot. Let's consider a minute."

Here Sanford rubbed his hands and puffed away at his cigar with great fury for a few seconds.

"I've got it," exclaimed he. "Here it is, gentlemen. The order of arrangements is made out. Day after to-morrow, seeing to-morrow is Sunday, we'll have it come off, for fear Abraham will get scared and cool down. I'll keep him practicing at a mark all day to-morrow, and I'll attend to keeping *him* straight. You two must practice tragedy between now and then, just sufficient to keep serious when the time comes. Charles, you'll have to prepare well on the dying part. Do it somewhat spasmodically, that is, jump up two or three feet, but without being too flustratious. Don't say that you are killed, or make any remarks of that sort. In a word, do it *naturally*. You know. You, John, load the pistols, give the signal by dropping your hat or handkerchief, while I will measure the ground and attend to Abraham. That last is the main point; leave that wholly to me. Don't even see Abraham, if you can help it. I'll do all that pertains to that individual.

hat's all, gents, I believe, and it's time for me to go over to the quire's and recite. I reckon we must let the old 'squire know, but obody else, excepting the Doctor and old Jones. Well, I'm off, gen-emen. Good-bye to you, and success to the cause."

Charles Turner and I then enjoyed a hearty laugh over the scenes f Thanksgiving night, and after carefully rehearsing our particular du-es, as defined by Sanford,—for we possessed very little personal know-dge of duelling,—we spent the rest of the evening in a pleasant *tete a te*, which chiefly regarded Ellen Mason, and certain other delicate ubjects, which it is quite unnecessary, kind reader, to report to you.

Abraham was awake very early on Monday morning: indeed, it is oubtful whether he slept any the night before. He was not at all ac-ustomed to these affairs of honor. The idea of standing up to be shot t, was entirely new to him in this *practical* sense. Every time the ld church bell across the way struck the hour, it sounded more fune-eal and dirge-like, and he often revolved in his mind the idea of ab-enting himself from the appointed exercises of the day. But then, he disgrace of such an action would rise up before his sensitive and oble spirit, and appear even worse than death itself. How could he ear to hear the broad laugh of Charles Turner,—to feel the scorn of Sanford! No, the die was cast. The rascal who meddled with his rig must be shot.

Abraham rose as soon as he could see, with a melancholy but deter-nined air, and went out behind the barn, to practice pistol-shooting.

The appointed hour (10 A. M.) had arrived, and Charles Turner and nyself were on the ground. Abraham had not yet arrived. The place hosen was an old pasture, about a mile from town. An unfrequented oad led through it, which connected with the Worcester turnpike, so hat we were able to ride to the scene of action. A light snow was alling, and both the day and scenery were as cheerless and desolate as they could well be. No sounds broke the stillness but the occa-sional screeching of a blue-jay, and the rumbling of approaching wheels on the frozen ground. Soon the crack of a whip, and the loud and cheerful voice of Sanford, as he drove furiously up, evidently exerting his colloquial powers to keep up Abraham's spirits, announced the pres-ence of those gentlemen. Abraham seemed very solemn and absent-minded. He shook hands with me, and nodded slightly to Charles Turner.

"Gentlemen," exclaimed Sanford, "as the parties appear to be all present, and the weather is growing inclement, we will proceed at once to the preliminaries. I hope this unfortunate affair will be shortly ad-justed to the complete satisfaction of all concerned. Twelve paces, if I recollect aright, was the distance contemplated."

While the ground was being measured, and the pistols loaded, Abra-ham vainly endeavored to conceal his anxious feelings, by whistling "Yankee Doodle," while Charles Turner employed himself in con-tinually buttoning his coat and arranging his collar.

"Take your position, gentlemen, if you please," said Sanford, "I believe every t..er, a rap announced visitors are well primed, sir, I suppose," at the ..dward Sanford. They se..my hands and examining the lock, to conce.. comic demeanor, as if, which had been strongly excited by Abraham ..mmunicate. ...s. I meanwhile examined the other, and reprimed t..nen," said I, " ..er to gain time for recovering my own gravity. ..d'" replied Sa..

" All correct..own since t..ngth remarked, at the same time handing the pistols. going to c..

" Attend the assistan.. gentlemen, and fire at the word *three!*"

" *One! two!!* THREE!!!"

At the instant, Turner's pistol snapped and missed fire. Abraham trembled so much that he did not succeed in pulling the trigger, until we began to advance, when the charge went off in no particular direction.

Abraham was evidently trying to say that he was fully satisfied; but Sanford, with a bland smile, interrupted him with—" I perceive, gentlemen, that you are not satisfied, and, according to the code of honor, I suppose a fair shot must be passed." Abraham stared rather vacantly at Sanford for a moment, and then calmly acquiesced, as a matter of course. The pistols were loaded again, and very carefully primed. At the word, they went off instantaneously, causing but one report. Turner dropped his pistol, leaped up, turned a somerset with extraordinary agility,—the result of much practice,—and fell heavily upon the ground. Abraham grew pale, and immediately rushed towards the murdered man, groaning aloud, but Sanford seized him at once, and hurried him by main force into the carriage, telling him that immediate flight was the only possible way of escaping apprehension, in which case we should all suffer the penalty of the law. Off he drove with furious speed towards Worcester, to meet the stage which was to convey them to the next railroad depot. Meantime Sheriff Jones was just stepping into the stage at the Mansion Hotel, in order to meet Abraham at the next village. ..r waiting till they were fairly out of sight, Charles and I proceede.. ..isurely homewards.

It was near night-fall when Sheriff Jones returned to M——, having in safe custody the ill-fated Abraham. Meantime the news had spread through the village, and quite a crowd had collected at the Hotel. My room had been transformed into a hospital. Charles Turner was bolstered up in an easy-chair, his face nearly hid in a large night-cap, and his breast covered with bandages. Surgical instruments and phials were displayed upon the table. The room was darkened, and a small candle in one corner shed its pale and flickering light upon the face of the pseudo-dying man. Upon being told that Turner was in my room, Abraham begged the sheriff to allow him the privilege of seeing his poor victim before he died. Several bystanders joined in soliciting the sheriff to release him an hour or two upon his parole. The old man readily consented, and I accompanied poor Abraham up stairs. We met Dr. White upon the landing, who informed us that the case was a very bad one. He " feared the man couldn't live an hour. He might, but it was quite uncertain." I slowly opened the door. Squire Mason

nd one or two more r[illegible] in mournful
mood by the wounded man, an[illegible]other. Abra-
iam fell on his knees before hi[illegible] humbly beg-
ed his pardon. He hoped for on[illegible]orld, and that
was that he would forgive him. Tur[illegible] that he would,
nd poor Abraham rushed from the room. [illegible]im at the door,
nd informed him of a plan of escape whic[illegible]ncerted by his
riends. The sheriff had gone home for a s[illegible]d a fleet sad-
lle-horse was at the door, which would carry [illegible]e nearest rail-
oad depot, just in time to take the New York ste[illegible]at train. Now
his horse was the most unruly beast in M——, and it was well known
hat Abraham could never, by any exertion of whip and spur, ride in
ny direction more than a hundred rods from the tavern stable. But the
ulgar crowd, who had gathered on the piazza to witness Abraham's
questrian performances, were disappointed; for just as he was placing
is foot in the stirrup, his heart misgave him: he resolved that he must
ee Turner once more before he died, and be doubly sure of his for-
iveness. We began to pity poor Abraham in truth, and allowed him
o return. But the dying man was not at all prepared for this second
isit. He had supposed his part acted, and was merrily engaged in
lancing a horn-pipe in his night-clothes and bandages. Abraham stop-
ed upon the threshold in mute astonishment. He rubbed his eyes, and
ooked earnestly at Turner, as if he were awaking from a dream, or
eared that the scene before him was merely an optical illusion. But,
s the dying man began to roar with laughter, Abraham was convinced.
His natural color rapidly returned, and his harassed and care-worn look
as exchanged for one indescribably foolish.

"Ain't you ashamed of yourself, Turner," exclaimed he. This was
e signal for a roar of mirth, hitherto illy repressed, to hear what Abra-
am would say. The old Mansion Hotel rang again. Squire Mason,
who had hardly recovered from the side-ache which he contracted on
Thanksgiving evening, rushed down stairs, to escape the contagious
nfluence of the general risibility. Abraham follow[illegible]. Another peal
reeted him from the bar-room and piazza, and as [illegible] hastened down
e street, he began to feel most sensibly, for the first time in his life,
at he was indeed a fool. * * * * * *

Abraham Smith, Esquire, of New York, was seated one morning,
fter breakfast, in his easy-chair, nursing his lame foot, which kept
im, generally speaking, in a peculiarly irascible mood. His wife had
ust put an end to his scolding about "a late, miserable, good-for-no-
hing, nasty, unpalatable breakfast, not fit for a cannibal—heathen—Af-
ican," by sending in great haste for several morning papers. This
changed the old gentleman's tone from home thrusts and personal allu-
sions to growling about the public affairs. Every thing he read was
"*radically* wrong—unreasonable—badly expressed," until he came to
a brief notice of the sham duel, which he at once attributed to his son,
although the papers gave no names, merely stating that it occurred in
M——, Mass.

"Mrs. S.," exclaimed the old gentleman.

"Well, *Mr*. S., what do you want?"

"Want? I don't want *any thing;* did I say I wanted any thing? I should be glad if you wouldn't interrupt me when I am about to make a remark."

"Well now, Mr. S., bless your heart, my dear, I won't."

"You won't, will you? Well, why in the name of religion and common sense did you, then?" *Now*, if you are *done*, I'll go on. There's our son Abraham, he's such a natural fool, I'm willing to bet five hundred dollars cash it's *him* all the papers are full of. I never did consider him fit for any thing but College, and that only makes him worse."

"Why, Mr. S., what's he done?"

"Done! I'm going to write to Parson D——, and see what he's done; no good, I warrant, nor never will. What do you ask me what he has done for, when *every body knows* it, and it's all in the papers. I suppose you would like to have me commit all the papers to memory every morning, and say 'em off to you—eh?"

"Bless me! Mr. S." ——

"Don't interrupt *me*, Mrs. S. Why don't you ring the bell, and send John up with my writing materials? That good-for-nothing son of yours will fight another duel before I can get an opportunity to write and have him sent home. Here I have been waiting, Mrs. S., ever since an *early* breakfast, exerting myself to no purpose to obtain my writing materials. I'll pay off that stupid, rascally man-servant to-day. No I won't; I shall need him to help me thrash Abraham. I'll write to Parson D—— to have him thrashed there, in the first place, if it takes the whole town-meeting to do it, and if he ever comes home."—John here entered with the writing materials, and wheeled up Mr. Smith to his escritoire. The old gentleman's voice, which was raised to its highest pitch, gradually subsided into an indistinct growl, which appeared to be concerning the propriety of Abraham's living the remainder of his days in the attic, tied to a bed-post, and at last nothing was heard except the furious scratching of his pen, interrupted at short intervals by an excruciating twinge of the gout.

It was about dusk, one December afternoon, when Abraham reached the door of his father's house. As he stood in the porch, with his hand upon the bell-handle, trying to summon resolution enough to ring, he looked more like a street thief than a returning son. Nothing but the certainty of being disinherited, prevented him from turning away forever from the parental roof, to seek the nearest wharf, and try his fortunes upon the sea.

Nothing was seen of Abraham for several months after this time, but it is supposed that he was profitably improving his time in solitary reflection and self-examination. At least, such was the impression of Mr. Smith's next door neighbors, who heard their servants say, (who heard it directly from Mr. Smith's man,) that the smart young collegian had been unceremoniously divested of his wig, and other personal ornaments, by his enraged father, accoutred in his old cast-off clothes, and sent up to sojourn for a season in the attic.

Nothing more, indulgent reader, remains to occupy your attention, save the usual Q. E. D. of story writers, viz., a summing up of births, marriages, and deaths.

Many years have passed away since the memorable duel was fought, and many a change has come over its actors. Edward Sanford returned to the South, to commence a lucrative practice, and to give fair promise of standing at the head of his profession in his native district. But he put no restraint upon his reckless and daring spirit, and after being engaged in several duels, was killed in one which also proved fatal to his antagonist.

Charles Turner has become sobered down into a consistent and highly-respected Congregational minister, and now occupies the parsonage of M——.

Ellen Mason is looking over my shoulder, and as my eye meets her's, that same "wildly witty," truthful look, which first thrilled my heart at the Thanksgiving dinner, fills it now with a still deeper and worthier delight.

But Abraham is changed yet more than all the rest. He is now a very worthy and respectable merchant, and you may see his neat sign in upper Broadway, a long way out towards Haarlem, "A. F. SMITH's *Eng. and Amer. Fancy Goods.*" His college education was cut short in time to save him from a life of folly, and to place him in the situation best suited to his capacities. He wears his natural hair, and is one of the Alms-House Commissioners, besides being a great comfort to his widowed mother, to whom, (being an aged and infirm old lady,) I often administer my professional services in the capacity of Mr. Smith's family physician. One of my especial favorites is Abraham's bright little boy, who bears the paternal name, (minus the Fitz-Henry.) His father has fully decided to train him up to industrious business habits, and especially, never to send him to a classical school.

JUDAS SOHN.

This singular poem was composed by Sigmund Wassermann, a German Hebrew. The English was first written, and is mainly remarkable as the composition of a foreigner little conversant with our tongue. By request it was translated into German, and both are here presented.—ED.

JUDAS Sohn soll wandern, in Aseh und Sak nicht mehr,
Wo sich die sonne neiget, *dort* winkt es freundlich her
Da liegt 'ne liebe Küste, da leigt das heil'ge Land,
Das reicht dem müden Pilger die treue Bruderhand.

Er grüst den strand mit Thränen, der Freiheit heil'ges zelt,
Ein süsser, höher, Fühlen, die Mannesbrust ihn schwellt.
Im warmen inn'gen Flehen, Kehrt er empor den Blick,
Er singet Dankeslieder, er prieset das Geschick.

Er legt den Trauer-Talar, den staub'chen stab beyseit,
Er schlürft den Freiheits Aether, sein Herz wird ihm so weit.
Er steht erhoben männlich, erlöst, im Freiheits licht,
Es strahl't der Himmel wieder, des Wütherichs Kette bricht.

Friede sei dir Pilger, Sohn Judas wein' nicht mehr,
Nicht Formen trennen Brüder, wo Freiheit waltet, höhr.
Komm bau das Haus des Herrn, laut eine stimme spricht,
Jehova ist dein Retter, und er vergisst dich nicht!

JUDEA'S SON.

Judea's son shall wander in sackcloth wrapt, no more;—
Where sets the son of Heaven there lies a friendly shore,
Surrounded by two oceans there lies the happy land,
That to weary pilgrims stretches forth the brother's hand.

With tears he greets the country where holy freedom dwells,
In new and sweeter feeling his beating bosom swells,
In warm and fervent prayer he turns his eye above—
He sings the song of blessing, he sings the song of love.

He lays the mourning Talar, the dusty staff aside,
He breathes the air of Freedom, his heart grows full and wide,
He stands erect and manly, redeemed in freedom's light,
The tyrant's chain is broken; the sky is clear and bright.

Peace to the weary Pilgrim, let Judah weep no more,
No form divides the brethren on Freedom's happy shore.
Come build the Lord's own temple, the voice resounds on high,
Jehovah is thy helper, the One forever nigh.

PHYSICAL IMBECILITY OF EDUCATED MEN.

It is a melancholy fact, that a large proportion of that class of men on whom rests the greatest weight of responsibility, are, physically speaking, least capable of enduring the wear and toil necessary to the faithful discharge of the duties expected at their hands. Especially is this true of the present generation of educated men; and to some extent will it admit of general application. Indeed, so universally is it acknowledged, that the pale face of the student has long been proverbial. And when here and there one has had the resolution to mingle with the laboring class, and secure health and hardihood at the expense of a sunburnt complexion, he has been the subject of wonder and remark, from the inflexible Cato of Rome, even down to the present day. The frequent entire failure of health among literary men, and the great numbers, comparatively, who sink into a premature grave, are constant witnesses to the fact, that a life of study is peculiarly hazardous to our physical constitution. And doubtless the numerous cases of mental derangement which have occurred within the last few years among the same class of men, may most of them be traced to physical causes, or at least to the neglect of the physical, while the mental has been taxed beyond reason.

It is a general rule, that those employments which are the most necessary and useful, are at the same time the most healthy; while many of those which are unimportant, or even injurious in their results, are stamped with the divine displeasure. Shall we then conclude that the extensive cultivation of the intellect, since generally attended with a diminution of health, and consequently of happiness, is in any manner disapproved of by our Creator? The most ignorant and superstitious would not hazard an assertion of this kind. We may therefore with reason infer that the present is not a necessary result of the pursuit of knowledge. But that this imbecility may be traced to one or more of the three following causes: First, an injudicious selection of the individuals to be educated; second, an undue amount of study crowded into the present system of education; or third, a neglect of the necessary precautions, on the part of those who follow this pursuit. Whatever be the true cause, it becomes those most nearly concerned carefully to search it out, and if possible to apply a remedy. For the man of letters, in whatever literary occupation engaged, of all others needs good health and a sound constitution; especially at the present time, when the field for mental and moral cultivation is so extensive, the facilities so great, and the laborers comparatively so few.

In reference to the selection of those who are to obtain an education, it has been remarked, that if a man had several sons, but one of whom can be sent through college, he is wont to select the most puny, because the others can gain a livelihood by labor. So far as this is true, it serves to account for the imbecility of literary men. Yet I am inclined to think but few, compared with the whole, are thus selected. Oftener the one that has the strongest inclination for study is chosen; which may or may not be the most robust. The plan of selecting the most feeble, would be an exceedingly unwise one; for the odds against a *healthy* man are quite sufficient, in a life of study: what then must be the fate of one who starts on this race far in the background? Nor is the plan sometimes pursued, of putting the laziest one to study, any more worthy of recommendation; since, though he has the intellect of a giant, without the requisite energy to secure bodily exercise, he must soon sink under the power of disease, and both mental and physical faculties be wasted. But in the case of the self-educated, these remarks can have no bearing, and among the rich little or none. Inasmuch then as far the greater part are governed by other motives in the choice of a literary life, than a reference to their physical powers, we must look to some other source for the main cause, why so many literary men are laboring under disease.

Is the system of education chargeable with fault in respect to this thing? Many even of the sufferers themselves are disposed to lay the blame here. We hear it said that students are crushed under the weight of labor imposed upon them by some of our colleges. But all will agree that it should be the aim of the system, to give the students the most rigid training possible, and not actually infringe upon the necessary hours of exercise and refreshment. In other words, that the student be made constantly to feel such a pressure of duties, when he sets himself to the performance of any given task, that every dormant energy of the mind shall be called into action. Thus will be acquired a concentration of thought, and an intellectual momentum, so to speak, capable of overcoming every obstacle. Without feeling this necessity upon him, the student will, as is now too often the case, sit dozing and nodding over his book, scarcely knowing whether he is in the body or out of the body. Such studying may make intellectual pigmies, but men never. Now every one acquainted with the facts in the case knows that after lively bodily exercise, the mind is in a much more vigorous and active state, and that while in this state, it will accomplish double the amount of labor in the same time that it will under contrary circumstances. He knows, furthermore, that but a very small fraction of the students in our colleges and seminaries, rigidly employ all, or any considerable part of their leisure moments, in vigorous bodily exercise. If the student were allowed no vacation, it might seem hard to insist upon such constant exertion, either of body or mind. But while almost one fourth of his time is given up to him expressly for recreation and the recovery of his exhausted energies, we may reasonably expect untiring application during the remaining three fourths. For we want no half-way students in the field, and would designedly encourage none but such as are willing to sacrifice ease and indolence at the shrine of literature. If therefore more time was devoted to exercise, less would be required for performing the same mental labor now perfomed, while the lessons would be more thoroughly mastered by the consequent vigor and concentration of mind, and the amount of mental discipline would be far greater. Hence the reason why students who have spent several hours a day in teaching or other employments, have often been perspicuous in their class, if not for superiority in the recitation room, at least for depth of thought, and ability for surmounting every difficulty occurring in their lessons. The necessity often of mastering a given task in a very limited time, gives them a power of application to which they otherwise would have been strangers. Hence, too, the reason why many of our greatest and busiest public men have been able to perform such a vast amount of private labor. As the fruit of this labor, we may point to some of our most valuable commentaries on the Bible, and to many of the works that adorn our public and private libraries. In view of these facts, who that is a friend to literature would be willing to see the amount of study in our public systems of education in any material degree diminished? The minds of the young in general, will not act to any purpose, except when under pressure. And as soon as the rigor of our colleges is to any considerable extent relaxed, we may look for serious deterioration in the standard of education through the land. If we have not erred in the foregoing remarks, loss of health is not a necessary result of our system of liberal education.

We have one remaining source to examine, which we approach with the greater reluctance, as it comes too near home to be properly relished or duly appreciated, either by ourselves or our friends. It is the negligence of students in regard to the preservation of health. Time will not permit us to touch upon the thousand irregularities and excesses, indulgences and neglects, which characterize a student's life. But as a word to the wise is sufficient, we trust that merely calling attention to the subject will lead some, at least, to stop and consider for themselves. We have already hinted that want of exercise is an important item. The body and the mind were made to act in some reasonable proportion. The severer our mental labor, the more need we have of bodily exercise. This fact is established by the concurrent testimony of writers on this subject, by our own experience, and by the dictates of common sense. But many students reverse this rule, and when they have had a harder task than usual to perform, instead of resolutely overcoming the feeling of languor that is brought on by fatigue and exhaustion of mind, they settle listlessly down into a rocking-chair or upon a bed, and give themselves up to sleep. Following pursuits which are acknowledged by all to need the most assiduous care in order to preserve health, and yet seemingly the most careless of the whole human race in regard to health. The only wonder is, that the results of such a course are not felt much sooner than they are. But a sound constitution will endure abuse long before it apparently begins to yield. A person may indulge in a little too much sleep, a little too much food, a little too much drink, a little too much indolence, a little too much of almost any thing, a great many times even, before the effects are perceptibly felt. Yet where so many littles are constantly at work, they will finally undermine the firmest constitution, as surely as the student goes on thus reckless of health. He may pass some years without any symptoms of settled disease, but his frequent headaches, his morning dizziness, his occasional colds, his disagreeable feelings at the stomach, his phlegmatic throat, his nauseous mouth and fetid breath, are sure forebodings of that more formidable disease, which is already like a hidden canker beginning to corrode his vitals, and which will ere long show itself, the destroyer alike of his happiness and his usefulness. A day of reckoning will surely overtake every transgressor of the laws of his physical nature. No sins of ignorance are winked at here. As long as effect follows cause, so long will error in this respect be its own punisher. What a man soweth, that he must expect to reap. If we will scatter all our future path with thorns, rather than forego the gratification of the present moment, when we begin to feel the pain they inflict, we shall have none to blame but ourselves. Could we occasionally cast a gl the curious and delicately wrought machinery within, and s effects produced by every little irregularity in our habits, we sho startled at our own rashness. Would that physiology, or at lea part of it which relates to the human frame, might be among t studies introduced into our common schools, and the last to be out of our academies and colleges. Then peradventure the ig might learn wisdom, and the negligent be compelled to look a own folly. In conclusion I would say, that while we have be examples without end, of those in kindred pursuits with ourselve by imprudence have brought upon themselves hypochondria, derangement, horrors, blue devils, and ten thousand other n diseases too numerous to mention, and too horrid to think of, it us in hand to guard well our footsteps, lest we be caught in the snare. DE

MY MOTHER'S BIBLE.

A SONNET.

My Mother's Bible: dearer to my heart
Than any thing beside is this worn book.
With reverence always on each page I look,
And never, never with it will I part.
The many texts so often marked, I find,
And notes close written the broad margin o'er,
Bring up that mother's image to my mind,
And cause my heart to think of her the more.
Although for many years she has been dead,
Her influence even yet is o'er me stealing,
And when I stray from God it there is shed
Upon me, my ungrateful soul revealing;
Oh! may her Bible be my constant guide,
Till I awake in heav'n, there to abide.

LITERARY NOTICES.

AN ADDRESS TO THE PEOPLE OF THE UNITED STATES IN BEHALF OF THE A COPYRIGHT CLUB. Adopted, at New York, October 18th, 1843. New Yor lished by the Club, MDCCCXLIII.

WE have received a pamphlet with the above title, from which it appears, organization has been formed in the city of New York, under the name o American Copyright Club," whose object it is "to procure the enactment of or laws as shall place the literary relations of the United States and foreign c eference to Copyright, on just, proper, and equitable grounds." The President of Association is William Cullen Bryant, and its list of members comprises not the rank and file of American authors, but several of our most distinguished esmen. The Address is a well written and forcible appeal to our countrymen, set forth in plain terms the necessity of their immediate attention to the subject of pyright, and earnestly entreating them to remove the restrictions, which at present er the energies of our literary men, by a legislative recognition and protection of rights of all authors, native and foreign, in their own productions.

This movement has our warmest sympathies The object in view is of national cern, and is daily becoming of more pressing importance. None, but the blindest greediest of literary gourmands, can fail to perceive, that in permitting our publish- to pirate with impunity from foreign works, and to inundate the land with their ap pulications, we are thinning the ranks of American authors, crushing our infant ature, and in all that relates to Thought and Intellect, forcing ourselves back into ate of worse than colonial bondage. But the Address speaks in better words than can use:

Do you know, have you marked how authorship in any worthy sense is almost utterly nced throughout the land? How, day by day, and dollar by dollar, the revenues writers known far and wide as American, as yours, have shrunk to nothing, and t they watch with hope and trembling, what you in your discretion shall next do in ir behalf? A year or two more of neglect of their interests, a year or two more of reproduction of foreign books, a year or two more of brown paper and cheap ropriation, and the craft of American authors is dead and extinct. At intervals, ces, faint and far apart, may be heard, but the winter will not waken with one eam or two thawed in the sun by chance. The popular mind will be in full and disturbed possession of foreign writers, to shape and mould it as they choose. A asant prospect indeed! Speaking our own tongue, yet babblers of the language of angers: at home, yet abroad: free, yet servile as the dog that whimpers in his mas- 's track! Forethought glorious beyond measure! That the hour is not too distant, en one may walk the streets and highways of his country, and be pointed at, still sisting as he does in the framing of books, as a natural monster, whose business is ntraband, and forbidden by the law of the land."

It is to be hoped that our legislators will find it convenient during the present ses- n to forget for a while their partisan animosities, and cordially unite in some plan avert the dangers that are threatening our literary interests. This is a matter that ncerns the whole country, affects every department of society, and is, perhaps, of gher importance than any of the great questions of public policy that now agitate r people. Certain movements lately made in our national councils, speak words of eering to the heart of the author, giving him reason to expect that this subject is out to receive, what it has for a long time demanded in vain, a serious and just nsideration.

---

r Address, on the Origin, Progress, and Present Condition of Philosophy. Delivered before the Hamilton Chapter of the Alpha Delta Phi Society, on its eleventh anniversary, at Clinton, N. Y By I. N. Tarbox. Utica, N. Y., R. W. Roberts, 58 Genesee street; 1843.

This pamphlet has just found its way to our table, and we have time only to glance its title. The name of the author, who is a gentleman well known in this commu- y, will give it all needful recommendation. We shall endeavor to notice it more at gth hereafter.

EDITORS' TABLE.

We have received a letter from an esteemed subscriber in South Carolina, forcibly directs our attention to a subject that has occupied our thoughts for months past. Our correspondent says, "will you allow a member of the class that established the Magazine which you conduct, and of which our venerable Alma Mater has reason to be proud,* to suggest with all kindness, what I have every reason to think would make the Magazine more interesting to the *Graduates*, who have left, and who annually will leave those scenes and that spot so endeared and hallowed to them. I judge from my own feelings, and suppose that all who leave those walls feel as I do—an anxious desire to know all that is going on in College—how the societies prosper—the exhibitions—commencement—the society anniversaries—and above the little chit-chat of the day, concerning Yale and all connected with it. And what I would respectfully suggest to your consideration is, that an article in every number should be devoted to College news, and to any interesting topics occurring in New Haven."

Now, the truth is, there is much difficulty about this matter. We live in a quiet place; little could be found at any time to fill such an article. News is a rare condiment here. Still, we shall endeavor to act upon the hint given by our correspondent so far as lies in our power, for the future—at this present moment there is nothing to be told; but whenever the anniversaries, of which he speaks, occur, whether of the societies or of College, we shall endeavor to give a sufficient account thereof. . . . . . .

We have noticed, in different quarters, severe strictures upon our remarks respecting Mr. Mathews' poems in our last number. Still, our opinion is not changed, and we cannot feel any inclination to say any thing different from what we have already said. It is the work of such attempts at versification as the "Poems on Man" that has produced in the public mind a sort of contempt for poetry, and we cannot blame those who may chance to fall only upon such productions, if they pronounce all rhyming detestable. If others have different opinions from ours, they are welcome to cherish and express them, but we have no desire either to puff or ridicule, because higher authorities have done the same. . . . . . .

Our correspondent "Thou and I" is as singular in his style as in choice of a cognomen. We have space for but a specimen of his article, which we will give and leave himself and others to ponder thereupon.

"31 *Dec.*, 1841.

"The hour is past eleven. It is a cloudy winter night. The sighing of the wind among the leafless branches, comes to my ear as if it were THE DYING VOICE OF THE 1841st DAUGHTER OF OLD FATHER TIME. The gray-headed, though yet powerful spirit stands by her bedside and her god-father, Jove himself, makes the earth and muiscal spheres to sing her requiem. *The bells that hang in the great Cathedral of the Universe* chime sweetly as they tell that she is going, going whither her thousand sisters have gone before. THE SEXTON IS DIGGING HER GRAVE AMONG THE RUBBISH IN THE POTTER'S FIELD OF ETERNITY. HUSH! I HEAR THE CLINK, CLINK OF HIS SPADE, LIKE THE RATTLING OF HAIL UPON THE PAVEMENT!!"

"Thou and I" will receive his communication by calling for it. . . . . . .

"A Day in Vacation," "The Rescued Bride," "Esdras, 2, 10, 11, 12," "Mutual Love," "The Whippoorwill," &c., &c., are rejected.

We were obliged to curtail the sixth chapter of "the Witch" in the present number to make room for other articles.

---

* Gammon.—PRINTER'S DEV.

THE

YALE LITERARY MAGAZINE.

VOL. IX. FEBRUARY, 1844. No. 4.

ENGLAND.

THE elevated position which England occupies at the present time, her vast influence and power, and the part she is acting in the world's affairs, tend to attract towards her the attention of all reflecting minds. Her political and social condition is the subject of much thought in these times, and not a few dark forebodings are uttered now and then concerning her destiny. What are her prospects and what is to be her fate? Will she continue to maintain the rank which she now holds among nations? Will the complicated machinery of her government move on with regularity, amid the troubles that surround her, imparting no check to the enterprise of her subjects, and producing no diminution in her capital and resources; stimulating her industrial and commercial energies, encouraging the arts and sciences, and increasing the refinements of civilized life? Does she possess within herself elements that will enable her to defy the tempest and the storm; to endure the shocks of war and the certain but insidious effects of time?

Though some of her politicians tell us, that she was never in more skillful hands, and that there is no cause for alarm; that from "the nettle danger she will pluck the flower safety," and out of existing disorders derive the means of advancing and establishing her power for ages; yet on the other hand we are assured, in tones neither feeble nor ambiguous, that the present condition of England is one of the strangest and most ominous ever seen in this world, and that the legislative incapacity and corrupt and miserable policy of the dominant party is tending to work out the ruin and disorganization of the State. Indeed, the opinion that England has seen the meridian of her greatness, and is now hastening to decay, has been held, and in various ways expressed, not by politicians merely, but by men who are free from the influence of party spirit, who are not alarmists, and who have watched and weighed well the signs of the times. When such predictions are uttered concerning a country with which we are so intimately connected, and in whose prosperity we naturally feel much interest, it may not be amiss, nor prove uninstructive, to speculate somewhat upon her present condition and prospects.

In directing our attention to the affairs of England, we first remark the vastness of her wealth and power. It may well excite our admiration, that this little island—"a fragment," as it has been called, "chipped off from the continent,"—a small spot of earth peeping above the waves of the German Ocean—should become the repository of more power than was ever possessed by any nation, ancient or modern, and should acquire and exert an influence that is felt in the remotest part of the world. The territorial possessions of England encircle the globe, and are found in every clime—in Australia and India, among the islands and ports of the Mediterranean, in Africa and America; her subjects amount to no less than two hundred millions of souls, of every tribe and nation, differing in complexion and language, in manners and customs, but all acknowledging the sovereignty of the "Ocean Queen." In her navy she admits no superior, nor even a rival; in commercial pursuits she is the mistress of the seas. Wherever a ship can float, there may be found her "wooden walls," and wherever man can exist, she has extended her trading interests, thus by an interchange of commodities and benefits, binding all nations together, and making her own prosperity the prosperity of all. Her bold mariners are found in all seas; her ports and harbors are ever crowded with fleets of merchantmen, richly laden with the products of her distant colonies; in her marts may be seen an enterprising and sagacious, if not a contented people, earnestly engaged in increasing the wealth, and promoting the prosperity of the nation. Her manufacturing towns are filled with multitudes, toiling at their useful employments, and her mines are constantly yielding up their rich and abundant treasures. She likewise carries off the palm in her magnificent works of art and of extensive utility. The nations of the continent envy her proud career, and fear her potent arm. In short, with a dense and hardy population, all anxious for their country's welfare, and ever ready to take up arms in her defense; possessing the noblest language and the noblest literature in the world; foremost in science and art, in discovery and invention; every muscle swelling and every pulse beating with indomitable energy, this little sea-girt home of the Englishman exhibits much that may well feed his national pride and vanity.

Such would be some of the thoughts of an observer on a superficial and careless survey of the British Empire. He would see many indications of prosperity, and would perhaps conclude that there was no cause for fear. But there is another side to this picture. We need not look far to find much that is calculated to excite the compassion of the benevolent, and the zeal of the reformer, and that ought to awaken alarm even in the mind of the conservative. There is scarcely a portion of the British Empire, where there have not been within a few years symptoms of rebellion, or at least of discontent, and the demand has been loudly made, and oft reiterated in vain, for the abolition of oppressive laws and a redress of wrongs. It is needless to point out examples. Every one has heard of the charge of treachery and poison, urged by the Chinese; of the ineffectual supplications of suffering Irishmen, and of the almost universal cry of oppression and misrule. The fact cannot be denied or disguised, that England is a proud and avaricious nation, and seldom fails, when occasion offers, to make an exhibition of her insolence. She may yet have to learn, that she is not omnipotent; that her grasping avarice will neither do her credit, nor promote her welfare; that her haughtiness and pride will not satisfy the wants of her people—will not crush a single foe, nor add to her crown a single laurel.

English writers are accustomed to boast much of the freedom that their people enjoy—of the rights and privileges conferred by their 'matchless constitution'—and we hear it arrogantly proclaimed, that England "has to think and act for mankind, to supply their wants, guide their labors, and cultivate their minds." She may indeed have done more than any other nation, in benefiting and enlightening the world, by means of arts and civilizing energies, and by her wonderful enterprise and skill, yet when we hear such boasts as these, we would turn and ask, what is the condition of her *own* people, and how are their wants supplied, their labors directed, their minds trained and cultivated? Sad indeed must be the answer. For years almost every rumor that has reached us has spoken of the wretched and degraded condition of her laboring classes. Who does not not know, that squalid misery and starvation has been and is the lot of the poor man in England? The groan of the coal-digger comes up from her subterranean vaults; the operatives rush from her crowded manufactories, and, half demented by suffering, ask in vain for relief; the inmates of her workhouses, and paupers innumerable, with looks of gloom and despair, are also making earnest demands, and among her agricultural population there likewise exists misery, deep, incalculable, and almost intolerable. How idle then it is, and how little does it become her eulogists, to proclaim that freedom is enjoyed by the English, and that the slave cannot breathe in England, when there can be found vast masses of human beings, collected in her large towns and scattered over her fields, moors, and mountains, who are enduring, if not slavery, the tenfold worse horrors of pauperism and starvation!

That the lower classes in England are ground down by the iron hand of want, and by searching poverty, and that the middle classes have suffered much from pecuniary embarrassments, depression, and derangement of business, and in various other ways, while an idle, *soi-disant* nobility possess the wealth and consume the products of the industrious, are facts universally known. It is perfectly sickening to read the details of the poverty and misery which English statistics afford. "Our Factories," says one, "are daily scenes *even now* of hecatombs of youthful victims, sacrificed not only without remorse, but with a stoical indifference, to which it is difficult, we should imagine, for human nature, in its most depraved state, to attain." "It is a monstrous thing," says the Quarterly Review, "to behold the condition, moral and physical, of the juvenile portion of our operative classes, more especially that which is found in the crowded lanes and courts of the larger towns, the charnel-houses of our race. . . . Emerging from these lairs of filth and disorder, the young workers—'rising early, and late taking rest'—go forth that they may toil through the *fifteen, sixteen, nay seventeen relentless hours*, in sinks and abysses, oftentimes even more offensive and pernicious than the holes they have quitted." Had we room and inclination, we might easily fill our pages with horrible accounts of human suffering and degradation. In a land of wealth and plenty, of learning and religion, we hear that human beings are actually *starving* for want of bread; that nearly twenty millions of workers are living from "hand to mouth;" ill-clothed, ill-educated, if educated at all, depending upon the most precarious means for subsistonce, deprived of the rightful reward of their labor, and destitute of the common luxuries of life. Men once strong and robust have become pale and haggard; human faces are lit up by the smile of happiness no longer; hearts that once bounded with joy and hope have been withered by despair; and cottages that formerly rang with the song of gladness are silent and mournful. In short, we are told, that as far as direct education is concerned, "not more than one half of the working classes are in a condition very much better than barbarians." Verily, it would be well for our Missionary Societies to remember England.

And yet England possesses an abundance of all that would satisfy the wants of her people. Her harvests send forth their annual supplies; her mines do not fail; from her manufactories, from her distant colonies, and from other nations comes profit and multifarious produce; opulence and abundance are in the land; still the poor man is vegetating upon crusts and crumbs, doled out by the cold charities of the world. Is it strange, then, that he sometimes murmurs? Is it strange that we hear now and then of a Manchester insurrection, and of fearful outbreaks? Man can endure long and grieve much—the human heart is slow to break, and will bend beneath a load of suffering before it yields, but there is a turning point. If we are to believe all accounts, the people of England are not far distant from that point at the present time. If the governing party do not do something for their relief, the people, driven by despair, will take the matter into their own hands. The ignorant man can tell the difference between right and wrong, justice and injustice, as readily as the most skillful casuist.

In searching for the causes of the wretched condition of the English people, we must look first at the peculiar constitution of their society. In regard to wealth, education, and habits of life, the higher and lower classes are widely separated. The soil of England, stations of honor, and offices, with their emoluments, for the most part are possessed by the nobility and gentry. Their coffers are overflowing with treasure; many of them indeed have incomes, that amount in one day to a sum "more than sufficient to support a hundred poor families through the year." The pride of ancestry serves to separate them still more from the lower classes. They may be, for aught that we know, a noble class of men, may have high notions of honor, and may be governed by an unwavering devotion to the peculiar institutions of their country, yet still their position and mode of life must prevent them from possessing those popular sympathies, which would give them a just appreciation of the condition of the lower classes. Hence, as might be expected, the causes of existing grievances are charged upon them. Their 'fox-hunting' clergy, with their rich livings, sustained by the poor man and widow, must likewise come in for their share of the blame. How many curses have filled the air, which, but for their sacred profession, would have remained unuttered! While these are living in luxury, surrounded by "down-bolsters and gilded appliances;" while corruption and intrigue are at work in high places, and ambition is struggling for power, and while political parties are contending and carrying out their idle schemes, fatal evils are silently but surely creeping into the very vitals of the State Though the surface of society may appear calm and peaceful, yet beneath there are potent elements, which but a touch will bring into fearful action. The hydra-headed are struggling for release, and like the giant, "whose sighs are the hot breath, and whose groans are the mutterings of Etna," are endeavoring to throw off the weight that is crushing them down. We do not believe that the classes of English society are so completely fused together, that both the middle and lower classes would not rejoice at the explosion of the cherished privileges and fallacies of the aristocracy.

Another cause of the disorders in England is found in her immense National Debt. Thirty million pounds of annual taxes are required to pay its interest, while nothing is reserved that will go to liquidate the principal. We can from this form some opinion of the severity with which the English people are taxed; we can see to what end the product of the laborer's toil is appropriated. Again, they have odious and oppressive laws, and the demand is loudly made for their correction and reform. The people are beginning to think that they ought to have a little more to do with matters that so intimately concern themselves. They are anxious for more liberal and republican principles, and are endeavoring to obtain an acknowledgment of their rights, and an amelioration of their political and social condition. The question now to be discussed is, whether the pleasures of the Few shall remain undisturbed at the expense of the Many.

We are aware that we have given but an imperfect account of the condition of the English people, and of the evils that they are suffering. Other causes, such as an increase of population, and a consequent diminution in the labor and wages of the poor man, have tended to increase the burdens under which he is groaning. Various remedial propositions have been presented for counteracting the diseases of society—Emigration, Education, Abolition of the Corn-Laws, and the five points of the Chartists. Societies have been formed,—"Anti-Corn-Law Leagues," the "Complete Suffrage Union," and others, numbering among their supporters some of the leading and most influential men in the United Kingdoms. It is evident that radical changes must occur. The minds of men are becoming fully awake to the monstrous grievances and wrongs caused by some of their existing laws. "If I were the Conservative party of England," says Carlyle,

"I would not for a hundred thousand pounds an hour allow those Corn-Laws to continue! Potosi and Golconda put together would not purchase my assent to them." Argument indeed is used no longer; the keen edge of ridicule is now employed. The tide has turned strongly in favor of free trade; and its enemies are giving away before the irresistible movements of public opinion. The middle and the lower classes are united in interest and in purpose, and now that their energies are becoming aroused, and their minds enlightened, we may expect that deadly blows will be dealt, not merely against the interests of the landed gentry, but against their splendid aristocracy itself.

It is a distinctive feature of the English character, to be slow and cautious in action. They are by nature conservative, and even when surrounded by evils will deliberate long before they take measures for their relief. "In our wildest periods of Reform, in the long Parliament itself, you notice always the invisible instinct to hold fast by the Old; to admit the minimum of the New." Old and time-honored customs are revered; institutions gray with the dust of years are bound to their hearts by the most sacred associations; every spot of their country, even its barren rocks and cliffs of chalk, are objects of veneration. They are content to walk in the ways of their ancestors, to endure the inconveniences that they endured, and they will hesitate much before they adopt new opinions, or venture to walk in new paths. But John Bull, with all his patriotism and sturdiness of character, and with all his dislike of change, has also much good sense, and can be taught, as he has been to some extent, though it has been a terrible lesson, to become a Reformer. Legislation for privileged orders and class interests has taught him that he must act or die; that he must manfully assert his independence and his rights, or endure the evils and degradation of slavery. Hence it is that we have seen those violent insurrectionary movements among the lower classes, and hence also have their employers and friends, men of rank, of wealth, and of influence, taken up on the side of those great and momentous measures, which are destined to promote the well-being, and to work out a more tolerable mode of life for the people. These are but skirmishes in the war which is now going on between the Aristocracy and the People, and which will result, we verily belive, if not in the downfall of the former, at least in the loss of many of their rights and privileges.

It may seem extravagant to talk of the decay of England. We hope that it may be, and that all predictions of her decline may fail of accomplishment. With one of her own writers, we hope that "she is but in the morning of her existence, bursting into light, and betokening a golden harvest, not only for those of her own race and lineage, but for all who desire the inappreciable blessings of a Christianized civilization." But when we regard the evils in her government, deep-seated, if not ineradicable, when we see her governors resorting to temporary expedients instead of remedies, and wasting their time in the bitter and acrimonious strife of party; when we behold a country, whose social edifice, if it is not built of human skulls, cemented with human blood, like the temple of Tescalipoca, the Mexican deity, is composed co-

ainly of very discordant materials—a country that has acquired its vast power and greatness, its almost unbounded territorial and oceanic supremacy, at the expense of the groans and woes of its subjects,

> "By bartering freedom and the poor man's life
> For gold as at a market!"

we begin to think it is time for birds of strange augury to appear in the air, and that a crisis of some sort is approaching. And who is there who would not welcome any event that may tend to elevate the poor man, and bring about a better organization of labor?

The times are indeed full of change. A band of men, neither few in number nor insignificant in character, have arisen, who are the zealous advocates of popular rights and political reform. The people heretofore, through want of leaders to concentrate and direct their energies, have acted blindly and to little purpose. Their measures may have been rash and ill-advised, but they have had one good effect; the minds of men have been directed to their condition and wants. They have obtained leaders from the higher and wealthier classes, and those too who are by no means weak and ignorant; who are not extravagant dreamers nor rash enthusiasts; who are not advocates of vain shadows or plausible sophisms, but are sound and practical thinkers, energetic and determined actors. They are not seeking to injure their country; on the contrary, they would peril their lives in her defense; and in aiming to promote the cause of popular education, and bring about the consummation of a freer and nobler system of commercial policy, they are advocating not only the true interest of their own country, but of the world.

As Americans we can but sympathize with the efforts of these reformers, nor do we think that the true friend of man has cause to apprehend danger from the democratic feeling that exists in England. In the existence and growth of this feeling, we recognize no tendency that can be promotive of evil or destructive of good, no wild radicalism that will sweep away all the bulwarks of law and order, and introduce vague and unsettled notions of government; but we see in it the progress of those high principles of liberty, which animate every free, manly heart, and an indication that men are obtaining truer perceptions of their own nature and destiny. The end that is aimed at is merely the removal of evils that are to be found in existing institutions, by peaceable means, and the result will be, as we trust and hope, an improvement in the individual and social well-being of her subjects.

THE BIRTH OF THE STARS.

There was no Sun in Heaven; no moon looked down
With pensive ray upon the lonely world,
Nor any star burned on the brow of night;
And one might deem no heedful Seraph's eye
Watched o'er the weal of this neglected earth.
From pole to pole a concave vast and black
Hung as some pall might hang o'er Nature's grave;
And old gray Ocean with a hoarse loud moan
Rolled round the central globe his sleepless wave:
The voice of many waters! Not a sound
Of bird, or beast, or whispering zephyr's sigh,
Or Angel's song, or man's profaner lay,
Blent their low notes with the eternal anthem.
The world was Ocean—in his circuit vast
He found no shore to chafe his hoary mane
And change his sad song to wild breaker's roar,
Save that, where now the great Sahara lies
Under the blazing equatorial sun,
A mountain ridge rose beetling o'er the sea.
A thousand miles in front a rough-drawn profile
Swung in the tide that laved its rocky base.
And mountain piled o'er mountain backward stretched
To where old Nile his annual tribute pours
Of golden plenty o'er Egyptian fields—
Names known in after age when time began,
Andes on Andes piled, and Alps o'er Alps!
As 'twere a structure built by rebel Titans
To climb away from "Chaos and old night."
An unnamed continent of desert gloom—
The sky was crowded with its mountain peaks
Like aged hemlocks on some barren hill
Lifting their withered arms in silent air,
Deep scarred with thunder and red lightning's breath,—
Sad witnesses of elemental strife.
Up the dull sky, all tremulous and red,
Aurora darts her wavering streams of flame
Like angry serpents springing on their prey.
In her disastrous light the sea was blood;
The savage landscape stands distinctly forth—
Cape, promontory, mountain—all on fire—
Each precipice and valley to its utmost depth
Brighter than noon-day. Suddenly she starts
And swifter than the wing of thought flies back

To hide herself by her own northern pole,
And twilight spreads again o'er land and sea.
The mighty sweep of the advancing main
Vented its vain rage on the granite shore;
The refluent wave beat backward by the rock
In parted stream rolled bellowing round the isle,
To make again the circuit of the sphere.
Thus while eternity's slow ages passed,
The assailant waves made war upon the rock,
And ever and anon some beetling cliff
Or promontory huge sank in the deep.
Oft Spirits, bound on speedy errand-wing
To distant worlds, paused, hovering o'er the deep,
And wondering saw, shook from their seated base,
Whole mountains plunge into the sullen main,
Like fragments broken from eternity!
Then, while in Heaven the everlasting song
Through many a circling age its measures filled,
The angel-messenger with laboring wing
Above the sea staid his swift flight again—
Again beheld another rocky cliff
Bow his bald head into the rushing wave;
Till in his thought the crumbling continent
Became a kind of horologe, whereon
The Sea notched cycles of eternity.
Let computation take most rapid note,
And let each unit be a century,
Or every number be a space as great
As all earth's years have been—in vain! in vain!
The baffled mind turns back upon itself,
Aweary of its fruitless zeal to reach,
What thought of man or angel cannot grasp—
The ages that elapsed ere the last shore
Sank to its grave. * * * * *
* * * * The world was water only.
It was a sepulchre in which lay buried
All form and substance, and all hope of life.
Full many an age in darkness circled round
Beyond all thought and number to compute,
Save thought of Him who knows and numbers all.
Sudden in Heaven, bright, tremulous, alone
A star came forth from the Almighty's hand;
She was all eye, all hearing, soul, and sense,
And onward, through ethereal path prescribed,
Moved with a calm and boundless consciousness,
Making wide inroads on old Night's domain,

With her still brightness—singing all the while
Unto herself a low sweet melody
That gushed spontaneous; such the joy young life
Feels in its fresh and spotless purity.

At the far confines of her radiant realm,
Above, below, on every side she saw
A mighty sphere of Darkness bended round,
And on its mystic wall her struggling ray
Fantastic played: vacuity unknown, and dread;
As when within a cave of boundless gloom
One little candle throws abroad its beams,
Waging vain war with the surrounding Dark,
Brief space of light hemmed round by Infinite!
Long time she gazed upon the void expanse,
Waiting some spirit's eye, or tongue responsive,
But waited long in vain, till her glad song
To plaintive cadence sank, then fell to silence.
So when, amid the briny waste of waves,
The ravening sea hath gorged his hungry maw
With a whole fleet of stately galleons,
One sad survivor from the billow's crest
Climbs up a lonely rock and looks abroad:
Alone amid the elements! the wave and sky
Are round about him with their solitudes.
Oh! how his heart unutterably longs
For some kind ear to list his latest breath,
Some friendly eye to mark his watery grave.
Thus on her joyless course the sprite was passing,
And busy thought with a most fruitless zeal
Sketching her sad and solitary future,
When on her startled ear, with gradual growth
Did steal the voice of waters—yet afar
Beyond her light arose the wild uproar,
As 'twere a buried earthquake's awful voice.
Then slowly heaved from out the rayless void
This pendulous round world, with the black wave
Swift rolling o'er her sunken continents,
And deep within the bosom of the sea,
The orbéd radiance of one bright star
Looked forth with spiritual ray serene;
Hope cheered her drooping heart once more, and Joy
Relumed her waning eye to find herself
In the wide universe not all alone.
Then, with unutterable longings filled
To hold communion with her sister spirit,
Oft she accosted the vain watery image,
Till baffled Love resigns his vain attempt.

Lo! far away upon the twilight main,
Another imaged star came slowly forth,
And by the first its steady station took.
Now sweetly stole upon the stilly air
A gentle song, articulate with words
Of wondrous melody. Another star
All eye, all ear, intelligence, and soul
Moved by her side, in heavenly path prescribed.
Joyous, as round the earth they held their course,
Star after star through all the vaulted sky
Sprang into being—mingled in the dance,
And raised the according song to utmost Heaven.
As upon earth in some old castled hall,
Where Beauty and high Chivalry together meet,
And on the wanton air sweet music swells;
Some stately courtier with his partner fair,
In graceful, measured tread begins the dance;
Soon others, won by the soft viol's tone,
Join the deep maze through many a devious round—
They meet—they pass—return—divide again—
Such guidance dwells in music's flexile tones.
Now soft, yet loud the anthem of the stars,
Through all the empyréan rang full high,—
Soaring sublime to Heaven-gate ascended,
And the Almighty Father heard, well pleased.

Rising and silvering o'er the eastern wave,
Uprose another orb to deck the sky—
The stars around her hid their fearful heads,
Abashed beneath the radiance of her beams,
Soon tendered their allegiance to their queen;
All sang with loud acclaim unanimous—
God the Creator of all things that are—
The sole proprietor of all that live—
The moon, fair queen of all the starry hosts.
Now in the Orient, the first glad morn
Began to dapple, and the morning stars,
Who have their station by the gates of light,
And herald the approaching King of day,
Joined in full chorus with angelic voices;
"Glory to God they sang in the highest,
And on earth peace and good will to men,"
Who soon around the renovated ball
Shall sing thy praise innumerous. Their song
Was echoed and re-echoed through all Heaven,
Till on the wave a flood of sunlight rolled;
Sudden the song surceased, and all the stars
Fled from the brightness of his rising beams. HERMENEUTES.

THE SPIRIT OF HUMBUGGERY.

We do not enter upon this subject with that degree of pleasure and hearty good-will, which is requisite, perhaps, to insure success in a literary essay. It is taken from one of those chapters in the History of Man, which present his character in a most unfavorable light, and is taken up with reluctance, because we dread nothing more than being classed among those unhappy beings who are forever finding fault with men and things. We envy not, nay, we pity from our very soul, the man who, through short-sightedness or willful obstinacy, looks only on the dark spots which are scattered here and there over the picture of human life, and is blind to every beauty. Deliver us from such a disposition as he possesses, who is forever ringing the changes upon the infirmities of men and the miseries of life. We prefer to look upon and enjoy the brightness, and whatever of excellence there is in the picture, and to hold our hand before our eyes as we pass the *blotches*. We would make the most of life, and be as well pleased with every thing and every person about us as we can. To do this always, however, is impossible. In studying man and his history, "Past and Present," we discover in his character disagreeable traits of such importance, from their universality and influence, that, although we may not be *pleased*, we cannot but be *interested* in tracing out their effects. Aside from the interest attending the consideration of such constitutional weaknesses, there is an immediate advantage, not to say an absolute necessity, connected with it. Flighty sophomores and sophomoric undergraduates in general, from the frequency with which they are called to expatiate upon the genius, dignity, power, and other tremendous, overwhelming attributes of man, are in danger of falling into error with regard to his character; and indeed he is oftentimes elevated to a region from which a survey, now and then, like that which we are attempting, is requisite to lower him to his proper level. If we succeed in causing any of the bold and soaring writers, who pour forth their semi-monthly lucubrations in the Division Room, to pause and ponder whether man is *in all respects* the greatest, noblest being that treads the earth, we shall not deem our time and trouble thrown away.

We have placed the word *humbuggery* at the head of this article, and may be tempted to use this and its parent *humbug* more frequently than will be pleasing to our classical readers. In this we beg their indulgence. We deprecate, as much as any one, the introduction and frequent use of those vulgarisms and new-coined phrases which, on account of their number, are making sad work with the purity of our vernacular, now-a-days; but when words with such happy and peculiar force as these present themselves, we welcome them, and say, "God speed you!"

Our subject is, the universality and influence of the Spirit of Humbuggery. There are two very prominent features in the human character, from which we have drawn it—deception and credulity. The effect of these two traits coming into contact, it is our design to view under the term humbuggery. Neither credulity alone nor deception alone is what we wish to speak of. To use both terms would give us two subjects. We therefore gladly take the only word we are acquainted with to express the desired combination. Every person knows what humbug means. Every day's observation and experience have made its import as familiar as the most common household term. Humbuggery is the perpetration of a humbug—the process of deception working upon credulity. If any one, dissatisfied, can furnish us with a word which will express our idea with a better regard to euphony, we shall thank him, and substitute it for our own in the next edition of the Magazine. Some may be disposed to smile at the "Spirit of Humbuggery." We would remind them that, spirit though it be, this is one far more real and substantial than the Spirits of the Age—of the Past—of Philosophy, and the like, sent forth by those lecturers who endeavor to "call spirits from the vasty deep" of their own imaginations, but which do not always come when they are called for. It is a spirit which has hovered over even themselves, for its influence has been freely shed by the Great Enemy of the race upon all the sons and daughters of Eve. It came into the world, there is every reason to believe, when Eve was humbugged by the serpent in Eden, and from the time of our great ancestress down to the last case of conversion to Millerism, it has been busy at its work, and we shall see how faithfully this evil visitor has been accomplishing its mission. As in the case of all the crimes which are numbered in the criminal code, and in wars and fightings, men injure themselves, so man is the instrument of this spirit's operations. He is the persecutor and inflicter, as well as the victim. The spirit is confined wholly to man: not wholly, either, when we think of it, for it is obviously just to allow to devils and foxes a considerable share. These with men constitute the greatest impostors in the animated world. As to which of them deserves the first place for dexterity and success, it lies, doubtless, between the men and the devils: if, however, an accurate history of the impositions on both sides could be obtained, and an impartial judgment given, we verily believe that Old Nick and his impish retinue would withdraw from the contest in despair. One who understood the matter perfectly has said,

All the world's a stage,
And all the men and women merely players.

And capital "players" they are, too, if a complete mystifying of the spectators constitutes good playing. The excellence of the histrionic art depends upon successful deception, and depriving the spectators of all knowledge of their condition and whereabouts. Certainly, then, Covent Garden or the Park never afforded better acting than that with which neighbor favors neighbor in this obliging world of ours.

Let us now take a glance at some of the most prominent instances in which this spirit has displayed itself. What stupendous—and, as curious productions of man's genius—what magnificent pieces of imposition are some of the systems of false religion which have flourished or are still existing! The first to suggest itself is, of course, the Mythology of Greece and Rome—the religion of the two most enlightened nations of antiquity. The millions of these two countries, notwithstanding their stores of knowledge and the full blaze of their own wisdom, were deluded into the belief of a system the most absurd and unworthy of an intellectual people. The fabric was of an exceedingly slight and loose frame-work, built up merely of improbable and monstrously absurd, together with some absurdly monstrous fables and traditions, heaped one upon another. The number of deities increased by this means, till no fewer than thirty thousand gods and goddesses, sailing in the air, perched upon mountain, sporting in valley and stream, scattered everywhere, kept watch over the interests of Greece alone. Over these presided Jupiter, distinguished from the rest by the infamy of his character, and elevated far above them by the number and blackness of his crimes. Those who imitated him with most success came next in rank. Mars played the villain, and Venus the wanton, in so *superior* a manner, that they, of course, were placed high up in the scale of *Dii Superiores*. These deities were all of flesh and blood, palpable to the human senses, and they were constantly making visits to the earth, and mingling with men; yet in all the volumes of sober history which have come down to us, we cannot find a credible person who says that he himself saw any of these heavenly visitors. All knowledge of these beings in ancient times must have been—like that of ghosts in modern—second-hand. Yet in this system, unsupported by any evidence, internal or external, such noble spirits as Demosthenes, Cicero, and Virgil, reposed their faith, and in these deities they placed their hopes of future happiness. When we think of such men passing through life in submission to this jumble of gods and heroes, oracles and oxen, must we not blush in view of the humiliating exhibitions of human nature which this spirit has afforded? Indeed, the nations we have mentioned present us with these exhibitions in more perfection than the most degraded of our modern heathen. Taking intellectual light into consideration, the Hottentot is superior to the Roman—the New Zealander deserves more praise than the polished Greek.

Mohammedanism, that vast structure which arose so suddenly and rapidly in the East, stands a towering monument of the credulity of man. A self-constituted prophet appears, and with the assistance of a fertile imagination and gleanings from existing forms of Religion, he frames the most unreasonable system, presents it to the world as if direct from Heaven, and as the common sense of men causes them to linger in their acceptance of it, he issues forth, sword-in-hand, and by a keen and pointed mode of reasoning, hastens them in coming to a decision. A specimen of his humbuggery, and it is one of the finest specimens extant, is his account of a night-journey in company with Gabriel through the seven heavens. The gigantic cock in the first heaven, whose head was five hundred days' journey from his feet, is an excellent creation. The angel in the second heaven, the distance between whose eyes was seventy thousand days' journey, is a greater wonder still; but the crowning glory of the prophet's abilities in the imaginary line, and an unequaled attempt, is the angel in the upper heaven, "who had sev-

ousand heads, in every head seventy thousand mouths, in every seventy thousand tongues, in every tongue seventy thousand , with which day and night he was employed incessantly praising These stories speak volumes upon Eastern humbuggery and cre- and will render any further remarks, we presume, unnecessary. thstanding these indigestible traveling sketches the religion is es- ed to hold in bondage millions of the race for centuries, to render te the fairest portion of the globe, and serve as an almost insur- able obstacle to the progress of light and truth.

the influence of the warrior-prophet over the restless, warlike inasmuch as exerted over Eastern ignorance, is not half so stri- n instance of man's credulity, as is displayed in the yoke which y has for ages pressed upon the neck of Europe—Europe, in her t hour, the abode of some common sense, valuable knowledge, ie religion. Here we have the spectacle of *men* believing a *man* ble of erring, and of *Christians* deluded into the belief that i is to be gained through priests and their absurd mummery, more and certainly than through the Bible and its simple teachings!

s we might proceed to notice system after system, until the riendly disposed and persevering reader would be frightened by midable catalogue. Rather than bring about so unpleasant a re- e shall make no use of the admirable materials for our subject, ied in the many false and wretched systems of ancient and mod- nes, less noted than those already mentioned. By way of variety, view this spirit as manifesting itself in a manner very different nat of palming upon the world Popes, Prophets, and Jupiters. ve been speaking of wholesale humbugs. Although the exam- bout to be presented are not on such an extensive scale, yet in ig out and developing this weakness in man, they are not less ant and satisfactory than the former. Little, scattered influences, collected and placed in the scale with the great and settled, gen- preponderate. Uncared-for and almost unnoticed habits build up s character, and exert the greatest influence in deciding his des- So it is with a nation's character. We should therefore look to i thousand little pieces of imposition, which men are daily playing on each other, for the best evidence of this spirit's supremacy an.

child comes under its influence, when, in his first literary pur- ie receives as gospel truth the marvelous tales of Jack the Giant- and the terrible Blue-beard, and when he is lost in wonder, and es in his memory as real, the strange and startling events nar- n the lines—

Hey, diddle, diddle!
The cat's in the fiddle,
The cow jumped over the moon,
The little dog laughed to see the fine sport,
And the dish ran away with the spoon.

The boy, having left the wonderful and romantic for the practical, discovers its existence, when upon a holyday he pays too much for a whistle, and he feels what it is to be its victim when returning home, he runs the gauntlet of the laughter and jokes awaiting him. When grown up and ripened into a philosopher, he will see that the human family is a company of brothers and sisters laughing at the credulous whistle-purchaser, and each one in turn the victim and the laughed-at. The young man sacrifices, upon the altar of some fickle beauty, the finest feelings of his heart, his peace of mind and happiness, and he learns that this foul spirit has a place even in woman's breast. The artless maiden has the truth impressed upon her heart in deep, enduring marks—in feelings of remorse and despair—and she bears it traced upon her brow, in blood-red characters of shame, when she has once listened to the artifice of man and become its victim. Thus step by step we might mount the ladder of life, till we could hear the old man on the top round railing against the humbuggery which he has experienced, observed, and perpetrated on his upward way, cursing in too many cases his fellow-travelers as a selfish, crafty, injury-inflicting race, and awaiting not unwillingly the jostle which will dash him to the earth from whence he started.

Whether we regard man as a friend, stranger, business-man, ruler, or philosopher, we shall find him making use of this propensity to assist him on his course. For instance, some men, actuated by principles of the purest benevolence—men, in whose hearts the milk of human kindness is bubbling up and running over—devote their time and efforts to the discovery of latent power in drugs, whereby the world may be blessed with all-powerful remedies for mortal ills. Pills enough, it is reckoned by shrewd calculators, have been rolled and swallowed within the present century, to form huge mountains, if men could only be persuaded to stop swallowing them long enough to make a trial of the experiment. Oceans of liquid medicines have flowed from the never-failing springs within the breasts of these same benefactors. Amid the great abundance of these things the world is left in a sad quandary, each new proprietor swearing, with all emphasis, that his production is "the sovereign'st thing on earth" for each and every ill that flesh is heir to.

Enterprising men get up a science. Scientific men are alarmed and people generally carried away with excitement. An astonished world —a blazoned name—listening crowds catching up their every word—staring—holding up their hands, and shouting "wonderful!"—above all else, a full and comfortable treasury—with such assistances as these they have a glorious time, they chuckle inwardly over an easily duped world, until, when at length the mist which a morbid love of novelty has thrown around the public eye begins to clear away, they sink into oblivion, and "their works do follow them."

Others, by keeping aloof from the world of common sense around them, and communing with musty books and their own more musty minds, conceive the idea that men and things have been moving along in a marvelous hap-hazard way, and that they are the first to discover the true philosophy by which the mysteries of nature may be unfolded. They then start forth to collect a crowd at their heels, to confuse the ideas of all who hear them, and to make fools of many. These philosophers were particularly busy in ancient times. One gave to thousands of men the name and disposition of the dog; another told them that the living soul within them might have been in former time the nobler part of some snarling cur; whilst another still taught that to live and die in imitation of this same animal, or better yet, of swine, was 'man's chief end;' to eat, drink, sleep, and lie in the sunshine of ease, and pleasure, this life's *summum bonum*. And did these credulous disciples oppose this degrading transformation as beneath the dignity of human nature? Not in the least; but when new teachers came along they, forgetting past ill-treatment, began to fawn, and lick the dust, and whine most piteously for another change. Kings and princes humbug their subjects, they cheat them of their liberty. The fame-seeking Cæsars of the earth by humbug gain the blood, treasure, and lands of men; they are in turn deprived of the influence and glory upon which they had congratulated themselves, and at death discover that they have cheated themselves of self-approbation, honest fame, and heaven.

There are still other and not less extensive manifestations which we shall notice very briefly. The dying groans of the victims in the days of witchcraft, as they rose to heaven, bore witness against this spirit. By it, too, are our graveyards made populous on dark and dismal nights with wandering spirits. The horror-struck visage and trembling limbs of the solitary traveler well attest its power. Banish this spirit and fortune-tellers will starve, jugglers hang themselves or commence an honest business, gipsey bands become a shaking of the head to every nation, and dream-interpreters no longer be regarded with reverence and awe. This it is which lights the evening Jack-o'-lantern which leads the solitary wanderer a weary chase, through woods and swamps, into an inextricable labyrinth. Insinuating its etherial substance into his breast, man becomes a hypochondriac and boils as an imaginary kettle, in a most distressing manner, or transformed into a basket of eggs or vessel of glass, he is in a state of perturbation upon every demonstration of an approach, lest a general crash may ensue. Fashion (we mean *ultra-Broadway fashion*) is a child of this most prolific parent. If we attempt to imagine the number of pinches, pains, and vexations—to weigh the expense and sorrow—which are encountered in her service, a vivid idea may be formed of what humbuggery can accomplish. There is a vast deal of the ludicrous and the miserable between the two conditions of a toe in the tender mercies of a tight boot, and a family ruined or State overthrown. A wretched martyr in the cause of Fashion, and a pitiable spectacle of human weakness is a Chinese belle, tottering on a pair of feet whose bases would scarce support an ordinary baby. A flat-nosed Indian suffers in the cause; but our pretty countrywomen require the greatest draught upon our sympathies. The Pekin maiden might look upon her little feet with pleasure, and thank her stars for having cast her lot in the Celestial Empire, if she could see the wasp-like form of a N York promenader. She would certainly think her wooden shoes trifling weight, when compared with the huge articles which our ladi to create a bustle in the world, endure with such a stern spirit of ma tyrdom.

Such are a few of the ways in which the Spirit of Humbugge manifests its presence in our world. "A few," we say, because v did not design, nor have we tried to give specimens of all its mod of operation. A dozen or two folios might probably accommodate tl whole of such a narrative, though we should greatly fear their incap city. Sufficient have been given, it is hoped, to exhibit our idea this mighty power moving among men. The active minds of our rea ers, taking advantage of our brief hints, have doubtless anticipated u and made the reflections which the subject naturally suggests, so th the usual application would be superfluous. If *all* that we have sa is not sufficient to exhibit the universality and influence of Humbugg ry, we are satisfied that we could do absolutely nothing within the limi of a closing flourish.

QUIS.

LINES,

SUGGESTED BY A FREQUENT AND EARNEST CONTEMPLATION OF THE CELEBRATED BE OF BEETHOVEN, IN THE IMPERIAL PALACE AT VIENNA.

Those who are familiar with the history of Beethoven, will readily appreciate the allusion his character and career—the sensibility and genius so evident in his countenance and air—the i cible and passionate temperament of the great composer, aggravated by unsuccessful love, and base ingratitude of an adopted son—the deep dejection which settled upon him, as the sense of h ing, originally so exquisite and so prized, gradually decayed and became extinct—the intense sy pathy which his presence excited, at the performance of his sublime productions—himself utt excluded from the gratification he so richly afforded to others—last, his premature and melanc end.

Thou hauntest me! Amid my dreams
Thy wild, unearthly aspect gleams:
The massive brow; the locks of gray;
The eye, whose fierce and fitful ray
Stares from beneath; the rigid lip,
Wont from the mingled bowl to sip
Its heated draught of joy and pain,
Till frenzy fired the fevered brain.

I dare not pity! yet my heart
Hath bled for thee: thine was a part
Mournful and varied in the show
Of life; the ceaseless ebb and flow
Of love and hate, of light and gloom,
Reached from the cradle to the tomb.

She, who around thy trusting heart
Had wound her web with fatal art,
Betrayed! The *orphan*, whom thy care
Rescued from want—the destined heir
To hard-earned gains—lived but to brave
The love that suffered and forgave!
Last, came the *mighty grief* that bowed
Thy spirit to the vulgar crowd!

'Twas not the rending bolt, that broke
In thunder down the rifted oak,
Leaving its seared and blasted form
The fury of the vengeful storm;
Rather the secret worm, that preyed
Unknown, save by the wreck it made.

Fainter and fainter came the din
Of the loud world—its sounds within
Died, one by one, until no breath
Disturbed the ever-living death;
The tinkling brook, the moaning surge,
The matin hymn, the evening dirge,
The cry of fear, the voice of love,
Grew silent as the stars above.

The wild-wood birds, whose carol sweet,
Once, a responsive smile would greet,
Pours forth her liquid lay, in vain,
The tribute of thy love to gain;
The choirs of sky, and earth, and sea,
Awake, in vain, their minstrelsy.

So, 'mid the loud-applauding throng,
Whose shouts the mighty notes prolong,—
Where the sonorous trumpet rings
Clear, 'mid a thousand quivering strings;
With roll of drum, and clang of steel,
And clarion's wild and wakening peal;
While, o'er the organ's heaving swell,
Floats woman's soft and wildering spell—

The master genius of the scene!
We watch thy dark and mournful mien:
Within thy soul, in depths profound,—
The grave of every *earthly* sound,—
Flows on the mighty tide of song,
Whose waves, in ceaseless notes, prolong,
With varied tone of dirge and glee,
The music of *Eternity*.

Yet, no!—the troubled scene is o'er;
The dregs of earthly woes no more
Thy lips shall quaff: thine ear again
May listen to the melting strain
In boyhood heard. Death hath set free
The minstrel from his misery:
The Harp, that held a world in chains,
Now thrills to the seraphic strains!

Vienna, Nov. 2, 1843.

ANACREONTIC.

'Twas said that rosy wine had power
To cheer all loneliness of soul;
So quick I sought the jovial hour,
And filled the bright and sparkling bowl;
And Bacchus with his jocund train
Essay'd sweet Eros to dethrone,
And drive him from my heart again,
To wander wearily alone.

'Twas vain—I quaffed the ruby tide,
And wreathed my brow with sweetest flowers;
I thought of love, and nought beside,
So sadly passed my jovial hours.

I heard that music with its spell
Could surely quench the burning fire;
So quick I seized the magic shell,
And tuned my unharmonious lyre.
Then Phœbus touched each tender string,
And woke a sweetly soothing song,
Bade rock and hill with echoes ring,
And woody groves the sound prolong.

'Twas vain—I took the lyre again,
And bold essayed its chords to move,
To wake some careless pleasing strain;
But ah! it spoke alone of love.

THE WITCH.

A TALE OF THE LAST CENTURY.

BY CUJUS.

"The earth has bubbles, as the water hath."—MACBETH.

CHAPTER VII.

WHEN the Indian fell, as if killed by the shot of the negro, he was in reality but slightly hurt, and after Brownhead and his companion, deceived by the stratagem, had hastened away on the track of the Tory, he arose cautiously and walked to the entrance of the dell. Here he found the slain whites, Morris and Treadway, and scalped them with savage delight. He then collected a few plants growing near, and having bruised them between two stones, bound them upon his wounded side, with a piece of cloth torn from the hunting-frock of one of the corpses. In order to avoid being followed by his trail, he stepped carefully from one fragment of rock to another, back into the interior of the hollow, and by the help of roots and fissures, climbed up the southern side of the cliffs, and with much labor gained the top. Here he hesitated a few moments, as if uncertain which way to go, and at length started rapidly away toward the pond. As soon as he came in sight of the water, he turned and directed his journey to the west. He quitted the forest, and came out into the open fields, again plunged into dense woods, pursuing his course over rocks, through swamps, and across streams, as unerringly as if guided by instinct. At last, after traveling in this manner some eight or nine miles, he stopped on the margin of a pond, considerably larger than Rapaug, and perhaps still more beautiful in appearance. Its shape was triangular; not a plant or weed of any description disfigured its surface, and its waters were clear as crystal. Immediately around its edges was a beach of white sand about ten feet in width, next to which, completely encircling the miniature lake, rose the tall forest. A high, wild-looking mountain, covered with pines and hemlocks, from whose branches dangled the long, gray moss, overlooked it from the east, while the woody land on the other sides seemed but little elevated above the surface of the pond itself.

Near the southern base of this mountain stood the savage, and as he gazed around, his eye fell upon the fragments of an old canoe, partly immersed in the water, and partly lying on the beach. A scowl gathered on his countenance, as he looked at this type of a former generation: he might have thought of the fate of his tribe, and of his own lonely destiny. But the emotion quickly passed away, and, raising his hand to his mouth, he gave a shrill whoop, which rang across the water, and echoed through the forest like the cry of a demon. For a little while after he was silent, standing as if expecting an answering signal. But the stillness which followed remained unbroken till he repeated the yell, when it was responded to by a shout from the opposite side of the pond, and he discovered the form of the Tory emerging from that part of the forest whence the sound proceeded. The Indian turned quickly, and hastened around the edge of the water toward the object of his expectations. As he drew near, Martin sprang eagerly to meet him, exclaiming,

"Grahtimut! by ——! I never thought to see you again. I saw you fall; how did you come to life?"

"Panther old warrior; they think him dead, and run 'way to chase d—d Tory. No catch him, though, Cap'n Martin."

"No, no, old king of the woods! Reckon we both outwitted 'em this time. I had to run for't, though. Followed the brook a mile; found a horse in an open field, led him to the bars, tied a thistle to him, and sent him into the road; away he went, as though the devil was after him, and I took my track back to the brook, followed it into the woods, saw the d—d rebels when they found the horse's hoof-marks, laughed softly, and here I am, half tired out."

"Ugh! Cap'n Martin," said Grahtimut, holding up the scalps.

"Aha! I wish you had two or three more, though."

"Have 'em, Cap'n, by and by. What we do now?"

"Well, Panther, I don't hardly know; I mustn't go to New York yet, and I can't go back to Rapaug, for they'll hunt for me there day and night. Why not stay here awhile? They'll not come here, unless, indeed, they follow your trail."

"They no do that," said the savage.

"And why?" inquired Martin.

Grahtimut laconically explained the manner in which he left the dell, adding,

"They no think of that, Cap'n Martin."

"Ha, ha, ha! they won't, that's a fact," replied the Tory. "Well, then, we must build a wigwam off against one of the corners of the pond, and see if they can hunt us out again. Stop, though," he continued, seating himself at the foot of a huge tree, while the Indian followed his example; "no, no, we can't go back to Rapaug, any how. Damnation! all that we can do is to sit still and watch our chance."

The savage made no reply, and both for a time were silent. There was something noticeable in the characters of the two men. Though coadjutors, partners apparently in the same schemes, they were totally unlike in disposition and expectation. Martin was a villain, because he chose to be so. He had selected his own course deliberately—had cast himself out of the society of old friends and acquaintances, to wage treacherous and relentless hostility against them. He had rejoiced in the outbreak of war, because he thought it might further his ends; he had never dreamed of the possibility of the colonies withstanding the mighty power of England, and he became a Tory, that he might grow rich by confiscation and plunder. He was selfish, simply, coldly, calculatingly selfish, in all his motives and desires. Another and yet fiercer passion than avarice now burned in his bosom also. He had seen Orra Stanfield, and the sight had filled him with such love as his coarse nature would allow. He knew that she was beloved by Hugh Warden, too, and thus he fancied that he had found an opportunity for the gratification of revenge and lust at the same time. To gain these ends, he was willing to go all lengths, to betray his native village to destruction, and to consign the house which sheltered his infancy to the flames.

The Indian was of a different stamp. His ancestors had been powerful chiefs among the Pequots, and he brooded continually over the lost glories of his race. The little portion of his tribe that remained was now beyond the Hudson, almost confounded with other once hostile nations.* *His* wish was to bring them back to the territory of their fathers; though, till Martin crossed his path, he had given up all hope of its accomplishment. When the Tory secreted himself in Rapaug forest, he needed some coadjutor, and as it happened that Grahtimut had just returned from one of his excursions to the west, he found in the Indian an individual suited to his purposes. By assuring him that the Americans immediately around were the cause of the extirpation of his race, and artfully promising that when England should have conquered her rebellious children, a place should be allotted to him and his tribe, out of the lands that had been wrested from them, he succeeded in drawing the simple-minded savage over to his interests. Grahtimut loved the ancient territory of his race, with all that affection so conspicuous in the Indian character. He hated those who now enjoyed it; perhaps justly, for the native inhabitants of this country have had no historian to tell *their* tale.

"What's that across the pond there, Grahtimut?" said the Tory, at last, pointing to the broken canoe, which at that distance looked like some living object on the opposite beach.

"That old Indian boat," replied his companion.

"And its owners, Panther?"

"They gone, Cap'n Martin. Pequots great tribe once; but Great Spirit get angry at them. Then come pale-face. First, he only want one, two, three land; then he want more; but Pequot see that he cut down forest; bear and deer all run 'way; and he no give pale-face more land. *He take it;* then come war; Pequot no match for him. They die, Cap'n Martin; one after another shot. Onosag killed at Unquowa, great many moons ago. Manepah, Onosag's son, go out to big lakes; he Grahtimut's grandfather. When Grahtimut's father die, he say, Go back to Onosag's hunting-lands. I come; find pale-face cut down the big woods, ploughed over the pleasant fields. I saw old Indian burying-ground; the bones of my fathers were dug up and scattered abroad, Cap'n Martin. My heart swell, and I swear by the Great Spirit always to hate white men,—to get many scalps for Onosag in the spirit-world. But Grahtimut old now; he no longer young Panther; his tribe all gone; soon he go too. But he always hate white men."

* I do not know but that I am here making a slight historical mistake; but it is of so little consequence, that I have thought correction unnecessary in a tale not purporting to be a strict narrative of facts.

"When the King has beaten the rebels, Grahtimut, he will give yo lands back to you," said the Tory. Again they relapsed into silen till Martin a second time resumed the conversation.

"Grahtimut," said he, abruptly, "we must discover what is going in D——. It is so situated up in the centre of the county, that might be made a place of some importance. They've got a hospi now, and it would be nothing surprising if they should make a depo of stores there. If they do, I'm right off for New York, and then w feather their nest for 'em with a vengeance. This Rapaug girl, to Hugh Warden will have her, will he? D—n him!"

"Cap'n Martin want young squaw himself?"

"Yes, he does;—reckon he'll have her too."

"Why not go get her, dark night?"

"Dare not risk it. That old hag frightens me every time I see h How the devil did she know I was down in the dell? And her inf nal cat, too. Look at my face, Panther!"

"Ugh! black cat great warrior."

"Yes, you're right; but I'll have the girl yet, in spite of the cat, witch, and the devil to boot!"

"Will ye, John Martin?" said a shrill voice behind them, and they leaped from their seats and turned around, they beheld the form of Mrs. Stanfield standing between the very trees against trunks of which they had been reclining; "ye will have the girl y continued she, passionately; "nay, point not your rifles at me. Gr timut, have you forgotten"—she spoke some words in the Indian lect, at which the savage instantly dropped his gun, and stepped b to the edge of the water, while Martin almost mechanically placed butt of his own piece upon the ground.

"Do you remember," said the old woman, fixing her eyes upon Tory's countenance, "that, many years ago, I wished you—*you*, J Martin, an untimely and bloody grave. It is a curse which hath ne yet failed, nor shall it now, unless you give up your evil designs agai me and mine. Look there!" pointing to the cat which had follov her out of the woods, "that is a better friend to me, aye, and an ab one, than you have. You possess not a single friend on this ear Grahtimut is not so much yours as mine. Beware how you make e mies!"

"Who the devil sent you here to lecture me?" said Martin, rec ering himself; "like a fool, you have put yourself in my power; let me tell you, old woman, it's easier to get into a trap than out of Stir but a single step,"—he again pointed his rifle at her breast,—"a as sure as you stand there, I'll fire."

"And a brave deed it would be," she replied, contemptuousl "Grahtimut, speak!"

The Indian came forward, and laying his hand upon the Tory's a exclaimed,

"No hurt old squaw, Cap'n Martin. She great friend to Grahtin many moons ago, 'fore you here. Shoot *her*," he stepped back a brought his rifle up fiercely, "shoot *you*!"

With a violent execration, Martin dashed his gun to the ground, and cried, "What in —— shall I do, then?"

"I will tell you," said Mrs. Stanfield: "forget your foul passion for my child; pursue your schemes as if you had never seen her; trouble not me and mine, and we will never more trouble you. One thing I will say, Orra Stanfield shall never be Hugh Warden's bride; she has another destiny. Will you be content now?"

"Let young squaw be, Cap'n Martin," said Grahtimut: "she do no good; old squaw do much, great deal hurt."

"I am satisfied," replied Martin, at length, "d—n the girl, there's plenty more." The old woman looked at him distrustfully. "I tell you," he exclaimed, angrily, "I'll never come near her again, or you either, if I can help it."

She turned to go, looked back, raised her hand, threateningly, and saying, "Beware of treachery!" hastened into the forest.

"If I can get Tryon with a couple of British regiments up here," muttered the Tory, "I'll outwit the whole of them, old woman and all!" then turning to the savage, he said aloud, "Well, Grahtimut, we must begin our wigwam:" at which occupation we leave them, and turn to another part of our story.

CHAPTER VIII.

About a week after these events, Mr. John Warden, having just finished his morning repast, sat in a comfortable arm-chair, before a pleasant fire in his parlor, apparently absorbed in contemplation of the huge smoke-wreaths which alternately curled upward from his lips, and from the bowl of his old-fashioned pipe. We have great respect for the opinions of Anti-tobaccoites; yet we must confess that we like to see an honest, hearty-looking old man, approaching to sixty or thereabouts, solacing himself with his pipe There is a quiet repose, an open-hearted simplicity about him at such moments, that attracts our love and commands our reverence. He is at peace with all men; he would not harm the veriest insect that crawls the earth; he is cheerful, contented, happy. At least so seemed Mr. John Warden on that November morning, in the year of grace 1776.

Suddenly his nephew entered the room at one door, and was passing, as if to go out at another, when the old gentleman stopped him by inquiring, "Hallo! boy, where now?"

"Into the woods, sir."

"What, hunting?" The youth nodded. "Well, then," continued the bachelor, "let me tell you that I don't see what the deuce you find to shoot. Every day here for a month you've been off hunting. You never kill any thing,—came near getting killed yourself, though; always go in one direction, and come back the same way; bring home a loaded rifle, fire it off, and so end all your *hunting* excursions. I don't understand it;"—he laid his pipe upon the mantel-piece,—"I say I don't understand it."

" Why, I am rather unlucky, to be sure ; but Richard often shoots enough for both."

" Oh ! ay ! yes, Richard does, does he ? Well, what do *you* go for then, hey ? Another thing—why do you go in uniform ? Why don't you put on a hunting *dress ?* A man would think, to look at you now, that you were going to pay your respects to the General."

" Well, then," said Hugh, taking a chair near his guardian, and suiting his language to the disposition of the questioner, " to tell the plain truth, I am in love."

" In love !" shouted the bachelor, jumping out of his seat, and giving a long, low whistle, " in love ? Who—where—when—how—what the devil did you get in love for, sir, without asking *me*—hey ? Tell me that, sir ; tell me that."

" Why, you see, uncle"—

" No, I don't see, I'll be d—d if I see, sir."

" Well, I have been waiting for an opportunity to tell you my circumstances for some weeks now"—

" Waiting for an opportunity to—what ? Han't I sat in this armchair and smoked this pipe every morning for the last ten years ? Why didn't you tell me yesterday—a month—a year ago, hey ?"

" But, sir, if you'll be cool a moment, I'll tell you all"—

" Cool ! I'll see you hanged first, sir. Cool ! zounds, I call that *rather* cool."

" May I go on with my story now ?" said Hugh, deferentially, for he was accustomed to these fits of impatience, and he believed that in the end his uncle would offer no opposition to his wishes

" Go on ? to be sure you may ; that's what I've been trying to have you do for the last half hour."

The young man now told the story of the rise and progress of his attachment, giving, in conclusion, an elaborate panegyric upon the beauty, amiability, intelligence, &c., of Orra.

" Whe-e-w !" whistled the old gentleman, as he finished, " so the boy's really over head and ears in love with the granddaughter of a reputed witch, of whose history, birth, parentage, and true circumstances, he knows just nothing at all : whew ! whew !" and he walked back and forth across the parlor in deep meditation.

" But," said Hugh, " I do not believe that Orra *is* the grandchild of Mrs. Stanfield, uncle, or any way related to her."

" You don't, hey,—then who is she ? Did she drop from the moon ? What put that notion into your head, boy ?"

" The way in which the old woman treats her, her own imperfect story, and some language which Mrs. Stanfield herself unintentionally used in my presence."

" Umph !—well, Hugh, you can follow your own inclinations in the matter entirely. I wish you would bring the girl down here, though ; I should like to see her."

" There's a difficulty about that, sir. Mrs. Stanfield makes, or has made, no objections to my coming there as often as I please ; but she has told me again and again that Orra can never be my wife, and"—

"The devil she has! Umph! she *shall* be your wife, though, if forty witches rise up and forbid it."

"I have asked Orra to leave her grandmother and become my bride at once; but she told me that Mrs. Stanfield had been her only protector from infancy, and that she could not thus abandon her."

"Good! why, Hugh, she *must* be a glorious girl; but I see you wish to be off. I've been in love once myself."—a shade came over the bachelor's face,—"go, Hugh, go, and God prosper you!" He stretched forth his hand to the young man, who gave it a hearty clasp, and left the room.

As Captain Warden came out into the avenue before his uncle's house, he there found Richard Brownhead, fully equipped for a hunt. As they met, the latter inquired—

"Wal! I s'pose you're goin' up to the pond now?"

"Yes, Richard, and I shall be very glad of your company, too."

"Pos-si-bil-i-ty! though," replied the hunter, as they walked toward the gate, "wal! I thought may be you'd like to have me with you; so I got myself ready aginst your comin' out of the house."

After they came into the street, they proceeded in silence, till they entered the lane mentioned in a former chapter. Here Brownhead seemed to be somewhat troubled, for he muttered to himself for some moments, and at last exclaimed aloud, "Blast his infernal pictur!"

"Whose, Richard?" inquired Hugh, looking at him in surprise.

"Why, you see, Captain, I was thinkin' of poor Morris and Treadway, and that made me think of John Martin, and that somehow made me think out loud. Wal!" drawing a long breath, "we buried 'em with the honors of war. If I ever do see that 'ere Tory agin,"—he clutched his rifle firmly, and muttered the remainder of the sentence in an indistinct tone. Again for some time they were silent. As they entered the forest, Warden accelerated his pace, and Brownhead said, half to himself, "You walk fast, Mister Hugh, but it's nat'ral; and a young man that had the love of Miss Orra, and wouldn't walk fast to meet *her*, would desarve hangin', he would." Hugh made no reply, and the hunter continued, "Let me see, it's more than—no matter how many years ago, that Richard Brownhead would have walked for many a mile to see Emma Parkinson,—but—wal! wal! it's all over now."

"I did not know, Richard," said Hugh, kindly, "that you had ever had a sweetheart."

"No, Captain, a man don't like to talk of such things, after they and their hopes are all gone. But somehow, when I see you and Miss Orra, it sets me a thinkin' about old times; and then Emma Parkinson comes up to my mind, just as she used to be when she was a gal, and I used to help her across the brooks and over the fences, when we run about in the fields in the summer time. But, though she always said she liked me, Mister Hugh, she told me she couldn't love me as she ought to love a husband; and then she married a man down in New York, who turned drunkard, Captain, and abused her, till at last she died, folks said, of a broken heart. He must have been worse than a brute, to have treated *her* so, Mister Warden."

"You are right, Richard; no brute does anything as bad as that"

"Wal, you see, I loved *her;* and when she was married,—though I knew she did right to take the one she liked best,—it was hard to bear; but when she died, and I heard of *that*, it was harder yet, and I thought I'd never court another woman, and I never have, and never shall."

"It was a sore trial, indeed, Richard," said Hugh, "but you have borne it like a man, and can look back to it now as to an evil necessary but past."

"Yes, and lately I don't often think of it—ah! there is Rapaug, Mister Hugh, and over yonder's the clearin' and the house; and Miss Orra, God bless her! is expectin' and waitin' for you there, I don't doubt. I'll take a turn in the woods, I guess, and come around to you by and by," and without stopping for an answer, he hurried away into the forest.

When our hero entered the hut, he found Orra alone, and as she sprang forward, with a smiling face, to welcome him, he passed his arm around her, and gently kissed her cheek.

We envy not the man who can sneer at the innocent familiarities of young love; if he be himself in the spring-time of life, that sneer betokens a heart dead to the sympathies of youth, nay, more, to all the finer feelings of our nature. If affection imparts to it no warmth, how shall vice and crime move it to indignation, or misfortune and suffering excite compassion? Such an individual is prepared to go through this world without a single friendship formed—to follow one unswerving track, be it right or wrong, without pity, without benevolence, without remorse. Has age whitened his locks and stamped his brow with wrinkles? heaven help him! his lot has been hard indeed. The love of woman never lighted up his young days; for if it had, instead of a sneer, a shade of sadness would come over his countenance, as awakened memory brought to his fancy the form once so dear, now perhaps mouldering in the grave; no wife or children consoled his manhood, and he is fast approaching a cheerless tomb, unlamented, uncared for. Or, for the sake of wealth or vanity, he may have wedded one for whom he never felt a single throb of affection, and his years have been years of contention and bitterness. Whatever he may be, rich or poor, in youth, in manhood, or in old age, he that makes mockery of the warm feelings of love, and ridicules their tokens, is worthy of pity rather than envy, of contempt rather than either.

"Your grandmother, Orra," said Hugh, placing himself by the maiden's side, as she sat down, "where is she?"

"She went out early this morning, and has not yet returned; indeed, she is often gone of late."

"Do you know, Orra," said the young man, "that I have for some weeks past had strange thoughts—suspicions perhaps I should call them—respecting Mrs. Stanfield?"

"You don't think her a witch, I hope, Hugh," replied the girl with a smile.

"No, no; but what reason have you for believing that she is really what she pretends to be—your grandmother?"

"None that I know of, except her own word," replied Orra, with a look of astonishment: "why, Hugh, what do you mean?"

"I mean what I say. Has she ever told you who your father was, or spoken of your mother?"

"Never," said the maiden, sadly. "I know not my birth-place even. My own memory goes no farther back than our residence in New York. I have never seen a single relative except her, or a single friend—except Hugh Warden."

The reader may imagine how the moment's interval which followed before Hugh spoke again was occupied, by conceiving what sort of a reply would be most appropriate to the last words which Orra uttered.

"Strange, strange!" said he, at length,—"it would not be thus, if she were the mother of either of your parents; it would not."

"What am I, then?" said the girl, leaning her head upon his shoulder: "Oh! Hugh, say not so; you would leave me alone in the world, entirely alone."

"Not while I live, Orra;—but why does she so oppose our union? what would she do? I do not believe she means well"—

"We know not her motives," said Orra, deprecatingly.

"Let her make them known, then, that we may judge of their propriety. Orra, why not become mine at once? I have pressed this, perhaps, too often already; but hear me. If she be indeed your relative, she need not be separated from you. You do not abandon her; you can give her a house in the society of others,—a home, at least more secure than this. If she be not your relative, what right has she to control your actions, or hinder your happiness?"

"Hugh, she would not accompany me to another home. She is, at all events, the only relative I have ever known. Many long and pleasant years we have dwelt together, and she has always, till I saw and loved you, been kind, even indulgent, to me. Would you urge me to forsake her now, in her old age, when she most needs a companion? No, no, dear Hugh, it may not be. We are young yet: she may cease her opposition, and then"—she stopped, and a blush overspread her countenance.

"God bless you, dear Orra!" exclaimed Warden. "You are right, always right, and I begin to think its only my own selfishness that would prompt you another way."

The maiden replied in a low tone, and as the remainder of the conversation, though doubtless interesting to the lovers, might be unpardonably dull to a reader, we transcribe it not.

Two or three hours had passed away in this manner, when Brownhead made his appearance. "I calculate, Mister Hugh," said he, "that it's about time to be goin'. The 'squire'll git awful touchy if you ain't home to dinner to-day. You know he expects the colonel." Hugh seemed to be of the same opinion; for, after a parting embrace, he arose, took his rifle, and departed with the hunter.

CHAPTER IX.

We must now pass hastily over a period of about six months. During this time, little of importance to our story had taken place in D—— or its neighborhood. A considerable quantity of military stores had been collected there, under the superintendence of Captain Warden; but so inadequate means of defense were provided, that both that officer and Col Cook had made several attempts to procure a more efficient body of troops, though unfortunately without success. Still, every thing had appeared so quiet during the whole winter, that little fear was now entertained either of domestic broil or hostile incursion.

Our hero was of course a frequent visitor to Rapaug; but, notwithstanding his conciliatory demeanor, he had found it utterly impossible to shake the resolution of the old woman: and, as Orra would not consent to take any decisive steps without her grandmother's acquiescence, he was obliged to see his suit stand still, without being able to devise any means of hastening its progress. Meanwhile, the patience of his uncle was completely exhausted by the obstinacy and repulsive carriage of the old woman, and after much irritation and vituperation, he had cast the whole matter out of his mind, leaving things to work out their own course.

Orra Stanfield keenly felt the difficulties of her situation. The language of her lover had infused a doubt into her mind as to the reality of the relationship between Mrs. Stanfield and herself, which all her efforts could not entirely remove. The conduct of the old woman towards her also was of late very unkind; and though she still met the urgent solicitations of Hugh Warden with a firm refusal, yet the uncertainty of her position and future prospects cost her many an hour of painful reflection. Still, the visits of Hugh tended to cheer her; and when in his presence, and assured of his love, she could not be unhappy. The Tory and his savage companion had not been heard of since the unavailing attempt at their capture, and it was commonly supposed that they had left the State, though Richard Brownhead repeatedly declared, that though "it wan't onpossible, yet they mightn't be a great ways off, a'ter all."

About two miles and a half to the southeast of that portion of D—— already described, there is a small village embraced within the limits of the town, but which, nevertheless, forms a distinct community. It is a thriving little place, and its inhabitants consider themselves not a whit inferior to their more central neighbors; and indeed it has often been observed, that there is no good reason why B—— (the name of the village) should not be constituted a separate town. Such, however, it is not; and to this day, the good people thereof are obliged to undertake a journey of nearly a league, in order to exercise the privileges of freemen at the polls. B—— is a romantic spot, and when viewed from the summit of a neighboring eminence, called Owl Rock, it presents, as it lies embosomed among the hills, with its white dwelling-houses and red shops, a very picturesque appearance. It is quite a bustling little place, too; equally noisy in its political and religious contests, and might probably—so at least its inhabitants think—exercise a powerful influence for the weal or wo of the whole country. It is peculiarly precocious in regard to fashions. The latest Paris modes, within six months after they have reached New York, are displayed to the greatest advantage on the persons of the belles and beaux of B——, and being particularly exhibited on Sundays, are thus made known to the various families settled about in its vicinity. But it is not now what it was half a century ago: it is larger, more learned, more enterprising, and, in every respect, makes more show in the world.

It was a pleasant night in the latter part of April, 1777. The moon shone quietly down on the few scattered dwellings which then composed the village of B——, and the stars shone out with the peculiar brilliancy of spring. Silence reigned undisturbed, except when some chanticleer, troubled with the nightmare, burst forth into a sleepy, hysterical crow. It was already past twelve o'clock, when two armed men might have been seen proceeding with cautious step along the main road which passed through B——. They walked in perfect silence, till they came opposite the village meeting-house. Here they paused, and seemed to be examining the construction of the edifice. It was of antique form, in shape nearly square, with the gable end standing east and west. In the middle of the side looking toward the south, and fronting the road, was the main entrance, though a huge oaken door afforded another means of ingress on the western end. The spire rose to a moderate height, over the eastern extremity. The men, after conversing a few moments in low tones, advanced to the lesser entrance of the building, and seated themselves on the rude wooden steps.

"By heaven! Grahtimut," said one of them, as he sat down, "if he don't come to-night, I shall be inclined to give over looking for him."

"We been here one, two, three night, Cap'n Martin, and he no come yet."

"Right, Panther; but Tryon himself told me, in New York, that he could not say for a certainty what day he should be here. He promised to land Riggs, however, the moment he reached shore; and as Riggs was brought up in these parts, he would not be likely to lose his way."

Our old acquaintances (for the reader has by this time recognized them) were little changed from what we have already described. Martin had the same restless glance in his eyes, the same forbidding scowl upon his features. The face of the Indian was streaked with war-paint, giving him an extremely repulsive look. The two sat in silence after the last remark of the Tory, till the quick ear of the Indian detected a noise as of some person moving along in front of the church."

"Wagh! Cap'n, what that?" said he, in a suppressed tone, as a low peculiar whistle came to their ears from the same direction.

"It's him!" exclaimed Martin, answering the signal by a similar note. The next moment, a small, wiry-looking man, dressed in the ordinary attire of a country farmer, came around the corner of the building toward them.

"Riggs!" exclaimed Martin, starting toward him.

"Hush! right; hallo! who's that?" said the new-comer, meeting him, and pointing to Grahtimut.

"The Indian that I told you about."

"Aha! let me look at him;" and walking forward, he stopped directly in front of the savage, and bent a scrutinizing gaze upon his painted countenance. Grahtimut sat as unmoved as a rock; not a muscle stirred; and the spy, having finished his examination, turned to the Tory, and said—

"He's game, John, I'll be hanged if he's not."

"Ay, ay! but what is your news? Has Tryon landed?"

"He came up with more than two thousand men; reached N—— in the latter part of the afternoon; I came at once on shore, sneaked along the coast half a dozen miles, cut through the woods, got into the road, and here I am. Tryon's on the march before this time."

"Good! he's got enough too to harry the whole country."

"Right; but do you know the situation of things exactly?"

"Yes; the d—d rebels have filled every thing with their stores; the church itself is stuffed to the galleries with pork, flour, and beef. They've got no force, though, and it won't be ten minutes work to finish the business."

"The quicker the better. I don't know but that we'd better start down to meet Tryon at once."

"I wish to —— you would, Riggs," said Martin, in a whisper, "and take this Indian with you. I've got a job of my own to do, which I might arrange by the time our troops got here, if he was not in the way. He's true to the back-bone, but in this matter of mine he's got some scruples. Can't you get him off?"

"Some woman affair, John, eh? you always *was* a devil among the females; well, I'll try it."

"Good! only get him away, and"—

He was interrupted by a shrill whoop from Grahtimut, who, with one hand, leaped over the rude board-fence, into the grave-yard adjoining the church, and disappeared.

"Run, Riggs, for your life!" exclaimed Martin, following the example of the Indian, though a couple of rifle bullets whistled close past him as he spoke. The spy was not quick enough: as he attempted to start, he felt himself seized by a strong hand from behind, and a voice exclaimed—

"Ki! Misser; you needn't try to get 'way; think Bill Armstrong no hold fast, hey?"

"Got one, have you, Bill, you etarnal nigger?" said a lank-looking personage, slowly climbing over the fence, after a short but ineffectual chase of the two who had fled, "wal! it's better than none; who is it?"

"Don't know, Misser Richard," said the negro, who had thrown his prisoner down, and was busy tying his hands behind his back, "spy, reckon."

"Let *me* look at him," said the other, walking up and bringing the of the captive into the moonlight, "Lord! Pos-si-bil-i-ty! Jim s, where on airth did you come from?"

ggs made no reply, and Brownhead, for it was our old friend, the r, continued,

Wal! Jim, I'm sorry for you; you always *was* a Tory, and you up here for no good, any how; who was them with you? Why, see, Bill and I ha' been huntin', and was jest comin' back 'long when we heerd you talkin' away; I heerd somethin' about the s, and I knew that wan't right; but two on you run, afore we ound the corner—whew! pos-si-bil-i-ty! he whooped! it must ha' the Injun, Bill, and John Martin, by thunder! Wal, wal, Jim s, I know'd your father, and p'raps if I'd known it had been you I might ha' let you go; but I can't now, can I, Bill?"

Lor! no, Misser Brownhead; we must take him up to Cap'n War-

Yes, Bill, we must, and—here come some of the B—— folks, too."

he spoke, several men, armed with such weapons as were at hand they were aroused by the report of the rifles, came toward them.

What are you doin' there, and who are you?" cried one of the ap-ching party.

Richard Brownhead," answered the hunter, "and Bill Armstrong, prisoner."

chard was well known in the neighborhood, and the surprised vil-s crowded around him, eager to hear the story. After relating the e matter some half dozen times, the hunter and his sable compan-accompanied by two volunteers from the village, set out on the road —— with their prisoner.

[TO BE CONTINUED.]

FAREWELL TO HOME.

I.

Oh! can it be that I so soon must leave thee,
  My own, my native home! What cheating thought
Has had the power so deeply to deceive me,
  And bring my dreams of pleasure all to nought?
The birds and flowers have come to make thy beauty
  More lovely than before: and can it be
That even now the sterner voice of duty
  O'erpowers the warbling birds' sweet minstrelsy,
And bids me leave thy passing loveliness,
Thy kind endearments, and thy power to bless?

II.

'Tis even so. The sun shall rise to-morrow,
  And gaze upon thy charms e'en as to-day;
But I shall be—O thought o'erfull of sorrow—
  From thee, and those I love, far, far away.

And yet, my heart, shouldst thou feel only sadness?
  Is there no gentle thought to soothe thy pain?
The parting hour may have e'en thoughts of gladness;
  For I but leave thee to return again,
Sweet boyhood's home! This is the "thought at parting,"
Which ever keeps the imprison'd tear from starting.

III.

Then fare thee well, my own loved village home,
  Ye green-clad hills—ye gently murm'ring waters—
And you with whom in youth I loved to roam—
  A kind "adieu" to you, earth's fairest daughters.
Thus friends part evermore, while part they may,
  And dearest friends doth Time the soonest sever;
Yet hope is left to cheer us on our way
  To that bright world where friendship lasts forever.
But on thy much-loved scenes mine eyes may dwell
No longer now. My own dear home—farewell.

C.

COMMUNION WITH GREAT MINDS.

'I SHALL not wholly die.' This thought animated the bard of Venusium in his literary toils, smoothed the asperities of the present, and lighted up the dark pathway to the tomb. He believed that his name would be repeated and loved in distant lands and in future years; nor was this belief groundless. Thousands of others have pampered their ambition on the same dazzling hope, through life, and died in the full assurance of a like glorious immortality. But the grave is not more greedy for its cold, silent occupants, than oblivion is tenacious of its victims. No sooner had one claimed their inanimate dust, than the other laughed at their day-dreams of eternal remembrance, and threw a pall of forgetfulness over the works of their hands.

But if we mark well the forms that flit across this stage of life, we shall note a few, a very few, lofty spirits, in each age, stepping out from among their companions, and writing their names on the record of the illustrious. They may be comprised in two classes—those who have been the most terrible scourges of their race, and those who have distinguished themselves as its most munificent benefactors. It is the extremes, the antipodes of humanity, who are remembered by posterity. For, one class carves the lineaments of its character on the fabric of society with the sword and battle-ax, or burns them there with the brand and faggot; the other interweaves them with it, by deeds of charity, philanthropy and patriotism. One, like the wrathful tempest, peremptorily demands notice, by the wide-spread havoc and desolation which mark its track; the other, like the mild zephyr of spring, sweetly allures atntion, by the life, and loveliness, and joy, which linger around its rogress.

With the last of these classes we are concerned at present, and hiefly with the literary part of this. Here, then, are, or may be, the cholar's daily associates—his bosom companions. Gathered together ut of every nation and people, they constitute an assembly, of which e is a conspicuous member; indeed, over which he presides, in the ignity of serious thoughtfulness. Here are philosophers and sages— gray old bards and gifted seers." Here, the sprightly Horace sits by he side of blind old Homer, or, with gentle hand, guides his uncertain teps, or, perchance, proffers him a sparkling goblet of his favorite Fa- smian, "for his stomach's sake and often infirmities." Here, Newton nd Galileo while away more thoughtful hours, in discoursing of the otions of the heavenly bodies, and the laws of gravitation. Here is synod, not of bickering bishops nor of embattled laymen, but of the evout priests of philosophy, and of the devoted followers of wisdom— n assembly—a congress—not of allied states, but of confederate na- ons, and not of nations only, but of generations—of ages.

Nor does the scholar sit in this council, and hold converse with its embers, through the perplexing, imperfect medium of biography. He ommunicates with them, without the interposition of such a clumsy nterpreter. Thought grapples immediately with thought. Heart em- races heart. This is as it should be. We are aware, however, that, hatever may be uttered against biography, runs an imminent risk of eing construed into treason against the republic of letters, as it most ssuredly is treason against the craft of book-making. But, neverthe- ess, we must say, that we deem it next to useless, so far as making ny really valuable acquaintance with literary men is concerned. It is o from the manner in which it is written, and, indeed, from its very ature. Let us illustrate our opinion.

A few years, or months, as it may chance, after a man of eminence as died, a host of long-faced, sanctimonious, biographical scribblers ppear, and, with many a profession of pious esteem, essay, by pon- erous quartos and folios, to set the good man's character right before e world. Thus we have lives, reminiscences, biographies, *memoirs* ritten by the editor, and posthumous papers, composed by the author fter his decease, in endless variety. Therein the dress, equipage, iet, habits, thoughts, actions, motives, successes, reverses, in short, all at appertained to the physical, social, intellectual and moral character f the departed, are, professedly, depicted with the most graphic mi- uteness: *professedly*—but we feel half-inclined to doubt the sincerity f professions in this matter; for we remember that it was said, of old, where the carcass is, there are the eagles gathered together." Doubt- ess, appeals to respect and love for departed worth have a mighty po- ency to enclose the purse-strings. Doubtless, an ostensible biography, ith the name of some distinguished man, now dead, mentioned once r twice in the preface, is a note of hand, which many a one will cash t sight.

But, grant that the motives which actuate biographers are indeed unimpeachable; what then? If a man has lived, and written, and distinguished himself, by his writings, might we not *infer* that he was born and educated somewhere, at some time, and under certain circumstances? Would it require a very excessive stretch of credulity to believe that the root of his pedigree extended back *several* generations, at least, even if his grandfathers and great-grandfathers were not specified, in regular line, up to Noah and his family? Do we really need a folio to make this matter plain to our comprehension? Furthermore, is it absolutely essential to the best interest of the literary public, or to mankind generally, to be informed whether the doublet of such an one was blue, white, or black; whether he wore a cue or a wig; whether he rose at five, or six, or seven in the morning; whether he lived on a strictly vegetable, or animal, or mixed diet; whether he studied in an upright or in a sitting posture?

Many, we are aware, would deduce rules from the habits of great men, to govern the life and conduct of young students. And so they may. But these rules will be either so obvious to all as to need no such illustration, or so diverse as to be valueless to others. Repeated attempts have been made to discover a royal road, a sort of "Northwest passage," to eminence; but, so far, they have proved repeated failures. And it will probably be found in the end,—what indeed might have been known at the outset,—that the man who has genius enough to become great, has likewise common sense enough to employ that genius aright. *Ten* individuals, we will venture to assert, have been led, by reading Boswell's Life of Johnson—a work perfect in its kind—to ape the habits of the sloven, the egotist, and the glutton, for every *one* who has thus been induced to practice the abstemiousness of the student, the virtue, the intense application and gigantic efforts of the literary Hercules.

Besides, what is this hankering for whatever can, and much that ought not to be said of the departed? Is it aught else than mere idle curiosity, perhaps we should say, the vulgar appetite for scandal? True, it is a little more fastidious than usual; but is it not also more insatiable? for it levies sustenance for its cravings from the cold tenants of the grave, and often, with more than Vandal ferocity, disturbs their last sacred repose. If we are to have works of this description respecting great literary men, let us have, not biography, but *auto*biography; not the dubious guess-work of strangers, nor the motley gleanings of insolent eaves-droppers, or of hollow-hearted friendship, nor yet the minute detail of every-day life and habits; but rather the bold, prominent, and faithful outline of intellectual and moral character. Such an autobiography does every man write, who publishes his thoughts on any subject to the world. In it, the expression of his mind, the lineaments of his soul, are portrayed with more than daguerreotype exactness. It is a portrait, in which the cheeks glow with life-tints, the eyes sparkle, and utter their own mysterious language. It is a Pygmalion statue; and, while we are gazing, the celestial fire descends to animate it, the heart throbs, the ruddy life-current leaps along the veins, the lips open with words of wisdom, and we commune with a living friend!

We deem it, then, evident, from what has been said, that, if we have not *biographies* of the great literary men of the past and present, we can yet, in their writings, commune with them on far more intimate terms than by means of these biographies ; and thus we can reap the richest harvest of advantages which can possibly spring from such a communion. What then are some of these advantages?

It is in this way only that any *actual* advance in knowledge can be made. Were the generations of men perfectly isolated, in point of knowledge, so that the acquisitions of a preceding should be hidden from the view of a succeeding one, the stature of the human mind, in all ages, like the dimensions of the trees of the forest, would observe the same uniform standard. It is this power of transmitting ideas from one generation to another, which imparts progress to knowledge. Nor is it a mere transmission of ideas in the same *form* and *number*, which makes knowledge progressive ; but, if we may use the illustration, the acquisitions of one generation become the *principal* in the hands of the next, which principal it is to transmit, with *interest*, to its successor. Thus, a truth, first detected in one age, and more plainly seen in another, is comprehended in its relations and bearings ; as the marble is first dug up from the quarry, a rude, misshapen slab, then reduced to the form of a regular block, then to that of a rough-hewn image, till at last it stands forth in the graceful symmetry and beautiful proportions of the exquisitely wrought statue.

There is a close analogy between the progress of an individual in knowledge and that of the race. The individual begins his progress by learning the alphabet of a language, and advances from that to simple sentences, from these to complex propositions, and so on. The race commenced its education in the infancy of the world, by learning the rudiments—the alphabet of truth—and from that time to this, it has been advancing, by successive steps, into the depths of art and science, and into the higher regions of philosophy and poetry. The present generation should therefore occupy the front rank in this march of knowledge ; but it must do so by making the acquisitions of past generations its own : for if it rejects them, if it throws away the previous steps of reasoning, in the solution of the various problems of truth, it will have to go back, and commence the process anew.

Doubtless, the greatest minds have often formed theories, now seen to be visionary ; and advocated systems of Philosophy, since shown to be false. But it is also true, that, intermingled with them, and shining with superior lustre, from a contrast with base materials, are many invaluable gems of truth. Much genuine wheat is growing among the tares. We sometimes regard these false systems of Philosophy as valuable, perhaps indispensable modes of arriving at the reality of things ; those mathematical theorems, in which a proposition is established by demonstrating the absurdity of its converse. At any rate, they stand as beacons to warn us of the rocks on which others have split. The Indian, who treads the pathless wilds of a North American wilderness, notches the trees with his tomahawk, as he passes along ; and, thus, *he* is enabled to retrace his steps, *others* to follow them. In these exploded theories, these false reasonings, are signs, made by those who precede us, to indicate where the path of true knowledge lies. Assisted, then, by the attainments of past generations, and guided by their experience, we are prepared for still farther advances—for still loftier flights in knowledge.

Whether the present age is actually making this advance, is quite another matter. To us, it seems not. Knowledge, although daily becoming more universally diffused, seems to have ceased, in a great measure, its aggressions on the kingdom of error. Indeed, from being progressive, it has become reflexive. It is regarded not as a *means* of farther advancement, but as an ultimate *end*. The human mind seems to consider it the paramount object of its being, to gaze intently at its own image as mirrored in the silent depths of its past achievements.

Perhaps, however, the progress of knowledge, from its very nature, must be intermittent and periodical; the periods between the different stages of advancement being employed in *reviewing*. If so, this, most assuredly, is one of the reviewing ages. Still, we frankly acknowledge we cannot suppress the fear, that, like a lazy heir, we have received our patrimony, and are set down to admire over and over again; to count and re-count, to view and re-view the golden inheritance; or, what is still more ridiculous, that we are endeavoring to increase its value by battering out the coin, or by mixing it with some base alloy. There is another view of this branch of our subject. That power, or mode, by which the works of Nature excite emotions of terror, beauty, sublimity, has often been termed "the Language of Nature"—a language un-written, addressed not to the natural or to the vulgar ear, but speaking eloquently to the inner perception of the sensitive and gifted mind. This language Nature hath ever spoken. In the dawn of the Creation it swelled forth in one full concert of harmony, when "the morning stars sang together."

Nature hath not existed these six thousand years, uttering this language from all her varied works, without exciting some response. Inspired bards have responded in every age. They have responded in the passionate gushings of overflowing hearts. They have responded with joy and with tears. Nature hath listened, as it were, and learned another language. It is the Language of Association. And many a wild note, many a tuneful strain, many a snatch of deathless song hath she treasured up in her memory.

Go forth, ye who, in like manner, have learned this language; go forth, with silent and thoughtful hearts, into the green fields, or upon the gray old mountain—she shall speak with you there. In the autumn, when the forest hath put on its many-colored vesture, and a dreamy haze hath gathered on all the gloomy hills, and the bird is caroling his plaintive farewell to his native vales—then shall she whisper to you in touching language,

"The melancholy days are come,
The saddest of the year."

ne shall address you in each returning season. She shall speak to ou, from every tree, and flower, and murmuring stream. Universal ature shall commune with you, and shall be an Instructor, a Compan-n, a Friend.

Again; this communion, of which we are speaking, invigorates and larges the intellect. This must be so from the Laws of Mind. Iind is susceptible of indefinite expansion. Action is the means of is expansion. And action, in its most efficient mode, does the mind perience, in communion with the highest orders of intellect. Who, at has set down to peruse the works of a Milton, or of a Dante, and iven himself up to the full influence of their mighty creations, has not risen, feeling within him the consciousness of being himself a greater nd a better man than before?

This communion, also, inspires enthusiasm in literary pursuits. It the Parent of a noble ambition. It is the Genius of lofty aims. It nparts acuteness to the perception of ideal beauty. Thus, it discov-rs to the mental eye a new world—a world of thought—radiant with right imaginings, instinct with the forms of lofty conceptions; a world here bubble perennial fountains of pleasure, and where the breezes re laden with odors more fragrant than the breath of Araby;—a orld which shall survive when these visible heavens shall have been olled together as a scroll, and this earth shall have passed away,—a orld whose existence is co-eternal with the mind—whose realities hall never fade—whose joys shall have no end.

A DREAM.

LAID me down on a bank one day;
was worn and weary and tired of play;
'Twas in a thicket of hazel deep,
Where Fairies might their revels keep.
A jessamine vine was clambering there,
And many a flower perfumed the air;
The breeze, with my locks it carelessly
played,
And then flew on through the forest shade.
On its viewless wings, so light and free
The breath of the flowers it seem'd to be.
The music of birds was sounding there,
But ere their notes half died on the air,
They mingled their strain with the voice of
the rill,
That prattled and danced and leapt down
the hill,
And dash'd on its banks its foam and its
spray,
As its life were an endless holyday.

I lay and slept on a bank so green,
It seemed a couch for a Fairy queen:
But as I slept, a maiden came,
A fairer form I cannot name:
Her locks were dark as the raven's breast,
Her eye as bright as a silvery star
That catches a tint from the fading west,
And shines alone in the blue afar.
Her step so light—'twas made to tread
But only on the rose's bed;
Her breast a veil but half revealed,
Which more enhanced what it concealed:
Her tresses to the breeze she flung,
That am'rous played her locks among.

All sounds were hush'd—the winds were
mute,
She placed her hands upon the lute,
And woke a strain as soft and sweet,
As that which might an angel greet,

When from some embassy of love,
He mounts to Paradise above.

She ceased—from many a feather'd throat
A voice of praise came swelling
Like the music strains that float
Round Peris' coral dwelling.
The woods in vain attempt essay'd
Those tones to hold in their forest glade;
Soon they fled on the breeze's wing,
Like the heart's fond imagining,
And left no more of trace behind,
Than did the fleeting summer wind.
I woke—ah! was it but a dream,
A fond delusion sent,
Like the spray upon the stream,
In its creation spent?

Ah! yet methinks at times I hear
Those magic tones so soft and clear,
Entrancing with a strange delight
The senses, till the soul takes flight,
And wings its way obedient to that power
That dwelt upon the lute in that sweet hour.

W. C.

RAMBLES IN SWITZERLAND.

Lucerne, situated at the head of a bay of the same name, in the lake of the Four Cantons, is a town of much note in Swiss history. It still retains some political importance, in consequence of being, with Berne and Zurich, a city in which the Diet of Switzerland holds its alternate sittings. It is also the residence of the papal nuncio. Within the walls of this city, which was one of the first to assert the independence of Switzerland in opposition to the formidable power of the Empire, are contained, at present, a population of as devoted adherents to Roman Catholicism, as any which the "Apostolic Church" can boast. There are 7500 inhabitants, of whom all but 180 are Catholics. The inhabitants are a lazy population, frequenting the churches in business hours, bearing their votive offerings which go to the support of an indolent priesthood. Its architecture is of feudal origin. On the side of the land, it is protected by a wall of strong but rude workmanship, containing seven towers, each of which is unlike the others in size and shape. Each of them seems to have been built at a different period from the others, and without any idea of symmetry. Several of these are surmounted by observatories. One sees here, as in every Swiss town of note, fountains decorating the streets, surmounted by some piece of statuary representing, most commonly, a warrior in the dress of the middle ages. From the balcony of the Hotel des Ballances we overlooked the River Reuse, which, flowing in a rapid current from the lake, passes through a portion of the town, on its way to unite with the Rhine.

Just without the walls of the city, in the grounds of Col. Phyffer, I visited a monument erected to the memory of the Swiss guards who died in defending the Bourbons, at Paris, in the revolutionary struggle of August 10th, 1792. A large niche is cut in the perpendicular face of a gray limestone rock, in which is carved in full, a lion, which, having received his mortal wound, and in the act of dying, holds his paw upon a shield, on which is carved the *fleur de lis* of the Bourbons. The shaft of the dart that inflicted the fatal wound, is seen projecting from his side. The guards numbered one hundred and fifty, and were nearly all natives of Lucerne. Like true Swiss, they remained constant to the last, and met, as heroes, the fate in which they were involved by their fidelity to Louis XVI. The lion measures twenty-eight feet in length and eighteen in height. Beneath it are the names of those, fifty-five in number, who fell on that occasion. The person who conducted us about the grounds was one of the guard, who had returned to his country. Habited in the dress of the old Swiss guard, he now passes his life in attendance upon the monument, reciting to visitors the particulars of that tragic event, which this monument is designed to commemorate.

The Cathedral of Lucerne is a building which has no pretensions to architectural merit. The altar is decorated with a profusion of tinsel, befitting rather a shrine dedicated by savages to their deity, than that of a Christian temple.

The *arsenal* of Lucerne is a repository of many interesting historical relics, besides the arms destined for the supply of the quota of troops furnished by the Canton for the service of the diet. There is the sword of William Tell, a huge weapon, with devices on the handle representing the leading incidents of his life. Near the entrance, spread in full view, is an immense Turkish naval flag, captured in the battle of Lepanto, and brought to Lucerne by a knight of Malta, a native of Lucerne, who was present in that battle. Over the door of one of the rooms, hangs a portrait of Leopold, Duke of Austria, who fell in the famous battle of Sempach, in which fifteen hundred Swiss defeated several thousand Austrians, well armed and protected by coats of mail. Leopold's troops were all cavalry; but as he approached to attack the force of the confederation, he learned that his enemies were all infantry and badly armed. Anticipating an easy victory, he ordered his men to dismount, and met the Swiss force on the field of Sempach, where the devoted courage of Arnold Winkelried enabled his countrymen to win the day. Leopold was found amidst heaps of the slain. His body was stripped of the coat of mail, which, with his armor, hangs in this arsenal. The coat of mail is formed of a great number of steel rings linked together in a manner to afford protection to the person against swords and spears. Among the trophies of victory, were an iron cravat destined for the neck of Gundoldingen, the commander of the troops of Lucerne, and a great number of Austrian flags, coats of mail, and spears. The shafts of the latter are of enormous length. I noticed also, a number of Swiss battle-axes and crossbows that were used in the battle of Mongarten. The stocks of the latter were about the length of those of our rifles. The bows were constructed of a number of steel bands, so disposed that the greatest strength should fall about the centre. These bows are so strong that they could not be bent except by a machine which the bowman carried with him. We also saw a number of Turkish muskets, captured in the battle of Tunis, which are very elegantly wrought weapons.

Early on the morning of September 23d, I took my place on board of the steamer, for the purpose of visiting Altorf, the capital of the Canton Uri; a place rendered interesting by being associated with the memory of William Tell. The lake, which is twenty-five and a half miles long, washes the territories of four Cantons, Uri, Unterwalden, Schwytz, and Lucerne. On which account, it is called the "Lake of the four Cantons." It is not exceeded in interest by any lake in Switzerland, whether we regard its historical associations or the beauty and sublimity of the scenery by which it is surrounded. From Lucerne, the river extends down the lake, on the left, as far as the base of the *Righi*, a mountain celebrated for the extended panoramic view afforded from its summit. On the right, the view from Lucerne extends to the bay of Alpnach, which is half concealed by the base of *Mt. Pilatus;* a mountain of about the same height as the Righi, whose bold precipitous front overhangs the lake. Tradition attributes its name to the fact that Pontius Pilate, stung with remorse for his participation in the murder of our Saviour, sought retirement from the world in these mountain solitudes, and put an end to his life by precipitating himself from the summit of this mountain into the waters below.

The usual assemblage of French, Germans, and English thronged the steamer, as we left the dock at Lucerne. An individual of a romantic temperament might have experienced annoyance from an unexpected source. Two scows, laden with cattle destined for the markets of Italy, had attached themselves by long cables to the stern of the steamer, and were towed down the lake. The lowing of herds, pent up in such narrow accommodations, was not sufficiently "rural" (to quote a favorite expression with the English,) to harmonize with an exquisite perception of the sublime and beautiful. The day was uncommonly fair; but Pilatus warned us that it was not to continue so till its close; for there was no cloud upon its summit, the absence of which is regarded at Lucerne as an unfailing prognostic of bad weather.

A large square tower stands in the bay of Kussnacht, which formerly belonged to the Counts of Hapsburg. At the head of this bay are yet to be seen the ruins of Gessler's Castle. The town of *Gersau* is picturesquely seated near the water, almost overshadowed by the enormous mass of the Righi. This place, with thirteen hundred and forty-eight inhabitants, maintained the rank of an independent republic, from the year 1390 to 1798, when the grasping policy of the French could not spare even poor neglected Gersau. Soon after passing Gersau, we came in sight of *Schwytz*. This town, now neglected and desolate-looking, originally gave the name to the whole confederation of Switzerland. It is now the residence of Shepherds and cowherds, and is secluded by barriers of mountains, impassable except to the wild mountaineer. But its name will live associated with the first dawnings of Swiss freedom. The battle of Mongarten was fought in its vicinity, in the year 1315, immediately after which event, the first alliance between the three confederates of Uri, Schwytz, and Unterwald enwas formed in Schwytz. The scene which opens before one entering the bay of Uri, is one of unequalled magnificence. At its entrance, an enormous rock is seen standing out of the water, like an obelisk, to the height of thirty or forty feet. Its mountains are grouped together in a manner to present the contrast of bleak and desolate masses of rock with hills and level spots crowned with verdure. A little green platform, at the elevation of several hundred feet on the side of the mountain, is pointed out as *Grutli*, the rendezvous of three conspirators, in the year 1307. A cottage stands at present, over three springs of water that are said to have issued spontaneously, marking the places where the three confederates stood during that conference. But the most interesting object on the banks of the bay of Uri is *Tell's Chapel*. This little edifice stands on a narrow ledge of rock, near the surface of the water, at the base of the overhanging mountain. Tradition says that upon this spot, Tell leaped from the boat in which Gessler was carrying him prisoner to his castle, near Kussnacht. Gessler, alarmed by the sudden rise of a storm upon the lake, was obliged to trust the piloting of his boat to his prisoner. Tell, by adroit management, brought the boat to land, leaped from the boat to the rocks, and made his escape up the steep ascent of the mountain. We had now arrived at *Fluellen*, a village at the extreme end of the lake. Here I left the steamer and took passage in an omnibus for *Altorf*, distant two miles.

Altorf, associated in our minds with the first dawnings of Swiss freedom, the home of William Tell, and the place where oppression first drove to revolt, is the capital of the Canton Uri, one of the poorest of all the Swiss Cantons. The whole Canton contains only thirteen thousand inhabitants. The town is a desolate lifeless-looking place of sixteen hundred inhabitants. At the inn, I found only one guest, a young gentleman of Milan, who was awaiting the *poste*. We soon made acquaintance, with travelers' freedom; an acquaintance particularly gratifying to myself, as he could answer as interpreter in the rambles I was proposing to make in the afternoon. To him, it seemed a matter of little interest that Altorf was the scene of Tell's adventures, while I was eager to examine every stone that might contain any reminiscence of him.

Before proceeding further, it may be necessary to revert, for a moment, to some of the leading characters of that period. William Tell, a name associated with that of Washington, among the friends of liberty, was born in a little village near Altorf, a short time previous to the commencement of the fourteenth century. He was of the humblest origin, and received no education, except such as was afforded to the poor peasants of that period. His ideas of liberty were innate, not acquired from the illustrious examples of the past. His country was a humble province of the German Empire, and was ruled by despotic rigor by the minions of the emperor. The unequalled feat of archery by which he evinced the nerve he possessed, in the presence of the heartless tyrant, who would have made a father the murderer of his child, his bold conspiracy and its successful execution, the assassination of the tyrant in the presence of his followers, and, in fine, his disinterested aims in these achievements, have endeared his memory to his countrymen; and have placed the name of a humble peasant of Altorf among those of the benefactors of mankind. His death did no dishonor to his life; for he was drowned in the year 1350, in the attempt to rescue a poor girl who had fallen into the stream near Altorf. Con[illegible] plating the zeal manifested by Tell in favor of libert[illegible] to inquire, had he lived two centuries later, in the days of Luther and Zwingle, would he not have embraced the doctrines of the reformation, and hastened to liberate his country from the thralldom of Rome? As it is, the patriot must lament that *one* Tell was not enough for Switzerland. The memory of Arnold Winkelried, of Unterwalden, is cherished with much respect. To his heroic self-devotion, his country owes one of the most brilliant victories that grace its annals—that of Sempach in 1336.

Early in the afternoon, I set out on a cruise with my Milanese friend. The language of the Canton Uri is a miserable patois German, which my friend found as much difficulty in comprehending, as a Londoner would in that of some parts of Yorkshire. We readily found the public square, an open space by the side of the road, in which are standing, at the distance of a hundred yards from each other, two stone fountains, marking the spots on which the archer and his son stood, when the apple was shot from the head of the latter. This distance will not be incredible when we consider the prodigious power of the crossbows in use in the middle ages. A prominent object is a square stuccoed tower, about eighty feet high, which the records of the Canton Uri show to have been erected before the time of Tell. It is covered with gay frescoes, (a method of recording much in vogue at that period,) representing various scenes in which Tell was the hero. We found, on inquiry of several of the peasantry, that tradition has yet preserved in their minds the remembrance of these events. The present inhabitants of Altorf are a degenerate race; but the historical associations of the town, and the magnificent scenery with which nature has invested it, render it a place of no ordinary interest.

Our next walk was to Fluellen to hire a boat, for the purpose of visiting Tell's Chapel, which I had beheld from the deck of the steamer. We procured the services of two men to row us thither.

Tell's Chapel is a small edifice, about fifteen or twenty feet square, thrown open in front by an arcade. Its walls are thick and stuccoed on the outside. It is surmounted by a little cupola. In back stands an altar, on which, mass is performed once a year. Gay frescoes cover the walls. This Chapel is said to have been erected in the year 1388, about thirty years after the death of Tell, in the presence of one hundred and fourteen of his countrymen, who had known him personally, as the records of the Canton show. I attempted to ascend the hill, up which Tell must have run from his pursuers; but, although a path is now made, I succeeded with difficulty, encountering, meanwhile, the risk of falling backwards.

On the following morning, I visited a little chapel, said to have been built on the site of Tell's house. It stands on an eminence overlooking Altorf and the valley. It dates back to A. D. 1522.

At twelve o'clock, I took the steamer at Fluellen, meeting my *compagnon du voyage*, Dr. H., on board, and planned with him an excursion to visit the Righi. The passengers consisted almost entirely of English and Americans, an unusual assemblage. My own language sounded finer than ever, after having listened for so long a time to French and

German patois. At the request of some of the company, a table was spread under an awning on deck, and we sat down to dine amid scenes that might inspire the highest enthusiasm in the lover of nature.

Our party to the Righi, consisting of Dr. H., a Prussian student, an English gentleman, and myself, landed at Weggis, and commenced the ascent immediately. About midway, we came to the chapel of the "Holy Cross." Further on, the path passes under a singular natural arch formed by an enormous mass of pudding stone resting in the manner of a key-stone between two other masses. Indeed, the whole mass of this mountain is of conglomerate rock; and consequently slides of large masses are not uncommon. In 1795, a slide upon the village of Weggis destroyed a large part of the village, and covered a number of acres of land with a deposition of stones. But as these accidents are common about the mountain, so the nature of the rocks and the friction they encounter mercifully prevent them from being instantaneous. In 1795 the sliding masses advanced slowly, like a current of lava, taking about a fortnight to reach the lake. On the flank of the mountain is a precipitous ledge of rock, which descends from right to left until it buries itself beneath the waters of the lake. We reached the summit at six, but were unable to catch a view of the sunset, as the western horizon was obscured by clouds. To secure this is a great object with travelers, in their mountain ascents. I had been so fortunate as to gain a fine view of sunset from the top of Faulhorn, a loftier ascent than the Righi.* I shall never forget that magnificent spectacle. On the one hand lay nearly the whole of the plain part of Switzerland; and one could take in at a panoramic view, the sizes and shapes of most of the principal lakes, the courses of rivers, and the natural boundaries of the different Cantons. I had watched from thence the lengthened shadows on the plains and lakes, until it was evident that to those living below, the sun must be set, as soon after it was to us; while, for some minutes longer, his beams were reflected brightly from the snow white masses of the Oberland mountains.† These enormous mountains bound the southeastern horizon, as seen from Faulhorn, and oppose the aspect of mountain grandeur and eternal snows to the verdure which is seen to prevail in lower Switzerland.

But to return to the Righi. Disappointed in the evening view, we sought the repose of the inn, where we found a company of thirty or forty assembled. Our guide had selected for Dr. H. and myself, a corner room, with one window looking out upon the eastern sky, for the purpose of viewing the rising sun, if the morning should prove clear, and another looking out upon the mountains of the Oberland chain.

In the evening, the guides assembled in a room adjoining the *salle-a-manger* (dining room) and sung, in concert with the girls of the inn,

* Faulhorn is 8140 feet high; the Righi, 5700.

† The Oberland mountains, or Bernese Alps, as they are frequently called, are the loftiest range of mountains in Switzerland; varying in height from ten to fourteen thousand feet. The names of the loftiest peaks are, Blumlis Alp, Jungfrau, (the Virgin,) Monch, Eigher, (the Giant,) Finster Aarhorn, Shreckhorn, (Peak of Terror,) Wetterhorn, and Wellhorn.

some of their mountain airs. Comic songs and love ditties were also in vogue, and interested Dr. H., who was familiar with the patois German.

On the following morning, we were summoned at an early hour, at the sound of the "Alpine horn," to see the sun rise. All the guests were soon assembled on the brow of the mountain, clad in cloaks and overcoats. The horizon was clear, though not far above it, a heavy bank of clouds was discernible. These were tinged with the most brilliant hues. The gradual illumination of mountains and valleys is a magnificent spectacle. First, the snowy tops of the Oberland Alps are reflecting the rays of the sun, while to our view the sun is not yet risen. And when he is visible to us, rising above the horizon, the surfaces of lakes and rivers are yet dark. The numberless small peaks visible from the Righi, are lighted up in succession. Finally, the masses of vapor begin to roll off from the lakes and valleys, as these feel the influence of his beams. The Righi is a kind of centre between the plain and mountainous part of Switzerland. The panorama of mountains is very extensive, embracing in the centre of the picture the Oberland Alps, and an infinite number of inferior mountains, varying in size from the white peaks of Glarnish and Mitres, to the smaller peaks of the bay of Uri and of the lake of Lucerne. The broad expanse of the latter is seen bathing the base of the Righi. Eleven other lakes are discernible; mostly small, however, except those of Zug and Zurich. The lake of Sempach is renowned for the victory won on its banks, and for the heroic death of Arnold Winkelried. Numerous cities and villages to the north and west, give the aspect of a country rich and populous. Among these are Lucerne, Arth, Zug, and Zurich. The latter, however, is scarcely visible, being fifty miles distant.

Near the Righi rises the *Rossberg*, whose side yet exhibits traces of a frightful catastrophe which occured in the year 1806. On its southern flank, the line of desolation left by a mountain slide is to be seen, leading down to a small lake in an elevated plain between a number of mountains. A small church and a house, both surrounded by heaps of rocks, are the only remains of a village that stood on the banks of the lake. The catastrophe, unlike mountain slides in general, was instantaneous. Four hundred and fifty-nine of the inhabitants of that village were destroyed. Of a party of eleven young men from Berne, seven, who were little way removed from their comrades, were overwhelmed, while the latter had time to escape, warned by the sudden oozing and pouring of water from crevices, the reeling of pine trees, and the breaking up of rocks. The effects were like those caused by a volcanic eruption.

"Mountains have fallen,
Leaving a gap in the clouds, and with the shock
Rocking their Alpine brethren; filling up
The ripe queen valleys with destruction's splinters,
Damming the rivers with a sudden dash,
Which crush'd the waters into mist, and made
Their fountains find another channel—thus,
Thus, in its old age, did Mount Rosenburg." MANFRED.

The whole mass that descended is estimated to have been a league long, a thousand feet broad, and a hundred feet thick. The Rossberg is composed of numerous strata of pudding stone rock, the seams between which descend in parallel lines, by a regular slope, towards the hollow between the mountains. These seams are so large as to be very perceptible from the side. At the time of the catastrophe, they are supposed to have been filled with water, in consequence of violent rains, by which intervening layers of earth were dissolved, and the adhesion of the outer stratum to that next under it was removed.

We commenced the descent from the Righi, at about ten o'clock A. M., purposing to walk to Lucerne by way of *Kussnacht*. This town has given its name to a bay or arm of the lake, at the head of which it is situated. Our course conducted us along a road leading inland from the town, between banks covered with a luxuriant vegetation. At about a mile from Kussnacht a spot is pointed out as the scene of the assassination of Gessler by Tell. After the latter had escaped from the boat on the lake, he had provided himself with a crossbow, and made his way over the mountains, a distance of about twenty miles, to this spot. He knew that Gessler would pass this place on his way to his castle near Kussnacht. He was not disappointed. Gessler, having lost his prisoner, rowed up the bay of Kussnacht, and was riding attended by his suite, when he was struck by an arrow from a crossbow. Mortally wounded, he exclaimed that it must have been Tell that shot the arrow. In commemoration of the deed, a small chapel was erected, which is yet standing. It is not unlike the one upon the side of the lake, and similar devices are frescoed upon the walls. Our guide remarked that this was "une place bien choisie" for the commission of such a deed. We arrived at Lucerne, well fatigued with our walk, and sought the repose of the Hotel des Ballances. J. H.

STANZAS.

Thine was the spirit of the dove—thou hast
Her heavenward pinion now ;—and cleaving far
The dark clouds which had wrapped thee, thou hast gone
Into thy native atmosphere of light,
Without a taint of earth upon thy wing.

As one, who from a dark and toilsome way
Emerges into light, and sees above,
The bright blue sky, and feels the balmy air
Inviting and assuring,—so hast thou,
Fair spirit, passed the narrow ordeal through,—
Surmounted all the rocks, o'ercome the heights,
And through the twining thickets that kept back,
Hast gone in triumph to another land.

The prize is thine. Thine eye beholds
The blessed path before thee. The blue sky,
Drawn wide, like some rich curtain that concealed
A richer object, opens,—and within,
Joint heirs of grace with thee, myriads of forms
All lustrous in their white, beckon thee on
To thy blest home and high inheritance. T.

EDITORS' TABLE.

This number of our Magazine makes its appearance later in the month than usual, but the great amount of interesting and attractive matter which it contains,—pardon our vanity, reader,—will, we think, make ample amends for the delay. We thank our correspondents for their generous attention to our wants, and would assure them, that if we have been unable fully to appreciate the merits of their productions, the fault lies rather in our judgment than will. An editor's life is surely one of considerable toil and drudgery, yet still he has moments of pleasure. An agreeable thought does now and then find its way into his mind, like a sunny ray struggling through the clouds of winter. O, how we have cachinnated and guffawed over some of these productions before us! Here, for instance, is a precious little scrap, a dingy, suspicious-looking half-sheet, crowded full of brilliant effusions, to which the following note is appended: "If the editors find any of the verses worth any thing, they are at their disposal. . . If they can publish them, either wholly or partly, all the verses or a few of them doctored up, they would very much gratify XIX."

We would inform our correspondent that we are not very much skilled in doctoring up verses, and would rather decline his proposal. We will, however, publish one or two verses, and let a discerning public judge of their merits, and doctor them up to suit their own taste. We select the lines "On the Death of Miss L." They are as follows, if we decipher the execrable chirography correctly:

And art thou gone? *O say not yes!*
But pity, O pity me,
And I thy name will ever bless.
Ever, sweet girl, think of thee.

Yes, thou art dead! O what a word
For me to say—*that* one, *dead*.
It makes me chill, curdles my blood;
Back bursts my throbbing head.

Poor fellow! He is in a bad way, certainly. We wish we could offer him some relief; but we must do our duty, painful though it is, and inform him, that his other articles, viz. "Prayer," "To the Moon," "Stanzas," &c., are decidedly rejected. We would also inform him, that if he will call at our room, we will give him a clean sheet of paper, a cake of soap, and perhaps a gratuitous lecture on the advantages of frequent ablutions. . . . . The lines "On the Death of my Pig," are, we think, a little superior to those quoted above. Indeed, we think they contain some real poetry, for we found the tears in our eyes several times while reading them. We have room for only one stanza, and would segregate the following:

O Piggy dear! thy limbs are stiff and cold;
Thou'rt free from mortal pain;
That tail, that once was rolled in many a fold,
Will never curl again;
For ah! the spoiler came and cut thy throat,
And when he saw thy life-blood flow,
He grinned—the miserable goat—
To see it go,
My Piggy!

He who can read these lines unmoved, must have the heart of a savage.

PROSPECTUS

OF THE

NINTH VOLUME

OF THE

YALE LITERARY MAGA[illegible]

[illegible]

[illegible]

THE

YALE LITERARY MAGAZINE.

Vol. IX. MARCH, 1844. No. 5.

THE REPUBLIC OF LETTERS.

It was a beautiful conception of classic mythology, which represented the shades of the poets and philosophers, as meeting together after death, in the happy retreats of the Elysian fields. Removed from the influence of the frailties and animosities to which they had been subject, during their mortal career, yet retaining all their individual traits and recollections, they were united in the calm enjoyment of innocent and exalted pleasures, and employed forever in their favorite themes of contemplation.

From the fortunate period when, by the invention of that "art of arts," the fleeting thoughts of the human intellect were stamped on a material substance, may be dated the beginning of a race, who, if their physical frames were destined soon to moulder into the dust, were yet endowed with powers and sympathies which never would cease to be active among mankind. Not in the realms of the shades, but in the cheerful light of this upper world, do we see clothed in forms of our own life the ideal of the Grecian fable. In the quiet study of the philosopher, in the libraries of the schools, in associations formed for the cultivation of good letters, in all the intercourse of mind with the master minds of the living and the dead, do we see this realization. We ourselves even may be permitted to enjoy the companionship of their immortal thoughts.

It is for the purpose of becoming familiar with the intellectual treasures of past times, and of making contributions of their own, that the scholars of every successive age are associated together, not always indeed by written pledges or constitutions, but by the more enduring bonds of kindred feelings, aims, and honors.

There is in the very nature of a principle of union, which traverses so wide a field and binds together so many hearts, that which speaks of the dignity of learning, and declares its high functions. It recognizes the obligations of its living patrons to all their predecessors, while it immortalizes the sympathies as well as the works of the dead; for it may be said, without extravagance, that wherein the living race of authors are indebted to their predecessors for some of the greatest productions of human genius, the ancients, in turn, are repaid by the veneration of the moderns, while both alike await the approving judgment of the future. Posthumous reputation indeed does not often concern him who rejoices only in the smile of present popular favor. Such are generally careless of future renown, whatever may be their professions, and for the same reason will they speak with contempt of the past. But he who truly prizes the liberal arts, will have a most anxious regard to the unbiassed judgment of the distant future; and at the same time he will reverence the Wisdom of History; for he cherishes that which the voice of true *humanity* approves alike in every age; and he knows that in the immortality of the good, the true, and the beautiful, in morals, art, and sentiment, his own fame will be secure. Such was the ambition, and such the confidence of Milton, when in early life he wrote to his Florentine friend,—"Hear me, my Deodati, and suffer me for a moment to speak without blushing in a more lofty strain. Do you ask what I am meditating? By the help of Heaven an immortality of fame."*

It is common to speak of the class devoted to the cultivation of letters, as a profession, and this may be sufficient in a popular sense to mark their general character and pursuits. And yet it is different in many respects from the ordinary professions. The latter are called into being by the necessary laws of the social condition. They have specific ends—they afford constant service—they look for present remuneration. In their distinctive character, their destiny is accomplished, when their specific duties are performed. But the literary profession, though coincident with others in their methods of promoting human happiness, has a higher nature, and ends of greater consequence to gain. It serves mankind by controlling them. Its proper domain is the empire of feeling and intellect. The habits of the literary men of our own country have given rise to a mistaken apprehension in the popular mind, as to the true character of their profession. Few find leisure to devote exclusive attention to literature; hence, many of our best writers engage in pursuits relating to their private affairs, or those passing events which are of no moment to the cause of letters. Thus do they fail to fulfill their proper mission.

Such a case our own poet furnishes, whose voice, after a long interval, has been recently heard once more. How brilliant the morning of his literary life! The recollections of it are still the pride of his native land, which was then, as now, the theme of his rich patriotic lyrics. Would that the dark days of "Genius Slumbering" had not intervened, when we saw him employed, with vision downcast to the earth, in search of fossils and strata. Nothing but the strains in which he wrote his own sentence of condemnation, and gave promise of a bright awaking, can pardon the silence of those years, when

* Familiar Epistles, No. 7.

"He slept, forgetful of his once bright fame;
He had no feeling of the glory gone;
He had no eye to catch the mounting flame,
That once in transport drew his spirit on."

How changed and cheerful the aspect again, as we now see him in the exercise of his high vocation!

We can properly estimate the functions, as well as the relative importance of the literary profession, when we glance at the wide field it traverses. Literature embraces Poetry and the Drama, Romance and History; the last department comprehending, in its full scope, the category of Dr. Channing, "whatever relates to human nature and human life." Its influence is commensurate with the range of its subjects. Literature, therefore, must take rank with forms of civil and religious polity, as a means of human happiness. Though a distinct element in enlightened civilization, it is often coalescent with the power of the State, and it has been called the Handmaid of Religion. But yet it has a sphere of action entirely its own. Its peculiar power has been often and conspicuously seen, in the operation of the LAW OF PROGRESS, which so strongly marks the civilization of modern times. Literary men acting in their own capacity, however much they may be tinged with the prejudices of antiquity, or at times with the spirit of partizanship, do precede the rest of the world in their onward march. This is their appointed destiny.

In a comparative view of the relative influence and offices of Literature and Religion, we would not be understood to give undue importance to the former. We refer not at all to the individual relations of mankind, under the latter, to the immortal kingdom of God. We speak of each, only as elements of the social constitution; and while we give to Religion the highest place of power, which in ordinary periods is always efficient and vitally conservative, it is also due to the cause of Letters to say, there have been crises in the history of civilization, when Literature performed more than the part of a Handmaid to Religion; when the purity and the power of the latter over the hearts of men, seemed for a time to depend on the predominant influence of the former. "Martin Luther," says Lord Bacon, in his Advancement of Learning, "conducted no doubt by a higher Providence, but in *discourse of reason*, finding what a province he had undertaken against the Bishop of Rome, and finding his own solitude also, was enforced to awake all antiquity, and to call former times to his aid, to make a party against the present time." If we should here be told that literature, instead of being the patron of Religion, has often been arrayed against it; that some even of the brightest names in Letters have been counted as enemies of the Christian Faith, we admit it; and, also affirm, that in their unholy warfare not one of their unfading laurels have been won.

With the field of literary investigation so widely opened before us, we shall not be surprised at meeting with bold features in the profession of Letters. In the stormy periods of revolution, and the conflict of great nations, as well as in the operation of more silent causes, which have nevertheless left in their courses deep imprints upon the character and destiny of succeeding generations, we should expect to see the man of Letters, no less than the prophet or the conqueror, perform the part of a hero. "Show me," says an elegant European writer, "what one or two great men, in the solitude of their chambers, are thinking of, in this age, and I will show you what will be the theme of the orator, the vision of the poet, the staple of the hustings, the declamation of the press, and the guide of the statesman in the next."

We would not be considered, by extending thus far the province of Literature, as invading the proper limits of the statesman, or of either of the so-called learned professions. We are aware of the distinction which ever should be made in the respective offices of each. It belongs to the Literary profession to explore, to defend, to perpetuate; while it is the duty of the latter to explain, to communicate, to apply to proper ends: and the distinction is as real and as wide as the essential difference between the word *instruction* and the word *education*, though they may be confused and considered as synonymous in the common apprehension.

This distinction is, moreover, a proper criterion in determining the credentials of those who are justly considered as belonging to the commonwealth of Letters. To discriminate between the power of acquisition and the power of invention, between the man of mere learning and the man of enthusiastic, passionate fondness for the higher departments of literary composition, is not invidious or unjust.

The object of many, the great majority even of persons of liberal education and of the most excellent attainments, is not directly the cultivation of literature, farther than as they award to it their general favor, and perhaps become the repositories of its most valuable treasures. They have other and important objects to secure, which lie in other fields of enterprise and ambition. Few comparatively among the great numbers who crowd the European universities, whether in an academical or professional garb, resort to those seats of learning to make contributions, but *all* to receive the benefits of instruction; few to extend the limits of human knowledge, but all to achieve, as they are able, conquests many times won by their predecessors: and the honors thus acquired in comprehending what is already known, do of right lead those who have won them, to stations of the most responsible service to the world.

But he who would aspire to literary eminence, must bring to the light the results of his own deep researches. The bright ideal must be clothed in forms of fit expression, and addressed to the universal heart of man. The productions of such minds constitute a literature, which controls while it delights mankind. It will receive the only meed of true renown—the admiration of the distant future.

The idea of a REPUBLIC, so long applied to the whole body of literary men, happily expresses those elements of power and social influence, which we have represented as belonging to the profession of letters. It seems to refer to the existence of some general restrictions or laws, which, though not expressed in written codes, and sanctioned in form by the learned universally, are yet always recognized in all associations formed for the cultivation of letters. It refers also to the existence of a common freedom and immunities, of common sympathies and pursuits.

Liberty is an essential condition to the full enjoyment of every other advantage; and liberty in the commonwealth of the learned is absolute, whatever may be the social condition or political complexion of the country, which happens to be the home of the scholar. In former times literature sometimes was said to be in bondage to patronage; but she will never more sit at the feet of princes, or wait for favor upon the smiles of the great and noble born. The human mind, when once free, cannot be again subdued by any force external to itself; and it will not long be oppressed by its own delusions, if truth be not hid from the understanding.

A republic implies a *community of priviliges.* The same hearty welcome is given to all who prove themselves worthy of admission to the brotherhood of scholars. The same facilities are provided for every aspirant in the career of a noble ambition. An entire equality exists, but it is one which has just as little to do with the pretensions of a "titled nobility," as it has with all doctrines and imposing declarations, announcing the non-existence of "nature's nobility." It is nevertheless recognized by all the learned, in the respect which is voluntarily and cheerfully paid to superior excellence, wherever it is found. In the republic of letters, the garret of Goldsmith is an audience chamber fit for a chancellor. The bard of Avon claims and receives homage in the courts of princes. Johnson legislates for nations while famishing for bread, and though his person be unknown and lost in a London crowd, he rules a wider empire than the monarch of the British Islands. And sometimes he will signally exercise his prerogative. He enters the palace of a noble lord, descended from one of the proudest and most ancient families of the realm. He solicits patronage, and is coldly dismissed, with a refusal, by the man whom the world of fashion adored as the paragon of politeness. He is left without aid to complete his work alone, and then does the scholar in turn reject the solicitation of the same proud peer, who is now inclined to be satisfied, if he may but occupy a niche in the portico of the temple Johnson had constructed. Chesterfield was vain enough to desire that his name might be identified with the reputation of one he had treated with contumely; and he obtained what he sought in such a rebuke, as, for severity and point, finds no parallel in English literature. Johnson only could have written it.

Nor is the intellectual superiority, wherein one star differeth from another, inconsistent with fair opportunities for literary eminence. It is not true, after all that has been said of the havoc of criticism, and the tyranny of master spirits, and the "crushing of genius in the bud," that injustice is ordinarily done to works of real merit. The productions of authors are generally appreciated according to their worth, and there is no better criterion than the judgment of those, for whose benefit or pleasure they are written. He who writes for the present, receives his reward in the present. He who writes for mankind, will sooner or later be read by all. His works cannot perish, not even by the ordeal of fire. But the cry of injury and complaint comes, for the most part, from

> "Infantumque animæ flentes, in limine primo;
> Quos dulcis vitæ exortes, et ab ubere raptos,
> Abstulit atra dies, et funere mersit acerbo."

Why should they be anxious for the future, when every thing designed to make an impression succeeds according to the "getting up?" The common lot should be met with becoming fortitude.

We would not be understood as defending the modern system of periodical criticism, which having become a regular trade, has adopted its rules as conducive rather to the convenience of the craft, than to the improvement of literature. A mere glance at the reviews shows the sad prevalence in our times of what Lord Bacon quaintly called "the three literary distempers. First, Fantastical Learning; second, Contentious Learning; and the last, Delicate Learning."

A third characteristic of a republic consists in the *mutual dependence and sympathy* of the members of the literary profession—a dependence which relates to common pursuits and common rewards—a sympathy which springs from high endeavors and belongs to the best and most refined sensibilities of our nature. It forms the basis of friendships which are pure without passion, sincere, permanent, and true.

We do not deny that the interests of individuals do sometimes clash, and that personal animosities often rage with an intensity proportioned to the mental endowments of the parties, in whose bosoms they burn. But they cannot become general. Strife is engendered in the heat of ambition, but how far removed is it, from all resemblance to the rivalry of conflicting interests in the common affairs of life! How utterly dissonant in the ends it seeks from the ambition we so often see in the camp and in the cabinet! The history of empires is but little else than the record of human sorrow; but, "in the history of letters," says Gibbon, "is written the glory and happiness of the human race." If, in achieving the triumphs of the human intellect, many run for the prize, literature is not at fault, nor does it suffer injury. If the successful competitor is honored, it is the vanquished who crown the victor and strew his path with flowers. We repeat it, that literary antipathies must ever be limited to a narrow circle in the republic of letters.

Nor is it true, as some have affirmed, that the habits of literary men naturally tend to misanthropy. There may be singular exceptions, like that of Junius, in whom it would seem for once, that transcendent abilities were joined with a pure hatred of the world; for had there been mingled with his malice against his rivals, any regard for the welfare of mankind, he would, ere long, have torn away the mask that conceals his real name. There may be also malformations of the mind, like that of a deformed limb, in what would otherwise have been a form of matchless grace, which rendered the intellect of Byron

> "A blighting star shot madly from its sphere."

But it is vain to generalize with a single or an imperfect specimen.

How cheerful in the contrast, is the moral temperament of such a mind as that of Wordsworth or Milton! The region where they dwell is like the home of the Attendant Spirit,

> "Before the starry threshhold of Jove's court,
> In regions mild of calm and serene air,
> Above the smoke and stir of this dim spot,
> Which men call earth."

What lessons of wisdom does the story of their literary life teach, as to the proper sympathies and aims of the scholar! How rich a tribute did Milton pay to the value of literary friendship, when he wrote his "Lycidas" upon the death of King, his fellow collegian and intimate friend!

We mention, as our remaining topic, that *community of purpose and pursuit*, which in general belongs to the republic of letters. This characteristic is the more interesting from the fact that in the objects sought for by the literary profession, their sympathies are coincident with the highest welfare of their contemporaries, and of all who shall come after them. We shall refer to only *one* of these common objects of pursuit, the general desire of literary men, to identify their fame with whatever relates to the permanent glory of their native land.

It is not less the duty, surely, of the scholar, than of every other man, "to be grateful to Providence for that state of society in which his lot is cast." This obligation would seem to be admitted as a settled axiom by the learned of almost every country. Hence we find them so careful to present faithful portraitures of national manners and renown. Hence the immortality of Burns' pastorals and lyrics. Even in Iceland, a literature has been found by modern scholars, said to be by no means deficient in vivacity, rich in heroic adventure, full of patriotic devotion; in short, a perfect picture of a people whose home, as Carlyle has expressed it, is on "the battle-field of frost and fire."

There are, however, some among our own writers who echo the sentiments of foreign reviewers and tourists, and speak in discontent and disparagement of American civilization as being detrimental to the cause of sound literature. Sometimes the idea is sanctioned by distinguished authors abroad. "In the United States," says Mr. Alison, in his chapter on American History, "the scholars are dissatisfied,—they complain of the superficial character of literature, and that it is progressively sinking instead of rising."

If Mr. Alison, or his informants, mean the literature of the fashionable monthlies, or the literature called *diurnal*, in the dignified phrase of the penny press, we shall not dispute the assertion, that it is "progressively sinking." If he means the light reading of the Harpers', or the twelve penny editions of the New World, his statement that it is not "rising," should be deemed a public misfortune. We hope some better invention than the mammoth sheets of the metropolitan press will be found, to render the process of evaporation more rapid.

But such accusations are not new, though they often are accredited by less respectable authors than Mr. Alison. There are those who judge of the character of a literature without estimating its aim; others estimate its excellence and influence by its antiquity, or the number of books it contains. There are others still, whose ideas of literary subjects are shaped by an almost exclusive devotion to classical studies, or the reading of foreign opinions. All these persons, in their admiration of what has been accomplished by other nations and at other times, do not search for fields of new acquisition, and they declare that we have nothing deserving the name of a *national literature*, and furthermore that we have no materials to form one, separate from that of the Anglo Saxon race.

It is indeed true, that our political separation from England did not take from us our joint heirship to the glory of English letters, previous to that period, nor has it since rendered those works of British authors exclusively national in any proper sense, which in their scope and design are essentially cosmopolitan. We still speak in its purity the language of Shakspeare. Bishop Berkeley, eminent as a philosopher, and a master also in English prose composition, wrote his celebrated "Minute Philosopher" at Newport, in Rhode Island, while residing on the farm, which, with his library, he afterwards gave to Yale College. But this work, though the author was an ardent friend to his country, and to the American colonies, contains no particular trait of nationality. Nearly a hundred years afterwards, Dr. Channing sought out the same delightful seclusion, where he composed some of his finest essays. Like Berkeley, he made himself to be remembered as a patriot, by the immortal productions of his pen; and like him, too he wrote some of his best works for the general welfare of mankind The "Character of Bonaparte," and the "Life and Writings of Milton," were designed and destined to an influence, irrespective of a particular period, climate, or people. Milton himself spent the vigor of his days in the service of his country; and his "Defenses of the People of England" may be said to give him almost the same rank among prose writers, which he enjoys as "Prince of the Poets." But if, at the close of his political life, he had been compelled to take refuge with the Regicides in the colony of New Haven, who shall say that the bright visions of his youth, which had passed before him at the University, might not have been revived here; and thus Paradise Lost, "the world's epic," might have had its origin, word for word, as we find it, on this virgin soil, breathing, as it actually does, as much of the religious tone of New England, as that of the parent land?

A literature, then, to be strictly national, may not include all the works written by native authors, as some maintain. We reduce the standard to more narrow limits, but there is a fairer prospect before us of doing according to our republican maxim, equal and exact justice to all. We believe it possible to possess a body of letters, which shall be properly and purely American. But what shall be its scope and design? What rule shall determine the long mooted question of boundaries, between the provinces of English and American mind, which often perplexes many of our young and patriotic literati? As in many other questions of diplomacy, so in this; the controversy ends, when the points in dispute are clearly stated.

A national literature is the imperishable expression of the national life and sentiment. Its office is, to record in creditable history the great events which mark its different eras, and the bright examples of its illustrious citizens, generals, and statesmen. It must paint the social character and traditions, and domestic manners of the people; and what is a more important function than all, it must reveal that which constitutes the inner life of a people, that noblest part of national existence not necessarily subject to decay, which animates every successive generation with the same patriotic impulses, the same sensibility to the national honor, the same pride in the national renown. If we have stated the proper functions of a literature distinctively national, the conclusion is favorable as to what American genius has already accomplished. We have a literature, which has done much to express and perpetuate the national character. Its influence is felt in other lands; it is honored by illustrious names, some among the dead, many among the living.

But what chiefly concerns us, is the bright promise of the future. It is not a fault or a misfortune, but our chief pride, that our civilization is yet in its early youth. It will certainly and nobly reach its destiny; and the period of its ultimate maturity and glory will be adorned and commemorated by the LITERATURE OF LIBERTY. This is the great work foreshadowed, which is to be accomplished by such as are to constitute the American republic of letters. The sympathies of the patriot and the scholar are united in a common object, and in a common reward. This object, as a stimulant to intellectual activity, is of priceless value. The presentiment of our coming glory, as a great nation, is a richer inheritance than the records of old renown. Would that all who love the liberal arts, might read aright the prophecy of the good English Bishop, the early and munificent patron of our beloved Alma Mater, who, long ago, foresaw in these "happy climes,"

> another golden age,
> The rise of empire and of arts,
> The good and great inspiring epic rage,
> The wisest heads and noblest hearts.

DIGNITY OF THE AUTHOR.

One great and kindling thought from a retired and obscure man may live, when thrones are fallen, and the memory of those who filled them obliterated, and like an undying fire, may illuminate and quicken all future generations.—Channing.

The chief element of Dignity is Power. This is an essential requisite of all the nobler qualities of our nature. Without possessing it in some form, no one can attain to great and admirable eminence. The highest style of Power is Self-control—that sublime, unconquerable energy of mind, which subdues all passions, endures all trials, and triumphs over all obstacles. Even the abhorrent character of Satan is clothed with an awful dignity when invested by Milton with this mighty spiritual power. We are compelled to admire that dauntless and vehement will, which enabled the lost Archangel to seize with proud defiance the burning sceptre of his dismal realms, and to hail with grim delight his horrid prison-house, bringing there

"A mind, not to be changed by time or place."

Next to self-government, is the power of mind over mind. This intellectual sway is nobler than any other which man wields over man. The power of creating immortal thought, of kindling it in other minds, and assimilating them to our own, is surely God-like, for it is such an agency in kind as the Creator exerts upon our rational natures. Under this form of power, we may comprehend the influence of the mind over the material universe. Having summoned physical strength to its aid, the intellect triumphs over nature, and makes the wild elements themselves its servants.

How noble is the unlimited dominion of the mind, which enables the solitary man of letters, from his humble retreat, to speak with a voice which millions will listen to and obey—giving new impulses to human thought, awakening kindred intellect, and leaving an ever-present and imperishable renown! Who are they that possess this kingly power?

The Poet—who, by his unseen and ethereal influence, refines and exalts our better natures—who reveals to us lovely forms of beauty and glory—who delineates our tenderest and profoundest emotions—who lifts us above this sultry and dusty world into a higher and purer atmosphere, giving us respite from care and weariness, and awakening the conscious hope of Immortality; thus fitting us for higher enjoyment in this world, and under the purifying influence of Christianity, preparing us to love Infinite beauty and purity in another.

The Philosopher—who explores new realms of knowledge, both in the material and spiritual universe—who soars into the heavens, and traces out the laws which rule the starry world—who sends forth from his little nook many a ray of light—one, to illumine the mariner on his dark and tempestuous way—another to describe the road to honorable wealth—another to teach the statesman in the Senate, or the king upon the throne—another still, to guide lost man to immortal happiness. The Historian—who shadows forth the scenes of all former times, and causes to pass before us in long review its great army of nations and their heroes, spreading out to our gaze unbounded treasures of wisdom gathered from the examples and experience of past ages. The moral, political or religious Reformer, whose energy of mind, diffused far and wide by his writings, leads the van of a new era in human opinions. These are the true sovereigns of the world.

There is another dominion which man exercises over man—viz: Arbitrary Power—which rules through force or terror. The Jesuit priest avails himself of this, when he inspires his ignorant subjects with a dread of the torments of Hell and Purgatory. The military tyrant exercises it, who controls men through fear of his arms. This is the lowest form of power. It has its origin in low, selfish ambition. Instead of creating, it destroys. Unlike that higher power of mind over mind, which awakens kindred energy in others, thus giving new impulses to goodness and happiness, and making men more free and God-like, it chills and enfeebles their nobler natures, by robbing them of that self-dominion which is the highest attribute of human nature. Still, arbitrary, power confers dignity upon its possessor, especially when acquired by his own genius and energy. It is our design to compare the dignity of the great Military Hero with that of the great Author.

The enterprise of founding a monarchy, it must be admitted, requires some greatness. We cannot but admire that intrepid energy and bold decision of purpose, as well as rapidity of execution, which enabled Oliver Cromwell, in the midst of trying reverses and disappointments, to become a soldier at the age of forty, and after calling into existence the bravest and best army Europe had seen, to lead it to conquest. Still more do we gaze and wonder at the dazzling greatness of the modern Cæsar who, an obscure Corsican, soon bestowed upon himself the titles of Consul and Emperor, made his name the terror of powerful nations, and his will—destiny: now thundering at the gates of Rome, now, beneath the Pyramids of Egypt—a second Mahomet—now, upon the throne of France, and, again, in the heart of Russia—last of all, the solitary prisoner of the Ocean.

His sublime energy, fully equal to any crisis, commands our admiration, while its dazzling effects have thrown a lustre around his name, which, like a blazing meteor, seems entirely to obscure the solitary star of unassuming genius. None occupy so splendid a place in history as these Cæsars, Cromwells, and Napoleons. Their glory is dazzling and seductive. It suits that depraved nature from which wars and fightings proceed, and lust for the power which they procure. But, notwithstanding all the seductive attractions which encircle such renown, our more candid and conscientious judgment must convince us that Intellectual greatness is far more pure and noble. Let us analyze the dignity of Napoleon's character. His ruling motive was a selfish and inordinate love of arbitrary power. The sword and the bribe were his agents. His wonderful genius for using them indeed created great revolutions; but did these revolutions accomplish any noble ends?

Was the increase of human weal and happiness their object? We glance along the events of his strange career for a cheering reply; but in vain. A long list of dazzling victories perhaps blinds our eyes. Look again. Beneath the waving plumes and standards, and gleaming arms, the earth is red with blood. Besides the wild, triumphant shout of victory, we hear the groans of the countless dying, while upon every distant breeze is borne the wail of the conscript's orphan and widow from numberless abodes of the poor and desolate.

A nobler army than the world had seen, follows this strange and wonderful man into the frozen regions of Russia. There was the glory and strength of France—her youth—her manhood—her pride. One pulsation throbbed the heart of that noble, unequaled host. It was that of high hope and ardent trust in the invincible power and unchanging fortune of Napoleon. But soon, a strange, unusual sound is heard. It is the signal trumpet of retreat!—a sound which Napoleon nor his army had ever heard before. A few months, and where is that splendid host? Broken, famished, fallen in heaps by sword and cold a few broken-hearted, straggling, desperate men return to their native France with the sad story of disaster. This was to gratify one man's ambition. His dignity was that of arbitrary power, obtained by force supported by enslaving fear, and leaving no trace behind of moral greatness.

Let us turn from the contemplation of such renown to the high and nobler dignity of the scholar. Whom shall we choose as o beau-ideal of the literary character, from the host of distinguishe names which present themselves? It shall be John Milton, the Chri tian, the patriot, the poet,—that divine old man, "who sang his immo tal song, far from ease and wealth and courtly power, with darkne and with dangers compassed round." It had not always been th Many of this world's honors surrounded his youth. He had been t champion of Liberty in Republican England. But when the sto came, sinking the republic, which it had been his glory to defend, l name was nearly forgotten. Embittering neglect and care-worn a advanced. Youth and health and honor left him. The fair face Nature departed from his view forever. No more to him was the light

"Day, or the sweet approach of Even or Morn
Or sight of vernal bloom, or Summer's rose,
Or flocks, or herds, or human face divine."

In this dark hour, Milton needs not our commiseration. Indignant his contemporaries for their neglect, we view with unfeigned reverer that noble and exalted mind which is a brighter manifestation of Pov than this world's honors can betoken. His spiritual nature sheds more glorious light around him, than that of the sun. In it, he co see nature's beauties in all their surpassing loveliness. He could v the scenes of antiquity and gather around him its heroes, poets, a philosophers. He could leave this little world, and soar away amc the Cherubim, loosing all griefs in the contemplation of the glories a terrors of the Almighty. He could solace his darker hours with the cheering thought that, however much despised and neglected then, he was creating for himself the esteem and reverence of future generations upon the earth, and the love and fellowship of the wise and good in Heaven. How has that prophetic hope been answered! How sacred now is John Milton's memory! How priceless do we hold the legacies of his immortal genius! How would we esteem the privilege with millions more to visit the divine old bard in his humble retreat, and pay him the homage due to Intellectual and Moral Greatness.

Let us consider a few of the qualities which make this power infinitely more dignified than arbitrary force. They do not lie upon the surface, obviously at once to the common eye. The solitary man of genius in his retirement is unseen; his influence, like that of the Deity, is spiritual. There are none of the trappings and baubles of thrones and courts about him to attract the vulgar gaze. Neither the thunders of cannon nor the shouts of mobs proclaim his dignity. But, though unseen, his influence is not unfelt. In the stillness of meditation, the great author is arranging materials, collected from the knowledge of every age and country, to instruct the public mind; or, from the resources of his own, bringing for thnew and hidden thoughts, thus stamping the times with his own impress, and paving the way for great reforms. 'He stands between the People and their rulers—thinking for them both—the true lawgiver.'

Again—this power is Immortal. "Words are the only monuments of human power which continue forever." As we look back through the long vista of six thousand years, what remains of human productions? Here and there mouldering ruins, already far consumed by the gnawing tooth of time. But the Poets, Historians, and Philosophers of antiquity yet speak to us of the renown and grandeur of their times, and through their immortal writings, yet maintain their sway over Mind. Though not a trace is left to mark the dust of Troy, Homer's story of its eventful siege remains unharmed by the lapse of ages. All monuments of Cæsar's glory have perished, save that one of his literary character—the simple record of his own great deeds, recorded by his own hand.

As we look forward, through the dim and endless future, the dignity of Intellectual Power is enhanced, while that of Arbitrary Force is at an end in that world where the din of arms is never heard, and the warrior puts off his strength forever. Then the exalted intellect, freed from the trammels of this lower world, and purified from its dross, will soar to that higher state, where the realms of Knowledge are boundless and Eternal.

THE PAST.

Thou hoary-headed Past!
Who sit'st upon thy throne;
And as the Ages, wheeling by,
Move in review before thine eye,
Dost call them all thine own—
My childhood's years—
Its hopes and fears,
Each in thy solemn train, to Memory appears.

Cruel thou art, O Past!
No pity lights thy breast;
The aged I was wont to see,
And youthful friends beloved by me,
O where their place of rest?
No longer mine,
Thou call'st them thine,
And bid'st around my brow the mourning wreath entwine.

Thine are the sheeted Dead,
Yea, Death itself is thine;
Death, Plague, and Pestilence, thy slaves,
Who pile thine altars, fill thy graves,
And worship at thy shrine;
Their service pass'd,
Then, then at last,
Thy victims they shall be, inexorable Past!

Where are the Heroes—where?
And Mighty of the earth?
Where are the armies, at whose tread
Proud Nations shook with mortal dread,
And Life bewailed its birth?
All gone to be
Subject to thee,
Lord of the slumb'ring Dead, thou Past Eternity!

A realm of dust is thine,
And mouldering decay;
The crumbling mast, the falling fane,
By artists ne'er rebuilt again,
There sink and melt away;
Nor Life throbs high,
Nor does the eye,
Kindling with joy and hope, survey the Earth and Sky

Life never lags behind,
Of hours, the fleeting train;
The flowers that blossom in the Spring,
The bird that soars upon the wing,
Are not for thee to gain;
Until that day
When grim Decay
Upon them sets his seal, they will not be thy prey.

Yes, boastful Tyrant, know,
How impotent thine arm!—
The lifeless form thine arms may clasp—
The soul—it will elude thy grasp,
Without or fear or harm;
Deathless and free,
'Twill fly from thee—
Find an Eternal Home in vast Futurity.

THE IMPORTANCE OF THE ENGLISH CLASSICS IN A LIBERAL EDUCATION.

"Cedite, Romani scriptores,—cedite, Graii."

To one, who has borrowed the rudiments and finish of his education from the pages of Grecian and Roman authors, the title we have chosen for the subject of our present essay may seem somewhat arbitrary. He who has been schooled from his youth in the teachings of Plato and Socrates, of Virgil and Cicero, and has consequently shaped all his ideas of a classical standard by the model of such minds, may at first seem disposed to dispute the high ground we claim for our English authors, and demand at least an exposition of the reasons that substantiate this claim. Our only apology, if we may term it such, will be in directing them to the *study* of the English classics, and leaving the subsequent decision with their own nicety of perception and taste.

It would indeed seem strange, if in this age, which has with propriety been termed the age of reflection ,there could not be gathered from among all England's heroes in the field of letters, some few of such noble proportions and astonishing power as to merit the distinction of *classic;* some who, by their bold originality and unwearied industry, may be grouped apart from those that were borne on in the common current. The high rank which literary taste and talent have already attained, is traceable back, for its source, to that somewhat rude state in which they existed in the days of Greece and Rome. Every subsequent age of the world's history has added to their lustre, and experience has only been effective to unite and consolidate them;

if they lay torpid in the overwhelming darkness of the middle ages, it was that they might emit with increased brilliancy that flame, whose source had not during long years been exhausted. On the old system of classics, as a foundation, rests what we term the new: the lovers of learning have in every age contributed their mite to its augmentation. Princes have erected, in support of the increasing fabric, many a royal pillar, and the charms of the Court of Chivalry and camp of War mantled its proportions with the richly colored beauty of romance. To pretend then that we must undo what labor and experience have so well done, in order to find some great desideratum for the mind of the present age, is no less than absurdity. Would we look at the bare canvas, to discern and admire the skill of the painter? or examine the quality of the foundation, if we would praise the symmetry and beauty of the superstructure? The simplicity, that in every other respect marks ancient mind, is by very many the subject of ridicule, or even contempt; their philosophy was too often mere child's prattle, and their ideas of skill in what are now termed the learned professions, too slender to withstand the test of scrutiny. Why then their attainments in letters should be of such disproportionate consideration among men, whom we would be the last to suspect of defective perception and judgment, is a matter of no little wonder. If simplicity or freedom from imperfection be a recommendatory quality, then we would assert for English authors the possession of such qualities to a marked degree, while they evince the additional one of learning and experience. We would look on the literary efforts of the Ancients not as on models, whose use they have already subserved, but with that feeling of reverence with which one of us contemplates the distant and receding shores of his Fatherland,—as on some huge pile of antiquity, which although it has suffered little from the hand of Time, is nevertheless better fitted for admiration than occupation. By no means should they be subjected to disregard; we would have them by us for occasional study or reference. Spirits should they be, to gather at our bidding around us, and reveal to us the depths of antiquity: we would regard them as old and well tried *friends*, pleased ever to commune with them in the stillness of solitude, and not ashamed to be found with them in our intercourse with the world.

But if enough has not already been said in vindication of the claims of English writers to the rank of models, we leave all that yet remains, to the discernment of any who will make them their study. Their merits are not to be set forth by any rhetorical skill, but by that deep conviction which acquaintance alone ensures. And with such a conviction on our own part, founded, we must confess, on a familiarity too limited and brief, we propose to devote our remaining remarks in urging the incomparable value their study has in the acquisition and use of a liberal education. It is not enough for the scholar of so enlightened and spirit-stirring an age as this, to go forth among men, weighed down with the mere lumber of a heathen mythology, or manacled by the limits their learning has never transcended. The dreamy musings he has enjoyed in the bowers of their Fairies or the grottoes of their Nymphs—

he reveries in which he has so frequently indulged at witnessing again nd again the battles of the Gods 'fought and won,' have silently woven round his imagination a spell, whose pleasure has been purchased at a ost no less than its strength. All his views are shaped to the changing tandard of ideality,—all his knowledge is mere speculation. Like hose of the old 'Antiquary' of Sir Walter Scott, all his possessions, ver which he gloats with a miserly pride, and whose origin he can race back even beyond a definite certainty, are mere trinkets to gratify he eye, fitter ornaments for the unmolested recesses of a museum than or any practical utility; while the most meagre attainments of the deroted student of English mind, like those of the 'poor maun Edie Ochiltree,' are every one useful and so happily at hand as on no occasion to be entirely valueless.

Were we required to select from the numbers who follow such a variety of paths in reaching their great end—'an education'—one in every respect equipped as well for the defense as the service of Letters,—one 'armed at all points' to grapple with the mind, whose contact he cannot avoid or even treat with, and yet with such beauty and grace about his whole form as at the same time to captivate and charm; such an one should be the confident of the spirits of England's past ages, their devoted student and judicious follower. Exemplars more worthy or capable than they we could not ask for, and our admiration of them should border so far on servility as to require an acquaintance with them for a passport over the very threshold of the temple of Fame. While unqualified devotion to *Ancient Authors* is yet in the mouths of undecided disputants, it makes much for the strength of our position, that English writings have ever, to a greater or less degree, had the primal influence in moulding our minds, in addition to their receiving the most liberal praises from the learned. The learning a heathen antiquity would tend only to obscure, or at best to ornament with a tinselry of questionable composition, could profit men only as a pastime, possessing in itself no immediate influence in shaping and directing thought. But the writers of pure, unadulterated English, clothing thoughts as chaste and vigorous as itself, have been schooled in English classics, and made them as well the objects of their relaxations as of their severer studies. To refer one to the ancient classics for models, and that too with the plea of their assistance in enabling him to master his mother-tongue, is, in the face of all these productions of our own, like another voyage for 'bringing coals to Newcastle.'

Commencing the English classic writings at the happy reign of 'Good Queen Bess,' we find there authors of whom any literature might be proud. There for a time stood foremost Jonson, with a pen like a battle-axe, which he wielded with astonishing effect to the discomfiture of the old castle of Barbarian Ignorance. Around him were congregated such spirits as Raleigh, Cecil, and Bacon, the stars of the courts of Elizabeth and James. Originality is the truest test of genius, and a subjection of the old English poet to this standard, fixes our opinion of him broad and high. Next, *numerically only*, rises the genius of Shakspeare, transcendent in its conceptions, in its composition too wonderfully complicated for strict analysis—the very personification of the world's entire ages; with a foresight that overstepped all boundaries, a perception that penetrated the most secret and hidden springs of human action, an imagination that could flit about on a wing of gossamer among the tenderest flowers of earth, or soar on a tried pinion into realms far beyond 'human ken.' It would seem as if the Deity had folded in his mind a mighty collection of power, as varied as excessive, and yet not of an excess to surfeit or weaken. As cant and gratuitous as it may be at this day to show any attempt at eulogizing Shakspeare's genius, it is one of those stupendous objects, '*rari nantes in gurgite vasto*,' which, as we could not in our course pass *over*, we must not even pass *by*, unnoticed.

Milton, too, who 'tried his flight' while the overtasked frames of Jonson and Shakspeare were hardly laid in their graves, stands forth conspicuous on the page of the History of Literature. In his occasional essays, which are too frequently of ponderous frames, he is justly chargeable with that bitter invective and scornful taunting, which scathes every thing in the path of the polemical writer, yet abating the necessity to which he was driven by the heresies and feuds everywhere springing up and ripening around him, his labors among England's loyal sons in the cause of Letters were Herculean—nay, more, God-like. And there were Hooker, Taylor, Barrow, and Hobbes. As we run through the list we unconsciously feel that if ever yet there existed any objects on earth, to which we might with justice pay idolatrous homage, they were the giant spirits of the time that elapsed from the middle of Elizabeth's reign till the Restoration. Such an age England or the world had never before beheld: the times of Leo X. and the Medici, of Charles V. of Germany, and of Louis XIV. of France, are all splendid colorings in the magnificent picture of European Literature; yet all their splendor and dazzle becomes but a mild brightness, when viewed with the astonishing variety that gilds the period we have described. The age of Charles V. may boast its Luther and Calvin, or Ferdinand of Arragon may doat on such a prodigy as his faithful Cardinal Ximenes; or Augustus may glory in those spirits, who guarded with vestal sanctity the literary character of his time; but England had accumulated all the valuable pearls of Learning that Time had wasted upon its shores. Such were the exalted geniuses, whose names only we have mentioned; on these does Britain proudly ask us to look, while she exclaims with the mother of the Gracchi—'These are my jewels!'

For upwards of half a century after these spirits had passed away, the turbulence of political factions and religious dissensions kept the Genius of Letters a wandering exile; she traversed the bleak hills of the North, and trode lightly over the deserted heathers of Southern Scotland; she visited Germany, hardly yet recovered from the bewildering excitement of the warfare of the Reformation, but at last returned to England and assumed her high station in the court of Anne. The age of Anne was one rather of improvement than invention—of polish than original labor. What the mind of the seventeenth century had extracted from the quarry by main strength, though it was 'rough and unhewn,' that of the eighteenth would seek only to beautify with the chisel; the former originated, the latter amplified and adorned; the one gave to mankind with their characteristic roughness and frankness what the benevolence of Heaven had given them; the other manifested a pride in the appearance of their gifts. Such was the stamp of mind in the famous reign of Anne, though not of that rough, and in some respects rude originality, which marked the preceding age, yet of such refined taste and nice discrimination as to deserve the title *classical*. Steele, Addison, Swift, Jonson, Dryden, Pope, Parnell—all are names too legibly written 'in the sands of Time,' to be forgotten. This was indeed the Augustan age of English literature, abounding with poets, satirists, critics, divines.

Thus hastily have we glanced over the noblest models we can propose for imitative study; to attempt now to eulogize their peculiarities would, we fear, be but trifling with the good sense and perception of our readers. Yet we must be pardoned for so far examining them as we are necessitated by our proposed design.

There is in the writings of these classic authors a strength of thought that would alone compensate for any occasional want of originality. By their unwearied and fearless efforts they acquired a wonderful tact at handling their subject, in however difficult a form it might come to them. Their labor was before them, and the great motive with them in bringing it to a grand consummation, seems to have been that satisfaction, which great minds alone enjoy in the search and discovery of Truth. They broke through the lighter filaments of the soil and sank deep their implements beneath the surface, laying open to the light of the human understanding all that by the dilapidation of centuries had been well nigh buried for ever. Thought so bold and original could be hemmed in by no honeyed expressions or nice turning of language. They wrote in good strong Saxon, as dashing and unguarded as their own free natures. The vastness of the mine they had opened led them to other considerations than those of any method in laying out their labor. Within any definiteness of rules they could never be confined, leaders as they were rather than followers. Nor do they exhibit any of that regard for economy in employing their means, which has strongly marked a late age; none of that fear of diminishing their strength, which betrays its very weakness.

In their language too we find a copiousness, a vigor and yet a flexibility, which the *speaker* as well as the writer of the present age may study with advantage. With their thoughts their language is so nicely interwoven, that a disunion would render each mere flimsiness; both are the coining of the noblest minds, and their union is the happiest consummation of all. Their expressions are employed not merely as rough receptacles for their conceptions, nor yet for any useless ornament with which to set them off; every word is pregnant with meaning, every sentence is linked by the strongest bonds, and they carry about them a compactness and a finish, that deservedly earn for them a classical rank.

In view of such profitable objects of study, the statesman and counsellor may calculate on a valuable possession. By familiarity with them they are fortified with originality and strength, armed with quickness and sagacity, and exhibited in a dress of superlative ease and beauty. The skill of originality, finishing and presenting an argument, the true exciting fervor of language, the vigor and chasteness of thought, the impulsive eloquence, which thrills while it charms and electrifies while it persuades,—with all these may the orator enrich himself by faithful labor in these mines of pure English.

But if the man of liberal education is not professedly to devote his talents to the distinguished callings of the orator, or the writer, in addition to the elevated dignity it imparts to his character, and the high tone it lends to his influence in life, an acquaintance with the old authors will form a most enviable solace for his declining years. Hope and anticipation are powerful ingredients in the youthful character, and to no object does youth look forward with more elasticity of spirit than to the comforts and calm enjoyments of old age. We remember it to have been the advice of our experienced old instructor, as we were about entering University retirement, not only to sharpen and polish there those weapons on which to depend in the 'hurly-burly' of life's battle, but also to obtain under no mortgaged conveyance an eagerness for the *solid food* of learning, which would prove our firmest friend in declining years. The picture of such an old age has been faithfully drawn by Cicero; the additional beauty a later period would give it, is the additional beauty of genius and learning and the purity of the Christian religion.

We can well imagine the exalted happiness of one, who has stood shoulder to shoulder with his comrades in life's struggle, and now that his work is finished, has retired to the calm seclusion of private life, surrounded only by the friendly spirits of past ages he has loved and cherished from his youth. The tastes he early imbibed have 'grown with his growth;' what were once the subjects of his severer study, now form the greatest assistance to his relaxation. The deep tragedies of Shakspeare move his passions or excite his sympathies, the comedy of Jonson smooths for a time the wrinkles Time has written on his brow; the caustic irony of Steele, or the polished elegance of Addison, shed over his soul a playful light. He in truth communes with the spirits of the world's ages. By the comfortable winter fireside, or strolling in the 'green lanes' in spring, or reclined on some mossy bank in summer, beneath

> 'the yew tree shade
> To listen to the brook that babbles by,'

or gazing with pleasure on the pure delights of the 'Harvest Home,' these spirits all accompany him: he courts them in solitude and talks of them in social intercourse: and 'ere coldness wraps his suffering clay' and he pillows his silvered head in the quiet of the grave, they stand about him a faithful band, the truest handmaids of Religion in offering him his last consolations.

ANACREONTIC.

A PLEA FOR INCONSTANCY.

The truant bee from flower to flower,
May roam at will the sweetest bower,
And ne'er content for aye to sip
The sparkling drop from Rose's lip,
He steals each leafy covert through,
And drinks from all the honey-dew;
Then off upon his gaudy wing
Away he flies—a careless thing.
Those shining orbs of beauty bright
Must change with every hour of night—
Must fade at last, and die away
Before the glorious light of day.
The dew that falls upon the flowers
Must vanish with the morning hours.
Yon heavenly bow, so bright and gay,
Must lose its beauteous array.
The rose may bud and bloom awhile,
But it must lose its sweetest smile.
Ah! what can these in nature be,
But emblems of inconstancy?
I am not, love, more light and free
Than the truant honey bee,
Not satisfied for an hour
To live on one though sweetest flower,
Unlike this ravisher of sweets,
Who steals from ev'ry bloom he meets,
And then, ingratitude to prove,
Forgets, at eve, his morning love;
Who ne'er returns unto the rose,
Bereft of quiet and repose
By his delusive, flattering voice,
Which swore it was his only choice;
Unlike this false, deceiving bee,
I oft return, my love, to thee,
And only by my rovings learn
With what an ardent flame I burn.
The many smiling flowers I see,
Lose all their charms, dear love, for thee;
And though I rove all Flora's ways,
My heart its constant homage pays
Unto a single budding flower,
That rules my every breath and hour.
Then let me roam for ever more,
Since I can learn but to adore.

W. C.

THE WITCH.

A TALE OF THE LAST CENTURY.

BY CUJUS.

"The earth has bubbles, as the water hath."—MACBETH.

CHAPTER X.

IT took but a short time for Brownhead and the negro, with their prisoner, to reach the central part of D——. As they approached the house of Mr. Warden, they paused to consult upon the proper measures for them to adopt. During the whole time since his capture, Riggs had not uttered a word, and he seemed determined to preserve the same obstinate silence. It was already nearly two hours past midnight, and Armstrong was at first inclined to take the spy immediately to the quarters of Col. Cook. Brownhead, however, insisted upon bringing him into the presence of Captain Warden, thinking that his tidings would thus be more speedily obtained. The negro finally assented, and passing through the avenue and around to the rear of the house, they entered by a private door, the key of which was left in Richard's possession for his peculiar accommodation. The hunter then struck a light, and having placed the prisoner in a chair, (his hands being still bound behind his back,) he left the negro in charge of him, and hastened to call our hero. In a few moments he returned, accompanied by Hugh.

"Riggs," said the young soldier, "I am sorry to see you in this situation;—by the laws of war, you have of course forfeited your life, but if you will faithfully reveal to us what knowledge you possess of the movements of the English, I give you my promise to do every thing in my power to save you."

For a little while the prisoner made no reply; but his features worked convulsively, and at last breaking silence he exclaimed,

"It is a hard thing to die, Captain Warden, and to die upon the scaffold harder still. But what I could tell you, can now do you no good, and for me to reveal it would be but cowardice;—no, no, you will learn soon enough without my aid."

"Jim Riggs," said the hunter, earnestly, "I told you that I know'd your father, and when you was a little boy, not more than so high, I use to see you about the streets and everybody thought well of you;—you was a bright boy, and if you'd taken the right side, you would have been a *man;* but you turned Tory,—so much the worse for you,—but arter all I can't bear to give you up—I don't want to see you hung, Jim Riggs—I dont. I liked your father, and your mother too—she died before you can remember; if what you've got to tell can do *us* no good, it can't do *you* any hurt,—and if Captain Hugh here stands up for you, it'll save you from the halter; and you can come round to the right side and make up for the past—you can, Jim."

The prisoner moodily shook his head.

"Look here," continued the hunter; "if it was daylight, from this very winder, I could show you the old house which your father used to live in; I could show you the *old* barn where you played hide and seek; and I could show you the men and the women here that were boys and gals with you, though now I think on't, some of 'em are dead and buried down in the grave-yard yonder—and there's the trees here, Jim, that you used to climb, and the meadows and the orchards and the brooks, that you used to know—and the Britishers—blast 'em—would spile the beauty and goodness of 'em all, if they could—and you, Jim Riggs—is it you that's goin' to help 'em to do all this?—you left the D—— folks in anger, I know—but, I calculate you never thought of this afore."

"It's enough, by ——!" exclaimed the prisoner, leaping from his chair, with quivering lips; "cut these cords, for Heaven's sake, and give me a musket;—Richard Brownhead—Captain Warden, I'm a Tory no longer—I'm not!"

"Hurraw!" shouted the hunter, springing to the side of Riggs, and severing the cords with his knife, "I knew you was sound at heart, Jim, a'ter all."

"William," said Captain Warden, who had been watching the scene with much deep interest," go as quick as possible over to the house of Col. Cook and ask him to come here."

The negro bowed and hastened away. Hugh then turned to the spy and said, "you know, Riggs, that it will be impossible for us to set you at liberty at once, however firmly we may be convinced of the integrity of your purposes. You shall, however, be as free as circumstances will allow, till you can have a fair trial, and I apprehend little danger of its consequences."

"I know, Captain Warden," replied Riggs, "how much I deserve, and I cannot blame the suspicion of your friends. But let me tell you that before twenty-four hours have passed, you will have need of every available man, and if Jim Riggs can do you any good, he's ready."

"Col. Cook will be here soon," said Warden, "and then we will hear your story and take what measures we can. Hark! I think I hear them coming."

As he spoke the last words, the negro opened the door and ushered in the officer they were expecting. He was a stout, middle aged man, with military whiskers and a searching eye, and a countenance whose general expression was stern and forbidding.

"What's this, Captain, what's this," exclaimed he, coming forward, "that you send for me at three o'clock at night for?"

"Richard and the negro have taken a prisoner, sir, who appears to have some news of importance to communicate. He has been with the enemy, but seems anxious now to atone for his past conduct by doing all in his power for us."

The Colonel advanced toward the captive and looked into his face. "Humph! Riggs, hey? A d—d Tory always;—Captain Warden, this man is a spy."

"I fear it must be acknowledged so," said Hugh, "but he can, nevertheless, render us good service, and I think him honest in his determination to change his conduct."

"Well, well, let's hear his story, any how."

"Riggs," said Hugh, "we are waiting for your news."

"I don't ask any favor of you," said the spy, "try me and see what I'm worth, and may be, you'll not be anxious to give me the halter. Nearly twelve hours ago, Tryon landed two thousand troops at N——, and is by this time far on his march toward this place. His intention is to destroy the military stores in D—— and to burn the town."

The two officers looked at each other in breathless silence.

"I left the vessels at N—— as soon as they reached the shore, to meet a Tory named Martin, who has been in these parts and has visited New York of late several times, bringing intelligence of the state of things here. I was with him and an Indian of his, when I was taken prisoner."

"I knew it, blast his pictur! pos-si-bil-i-ty! and he's got away agin, by the Lord!" exclaimed Brownhead.

"Col. Cook," said Hugh, in a suppressed tone, "will you step this way?" and taking a light he led him through the hall into another room. Placing the light upon a table, he turned and exclaimed, "for heaven's sake, Colonel, what shall we do?"

"Is that man telling the truth?" asked the senior officer.

"Undoubtedly, sir, he is."

"It's of no use, then, by ——! They'll do just what they please. But we'll *try* to stop their triumph: who can we send to Gen. Silliman, immediately?"

"Riggs, himself?" said Hugh, inquiringly.

"No, no, I dare not trust him. Let me see; there's Lockwood—he's just the man; knows every road and lane in the county."

"You're right, sir; I'll send Richard for him at once."

In the course of an hour the messenger was despatched, supplied with verbal communications to the General, urging immediate assistance and detailing the forces and intentions of the enemy. This being done, it was the next care of the two officers to see what measures could be taken for the defense of the place. Leaving Riggs in a kind of general custody with Richard and the negro, they hastened to collect what individuals they could find, to join the handfull of troops stationed there. After doing their utmost, they found it impossible to raise a force of two hundred men, and even for these there was no amunition. It was now toward sunrise, and the whole village had become alarmed. The small body of patriots had been hastily gathered together with such arms as they could procure at the moment. D—— at that time was built mainly upon a single street, running North and South, and about a mile in length. At its southern extremity this street or road turned to the East, and after proceeding in that direction a little more than a furlong, took a winding course over a considerable hill toward the village of B——. There were several dwelling-houses and a church belonging to the Episcopal denomination, along that part of the road which run due east, and these formed the lower portion of the town. On the corner which we have described, just at the end of the main street, were collected the scanty American forces. Col. Cook and Captain Warden were in earnest consultation with some of the inferior officers as to the most proper course to be adopted. Meanwhile, the women and children of the village, assisted by some few of the men, mostly the aged, or those who from some bodily infirmity were unable to join the troops, were making preparations on every side for flight. Wagons and ox carts, laden with such articles as necessity, avarice, affection, or whim would select, and often also with females and children, were hurrying through the street towards the North. The sun rose in cloudless splendor, and the meadows, forests, and pasture fields, clothed in the first verdure of Spring, glistened in the morning radiance. But amid the confusion of rattling, shouting, shrieking, and feminine terror, there was little opportunity to observe or think of the appearance of external nature. Mrs. Wilkins and Miss Lappet, who were so conspicuous in our first chapter, whom we had nearly forgotten in the hurry of narration, were particularly distinguished for their exclamations and their exertions.

"Oh! deary me!" cried the latter, as she was hastening up the street with some unnameable articles of female apparel tied up together, depending from one hand, and a large bandbox from the other, while she carried a looking-glass and a china tea-pot under her arms, "what *shall* we do! Why, law! there's Mrs. Wilkins," and she passed across the street to share her griefs with that lady, who was proceeding in the same direction.

"Massy on us!" said Mrs. W. making a full stop, and placing on the walk a large wash-tub and a blue umbrella, which she was endeavoring to preserve from British ravages, "is that you, Miss Lappet? oh! I'm so glad to see somebody to talk to."

"Pick up your things, Mrs. Wilkins," replied the other, "and we'll talk as we go along. Why," she continued, as the matron followed her directions, "did you ever hear of the like in all your born days? They're goin' to burn the town up, and kill all the folks—oh dear! oh dear."

"How many on 'em is there?" inquired Mrs. Wilkins.

"Oh! I don't know, they say there's millions on 'em—and they'll murder all the men, and they treat the women awfully—they say!"

"Miss Lappet," said the matron, solemnly, "they won't."

"There—there's a cart, and room enough for us on't too," cried the maiden lady, and shrieking for the vehicle to stop, they hurried to secure a place in it for their accommodation.

But we must return to the movements of the two officers. While they were yet consulting, Mr. John Warden came to the place of rendezvous in great excitement. "Look here, sir," exclaimed he, addressing our hero, "why the devil didn't you call me up with the rest? I might have remained in ignorance till this moment, if it hadn't been for Mrs. Barton—poor woman, she's horribly frightened. I've sent Armstrong off with her and such articles as she wished to carry away, in the old lumber wagon. Richard and that spy are talking over old times, and *I* want to know what we're going to do."

"Why, sir," said the Colonel, "we shall be obliged to evacuate the place, I fear."

"Evacuate! No, no, fight 'em, Colonel; give me a musket; zounds! evacuate!"

"But, uncle," said Hugh, "there are two thousand armed regular troops, to somewhat less than two hundred unarmed, unprovided men like these here." The bachelor muttered two or three execrations upon the British in general, and at last replied, "well, well, I suppose you are right, but it's hard, though."

"We have crammed the church full of stores," said Col. Cook, "and disposed of more in various places,—what is left we wish to carry away with us as far as possible. It will be necessary to procure carts and wagons for this purpose, and the sooner we set about it the better." In this opinion the other officers unanimously coincided, and it was speedily communicated to the troops. Men were sent in various directions to procure vehicles, which were speedily loaded with military provisions, and the little band were ready to depart. Richard Brownhead was sent for and Riggs guarded by him, and a soldier was placed near the centre of the troops. Two hours later, D—— was left almost desolate, a few only of the inhabitants, who hoped for safety from their inoffensive character, remaining behind.

CHAPTER XI.

The spy had correctly stated the number of the forces which were now approaching D——. They consisted of about two thousand men under the command of Gen. Tryon. It was nearly two hours past mid day, when the van of the hostile troops gained the summit of the eminence southeast of the place, on the road from B——. Tryon himself, mounted on a noble bay charger, was in front of the whole; on his left rode Sir William Erskine, and on his right walked—John Martin. As the General reached the top of the hill, and saw the village reposing peacefully in the valley beneath, he ordered a halt. Turning around, he surveyed for a moment his forces, which were slowly filling up the hollow behind him, and then looking again earnestly at the town, he exclaimed, pointing with his drawn sword toward the rustic dwellings,

"They'll soon be blazing, Sir William!"

The knight shook his head, but made no reply.

"Well, we must on," continued Tryon. "March!" then as they resumed their progress, addressing the Tory, he inquired, "which is the church you mentioned, Martin?"

"The one nearest us; the rebels have stuffed it full of stores, hoping as it belonged to the Establishment it might escape, and secure its contents."

"I think we shall take the liberty of removing those contents, however," replied the General, with a laugh, "though we spare the edifice."

Aware by the reports of the scouts who had been sent in advance of the troops, that the American forces had retreated, the English regiments made no delay in entering the town and commencing their work of destruction. Dividing into small parties, they ranged at will through the place, burning the dwellings and out-houses, and destroying every species of consumable property. The church, in which a large quantity of military stores had been placed, was broken open, its contents dragged out, piled into a heap and set on fire. In the short space of an hour, the village presented only a dismal scene of blazing habitations, and a lawless soldiery, glorying in their powers of destruction. Several of the inhabitants who had ventured to remain, were seen, denounced as rebels, murdered, and their bodies thrown into the flames.

Among the foremost in the work of ruin was John Martin. With Grahtimut by his side, for the Indian had also found his way into the British ranks, the Tory heaped up piles of inflammable materials against the devoted buildings, and fired them with fiendish delight. When they came to the house of Mr. Warden, he first entered it and rifled it of every thing valuable, and then consigned it to the same fate with the rest. He remained gazing at it till all his companions deserted him, even to the Indian, and he stood alone in the avenue before it, watching the flames as they played about its walls, and burst out of the windows. At last, as the roof fell in, he turned to go away. At that moment a hand was laid on his shoulder, and a low voice close to his ear said, "a pleasant sight, John."

The Tory turned quickly, gazed eagerly into the face of the speaker, and exclaimed, "Good ——! Riggs, have you escaped?"

"Ay, John, I was too much for them, and have got back in time to take my share of the sport."

"But how, man; how did you contrive it?"

"Hoaxed 'em,—but never mind that; the undertaking you spoke of, in which you wished to get rid of the Indian; what was it?"

"The devil, Riggs! I had like to have forgotten that; and Grahtimut's off now, too,—just in time. You've seen this Captain Warden, I suppose; well, he's got a girl off here in the woods, whom he's desperately in love with. I hate him, Jim Riggs, and I mean to carry off his sweetheart; ha! ha! a glorious plan, isn't it? She's a perfect angel too—will you go with me, Jim? It wants an hour and a half of sunset yet; she lives with nobody but an old woman."

"No, John, I want to stay here and see Tryon; you'd better go alone; you'll be sure enough."

"Perhaps I will, but I want to be more than sure *enough;* however, if you can't go, I'll get some of our friends here; there's plenty of 'em that'll go a dozen miles for a pretty face."

"Yes, yes," said Riggs, "you're right; well, I must be off—success to you;" he turned and walked hastily away. Proceeding at a rapid rate up the main street towards the north, he paused not till he reached the upper part of the town. Several soldiers met and recognized him, but as he was well known among the British troops he was suffered to pass without molestation. At last he stopped, sprang over the fence into the fields, and crossing several inclosed lots, came to an orchard, where a horse, ready caparisoned, was fastened to a tree. Loosing the animal, he mounted him, and rode through an opening in the rude fence, across another inclosure, and finally again entered the road. He now gave spurs to his horse, and advanced with great speed along the route which the retreating American forces had taken. In a short time he came up with the colonial troops, and dismounting, he hastened at once to the van, and saluted Captain Warden.

"You return quick, Riggs; how goes it in D——?" inquired the young officer.

"I had need be in a hurry, Captain," was the reply. "I've some rather particular information to communicate. D—— of course is in a blaze. I saw your uncle's house perish with the rest, and Martin stood alone, gloating over it."

"Let it go—let it go; a day of reparation will come sooner or later; but the information you mentioned, what is it?"

The spy briefly related his conversation with Martin, and when he finished, Hugh without speaking hastened to the side of the commanding officer, and exclaimed in a low voice,

"Col. Cook, I must leave the troops for a time, and I wish to take Brownhead and Riggs with me."

"We can hardly spare a man now, Captain," said the Colonel, with a surprised look, "much less *you*; is the occasion urgent?"

"My betrothed bride, sir, who I thought was in a place of safety, is in danger of falling into the hands of John Martin. I wish to save her, and rid the earth of him."

"Go," said Col. Cook "for heaven's sake, go; I know too well a young man's feelings to attempt or wish to hinder you. May you succeed in both your objects."

"Where shall I probably find you on my return?" inquired Hugh, "if I ever return."

"Not far from this neighborhood. The country will become alarmed, and I doubt not but that Gen. Silliman is already on the march in this direction."

Without further delay, Warden hastened back to the spy and said to him in a low voice,

"Riggs, I of course wish to defeat this Tory in his machinations; I know where the object of his schemes is, and I intend to hasten there at once. Will you accompany me?"

"You couldn't please me better, Captain, than by taking me with you—shall we go alone?"

"No, Richard must go with us; call him here."

Riggs speedily found the hunter and brought him to our hero.

"Wall," said he, "what's the matter now, Mister Hugh?"

"Are you ready to give John Martin another chase, Richard?" inquired Warden.

"Pos-si-bil-i-ty though! have we got a chance at him *agin*? Ready? I calculate so. Where on airth is the crittur?"

"Not far from Rapaug, I fear."

"Blast his infarnal pictur! a'ter Miss Orra agin; wal, wal, come along, let's go."

In a short time our hero, the hunter, and Riggs, mounted on fresh horses and armed with rifles, hurried away by a cross-road, leading around to the west of D——, toward the Rapaug hills.

[TO BE CONTINUED.]

PROGRESS OF CIVIL FREEDOM.

The "advancement of civilization" is a phrase often employed in the most trivial connections, but which, in its reality and importance, is deserving our serious consideration. Progression may be well termed a law of human society. *Onward* is the motto of life. In every department of the arts and of practical life, improvement has followed improvement in such rapid succession, that life now bears no resemblance to life in days gone by. In the profound researches of science, the investigations of philosophy, and in every species of human learning, the mind continues to advance nearer, still nearer to ideal perfection, with time its only limit, and disposition its only hindrance. And such indeed is the legitimate result of our mental constitution. Possessing a mind all-grasping and unlimited in its expansion, active and inquisitive; animated by passion and urged on by ambition, the course of man must be onward and his goal improvement.

The superiority of modern society over the ancient, in no way perhaps would appear in so favorable a light, as by making the moral influence exerted in each, the measure of their comparative excellence. The exchange of physical for moral power, is the chief purpose of all human instruction. Liberty cannot hope for a stable existence, or right for an universal acknowledgment, till morals are not only the result of our religious obligations, but also regulate all our social and civil relations. To unite civil with religious freedom, and to recognize private equality as the foundation of political power, has been the object, first in importance, but almost the last to be achieved in the past history of man. This has been the especial prerogative of modern times. Slavery no longer presents the plea of justice for its support, and tyranny hides her coward head in lands of semi-barbarism. Slavery, it is true, still pollutes the character of America, the freest land the sun shines upon; but as a damning legacy of former generations, which even the considerations of temporary expediency can barely tolerate. The unanimous voice of the enlightened world is in favor of civil freedom, neither through prejudice or preference, or as a favor granted to the crowd, but as an inborn and undeniable right. With this, the received opinion of society, better can never be succeeded by worse. We regard it as the chief bulwark of our own hopes of political prosperity, a bond of union to philanthropists, and the harbinger of a glorious era.

The very character of political truth may be considered the principal cause of its gradual progress. Immutable in its nature, and universal in its application to every social relation, it contains that within itself, which must convince mankind of its laws and their importance, whenever they rightly comprehend the object of their own existence, and their duties in promoting the natural peace and harmony of the world. Duty, as regulating the mutual intercourse of man, as constituting a motive to action universally received, is of such a nature, that the human mind can neither deny or forego its authority. Among the plains of Hindoostan, the African deserts, or the American forests, as well as in civilized communities, it is the prime mover of every religious feeling and action. But we are compelled to admit, that its precepts have but seldom been correctly understood, or the heart is far blacker than we would willingly believe. One of the chief advantages of the advancement of civilization is, to define the precise limits of duty, and enforce its dictates. By tearing away the thick veil of mysticism, which, as the garb of iniquity is wont to deceive the ignorant—leads them to believe virtue vice—it discloses the secret springs of action, and renders principle the moral governor of our race. Thus our true duty becomes our guide, without the liability of being perverted, and he who acts the villain must also possess the villain's character.

But this, which ought to embrace our whole conduct, has been generally, heretofore, and is too often at the present day, restricted to private morality. There are few truths of more importance to man than political truths, and they may be said to bear the same relations to his temporal that religious truths do to his eternal welfare. Yet for many centuries this principle of duty was rarely, if ever, applied to civil relations. True, politics have been confounded with religion, church united with state, and duty to God substituted for duty to man. A grievous mistake, well characteristic of human fallibility, and one which has clearly proved that if it is human to err, it is also our lot fearfully to atone for our faults. It is perfectly natural indeed, that the claims of religion should be recognized previous to the existence of civil freedom. For the existence of a creator is engraved on our very hearts, so that even the ignorant must believe, though he may not appreciate. He may neglect the loud calls of religion for justice to mortals, but can never overlook his own dependence on an immortal being. But liberty, we contend, cannot exist as a *right*, until our social duties are well understood, and possess the same influence as other moral principles over the minds of the virtuous portion of society. For such is the progress of society. In its earliest stages men are ruled by circumstances—in its more advanced, periods by principle. Nor can any institution be permanent in an enlightened community, which is not based on such foundations. Such we would believe is the basis of our own republic, constitutes its strength, and will alone ensure its success. If it perish, the same funeral knell may serve for liberty and hope.

We have frequently seen the freedom of the present traced back to he days of early lore. Greece and Rome are pointed out as the noble examples we should imitate. Far be it from us to detract ought from their fame. But we deny that the principle of universal equality—our own impregnable fortress—was ever acknowledged. Theirs was the freedom of might, not of right. The will of the small portion of the citizens who managed the government, restricted neither by conscience or duty, was as absolute as the tyrants, and often as unjust. Slavery existed in its worst forms, the *right* unquestioned. Encroachments upon foreign powers were deemed not only politic but laudable. And oppression at home, as well as conquest abroad, formed an essential part of their state policy. The security of walled towns, the habits of pastoral life, and the independence of mountaineers, have been looked upon as the great sources of human freedom—the means of its preservation—and the ultimate causes of those mighty revolutions in latter times. The important influence of these we readily admit; but like the investigations of the alchymists, they have led to the discovery of principles wholly unsuspected before, but now universally allowed, if not practiced. Then liberty was but a name for unrestrained license, now, it is the title of a sacred and inalienable right.

The progress of liberty must be, and has been, coincident with the progress of learning. There is no civilized nation on the face of the earth, which has not sprung from barbarian ancestors, except our own; and the course of improvement, thus far, is a good illustration of the principle we wish to establish. Knowledge needs but be once acquired, and it has an existence as real and stable as the everlasting hills. In the infancy of society, as nothing is known, chance and experiment are the only means of self-cultivation, and nations often continue long in this feeble state, before they learn the use of their intellectual faculties, and take the first step in the "march of civilization." This has frequently been termed the natural state of man; and in one sense it truly may be considered such; for natural causes and the crude uncultivated passions of the breast alone influence his conduct. If liberty exists, it is the liberty of accident, not of principle. The wandering Arab, or roaming savage, like the horde of bandits, are free, simply because no one has subdued them; and the power which constitutes their sole security to-day, may be the cause of their subjection to-morrow.

But after men are convinced of the existence, as well as of the importance of learning, and the period of youth has arrived—that period of society, when the enthusiastic student and visionary alchymist, consume day and night in their lonely cell, wasting life away in diligent thought and unremitting toil—advancement even here is necessarily slow. The little that already has been revealed, is easily learned, and like the light which penetrates the grate of the prisoner's cell, merely serves to render his darkness visible, and his confinement the more painful. This is emphatically the age of discovery—discovery both of the principles established for the regulation of the material world, and of those for the government of mankind. When leading minds point out the paths their successors explore—when physical and political truths become no longer imaginary, but real. Now a Galileo and a

Bacon penetrate and divulge the secret arcana of nature. Not far distant follow those terrible revolutions, which shook Europe to her centre—those mighty heavings of her populace, in their attempts to shake off the yoke of oppression, which have produced a change of opinion respecting their social rights, in no way inferior to that effected, by these scholars, respecting the laws of the world we inhabit. Taking his results from the study, and applying them to practical life, posterity reap the full advantage of the philosopher's investigations. Society rapidly advances into the full vigor of manhood. Knowledge becomes an essential characteristic of a noble man, and right of a noble government.

Such, in our opinion, is the present condition of the enlightened world, or at least soon will be. There appears to us, indeed, to be a close and striking resemblance between the enterprise of middle life and the multifarious projects, religious, moral, and political, which are now occupying the attention of every civilized people. We are no dreamers in human perfectability, but the natural order of things would certainly indicate, that a wise old age should succeed our present state. Experience is the only book which the great mass of men can read with profit to themselves. Its pages are now rapidly turning, and a lesson of wisdom must be the inevitable result.

The germ of political power was planted at the creation, and inherent in man, is now a wide-spreading tree that covers the earth. It has offered to our race many bright promises of universal happiness and prosperity, but, like the first blossoms of the fruit-tree, they have proved premature and unproductive. These blossoms have been succeeded by others less deceptive, and the fruit—political equality—is now, under the clear sun of general intelligence, rapidly ripening for a glorious harvest.

Z.

HOME.

How many are the tender chords that move
At mention of that fondly cherished spot.
'Twas *there* young life first dawned upon us. *There*
Intelligence peeped forth, a feeble ray
Of light divine; but destined yet, perhaps,
To span a boundless universe at once,
And fathom nature's deepest, blindest works:
And upward rising, scale those dizzy heights,
The boldest seraph's wing ne'er yet assayed,
While toiling to behold creation's bound.

The name of Mother, which we *there* first learned
To lisp, comes up with all its magic charms,
To add attraction to the place, and shed

A brighter lustre 'round each hallowed nook.
'Twas *there she* opened to our wondering minds
Those holy truths, so vast that Angels scarce
Can comprehend them, in their full extent;
And yet so simple that the merest child—
Enlightened from on high—can understand,
And learn the way to everlasting life.

The thought of *home* enkindles up afresh
The loves and passions of life's early morn.
The waking dreams of childhood's happy hours,
With all their numberless, enchanting scenes—
Like recollections of some fairy tale,
Of angel-forms and earthly paradise—
Come rushing through the mind; imparting life,
And joy, and hope, and warm affections, such
As in the spring of life are *wont* to fire
The youthful breast, before the chilling hand
Of time—the frosts of unrequited love—
The cold returns of misplaced confidence—
Have nipt the tender bud of hope, and shut
The avenues, through which affections flow.

Fain would I cast a parting glance at those
Transporting hours,—reflecting brightness, like
The cloudless beams of a May-morning sun,—
Ere misty darkness veils them from my eyes,
Or time hath borne me on, with rapid wing,
Beyond their sight. Each passing year obscures
The view, and makes their mem'ry more and more
Like some fond, fleeting dream, which leaves a faint,
Though lingering impression on the mind.
And yet they tell of young companions gone—
Of friends and playmates sleeping in the grave—
Of broken ties, and sundered bonds, which nought
But death could break.—Of happy spirits, free
To roam the fields of endless blessedness;
And sometimes, doubtless, wand'ring back to meet
Familiar friends on oft frequented ground,
To cheer their lonely pilgrimage, and help
Them on to bliss.

Who would not love at times
To steal from busy life, and linger near
His childhood's home? and revel 'mid the thoughts
Of by-gone days and early happiness?
When ev'ry grove was filled with richest strains

Of music, and each lawn wore freshness, like
Another Eden:—when the very flowers
That grew around our feet, fit emblems seemed
Of life; and Nature's self looked but to smile.—
When all the world was clad in friendship's garb,
And *knave* and *villain* were unmeaning sounds—
When ev'ry thing we saw, and felt, and heard,
To us was real as the ground we trod:
And men were judged of, not by inward worth,
But by the hollow forms of outward show,—
The only standard artless innocence
Had learned to use.

I envy not the man,
Who treads with stoic feet o'er scenes like these—
Whose heart leaps not, at sight of childish mirth—
Who does not, in imagination, love
To turn, and live again his boyhood o'er:
Nor like the eagle, feels his youth renewed,
When from long absence homeward bent, his eye
Espies each tree, and shrub, and rising knoll,
As when in simple innocence he first
Went forth, and thought he saw the bounds of earth.
His soul befits a monster, not a man.
And better might he seek some lonely haunt,
And lead a hermit's solitary life,
With no companions but the senseless brutes—
No friends to stand beside his dying bed,
Or bear his body to its last repose,—
Than mock his fellow men with human form,
While nothing human dwells within his breast.
There let him listen to the dismal owl,
Or start to hear the ill-omened raven cry—
Let croaking frogs disturb his troubled sleep,
And grinning witches dance around his couch;
But keep—Oh! keep him from the haunts of men,
Lest curses rest upon them for *his* sake,
Whose heart of steel knows no accord with *theirs*,
Nor harmonizes with the softest notes
That move the human soul.

DELTA.

REFORM.

The distinguishing characteristic of the present age seems to be an ardent zeal for reform. A Catholic priest inculcates the doctrine of total abstinence from intoxicating liquors, and immediately the sparkling cup is dashed to the earth; an Irish repealer excites a little *peaceful agitation*, and the mightiest empire in the world is shaken to its foundations. Wonderful indeed is the rapidity with which these great human regenerations advance, if we compare them with those of former ages. There we can distinctly trace the progress of the little curl cloud as it makes it way slowly, though steadily, above the horizon and advances against the numerous opposing currents; here, almost the first intimation we have of its approach, is in the rattling of the thunder and the confusion of the elements. Then it took centuries to effect the most indispensable reform; now, little more than years are requisite for the most radical changes.

We are not of those, who derive the greatest pleasure from censuring every thing which is done now-a-days, neither of those who imagine that man has reached the extreme point, the "ultima Thule" of his destination, whence he is soon to retrograde, or whence, at least, he is to hope for no further progress. We see that he has been steadily on the advance for the last thousand years, and can perceive no reason why he shall not continue so for a thousand more. Indeed, we think that such must be the case almost in his own despite. Yet where is the bold heart, the confident mind, that entertains no fears from this spirit of reform? Who is there that does not see in many of its manifestations the presages of troubles, dangers, and horrors, that threaten to vie with, if not to surpass any that the reign of terror ever witnessed? If there are any such, we are not of the number. It is impossible to behold, without apprehension, the enthusiastic ardor which pervades certain classes upon many of these subjects; and none, if we may judge of the blossoms, promises a richer crop of tumult and destruction than Liberty. It may excite some surprise, that an American should express doubts with regard to the beneficial effects which an ardor for liberty is likely to produce; yet it is even so. The most zealous Christian of the eleventh and twelfth centuries might have doubted the salutary consequences of the religious enthusiasm which distinguished that era. He might have discerned, in the enthusiasm that made the good Christian, the devout and pious man, or that girded on the sword in defense of the pilgrims to the holy shrine, the same feeling, that, a little perverted, was to assume the most hideous forms of fanaticism, to turn the lance against the breast of his brethren who might differ somewhat in doctrine from himself, and to make one vast funeral pile of the fairest portion of Europe. So it is with us. Reverencing in the highest degree the banner under which the reformers march, we cannot but fear that it will be polluted in scenes of blood, which nothing but its own sacred character will prevent from covering it with disgrace. Liberty is to us a real thing, and not a name, not a mere phantasm of the enthusiast's brain. Its constituent and essential parts are peace, good order, security, and we may add, that suggested by Mr. Carlyle, *bread*. If these are obtained under the despot's rule, then there does the eagle of liberty perch, rather than on the Pantheon of anarchical revolutionists. Much is said of the practical nature of the age. In relation to the physical sciences it undoubtedly is so. Few researches are made in them without an eye to practical utility. The chemist no longer wearies himself for years in search of the philosopher's stone, or the other dreams of alchemy, but rather employs the vast resources of his art in discovering the properties of steam; while the philosopher, discarding the idea of perpetual, inherent motion, is content to apply the mighty powers of nature to his machines. But far other is the state of the speculative sciences, and particularly those of politics and government, upon which chiefly reform is running madly through the world. In these we seem to be still theorizing with Aristotle, or rhetorizing with Plato. Neither has the experience of twenty centuries cast any satisfactory light upon the much-vexed question of the capability of man to govern himself; nor does the vast mass of facts which history furnishes, enable him to deduce any definite and well-established conclusion upon the important point. Indeed, in this, government appears to bear a close resemblance to medicine. The physician who, practising upon the Sangrado system, should prescribe in every case a remedy which has been successful in one, without regard to the constitution and habits of the patient, or the various symptoms of the disease, would deservedly obtain the reputation of a quack. So with the statesman; the phenomena which he observes in one country must be materially modified in their application to another. History may cast much light upon his course, but it furnishes him with no "Pocket Manual" of political medicine, by which he may heal the disorders of the state; no panacea, which is to remove all diseases, past, present, and to come. In truth, he who pronounces any single form of government or institution the best in the world, *the one*, is very like the quack who declares No. 6 to be "the universalest remedy in creation," and who administers it, on all occasions, alike to his horse and his son. Yet how often has this kind of quackery been introduced into politics? We have seen English measures ingrafted upon our policy, without the slightest regard to the differences which exist between the natures and the situations of the countries. That they were beneficial there, was considered as quite sufficient evidence that they would prove so here. Such, however, is the tendency of this reforming spirit. Either laying down some vain theory, it proceeds to act upon it, without reflecting upon the consequences, or it deduces its argument from cases in no way analogous. The results of such a course, it is evident, must be highly pernicious. To illustrate our remarks, we will cite an example—that of England, over which the storm is rapidly gathering in all its blackness.

A large party now exists in that country, which, deriving confidence from its success in ours, would there also indefinitely extend popular rights. There can scarce be two cases more dissimilar. The one is lemocratic in all its feelings and interests,—was founded upon these rinciples, which have "grown with its growth and strengthened with ts strength," and, moreover, enjoys advantages for their development, n the character of its inhabitants, the nature and extent of its territory, ossessed to an equal degree by no other people. The other has ever een accustomed to aristocratic institutions, and is oppressed with a relundant population, confined within the limits of a small island. Under hese circumstances it is, that they would proclaim the universal equality f man,—that they would open the ballot-box to the ignorant manufacurer of Leeds, equally with the intelligent merchant of London. This s evidently the course of events in England. Power is rapidly gliding rom the hands of the few to the many ; not an intelligent and welleducated, but an ignorant and degraded many. The contest is not one or the abolition of corn-laws, or the repeal of an oppressive and obnoxious ariff, (which, however, we are endeavoring to fasten upon ourselves,) r for the adoption of any measures which may tend to ameliorate the ondition of the poorer classes. Were this all, we should only say, ' God speed you!" But, although these may appear on the surface, f we look a little deeper, we cannot fail to perceive, that the real strugle is one for power. It is but the onward progress of that ball which he sans-culottes of Paris set in motion. "Democracy," says Carlyle, ' is everywhere the inexorable demand of these ages, swiftly fulfilling tself. From the thunder of Napoleon battles to the jabbering of open estry in St. Mary Axe, all things announce Democracy." We cannot ut doubt whether these principles can ever be applied with safety in Europe, but have no hesitation in averring, that they cannot at the resent time.

"Often," says some writer,—we quote from memory,—"have we een a child, mounted on the shoulders of his father, clap his hands nd cry that he was taller than pa." Such, we imagine, would be the tate of England, were the universal suffrage adopted. The people night boast of their liberty and equal rights, but they would still be lestitute, miserably destitute of the bodily or intellectual strength which lone renders it respectable. The height of which they were proud, would prove illusory, and they would have at last to descend to the level o which nature has allotted them. The possession of certain privileges loes not constitute the freeman; it is the safety with which these may e intrusted to him. It is not the universal exercise of the right of uffrage that elevates the American citizen, but rather the intellectual nd moral cultivation, which renders him capable of deciding upon he laws by which he will be governed. Strip him of these, and you convert his beverage into poison, his blessing into a curse. Indeed, lready have we experienced many inconveniences from granting this privilege to ignorant emigrants, although they constitute not a tithe of our population. Unable to appreciate its value, they are ready at all times to dispose of it to the highest bidder ; and thus a system of corruption and bribery is engendered, the effects of which, in some of our large cities, are severely felt, and which, were it to become general, would prove utterly destructive. That such consequences would ensue in a far greater degree upon its introduction into any of the European states, the mass of the people of which are of this character, none can reasonably doubt.

Another evil of this reforming spirit, closely connected with the one we have just been discussing, but of far greater magnitude, is its evident tendency to excite a war of classes, of all the most horrible, as it can only terminate in the extermination of one or the other. Passing by its advance to this in our own country, we again revert to the case of England. We can there plainly perceive the leaven of discontent fermenting in the breasts of the lower classes against the "unworking aristocracy," the gay and flippant noble, who, with his £100,000 a year, spends his time between the fox-chase and the race-field, or in exciting the admiration of gaping Londoners, by some new and splendid equipage. That there should exist such a class, that there should be men in society, who can boast that for twenty generations the hands of their ancestors have never been soiled with work, is, when viewed theoretically, a melancholy fact. Yet where is the country in which, to some extent, it does not exist? Where is the hive that has not its drones? Even in this "mammon-loving Yankee land" of ours, there are numbers, as he who will turn his mind to the Broadway D'Orsays, will readily allow. They are small imitations, it is true, a kind of breastpin likeness, but the features are impressed with the fidelity of the daguerreotype. But, could the English destroy, without a convulsion, their order of nobility, would it be well, would it be politic, to do so? Without entering into a discussion of this question in all its bearings, we would merely refer to the effects induced in France by the adoption of a similar measure. The revolution abolished all distinction of rank, and introduced the law of equal inheritance, than which none could be theoretically more just, but which in practice has proved a blighting curse to the land, the very locust of political legislation. Agriculture has in consequence been reduced to a miserably low state. Yet the one is the natural result of the other. To render the abolition of titles effectual, there must be devised some measure by which an aristocracy of wealth will not arise, equally proud, equally idle, and equally detestable. Indeed, speak as we may about the natural equality of man, there is not a country in which it is practically acknowledged; wealth, education, talent, must and will inevitably form distinctions in society. Sweep away one body of nobility, and another arises. Wealth will be obtained; this gives education, and education soon acquires power. Occasionally some mighty genius appears, who breaks the shackles of society; some Burns, to pour forth, behind his plough, the melody of heaven's sweetest music, or some Henry, to enkindle, by his deep-souled eloquence, the smouldering flames of independence. But these are rare exceptions, while the rule seems to be one established by nature; it may be modified, but never wholly abolished. This modification the English constitution imposes upon it to as high a degree as circumstances will allow. That the noble enjoys any privileges destructive to the peace, happiness, and welfare of the poor, we cannot learn. He is no longer, as in the reign of Charles II, or of good Queen mne, privileged to seduce the wife or the daughter, and then, if need e, consummate the crime by the murder of the husband or father. The xecution of Earl Ferrers has long since announced that a patent of noility affords no protection even against the ignominious punishment of he gallows. While then the English have much to lose by abolishing heir order of nobility, we cannot perceive that any solid advantage will ccrue to them.

But a feature of these reforms, more alarming than the things themelves, is the startling rapidity with which they are moving onward. We are taught in mechanics, that it is of the utmost importance that notion should be regular and uniform, and that all sudden changes of relocity should be carefully avoided, on account of their tendency to derange the whole machine. So we conceive it to be with government; ll precipitate alterations of existing systems must prove highly dangerus, and none more so than that by which a large body of ignorant and legraded people are elevated to power. Unaccustomed to the giddy height, they invariably rush into the most fatal extremes. In this may be sought the cause of the atrocities which almost disgraced the banner of popular liberty during the French Revolution, which sickened the hearts of the most philanthropic, and made them despair of man's ever ttaining the exalted destiny which their ardent imaginations had hoped for him.

We are also aware that the English claim for themselves an exemption from such terrors, on account of the temperate and steady character of the people. It will readily be acknowledged, that in this they possess a superiority over the mercurial temperament of their neighbors. How much such advantages will serve them in averting popular fury, is still to be proved. When, however, they point us to the revolutions through which they have passed, not only unscathed, but even improved, we must disavow the test. In none of their revolutions has the popular element predominated; in none have the people asserted their sovereign right to govern themselves, or to share to an extensive degree in the management of the state. They have rather borne the character of redressers of grievances, and have been decidedly conservative. It is true that the Long Parliament abolished the House of Lords, and centred all power in the Commons; but in this the mass of the people took no share, or claimed no authority for themselves. They had freed themselves from the burdens of ship-money and arbitrary imprisonment; they had punished a faithless king, and made examples of his ministers, and they retired to their homes quiet and content. They permitted, without a struggle, the power to pass into the hands of Cromwell, and they welcomed, with cheers and gratulations, the return of the ancient dynasty. Still more decided was the conservative nature of the revolution of 1688: it indeed was little more than the change of a popish for a protestant king. The "million-headed hydra" is, in truth, but lately arousing, and it remains yet to be seen whether the butcher of England will revolt more at the sight of blood, than the dancing-master of France. We hope, but can scarce believe, that he will.

We have used England as an illustration of our remarks; but it is by no means the only country which is threatened by this reforming mania. We cannot but fear that our own proud eagle is drooping under its insidious attacks, that patriotism is degenerating, and that the peace, safety, and very existence of the Union, is being sacrificed to its visionary theories. In France, too, it still has a powerful influence; and although at present it may be quiet, yet the whole world is conscious that its repose depends upon the life of a single old man, and awaits with anxiety the direction which it will take upon his death.

In conclusion, we will say, that undoubtedly the world is much indebted to this spirit. Often has it appeared in times of trouble and danger, rectifying the wrong, and making straight the crooked. It saved Europe from the merciless fangs of a vicious and depraved hierarchy, and dissolved the spell which had so long held it in a thraldom, more wonderful than that of which Rome had boasted in the proudest days of her imperial rule. It twice rescued England from the grasp of faithless tyrants, and has rendered her the most powerful of nations. Much it has done. Much, certainly, remains to be done. Without indulging in any fanciful visions of human perfectibility, or the establishment of democracy in all countries, we still believe that man is destined to advance to an elevation whence he will look down upon us as we now do upon our ancestors of the ninth or tenth centuries. But this ascent, to be beneficial, to be safe, must be gradual. The measures for his improvement must be conducted with temperate firmness, and are not to be sought in the immediate overthrow of existing institutions.

DEFECTS OF THE AMERICAN SYSTEM OF COLLEGE EDUCATION, AND THEIR REMEDY.

In prefixing to our sheet such a title as this, we would not have it supposed that it is our intention to furnish even a list of all the evils that exist under this system, much less to enter into a discussion of all the deficiences which occur in the discipline and character of the various colleges in our land; we would merely point out some of those blemishes which deface them all alike—and to which, therefore, the common attention of the literary world should be directed—with their cure; and to do this with the greater regularity and the clearer comprehension of our subject, let us take a single glance at its origin and history.

The sun of autumn was shedding his "last, lingering ray" upon the white church spire and the many colored foliage which adorned the young hamlet of Charlestown, in the year of grace 1638, and was lighting up, for the last time on earth, the fast-closing eyes of John Harvard, as with a dying effort he perused again the instrument which was destined to give to objects of benevolence those worldly goods he could not carry hence to the land of spirits. Dully and listlessly he pored over the details and distribution which filled up the greater portion of it; but when its last provision met his dim and failing gaze, all dullness and listlessness was gone at once—" death's hour of prophecy" inspired him; and with all the confidence of unshrinking faith, he looked forward to the period when light and education should flow, in glad and abundant streams, from the well of knowledge wherein he had hidden his wealth. Short, indeed, may have been his vision, but sure are we its triumph was complete; for his few last moments kindled with the smile of successful benevolence, with the joyful consciousness of accomplished good; and while it still played upon his pallid countenance, and lit it up with a glow of Christian exultation, "the silver chord was broken," and the soul, which had animated the father of America's first college, fled to its last account.

Years rolled away; and the tree of knowledge, planted by a dying hand, was carefully tended by the growing colonies around it. The storms of successive wars beat upon it; but, rooted on the rock of pious charity and good principle, it survived every shock, and extended the shadow of its beneficial influence farther and still wider. The colony of Connecticut for some time assisted it, until, called back by the foundation of a similar establishment at home, they turned their donations into a more domestic channel; guarded by wiser care, and prospered by better fortune, our own Alma Mater hastened rapidly onward in her intellectual growth, till at last, side by side with her sister institution, Yale College remains with but a single rival on the whole American continent.

Had we time, gentle reader, it would be amusing and instructive to detail, in the quaint language of colonial days, the singular incidents which fill up the early biography of our colleges, and enumerate the donations, of every imaginable sort, received from sundry generous hands, both public and private. But we must turn from such pleasant reminiscences to later and (alas!) more degenerate days—days, when rash denominational and sectional feeling studs the vast extent of our territory with imperfect and most defective colleges, whose influence (*as colleges*) is rather injurious than otherwise—days, when the misguided love of education sends forth multitudes of ill taught, almost uneducated men, with all the legal rank and dignity of high literary and classical attainments.

On a hasty consideration, it might appear that to multiply colleges—especially in the more ignorant parts of our country—would be to disseminate light and knowledge, and therefore to benefit the community; but it should be remarked that these institutions exert a twofold influence, one instructive and beneficial, the other entirely separate, and (as we think) unnecessarily evil. Could not a majority of them teach as successfully, if called schools? Would not the design of education be as well carried out, without the pompous and expensive array of Trustees, Professors, and Tutors, which is considered an indispensable appendage of such establishments? Might not a High School, with one teacher, and perhaps an assistant, give to its pupils all the good to be derived from a great portion of our "colleges?" It is the *unnecessary evil* of which we complain, and which we would remove; hailing joyfully the erection of schools, we would deprecate the superfluous increase of colleges.

One of the worst results of this reckless system, is the irregularity it introduces, by placing the partially taught on the same legal footing with the fully educated. Were it not invidious to particularize, we might mention a large number of institutions, whose course of study is as far below our own, as this is below that of Oxford and Cambridge; suiting themselves to the state of knowledge in the community, instead of elevating it, they lower their standard more and more, until they become mere classical seminaries in all but the name. It is true they advance the cause of education a little; but this advancement, (as was before remarked) is apart from their influence as *colleges*; yet in spite of their evident inferiority, the state laws make no distinction in favor of the better. The alumni of such institutions have the same privileges in pursuit of their professional studies as the sons of Harvard or Yale; but two years' preparation are required for the half-taught graduate, while the school-boy of perhaps higher attainments, must expend *three* in traveling over the same ground. Such have been the rash enactments of over-zealous and benevolent legislators, and surely the evil which results is great, calling for prompt attention and redress.

Another prominent ill effect of this system, is its tendency to inflame and perpetuate local, denominational prejudice. What calls into existence these literary fungi? What has led to this almost useless expenditure of funds and talent, so much better applied elsewhere? One grand cause, and one which operates more powerfully in the new states than it can here, is the wish of every sect to gain power for itself by prejudicing the feelings of educated men in its own favor, training up, as it were, an antipathy to its rivals, and a prepossession towards itself. As soon as one college has thus been established, the opposite sect drags into feeble and reluctant life an "antagonist institution," to be supported a few years by party strife and jealousy,—then fall back to idle uselessness, a dead weight upon the community.

But what becomes of the *pupils* thus educated? What effect is produced upon their denominational prejudices? Is it not probable that they will be strengthened and influenced by intercourse with minds of a higher class, which entertain the same feelings? Perhaps these strictures will be considered severe, but we must believe it were better to have a school with liberal, *general* religious instruction, than a college with such consequences and such an aim.

Again, it is a well known fact that the expenses of an institution do not increase in the same ratio with the number of students; if, for example, the number of undergraduates in this college were doubled, the outlay on the part of the corporation would not of necessity be twice as great as it now is. Suppose, then, the actual expenditure upon the ten colleges of Ohio to be three hundred dollars a year each; would not the three thousand thus employed promote more powerfully the cause of education, if concentrated upon one? A greater number of pupils could be supported, as we have attempted to prove; and the wealth of such an establishment would render it far more independent its discipline and exalted in its standard, than the ten could be; the ıction of such advantages would again give it new and increased pulse to extend its operations and perfect its means of instruction. at present situated, these colleges cannot possibly enforce the strict l salutary rules of morality and industry so carefully observed in the .er and better established; they have not, and cannot have, the con- l over public opinion or the internal firmness, which an accumula- n of their now divided strength could produce.

It appears then, that the great deficiencies which stain the American stem of college education, are poverty and consequent dependence, :tarian influence, and low standard in mental and moral discipline; d that these defects result in great measure from the *number* of such ablishments. Let us look, now, for the root of this evil, and we shall ready to search for the remedy necessary. Whence arises this super- undance? What drags these seminaries to their unnatural elevation, what void to they attempt to supply?

We think the true answers to these inquiries will be found in the want a *proper standard*, by which to legislate for colleges—of some fixed timate wherewith to value the pretensions of any institution to the me and immunities of a "college"—of some conspicuous landmark, whose direction bewildered legislators may direct their course, and rive at a safe result as to the necessary provisions on this important bject; and into the qualities which must characterize such a standard, will now briefly inquire.

It should be *national* in its establishment and support. Would it suf- e for our design, that Harvard or Yale should be called first rate stitutions by the law, and thus erected as the standard of government? ertainly not, if they remained as independent of the nation's rulers they now are; their course, uninfluenced by the progress of the untry, would still be that of private colleges, and local jealousies ould effectually prevent state legislatures from emulating them, or fol- wing in their path to high excellence and reputation. Besides, these stitutions, first endowed by private benevolence, could not be made tional, without so perverting their original plan, as to leave them no nger the same in nature,—and such a perversion would be an act of justice to its original founders. The nation, then, must create and eserve its own standard—enrich it by its own favor—govern it by its vn free and liberal principles—and establish a sort of literary execu- 'e, to exert a beneficial influence over the less patronized and power- l colleges.

This national institution should be free from all sectarianism; and ıre we see another cogent reason why no existing university should applied to this use. Each one is under the influence of some par- :ular denomination, and if patronized by government, the suspicion ould be excited, that our rulers, in the very teeth of their solemn oath, ere supporting one sect at the expense of the others. *How* this end uld be best attained, we will not take upon ourselves to decide; but atters might be so contrived, as to promote morality, and even Chris- ınity, without an unjust encouragement of any exclusive party. We would not have a Girard College, to put down religion; but an impartial beneficence to all.

The basis of our literary temple should be as elevated as possible. The offspring of a giant nation should itself be gigantic, alike at its birth and in its subsequent growth. All the knowledge of the world should be included in its compass; all the intellect of the nation should combine to strengthen its powers or exalt its fame. Holding up to itself a lofty standard—giving to its sons opportunity for deep and long continued research, it should stand in intellectual eminence beside the venerable institutions of the old world, and draw upward with it all the colleges in our own land which were able to rise, while the remainder, a truly wise and benevolent legislation would restore to their proper level as schools. Deprived of their borrowed plumes, they would return to the useful though humble rank for which they are fitted; and the graduates of those which had survived the test, would go forth to the world, thoroughly prepared for the station they were to occupy.

Though dependent upon government for support, and in some degree under its control, the institution whose erection we are advocating, need not, and indeed must not, be so closely connected with that government as to be influenced by the alternate ascendancy of parties, or the regular changes of administrations. Like the judiciary, whose very life is bound up in the existence of the constitution and the universal obedience to its provisions—yet remains unsullied in its purity and justice, amid the corruptions which at times has surrounded it, this *national university* (for such would be the establishment we propose) might exist, unchanged by the petty variations of the other departments; inseparable from the *spirit*, it should be unfettered by the outward and ever-varying *form* which our republican government might assume; exalted by the nation's wise and enlightened patronage of education to so lofty a stand among the guardians of her prosperity and the promoters of her happiness, it should, it must exist, like the famed tower on Boston's heights—unchangeable and eternal; far superior to this, however, in one most important respect—while the one is a *physical*, the other is an intellectual and moral monument; while the one remains unaffected by aught, either of joy or sorrow, in the nation's condition, the other is identified with her most vital interests, showing forth by its own character, the character and prospects of education among a people, whose very life as a republican people, depends upon their intelligence and enlightenment.

QUIVIS.

SONG.

FROM THE GERMAN.

SAYST thou, the Future is veiled in dread,
And dark with the shadows of coming sorrow?
That the sunlight of peace from earth is fled,
And clouds have shut out the evening-red,
And the tempest will break to-morrow?

Let thy heart be filled with trustful mirth,
And hope take place of dark misgiving,
For a brighter day shall visit the earth,
The day of the noble—when genius and worth
Shall be honored by all the Living.

Press on to the East, toward the coming day,
With the night-shades around, and the starlight o'er thee,
In faith and patience hold on in the way,
And count thyself blest, if the first faint ray
Of the morning glimmer before thee.

SCENES IN SCOTLAND.*

Valley of Keswick, August 12th.—My first movement, after breakfast this morning, was to inquire my way to the residence of the late Dr. Southey. The house occupied by this distinguished scholar and poet is in the town of Keswick, and stands about two hundred yards from the road, upon an eminence near the southern bank of the Greta. An alley leads up to its front, with a hedge upon the left, and an open space of sward on the right. Immediately around the house, and enclosed by a second fence, is an area, twenty yards perhaps in diameter, thickly planted with trees and shrubs, and embellished by flowers. The building is of stone, three stories in height, quite small, and of plain exterior. The scene was altogether domestic; and yet, there was a solemnity and desolation in it, partly perhaps from the associations connected with the melancholy end of Southey, that made a deep impression upon my feelings. All was silent as death. I looked in at the windows, but could see nothing save the bare walls; the trees and bushes looked mysteriously solemn; and the flowers overrun with grass, wore a sickly and decayed appearance.

Derwent Water lies at the southern extremity of the valley of Kes-

* An extract from the diary of an undergraduate, now traveling in Europe for his health.

wick, and about half a mile from the town. Its scenery is displayed in solemn and romantic grandeur, and no description can do it justice. The lake is about three miles long, by two miles in width. Upon its surface are several verdant islands, while lofty mountains rise abruptly from its shores, and extend back in unbroken succession as far as the eye can reach; and upon an occasional fertile margin between the water's edge and the overhanging precipice, appears a snug cottage or an imposing country seat. Near the centre of the lake is a circular island once inhabited by a hermit, the remains of whose hut are still visible. It is said that this hermit was cotemporary with St. Cuthbert, for whom he bore so great an esteem, as to pray that they might both expire at the same moment.

> "When with eye upraised
> To heaven, he knelt before his crucifix,
> While o'er the lake the cataract of Lodore
> Realed to his orisons, and when he paced
> Along the beach of this small isle, and thought
> Of his companion, he would fancy that both,
> (Now that their earthly destinies were fulfilled,)
> Might die in the same moment."

Near the upper end of the lake is an island of about the same size as the above mentioned, upon which is a gentleman's seat.

This island is thickly planted with forest trees, and the Manor House, just peeping out from among the foliage, has an extremely picturesque appearance. The other islands, although they add to the beauty of the landscape, are small and insignificant. The finest view of the lake and surrounding scenery is from the field called Crow Park, which from a considerable eminence upon the north, slopes gently down to the water's edge. It is said that this field, which now contains neither tree nor bush, was formerly part of an ancient forest; and that it was covered with fine oaks, which some avaricious landholder sacrificed to his love of gain, without any kind of regard to the beauty of the landscape, or the venerable remains of antiquity.

Aug. 14.—Left Keswick this morning for Carlisle, distant thirty-two miles, and on the direct route to Scotland. The country soon became rough and uninteresting. I was overtaken by the stage-coach which runs between Reswick and Carlisle; it was loaded with passengers, and drawn by three half-starved horses, which the driver kept upon a round trot, up hill and down, by the constant application of a heavy whip. The average coach-horses in this country are much inferior to those in the United States, and they are whipped and driven most unmercifully. At the end of the route, the coachman comes round to each passenger, bowing and cringing for his customary gratuity.

The gross ignorance and stupidity of the lower classes in this country are proverbial, and I had a provoking instance of it to-day. I came to three cross roads, and taking the one which from its direction I supposed to lead to Carlisle, walked on. In a few minutes I met a woman, of whom I inquired, "if that was the road to Carlisle?"

,, really she couldn't tell, but a little further on there was a ard, and that would tell me." I went to the guide-board, and *it it was just two miles and a half from Carlisle.*

eached Carlisle in the middle of the afternoon, I concluded to GRETNA GREEN, nine miles further north. In leaving the assed on my left the castle in which Mary, Queen of Scotts, fined for some time. The keep, or tower, which was Mary's 'as pulled down a few years since by order of the governor, it is said to have been the strongest part of the castle.

pproached the borders of Scotland, I was shown in the distance ent, erected by government to the late Sir Pultney Malcolm, n the English navy. This monument stands in the shire of ı, and on the highest ground in that county. Of the Malcolms re three brothers, sons of a plain Scotch farmer, each of whom istinguished himself, and was knighted. Of these, James alone

ı lies upon the north bank of the river Eske, which empties vay Frith, and forms the boundary between England and Scot- 'his place, being conveniently situated just within the borders nd, has been noted, for the past century, as the resort of RUN- VERS FROM ENGLAND; and here the marriage ceremony is duly ed. A few yards from the bridge which crosses the lake, is ıse where some of the marriages take place; but the greater performed at the village inn, half a mile beyond. The village e midst of a most beautiful country. It consists of half a dozen elling houses, with a church and inn; the latter is a large two ilding with projecting wings, standing upon the summit of a ninence, about two hundred yards from the road, with a spa- ıen in front and on each side. The whole appearance of the neat, respectable, and delightfully rural.

> "A parish church, some scattered cottage roofs,
> From whose secluded hearths the thin blue smoke
> Silently wreathing through the breezeless air
> Ascending, mingling with the summer sky—
> A rustic bridge, mossy and weather-stained—
> A fairy streamlet singing to itself—
> And here and there a venerable tree
> In foliaged beauty; of these elements,
> And only these, the simple scene was formed."

itting room of the inn is handsomely furnished, and adorned portraits of Mr. Linton, the present proprietor, who now offici- HIGH-PRIEST, and of his predecessor, who died in 1829. The ;, and even the window sashes and blinds, were completely l over with the names of aspirants after an unenviable immor- After tea, I requested to have some conversation with Mr. Lin- he was formally introduced to me. He is a good looking about forty-five years of age, and has evidently seen something of the world. He was very polite, showed me his marriage register, with comments and amusing anecdotes, and gave me an authentic history of Gretna Green. He gave me also a blank certificate of marriage, a duplicate of which is made, one to be given to the married couple, and the other retained by the person officiating.

No marriage ceremony is required in Scotland, except that the parties declare themselves husband and wife, before competent witnesses; while in England, besides the usual Church ceremony, a license must be obtained, and banns published three successive Sundays. When, therefore, expedition in these matters is important, there is a strong temptation to resort to Gretna Green. The very prevalent idea that a blacksmith performs the marriage ceremony, is erroneous, and originated in a caricature which appeared in London a number of years since.

The first person who officiated was one Joseph Paisley, a tobacconist residing at Meggs-hill on Gretna Green, and the office afterwards fell to a man named Elliot. Many persons of distinction have been married here, among whom may be mentioned the Lord Chancellors Erskine and Eldon. Under date of 1835, I was shown the name of Richard Brinsley Sheridan, grandson of the famed orator and statesman of that name. A couple were married in 1842, of whom the lady's name was JACOBA ALETTA CHARLOTTA EVERDINA VAN TRYLINGER VAN HENERICH!! Mr. Linton told me that he averaged 60 marriages a year. The parties come from England, Wales, Ireland, and even from Holland.

Aug. 15th.—Left Gretna Green this morning, for Dumfries, distant 25 miles. I however deviated a few miles from my route, to see a fine district of country in the vicinity of Headdom, and as the day was warm, I found the walk longer than I had anticipated. Supposing Headdom to be a village, I had fixed upon it as a place of rest and refreshment, during the heat of the day. It however turned out to be a single church and the name of the parish. This parish is in the celebrated valley of Annandale, a district renowned in prose and poetry.

On the summit of a small hill near the church is a tower, built of hewn stone, over the door of which are carved the figures of a dove and serpent, and between them the word "Repentance." It was anciently used as a beacon, and the border laws directed a watch to be maintained there, with a fire pan and bell to give the alarm when the English crossed, or approached the river Annan.

It is said that Richard Steele, while riding near this place, saw a shepherd boy reading the Bible, and asked him what he learned from it. "The way to heaven," answered the boy.

"And can you show it to me?" said Sir Richard, in a banter. "You must go by that tower," replied the boy, pointing to this tower of repentance!

T. W.

THE

YALE LITERARY MAGAZINE.

VOL. IX. APRIL, 1844. No. 6.

POLITICAL MASS MEETINGS.

From the quiet seclusion of our Academus, and the ordinary routine of our student life, it is profitable for us occasionally to look abroad into the busy world, and observe the changes there taking place. Absorbed as we often become in the pursuits of literature and science, we suffer these objects to engross an undue share of attention, while we neglect matters of the highest interest and concern. We forget that the great world still moves on around us, that society still undergoes its various modifications and changes, that important principles are constantly being tested and applied to practical life. Since such is the fact, it behooves us to mark carefully the developments of our social and political organization, that we may be prepared to act promptly our part in the great drama of life.

Within the last four years a new system of political measures has been adopted, truly note-worthy and remarkable. We refer to political mass meetings. Remarkable—not as an unnatural or unexpected development of our free institutions—but chiefly as an index of our political progress, and from their ultimate tendencies. So far, indeed, from surprise at the introduction of this new machinery into party tactics, we rather wonder that it was not sooner adopted. These meetings are the natural effects of causes which have long been in operation. They are only a manifestation, in a different form, of the universal rage for association, so characteristic of our nation. Every important change in political measures, is an additional test of the permanence of our free institutions. It is a new chapter in the history of our national experience, having all the interest of novelty—all the importance of the most vital practical truth.

The use of mass meetings, as a means for accomplishing party purposes, we consider one of the most important political changes since the establishment of the federal government. In their commencement, they seem to have been the result of accident, rather than any matured plan of operations. They have already, however, assumed a regular organization, and may now be considered as an important and permanent feature in the system of party tactics. Arrangements have been made in several States for a continued succession of these meetings during the approaching Presidential campaign, which we may expect will be attended with increased enthusiasm and excitement.

As an index of our political, and we may also add, intellectual progress, these meetings have, for us, a marked significance. They plainly indicate a rapid increase in the violence of party spirit, within the last few years. During the first thirty years, subsequent to the adoption of the Federal Constitution, with but few exceptions, party spirit was not carried to an unjustifiable extent. With limited means of information, yet in the exercise of sober reason and calm reflection, the people were able to form their opinions of political men and measures, and select those for official stations best qualified to promote the public interest. Important topics could then be discussed, and the characters and qualifications of public officers canvassed, in a mild and conciliating spirit. They needed not an assembly of thousands to arouse their patriotism or sanction the decisions of private judgment. And seldom did they mistake in the exercise of the elective franchise. It is, to us, a humiliating fact, that the race of American statesmen, during the infancy of the republic, was, in almost every respect, far superior to that of the present day.

A change has come over the spirit of our Democracy. The American citizen of to-day, is not the citizen of fifty years ago. Now, it is too often the case, that the interests of party are first in his affections—those of his country of secondary moment. To the imperious demands of party, he has surrendered, to a great extent, the privilege of independent thought, and the right of private judgment. He las lost the noble confidence of self-reliance, and feels himself strong only when according with the popular sentiment.

This is not an imaginary or falsely colored picture, but a plain statement of facts—facts confirmed by the immense political gatherings which we have witnessed during the last four years. These afford the means of forming a correct estimate of the extent and violence of party spirit, and its individual influence. We have seen the husbandman, amid the hurry and favorable opportunity of business, leave his plough in the furrow, and his golden grain unharvested, to join the ranks of his party, as they go up to the appointed place for sacrifice. The mechanic throws aside his tools, and generously foregoes the profits of business for the interests of his country. The laborer for his daily bread, and the avaricious miser with his income of thousands, alike forget their necessities, and spare neither time nor expense in responding to the appeals of party. With the earnest devotion and blind zeal of a worshiper at the shrine of Mecca, the political partisan often performs a wearisome pilgrimage, to pay an homage, scarcely less absurd, to the genius of party.

The place of rendezvous presents a scene of the most lively interest. A spectator, ignorant of the occasion, would suppose we were on the eve of a mighty revolution. The assembling multitude is numbered by tens and scores of thousands. The arrival of each fresh delegation, attended by martial music and flying colors, is welcomed by a new uproar of announcement, and the young patriot feels himself stronger than before, by a new thousand of eyes and arms.

Nor is it the sterner sex alone which participates in the excitement of these occasions. Woman, lovely woman, has so far forgotten the modesty becoming her sex, and the propriety due to her station, as boldly to mingle in the out-door promiscuous assemblage, and join in the mélee of political strife. Never did she appear to us less amiable and lovely, than when thus engaged. True, she has here, as everywhere, a most potent influence, which sometimes acts with magical effects. Of this we might cite many instances; one only shall suffice.

It was at the largest political meeting the world has ever witnessed. More than threescore thousand persons had assembled, from every part of the land, to listen to the greatest efforts of some of our most eloquent statesmen. On an elevated spot, commanding a full view of the speakers and multitude, had been erected a platform, on which were seated a large company of ladies. In front sat a beautiful young girl, of the most surpassing loveliness—indeed, a perfect Hebe. At her side stood her suitor, a distinguished leader in the party to which he belonged, of opposite political sentiments to her own and those of the meeting. Regardless of the speaker, he fixed his gaze intently on the face of his mistress, drinking from the heaven of her large, dark, melting eyes, deep draughts of eloquence—we suppose. Not so, however, his fair Dulcinea. With earnest and rapt attention, she watched each motion and gesture of the speaker, as he unfolded his argument and set forth the great principles of his party. As he warmed in his subject, pouring forth his thoughts in more impassioned language and gestures, her glowing cheeks and sparkling eyes testified the deep sympathy of her heart with the orator, adding, if possible, new charms to her person. The speaker became still more enthusiastic—the lady more intensely excited. She rose from her seat—advanced to the front of the stage—with inspired features and parted lips, leaned forward over the railing, until, at the close of an eloquent sentence, unable longer to restrain her feelings, she tore her apron from her waist, and waving it above her head, from her ruby lips burst forth the shout, "Hurra for Tippecanoe!" The effect was electrical. The air was rent with the applause of fifty thousand voices, in which none joined more heartily than the anti-political lover, who has ever since steadily and zealously supported the ticket advocated by his lady.

We relate this, not merely as an amusing incident, but as illustrating an important general principle. We have here an instance in which an individual suddenly changes his political sentiments from a supernatural influence. It is evident he was not convinced by the eloquence of the orator, for he heard it not. Nor, on the other hand, was it from the reasoning of the angelic creature at his side, for she used none. The only arguments used, were those of sparkling eyes and ruby lips—

arguments which, though almost always deceptive and fallacious, have ever been held unanswerable.

The endeavor to engage female influence in favor of their respective parties, is no new expedient with politicians. We find Addison, more than a hundred years ago, in a paper conducted by him, called the *Freeholder*, ardently engaged in this labor of *love*. He says: "Ladies are always of great use to the party they espouse, and never fail to win over numbers to it.

"Lovers, according to Sir William Petty's computation, make at best the third part of the sensible men of the British nation; and it has been an uncontroverted maxim in all ages, that, though a husband is sometimes a stubborn sort of a creature, a lover is always at the devotion of his mistress. By this means it lies in the power of every fine woman to secure at least half a dozen able-bodied men to his majesty's service. The female world are likewise indispensably necessary in the best cause, to manage the controversial part of them, in which no man of tolerable breeding is able to refute them," &c. Such arguments were doubtless consistent with monarchical principles in that age, but are by no means proper for a free government of the present day. We consider it dangerous in the highest degree, to permit this class of community thus to exercise a power, so directly affecting the vital interests of the republic. Grant that correct sentiments be thereby, for the time, promoted, we would not have even the cause of truth served by the establishment of false principles and unsafe precedents. We trust the time has not yet arrived, in which it is necessary to enter upon an extended argument, to prove the expediency of excluding ladies from political assemblies. We believe their own good sense will teach them the impropriety of such a course, and lead them to abandon it. Should, however, the time come when such a step seems necessary, a sense of duty to our country, and especially the fair sex, will impel us faithfully and fearlessly to expose the evils and dangers consequent upon the exercise of female political influence.

The annals of history furnish no parallel, in any nation, to the political mass meetings of the present day. We find the nearest approach to them in the gatherings of the Athenian democracy. But even these were widely different, both in their origin and object. The form of government in the Athenian republic was essentially different from our own. In addition to this, we remark, that the whole number of its free citizens was less than half that we have seen at a single political meeting of modern times. They had not then the press, by which to discuss the characters and qualifications of candidates for official stations. Almost their only sources of information, in regard to these, and affairs of general interest, were the forum and market-place. It was here they met to frame and enact their laws, and discuss the most important political measures. Here was their senate-house,—the people the senate. Here was the nation accustomed to listen to those masterly and sublime efforts of genius, which formed its taste to a juster and severer standard than has since been attained. Nor did the citizen neglect his ordinary employment, to attend the political assembly.

Another class performed for him the menial offices, and provided the necessities of life. The care of the republic alone was his duty. Least of all, were their females permitted to join their promiscuous assemblies, or take a part in political action. The noble matrons, who, with the shields presented their sons for battle, added the charge, "either with this or upon it," who regarded a well-trained family as their worthiest ornaments,—these rare and admirable virtues were acquired in the retirement of domestic life. They wisely left the management of state affairs to those to whom it appropriately belonged. In all these points, and others which might be mentioned, there was a wide difference between ancient and modern mass meetings; and, with all these advantages in their favor, we find these meetings in the old republics the source of innumerable evils. In these had the *ostracism* its origin,—an engine of evil which has only found its equal in modern times, in the cruelties of the Inquisition. In these were one day the most important treaties ratified, and public measures approved,—annulled and condemned the next. The fickle populace were swayed to measures of good or evil, according as the eloquence of the orator prevailed; until the splendid talents and unprincipled ambition of Pericles succeeded, under the specious name of liberty, in binding the chains of degrading and lasting servitude on the republic.

We frankly confess we have no very sanguine hopes of more favorable effects from political mass meetings of the present day. Their origin, management, and design, all tend to strengthen our opinion of their unfavorable influence. The limits of this article permit us to dwell but briefly on a few of the many arguments which might be urged against them. We notice that their origin is directly referable to the increase of party spirit. This again is the natural result of our system of government. As the country advances in population and wealth, the power of the executive increases in a corresponding ratio. It is evident, that the election of President must be a matter of much greater importance, now that he has ten or fifteen millions at his disposal, than when, as at first, he had only a third or fourth of this sum. Most especially is this true, since the adoption of the principle, within the last few Presidential terms, that "to the victor belong the spoils of the vanquished." We need enter into no argument to prove that our free institutions are in imminent danger from the violence of party spirit. Hence, as it is the natural and perhaps unavoidable effect of the operation of our system of government, to foster a dangerous evil, it is the duty of every citizen to oppose its growth by every possible counteracting influence. But the tendency of mass meetings is directly the reverse. The immediate offspring of party spirit, they, in turn, add fuel to the flame which gave them existence. Indeed, had it been the express purpose of the movers of these meetings to increase the rage of political excitement, they could have devised no plan better adapted to accomplish the object. To this end, the orator shapes his speech, aiming not so much to instruct, as excite the feelings, and kindle a glow of enthusiasm. To this end, the spirit-stirring music, the display of banners, the singing of popular songs. Were it indeed the chief object to extend political information, it would be attained at less expense of time and money, by placing the newspaper in the hands of every citizen entitled to exercise the right of suffrage. So easily are these now obtained, that even the humblest laborer, in the time which he would ordinarily spend at one of these meetings, may earn sufficient to supply himself during the year with all necessary information respecting political men and measures. And thus, at his own fireside, and in the social circle, will he best qualify himself to discharge the important duties that devolve upon him. These duties demand the exercise of cool reason and sober judgment, joined with candid and dispassionate investigation, and an earnest desire to benefit the whole country.

Another evil resulting from these meetings we notice, and have done—an evil of no slight magnitude, yet which, from its apparently remote and indirect influence, is often overlooked. We mean their prejudicial effects on true moral independence and self-reliance. Never, probably, did an individual leave one of these meetings with higher self-respect, with more confidence in his own mental power. He feels himself strengthened in his opinion, not from a candid examination of both sides of the question, not from the force of truth to which he has listened, but because he has met a score or two of thousands, thinking, speaking, and acting, like himself. All associations must be a compromise, too often at the sacrifice of that alone worth the preservation. A supposed temporary advantage has been gained—a certain infinite benefit lost. True, in the present state of society, perhaps never shall we be able to dispense with association. But it is proof of the weakness of human nature, not its strength. Just in proportion as we free ourselves from its chains, and rely upon our own strength, do we approach nearer the Divine nature. The sturdy oak, which grows upon the open plain, unprotected from the summer's scorching heat or winter's searching cold, strikes deep its roots and stretches broad its arms, bravely defying the winds and storms of heaven. So let the citizen learn to depend on his own unsupported strength. Not by innumerable mass meetings, conventions, or whatever political gatherings, is he prepared to discharge his social and political duties.

"Not so, O friends! will the God deign to enter and inhabit you, but by a method precisely the reverse. It is only as a man puts off from himself all external support, and stands alone, that I see him to be strong and prevail. He is weaker by every recruit to his banner. Is not a man better than a town? Ask nothing of men, and in the endless mutation, thou only firm column must presently appear the upholder of all that surrounds thee. He who knows what power is in the soul,—that he is weak only because he has looked for good out of him and elsewhere, and so perceiving, throws himself unhesitatingly on his thought, instantly rights himself, stands in the erect position, commands his limbs, works miracles; just as a man who stands on his feet, is stronger than a man who stands on his head."

Atwater

THE LITERARY WOMAN.*

A LETTER FROM ONE HUSBAND TO ANOTHER.

[Translated from the German of Schiller.]

And I should pity you! Is Hymen's band
With tears of bitter sorrow by you curs'd?
Wherefore? Because your faithless spouse doth seek
That in another's arms which you refuse
To grant her? Friend, unto a stranger's woes
Give ear, and learn to bear your own more lightly.

You smart, because *one* other doth enjoy
Your own peculiar rights!—Enviable man!
My wife to the whole human race belongs.
From Baltic straits unto the Mosel strand,
Unto the walls of lofty Appenine,
Unto the fashions' father-city, she,
In ev'ry book-stall stands expos'd for sale;
In coaches, packet-boats, by ev'ry fop
And ev'ry pedant, she must fain submit
To be review'd, with proper criticism:
Endure the townsman's spectacles, and then,
As any greasy critic may command,
On flow'rs or burning coals, to glory's temple
Or the pillory go.
A Leipzic villain,—may Heaven curse him!—
Of late survey'd her topographically,
Like a fortress, and offer'd, for a price,
Some portions to the public,—parts
Whereof I *only* have just right to speak.

Your wife,—thanks to the laws canonical,—
Is wise enough to call herself *your* spouse.
She has, perhaps, good reasons for her *acts*,
And doth conduct herself accordingly.†
But *I* am only known as Ninon's man.
Complain you that all tongues are whispering,
When at the faro-table you appear,
Or at the theatre? O man of luck!
That hath the chance to boast of such good fortune:

* Literally—The celebrated Woman.

† It is impossible to translate this passage literally. In the original it has great force, and is condensed in a single line.

"Sie weiss warum, und thut sehr wohl daran.

On me, my brother, *me*, a watering-place*
At last bestows this mighty happiness;—
The place on her left hand; no eye marks *me*,
But every countenance is fixed upon
My lofty better half.

Scarce is the morning gray, ere creak the stairs
With blue and yellow-coated messengers,
With packets, bundles, letters un-post-paid,
Addressed—*to the literary woman.*
She sleeps so sweet!—and yet I dare not spare her,—
"The papers, Madam—Jena and Berlin;"—
At once the eyes of the dear sleeper open;
Her first glance falls upon—*the last review.*
That sweet blue eye,—on me not e'en a look,—
She hurries through the abominable sheet,
(Loud crying in the nursery mean while.)
She lays it by at last, and makes inquiry
For her little ones.
The toilet waits already;
Her luckless mirror gets but half a glance.
A threatening, impatient, peevish face,
Gives wings to the affrighted waiting-maid.
From that toilet the graces long since fled,
And there, instead of sweetly-smiling loves,
Are to be seen the furies in attendance.

Next, carriages are rattling at the door,
And servants springing from their steps, to ask
An audience with *the literary one*
For the perfum'd Abbe,—the wealthy Count,—
The Englishman—who reads no German though,—
Grossing and Co.,† or for Herr Wundermann.
A thing, which meekly to the corner shrinks,
And sometimes is call'd *husband*, is scarce glanc'd at.
Here dares—will *your* house-friend venture so far?—
The dullest blockhead e'en, the poorest wight,
To tell how very much he doth admire her,
And dares to do 't before my very face.
I wait near by, and but to be polite
Must ask the dunce to stay to dinner.

At table, friend, my woes begin anew;
There, for my bottles, inwardly I groan.

* In the original, "Molkenkur," a word signifying a place of resort by invalids, for the drinking of *milk*. It is used much as we use the expression, "the Springs."

† A celebrated publishing establishment in Germany.

With wine of Burgundy, to *me* forbidden
By the Doctor, I must wash the gullets
Of *her* flatt'rers; my hard-earned livelihood
Becomes the prey of hungry parasites.
O! this detestable, this thrice-accursed
Immortality will prove the ruin
Of my stout old Nierensteiner,*
And plant the whitloe on my every finger.
What, think you, are the thanks I get? A shrug,
A mocking glance, unmannerly compassion—
Do you not take? I understand full well?
Pity, that such an uncouth dunce as I
Should bear away this jewel of a woman.

The Spring-time comes. On fields and meadows wide,
Nature her variegated carpet spreads;
The herbage clothes itself in living green,
The birds in ev'ry budding grove are warbling.
To *her*, the Spring has not a charm. The songster
Of the sweetest note, the pleasant wood,
The witness of our early happiness—
Speaks to *her* heart no more. The nightingales
Have never *read*,—the lilies ne'er *admir'd*.
The universal jubilee of Nature
Inspires *her*——to an epigram.
Yet, no! The season is so fair,—to travel.
How crowded it must be in Pyrmont now.
Yet ev'rywhere one hears them praising Carlsbad.
Quick she's there—in each honorable rank
Where puppet scholars intermixed with sages—
Celebrated men of ev'ry stamp,
Familiarly, like as in Charon's boat,
Pair'd off, together from one platter eat.
Where, gather'd from afar, tatter'd virtues
Of their wounds are heal'd, while others yet—
With honor to resist, right earnestly
Seek out temptation. There, my friend,—O learn
To prize your destiny!—wanders my wife,
And seven children leaves at home,—with me.

O! thou first happy year of my young love!
How quick—alas! *how* quick art thou flown by!
A woman, like no other woman, past
Or present,—with the graces of a goddess

* A superior kind of wine.

Deck'd,—with spirit pure,—with heart ingenuous,—
And gentle, quick-mov'd sensibilities;—
Thus saw I her, the dear heart-fetterer,—
To me a May-day, shining round my path.
The sweet words,—I love you! spake from her eyes;—
Thus I led her to the bridal-altar.
O who was happier than I!
A flower-field of happy years, unclouded,
From out that mirror smiling on me looked.
My heaven was open'd to me.
Already
I could see my children sport around me;
The fairest in their circle, *she*,—of all
The group, the happiest, *she*. And she was mine,
Mine, through the harmony of souls, and through
The ever-during bond of loving hearts.
And now appears—may he obtain his meed!—
A great man—an extraordinary genius.
The great man did a deed, and overthrew
At once my heaven-reaching paper-castle.

Whom have I now? most pitiful exchange!
Waked from my dream of bliss, what is left me
Of this angel? What *is* left? A strong mind,
In a body weak; a mongrel being,
Betwixt man and woman, for rule unfitted
As for love; a child in giant's armor;
A thing but half philosopher—half ape!
With trouble having gained a place among
The stronger sex, abandoning the fairer,—
Precipitated from the throne of love,—
Driven from beauty's holy mysteries,—
Stricken from Cytherea's golden book*
For——a newspaper notoriety.

* Golden Book: in a certain Italian state, a book is thus called in which the names of the noble families are enrolled.

THE WITCH.

A TALE OF THE LAST CENTURY.

BY CUJUS.

" The earth hath bubbles, as the water hath."—Macbeth.

(Concluded.)

CHAPTER XII.

It was one of those magnificent days in the latter part of April, when the sky has assumed the deep hue which it wears in May, while the landscape still retains the delicate tints of the earlier season. The sun, already fast approaching the western horizon, was gleaming through a mass of broken clouds, whose dark masses, fringed with a silvery lacing, presaged a coming storm. Immediately overhead, and to the east and south, the heavens were unobscured by even a passing vapor, and as the eye turned toward them, it seemed to pierce far into their blue depths, till sight became almost painful. There was a slight breeze, which rippled the surface of Rapaug pond, and breathed through the surrounding forest, bearing to the ear the sound of singing birds and murmuring brooks. The old woods, clothed in their spring garments, looked young again, and at times tossed their huge arms, as if in juvenile sportfulness. A faint smoke was curling lazily upward from the chimney of Mrs. Stanfield's dwelling, and it seemed as if, in that sequestered spot, the spirit of peace and innocent repose had taken its abode.

Of this scene but one human spectator was visible. The reader may remember the rock, which we have described, as, in one place, reaching to the verge of the water on the western side of the little lake. On this rock sat Orra Stanfield. A small basket of mountain plants stood near her, and she held in her hands some unknown flowers, whose purple-spotted petals she was examining. Her cheek was flushed, and her bosom heaving with exercise, and as her wild sun-bonnet fell back upon her shoulders, disclosing the graceful contour of her neck, and giving freedom to a profusion of glossy curls, which shaded her temples, and half-concealed the animated expression of her eyes, her extreme loveliness might have warmed the coldest heart, and bewildered the strongest head. For some time she continued her occupation, but at length she dropped the blossoms, and sat gazing thoughtfully at the water, whose tiny waves were beating against the rock a little below and beyond her. Suddenly she started, as she thought she heard the sound of approaching footsteps. She listened attentively for a moment, and a smile played on her lips, and a faint blush tinged her countenance, as she exclaimed, in a low tone,

" It must be Hugh;" but the smile and the flush vanished, as she recollected herself, and saying, " no, it cannot be; he always comes from the other direction; it was nothing;" she turned once more to the plants. There was a foot-path which passed from the clearing, quite around the western side of the pond, and finally turned off to the north. The rock on which the maiden was sitting, was not more than three yards in width, and shelved down some five or six feet till it projected beneath the surface of the water. Immediately behind it, the gradually ascending soil was covered by the old forest trees, through which, at about a rod's distance from the rock, ran the path which we have described.

In a short time, the girl again caught the sound of footsteps, now more audible, and she sprang up in some alarm. Her first impulse was to immediate flight; but, though the steps were coming from the north, and she was herself between the person approaching and the clearing, she feared to enter the only track there was, lest she should be overtaken before she could reach the hut. If she remained where she stood, she could hardly hope to escape his notice; but at last, saying, in a suppressed tone, "What have I to fear? I have harmed no one," she resumed her seat, and endeavored, though with a painfully throbbing heart, to continue her inspection of the plants. But the flowers fell from her hands as the unwelcome visitor drew nigh, and paused in the path immediately behind her, exclaiming,

"Hallo! what is this? By ——! better than I hoped." Instinctively the maiden arose, and turned toward the voice, and the next moment, John Martin, advancing between the trees, stopped close before her. For a short time, the Tory stood as if half-abashed; then, recovering himself, he said, sharply,

"Well, girl, your rebel hero is not at hand just now, with his lank follower, nor the old witch, with her infernal tongue."

"Who and what are you, sir," said Orra, with dignity, "that addresses me thus?"

"One John Martin, madam, pretty well known in these parts, I believe." Then suddenly changing his tone, he exclaimed, earnestly, "Orra Stanfield, I have no time now to spend in idle talk. I have long been near you,—have seen, have felt your exceeding loveliness; maiden, I love you as well as my nature will allow: I offer you my hand and my protection; I make no idle pretensions. Be mine, and I will not take you to a rebel's home and a rebel's fate, but you shall live in affluence and uninterrupted security. Be still; speak not yet! I know that Hugh Warden loves you, and you may think you love him. Discard the vain fancy; forget this rebel to his king, this foe to his country,—this renegade"—

"Stop!" exclaimed the maiden, her form dilating, and her eye flashing with indignation, "pollute not *his* name with your foul lips. I *do* know you for a traitor to your native land, a disgrace to your native State. I disbelieve your hollow professions, I scorn your lying promises; and, were no Hugh Warden in existence, I would sooner lie down in my grave than become your bride. Away! let me pass!" and she started, as if to gain the path. Martin, however, held his place, and motioning her back with his hand, said, fiercely,

"Not so, girl, not so; remember you are in *my* power now; drive me not to extremities; I wish you no harm; I speak to you fairly; but if you will not be persuaded, you *must* obey."

"I have protectors more powerful than man,—God and my innocence; I fear you not;" replied Orra, firmly, though her pale cheek and quivering lips seemed half to belie her words.

"Be it as you will, then," exclaimed the Tory, "you scorn my offer, you despise my love. I am not now to be foiled; I have told you that no Hugh Warden can assist you now; I told you not all," his voice grew almost hissing, and his face was red as blood, as he uttered the lie, "I saw his mangled corpse lying among the ashes of his uncle's dwelling."

"O God!" shrieked the unhappy girl, and she fell fainting at his feet. He seized her in his arms, and was turning to bear her away, when a hand was laid upon his shoulder, and the shrill voice of Mrs. Stanfield exclaimed in his ear,

"Be not too sure, John Martin, be not too sure."

"Damnation!" shouted the Tory, "you here again?" He placed the senseless maiden on the ground, near the foot of a tree, on one side of the rock, and drawing a pistol from his belt, he faced the old woman, and continued, "witch, you have crossed my path enough; force me not to murder you; stand aside!"

Mrs. Stanfield, without heeding his command, replied, in a tone almost mournful—

"Martin, twice already have I warned you; you can never carry your intentions into effect, and I would, if I could, save you from your approaching fate. Once more, for the last time, I bid you depart; seek not to tear my child from me, you cannot do it; your friends will need you before twenty-four hours have passed,—go join them."

"Old woman," said Martin, "I am no longer to be intimidated by your wordy threats; I have almost gained my prize—you cannot wrest it from me; yet, it's a cowardly deed to kill a woman, and I would not do it; return to your hut, and if you want aid, call the devil."

"It is done," screamed Mrs. Stanfield. "I tell you, lay not your hands on my child; a feeble woman can do little, but that little I will do. And now look up at the daylight, John Martin; look well—it is the last you will ever see!"

"You force me to it," exclaimed Martin, and he raised the pistol to her breast. As he did so, the cat, which had stood unobserved by the side of Mrs. Stanfield, sprang upon his shoulder, and fastened her teeth into his throat; the shock forced him backward—his weapon exploded, and at the same instant the sharp crack of a rifle sounded through the forest. With a wild cry, he leaped up, grasped the cat convulsively with one hand, and fell reeling into the dark waters of the pond. The fierce animal relinquished not its hold, and with a few bubbling groans and a shrill yell, both sank together to rise no more.

The sound of footsteps approaching from the direction of the clearing was now audible, and in a few seconds Hugh Warden, followed by Riggs and the hunter, sprang upon the rock.

"Orra, dear Orra," exclaimed Hugh, raising the maiden in his arms, "thank God! you are safe."

The girl opened her eyes faintly, and shuddering, murmured, "dead! he saw him—dead!"

"What mean you, Orra," said the young man, "it is I, Hugh Warden."

She looked wildly into his face, for a moment, and then, her features suddenly lighting up, she threw her arms impetuously about his neck, exclaiming—

"It is, it is! dear, *dear* Hugh, it was a horrible dream."

"What was it, my sweet girl?" said the young man, pressing his lips to hers, "what dream, Orra?"

"That you"—

"Mister Hugh," said the hunter, touching the arm of the person addressed, "look this way a minute."

Warden turned about, and saw Riggs supporting Mrs. Stanfield on one knee, while the blood poured profusely from a wound in her side. The bullet of the Tory had done its work, and the old woman seemed as if in the agonies of death. As the eyes of Orra turned toward the sad object, she sprang from her lover, and exclaiming, "My grandmother, my poor grandmother!" threw herself on her knees by the bleeding form, and clasped it franticly in her arms.

"Good heaven! Richard, I saw not this," said Hugh; "quick, let us stanch the blood and bear her to the hut."

"It's of no use, Captain, she may live a few hours, certainly not longer."

"Orra," said the young man, gently detaching the clasp of the maiden, and raising her from the ground, "let us bear her to the hut; there may yet be hope."

"Oh! Hugh, it is terrible," exclaimed the girl, clinging convulsively to his side—"but—let us go, let us go."

As she spake, the hunter lifted Mrs. Stanfield in his arms, and holding a handkerchief tightly over the wound, bore her away to the path towards the hut. Riggs departed in the same direction, and Warden, supporting the half-fainting Orra, followed them.

CHAPTER XIII.

About an hour after the events described in the preceding chapter, a mournful group was collected in that small apartment of Mrs. Stanfield's dwelling which we have formerly mentioned. The light of a single lamp revealed the form of the unfortunate woman, stretched upon the couch, mortally wounded—her few remaining moments of life rapidly gliding away. The ball had entered her right side, and though the blood was now stanched by a firm bandage, yet the pallid features and glassy eyes spoke of approaching dissolution. She had not spoken a word since the hunter first took her in his arms and bore n the rock; and an interrupted gasping breath only served to ow near was the death struggle. Kneeling by the bedside, her wed down to the coverlid, was Orra Stanfield; she spake not, not, except when now and then a half-suppressed sob shook her ted frame. By her side, holding one of her hands in his, and s bending forward to whisper some words in her ear, stood Warden, while behind these, standing with saddened counte-, were Riggs and the hunter.

ngth the old woman turned convulsively toward the group and ed, wildly—

ra—my child—where is she?"

m here," said the girl, taking the hand of the sufferer in her here; oh! grandmother, that you should be murdered for my

is too late to complain now," said Mrs. Stanfield, "I have lived nough—let me do *you* justice before I die; water—bring me rater."

hunter complied with her demand, and after simply touching the her lips, she continued—

ave never told you, Orra, of your origin, your parents, and of fancy, and I never would have done so, but for this accident"— cents grew more wild. "Who ever dreamed that my plans all be frustrated by this accursed Martin—they shall not—Hugh n—where is he? You shall not take my child from me—away, away!"

voice sank to an inaudible murmur, and for a few moments a ike stillness pervaded the room. Suddenly, the old woman again.

ra, you have always been faithful to me, and sometimes I have d of my resolution—but when I remembered *him*—I was firm -but it's too late, now—too late. Hear my story—and when I d, may you find a better friend."

annot, grandmother," said the girl, "I cannot—you have been me—all my life long—I have known no other relative, and must lose you."

u must, child, you must—but—my time is short, and I must be listen well to what I say."

ould weary the patience of the reader to give the story of Mrs. ld in her own language, rambling and incoherent as it was, and ntly broken by wild exclamations. It was, in substance, as fol-

about twenty years before, she had lived in England. Her na- ace was a small town on the Thames, some thirty or forty miles ondon. Here she was married to a man in opulent circumstances, n 1755, died, leaving her a widow, with an only daughter. This was then a beautiful girl of sixteen, and her innocence and loveli- were the chief solace of the widowed mother. Near where they dwelt a wealthy gentleman, whose only son became the constant nion of her daughter, and finally, unknown to the parent, won her heart. Two years passed away in this manner, when the father of the young man died, and the latter succeeded to the family estate. Immediately, without even informing Mrs. Stanfield and her daughter of his intentions, he set out for London. Weeks and months passed away without any tidings of the wanderer. The widow saw the eyes of her child grow dim and her cheek pale, without knowing the cause, and she began to fear that some lingering disease had marked her for its victim. At last, one pleasant autumn evening, as they were sitting near the trellised window, after she had remained some time gazing in silence upon her daughter, who was looking out, with saddened countenance, upon the glorious hues of twilight, she asked her what it was that had of late so altered her demeanor. The girl at first made no reply, but upon being questioned a second and a third time, she flung herself impetuously upon her mother's bosom, and, bursting into a flood of tears, exclaimed—"George Winston—mother—I love him!"

"And why, my child, should that cause all this grief?" inquired the parent.

"He told me," said the poor girl, sobbing, "that I was dearer to him than all the world beside; and before his father died, he said that he would never leave me for another—never; and now, mother, he has gone, without even coming to bid me farewell; and where he is, or whether I shall ever see him more, I know not."

The widow's eyes were now opened. George Winston was one who thought only of the pleasure of the present moment; a proud, ambitious, selfish man; and he had sported with her daughter's heart, till circumstances called him to another circle, when he departed, careless of the sorrow and bitter anguish which he was working. Still, Mrs. Stanfield tried to console the poor girl, by prophesying the speedy return of the wanderer. And he did return. Suddenly, after the lapse of a year, he came back to the place, to the family mansion, bringing with him a beautiful but haughty bride.

"When my daughter first heard the tidings," exclaimed the old woman, in this part of her narrative, "she fell, as if dead, at my feet. With long and painful attention, she was awakened from that fearful swoon—but not recovered from the blow. Day after day I watched her, as her step grew more and more feeble, and her form wasted away beneath the withering grief. She died!—in less than three weeks she died;—and when I saw her a corpse—I cursed *him*—I cursed his young bride; and I vowed a vow, that should a child ever be born to them, I would, through that child, wreak my vengeance on their hearts. I buried my daughter, and then sat down to wait my time. Another year passed away, and I was told that George Winston and his wife were blessed with an infant girl—aye—blessed—so they thought. Still, I waited till the beauty and innocence of their child had filled their bosoms with that love which a parent only knows, and had made their household the abode of joy, and then I completed my preparations. Every thing that I possessed, I sold; I entered the Winston mansion by night and carried off their child, and at once, with the proceeds of my property, embarked for America."

They arrived at New York—Mrs. Stanfield and the infant—and took up their abode in a rather elegant dwelling in one of the principal streets of the city. Years rolled away, and the child gradually won the affection of the lonely widow. She named it Orra Stanfield, and professed to be its grandmother. At length, news came to her from England, which seemed enough to satisfy every feeling of anger that might still be lurking in her bosom. George Winston had entered into rash speculations, had lost much of his property, had had recourse to the gaming table to retrieve his misfortunes, and had finally become utterly ruined. His wife died, it was said, of a broken heart, and he himself embarking for America, had perished by shipwreck.

Orra was then some eight years of age. The widow had given her the best advantages for education which the city could afford, and they had not been lost upon the girl. Her childish beauty presaged the loveliness of the woman, and Mrs. Stanfield resolved to withdraw her from the crowded town, before she should be of an age to attract the admiration of the other sex. She had a feverish apprehension of losing this last solace of her declining years, and she hoped, by removing her to some secluded spot to keep her affections fastened upon herself, as her only protector. Hence she removed to D——, and hence she chose her strange residence among the Rapaug woods.

"They called me a witch," continued she, "and I rejoiced at the superstition, for I thought it would render us more entirely solitary. But it was all in vain—before I hardly suspected it, the heart of my girl was won. Hugh Warden, I would not then give her to you, for I wished her to be all my own. I would have gone back to England with her at the end of the war, but my hopes are defeated, my projects destroyed by the hand of fate. Take her, now—here kneel down by her side and join your hands"—the young man obeyed her wishes, and she continued—"she is yours, Hugh Warden, for better or for worse. She loves you, for I know her heart, and you have sworn to love her also. Cherish her well, for she is worthy of it—she has been faithful to me, even when sore tempted to desert me; be you as faithful to her."

"I will," exclaimed Warden, pressing the tearful girl to his bosom, "God be my judge, if I ever falter in my love."

"Grandmother!" said the maiden, suddenly raising her head—"father—mother—both gone; and I—whom have I left? not one!"

"Orra!" said the young man, reproachfully.

"Forgive me, Hugh," exclaimed the girl, leaning her head upon his shoulder, "but this terrible story has almost crazed me."

"Away!" said the old woman, raising herself partially from the couch, and glaring wildly around. "George Winston—gaze not at me—there is your daughter, take her!" She fell back exhausted—the hunter sprang to the bedside and applied a restorative to her lips—she turned her head away—a convulsive shudder ran through her body, and—she was a corpse. The maiden rose to her feet, looked upon the senseless form for a moment, and with a faint cry fell swooning into the arms of her lover. Warden hastily bore her into the adjoining sitting-room, followed by Brownhead, which latter, without speaking, lighted the lamp upon the mantel, and returned to watch with Riggs by the couch of the dead.

It was now late at night, and the storm, which had been gathering since sunset, was at its height. The wind howled through the hemlocks which covered the rear of the hut, and the rain beat incessantly upon the roof.

On the third day after the events just related, a funeral procession entered the small grave-yard adjoining the Episcopal church in D——. The coffin covered with its black pall, was borne upon a rude bier by four of the villagers, and immediately behind these, as chief mourner, walked Hugh Warden and Orra Stanfield—or, as now rightfully called, Orra Winston. Mr. John Warden, Richard Brownhead, and Riggs, were also there, and such other of the towns-people as sympathy or curiosity had drawn together. When they reached the grave and the coffin was placed on the ground for a moment before lowering it into its allotted place, there might have been seen on its lid a simple plate, on which was inscribed

"SARAH STANFIELD, APRIL 26TH, 1777."

Reader, our history of THE WITCH has drawn to its close, and it only remains for us to tell what can be told of the subsequent fortunes of those who have been connected with her.

Hugh Warden, in the space of a few months, became the husband of the orphan girl, Orra Winston. That they lived happily together and that their love increased as years rolled by, will be readily inferred by all who have read the preceding pages. Of the bachelor, we need only say that he lived to a good old age, and after the war was ended often delighted the children of Hugh and Orra with his wonderful tales of the Witch. Brownhead remained in the family of the Wardens for many years, and we ourselves remember traditions of his marvelous exploits as a hunter, and of his extraordinary services in the war. We have not learned the fate of Riggs, but it is thought that soon after these events he joined the American army and perished in one of the battles at the South. The Indian was never heard of again. It was supposed that he left the State and sought a final home in the far West. Mrs. Barton continued as a favorite domestic with Hugh Warden to her dying day. Of Mrs. Wilkins and Miss Lappett we hear no more; they pass across our vision, and disappear in the mists of antiquity.

D—— itself speedily recovered from the effects of the British invasion, and in a few years assumed an appearance even superior to that which it formerly wore. From that day to this it has thrived and increased in population and prosperity. Rapaug changed its name in the lapse of time to MOUNTAIN POND, and under the latter title is known to all the surrounding people. The old forests are cut away, and a new growth has sprung up in their place; the traces of the original clearing are gone; the hut has utterly disappeared, not even a ruin being left. Yet the beauty of the spot remains almost the same. The waters are as placid as of old; the wild birds sing as sweetly; the sky above is as beautiful; and many have been the pleasant hours that we have enjoyed sitting upon the rock and gazing at the soothing scene before us. The tale which we have related is known only to a few, and to the mere spectator, who looks upon that peaceful prospect, the breezes which fan his brow, and the tiny waves which break at his feet, can tell no tale of love, and fierce conflict and agonizing death.

WHAT IS IT TO BE FREE?

Where beetling cliffs hang threat'ning o'er
  In fearful, awe-inspiring height,
The thunder of Niagara's roar,
  I saw an eagle take his flight;
He dashed from his proud wing the spray,
  The mist grew azure in his sight—
While hovering glanced his plumage gray,
  One moment in the rainbow's light;
Then in broad circles wheeling high,
  Soared upward from my wondering gaze,
As fast, with eager joy, his eye
  Drank in the Day-god's noontide blaze.
A sportsman saw the eagle fly,
He shot and brought him from the sky;
  Stoop'd the proud bird to meet the ground,
  With bleeding, yet not mortal wound;
His captor held him fettered fast
  In bondage vile, and placed him where,
With servile chains around him cast,
  He breath'd the tainted prisoned air,
And thought, but vainly thought, that so
  His free-born spirit he should tame—
Knew not, the bird could never know,
  Such lasting infamy of shame.
Weeks, months, and years, slow circling by,
  No change wrought in the captive's fate,—
Flash'd ever from his fiery eye
  Unconquer'd pride and deathless hate,
And that wild scream, which oft before
  Woke forest-echoes far and nigh,
Ringing as wildly as of yore,
  Startled the careless passer by:

His scornful eye and bearing proud,
His fearless voice, as trumpet loud,
Prov'd that his heart had never bow'd
  To Fate's stern destiny:
But mid gray rocks and mountains steep,
Mid sunless shades of forests deep,
His eyried home did ever keep—
  Still Freedom's bird was free!

Hard by where Tiber's waters flow,
  Mid hoary piles of crumbling stone,
Chained in a loathsome dungeon low,
  A wearied prisoner sat alone;
How such unseemly fate befel
  The captive, here I may not say,
Suffice it only this to tell,
  He would not own the tyrant's sway.
Of noble birth, unsullied fame,
  Unstain'd by shade of guilt or crime,
He wasted in that den of shame
  The gladness of his youthful prime.
Three weary years dragg'd o'er his head,—
  'Twas if an age had passed away,—
Entomb'd among the living dead,
  He never saw the light of day:
Nor human voice had bless'd his ear,
  Nor human form had cheer'd his eye,
But o'er his heart there stole the fear
  That all forgotten he must die.
Darker the prison'd darkness grew,
  To icy chillness turn'd the air,
Till Nature to his wilder'd view
  Seem'd one cold night of deep despair.
He heard his sentry's step no more,
  And death-damps, on his dungeon floor,
Crept nearer and more near, till now
  He felt them on his very brow.
Then fiends in human form came nigh,
  Unlock'd his dungeon door, and led
The captive to the open sky,
  A resurrection from the dead.
He looks on the sweet heaven above,
  Looks on the glad green earth below,
Hears tones of melody and love—
  Sweet singing birds and water's flow.

New life into his veins once more
Pour the free mountain breezes bland,
As blessed angel breathing o'er
The wasteness of some desert land;
And like an infant he did weep
Half sad and yet half joyful tears,
As woke within his heart the deep
Rememberings of by-gone years.
All sounds, and joyful sights to see,
All blessed thoughts which he could feel,
They promis'd him for aye, if he
Would to the haughty tyrant kneel.
At once a wild unearthly fire
Flash'd from his wasted hollow eye,
Dark lower'd his brow with sudden ire,
The fountain of his tears was dry:—
"Deem'd ye I was so base a slave,
Or lov'd the joys of earth so well,
A life of wretchedness to save
My soul's high birth-right I would sell?
Give back, give back my dungeon drear!
Come back ye death-damps to my brow!
Frozen this heart, ere ye shall hear
My lips pronounce your cursed vow."
The words upon his white lips died,
Choked by immeasurable pride,
The last his haughty soul replied,
Worthy the last to be;
As closed on him the dungeon door,
Life's fitful strife with him was o'er,
He knew its joys and griefs no more,
His mighty soul was free!

Fetters and servile chains may bind
The earthly body down to earth,
Scorns their control the godlike mind,
Which claims a higher, nobler birth;
The soul, which, wiuh high purpose true,
With earnest faith, keeps still in view,
And steadfast courage doth pursue
Life's glorious destiny,
Which Fate and Fortune both defies,
Which firm in its own strength relies,
And outward semblance doth despise,
Dwells ever with the free.

AN ADVENTURE ON THE PRAIRIES.

READER, hast ever seen a prairie? Hast ever stood on a plain—the bright blue sky above—while below, around, a vast sea of green stretches far, far away into the blue distance, until its edges mingle and are lost in the misty haze of the horizon—its undulating billows gracefully sinking and rising to meet the kisses of the wanton breeze—the brilliant hues of the many-colored flowers flashing in the sun-light, like diamonds on emerald ground? Hast ever gazed on the indescribable grandeur of the scene, or *felt* the deep awe-inspiring silence, unbroken save by the thundering *stampede* of a herd of some thousand buffaloes, as they rushed madly by, or the wild scream of the great gray eagle, as with talons filled with prey, he soars away to his eyerie, mid the craggy rocks of the North? No? Then hast thou in store for thee a rich treat—a feast of enjoyment of which thy mind can but faintly conceive, and

> "There are more things in heaven and earth
> Than thy philosophy hath ever dreamed of."

For *thee*, we say—for in four days, at farthest a week, from the time you leave the halls of Yale, you stand in a new world. And dost thou begrudge the trifling expense so richly repaid? If so, wherever else thou hast traveled, whatever thou hast seen, think thyself but a novice in American scenery. Thou hast, perchance, looked, in wondering astonishment, on the grand and picturesque scenery of the "granite state mountains"—hast gazed in speechless, reverential awe, on the sublime grandeur of Niagara—thy soul in a transport of delight has drank in the surpassing loveliness and beauty of the romantic scenery of the upper lakes—all scenes unequaled in their kind, and worthy of their world-wide fame, but none of them producing *such* sensations as the boundless prairie of the West!

But we wander. We proposed not, kind reader, at this sitting, a particular description of a prairie—only, with your good leave, to relate an "inkling" of an adventure, which it was our fortune to meet thereon, some few years "syne."

It was on the 25th of November, '39, that we found ourselves on the east bank of the De Moine, some fifty miles from its mouth. How we came there—with what object—what adventures we met with—how many deer and buffalo we slaughtered in that vicinity—each and all these matters we consider entirely irrelevant to the subject, and accordingly leave them untouched. Should we at some hereafter feel in the humor, they may, perchance, furnish *materiel* of an article for Maga. For the present, turn we to another subject. As remarked, at the time and place above mentioned, we found ourselves (that is, myself and a hardy, sensible *mustang*, who dated his origin from the plains of Arkansas) after a morning ride of some twenty miles, at a dead halt, holding a council respecting future operations.

The reader (who is supposed to be acquainted with the science of geography) will remember that the De Moine empties into the Mississippi, forming, by its junction with that river, an acute angle, rapidly widening towards their sources. He will also remember, that in the intervening space lies a part of the great Platte prairie, stretching far, far away to the north and west, beyond the utmost limits of civilization. Now, our purpose was to reach a settlement some fifty miles northwest of the spot we then occupied—the object of the council, to consider how this might best be accomplished. Two routes offered themselves, each attended with difficulties. The first, the ordinary circuitous road following the course of the rivers, making a journey of more than one hundred and fifty miles, the most of it over the most detestable of all roads in those parts, at that season, where each is so bad as to admit no comparison for the worse. The other, a delightful gallop across the magnificent prairie, its hard, plain surface, and clear, level expanse, presenting a tempting contrast to the mud, bogs, and forests of the first mentioned route. Unfortunately, however, it was a way never traveled, uninhabited, affording no means of ascertaining the direction of the place we wished to reach, except a slight Indian foot-path, which would soon, perhaps, entirely disappear. Here, then, was the choice. On the one hand a wearisome journey of several days, through mire, almost impassable swamps, and gloomy forests; on the other, a single day's ride over the glorious prairie, yet with the risk of losing our way, and perhaps falling a prey to savages and wild beasts. What was to be done? We were completely in a fix—a dilemma, scarcely less perplexing than that of the countryman giving directions to the traveler. "Go," said he, "directly forward, half a mile, and you will come to what may seem the end of this road; but it is not. One part turns to the right, and the other to the left. The right hand road is traveled most, and considered most direct to the city; but the left hand road is *certainly* the better way; for the right hand road does not lead to the place at all. But, I don't know, I declare. The left is not much traveled. I think, on the whole, you'd better take the right hand road. Stay! Let me see! Be careful, Mister, not to take *'um both!*"

Luckily, at this moment, a thought suggested itself, which relieved us of the inconvenience of taking *both.* At the place of our destination, a fair cousin, with whom we had carried on sundry pleasant flirtations, was, on the morrow, to take the bridal veil, on which interesting occasion we had a special invite to be present,—a circumstance which had been forgotten amid the sports of the chase. By the river route, we should be several days after the fair; by prairie, with luck, we might arrive at the settlement before twelve that night. One glance at the miry sloughs which lay before, one thought of the first sweet kiss from the ruby lips of the blooming bride, (we always take the *first* on such occasions,) together with the infinite variety and abundance of good cheer, and unbounded fun and jollity of an expensive Hoosier wedding, decided the question, and putting spurs to our mustang, we dashed away over the prairie.

But hold a moment,—not too fast,—take things coolly. A gallop of fifty miles, (in addition to a 'step' of twenty performed the same morning,) across an uninhabited prairie, should not be rashly undertaken, without due provision for the wants of the inner man. This proposition appeared the more evident from the fact, that although considerably past mid-day, neither myself nor friend (i. e. the mustang) had tasted food since early morning. So forcibly, indeed, was the idea presented, that we had scarcely proceeded half a mile, when we drew rein, wheeled about, and retraced our steps to an inhabited shanty, standing near the place at which we struck the prairie. Now in most parts of the country, where a person sees a dwelling inhabited by human beings, he very naturally and correctly supposes they must have provisions for their subsistence. Such a supposition, however, in regard to a Hoosier family, would be entirely gratuitous, not to say often decidedly erroneous. Whether this is only the natural and practical result of Ralph's theory of the "inevitable dualism which bisects nature," or referable to some other principle, we know not. For ourselves, we consider the simplest explanation the most satisfactory, namely, that the excessive richness of the soil supports animal life, without the ordinary intromission of food. However this may be, the fact itself is well established, which may be demonstrated from the "recent preparation."

The inmates of the shanty afforded a fair specimen of the Hoosier family in its natural, healthy state. The husband, of course, was absent at a shooting-match. Advancing to the door, I was met by a dame of goodly proportions, surrounded by some ten or twelve young Hoosiers and Hooshierina's, all nearly of a size, with long yellow hair, a peculiarly wolfish expression about the mouth and eyes, while their faces and persons afforded a fair index of the color and depth of the soil.

"Couldn't we obtain a peck of grain for our nag?" inquired we of the lady.

"Well, I allow so; jest lead him to the barn, and help yourself."

We proceeded to the spot indicated, (which, by the way, consisted merely of four upright posts, with poles laid across, covered with bark,) where we found a plentiful supply of beautiful wheat, of which, having furnished our poney with a *quant. suff.*, we returned, to ascertain what fare could be obtained to satisfy the cravings of our own appetite.

"My good woman, would you be so kind as to accommodate a stranger with a bowl of bread and milk!"

"Well, I allow I couldn't, no how you can fix it; han't had a drop of milk fur five years."

(We started in surprise at her numerous thrifty offspring, the youngest of which might have had ideas of three or four weeks' growth.) "Well, no matter," we are not particular; a slice of bread and butter, or any thing that's handy."

"No, ye ain't partic'lur, be ye? How d'ye s'pose I'm a goin' to make butter without milk?"

"Oh, ah! true; but at least you can give us some crackers and cheese, or bread and molasses?"

"Well, I tell you what it is, strangur, I'm sentimentally a sort of pinion, if you're a goin' to be so powerful nice about your vittals, ou'll have to go down to 'square Jones's, where they keep them fixins, r I'm teetotally blamed if we've had any sich indulgences since we am on the prairies."

Now, to reach 'square Jones's, we must travel at least six miles out our way, a thing at that time entirely out of the question, even were e certain of being regaled with the 'nice fixins' we had called for. Ma-y would have called the woman a hard-hearted, inhospitable vixen, and linquished the attempt in despair; but it was evidently not our inter-st, in the circumstances, so to regard her: besides, we were too well quainted with western character, not to know, that a heart of genuine ospitality was concealed under the rough exterior. We must try an-her tack; a new chord must be touched; an apology must be made.

"Beg pardon, ma'am; meant no offense; hope you'll overlook—but e are most powerful hungry, and can eat any thing you have, even to raw buffalo's hide. You surely would not send a fellow-creature a urney of fifty miles across the prairie, without a mouthful of food?"

"Law me! now don't take on so. I allow no man could ever say e went away hungry from Ned Stanley's, when he could eat sich as e family. But you wasn't raised on the prairie, I take? Don't look s if. Howsomever, if you'll set up, and eat hog and hominy, which e have, you're welkum."

We assured her we regarded the dish as a perfect luxury,—that, in-eed, we preferred it above every other, and should have mentioned it first, only fearing it might be inconvenient to furnish the article. Here a slight twinge of conscience indicated a trifling deviation from e strict truth, as we had a mortal aversion—a perfect Jewish abhor-nce of swine's flesh, and, moreover, knew it was the only indispensa-e and ever-present dish in the frontier settler's bill of fare.) The dy was now, however, restored to good humor, and, with many re-ets and apologies for "sich powerful poor fixins," our dinner was on ready, and, with the customary invitation, "Wal, come, set up!" e prepared to discuss its merits. The flitch of bacon—evidently the mnant of several previous meals—had certainly the appearance of eing *rather* old and rusty, and the hominy an indefinable compound etween a Yankee "johnny-cake" and Indian-pudding, and about the nsistence of a brick-bat, was of *rather* a *dubious* texture and color; it we had little time or inclination for practical observations. We ad an excellent appetite, both retrospective and prospective, and if we ad before done violence to conscience by our assertions respecting oice of food, we now made ample amends, by desperate infractions our ordinary habits in regard to its use. Besides, we wished to ex-ress to our hostess our deep and grateful sense of her kindness, in so eerfully ministering to our necessities from her limited means, which e could effect in no way so well, as by doing full justice to the *sub-antial* fare before us.

[And here, as perhaps the force of the last observation may ot be clearly seen by all, we beg leave to digress a little from e subject to suggest some hints, which may be of use to our readers in their future peregrinations. And should you, kind reader, be at any time traveling in the South or West, and ask entertainment at a private residence, never think of offering your entertainer a pecuniary compensation. You not only run the risk of being thought "decidedly green," but will very likely receive another *sobriquet*, which will add neither to your respectability or comfort, while sojourning in those regions. Partake heartily of the refreshments set before you, thank your host, frankly and sincerely,—your obligations are all canceled. It is the more necessary to speak of this, from the fact, that in some parts of the country a very different custom prevails. We have known frequent instances in which the traveler, tired and faint, calls at a wealthy farmer's house, to rest a few moments his wearied limbs, and asks for a bowl of milk to drink. It is brought and drank.

"Very much obliged to you, Ma'am ; how much is the damage ?"

"Well, I don't know, I *guess* nine-pence would be about right."

Reader, can you by any, the utmost stretch of your imagination, conceive that such beings have souls ? Yes ? Then, whatever be your occupation, we advise you to relinquish it at once, and turn poet. Such powers of the imagination give promise of the most complete success in the art, and should not be lost to the world. For ourselves, we boast no such imaginative gifts. We have been engaged in a minute and careful examination of these beings during the last four years, with reference to an important theory, and shall give the result of our investigations to the world, in the next number of Silliman's Journal.]

Thus prepared, we again started on our expedition, with fresh courage and animation. The air was cool and bracing, the Indian trail smooth and easily traced, and the effect of the lunch upon my friend's spirits and heels of the happiest description. As we galloped gaily on, we often congratulated ourselves on the wisdom of our choice, and indulged in sundry pleasant reveries of the joyous festivities of the morrow, in which we were to participate. The prospect was magnificent. A few hardy flowers, even at that late season, were in bloom ; at wide intervals were seen the 'oak openings,' the mighty moss-covered trunks, and giant branches crowned with the most gorgeous foliage, towering far, far up, as if they would embrace the very clouds, so antique, so quiet, so covered at the roots with fresh green sward, they seemed of all others the very abodes of fays and fairies. Now and then a herd of deer would start up in fright, and bound gracefully away over the rolling surface, until lost in the distance, while more seldom, a drove of buffalo would raise their shaggy heads, gazing in stupid astonishment, until, as we approached nearer, they moved more sluggishly away some short distance, again to resume their grazing. We had thus pleasantly accomplished, as we conjectured, near half our journey, about sunset, when appearances began to assume an ominous and forbidding aspect. The sun, which during the afternoon had shone but dimly, wading, as it seemed, through banks of snow, and surrounded by a dense circle, in that climate a sure precursor of a storm, sank to rest behind a thick mass of dark and threatening clouds. The path, which had hitherto been easily discerned, grew each moment more and more indistinct, so that we were often obliged to proceed entirely at venture. The wind was rising, and blowing colder, and all things betokened an approaching storm. Confident, however, that we were pursuing the true direction, we held boldly onward, 'abating not a jot of heart and hope.' We had thus proceeded some two hours after sunset, when suddenly, in the far northeast, the clouds were seen rolling on in massy white folds, a dense mass of fog seeming to descend to the earth, while the wind swept madly by, in wild and fitful gusts. We knew too well the indications of a prairie storm, to need further warning. Turning from our course in the direction of an 'opening,' which we knew, from the howling of the prairie wolves, was some two or three miles distant, we put spurs to our mustang, and pushed for the grove. We were not too soon. Before we had reached a place of shelter, we were completely enshrouded in what seemed almost a solid sheet of snow, completely obstructing our sight, and almost instantly covering the ground. The instinct of our sagacious animal soon brought us to the wood, where we found a comfortable shelter under a friendly group of pines.

Here then we found ourselves, against our will, holding a council of a somewhat more serious nature than that of the morning. It was, however, of short continuance, as only one side was open for discussion. To proceed in the snow-storm was impossible: our only alternative, therefore, was to pass the night as best we could, in the grove. The alternative seemed the less objectionable, as we were confident that a ride of a few hours in the morning would bring us to the place of our destination. Our arrangements were soon made. By the side of a dry oak, which fortunately lay near, we soon kindled a fire, which afforded security against the attacks of wild beasts. A few pine boughs formed our couch, our saddle our pillow, and thus, supperless, and with the howl of the wolves for a lullaby, we laid ourselves to rest, to await, with what philosophy we best might, the events of the morrow.

[TO BE CONTINUED.]

ORIGIN AND MODES OF SUPERSTITIOUS BELIEF.

SUPERSTITION is the offspring of that feeling of reverence which was originally planted in the breast of man by the hand of the Creator. Or, if this be not one of his innate moral faculties—and that there are such, none can doubt—the beautiful and sublime objects in nature, which greet his eye upon his first entrance into the world, the manifestations of superior wisdom and power which everywhere surround him, impress upon his mind, at so early a period, the idea of superhuman agency, that it is impossible to solve the question of its doubtful origin. But whether the religious feeling which is universally found in man be innate, or whether his ideas of God are derived from the contemplation of his works, is equally unimportant to the truth of the position which has been advanced. We propose, then, in accordance with this premise, to trace out, so far as we are able, though necessarily in a somewhat desultory manner, the origin of superstitious belief, as exemplified by the religion of the ancients, and to notice, briefly, some of the principal forms in which it has been embodied among the moderns.

This principle of reverence, which has been spoken of, would, it is evident, prompt to the worship of *something*, and in the absence of a religion really or supposed to be directly received from heaven by revelation, the uninstructed mind, "leaping from nature up to nature's God," would naturally strive to people with imaginary deities, that unknown and invisible world, which we instinctively believe to be inhabited. The existence of evil as well as good, of misery as well as happiness, would be attributed to the agency of two antagonistic spirits, the one opposed to the interests of man, the other humane and benevolent. This idea, in fact, with various modifications, we find to be the ground-work of all false religion. In subsequent times, various subordinate deities would be added to these, and accordingly, as they were supposed to be subservient to the one or the other, invested with good or evil powers and inclinations. Heroes, whose eminence in arms, the chief employment of a barbarous age, have gained the admiration of their contemporaries, while their martial achievements are exaggerated by tradition, lose their mortal character in the lapse of time, and are worshiped as superior beings. By another advance the Earth, Sea, and Air have their peculiar deities. Neptune, with his attendant Nereids and Tritons, rules the vast realm of ocean. Jove, "the thunderer," surrounded by the Celestials, reigns on high Olympus; the Naiad dwells in the limpid waters of the fountain; the Faun inhabits the fields and groves, and the "great-footed Satyr" frightens the incautious wanderer into the solitudes of the forest. With the advance of intelligence and refinement, the creative imagination of the poets, who are always found in the earlier stages of society, would continue to multiply divinities, and to assign to each their sphere of action. The passions would be deified, particular pursuits receive their patron gods and goddesses, and finally, abstract virtues come to be worshiped. The superstition of the Greeks and Romans has been spoken of, both because it presents a striking illustration of the preceding remarks, and for the surpassing elegance and beauty of the whole system.

Let us now turn to the barbarian conquerors of the Roman Empire. Here, too, the same radical idea of the existence of two conflicting spirits prevails, and there appears such a remarkable similarity, in some other respects, between the Northern and Classical mythologies, as leaves little room to doubt that there is an innate tendency to superstition in the human mind, which, when left to itself, produces essentially the same creations. Such, for example, was the striking analogy between the sorceress of the Romans and Scandinavians, the latter, however, being supposed to possess inferior powers, which were also used for less malevolent purposes. More marked still was the resemblance between the satyrs and woodland deities of the two creeds, extending, in some instances, not only to the disposition and character, but even to the outward form.

Nor is it an uninteresting task to contemplate their points of difference, showing as they do, the great influence of incidental circumstances upon superstitious belief. The Norse mythology, considered merely with regard to beauty, does not compare to advantage with the highly elegant fictions of Greece and Rome. The Classical system was such as we might expect from a people who have left behind them such glorious monuments of their genius and refinement in literature and the arts. Beautiful in every part, complete in its whole structure, it would seem that none but a poet's hand, guided by the purest taste, could have fashioned its admirable and finished proportions. The Norse, on the contrary, was rude and ill-constructed. It wanted that completeness as a system, which characterized the mythology of the Classics. Though highly imaginative, and even poetical, in some of its features, it did not display such superiority of fancy. Its divinities were coarser and more malevolent, and its whole complexion sullen and gloomy.

But these differences are only what we should be led to expect from the diversity of character and situation, which obtained between the two people. The Greeks and Romans were by far the most polished nations of antiquity. In literature, it is probable that they fully equaled the moderns, while in refinement of taste and strong poetical temperament, they far excelled them. They lived, too, in a land which in richness of scenery, softness of climate, and a delightful sky, stands unrivaled, even were its shores not washed by that magnificent sea, whose very *name* is associated with all that is beautiful in the outward world. But the home of the rude Scandinavian was in a land of dismal morasses and dreary forests, upon whose sombre foliage not even the enlivening presence of summer could cast a smile. "Amid the twilight winters and overpowering tempests of those gloomy regions, he did not unnaturally attribute to his gods the same sullen character which he saw stamped upon the face of nature around him. His stern soul was attuned to no note of softness. No poetic fire glowed in his daring breast, save when he sang, in verse rude and unpolished as himself, some bloody feat of arms. Martial eminence and a fame for courage which not only quailed at no danger, but even sought it for the sake of the venture, were the only objects of ambition among these "sons of the sword and spear." They even dared to challenge the gods themselves, rather than admit that any thing was capable of intimidating *them*, and many of their fabled heroes, as Diomede, in the conflict with Mars, were supposed to have come off victorious from the unequal contest. Can we wonder, then, that instead of the refined enjoyments of the Classical Elysium, these Northern warriors should have destined for the use of the brave on earth, a heaven, where, in the presence of Odin and his associate gods, probably himself some deified conqueror, who, like Tamerlane, had piled his pyramid of human heads, they drank wine from the skulls of their enemies, and indulged in an unceasing round of beastly revel?

There is an interesting fact connected with the Classical mythology, which shows most strikingly the effect of national character in modifying superstition. Though the religion of the Romans, like their literature, was borrowed from the Greeks, and almost exactly similar in all its details, it differed in the important particular of being far more elevated and dignified. Whence this difference? We conceive it to be clearly owing to the following difference in the character of the two people. The Greeks probably excelled all other nations in the appreciation of *external* beauty. In every thing which addresses itself to the eye, their genius was unsurpassed. Nothing can exceed the elegance of their conceptions, as they have been embodied and handed down to us in the remains of their sculpture and architecture. But they were comparatively deficient in the perception of *moral* beauty. The Romans, on the contrary, with less taste in *externals*, were peculiarly sensitive to the *morally* beautiful. Their perceptions of the dignity of man's nature and of the sublime as exhibited by his actions, were vivid and clear. Cato the elder was but a strong personification of their stern and unyielding virtue. Those qualities of mind which made them the noble and high-souled people that they were, caused them also to attribute a more exalted character to their gods than was given them by the more volatile Greeks.

Having spoken of the origin of superstitious belief, and of some of the causes which tend to modify it, as illustrated by the mythological systems of the ancient nations, we will now proceed to notice some of the forms it has assumed in later periods, and more particularly in Great Britain, many of which have descended even to our own times. The first and by far the most important of these—the Fairy Superstition—was so deeply ingrafted into the popular mind, that it was not eradicated until the commencement of the eighteenth century, and even in the last generation, some lingering remains of it might be found in a few sequestered and romantic spots of England and Ireland. By some writers it is thought to have been derived from a fiction of the Northern nations, somewhat similar, indeed, but much inferior in beauty. But the belief in subordinate woodland deities of this kind, is known to have been entertained by the Celtic, as well as the Gothic tribes, at the earliest period to which our knowledge of these barbarians extends, and though the two creeds may have coincided in some points, there is reason to suppose that this idea was original with them.

The first particular which attracts our attention in the character of the Fairies, is their strong resemblance to the *Dii Campestres* of the Romans. Nor, if we divest them of the coarser traits which were attributed to them in later times, is the Northern fiction inferior in elegance to the classic. When we consider that the one was the invention of a people but few degrees removed from barbarism, and the other of a nation far advanced in learning and refinement, the comparison is highly favorable to the imaginative faculty of the ancient inhabitants of Britain. Indeed, this appears to have been the predominating principle in the intellectual constitution of the Celts, as is shown by the passionate fondness for music and poetry which is felt by the Welsh, Irish, and the Highlanders of Scotland, even at the present day. Until very lately, a professional bard, or piper, attached to some important family, was of no infrequent occurrence. How great their influence over the popular mind was in former times, is shown by the massacre of the Welsh bards, at the command of Edward I., lest their soul-stirring songs should arouse among their countrymen a spirit that would not "down at his bidding." The author of Waverly, whose patriotic pen has done so much to rescue from oblivion the primeval customs of his native land, has given us, in McMurrough nan Fonn, an unfading picture of a class which has now entirely passed away.

But, to return from this digression, many circumstances combined to change the original character of the Fairy, nor was it rendered more agreeable by the additional qualities which it received. In truth, they borrowed most of their disagreeable attributes from other subordinate members of the Norse mythology, whom they survived, when that system was overthrown by Christianity. From this source especially they derived their reputation of abstracting young children, and, in some instances, even adults. One of the finest ballads in the Border Minstrelsy commemorates the rescue of a gallant knight, who has been thus kidnapped, through the courage and constancy of his "ladye love." Upon the introduction of Christianity, the Fairies, in common with all the deities of the heathen mythology, were regarded as infernal spirits, and hence much of the malevolence ascribed to them originated.

It must not be forgotten, that the military spirit of the middle ages, which assimilated all things to itself, mounted these diminutive beings upon gallant chargers, and arrayed them in "all the pride and pomp and circumstance of glorious war." Many instances are related by the writers of that period, of single combats between these Fairy knights and mortal antagonists, with various success. To this current of "warlike ideas," says an author, "we may safely attribute the long trains of military processions which the fairies are supposed occasionally to exhibit." On Halloween especially,

—"that night, when fairies light
On Cassilis Downans dance,
Or owre the lays, in splendid blaze,
On sprightly coursers prance,"

the whole Elfin court were thought to have a grand annual procession, and at this time alone could stolen mortals be recovered. Upon this night, too, if we mistake not, witches and evil spirits of all kinds are out on their mischievous enterprises, though, from Tam O'Shanter's ludicrous adventure at "Alloway's auld haunted kirk," it is to be inferred that they did not confine their revels to any particular occasion.

That the Scotch fairies were much less agreeable than the English, both in appearance and disposition, setting aside the influence which diversity of scenery may have exerted, is mainly to be attributed to the new and more amiable qualities which Shakspeare and the poets of his age assigned them in their productions. These, however, assimilated them too much to the Peris of the Persians,—the most lovely class of ideal beings to which the imagination of man has ever given birth,—who are supposed to live in the colors of the rainbow, and subsist upon the fragrance of flowers. "If the Irish elves," to use the words of Scott, are anywise distinguished from those of Britain, it seems to be by their disposition to divide into factions, and fight among themselves,—a pugnacity," he humorously remarks, "characteristic of the Green Isle."

It may not be amiss to notice here two classes of imaginary beings, who, though somewhat unlike the fairies, appear to have been originally derived from them. The least attractive of these is the Scottish household spirit, called the Brownie, who was believed by the peasantry to perform various domestic services for the family to which he had attached himself, while they were buried in sleep. It requires no great penetration, however, to find the source of this fiction, in the parsimonious spirit of the prudent Scot. The other, the Banshie, is highly imaginative, and invested with a kind of mournful beauty. It is an attendant spirit, supposed to be attached to the most ancient and noble families of pure Irish descent, which, clad in the habiliments of woe, announces by its appearance the near approach of death. Similar to this, but more awe-inspiring, was the apparition of the Bodach Glas, in Waverly, described with such thrilling power by the "magician of the North," which appeared to the Vick Jan Vohr of the time on the eve of some great calamity. The family of McLean of Lochbuy, as we are informed by Scott, have an ancestor who performs an office analogous to that of a Psanchie. "Before the death," he says, "of any of his race, the phantom chief gallops along the sea-beach, near to the castle, announcing the event by cries and lamentations. The spectre is said to have rode his rounds and uttered his death-cries within these few years, in consequence of which, the family and clan, though much shocked, were in no way surprised to hear, by the next accounts, that this gallant chief was dead at Lisbon, where he served under Lord Wellington."

"The Fairy Superstition," says a distinguished author, "as received into the popular creed, and as described by the poets who have made use of it as machinery, is certainly among the most pleasing legacies of fancy. "So fascinating is the influence of such ideas upon the mind, that we almost envy the credulity of those ages, when, on the green sward,

> "The nimble-footed fairies danced their rounds
> By the pale moonshine,"

or held incessant revels in magnificent palaces beneath the grassy hillocks of "merrie England." Did superstition present itself in such aspects alone, we could not wish to have it dispelled. But it has other and more gloomy phases, which more than compensate for its occasional beauty.

From these comparatively innocent and harmless delusions, we turn now to a darker page in the history of human credulity—the subject of witchcraft. This superstition, as that of the fairies, was a legacy from the Northern nations, but unlike that in other respects, it was foul and disgusting in all its features. The heathen archetype of the modern witch, so far from being an object of detestation, was honored and revered, in proportion to the claims which she set up to supernatural power. Odin himself, in addition to his other qualities, was considered the especial patron of magical pursuits. But upon the introduction of Christianity, he and his associates were indiscriminately regarded as evil demons, and corresponding odium attached to the sorceress, who pretended to derive her skill from their favor. By a natural transition, losing sight of these demons, she was supposed to render allegiance to the arch fiend himself, and to be a willing instrument in his hands for the injury of the human race. Finding both confirmation of the existence of such a crime, and an excuse for its punishment, in the denunciations of the Scriptures against the witch—which term there signifies nothing more than a fortune-teller, or diviner—the most cruel persecutions were entered into against those unfortunate creatures who fell under this horrid suspicion. Evidence the most unsatisfactory and tests entirely absurd, were considered sufficient to convict of a crime, which scarcely any proof can establish. It is not surprising that the belief in witchcraft itself should have prevailed at the time it did, for knowledge of all kinds was then in its infancy, and even physical science was so imperfectly known, that many of the most ordinary phenomena of nature, which are now easily explained by the laws of chemistry and mechanical philosophy, could only be accounted for, by attributing them to the direct agency of supernatural beings. But, after making every allowance for the influence of superstition, it *is* surprising that men of ordinary intelligence, much less of the acquirements which Sir Matthew Hale possessed, could regard for a moment such trivial and ill-supported charges as sufficed to consign multitudes of people to the stake and the scaffold, both in Great Britain and upon the continent. The disgraceful laws, whose existence tended to create those periodical fits of popular frenzy, which appeared frequently in Europe, and once, in an aggravated form, in this country, are now, it is believed, erased from the statute-books of every nation in Christendom, and the repetition of such scenes of cruelty, as were often witnessed in days of yore, effectually prevented.

Superstition, driven from every other strong hold, in the minds of the educated at least, appears to have intrenched itself in one position, where, even yet, it maintains, in some degree, its footing—the belief in the occasional appearance of departed spirits. This, the most plausible of all delusions, if indeed it be a delusion, has been entertained by mankind, in all ages and in every region of the world. It had its origin in that innate consciousness of the soul, of its own separate and immortal being, which exists in the breast of even the rudest savage, and which no effort of the reason can entirely extinguish. What conclusion, then, is more natural to the reflecting mind, than that the disembodied spirit should continue to frequent those places, and attend the footsteps of those persons, who were intimately associated with it in life? There is even a kind of melancholy pleasure in the thought, that those we have loved when on earth, are not indifferent to our fortunes, in their new state of being; that they look down upon our good deeds with a smile of approval, from their abodes above, or grieve at our fall when seduced from the path of right. Such a reflection, it would seem, were an irresistible incentive to virtue, and a double safeguard from the syren song of temptation. How know we that this is not so? Who has so far penetrated the mystery in which we are enveloped, as to pronounce with certainty, that we are not ever attended by guardian spirits, who, though unseen and unfelt, watch over us with a care that never tires and a vigilance that never sleeps. To use the words of another, "If we cannot believe, we cannot entirely disbelieve. Our whole being is a mystery. Above, below, around us, all is fearful and wonderful. The shadow of a solemn uncertainty rests over all. Who shall then set limits to the capacity of the soul, when its incarnation has ended, and it enters, unfettered, unconfined, into a new state of being?" This language has a responsive echo in every breast.

While it must be acknowledged that superstition, in earlier ages, has lent to poetry some of its loftiest inspirations, and, in many of its features, is exceedingly beautiful and pleasing, still it cannot be denied that its general aspect is gloomy and forbidding. Those frightful spectres, with which sinless and untutored infancy surrounds its pillow in the darkness of night, are merely illustrations of its natural tendency. This alone were sufficient to make us deprecate its sway, even had it not kindled the fires of persecution, and given rise to some of the bloodiest wars that have afflicted man. Let us rejoice, then, that the advance of knowledge is gradually driving off its gloomy fantasies. But let not that supreme national vanity which is attributed to Americans, *par excellence*, prompt us to believe that our own land is entirely free from error on this point. True, the Elfin Court, and its gay followers, have passed away—almost from the memory of man—and many of its contemporary delusions, which were the terror of our stout-hearted ancestors, have now become food for mirth in the nursery—"to such base uses do we come." But others have survived, and new fictions have been created to fill the void, which was occupied by the old. It is far from true, however beautiful the expression, that

"The last lingering fiction of the brain,
The church-yard ghost, is laid at rest again."

In many of our quiet and secluded villages, remote from the bustle and tumult of the busy world, where the noise of the locomotive—that great revolutionizer of opinions as well as of commerce—has not frightened off the creations of the fancy, the belief in the appearance of departed spirits. if not still entertained, is at least not rejected; nor have the suspicions of the vulgar yet ceased to attribute to the ill-favored and solitary woman, whose temper has been soured by age and destitution, the mischievous inclinations and dreaded power of the witch. Other and marked manifestations of the natural tendency of the human mind to the supernatural, have, even of late, appeared among us. To what else can we attribute the success which the swarms of lecturers upon Mesmerism have met with, in their career of imposture through the land? Look at the extravagancies which were enacted, during the past year, in *New England itself*, by the disciples of the second advent.

Would that the ridiculous were all connected with that delusion. But no, its effects have been too terrible to provoke our mirth, and now—from the crowded mad-houses, which contain the unfortunate victims, whose reason this fanaticism has driven from its seat—attest the fearful power of the imagination in the economy of the intellect. Look yet again at the deluded thousands who throng the streets of the Mormon city of the West. These facts proclaim that futurity alone can decide whether superstition be not a hydra-headed monster, which cannot be entirely destroyed. The present, at least, is unable to determine.

THE PEOPLE.

There seems to be at the present time, and especially in this country, a kind of charm connected with those two words—'*the people.*' They are found in every man's mouth; they are uttered from the pulpit; they are the favorite theme of the orator; the patriotic candidate for office loves to dwell upon them; they form the title of half the editorials in our daily and weekly papers, and have become the watchword of both the great political parties of our land. Such being the general fact, it becomes a matter of interest to us, who from the quiet seclusion of a literary institution, can look calmly forth upon the turmoil of faction, and can decide without prejudice what *we* ourselves shall strive to accomplish when called to the active duties of life—to inquire, what is meant by all this outcry? who, now, are *the people?*

It is not easy to give a satisfactory answer to this question. Men, in different ages of the world and in different countries, have cherished widely-varying opinions upon the subject, and it is difficult to collect from the chaos of contradiction materials for an adequate definition. In ancient Persia, there were no *people* as an influential political body; in ancient Athens, the whole population claimed the title, and under its sanction exercised all the prerogatives of the most sanguinary despot. In the Roman Republic, a distinct class of the inhabitants adopted the name, and gaining the chief sovereignty, threw themselves, their property and the liberty of the State, at the feet of a military despot, and thenceforth lived as mere cyphers in the empire. Europe in the Middle Ages had, properly speaking, no people—nothing corresponding to what we now understand by the term. In England, we find the earliest distinctive action of '*the people*' in modern times. From the reign of Edward the Fourth, there was a gradual rising of the middle and lower classes; an increase of their influence, their intelligence and their power, which nothing could retard. The mad despotism of the eighth Henry and the equally firm resolution of his daughter Elizabeth, were unavailing against it. During the weak administration of James it acquired a might at the time invisible, but also irresistible. It was the great fault of Charles I. that he did not perceive this, and he necessarily perished in his foolish endeavors to retain the exercise of prerogatives which had been *allowed*, but never given as a *right* to his predecessors. The Revolution of 1688 was but the carrying out of the same great principle, and at the present day avowedly, as for the two last centuries in reality, the governing power in England has been her people, as represented in the House of Commons.

The mighty upheaving of the people of France in 1789, is familiar to every one, but it is needless to look to European countries for a definition of this term, which could be made applicable to the United States. It is not employed here, as it is there; we have a wider meaning, a more extensive signification. There, it is a separate class of the community; here it represents, according to common ideas, the whole nation: there it has antagonistic bodies to contend against; an aristocracy, titled and hereditary; here, it is called sovereign, and has nothing but itself to struggle with; there, it is feared, and in many instances kept in check by standing armies; here, it is courted and caressed.

With a certain class of politicians in this country, it is highly fashionable to extend the privileges and exalt the powers of this republican sovereign—the people. The Declaration of Independence, say they, affirms that "all men are born free and equal." Hence the American people are the whole body of the inhabitants of the land. All power originates with them; they are the arbiters of law and justice; they rule their magistrate, not their magistrates them. As collective bodies must act by majorities, the majority of the inhabitants of the Union have the undoubted right to sovereignty; they are more powerful than statutes and constitutions; they can build up and pull down, can create, alter, and remake at their own will and pleasure. Now, the latter part of this proposition negatives the former. If the right of governing resides with the whole body of the people, no part of that body, great or small, majority or minority, is entitled to make enactments for any other part. The principle does not admit of such a construction, and as it can be made practical in no other way, however good in theory it may be, it must fall. But this is not the only defect of the proposition. It has an inherent weakness. If "the people" be *all* the inhabitants of the land *born* free and equal, then the veriest infant, the child of six or ten years, the idiot—nay, may we not say, women—should have an equal share in this sovereignty with the profoundest statesman or the most learned politician of whom we can boast. To refuse to admit this consequence is to deny the antecedent, for the same remark which we have formerly made, holds good here—that the rights of a collective whole cannot be justly usurped by any of its parts. It may be urged that the body, as such, may *delegate* to the majority the powers of government; true; but if it be a constituted majority, its individuals remaining the same at all times, then either *the people* no longer rule, or the delegated portion is itself the people; if it be a mere majority, its individuals varying according to whim or personal feeling, in this case, the right has no fixed abode, but it still dwells with a part, and, what is worse, is continually changing owners, effectually destroying that which is essential to all good governments, stability.

But it may be deemed useless to contend against a proposition so manifestly unfounded. We do not imagine that even those who hold the doctrine that the people are the rulers of the land, would assert that in that body are comprised the women and children, the criminals, the insane and the slaves, and that we are governed by such a motley multitude. The people then are not the whole nation, but a part. What part? we ask. The entire male population above the age of twenty-one? This category would admit three objectionable classes—the criminals, the insane, and the slaves. To conceive that the laws of the confederated union and of the several States furnish the only decisive explication of the matter. If we assume for granted that the people *are* the rulers of the land, then by the term nothing more or less can be meant than *the legal voters of the whole country*. No other large body of individuals, that is, no other miscellaneous mass of men, can be said, to employ the expression as figuratively as we may, to be the governing power. They comprise the only persons who can with any propriety be said to have a voice or an influence in the administration. If our officers are the servants of the people—as they are, at all events, the servants only of those by whom they are chosen—we must admit that those who do choose, are the people.

But there is another sense in which the conclusion to which, by adopting a particular opinion, we have just arrived, appears almost irresistible. In this land we acknowledge that the people are the source of all power. Whatever privileges our magistrates may have—whatever *powers* they may possess, are derived from this common fountain. Not directly, however; but through their assent as expressed in the Constitution of the land. Our legislators can neither gain or lose any rights from a sudden movement of the popular fancy; these rights are secured to them by written and printed instruments, unchangeable except according to prescribed modes. Surely, we cannot say that our Senators and Representatives receive any thing, in any manner, except from those whose privilege it has been, or is, to act through the ballot-box. The women, the children, the non-voters, confer nothing upon them; it is the voters, the people as such, who do this. The Constitution itself originated from the wisdom of men delegated by the qualified *voters* of 1788 and 1789, and from the deliberate consent of those voters themselves. But in what manner did the latter class acquire the sole right of suffrage? The women and children, the criminals, insane, and slaves, never met in convention and delegated it to them. We answer, from the natural fitness of things:—it was necessary for the preservation of law and order, necessary for the general welfare of society, necessary for the best interests of mankind, that the right should be legally vested somewhere; and equally necessary that it should be vested in such a portion of the inhabitants of the country as were best qualified to perform its duties: that those who in this Union are the legal voters, are also thus qualified, and, that by the very constitution of the human race, it does, and ought to belong to them. Hence the conclusion appears incontrovertible, that by *the people* of this country, politically, nothing is, or can be meant, but its great body of legal voters.

It may not now be utterly useless to inquire into the validity of the principle, which we have already once or twice stated—viz: that the people are the ruling power of the land, and that our legislators are simply their servants. There may be a sense in which this is true; a sense which we have already intimated. The Constitution is in reality the formal and decisive '*will of the people*,' and that all our civil officers are bound to proceed according to its prescriptions, none, we presume, will deny. The people, moreover, when they become dissatisfied with this instrument, or even with the present form of government, have the power to alter, amend, or even to overthrow and re-construct as may seem best. But this is not to be done lightly, at every popular excitement, or at all, except according to known usages, and by methods laid down in the statute law. Were the doctrine carried no farther than this, we would be content; but when we find influential men abroad promulgating such views as these; that in the ordinary process of legislation, the chosen law-givers are to be esteemed as simply servants—that they are bound to conform in all things to the will or fancy of their constituents or masters—that constitutions or statutes are of inferior obligation, when not suited in every respect to the changing desires of the multitude—that an illegally assembled convention of large numbers of individuals can destroy, or render invalid at its pleasure, the instruments or the laws, by which our Congresses and State Assemblies are guided, and upon which the whole structure of our civil polity rests,—then we think that it is time for serious consideration. We imagine that we detect absurdity upon the very face of such propositions, and imminent danger to the whole country, should there be an earnest attempt at carrying them out.

If we understand the expression, that "our rulers are not rulers, but servants"—rightly, according to the plain English signification, it can mean nothing more nor less than this; that they are to obey implicitly the will of their masters—that the latter are not bound by any of their acts, which, at the time, may be unpopular; and that the proper method of counteracting the influence of any legislation which may not suit the fancy of the constituents at the moment, is, to refuse obedience; and not to apply the proper remedy through the ballot-box. The danger of such a principle is too obvious to need much comment. It strikes at the root of all social order; it undermines the foundation of all law; it overthrows the power of any Constitution; it destroys national faith and national honor, by depriving national contracts of their only security—the validity of national statutes. Such a state of things was never contemplated by the fathers of the revolution, or by the wise men who composed the convention of 1787; and its only shadow of support is to be found in the wild dreamings of Jefferson, when he declared, that "no Constitution could be binding for more than a single generation." Such a state of things has never existed, except in ancient Athens, and the condition of that city, as described by an enlightened scholar and patriotic writer of our own country, is so much to the point, that we cannot forbear a short quotation. "A community," says he, "deciding in the weightiest matters upon the spur of the occasion, incessantly excited by unprincipled agitators, living by forfeiture, confiscation, and plunder, *without a constitutional barrier or guaranty*, where no bills were required to be read three times in two houses, where the departments of government were all confounded in one tremendous mass of arbitrary power, where, in short, there was no time for reflection, no *locus penitentiae*, BUT THE DECREES OF A PASSIONATE AND TUMULTUARY MOB, MISINFORMED, MISGUIDED, SUPERSEDING ALL LAWS AND CONSTITUTIONS, WERE CARRIED INTO IMMEDIATE EXECUTION !"

From a condition like this, the institutions of our republican government have thus far happily preserved us. The power, whose source is the people, flows from them to our legislators, and becomes the right of the latter, so long as they retain their official stations, to be exercised according to the *will* of the people as expressed in the great charter of our liberties, the Federal Constitution. Exercised, not according to the desires of a part, but for the general good of the whole ; exercised, not according to the clamorous outcry of an excited mob, but in conformity with written statutes, and the great principles of general justice and general expediency.

Neither does this detract from our position as a self-governing people. We *are* such ; we have been free to choose between all forms of civil polity, or to choose none at all ; to govern ourselves by laws and lawful magistrates, or to remain every man independent of every other man. We have decided deliberately upon the former ; we have made our own constitution, elected our own rulers, according to a method prescribed by ourselves ; and it is the noblest proof of the high capabilities of human nature, that while for more than half a century we have claimed the power, *as a people*, to overthrow this Constitution and to do away with these methods, we have still preserved them of our own free will and pleasure. Those who urge us then, to exert the superiority of mere numbers and brute force over those whom we choose to be our legislators, are, at the same time, urging us to destroy the good work which we have accomplished ; to put a sudden end to what we have so well begun ; to render ourselves, our fellow-citizens, and our country, a bye-word and a mockery to the nations of the earth ; to deliver up all we hold dear, to the terrible dominion of civil anarchy. We close this brief essay with a quotation, whose pungent truth must, we think, be acknowledged by every intelligent mind. " If every American feels, as he must, a deep and fervent gratitude to Heaven, for having cast his lot in this most blessed of all lands, where perfect liberty has hitherto been found united with the dominion of the law, and the reign of order, let him be penetrated with the conviction, that he owes it to the institutions of our fathers, as they were originally conceived. Let him be assured that their glorious work needs no reforming, and that the base flatterers of the sovereign people, who preach to them of their infallibility, are here, what they have ever been, the ambitious, the vain, the unprincipled, the aspiring, who would bow down and worship any other power that could promote their own. History is written in vain, if mankind have not been taught that the demagogue and tyrant are synonymous ; and that he who professes to be the friend of the people, while he persuades them to sacrifice their reason to their passions—their duty to their caprices—their laws, their constitution, their glory, their integrity, to the mere lust of tyrannical misrule—is a liar, and the truth is not in him."

CONVERSANO,

A ROMANCE IN HISTORY.

CHAPTER I.

E non minor che duce e cavaliero;
Ma del doppio valor tutto ha le parti.— Tasso, Gerusalemme.

Peerless in fight, in counsel grave and sound,
The double gift of glory excellent. Fairfax.

The last rays of the sun had for some time ceased to gild the summits of the Appenines, and the moon was rising in the east, with a glory and beauty which none but those who dwell under an Italian sky can know, when a band of Christian warriors might have been seen riding at a rapid pace along the shores of the Adriatic. They were a fragment of the immense host that had engaged in the first crusade to the Holy Land, and were now on their return, after years of absence, and the endurance of great toil and danger. The effect of unremitting exertion upon the human frame was evident from the gaunt and bony forms of the knights, and the ghastly scars that appeared upon their weather-beaten visages, told how well and surely the keen scimetar of the Saracen had done its work.

The men were not all of one nation: the standards of Maine, Ireland, Brittany, and England, were waving over their respective people, but highest of all floated the broad banner of Normandy, and most conspicuous rode the Norman leader. He was a man of no more than medium height, but possessed of a depth of chest, and compactness of frame, that gave promise of great physical strength. He was cased in armor, from head to foot, of burnished steel, which possessed so bright a polish, that his coat of mail, breastplate, helmet, and even the plating of his gauntlets and shoes, shone in the light of the moon like silver. The steed which he bestrode was of the Arabian breed, and plainly evinced, by his bearing, that no cross of baser stock had reduced his high blood. Although the other horses were jaded by the length of the journey they had performed, and dispirited by the travel of the day, he was fresh and gay as a lady's palfrey, and, as he moved forward, seemed, by the arching of his neck, and the pricking forward of his rabbit-like ears, to testify the delight he felt at the rattling of his own and his rider's armor.

The band had proceeded for some time in silence, when an abrupt bend of the shore brought them suddenly in view of a stately castle, situated upon a hill, and less than a mile distant. The hill was covered to the top with olive-groves, which, as they moved to and fro in the night breeze, exhibited every variety of shade and color, while above all rose the castle, with its battlements, walls, and projections, even to the minutest turret, imprinted in clear characters upon the sky beyond. The sight was a pleasing one, and, as the warriors beheld the termination of their long day's journey, a murmur of delight ran through the ranks, and each involuntarily grasped the rein tighter, and spurred on his weary charger to a yet swifter pace than before.

When they had reached the foot of the hill, a few hasty words of command were given by the leader, and the main body filed off around the base, while the Norman chief, with a few of his immediate followers, kept on to the castle. As they approached, the hoarse call of the sentinels was heard, passing from mouth to mouth, and soon an aged warder appeared upon the walls, and hailed them,

"Ho, there, without! Halt!"

The band drew rein, in compliance with his order, and a knight from immediately behind the leader, riding forward to the edge of the moat, the warder addressed him,

"By St. Dennis, sir knight, but how shall we receive you? A friend, methinks, might in courtesy have been preceded by some messenger."

"Ha, old man!" replied the knight, "have your ears been sealed, or have you burrowed in the granite of your walls the last month? We had the presumption to think that the fame of our leader might suffice for his herald. But keep us not waiting. ROBERT OF NORMANDY, from the Holy wars, stands at your gate."

At the mention of that well known name, the gray head of the keeper sunk from the walls with more haste even than it had appeared, and, with an alacrity and quiet which betokened the strict discipline that reigned within the castle, the draw-bridge fell, the portcullis flew up, and the crusaders rode into the outer court. Here, having dismounted, and resigned their steeds into the hands of the menials, they passed through the inner court into the great hall.

The castle, into which we have introduced our adventurers, was one much celebrated in history,—that of William, Count of Conversano, the most powerful chief of all Lower Apulia, and grand-nephew of stout Robert Guiscard, who laid the foundation of that Norman power in Naples, which afterwards spread over the fairest portions of Italy. Here were gathered, at the close of the first crusade, the brightest stars of Europe, and the right noble host spared neither trouble or expense to render their sojourn agreeable. Horses, hounds, and hawks, in any number, were free to all, and the wild-boar and other game that roamed the vast plains of Apulia, found them ample employment during the day; whilst minstrels, jongleurs, and dancers, enlivened the evening, and gave zest to its enjoyments. But by no means the slightest attraction to the castle, and by no means the least inducement to a protracted tarry there, was the beautiful maiden Sibylla, the old Count's daughter. Her charms, which even history has deemed worthy of record, were celebrated far and wide, and suitors, old and young, gay and grave, sought to win the favor of the father and the smiles of the daughter. Thus the castle came to be a rallying point, as it were, for the most noble and chivalrous of the age. Here the bold knight, who had warred with the infidel upon the burning sands of Syria, and, for months, known no rest from toil or respite from watching, unbent from the austerity of his life, and once more cultivated the refinements of the court, once more mingled in the society of polite men, and tuned his rough voice to whisper words of love. Hither also came monks and priests, and even mitred prelates gathered at the hospitable board, and evinced their full appreciation of the gifts of Providence, by quaffing stoutly, at the evening feast, the hippocres and richer wines of Gascony.

But of all, cavaliers, and statesmen, and wily clergy, that had graced these walls, none could vie with Robert, in eloquence and knightly feats of arms. Indeed, not one of all the crusaders who visited the Holy Land, save afterwards him of the "Lion heart," attained to the renown of this prince. Palmers, toiling homeward from the wars, told, wherever they tarried, of prodigies of valor and matchless deeds of strength performed by "Bold Duke Robert," so that all Europe rung with his fame, and monk and minstrel vied with one another in awarding him his meed of praise. Such was Robert of Normandy, and such as has been described, the state of affairs in the castle of Conversano, at the time of our narrative.

The reception room was thrown open, and a blaze of light from the torches of the attendants shone out into the wide hall. William, who was seated upon a *dais*, at the upper end of the room, descended, as his noble guest entered, and, grasping him by the hand, gave him a cordial greeting. "Welcome, brother of Normandy, welcome to our poor abode. We have to crave your pardon for our seeming lack of courtesy, in not going out to escort you hither ourselves; but we had certain information, as we thought, that you would not be with us until the morrow."

"Nay, sire," said Robert, as the old count led him to a seat under the canopy that extended over the centre of the dais, "but we are ourselves in the fault; we should not have reached this until the morrow, had we not, in our impatience to see you again, after so long a lapse of time, disregarded the fatigue of our beasts, and outstript the course of our own plans. We have journeyed a weary way since dayspring."

"Truce, then, to excuses," said the count, and then turning gaily around to a maiden by his side, "Ah, pardon me, child,—sir knight, my daughter, the Lady Sibylla." Robert arose, and as he bowed and saluted the hand of the lovely being before him, felt that his doing so was rather an act of involuntary homage to her charms, than an observance of etiquette. The moment he looked upon her, he was charmed by her extreme beauty, the effect of which was heightened by the simple yet attractive style of her dress. A tunic of white, gathered at the waist by a girdle, displayed to the finest advantage her voluptuous form; her hair, instead of being plaited in the unbecoming fashion so prevalent at the close of the eleventh century, was encircled by a fillet, and fell in dark masses over her neck and shoulders, like clouds upon a summer sky. Her carriage was in the highest degree gentle and winning, yet the red, pouting under-lip, and eyes black as night, told of a volcano of passions asleep under that placid exterior.

The duke paid his compliments in the pompous language used towards ladies by the cavaliers of the day, and then resuming his seat, conversed upon various topics until the announcement of supper.

"We boast at our board of no dainties," said William, as they seated themselves at the head of the long oaken table, "yet we trust that hungry men will find enough of the substantials of life to satisfy their appetites."

Robert cast his eye over the smoking lines of venison, fish, and fowl stretched out before him, as he answered.

"To men who have been wont to carve their meat, such as [illegible] may send, in gloves of steel, and eat, at morning dawn, [illegible] may be their shrouds before nightfall, any one of the dishes displayed here in such variety and profusion, is a very luxury."

"Your retinue," replied the count, "[illegible] of great strength and endurance. I am told that the fierce rays of the Syrian sun are like the potter's fire, either to harden the clay or [illegible] or shatter it to nought."

"True for it," answered Robert, "for men of [illegible] and iron strength commend me, before all Europe, to the [illegible] whose feet have trod those burning sands, and [illegible] back to their native land."

"Yet," said William, with a complacent smile, "[illegible] as your men must be, I doubt not that we have within our [illegible] who can hurl the stoutest of them to the earth."

The duke's eyes glistened, and he answered [illegible] "[illegible] my good steed against the golden chain about your neck, that we find him his match, nay, his better, before he break his fast to-morrow."

"Softly, softly, noble sir," said William, with perfect [illegible], "consider the matter again, before we close the wager; [illegible] ready when you have seen the man. Ho! there! [illegible] the [illegible] knave, who wrestled yestereven with the [illegible]."

"Were he another Hercules," [illegible] "[illegible] will find a Norman wrestler who shall make him [illegible] continued he, as the man appeared before them, "[illegible] fellow; plainly no trifling antagonist for any one."

And indeed the man was a very personification of strength. [illegible] gi-ant in size, there was not upon his frame the least superfluous flesh; his limbs were masses of thews and sinews, and his coarse hair hung in shaggy locks over his eyes, gave him an extremely [illegible] appearance.

"How now, sirrah!" said the duke, "dare you adventure a fall on the morrow, with some of my followers?"

"Methinks, my lord duke had better ask them if they care for the trial; the man was never born of woman that I [illegible]," answered the giant, in a dogged, yet respectful manner.

"Well, well, fellow," said the duke, [illegible] "[illegible] and to-morrow we will find you one who shall test your strength; and mark me, you are to expect no child's play."

"By the mass, then," muttered the [illegible] between his teeth, as he departed, "let him look to himself, for he must be a good man and true, if he ever walk again."

The supper was now far advanced, and the [illegible] at the middle and lower end of the table, excited by the fumes of the wine, could scarce contain themselves, so far as to allow proper respect to the noble guest and host at the head, when all restraint was removed by the departure of these two personages, accompanied by a third, whom we have not yet introduced to our readers. This was no less a personage than the notorious Odo, Bishop of Bayeux, and half-uncle of Robert, whom he had accompanied to the wars,—a man of great native courage and energy, yet rendered in a measure odious by the ferocity of his counsels. The three now retired to the conference-room, to converse at their leisure upon the all-absorbing topic of the day, the result of the crusade.

"I have been anxiously waiting for an opportunity, my lord," said the count, as they seated themselves, "to ask you, why your return to Europe tallies so ill with the reports which have reached our ears."

"Reports, my lord?" answered Robert, "to what reports do you refer?"

"To those that told us you had taken up your abode in the East," answered the former.

"And why, sire," said Robert, "should I make my home among the followers of the false prophet? Have not the infidel dogs been driven from the Holy city? And have I not possessions, power, and above all, a home, in our sunny Normandy?"

"Nay, but what are all the vineyards of Normandy, compared with the brightest diadem in Christendom?" rejoined William.

"You speak in parables, my lord," answered the duke; "I do not understand you."

"Well, then," said William, "we are told that you had been proclaimed 'King of Jerusalem,' and, by my troth, were greatly rejoiced to think that the keeping of the Holy city had been intrusted to so goodly a warder."

"Ah! you do but jest, my lord," said Robert, "what claims to such high honors could I prefer, that would compare with those of Godfrey of Bouillon, a knight whose surpassing wisdom, prudence, and bravery, will so well defend and grace that high station? It is with me, I believe, even as this our reverend bishop says, 'I lack the prudence necessary for such a trust.'" And then, as if anxious to change the subject, he continued, "But of this sport to-morrow.—Will the Lady Sibylla"—

"Nay, but bear with me, my lord," interrupted the bishop, "if I inquire a little farther into this matter. There is certainly more in this report than ye wot of. Are you sure, my lord, that it came from the East?"

"From the East, of course," answered William; "but stay, let me think,—ha! a monk from Brittany; I remember him well, for a dark-browed knave first told me the tale, and though it was not confirmed by the stragglers that came from the East, I believed it. 'Tis strange that this inconsistency never struck me before."

"Yes," said Odo, thoughtfully, "from the west, from Brittany,—evidently a forged tale; the author must have known it for a lie. My lord," continued he, turning suddenly around to Robert, "why will you repose so much confidence in the promises of ambitious men? My life upon it, there is treachery and plotting against you at home. Why this story, if not to quiet the people, and seduce them from your interest?"

Robert laughed, and, turning to the count, said, "Well, I am sure that if I lack prudence, it is more than compensated by the discretion of this my most wary uncle. I do verily believe that he would try to make me think my good brother Harry set that report afloat. 'Happy is the man that feareth always,' is his motto; for my part, I put my trust in that most comfortable proverb of the Persians, which tells us, 'We must believe nothing we hear, and only half we see.'"

And this was all that Robert said or thought about a circumstance so suspicious, until months afterwards, when his just claim to the throne of England was disputed by this same "good brother Harry," when ingrate friends were deserting him, and the grim calamities of unsuccessful war gathering about his path, he recalled the admonitions given by his cautious uncle in the castle of Conversano, and rebuked himself, in bitterness of spirit, for his apathy and want of foresight.

CHAPTER II.

Ros. But is there any else longs to see this broken music in his side? Is there yet another doats upon rib-breaking.—AS YOU LIKE IT.

The sun arose on the morrow in a cloudless sky, and shone down warm and cheerily upon the goodly company of knights and ladies and men at arms who had assembled in the open space before the castle, to witness the encounter planned the night before.

Elevated seats had been prepared for the spectators of rank, whilst their numerous attendants stood together in a more humble position on one side, awating the coming sport with impatient and anxious looks. William and Sibylla occupied a conspicuous place, and by their side was Robert, who had already become half enamored of a lady so gifted in mind and person.

The German was ready for the contest, and with his huge form extended upon the sward in a half-reclining posture, waited, in seeming surety of success, for any one who should have the hardihood to face so formidable a foe. He had never yet found his equal in wrestling, and only a day or two before, had sadly broken the bones of a lubberly mass of humanity from Bari.

At a signal from the duke, a young man advanced into the arena, accoutred for the contest. He was of much more than medium size, but not by any means possessed of the giant proportions of his antagonist; yet he at once enlisted the sympathies of the spectators, for his countenance was open and handsome, and his whole bearing so noble and engaging, that some cried out, "it was a shame for him to be matched against so unworthy an adversary."

"A right noble fellow, my lord," said William, "tell us, who is he?"

"A youth of gentle blood," replied Robert, "who followed our fortunes to the wars, one always first in battle, and whose arm hath ever kept pace with ours in giving blow for blow upon the enemy."

"Ah, recall him, I pray you, sir," said Sibylla. "Think you it is well for one so generous to be sacrificed to the wantonness of yonder brute ?"

"Fear not for him, lady," replied the duke, "his arm is strong, and hath never yet failed him. Yet would I gladly recall him, in obedience to your wish, were it not now too late. See—they close."

As he spoke, the German, clasping the youth in his huge embrace, raised him high from the ground, and strove to throw him on his side; but the Norman, with wonderful strength and agility, turned himself as he neared the ground, and struck upon his feet, yet with such force as seemed enough to have shattered to atoms a frame of less compact materials. A second attempt of the same kind had well nigh proved fatal to the success of the German; for the youth, as he came again to the ground, catching him off his balance, swayed him around, and almost won the victory, by bringing him to the ground. The giant, stung to madness by this second failure, grew black with rage and vexation; yet the Norman stood undaunted, and ready for a third struggle, when Sibylla, whose warmest sympathies had been from the first awakened for the youth, called aloud to her father, in a supplicating tone—

"Oh! stop, sir, stop, I pray you, this sport! I know that death will come of it. See, look at yonder villain, there's murder in his very eye."

The old man heeded her not; wholly engrossed in the spectacle before him, he was deaf and blind to every thing else. His blood was up, aye boiling with excitement, and stretching himself forward so as almost to lose his balance and fall from his seat, he cried—

"Now for 't, now for 't. To him, you knave, to him! Now, by all the saints, your steed is lost, my lord."

Ere the last words passed his lips, the German had caught his luckless foe in his iron grasp, and stiffening every sinew until they stood out like ropes from under the skin, swung him from the ground and hurled him away, clear over the low barrier, to the very feet of the spectators, where he lay stunned and bleeding. So carried away was the old count by his feelings, that, springing from his seat, he gave a shout that was echoed long and loud by every inmate of the castle. But, immediately bethinking himself of his uncourteous conduct, he turned to Robert, who sat with a flush upon his brow, and said—

"'Tis idle, my lord, for a gray head to be thus overturned by a silly bout at wrestling; yet it does seem as if, in a strife like this, one's feelings became even more enlisted than in the noble tournament, where the attention and interest are distracted by the number of combatants."

"'Tis so, 'tis so, my lord," answered Robert, in a mortified tone, "but the foul fiend take the German dog; I would lose half my army, sooner than that good fellow should thus be harmed. St. Dennis! but yonder scowling knave shall rue it. Ho! there—summon the other man."

This was a burly wight from Brittany, who, although possessed of enormous size and strength, lacked entirely that agility and quickness of motion so essential to the good wrestler. Hardly had his brawny foe grasped him, ere he came lumbering to the earth, like a great, top-heavy wain.

The German, proud of his success, first swaggered up and down, challenging any and every one: "Are ye all frightened out? Come on, now, an' ye dare; come on, Barian, Norman, and Brittain, and choose the ground ye would lie on;" and then seated himself, in great complacency, upon the grass, with his knees drawn up to his chin, and his hands clasped about his shins. The assemblage, after waiting for a space, was about to break up, in despair of farther sport, when a new candidate for honor appeared in the arena. He was, in point of size, less than any of the other wrestlers, yet were his limbs well knit together, and he entered the ring with a firm tread and fearless bearing. The German sluggishly rose up, like a huge mastiff, as he presented himself, and, scanning him from head to foot, said, sneeringly, "'Tis better for you to go, I'll not wrestle with you; the eagle of our mountains does not prey upon sparrows."

"Silence your boastings," answered the new comer, "I need none of your advice; look to yourself."

"This, then, for your fool's obstinacy," said the other, as, seizing him around the middle, he raised him from the ground. But the victory was not so easy as he expected; thrice he raised him up and essayed to fling him on his side, and thrice were his efforts vain. Then, enraged at this unlooked for resistance in an adversary apparently so inferior, he gathered all his strength and tried to hurl him off, as he had done the Norman; but his adversary clung to him as though his arms were bars of iron; nor did he act entirely upon the defensive, for, striving also to trip and throw his adversary, the struggle became great. With limbs entwined and swollen veins, they strove, now here, now there, as if for very life. First one and then the other seemed to have the superiority, and the contest was at least doubtful, when the German began to show signs of exhaustion, his breath came thick and fast, his face grew first red and then purple, and his efforts began to relax. But now his opponent, who appeared to be untiring as he was skillful, summoning up his strength for a final struggle, caught him upon his hip, and raising his huge form, with giant strength, high over head, held him balanced there for a moment, and then, with "This for vengeance," brought him, thundering upon his head and shoulders to the earth. A simultaneous shout of exultation from the Normans rent the air. Even the old count seemed pleased, and turning smilingly around, he was about to address Robert, when he saw that he had left his seat. "Call hither the duke," said he, "where is his highness?"

"He is here," answered the victor, as he threw off the slouched hat, which had hitherto concealed his features, and the rich flaxen curls fell from under it around his face.

"Long live the Duke of Normandy!" burst from every mouth. And the conquered giant, as he slowly rose from the ground, the blood rushing from his mouth and nose, swore that "when he first felt that gripe, he knew it must be Robert's or the devil's."

[TO BE CONTINUED.]

EDITORS' FAREWELL.

The lapse of a brief twelvemonth finishes our editorial labors, an
we resign to other hands the care of this Magazine. We do this wi
mingled feelings of regret and pleasure—regret at dissolving our co
nection with the Magazine in which we have taken so deep an inter
which has occupied our thoughts during so many of our waking a
sleeping hours, which has become, indeed, a part of our existence. O
the other hand, we are not unwillingly relieved from the load of anxi
labor, and responsibility, which has been imposed upon us, in the di
charge of our editorial duties. Our eye now rests upon the promi
made to our patrons at the commencement of our labors—whether
has been fulfilled, is not for us to say. This only can we honestl
affirm, *we have tried;* if we have failed, we pray you ascribe it rath
to lack of ability than inclination.

To the members of all the classes for their unusually liberal sub
scription and noble stand in support of the Magazine, we return o
sincere thanks. Those who have cheered from time to time our labo
by a word of encouragement, a favorable notice, we remember wi
gratitude—while even against those who have greeted our monthl
visits only with cynical criticisms and animadversions, we harbor n
a single feeling of unkindness or ill-will,—to one and all at parting
we add a hearty "God bless you—Farewell."

I. Atwater,
J. W. Dulles,
O. S. Ferry,
W. Smith,
J. White,
Editors of the Class of 1844.

Yale College, April 13, 1844.

TO OUR READERS.

We beg leave, kind reader, to present to you this, our first number, with the familiar nod of old acquaintance-ship, rather than the formal and distant bow. Regarding our Magazine, there is need of saying but little. The history of its success through nearly nine years, is well known to you—the past speaks for itself, the future depends upon our exertions. This truth the experience of the last month has fully proved. To use *the* figure employed on occasions like this, "our good ship" we found well anchored and sea-worthy; but a dead calm prevailing, when the tardy breeze came at length, inexperienced hands made some delay in getting her under sail. This accomplished, we have no doubt of a pleasant and prosperous cruise.

But leaving for the present, any further attempts at rhetorical address, we simply ask, Fellow Students, the same kind wishes and assistance which have been bestowed in time past. With the undoubting hope that this reasonable request will be fulfilled, we enter most cheerfully upon the toilsome responsibilities of our office ; at the same time, taking this opportunity to return our acknowledgments for the honorable trust which you have seen fit to place in our hands.

We remain, Classmates and
Fellow students,
Respectfully,
YOUR EDITORS.

YALE COLLEGE, JUNE 26, 1844.

THE

YALE LITERARY MAGAZINE.

VOL. IX. JUNE, 1844. No. 7.

TASTE AND MANNERS.

THE American people are far from being disciples of that ancient philosophy which associated the beautiful with the good. Quite in contrast are these bustling and practical times with the age of Pericles, when Beauty ruled in Athens. If we now and then do homage to the superior taste of the old Republic, by bringing from among its shattered, yet noble ruins, some faultless model of architectural elegance, the spirit of our political economy prompts us to daub its fair proportions with untempered mortar, and adorn them with flimsy ornaments of stucco. The great national maxim, of practical, tangible utility, obscuring our nobler perceptions of the spiritual and the beautiful, has fixed our eyes too constantly upon the dust beneath us, where, like the man in "Bunyan's Pilgrim's Progress," we grope and rake about, for the 'useful and the good.' With very many, beauty is considered a worthless commodity, and the culture of good taste, since it produces no marketable fruits, as the peculiar occupation of the idle and effeminate, if not quite contrary to good morals. They seem to believe that the lessons of perfect taste and beauty, with which the garden of Paradise was fraught to its first inhabitants, were not designed by the great Teacher for the race, it being only left for them after the fall literally to fulfill the curse. Perhaps the peculiarities of our political condition may have something to do with these prejudices. It ill suits the ultra spirit of democracy to cherish those refining and elevating influences, which surrounded the original perfection of our being. Its restless and envious disciples would rather blacken the faces of all, than that any dissimilitude should exist in the moral or physical likenesses of the "dear people." Then, again, though we would speak it reverently, the stern and simple faith of our puritan ancestry hardly recognized, in its hatred of a formal church and a kingly court, the doctrine of external beauty, or the alliance of Taste with Religion. The shaven crowns and buff surtouts of Cromwell's court, marked their dislike of worldly display, and to escape the tainted air of lofty cathedrals, they sought, in this dreary wilderness,

"A Church without a Bishop, and a State without a King."

This peculiar hostility towards every form and symptom of prelacy and royalty, which persecution cherished in the hearts of our ancestors, seems yet to live in the warfare which many among us continue against all the beauties of art, as if they were tainted with some influence of the evil one; as though, since the Devil has in his wisdom found access to the hearts of men through those arts which delight the eye and please the ear, to him only must belong the architecture, the music, and the painting!

What is Taste? Let mental philosophers attempt to define, in their set phrase, its varied and delicate emotions. Such an analysis comes neither within our wishes nor ability.

The view of a beautiful scene once awakened in a highly gifted mind, a strain like this:

"It was the night—and Lara's glassy stream
The stars are studding, each with imaged beam;
So calm, the waters scarcely seem to stray,
And yet they glide like happiness away;
Reflecting far and fairy-like from high
The immortal lights that live along the sky:
All was so still, so soft, in earth and air,
You scarce would start to see a spirit there,
Secure that naught of evil could delight
To walk in such a scene on such a night!
It was a moment only for the good."

Who can read this without emotions kindred to those which gave it birth? These emotions constitute Taste; a word, however, far too feeble to convey to our minds a just idea of that faculty by which we appreciate whatever is glorious and beautiful in the great realms of divine and human creation.

Without usurping, then, the dull prerogative of the mental anatomist, let us consider the objects of Taste to be all comprised in this one term—THE BEAUTIFUL—whether it is found in the works of nature, of art, or in the nobler qualities of the soul. The Cartesian philosopher notes with learned gravity that the objects of taste are always sensations, and have no residence beyond the precincts of the mind. It is sufficient for our purpose, however, to follow the doctrine of our common sense—that beauty exists wherever the hand of the Creator has been. We read this in the creation of the fair world which we inhabit—the conception of perfect taste—hung without hands in boundless space, and adorned with all its glorious ornaments; "its ocean of air above, its ocean of water beneath, its zodiac of lights, its tents of dripping clouds, its striped coat of climates, its fourfold year." "Look upon the rainbow," exclaimed an admirer of beauty in ancient times, "and praise him that made it; very beautiful it is in the brightness thereof. It compasseth the heaven about with a glorious circle, and the hands of the Most High have bended it."

We turn now to the fine arts, the second creation of beautiful forms and thoughts, the reflection of natural beauty in the mirror of man's creative genius. All the harmonies of sweet sounds, the magic delineations of the pencil, the life-like statue, the ornaments which architecture and gardening lend to nature's hills and valleys, the wonderful treasures of poetry, gathered from all times and realms of human thought; these, also, contribute to the delights of Taste.

Although the susceptibilities which enable us to love the beautiful, are, to some extent, innate, we have already, in enumerating the objects of Taste, included those beyond the capacities of that intuitive knowledge which the Creator has bestowed. A just appreciation of the fine arts requires that our natural susceptibilities should be educated and improved, until, united with maturer years and enlarged experience, Taste becomes a critical faculty, not only perceiving and appreciating, but judging and distinguishing the true from the false. Like the bodily sense from which it derives its name, it may be vitiated, and as the palate naturally chooses proper and nourishing food, so does our internal taste commend to us what is in itself beautiful and excellent. If this is true, that in nature there exists a standard of true beauty, and consequently of good taste, the old maxim, "There can be no disputing about Taste," is incorrect. The variety of tastes departing from the true standard, must be accounted for in the force of prejudice, wrong habits and associations.

But Nature has not been so impartial as to bestow upon us all alike a love for the beautiful. There are some of minds so dull and gross, that even external Nature, in her gayest or most sublime moods, fails to awaken a single emotion of joy or wonder. To such, mental discipline and extensive knowledge cannot ensure a refined Taste. The maxim "*Poeta nascitur, non fit*," applies to them. Many a scholar, who has spent long years in the pursuit of abstract truth, fails to appreciate the true value of a beautiful poem, even though just rules for its criticism may be duly stowed away in the labyrinths of his learning. He may behold a splendid prospect in Nature, and yet feel no emotion, unless it be the satisfaction of measuring its area, or surveying its geological structure. Meanwhile, the youth, unpractised in criticism, but full of ardent sensibility, steals many an hour of true delight from his irksome syntax, to read and enjoy that same poem; and the untutored savage pauses in his chase to view, with like emotions, some magnificent display of Nature's wild scenery; though neither can state the reasons of his enjoyment.

We have considered the beautiful works of nature and art as the objects of Taste. The beautiful in morals, also, it is her province to discover and admire, not indeed of herself alone, but aided by the arbiter of morals, a good conscience. It was the school of Shaftesbury, we believe, who considered virtue as beautiful rather than obligatory, and regarding it as a mere sentiment or emotion, have failed to give it the sanctions of Law and Duty. On the other hand, there are some good men, who, going to the opposite extreme, will not acknowledge any connection between good Taste and good Morals. They pursue, with stoical precision, the straight and narrow path of stern duty, neither turning aside to gather flowers, nor delaying to heed the beauties of the prospect. In the character of the men themselves, we are apt to see the influence of their mistake. There is more in it to approve, than to love and admire. They perform well all the great duties of life, and through their good works appear to advantage in the distance, but on near approach fail to win our affection, through negligence of the minor duties of daily life. In the beautiful words of President Hopkins, "They seem like stately trees, in the trunk and main branches of which the sap circulates vigorously, but does not reach and animate the smaller twigs, and give to the leaves their perfect green."

It is over that department of morals which relates to our social intercourse, and in which the proprieties and courtesies of life are comprised, that good Taste presides. Its virtues are the "*petites morales*" of the French, that nice regard for others' convenience and feelings, and that sympathy for their ills, which constitutes true politeness. The emotions of beauty, then, which moral actions awaken, must proceed from those warm and generous affections, which command not merely our respect and approval, but our admiration. Duty draws the bold outlines in the picture of life, while the perception of moral beauty which we call Taste, bestows the rich and mellow coloring. And here we may notice the fact, that with moral Taste, as with intellectual, Nature has not bestowed impartially those finer affections and sympathies which clothe the soul in her beautiful vesture. There are some men so dry and coarse and so hard-visaged, that we are at once repelled from their closer acquaintance, while others in each look and gesture evince those acute susceptibilities and ardent emotions, which draw us to them at once. The one class duty leads on, as with a halter, while with the other, good principles are so aided by impulse that it seems almost to supply their place.

"A man's manners commonly makes his fortune," is one of those maxims of common school philosophy, inculcating at once a lesson in ethics and penmanship, which the school-boy has often seen inscribed in running-hand upon the top of his copy page. Whether it was the hasty conception of the pedagogue's own brain, or a stolen gleaning from some other sage, it is, like most of its class, about half true. To adopt it unqualified we should promise the world to be commonly either courtiers or dancing masters. We cannot doubt, however, that one's manners commonly aid or hinder to a great extent his progress through the world. To say that they designate a man's fortune, would perhaps give more veracity to our adage. So plainly is the inner man mirrored in the outward demeanor, that a nice observer will generally discover by it an individual's character and station in life. Much is betrayed in the minutest action, look, or tone of voice. Although the mere forms of etiquette are in some degree arbitrary and conventional, and taught with technical precision to those who lack experience, in many small duodecimos, yet the true gentleman is always recognized, while vulgarity, though varnished and plated ever so much, soon discovers itself. Let us inquire who is the true gentleman, lest he be supposed to belong to the school of Chesterfield, whose guiding principle was selfishness, under the garb of a false-hearted and hypocritical benevolence, and whose polished manners, like the bloom of waxen fruit, were put on to deceive. True politeness has its source in the heart, and needs the kind and generous emotions to give it life and beauty. It is the showing forth of a cheerful, pains-taking good will in every action. To confer pleasure, by rendering our social intercourse happy and agreeable, is its only end. This must be accomplished by the habitual exercise of the social virtues. A blind obedience to Fashion will not do it, for Fashion owes no particular allegiance either to Morality or good Taste. It is merely the current stamp given by the arbitrary whims of dress-makers and courtiers to the external life, neither enhancing nor diminishing its real value. A man's dress does not represent his tailor, nor his bow his dancing master, but himself, his own good taste and kind feelings. By nearly the same outward action men express far different emotions. In the warm grasp and the beaming eye we know full well the indications of a friendly heart, while in the stiffly extended arm, and the insipid smile of a formalist, there is nothing to admire. Still the former may be as far from being truly polite, as the latter from being amiable. Good feelings, though the indispensable source of truly good manners, do not of themselves create them, for as men with the best intentions often err through lack of common sense, so the kindest feelings may be expressed in the most awkward and embarrassing manner. A good heart very often lies concealed beneath a rough exterior. The influence of a correct taste, is needed to refine and chasten its sterner qualities. It is like that which architecture and gardening lend to Nature, clearing away the wild forests, laying out the green slopes, in their dress of fruits and flowers, to the genial sun, and adorning the hills and valleys with beautiful works of art. And not only does Taste chasten and improve the dispositions to virtue, but it enlarges their number—creating new objects of affection, and new ties of sympathy. It educates the soul to the knowledge of its finer nature. To the man who combines with his natural love for the beautiful, an intimate and scientific knowledge of the Creator's works, a thousand associations arise to give ever fresh delight, in contemplating the skill and wisdom displayed in every part. Thus, he whose moral taste is cultivated, beholds human character with keener discernment, and a nicer perception of the beautiful in conduct.

We have thus endeavored to point out the connection between taste and manners. "*Cui bono,*" is doubtless the question of many a practical, judicious reader. We have no time, say they, for the fascinating pursuits of Taste, or the acquirement of refined and graceful manners. The world calls us to active, arduous exertion, and to meet its heartless strife, we have little need of the fine arts, and must use other arms than Cupid's, and stouter armor than the exquisite sensibilities and delicate sympathies of a refined Taste. Let others, whose time and means permit them to glide gracefully through the world, learn to be its gentlemen. Duty, and not pleasure, is our aim—to perceive truth, and not beauty, our desire.

Now, this self-denying, heroic stoicism, which would dissever goodness from beauty, is neither consistent with the constitution which God has given us, with the teachings of his word, nor with the promises of an hereafter. As man's first residence was adorned with all things good and beautiful, so do we know, that the last Paradise shall be the city, whose foundations are garnished with all manner of precious stones—whose streets are of pure gold—whose gates are of pearl, and whose white-robed inhabitants attune forever, in melodious strains, the praises of their King. In his journey thither, the pleasures of Taste strew flowers along the rough path of life, and unfold prospects of beauty and loveliness to his view, which those of grosser nature can never see. But especially is the influence of good Taste upon the character important, inasmuch as it confers upon its possessor new power of doing good to others. If his influence is confined to private and domestic life, where a strict attention to the minor duties, which we have comprehended under good manners, can alone ensure the love and regard of friends, by a neglect of these, he may well-nigh bury his only talent. As our sphere of action is extended, and its ends more important, the importance of good manners is enhanced. Lustre of talent and strength of character, though they may conceal many defects, never atone for them. These defects are the minus quantities to be subtracted, not canceled, in the general account. Washington might have accomplished his great ends, had he not been the dignified and polished gentleman; but much of his good influence, little heeded perhaps by the general observer, would never have been exerted. Whitfield and Wilberforce, though their pious philanthropy and wonderful eloquence were the great causes of success, owed very much to refined taste and scrupulous propriety of manners. While the lawyer knows full well the convenience of an affable and engaging address, and the physician makes his remedies effectual and his name distinguished, by winning the confidence of his patients, more than either should the clergyman, whose business it is to reach the hearts of men, remove the obstacles which severity of mien, unguarded speech, and vulgar demeanor, will certainly throw in the way, and often to render his best intentions completely ineffectual.

It remains for us to inquire, How shall a correct Taste be acquired? It is unnecessary to dwell upon the truth so often and fully explained by the essayists, that youth is the time, and the only time, for its cultivation. If in the spring time of life, the tender and ardent emotions of the soul are left uncherished, grosser passions will grow apace, and the withering influence of the world complete their destruction; or if kept alive by purity of heart, yet their growth will be stunted and unseemly, unless cared for by some fostering hand.

Who then shall educate the youthful Taste? We answer, the classical authors of Greece and Rome.

We refrain from entering upon the well-worn college theme of Classical Study. Suffice it to say, that its higher advantages as a means of cultivating Taste, are rarely appreciated by scholars here. The toil and drudgery is too often bestowed, without enjoying the harvest. It is not in the grammar and dictionary of a language that we find anything to cultivate and refine the Taste. These are the mere props and braces to be dispensed with when the structure is complete. How often is it left rough, useless, and unfinished. In the preparatory schools of England the drudgery of classical study is nearly all accomplished in the thorough apprenticeship of many years of severe and patient discipline. Then at Oxford and Cambridge, the classics are a pastime, read to cultivate style and improve taste.* With us, on the contrary, the college course is hardly preparatory to a just appreciation of the beauties of the classics, and after this they are thrown by for life. Consequently, their important end, to polish and refine the mind, is never accomplished. We see the ill effects of this immature scholarship in the national manners. Taste is not the guide of those who direct public opinion. In our Congress, the dull, prosy speeches, measured off by the day, seldom tell of Tacitus or Ciccro, unless perhaps in an occasional quotation. Neither does the angry confusion which often fills those halls, speak of courtesy and propriety. "The people" are seldom in advance of their legislators. The French are no longer the politest nation of the world, since their "citizen king," in obedience to the leveling spirit of democracy, has dispensed with the courtly manners of the old Bourbon school.

It belongs then to the scholars of this country to erect the standard of National Taste. Let them early appreciate the value of liberal and humanizing studies, and as each year sends its generation of educated men from our institutions, to occupy the places of influence and trust, let them go forth, good exemplars of their training, to unite the character of the scholar with that of the polished gentleman.

* "Cambridge University," page 321.

CAIN'S SOLILOQUY.

Scene.—A mountain in Assyria. A storm raging. Cain standing on a crag of the mountain.

Here let me stand and gaze! this mountain storm,
This wild uproar of nature's elements,
Mingling tumultuously in battle fierce,
Makes concord with my heart. 'Tis a fit scene
For one so lost as I to contemplate.
List to the thunder's voice, the voice of God,
Which peals terrific through these mountain hills—
How like a cataract the heavens pour down
Their sheeted waves! Wilt Thou, oh injured One,
Deluge thy new created earth! Mark how
Yon swollen flood leaps from its lofty source,
And dashes roaring to the plain below.
The mountain peaks, the pillars of the clouds,
By the fork'd lightning's glitt'ring bolt are riven.
The rent rocks topple from their giddy base,
And crashing, thunder down the mountain side,
Spreading wide ruin round. Among the hills
Echoes the whirlwind's voice, and on the blast
Come hollow sounds of mirth, as if the fiends,
Reprieved from hell, were riding on the wind,
And this a theatre of giant sport,
Where spirits fierce are mingling in the game.

I stand alone—unterrified, unawed—
I cannot tremble at a scene like this,
Who *feel* a fiercer storm. This is the war
Of elemental nature—mine the strife
Of passions dire, beneath a tortured breast,
Waking the spirit's hell within my soul.
Hope has forever fled, yet I feel not
Even the calmness of Despair—guilt, deep
And damning guilt hath scathed my soul—my heart
Is like a cavern dark, where passions foul,
Like angry winds, contend for mastery.
I'm but my nature's wreck, a mortal breast
Sheathing the lightning of Omnipotence.

Abel! thou art avenged! Yet he was pure,
And beautiful, and good; the winning smile,
Which ever dwelt upon his peaceful face,
Betokened that his gentle soul ne'er knew
The angry strife of passions rude. His voice
Was music's melody—to its sweet sound

The deer would hasten from his covert wild ;
The untamed lion and the tiger came,
And round his forest path would sportive play,
As erst in Eden's fields ere Adam sinned.
All Nature loved him—ev'n the lamb he slew
For sacrifice, seemed conscious 'twas his hand
That dealt the blow, and bowed submissively.
The favorite of Heaven, he entertained
The angels in his tent. At twilight hour,
I've seen the seraph bright come from the skies
To visit him ; and ere they part, beneath
The starry canopy they stand, and pay
Adoring homage to the Lord most high.
And as the altar's smoke went up to heaven,
I heard the approving voice of God, like sound
Of mighty music from afar, whose tones
The echoing mountains rev'rently proclaimed,
While all the forest trees bowed down their heads,
And animated nature silent stood.

To me no token of approving love
Ere came, nor mark of approbation kind.
I laid my bloodless gift upon the shrine,
And offered to the Omnipotent the fruits
Of earth. No kindling fire from heaven came down,
No angel visitant communed with me,
Nor ever did I hear the voice of God
At evening hour, majestic from the sky.
He was the chosen of God. For this he died !
Could I endure that he, the younger born,
Should gain the smile of partial Heaven, while I,
The eldest, the primeval son of man,
To whom the birthright of creation was,
Must stand aside to give the youngling room ?
In childhood's early hour I hated him,
For then I saw his mother look on him,
And smiling, gaze as she ne'er gazed on me.
She fondly dreamed he was the promised seed
Whose hand should bruise the serpent's head accurst.
At every step of life he crossed my path
And thwarted me ; supplanted me on earth
And cheated me of Heaven's regard. For this
I slew him. Yet was he not a brother kind ?
Ah yes ! he e'er repaid for evil, good ;
Smiled on me when I frowned, loved when I scorned,
And often wept for me at Mercy's shrine.
Abel ! I hated thee without a cause,

Viewed all thy holy deeds with envious eye,
And charged thy goodness on thee as thy crime!
Whene'er the look of holy love would light
His beaming eye, and throw a smile of joy
Celestial o'er his seraph brow, that smile
Spake but the contrast of superior bliss;
And waked the vengeance sleeping in my soul.
I fed upon my fevered thoughts, and nursed
The growing flame; watched all his actions,
Every feature watched, and evil saw
Where only good was meant, till malice strong
Possessed my soul, and concentrated hate
Drove each inferior passion from my breast.
As in some woody grove sequestered deep,
When meaner forest beasts for empire fight,
Should some huge Lion suddenly appear,
Straightway the frightened herd forsake their strife,
And leave the field to him—so in my soul
Hatred to Abel quelled each meaner thought,
Till maddened by the demon spell, I struck
The fatal blow, and made this gory hand
Red with my brother's blood.

Methinks again
I view the fearful scene—that pallid form
Lies stretched upon the sod—the blood-red stream
Flows from the gory wound; with failing eye
He looks to heaven, and with uplifted hand
And quivering voice he prays, 'Oh God, forgive him!'
And now he turns to me, and with a voice
Soft as the trembling note of some faint lyre,
He says, 'Cain, I forgive thee.' Would he had
Cursed me! I'd rather hear the rattling of
Ten thousand thunders, or all the groans
That shake th' abyss of hell, than once again
To hear that gentle voice, 'Cain, I forgive thee!'
And now above him bends his father's form.
With clenched hand he smites his burning brow,
And with glazed eye looks on his murdered son,
While agony, too big for utterance,
Shakes all his manly frame. My mother comes!
How shall I meet her gaze! She pauses now—
Hark! what a shriek! the distant hills give back
The sound. She clasps the dead within her arms—
"Abel! awake, awake, my boy! my boy!
Oh! he stirs not—alas! he does not breathe!
Can this be death? this wound? who has done this?

Cain, this is not thy hand! hast thou done this?
Thou hast! thou hast! now curst be thou! may all
The plagues—but oh! thou art my son, and now
My only son—God pardon thee this deed!"
But hark! I hear again the voice of God.
How my heart sinks! where shall I hide! how flee
The scathing lightning of that awful eye.
"Where is thy brother Abel, Cain? The voice
Of his shed blood cries to me from the ground.
And now art thou accursed, a fugitive,
A wanderer forlorn, henceforward thou
Shalt dwell on earth; the ground thou till'st
Shall not yield unto thee her strength,
For she her mouth hath opened to receive
Thy brother's blood shed by thy impious hand.
Therefore depart—cursed, thrice cursed, shalt
Thou be; cursed at morn and eve,
Curs'd when thou risest up, and liest down."

Oh God! how shall I bear my agony!
Thy glorious face is now forever hid,
Nor shall I look on thee again, in peace!
The sealing mark of shame is on my brow!
Where shall I go for rest! upon what spot
Of earth's wide bosom shall I lay me down!
On every breeze is borne my brother's groan,
I hear the shriek of Eve, in every wind!
At night's dark hour the stiffened corpse appears,
And the cold eye glares on me horribly,
While in my ear some voice with demon yell
Shrieks "murderer," and starting up from sleep,
Conscience gives back again the dreadful word.
Is there a hell? I've heard my father say
There is a hell. Can it be worse than this?
Ye toppling rocks, why pass ye by my path!
Oh! fall and crush me! hide me from the face
Of Heaven! But wherefore do I live? one bound
From yonder precipice and I am gone—
Gone! whither gone? I dread to think, alas!
I've not a hope in life, and dare not die.

R. A[illegible]

CONVERSANO,

A ROMANCE IN HISTORY.

CHAPTER III.

"Natural to love are all these evils—injuries, suspicions, enmities, conciliations, and alternate war and peace." TERENCE.

THE incidents of our tale carry us for a while from the castle of William to another scene. On the west of Conversano, quite far inland toward the other sea, lay the province of Luciana; a sunny land, where hill and plain diversified the surface, and rich vineyards and olive groves delighted the eye. A scene so fair and tempting was by no means calculated to escape the notice of the Norman wanderers. Here, too, had their lance prevailed, and here, at the close of the eleventh century, Ralf Guiscard ruled, a baron who boasted his descent, in an unbroken line, from one of the famed Twelve Brothers.

The strong hold of this high-born lord stood near the eastern boundary of his lands, and a mile or two to the westward was the humbler abode of one of his vassals, a place to which we wish to call the attention of the reader.

A description of the situation and construction of this house will give a correct idea of the style then used by the Normans in the erection of their secondary class of dwellings. It stood upon an eminence that had, evidently, in former times, been crowned with forest trees, but which were now cleared away for a considerable distance about the dwelling, so that in case of an attack, they might not afford a cover under which the enemy could come up to the walls, without danger from the missile weapons of those within. The house itself was built of stone, in the form of a square, with walls of great thickness and strength, and for the further security of the inmates, the part intended for habitation was raised above the ground by arches, leaving below a vaulted space, into which the cattle and horses were driven, for security, whenever an incursion of the enemy was expected. The second story, attained by a moveable staircase placed upon the outside, was divided into two rooms, the bare stone walls and rough oaken floors of which, would but ill accord with our modern ideas of comfort. In one, only, of the rooms, the dreary and inhospitable appearance was relieved by a wide-mouthed fireplace, with projecting funnel, which was generously supplied with fuel, in summer as well as in winter, the year about. A huge oaken table, with clumsy settles of the same wood, formed the principal articles of furniture, while shields, crossbows, quivers of arrows, and hauberks, formed of iron rings sewn upon woollen or leathern foundations, supplied to the walls the place of tapestry. A kind of staircase, or rather ladder, led to the sleeping apartments above, and here the gaping chinks of the roof promised the inmates but sorry protection in rainy weather.

In the outer room of the second floor, at the close of a summer's day, might have been seen, at the time of our narrative, two persons standing near the narrow window that looked towards the west, and engaged in deep conversation. The one was a maiden of the middle class of life, young, fair, and beautiful, with a winning smile and confiding look, that told at once of ignorance of the world and freedom from guile. The other was a knight, whose dress and bearing betokened his high rank and station; he was tall and well made, with dark complexion, and those piercing black eyes that are sometimes pleasing and beautiful, and sometimes rendered terrible by the gleamings of awakened passion. A coat of mail was his only defensive armor; a scarlet cap, which he had worn in place of a helmet, lay upon a bench by his side, while a long riding cloak, of thick Flemish cloth, thrown with careless grace over his shoulders, set off to advantge his manly form. The knight was holding one of the maiden's hands between his hardened palms, and had seemingly been urging some request which gave her no pleasure, for a cloud came over her sunny brow, as she answered, with spirit, at the same time withdrawing her hand:

"Nay, then, my lord, though I love you, as you know, truly and well, I can see you no more, if these are to be the conditions of your return of my love. Did I not tell you, when first we met at the Saint's well, in the forest, that we could not meet again, that you were too good, too high and noble, for a dowerless maid like me? And did you not answer by telling me of many instances where high-born lords had been joined to the lowest of their vassals in honorable wedlock?"

"Marry, then, sweet Joan," answered the knight, quickly, "what else but 'honorable wedlock' have I offered thee now? Such wedlock as I then meant, and which hath at all times been esteemed of good report. In what but the name does the left hand differ from the right? And if I give to thee my love and my left hand, in return for thy love, and then to some noble dame, my right hand without love, in return for her dower, which, think you, hath the better bargain?"

"Aye, sir," answered the maiden, "aye, sir, which? A little more experience had tóo well taught me how to answer that. Ah, fool, fool that I was, to look so high or hope so madly!" and the poor girl wrung her hands and paced the floor in agony; then, as if suddenly regaining her self-respect and native pride, she drew herself up before the heartless baron, and continued, "But think not, my lord, that I, low and friendless though I am, will thus sacrifice to your pride my happiness and peace of mind; to become thy plaything of an hour, caressed to-day, and thrown aside for another to-morrow; to be prisoned in the castle turret the livelong winter days, and then, if tired of, mayhap before another summer's sun shall shine, the castle dungeon will shut out, with the light of day, the eyes and ears of the world. Ah, laugh not, thus scornfully, my lord! such things, and worse, even, have I heard, how that——

"Ha!" interrupted the knight, with a sudden start, "and whence, in Heaven's name, should a simple girl, like you, know all this? Maiden, you have broken faith and promise, you have prated, to some one, of our meetings;" and the lawless man fixed upon the girl a look so dark and piercing, that her honester eye quailed and sunk beneath it. "But, by my troth," continued he, "how thought you the lord would wed the offspring of his vassal? You have played the fool, you say; fool thrice cursed with folly you must have held me, if you thought that I would compromise my dignity and station, or sully the brightest name of Normandy, for the fading beauty and fickle love of any woman. By faith, an your hopes prove but true, these must be piping market-days for bright eyes and pretty forms. But know, now and for all, that mine you must be, upon the conditions named, if mine at all."

"Then, Ralf Guiscard, proud lord, depart," answered the maiden, "stay not to tempt me with your flatteries, or to taint with your foul spirit a heart that is weak and sinful I know, but, thank my God, free, as yet, from crime. Too nearly, too nearly had you ensnared a silly, doting girl; but, my mother—aye, sir, start not, I have told her all—my mother, I say, has pointed out to me the dangers and trials of the fearful path I had well nigh taken."

The brow of the knight grew black, and, like lightning from the cloud, the fearful gleamings of passion shot forth from his eyes, as, with a voice hoarse from rage, he cried, "Then, for thee and that old beldam, may the curse"——

"Ah, stop, sir, stop! speak it not," shrieked the maiden, as she grasped his arm convulsively. "Oh, that dreadful look! The saints defend us! Believe me, on my knees I swear, I meant not to anger you; stay, oh stay your wrath, we can ill bear it; remember that we are unprotected, that my father and brothers went for you to the holy wars. They are dead, all dead, their bones lie upon the plains of Palestine, and your anger kindled and turned against us, whither can we flee for protection. Oh, spare us, in Heaven's name, spare us!" And the maiden, overcome by her feelings, burst into tears, and would have fallen upon the floor, had not the knight caught her in his arms.

For one moment the haughty lord wavered, and his proud spirit dictated that he should cast her from him and return to his castle; but her soft hair was brushing his cheek and the warm tears falling upon his neck, and humanity prevailed over the worse feelings of his nature. He raised her up and spoke encouragingly: "I meant it not, sweet Joan, I meant it not; by Heaven, I would brain with his own halberd the coward knave who should dare even to lift his finger against you or the old dame. But, come, weep not, cheer thyself up, and let us speak calmly; believe me, you will soon think better of this."

"Ah, my lord," answered the maiden, "if you have any pity for me, any respect for yourself, leave me, forget me, let me be that happy creature I was only a short twelvemonth since, when my days were blessed with peace, and my sleep at night sweet and unbroken; and though I have loved, too deeply loved thee, I will drive that image from my mind, though every heart-string break."

As the knight heard this answer, the quiver of his lip and the knitting of his dark eye-brows told of the host of conflicting emotions that were agitating his breast; he paced the floor with a tread so heavy that the windows shook again, and as he walked, unconsciously muttered his thoughts. "Curse this folly, curse the mummery of these infernal priests, who have lavished their religion upon girls and grannies, and kept not a tittle for themselves. By St. Paul, an the girl's not a witch may I be hanged for a knave; I could not go when I tried, the horse turned back with scarce any of my direction. But, by faith, she is a noble maid, though not of noble blood; fit wife would she be for any prince; I knew not that such high spirit could dwell in one so gentle. And then, too, she is beautiful—yes, very beautiful; and now, if I were to marry her, as she wishes, what boots it? If tired of, she need not be for ever tied to me; the knot could be easily loosed; a word to my men, or a bezant to some unknown losel, and with a push from the turret, the slip of a rope, or thrust of a poignard, she troubles me no more. By the mass, come what may, I will have her. Maiden," said he, aloud, and turning suddenly toward her, with a look of wild exultation, you are mine; come, we will wed as you wish. Why, what now? What aileth thee? Art crazed? Speak."

The poor damsel had marked the struggle of contending passions that was going on within the breast of the knight, and though she had not heard enough of his mutterings to learn their dreadful import, yet a vague terror, a horrible fear of something, she knew not what, had gathered over her mind, and when she heard him speak more loudly of 'a poignard," she shuddered at the thought that his ungovernable passion might be leading him to violence and murder; so that when he turned upon her with such vehemence of action and language, she could only answer him with a fixed stare of terror, and a few incoherent words that died faltering on her tongue.

"Come," said Guiscard, "do you not hear me? I will wed you, I say, wed you as my lawful bride. By the rood, I meant it all the time; this foolery has only been a test of your virtue, a trial to see whether you would do for the wife of a Guiscard, and, by my faith, nobly have you passed through the ordeal; that pride and firmness of thine would not set ill upon a queen. Come, then, let us away to the holy man."

"Oh, my lord!" answered the maiden, "I know not what to think or how to act; my brain reels, and my poor mind is but a broken, withered bough, driven hither and thither by every passing wind. At least give me until the morrow to collect my scattered senses;—and, see, there is a dreadful storm coming on; saw you not that flash? and hark, that awful peal! Stay, stay, I cannot go to-night."

"Beshrew thy silly fears," answered the knight, impetuously; "would you drive me mad? Come, now—now or never—and by Heaven, it shall be now! Think not that I will stoop to offer you my name and fortune, and then have you hesitate, waiting, like a spoiled child, to be urged. Come, on with thy robe and veil, and let us away."

"Well, well," said the maiden, scarce knowing what she said, "I will obey you—any thing—only be calm. I place my trust in God to him I look to guide me aright in this fearful strait. But, at least, I may see my aged mother before I go from her house for ever?"

"No, no!" cried the knight, with an oath so fierce and blasphemous that the timid girl shrunk as though stricken by the forked lightning that was playing without, and would have fled away from him into the inner apartment, had he not caught her in his arms and borne her off; and the while, as if in revenge for the step she had, as it were, forced him to take, he terrified her with wild and fearful expressions, and fiendish bursts of laughter. But half his hellish words were lost, for before he had placed the poor maiden upon his horse, she had swooned away, and he bore her from the home of her fathers, a senseless burden in his arms.

CHAPTER IV.

"They shall be married to-morrow, and I will bid the duke to the nuptials. But, oh, how bitter a thing it is to look into happiness through another man's eyes."

As You Like It.

Let us return again to the castle of Conversano. Several weeks had elapsed since the events related in our first chapter, and Robert was still an inmate of the castle. Twice he had yielded to the solicitations of the uneasy Odo, and prepared for an immediate departure, but some new scheme of pleasure for the morrow had detained him one day longer, and yet another, until at length, with the natural mobility of his disposition, he had accommodated himself to his situation, and become transformed from the active warrior to the careless and idle courtier.

One afternoon, as Robert was listlessly pacing the hall, when all had been detained from their usual field sports by a storm, Odo approached and proposed a turn upon the battlements, as he said the clouds had passed away, and the sun was setting in great splendor. Robert gladly consented, and they accordingly ascended the great staircase and went out upon the walls. Here they were agreeably surprised at finding the battlements occupied by the ladies of the castle; they were clustered around one of their number, who was singing to the lute an eastern ballad. But the first object of our hero's attention was the beautiful and impressive prospect which presented itself. In the west all was bright and beautiful; the sun had just set, and day was fading away in that mild, sweet light, which always sheds a calmness over the soul, and fills the free heart with thoughts of heaven and of God. While in the east, the black clouds of the retiring storm hung like a pall over the Adriatic, casting upon its deep waters a hue so dark and ominous, that one might almost distinguish the sounds of howling tempests and maddened waves, and fancy he heard the last voice of the sailor borne upon the wind.

One of the ladies had withdrawn herself from the careless group, nd as she stood gazing out upon the beautiful scene that presented itelf in the west, seemed to be communing with her own thoughts. obert immediately recognized the faultless form of Sibylla, arrayed a her usual dress of white, and approaching, addressed her:

"What, lady! musing, and sad, too? That brow, methinks, were ather formed for sunshine, than for clouds."

"No, my lord," answered Sibylla, "I was not sad; and yet, a nade of melancholy had stolen over my spirits, for I thought of childood, and the recollection of its teeming joys and hopes always makes e somewhat sad."

"Pardon me," said the duke, "but what, pray, may I ask, can there in your present life, which leads you to regret the past?"

"Ah! I know not how it is," answered the lady, "but sure I am, at the present is not, and the future cannot be, blessed as were the ays of my childhood, when I was a merry, thoughtless girl, free om care and elate with hope, when to find a bright berry or a new ower in the wood was an era in my existence, and the sweetest easure to ramble unrestrained through the olive-groves on the hill."

At the recalling of these old associations of her childhood, the lady's som heaved, and a tear started to her eye which she could not reess, and she turned again to the scene before her, to conceal her notions, so that she lost the piercing look of love that Robert gave r, as he answered—

"Did you never imagine, lady, in your day-dreams, that these sweet ars might be renewed? Know you not that there is an era in our es, brighter, even, than the halcyon days of childhood?"

The maiden, though formed for love, was as yet but a novice in e's language and wiles, and she answered, with perfect artlessness, she turned towards him—

"You are a true knight, my lord, to whom the neighing of the warse and the clash of steel are the sweetest sounds. I have been told the wild pleasure of the rush and excitement of battle, and of vicy, to which you doubtless refer as that brighter era. He who fought Paynim can indeed speak from proud experience. But from all se scenes our sex are free, and for that I thank Providence, as for a ssing, for the carnage and anguish of the battle-field would be but e pleasure for me. But, hark!—is not the storm returning; or is t noise the sound of the swollen brook, borne by the breeze to our rs?"

The knight listened for a moment, and then answered, with a smile, You have not, indeed, the ear for a soldier, or you would distinguish that sound the clash of armor, the rattling of the mail of knights and trappings of steeds."

"Ah, yes!" answered Sibylla, "I do now know that sound, like the off tinkling of a thousand little bells; often have I heard it before. t who, I wonder, can they be?"

"Aye, and there they come," said the knight, as a small band of valiers issued from the wood, and came gaily prancing up the steep. And now, for you must know better than myself, I iterate your question, 'Who can they be?' Their careless movements, and their shields hanging at their backs, betoken them friends."

"Oh, yes," answered Sibylla, "I know them well. That is the banner of our neighbor, Lord Guiscard; he is my"—the maiden hesitated and blushed—"my kinsman—our cousin."

A cloud came upon the brow of Robert, but it instantly fled, and he answered, with assumed carelessness, "A goodly train, indeed, your kinsman brings, and that noble fellow in the green armor, I would be sworn, is the leader, Guiscard himself; he is not altogether unknown to fame."

The band had now almost reached the castle, and our two friends stood in silent admiration of the movements of the leader. Evidently proud of his superior horsemanship, he came caracoling on, managing his noble steed with perfect ease, and as it were by his own will, rather than by any movement of the bridle hand; his visor was up, and the short black curls that straggled from under his helmet and fell about his face, set off to fine advantage his high, proud features; while, to enhance his beauty, his eye beamed brighter and his lip curled yet more haughtily with the excitement of the moment. Sweeping swiftly forward, and clearing the bridge at a single bound, he sprung gaily from his horse, and entered the castle, with the easy familiarity of one who was well known and respected.

"Well, by my faith," said Robert, "a nobler man cannot be found in Europe, whether for couching lance upon the battle-field, or whispering love in lady's bower, and I would stake my life upon his success in either."

"His name and his deeds, my lord," answered Sibylla, with a sigh, "do not altogether belie his looks; but pardon me, sir, I must leave you, to receive our guest."

"Nay, but stay one moment," answered Robert, hastily; "I have something of the last importance to say. and this may be my only opportunity, for soon I must away to other lands and ruder scenes. My looks, my words, my love, sweet lady, cannot have been unheeded by thee. From the first moment of our meeting, I have adored thee each hour, with an ardor that has only been surpassed by the increased love of the succeeding. Lady, you are the day-spring of my hope, the star of my fate, and at thy feet I lay my name, my fortune, my kingdom, my all." And assuring himself, by a glance, that the rest of the ladies had descended from the battlements, the knight caught her hand in his, and, kneeling, impressed upon it a burning kiss of love. Once he thought those soft, taper fingers returned his ardent pressure, and then, in his moment of hope, her hand was hastily withdrawn, and the lady turned from him and burst into a passionate flood of tears.

"Ah! tell me, tell me," she sobbed, "that I have not encouraged you, that I have not led you on to this, and I shall be happy."

"Dearest lady," answered the duke, "it has caused me weeks of anguish, that you have not returned my looks and signs of love; but hope whispered that nothing but maiden modesty and reserve was the cause, and with thy matchless beauty beaming before me, how could I cease to hope and love. Tell me, lady, by one word, one sign, that I have not loved in vain."

"My lord," answered Sibylla, "think of my situation, and you will desist from your suit. I am the only child of an aged father, I might well say, his only stay and companion; and think you I could leave him? No, not for sceptres and jewelled crowns. Others there are, far nobler and more beautiful than I, that would be proud and joyful at thy suit; but I, oh! I cannot leave my worn-out sire."

"And is that all?" said Robert, springing to his feet, and again catching her hand in his, "an that be all, I will bide here, or, stay—the good old count shall go with us, to even a sweeter home than this; he shall spend the evening of his life by the graves of his fathers. The skies of Izan are not more bright than those of Normandy, sweet lady, nor the plains of Yeman half so pleasant; we will away to Normandy."

"Ah, my Lord, you do but afflict me," answered Sibylla, with averted face; "I must not deceive you, I can never be thy bride—from my cradle I have been affianced to another."

"And that other?"—

"Is the knight who just entered the castle."

"I feared it, I feared it," said Robert, with a most sorrowful tone and look; "his claims are before mine, and your constancy I can but respect, while at the same time I regret it. Had that knight, lady, come hither as my rival, his lance had needs been strong and his sword keener than blade of Damascus, but now I yield. Your happiness, in this, as in every thing, is all that I desire, and while I resign you gladly, and yet with sorrow, to another, I only pray that his homage may be faithful and ardent as mine has been. Lady, I shall never love another, and by this token I swear never to wed." So saying, he pressed her hand respectfully to his lips and left her to descend with her maids.

"Ah!" thought she, as she slowly passed down the staircase, "how much more noble and magnanimous than *him*. Oh, the hated espousals! I am sure that I can never love Ralf Guiscard, sure as I am that he loves not me. Fear and love can never be mated, and his very look I dread as it were a serpent's glare. If only"—

"My lady," said a pert page at her elbow, whose approach she had not, in her reverie, noticed, "my lord count, your father, desired me to say, your presence would not be needed in the reception room; he is closeted with lord Guiscard, who sends his respectful compliments, and wishes you good health."

"I return the count my thanks," said Sibylla, "but, stay, know you—or, nothing, nothing; if wanted, I shall be in my chamber."

"Well, well," said the page to himself, as she departed, "what can be in the wind now? Certes, I never saw my lady sad before. St. Peter, but if I were a lady, I would not be so sorrowful that I could not see my lover, an he were such an one as that."

As Sibylla entered her chamber, she was met by her tiring woman, who, with the clattering officiousness allowed her station, began offering her services.

"Which dress will my lady please to wear this evening? Here is the new one brought over the mountains from Florence by the merchant, a fabric rich and fine; and here, too, is the bright Venetian silk, that we bargained for with the shipman, a queenly dress, and of brave colors; was not that a right good bargain, my lady? But I was always too sharp witted for these traders; my life upon it, he lost by that sale. Well, we will have this last for to-night; it will become you well, my lady?"

"No, no, do not trouble yourself, good maid, answered Sibylla, "I shall not need your services now."

"But, my lady," answered the woman, "I may at least arrange your hair; the good lord of Lucinna, you know, is in the castle. I saw him as he came up the hill, riding on his gallant black steed, and, faith o' me, how beautiful and like a king he looked. But I will dress you, my lady, so that you be not behind him in beauty, I'll venture."

So saying, the garrulous tiring woman commenced arranging her lady's hair. But Sibylla, in a tone of petulance that she was never wont to use, declining her services, bid her retire, and then threw herself upon a couch, and was soon lost in a mournful reverie. She could not but make comparisons between the duke of Normandy and him who was soon to be her liege lord and master, and every light in which she viewed the subject, only made the virtues of the noble Robert seem more bright, and the character of the haughty and arrogant Guiscard appear more and more repulsive. The latter she had known from her childhood, and his imperious temper and fearful bursts of passion had terrified her from perceiving and loving the few redeeming traits which he possessed. Robert, the favorite of fortune, and most famed of all the famous knights of his day, had appeared to her in the romantic period of her life, and with his engaging manners, noble person, and brilliant conversation, had more than realized that beau ideal of masculine excellence which her youthful fancy had painted to her. Against her will she loved him, and, what she dared not own to her own mind, she *could not* love, nay, she cordially disliked, his more fortunate rival. Revolving these thoughts in her mind, she was so lost in the consideration of her troubles, that she heeded not the bustle of the departing visitors, nor even the sharp clattering of their horses' hoofs upon the pavement below, and a knock at her door was twice repeated before she heard it and bid the applicant enter.

"I wish you joy, my daughter!" exclaimed the old count, as he appeared. But how is this? What a long, sad face! And you have been weeping, love—what, what! Nay, but I'll make those pretty eyes sparkle again. The time is fixed—one week from this, you are to be wedded; it is all arranged. Is not that good news for you, ah, my daughter?"

But little joy did the words the kind old man deemed so acceptable, bring his daughter. They fell upon her ear like a death-knell, damping her heart's last hope.

"But, father," said she, "I am young yet, too young to marry; and how can I leave you, dear father?" And she twined her arms about the neck of her old sire, and buried her head in his bosom, to hide the tears that would gush forth.

"Nay, child, you were seventeen a half year since. But is that all? are you sure you have no other reason for delay?" asked the father, as he raised her up, and regarded intently every motion of her countenance.

"But what matters any other reason, my father?" answered Sibylla, "I am betrothed to Ralf, and his I must be, come what will, what may; what boots it to object?"

"What boots it to object?" iterated the old man, impetuously, "what boots it to object? Think you, if you disliked, nay, if you did not love the Guiscard, that that old compact should bind any more than flimsy web of spider? He might fume, he might threaten; nay," said the old man, his blood rising at the thought, "he might fight, and he should find one who could repay him blow for blow and blood for blood. I would myself hurl the gauntlet in his face, my old armor should be cleared of its rust and once more buckled on, and the thought that I was striving for your happiness, daughter, would nerve my arm and give me success in my last fight, and, by this head that never bent to foe, I would conquer for thee."

"Nay, father," cried the maiden, hastily, alarmed at the very thought of his danger, "but did I say I loved not Ralf? What could make you imagine I disliked our handsome cousin? If I be old enough, let us have the wedding quickly; what maid would not wish to marry?" And she laughed a strange laugh in her hollow attempt at gayety. But this, the old man, in his agitation, did not notice; and his suspicions lulled into rest, the happy father went on to tell his plans—how that the good duke of Normandy had intended to have departed in the morning, but had been kindly forced to stay—how that the noted bishop of Bayeux was to officiate in the coming ceremony—that a new band of musicians was to be summoned from Florence, and gay dresses and bright jewels brought from Naples. And thus the kind old father forgot his fighting and became all happiness in planning schemes of supposed happiness for his daughter.

Soon supper was announced, and the lady Sibylla remained in her room, pleading want of appetite as her excuse; but the old count made up for her absence by his joyous and even noisy hilarity. "Ho, there!" he cried to the attendants, "another cask of wine; none of the poorer sort, as ye value your lives, but a barrel of the mellow Gascony, sealed a half century ago. Move cheerily, ye knaves; we must have nothing but pleasant faces for the next three moons." The generous wine flowed without stint, the jesters, as if inspired by the humor and gayety of their lord, loosed their tongues in bright and ready wit, and the song of the harper, and the oft repeated lay of love and chivalry, protracted the joyous feast to a late hour.

CHAPTER V.

"The bubble bursts—and we are what we are."—Wordsworth.

The intervening week, a week of pleasure to some, but of sorrowful anticipation to one, at least, had at length passed away. The marriage was arranged to take place at noon, and according to custom, a sumptuous feast was to follow.

On the morning of the eventful day, the lady Sibylla was yet sleeping in her chamber, when the door was carefully opened, and the laughing face of a girl of sixteen peered in. She was an orphan of noble birth, who had been adopted by the count in her infancy, and reared as the companion of his daughter; she gazed, for a moment, on the placid and beautiful features of the sleeper, and then, bounding lightly as a fawn across the room, threw herself on the couch by her side, and awoke her. "Why, sister," said she, as she played with the dark ringlets that strayed about the neck of her companion, "why so indolent on your day of marriage? The sun has risen and climbed a long way up the sky, and here are you, the most important character in the castle, dreaming of, Heaven knows what. You should see all the preparations that our kind father is making for you, below. And then, such a laugh as I have had at the confusion and noise—upon my faith, it is worse than Babel. There is poor old Hurd at the gate, with his head half turned by the noise of the minstrels and dancers and merchants, who are clamoring for admittance. Then there is the new steward of the kitchen, with the long name, I forget what, marching about, with as much dignity and importance as a young cavalier just knighted; now rating the cooks, now tending to the arrangement of the great table in the hall, and now chaffering with some peasant at the gate, for his cranes and peacocks. The count has not yet"——

"Oh, my dearest friend," interrupted Sibylla, "why did you wake me to all these hateful realities? The anticipation of them kept my eyes unclosed until almost day dawn, and I would fain have forgotten them, as long as possible, in sleep. No one without the experience can realize how it wrings the heart, to think of breaking all the ties that bind one to home, and to bid adieu forever to the objects and sweet associations of childhood."

"Nay, dear Sibylla," answered her companion, "but do not weep; I know full well the true cause of your distress. You think that Ralf loves you not; but, beshrew me, if I think he can do otherwise. He is proud, I grant, but then I am sure he loves you; and though you do bid farewell to home, it will only be to obtain, if possible, a happier home. Loved ones you must leave, but then it is for one who will love you yet more."

"Ah, my sister," answered Sibylla, "little do you know of the secret springs of the human heart; if Ralf be capable of love, he never will, and never can, love me; and in leaving all for him, I shall find no one to love—no congenial spirit, to whom I can cling for sympathy. Sympathy, forsooth! I would sooner seek it from a rude savage of the north. But I forget myself. I must shake off these thoughts, and at least before my poor father, appear happy. On your life, my gentle sister, remember your former promise, and tell him not of my feelings and my fears; but I will arise and prepare for this dreaded ceremony."

Leaving the Lady Sibylla to the attendance of her maids, which, while at her toilet, would perhaps be more proper than ours, we will descend to the less quiet scenes below. Here all was activity and bustle. In the outer court were the attendants of the cavaliers, some engaged in noisy conversation, some playing at dice, and others assisting the menials of the castle in dressing the horses of their masters, or relieving of their equipage those which had just come in. Most of the guests had arrived, but he who should have been there first, the Lord of Luciana, had not yet made his appearance. The time wore on, the appointed hour for the ceremony was drawing nigh, and yet he had not reached the castle; noon arrived, and gradually the shadows turned towards the East, and yet he did not come. What could delay him? was it accident? could it be careless indifference? The dependants, who almost venerated their mistress, began to murmur at this apparent slight, when at length, after the patience of the old count himself was nearly exhausted, and two hours later than the proper time, Guiscard appeared, hurrying up the hill at full speed. The horse which he rode was covered with dust and flecked with foam, while the blood from the spurs of his master, trickled off from his reeking sides. The dress of the knight was very much soiled and disordered, and upon his wrist was perched a young hawk, the plumes of which were quite as much ruffled as those of the owner. But one attendant accompanied him, and he was even in a worse plight than his lord—his riding cloak displayed a wide rent from the top to the bottom, and the gay cap which he had donned, was begrimed with dust, as though it had been trampled under the feet of his horse. As they came on, spurring up the hill, their horses strained and labored, as if completely blown by a severe ride, and their whole appearance was rather that of mad bacchanals at their orgies, than of a bridegroom and his train coming to claim their mistress.

They were met in the court by the old count, and to him, Guiscard with some shame and hesitancy, commenced his apologies: "I must beg your forgiveness, kind sir, and on my knees crave ten thousand pardons of my fair lady love for this delay; but the fault after all was with this fiend of a hawk; a brave young eyas never before flown, that I received of late from Mercia. Coming out with her upon my wrist, a noble crane started up from the pool on the other side of the hill, and by the mass, I could not but unhood and let fly at him. But the quarry, as if the devil sent it, would not mount forsooth, but must lead us off, a wild chase over hill and dale, that had well nigh ended in breaking all our necks. For my bold eyas striking the quarry and bringing him to the earth, we crowded on in hot haste to her assistance, and in mid career we all went, hurry-scurry, master and man, over a steep, so hidden from the view, that by St. Dennis, one with the eyes of the devil's Mercury could not have foreseen it."

"Methinks, if you had come straight on your way," answered William, dryly, "you had needed no such devil's eye, or devil's driving, for the doing of your proper errand"

"Nay, sire," said Guiscard, "but I pray you be not angered, for who could have thought, when I unhooded the hawk—the foul fiend take her—that she would give us such a race. And then, beshrew me if I do not think the worse if it hath fallen to my share, for we have left, stranded there upon the rocks, a score of my goodliest steeds, that will never take field more; one with broken knee, another with his bowels gushing out; and, by my life, may I never mount horse again, if my own noble Arabian did not lie in such mortal anguish from the crushing of his ribs, that out of mercy I pricked him with my spear, and so let his soul fly out, to find some more comfortable resting place."

"Well," answered William, "thanks be to the saints that it was no worse, and that you yourself were not injured. But our guests have been waiting with impatience—let us not delay the ceremony longer; and so, if it please you, repair some of these mishaps to your dress, and let us to the chapel."

A few moments delay found all the parties, which, with the guests and dependants, filled the building to overflowing, assembled in the small and rudely furnished chapel. They were a motley group, of both high condition and low, meeting here upon a common level, and most aptly illustrating the fact, that in those feudal times but a single step intervened between the two orders of society—the rulers and the ruled; that one step which marked the difference between tyranny and slavery.

The group in front of the altar was an interesting one; the bishop, arrayed in his splendid robes; the Lord of Luciana, with his stately form towering up in its commanding height, his countenance beautiful and faultless in every feature, yet wearing an expression withal, which one cannot look upon without dislike, or even fear; his bride by his side, fair and beautiful as ever, yet deadly pale, and with difficulty supporting herself upon her feet. The old count, erect with a father's natural pride, and happy in the seeming happiness of the occasion, and the duke of Normandy, with his graceful and noble figure, completed the picture. The marriage ceremony of the Normans, at that time, was very simple; the principal matters, indeed, connected with it, consisted of the preliminary arrangements of the *morgen gift*, etc. These having been previously arranged, it only remained to set a seal to the solemn rite, by the blessing of the divine, implored upon the union of the parties. After a short exhortation, he was about, with outstretched hands, to conclude the brief ceremony, when a great confusion was heard near the entrance, and loud shrieks of, "stay, stay, unhand me, vassal, I will be heard," caused him to stop, and demand in an imperative tone, "What is the cause of this sacrilege; who dares the divine anger, by attempting to break in upon this holy exercise?"

"Withhold, I pray you, reverend sir, that blessing, for if there be vengeance in heaven, it shall turn to a curse;" and bursting through the crowd, her dress torn and disordered, and her hair dishevelled and falling about her pale, wan cheeks, the dependant maid of Luciana appeared, and thrust herself between the parties who were about to be united. "Fiends and furies," thundered the knight, in a voice hoarse with rage, turning to address his attendants, "ye halter knaves, why in Heaven's name did ye suffer this?" and then, reminded by their absence, of the place where he had left his train, he turned to the old count, and with more calmness continued, "Ha, gramercy on this unseemly accident, what devil could have driven this wild woman here, at this time of all others? A crazy dependant, my Lord, that we have kept under bolt and bar in the castle keep for months."

"'Tis marvelous, indeed," answered the old man, who stood so bewildered by the strange and hurried scene, that he scarce knew where he stood or what he said, "but bear her hence, men: ye knaves, ye shall answer after this, for letting her in."

"Back, minions!" cried the maid, in a lofty tone, as with heaving breast and flashing eye she waved off the men who were advancing to take her—"away, do not violence to your manhood, by laying your hands upon a friendless woman; and you, old man, if ye be not void of a mortal's common mercy for his fellow mortal, yield not that fair form into the arms of yonder fiend incarnate, whose only impulse is his lust—his highest ambition, the deepest sin. Oh sooner, an ye be a father, nay, a man, thrust your daughter into the jaws of the desert lion. Aye, scowl on, son of darkness. Let that black front lower and threaten; I have seen it, ere now, flash forth the very fires of hell; and though I trembled then, and quaked to the heart's core, I shrink not now. The hand that aided hither my tottering limbs, is supporting me now—the God of justice, the God of the innocent and weak. Here," continued she, as she assumed a yet loftier tone and bearing, and every gesture seemed instinct with eloquence, "here are proofs that attest thy baseness, proofs even by the proofs of my own ruin. Aye sir, the injured woman, the despised dependant, comes, the herald of thy infamy! I hurl it on thy name, I brand it on thy front; wear it there forever; bear it through life, bear it to thy accursed grave, bear it"—

"Infernal Hecate!" shrieked the knight, in horrible tones, as the pent up flames of his rage burst forth in awful fury, "false witch, before that tongue has time to utter another lie, I'll tear it from its roots, and cut thy withered soul from out thy body. As thou canst not live like a woman as thou should'st, die, like a beast, as thou art." Ere he had finished speaking, his blade had left its scabbard and was flashing in the air, as with the yell of a fiend he sprang towards his victim—the next moment, and his sword had been sheathed in the body of the unfortunate woman, when a giant grasp was laid upon his neck, and the arm of Robert thrust him back, with such force, that he fell with violence upon the pavement.

"Foul craven!" cried the knight, as he rose to his feet, every fibre of his body quivering with fury. "Cursed dog of Normandy, must thou too interfere to keep the devil from his due? Go, sup with her in hell." Never was Robert in more perilous situation than then, for ere he could draw his sword in defense, the keen blade of his antagonist came flashing down like lightning, threatening to cleave him to the chine; but his wonderful agility served him here, and saved his life, for springing nimbly aside, he only received a slight wound upon the shoulder, and before the sword could be raised again, the arm that swayed it had received a blow from his clenched fist that shattered it, as it were a reed, and left it hanging from its socket, a useless member. The next moment, the unruly knight found himself pinioned by those powerful arms, whose terrible gripe the German wrestler had well imagined might be of the devil himself. His fury now knew no bounds; he raved and foamed at the mouth, demanding to be released, with oaths and imprecations so blasphemous, that the ladies fled, terror-stricken, from the chapel. * * * * * "God of Heaven, an there be a heaven and a God, help me now! Fiends of darkness! release me from this foul dog's arms, and by — I'll send his soul to thee this night:" and as he spoke, with a fearful convulsion he burst from the grasp of the knight, and springing high from the ground, fell at length upon the floor, the blood gushing in torrents from his mouth and nose. He never rose or spoke again. In his uncontrollable rage he had burst a blood vessel, and that awful promise had gone out upon his dying breath. He lay there, an appalling sight, the wreck of a noble form, stricken down by the visitation of the high God, he had so often insulted; and to render the spectacle yet more revolting, even in death, the demon that ruled the soul had left its characters upon the distorted features. For a space all was as still as the grave—no one moved, for all knew that life had fled, and naught was heard but the suppressed breathing of the men, and the purling of the life's blood, as it kept flowing out, while the dark locks of the dead man played up and down in the ebbing current. The old count seemed completely paralyzed by the suddenness of the scene, and its awful conclusion, and with folded arms and glazed eye, he stood gazing in speechless horror upon the form of the knight, until the duke took him kindly by the arm and led him away, after having first ordered the men to raise up and carry out the lifeless body. * * * * * *

In conclusion, it will no doubt please the reader to hear that the unfortunate dependant of the departed Guiscard, found friends and kind protection in the dwelling of Count William. To those acquainted with history, it will scarcely be necessary to add, that in a short time Robert and Sibylla were united, and bidding farewell to the hospitable castle of Conversano, set off for Normandy; and surely, no royal bride was ever honored by a better or more devoted train, than that goodly army of brave knights and noble cavaliers, which Robert was leading back, in all the triumph of victory, from Palestine.

We will now leave them, at a time when all in their future seemed bright and full of hope. We must acknowledge that their sky was but too soon clouded; yet being of those who are inclined to look upon the brighter side of things, and having seen Robert, at a period, perhaps the happiest of his life, we will be satisfied to leave the description of his subsequent misfortunes to those Timons, who are forever harping upon the depravity of human nature, and the ills of life, thus endeavoring to make every one around them as miserable as themselves.

J. *. *.

CAMBRIDGE UNIVERSITY.

BY A VISITOR.

Few objects in England so attract the attention and engage the interest of the American traveler, as the Universities of Oxford and Cambridge. Familiar as their names have been at home, he desires to know them more intimately, to compare them with similar institutions in his own land, to examine the system and its details, to study and admire their architecture; in a word, to amuse himself with a view of all that pertains to "English College Life." Nor will his expectations, though highly raised, be disappointed. Ample resources will be found to gratify curiosity, and render a visit extremely entertaining and useful.

While the two Universities resemble each other in general, they have each distinct characteristics. Oxford is more distinguished in classical studies and literature, but yields the palm in the natural and exact sciences. Its collections of antiques and curiosities are perhaps unrivaled. The Arundelian and Elgin marbles are among its choice treasures. In appearance it is highly picuresque, its buildings are venerable, and the whole air of the place is quite monastic. Noble spires and the dome of the great Radcliffe Library render the distant view imposing. The surrounding country is bold and romantic, and presents a fair specimen of the beautiful park-like scenery, so peculiar to England. Two of the noblest seats in the kingdom, Stowe and Blenheim, lie in the neighborhood, owned respectively by the dukes of Buckingham and Marlborough. In the park of the latter is the Fair Rosamond's Well, and Woodstock is immediately adjacent.

But leaving Oxford, whose numerous attractions merit a fuller description, let us now turn to the sister University. Were "dreaming chroniclers" to be believed, we should confidently affirm that it was founded by a Spaniard rejoicing in the name of Cantaber, at some invisible period of dim antiquity, that is to say, about the year 540, A. D. We should entertain no doubt that the venerable Bede and the learned Alcuinus took their degrees as Doctors of Divinity, in due course of time, at this institution, and that disciples of the former founded the University of Paris in the reign of Charlemagne, thus making the latter, in comparison, quite a modern establishment—all of which statements are very credible to those who believe them.

But certain it is, that under the fostering care of the Great Alfred, a school arose and flourished, and at the time of the Conquest had acquired such fame that William the Norman sent thither his son to be educated. The young prince showed himself so apt a scholar as to receive the title by which he is distinguished in history, Henry "Beauclerc."

After the lapse of two centuries, Colleges began to be separately established and endowed, as at present. Previously there had been one great school; but upon its gradual increase, it was divided.

At this time, and long after, the professors were monks, and the chief object of the institution was the support of religion, while learning was secondary in importance. This character, though since greatly modified, attaches to it even now. It forms a strong connecting link between Church and State. The restrictions were formerly so severe as to prevent the entrance of foreigners and dissenters, and a law generally obtained, not yet, we think, entirely abolished, by virtue of which all who could not subscribe the Articles of the Church of England, were incapacitated from taking any degree whatever. Dissenters have consequently been obliged to found their own establishments, of which University and King's Colleges, in London, are the most celebrated.

The University of Cambridge is a corporation in itself, governed by a Chancellor, generally a nobleman of the highest rank, who is chosen biennially, though often continued for life. The Duke of Wellington has been for many years Chancellor of Oxford. It is an honorary office, as is the next, that of High Steward. The Vice Chancellor is the highest resident officer, elected annually, always the Head of a College, and to all intents and purposes the President of the University. He is a Justice of the Peace, armed with full powers, and exercising jurisdiction over the town and county. The Senate, or general council, is the legislative body, composed of the higher officers and all resident members who have taken the second degree. It has the direction of all public affairs, and elects two representatives in Parliament, for the University, a privilege granted by James I. These are always men of rank and influence, worthy sons of Alma Mater. The Vice Chancellor's agents are the Proctors, Masters of Arts, who acted as peace officers, and being omnipresent, omniscient, and argus-eyed, patrol the streets in cap and gown, accompanied by their faithful attendants, familiarly ycleped "the bull-dogs." If a student, disregarding college laws, venture abroad without his academic dress, he is immediately espied, pounced upon, required to give his name and College, and ordered to his room. Or should a simple youth, at evening, after making libations to Bacchus, deviate from the perpendicular on his return, the Proctor's keen eye would note, with mathematical precision, the angle of inclination, and punishment is administered accordingly. The penalty is an "imposition," it may be, of half a dozen pages in Virgil or Homer, to be learned by heart, a paper in the Spectator or Rambler to translate into Latin prose, or, perhaps, by way of variety, a book of Euclid to be written out.

We are reminded here to relate an amusing incident, by way of illustrating the vigilance of these officers, and the annoyance to which the students are consequently liable. "Hal," said a gownsman to his companion, while enjoying their afternoon walk in the High street, "I'll wager my head against sixpence you dare not kiss the first lady we meet." "Agreed," said the other; and encountering a fair girl at the angle of a street, without ado, he fairly won the wager. Then pulling off his cap, and bowing to the earth, he was about to make a thousand and one apologies for such unpardonable behavior, mingled with compliments to the irresistible beauty which had compelled him to the act of rudeness, when, to his utter dismay, the wrathful visage of the Proctor appeared. In tones of thunder, he ordered the culprit to his room, there to await punishment, but afterwards, on learning the facts, with wonderful generosity, suffered him to escape with a reprimand, together with an injunction never to repeat the offense.

The undergraduates are divided into four distinct classes. First are the Fellow-Commoners, men of rank and fortune. Next, the "Scholars," who, on account of merit, enjoy certain advantages, as the receipt of an income, or exemption from charges for board and lodging through the course. Then follow the Pensioners, who compose the mass of students. And lastly, the Sizars, men of limited means, who usually have their commons free, and are partially dependent on the bounty of others.

The whole number of students averages about seventeen hundred, distributed among seventeen Colleges. Trinity has about four hundred. It stands first in mathematics. Newton's name is on the books, and the instruments used by him while professor, are still preserved. St. John's bears the palm in classics. All alike wear the cap and gown, which serve to distinguish members of the different Colleges, and the rank of each, by peculiarities in the style, color, and material. The commons are held in fine old gothic halls, and the fare is excellent. The tables groan beneath the weight of substantial dishes; flagons of foaming ale, and port, "the milk of Alma Mater," grace the board. After dinner, the older students retire with the Fellows to the Conversation-room, and have an hour's sociable chat.

Nine tenths of all the members room in their respective Colleges. The apartments are spacious and comfortable, and some are very elegant.

There are three terms in the year. Michaelmas, continuing from October 10th to December 16th; Lent, from January 13th to the last week in February; and Midsummer, from the eleventh day after Easter to the first week in July. The vacations thus amount to just five months—a very agreeable feature in the system.

Commencement occurs on the first Tuesday in July. Of the three or four hundred then graduated, all who contend for University honors, present themselves for a general examination, either in Mathematics and Natural Philosophy or the Classics. It is conducted in the Senate-house, with the utmost strictness and impartiality, before a promiscuous audience. The successful candidates in each department are divided into three classes. In the Mathematical Tripos* there are Wranglers, Senior Optimes, and Junior Optimes. The Senior Wrangler is the first man of the year, and his name resounds throughout the empire. He has made his fortune for life; the Government have an eye upon him, and the highest posts in Church or State are within his grasp. In the Classical Tripos, there is a first, second, and third class.

* A word meaning, originally, the three legged stool upon which the candidates were examined, and now used to denote all who receive the University honors.

The best scholar is Senior Classic of the year. All not included among these, facetiously designated the "οἱ πολλοί," receive degrees merely if they are qualified, otherwise, they are termed, in college phrase, "the plucked."

It has been thought very desirable that men who have distinguished themselves during the course, should be induced to remain, and pursue their studies as resident graduates, for the sake of mutual improvement, for the facilities and advantages which they may enjoy, and in order to have a body ready and competent to fill vacancies in the Professorships or other offices. For this purpose, Fellowships, four hundred and thirty in number, have been attached to the various colleges. They entitle the holders to a certain income, varying from one to four hundred pounds sterling, to a handsome suite of apartments, commons, access to the Libraries, in short, the "freedom" of the University. Should any one of the number, however, commit matrimony, he is immediately struck off the list, a regulation highly proper and necessary to prevent the accession of young "Fellows."

Here it may be well to notice the system of study, and glance at the habits, manners, and pursuits of the collegians. Every one who is able has a private tutor to assist his studies, and to hear his daily recitations. The college tutors pay especial attention to the poorer students. Lectures are delivered by the University Professors, where all attend and take notes. There are, also, lecturers in each college upon the several branches of study. Examinations occur three or four times a year. The tutors prepare their pupils to pass, creditably if possible, or if the case be desperate, "cram" them, as the phrase is. The time of the studious is fully occupied—they have little leisure for visiting or recreation, unless it be a proper degree of exercise. In this respect, the English differ very much from our own countrymen. They are trained to take care of health, as they are to observe punctuality, and to form good habits in general. Two or three hours, at least, must be devoted each day to athletic sports in the open air, either walking, riding, fencing, cricketing, quoiting, gymnastics, or boating. In the latter, the Cantabrians are very celebrated, and quite superior to the men of Oxford, though the latter have a larger river, the Isis, a branch of the Thames. There is an annual trial of skill, but the mathematicians almost invariably surpass their classical rivals. The boats are four, six, or eight-oared, and very sharp built, unlike anything we see at home, but nearly resembling the Thames wherry.* Students not unfrequently walk to London, a distance of fifty-four miles, in the day. The climate, though somewhat damp and foggy, is exceedingly mild and favorable, neither too warm nor cold. Footpaths, smooth as a gravel walk, skirt all the roads, so that there is every inducement to pedestrian exercise.

The average age for entering the University is seventeen or eighteen. In the intercourse of men with each other, etiquette is strictly observed.

---

* See "Jacob Faithful," by Capt. Maryatt.

here is a strong party feeling in the different colleges; each man, of urse, is proud of his own, and regards the member of another with a fferent eye. It is amusing to observe their extreme taciturnity in aveling to London by coach. Hardly a word is exchanged during e five hours of the journey. Without an introduction, no one premes to address another. There is a caricature story told of a Triarian, who, seeing a Johnian in danger of drowning, stood on the nk of the river wringing his hands in the greatest distress, and exaiming, "Oh! Oh! Would to Heaven I were introduced to that genman, that I might have the pleasure of saving his life."

The discipline of the colleges is strictly maintained. Students e required to be in their rooms at certain hours, and within the tes at nine in the evening, as they are then closed for the night. he porter marks all who come in at a later hour, and reports them to e Dean, unless they manage to get privately to their rooms, by scalg the garden wall. They are required to uncap to professors and gnitaries, and to attend prayers, usually performed at seven in the orning and five in the afternoon, in the several chapels. They appear d in the surplice, and in succession read the daily Psalms, while a aplain officiates. Choristers and chorister boys chaunt portions of e service, with an organ accompaniment, as in the cathedrals.

There is a great diversity between the systems of education adopted the English and American colleges. Students in the former enter an age comparatively mature, after having been thoroughly drilled d whipped for a long course of years, in the best schools. Boys at early age are sent to Eton, Harrow, or Westminster, and there ually remain till fitted for college. In reading the classic authors, e lessons are short, and it is required to scan, parse, translate, and arn by heart every word which occurs. In studying Euclid the prinpal diagrams are drawn upon their backs with the rattan, and to assist em in crossing the "Pons Asinorum," they are frequently "horsed."* ey are absolutely compelled to study, and if not idiots, must needs tolerable scholars when dismissed. When the Freshman enters e University, he is supposed to be a gentleman, and is left in a great easure to take his own course. If he prefer, as many do, to neglect udy, to follow the hounds, to course, to attend Newmarket and become sporting character, he can find means to do it, and by judicious cramming," can scramble through the examinations. But if he wish excel as a scholar, having already acquired an accurate knowledge of reek and Latin, he now reads the best classics, as he would critically udy Addison or Corneille, as models of style and composition. He ltivates Greek, Latin, and English poetry and prose, and writes for e numerous prizes which are offered.

With us the case is different. Our institutions seem to occupy a ace midway the schools and the university. The students often enr too early to appreciate what they read, and at an age when a more

* The "horse," an instrument of torture, is a wooden quadrupedal cylinder on hich the boys receive punishment.

rigorous discipline is needed to make them perform their duties. If not well trained previously, they are very apt to neglect study. Certainly to elevate the standard of scholarship in our colleges, the character of our schools must be raised, and the system made to conform, in some measure, to the English pattern.

Between the town of Cambridge and the University, or, more concisely, between "town and gown," a deadly feud has existed from time immemorial. In former years, pitched battles were not unfrequent, in which the pates of the young patricians were cracked, their countenances marred, and the whole outer man so grievously maltreated, that some have actually died in consequence. Yet on the whole, they have been victorious, and manage to keep their inferiors in subjection. The latter are in reality altogether subservient, so great is the power and patronage of the University. If a tradesman becomes obnoxious to the authorities, he is a marked man, and cannot prosper. The breach between the parties is widened by their difference in politics, and the elections for members of Parliament are consequently very exciting. The unfortunate voters are bribed, flattered and brow-beaten to make them support the Tory candidates. The students enter into the contest *con amore*, and move heaven and earth to defeat the opposition. Each party has its poll, so that every man's vote is known. The two candidates occupy the same platform, and in turn address the people. Any one who will read in the Pickwick Papers, Dickens' very clever description of an Election at Eatanswill, will have the scene drawn to the life. The ballot-box affords the only remedy for the evils of the present system. The election continues two days. It is held on a large green, and nearly the whole population of twenty thousand turn out thither to witness the affair.

Commencement is held for the University at the Senate House. It is the high day of the year, an occasion surpassed in interest only by one other, to which we shall advert. The building where it is celebrated, was erected for the purpose of holding meetings, congregations, conferring degrees, the performance of ceremonies, and the reception of distinguished personages. It is very spacious, and will accommodate an audience of three thousand. Once a year the friends of the students repair thither from the various parts of the kingdom. From far and near, the ladies fair congregate in this most fortunate spot, till it is radiant with smiles and Saxon beauty, which we will not trust ourselves to describe. The University is metamorphosed, books are flung aside, bookworms, literary reptiles, shed their coats and appear in gay attire. The student becomes the gallant knight. He conducts the fair strangers through the spacious gardens and academic groves. At evening, when the sounds of song and dance resound through the ancient halls, assuming the courtier dress, he abandons himself to gayety and hilarity, and in the eyes of the ladies themselves, eclipses his more dashing rivals of the Army and Navy. The exercises of Commencement are quite unlike our own. Certain subjects for poems in Greek, Latin, and English, are proposed awhile before by the Chancellor. The best writers take the prizes, and some eight or ten have the honor of reciting their compositions, in presence of the audience. The speaker occupies a rostrum in the middle of the house, near the side wall. The platform at the upper end is thronged with bodies of distinction, heads of Colleges, Bishops, noblemen, Doctors, and the "illustrious" generally. Rows of seats extending along the side walls also accommodate the ladies. The space between is open, and is held by a solid phalanx of Fellows, Masters, and Bachelors of Arts, and students of law and divinity. The undergraduates squeeze themselves into the galleries above, and whenever there is an opportunity, cry out lustily, "three cheers for the *press*," for "lunch," for "ourselves," six for the "Queen, Prince Albert, and the Duke of Wellington," nine for "the ladies," with occasional groans for "O'Connell, the Proctors, and bull-dogs." The Chancellor presides, and honorary degrees are conferred. Three days after, the term closes, and the students disperse themselves in every direction, some to pass the vacation quietly at home, others to roam through foreign countries, to catch trout and salmon in Norway, to visit the lakes and romantic scenery of Sweden, to indulge in the gayeties of the French capital, to ascend the Rhine, "the great thoroughfare of Europe," to make pedestrian tours in Switzerland, or in other ways to kill time till the three months vacation has expired, and the bell of Great St. Mary's tolls for prayers on the evening of the 10th of October.

It is somewhat singular that so many of the great English poets have been bred at Cambridge, though the art is rather more encouraged at Oxford. The names of Spencer, Waller, Cowley, Dryden, Gray, and Milton, grace its calendar. Perhaps the pure and unmitigated mathematics have driven them in desperation to the opposite extreme, to wander unrestrained in their own imaginings, to write what need not be "proved," and would not be true if it were. Milton was a student of Christ's College, as was also Sir Philip Sidney. The mulberry tree planted by his own hands, yet stands, decayed by age, bound around with sheet lead and propped by beams.

The architecture of the Colleges is, as it should be, Gothic, a style best suited to the climate, sky, atmosphere, and associations of England, awakening in the mind thoughts of all that is venerable and time-honored, producing involuntary awe, full of poetry, modeled from nature, her own device. They are built in quadrangles, or hollow squares, opening into each other, and into gardens in the rear, with castellated fronts and lofty gateways, over which are carved in stone, the College arms, and an effigy of the founder. The Cam, a gentle, placid stream, leisurely meanders through the principal gardens, crossed by light and airy bridges; his banks grassed, rolled and shaven, invite the fair to sit and watch his progress, while he, yet lingering, would fain stand still to view their loveliness. Cutters, gaily painted and adorned, manned by athletic youths in aquatic garb, cleave his surface, shooting with occasional stroke up or down the stream. On an afternoon in Midsummer the scene is fairy-like and enchanting.

Among the more remarkable edifices, the Libraries of Trinity College and of the University deserve to be described, but we will not fatigue the reader with an enumeration of their merits. They are filled with treasures of learning, ancient and modern, English and foreign, classical and oriental, choice manuscripts, and adorned with busts and portraits of many distinguished members.

The Fitzwilliam Museum is a very costly and magnificent structure of white marble, just completed. It was intended, by the noble founder, for the reception of the paintings, statuary, books, drawings, and curiosities composing his own collection, and all others which might hereafter be added. It forms a splendid addition to the University, and is even now triumphantly thrown into the teeth of the Oxford men.

But the building most admired, curious and deserving of attention, is King's College Chapel,* esteemed by connoisseurs the most perfect specimen of Gothic architecture in the world. Its lofty turrets are the first objects seen by the traveler in approaching Cambridge. Fuller speaks of it as "one of the rarest fabrics in Christendom, wherein the stone-work, wood-work, and glass-work contend which most deserve admiration." There are two roofs; the inner one slightly arched, and unsupported by a pillar, is "so geometrically contrived, that voluminous stones mutually support themselves in the arched roof, as if Art had made them forget Nature, and weaned them from their fondness to descend to their centre." Its construction puzzles the best architects. Sir Christopher Wren was accustomed to go once a year to survey it, and said, that "if any man would show him where to place the first stone, he would engage to build such another." Massive towers and flying buttresses strengthen and support every part of the building. The interior is grand and imposing, elaborately carved and adorned with quaint and grotesque devices from roof to pavement. Its twenty-six windows, the finest in Europe, are all richly painted, except that at the western extremity. And when at vespers, arrayed in robes of white,

"Assembled men to the deep organ join
The long resounding voice, oft breaking clear,
At solemn pauses, through the swelling base,"

the effect is indescribably solemn and fine.

It was the good fortune of the writer to be present at the most interesting and important occasion which ever occurs at Cambridge—the installation of Chancellor. Indeed, in display and magnificence it rather resembles the coronation of a Prince. The ceremony is performed on the day preceding Commencement, when there is always a crowd of visitors. At this time, the place was full to overflowing. For some days previous, excitement had risen to fever heat, and every preparation was making in the town and colleges suitably to entertain their noble guests. As the time drew near, coronetted carriages, with postillions and four, and from every quarter coaches heavily laden, thundered through the streets.

* From this building the central part of the new Yale Library was modelled, though there is a great difference in their comparative dimensions.

On the morning of the "fourth of July," 1842, at nine o'clock, the doors of the Senate House were besieged by troops of people, armed with tickets, resolved to do or die, to effect an entrance, or sacrifice their coat tails in the attempt. For an hour, they stood like martyrs, keeping up their spirits by treading on each other's toes, elbowing their neighbor's ribs, and other innocent amusements, till the clock struck ten, when they were admitted, and 'installed' themselves without delay. Time passed rapidly away, enlivened by strains of martial music, and the firing of cannon, but especially by the presence of numerous ladies, dressed for the occasion with infinite taste and elegance. At twelve o'clock, the trumpets sounded, and the Chancellor elect, Hugh Percy, Duke of Northumberland, entered with his suite, supported by the Dukes of Wellington and Cambridge. He ascended the platform, where the ceremony of installation was performed, and the oaths administered. He was then invested with the robes of office and the Chancellor's cap. Immediately after, the venerable Lord Lyndhurst, son of the American painter Copley, was inducted into the office of High Steward. The platform now presented a gay appearance. The proudest of "Albion's haughty dames" were there, with Bishops and Archbishops in sacerdotal dress, foreign ministers, officers of high rank, and statesmen; in short, the highest in the land had assembled to honor the occasion with their presence. All appeared in the rich dresses peculiar to their rank or profession, a sight very novel to a republican eye. An Indian prince, with his nephew, in oriental costume, attracted great attention. The elder was a noble looking man, and comported himself with the highest dignity. Young Lord Nelson, nephew of the naval hero, and a student of Trinity, was conspicuous in his nobleman's gown of purple, embroidered with gold. Among other distinguished strangers, the Hon. Edward Everett was treated with much consideration, and seemed to take a lively interest in the scene. The students recognized him, and gave "three cheers for the American minister." The Public Orator then mounted the steps of the platform, and eulogized the Chancellor in a long Latin speech, the end of which was universally admired and applauded. Scarcely was it over when an express arrived with intelligence that the Queen had been fired at. The house was in great commotion. The Duke of Wellington left immediately for London. Soon after, the exercises concluded, and the audience dispersed. In the evening, a Concert was given in the Senate House, and a magnificent *fête champêtre* in the gardens of Trinity, whose fountains, on these occasions, actually flow with wine. Commencement was celebrated next day with unusual *éclat*. The performances began with tremendous cheering from the undergraduates, who appeared to be in extraordinary spirits. Then the prize poems were recited, and honorary degrees were conferred. The Duke of Cambridge, the Queen's uncle, was made Doctor of Civil Law, and seemed mightily pleased when the scarlet gown was put on over his Field Marshal's uniform. He is one of the merriest, best-natured men imaginable, at home everywhere, and quite unconscious of attracting attention. At church, on the previous Sunday, when the officiating priest had finished the exhortation, "Pray ye for the Royal Family, for the Church, for the Universities," the old gentleman started up with great alacrity, responding in a very audible voice, "Oh! yes, certainly, by all means," much to the amusement of the congregation. The Installation Ode, written by the University poet, and arranged for voices and instruments by the Professor of Music, was then performed by the best musicians of England. Lastly, was sung the national air, "God save the Queen," whereat the Duke of Cambridge, thinking, doubtless, of the danger to which his royal niece had been exposed, began to rock his huge form to and fro, beating time with hand and foot, and adding a loud bass accompaniment.

A grand ball in the spacious saloon of the Fitzwilliam Museum, so crowded that dancing was impossible, and prolonged till two or three in the morning, terminated the celebration which Cambridge may not witness again for many a day.

Kankin

A REVERY BY NIGHT.

I.

How gently breathes the air to-night,
  Among these silent hills;
And in the pale moon's quivering light,
  How gaily dance the rills!

II.

In such a night as this, I ween,
  On many a dewy lawn,
The fairy elves of old were seen
  In revel till the dawn.

III.

But now, to my attentive eye,
  No festive sights appear;
No faery song nor dance is nigh,
  No revelry is here.

IV.

I sit upon the verdant sod,
  And gaze at yon blue dome,
Till, in sweet commune with her God,
  How pants my soul for home!

V.

Beyond those ever-radiant spheres,
Whose beams no clouds bedim,
My soul, entranced in rapture, hears
The songs of Seraphim!

VI.

Around His throne they bow the knee,
With bliss none others know;
And in those shining ranks I see
The loved ones lost below.

VII.

This fair, green earth, that once they trod,
Enslaves their powers no more;
But in the presence of their God,
Those souls, unchained, adore.

VIII.

Oh, blessed is this place to night!
In this calm hour of even,
The spirit bears its upward flight,
On angel wings to heaven.

IX.

And when is loosed life's silver band,
And breaks the golden bowl,
In such an hour, thy wings expand,
My weary, longing soul!

Saturday night, June 22d, 1844.

AN ADVENTURE ON THE PRAIRIES.

[CONCLUDED.]

At dawn of day I awoke, after a fitful and unrefreshing sleep, and took a deliberate survey of my situation. The prospect was any thing but pleasant. The storm yet continued—the snow had fallen to the depth of more than a foot, and even lay in considerable thickness under the trees of the 'opening,' except close to the fire. The wind still blew fresh, and the thick masses of dark threatening clouds which it drove across the heavens, or rather swept from thence, for they seemed but little above the tops of the trees, gave faint hope of a favorable change of weather. I was entirely unable to determine the points of the compass. My track in entering the grove, was of course completely concealed by the snow, and unfortunately I had neglected to notice the direction. My 'position' it would have been somewhat difficult to 'define,' but it was by no means enviable. In the midst of a vast prairie, covered deep with snow—exposed to the fury of the storm—wild beasts howling around—ignorant of my way—supperless, breakfastless, wet and cold, I began most heartily to wish myself safely back on the river road. But the die was cast—there was no retreat—the only alternative to take courage and go on. My unpleasant situation did not, however, prevent my making some valuable practical observations, regarding the influence of external circumstances on the power of imagination.

The warm honied kisses from blooming Hebe's, which I yesterday felt melting on my lips, now seemed changed to the embraces of icy statutes; and in place of tables groaning beneath roast turkey and venison, I could at the utmost only summon up the rusty flitch of bacon, on which I had so recently regaled myself. Eheu! little did I think that I should consider even this luxurious fare, before other could be obtained. In fifteen minutes after I awoke, my arrangements were made, and I was again on my way over the prairie. For one glance of the sun, as a clue to my course, I would willingly have forgone the pleasure of a hearty breakfast, but as there seemed little chance of such a God-send, I thought it safest to take the wind as guide, and accordingly pushed on in the teeth of the storm, this having been my direction the last evening. Although the violence of the storm and the depth of snow impeded my progress, I yet held on several miles at a fair pace, and in good spirits. For some hours I indulged the hope that I should arrive at my destination in time for the marriage ceremony; yet, as the forenoon wore away, and the appointed hour arrived, and still, on every side, as far as the eye could reach, nothing was to be seen but the boundless prairie—I was compelled to relinquish the hope, and even think myself fortunate, should I reach a place of shelter before night-fall.

The prospect was gloomy in the extreme. The snow storm had changed into a driving sleet. At intervals was heard the peculiar mournful cry of flocks of wild geese, passing from the northern lakes to a warmer climate, while ever and anon was borne on the sighing wind, the discordant croak of the prairie crane, evidently enjoying highly the rage of the elements. Here and there, beneath the shelter of some grove, might be seen herds of buffalo, quarreling with each other, crouching and shivering with the cold, while hard by were noble red deer, pawing away the snow to obtain a scanty sustenance of dried grass and leaves. The very desolateness of the far-reaching prairie, without sign of human habitation, sent a chill to the heart; and altogether the scene was as cheerless as could well be imagined. Nor did the state of things within present a more favorable aspect. My appetite, which had been well whetted since morning, now began to make the most importunate demands for food; and the constant gnawings of hunger, I was fain to pacify for the moment, by eating large quantities of snow.

It was thus that the afternoon wore away, in the vain hope of reaching the river, or at least some human habitation. The shades of evening were gathering round, and there was every prospect of spending the dreary night on the prairie, without fire, food or shelter—no very pleasant reflection—for although the storm had ceased, the cold was rapidly increasing, and already my garments were stiffening with frost. Though hope was well nigh extinct, we still held slowly on our toilsome way—for to stop was certain death—to proceed could be no more.

It was shortly after dark, at the distance of two or three miles ahead, that I saw a bright light. Heaven be praised! I was at least safe—had arrived in the neighborhood of human beings—should obtain food and shelter, and be put on the direct road to my destination. Many pious reflections passed through my mind, and grateful ejaculations escaped my lips, as I hastened onward, at this Providential interposition. Upon nearer approach, I noticed it as somewhat strange, that there were no enclosures, such as were usual around the dwellings of settlers; but it was easily accountd for, by supposing this the habitation of a squatter, recently located.

As I approached nearer the grove from which the light proceeded, I observed, with a little anxiety, no house apparent, nor was my presence announced by the customary bark of the watch-dog, the inseparable attendant of the western settler. Still, there must be some person near, as the fire could not have been the work of chance. I arrived at the grove, entered—no signs of life; but surely the place looked familiar. A dread presentiment, a strange chill came over me. I approached the fire. Good Heavens! It was too true—the very same spot I had left in the morning! What I had heard of as sometimes occurring on the prairies, but had ever ridiculed as a mark of consummate folly, had actually happened to myself—I had been traveling all day in a circle! My reflections, upon making this pleasing discovery, and the precise expressions which escaped my lips, are forgotten, but they were widely different from those in which I had a short time previous indulged, in the new hope of my speedy deliverance. My heart sunk within me as I found myself, after the long and painful day's journey, no nearer my escape from the prairie than in the morning. But I had found a fire—at least a cause of gratitude in the circumstances—and at once determined to spend another night on the ground. My hardy mustang (which had borne his long abstinence with the most admirable stoicism) I turned loose, to provide as best he might for his own sustenance. I replenished the fire, and thawed my saturated, stiffened clothes. The clouds had cleared away, but the piercing wind, from the icy summits of the Rocky Mountains, swept unobstructed over the prairie.

I had endeavored to keep up my spirits during most of the day with the idea, that the trip would prove only a romantic adventure, which would form subject of merriment and pleasant jokes for the evening, while with jovial friends, around the cheerful fireside. My situation now, however, was becoming fraught with too real danger to partake of the romantic. I used to read, with peculiar zest, narratives of terrible disasters, dreadful accidents, hair-breadth escapes, etc., especially where the victims were reduced to the last extremity of suffering, but escaped with life. Such accounts, however, are far pleasanter in the reading than in practical experience. Although not in the last extremity, circumstances began to look quite ominous, and it was hard to say what might happen! The wolves appeared to have increased in number and boldness since the preceding night; and one fellow in particular I noticed, of most enormous size and peculiarly fiendish leer, evidently leader of the gang, pacing back and forth so near that I could almost feel his fetid breath on my cheek. A rifle would have afforded full protection against all such unwelcome intruders; but, unfortunately, I was armed only with a jack-knife—a weapon very serviceable in its place, but of little use in those circumstances. In spite of my efforts to keep awake, the soporific effects of the fire, after the exposure of the day, soon induced a broken slumber, in which I suffered even more from the frightful images of fancy, than the waking reality. At one time, like Prometheus, I was chained to a lofty rock, while a hundred vultures were tearing out my vitals—the yells which I attempted to utter, to frighten them away, dying in whispers on my lips, a gang of demons hovering nigh, whisking their tails in my face, and laughing in fiendish glee at my impotence. At another, I found myself seated at a table, covered with the most luxurious viands, which ever, as I put them to my lips, melted into thin air, satisfying the sense of sight and smell with the most delicious repast, but tantalizing the taste and keen appetite with shadows. Now I was whirled swiftly away to the frozen regions of the north, until I stood on the polar iceberg, and felt limb by limb congealing by the frost, until, at length, I became completely assimilated to the frozen mass, yet with all the powers of consciousness entire; and anon, was withering under the scorching heat and insufferable thirst of the torrid sun of Zahara; while on every side, from the ground on which I stood, seemed to rise innumerable monstrous scaly serpents, from which I vainly struggled to escape—the circle each moment narrowing closer and closer, until at length I felt the green poison from their hissing tongues fall on my quivering flesh. In such pastimes, passed that long, dreadful night—a night of horror never to be erased from the memory.

It was Sabbath morning. A more magnificent spectacle than was presented with the rising sun, imagination cannot conceive. Not a cloud dimmed the deep blue of the ethereal expanse—not a breath of wind stirred among the trees—not a single sound broke the deep stillness of the boundless prairie—a silence so profound that it seemed oppressive. The clear, unspotted whiteness of the vast extent of snow, strewed with glittering frost crystals, flashed in the rays of the morning sun, like a sea of molten silver. The rain of the preceding day had frozen on the trees, until, from almost every limb, depended countless icicles of every size and shape, flashing like diamonds in the morning sun, and presenting a far more magnificent spectacle than any Aladdin's palace, or fairy grotto. When these began to thaw, as I saw them later in the day, beautiful rainbows were formed among the trees, most novel and curious to behold.

Delighted, as I should have been, with such a prospect in any other situation, I now regarded it with utter indifference, nay, I should rather say, with loathing and disgust. It seemed like the cursed enchantment of some demon, got up in mockery of my sufferings. It was now becoming with me a question of life and death.

The incessant and inordinate craving of the appetite for food, and the constant dwelling of the mind on beef, bread, venison, and other substantials, was giving place to a sinking and weakness of the stomach, accompanied by nausea. The desire for food, indeed, still continued, but not that intense and eager craving for it as before.

Later in the day, I ate two or three acorns, picked up by chance, but only to increase my sufferings. The momentary alleviation which they gave, was followed by a more intense pain, seeming as though I had swallowed live coals. My faithful mustang was at my side, and the thought often passed my mind to apply my knife to his throat, and satisfy my hunger from his flesh and blood. But he was now my only hope of escape, and, besides, gratitude forbade. Nor would my danger scarcely have been lessened, for the keen-scented prairie wolves, like ravenous tigers, would have gathered in scores to the repast.

But another effort must be made to escape from the prairie. It was the Sabbath, but I had few scruples just then, in regard to its violation by traveling. I saddled and mounted my horse, although scarce able to retain my seat. With the sun as guide, I now plainly saw that on the preceding day I had taken the wrong direction. On emerging from the wood, appeared another difficulty, almost insuperable. The damp snow had been congealed by the keen frost into a thick icy crust, which, at almost every step, dreadfully lacerated the legs of my horse, leaving his course marked with blood. Notwithstanding, the hardy, faithful animal held on some miles, though slowly, and with the most painful consequences. Some time after midday, he came to a dead halt, and turned his head with a most imploring look, as much as to say, "it's no go!" I looked at his gashed and mangled legs and hunger-stricken frame, and had not the heart to urge him on. I dismounted, took the bridle in my hand, and broke the path some distance in advance; but my strength soon failed, an utter indifference to life came over me, and I sank exhausted to the ground. Just then, I saw, or thought I saw, the blue smoke of a log hut rising in the distance, and made one more effort for life. It would not do. My legs refused to support their burden—my sight grew dim—a giddiness seized my brain—I remember no more.

* * * * * * * * * * * *

When consciousness returned, I found myself in a strange room, surrounded by strange faces, by whom the circumstances of my situation were soon told. I had suspended "operations" near the dwelling of a Hoosier, by whom I was soon after discovered and taken to his house, where I had lain sick two weeks in a delirious fever. Through the kind care and generous hospitality of my new friends, I rapidly recovered, and was soon able to pursue my course. Only ten miles distant was the residence of my fair cousin, who had taken the bridal veil; but I carefully concealed from friends my whereabouts, nor made them a call, as I was sure of being bantered most unmercifully for my ridiculous trip, and its tragical result. My arrangements were soon made, and I was on my way east—grateful for life preserved, and fully determined never to attempt another "short cut" across a prairie.

THE MONTH OF ROSES.

I.

The smiling spring now closes,
And early summer 's seen,
In bowers of opening roses,
And woodlands deepening green.

II.

A warmer sun is glowing
Within the clear, blue sky;
And sparkling streams are flowing
In gayer melody.

III.

Oh! what can cities render,
Of beauty, or of bliss,
To match the summer splendor
Of Nature's loveliness!

IV.

Then banish every sorrow;
Away with gloomy care,
And gladness let us borrow,
From scenes so bright and fair.

V.

Soon worldly care will find us,
And sunshine, song, and flowers
We then shall leave behind us,
In this dull world of ours.

VI.

But yet no cloud is glooming,
To dim our radiant noon,
And joy and hope are blooming,
This merry month of June.

C. A. W.

EDITORS' TABLE.

Our Magazine is often complained of for being lifeless and prosaic, both in its subjects and style. This fault arises in a great measure from the choice of subjects. Who can write *con amore* upon "English Literature," "Shakspeare," "The Crusades"—themes completely exhausted by many great writers years ago, and whose ideas have taken up their constant residence for generations back in the college division rooms? To bring them forth from this quiet resting place into the world again, to instruct the public mind, is certainly preposterous. To be sure, we cannot hope to afford our journal the spice and raciness which an acquaintance with the world, and constant practice in writing, gives the popular magazine writers of the day. The easy, flowing style which pictures character and manners to the life, is very difficult to acquire. Shut up too within college walls, we have small acquaintance with the outward world, even if we could describe it. Still we can find material enough in our literary life to render the Magazine acceptable to reasonable persons, without continually thrumming upon these old topics. Literary information concerning the various systems of education; notices of the past history of Yale; correspondence with other universities; a record of the principal events in our quiet life; such subjects as these would give the Yale Literary a character of its own, never tempting us beyond our depth, nor to make vain efforts to astonish the world. It might puzzle some ignorant persons, were the Magazine divested of its cover, to tell where it came from, and by what class of men it was composed. We shall endeavor to convey some idea of its origin and design, at least, in this last page of ours, where you will find, respected reader, all the odds and ends; a curious medley of items; some facts, some fictions; a mingled tissue of the grave, gay, and profitable. It is moreover most exclusively our own property. No one else is responsible for its style, or contents, and though written with a sincere desire to offend nobody in particular, it is intended more especially to please ourselves.

The Captives.—The following extract of a letter from an American gentleman in Germany, written in April last, to a correspondent in New Haven, will interest such students as are familiar with the *Captivi*, and have laughed over it.

Before leaving Berlin I had the pleasure of witnessing a representation of the *Captivi* of Plautus in the ancient style, and in the original language. It was given in one of the small theatres to a select audience of gentlemen, who were invited to the number of perhaps three hundred. I obtained my ticket through Dr. Zumpt. The director of the play was a *privat-docent* and Doctor of Philosophy of the University, and the actors were students. The audience consisted chiefly of scholars—a majority of them more advanced than students. There was Humbolt, Boeckh, Lachmann, Zumpt, and I judged nearly all the professors of the University, teachers of the Gymnasia, and the like. There were also many students; for the tickets, although perhaps in some instances given, were generally paid for. The Prince of Prussia came a little before eight; and on the arrival of the King, at eight precisely, the curtain rose.

The scene which it revealed, was of course the section of a street. This section was rectangular, the fronts of the houses on either side appearing on the right and left of the stage; among which, on the left, as indicated by the name over the door, was the house of Hegio. On either side of the street stood marble statues, a Medicean Venus, a bust of Bacchus, etc. To the Bacchus, the captive pointed, as he uttered

"Non equidem me *Liberum*," etc.—(III, 4, 46.)

In the background, a hanging scene represented the street as continued and divided into two streets, which were soon lost among the houses of the city; behind all which appeared hills, with here and there a temple, and the sky and clouds. The spot itself, where the play was acted, was imitated from a street in Pompeii. The actors were already on the stage, when the curtain rose; and after the herald had come forward and given a few blasts with his trumpet, and retired a little, the prologue was spoken by the master of ceremonies. All wore sandals and tunics; and the speaker of the prologue, Hegio and Ergasilus, the *toga*, or rather the *pallium*. For seeing the shape of this last, and the manner of folding it up, so that it may not encumber one who wishes to be active, a favorable opportunity was given in the scene, in which Ergasilus, in the ecstasy of his joy at the good news he had to bring to Hegio, took off his *pallium*, spread it out on the ground, folded it up into a roll of half its proper length, and put it round his neck.

This Ergasilus of course corresponded by no means with the description which he gives of himself, when he says,

"Ego, qui tuo mœrore maceror,
Macesco, consenesco, et tabesco miser,
Ossa atque pellis sum," etc.—(I, 2, 24.)

but gave every indication of a well fed epicure. Hegio was a tall, stately, imposing personage, ever speaking with gravity, and moving with dignity, and was aided in maintaining this character by his white hair, his long silvery beard, and white pallium, bordered with purple. He never appeared with his head covered. The whole play was very finely acted, and particularly the second scene of the fourth act, and the fourth scene of the third. Ergasilus performed admirably; but it is difficult to say whether he, or Hegio, or Tyndarus, bore away the palm. The contrast between the frenzy of Ergasilus, in one of the scenes above alluded to, and the imperturbable gravity of Hegio, was very laughable. In the epilogue, all the actors appeared again on the stage, and when they retired, with the request,

"Nunc vos, si vobis placet,
Et si placuimus, neque odio fuimus, signum hoc mittite;
Qui pudicitiæ esse voltis præmium, PLAUSUM DATE,"

the response on the part of the audience was sufficiently hearty. The curtain did not fall during the play, but the scenes succeeded each other rapidly. The prologue, however, was followed by Horace's ode *ad Lyram*, sung by a choir of ten young men, who stood before the stage. The second act was followed by the ode *ad Mercurium*, and the third by the ode *ad Aristium Fuscum*. I need not say that I was highly pleased with this chapter of antiquity.

THE DARTMOUTH, for April and May, has been received. Its appearance does much credit to the good taste of our student-friends of the "Granite State." The royal emblems of heraldry, however, displayed in the vignette which graces its cover, puzzle us somewhat. Such a coat of arms seems hardly consistent with the democratic principles of Dartmouth. The contents, especially of the May number, betoken much attention to good writing, evincing an unusual degree of manliness and spirit.

We acknowledge, also, with much pleasure, the receipt of the June number of the "NASSAU MONTHLY."

A new College periodical, "THE WILLIAMS' MONTHLY MISCELLANY," has to-day found its way to our table. The following are extracts from its "Prolegomena:" "Congregated within the walls of a rural institution, in a town not so prominent on the map of the world that it may not be easily passed over; where the hum of busy life is low and almost suppressed; where the noises of the world's great theatre are heard only in faint echoes, while the actors, hid from observation by the green hills that encircle our silent valley, are almost as if they were not, we lift up our voice, not knowing if any, in a world where so many are talkers and so few listeners, will stop for a minute to hear." * * * "We tender them a rustic wreath; and though the mountain flowers may not be as gay, or as fragrant, as their more favored sisters of the garden, their very rudeness may make them, for the hour, more acceptable." Our best wishes for the future success and long life of the "Miscellany." The articles on "The Nebular Theory," and "The American Seventeen Year Locust," speak well of the scientific interest which characterizes the "rural institution."

TO OUR READERS AND CORRESPONDENTS.—In our next, we hope to lay before you some further information respecting foreign University education, from the pen of an alumnus of Yale, who lately completed his course of study at Edinburg.

The present number was unavoidably delayed by certain unforeseen circumstances. Our efforts shall be redoubled to ensure punctuality hereafter. Seldom, however, has the first number of the summer term been issued before July, as will be seen on reference to old volumes.

A College periodical rests on no sure foundation. If no one happens to feel disposed to write, and circumstances now-a-days are peculiarly adverse to such a desire, the editors hope in vain for any aid.

Communications for the July number must be sent in *immediately*, or be put over till October, since our August number will be chiefly occupied with the "Townsend Prize Essays." It will also contain a portrait of Prof. Olmsted.

"The Huguenots," by a Carolinian, was received too late for this number, but will probably appear in our next.

"A graduate and former contributor," (?) who "only asks that if his muse does not find favor, she may die in peace, and that sarcasm may not scoff over her grave," is respectfully informed that the funeral rites were enacted with due solemnity.

"King's Mountain," a historical epic of some few hundred lines, is undergoing a course of reading by several editors. The indefatigable industry of the author merits a reward, but the limits of our Magazine will not allow its insertion. The tide of poetry which has flowed in during the past month, has been perfectly overwhelming; but, while the "Mournful Lamentation" for the young man who "died from the bite of a rattle-snake," on "*Springfield* mounting," is still extant, we think it answers every practical purpose to quote it, as a familiar specimen of its class:

"On Springfield mounting there did dwell
A likely youth, and known full well;
Leftenant Carter's ondly son,
A likely youth, nigh twenty-one.

"He went on to the mounting high,
A rattle-snake he did espy!
And all at once he then did feel
That p'ison critter bite his heel."

Much valuable time is spent hereabouts in making rhymes far inferior to these, and often by those who might, with the same "genius" and painstaking, write very good prose.

College Record.—The following gentlemen were chosen as officers of the Literary Societies, on Wednesday evening, June 25th.

Brothers' Society.—*President,* Thomas Kennedy; *Vice President,* Alvan Hyde; *Secretary,* John D. Potter.

Linonian Society.—*President,* Ira B. Wheeler; *Vice President,* Francis Ives; *Secretary,* Thomas D. Sherwood.

Calliopean Society.—*President,* James N. Brickell; *Vice President,* Leo[illegible] E. Wales; *Secretary,* William R. Nevins.

Mr. I. N. Tarbox, Tutor of Latin, has just resigned. He leaves the University with the warmest benedictions of all. Mr. George Richards, of the class of '[illegible], has been appointed to fill the vacancy.

The Ciceronian.—Under this title, we have a little volume, republished from the German, by Mr. Sears, of Boston. It exemplifies the Prussian method of teaching the elements of Latin, adapted by the translator to the use of American schools. The plan of the work is excellent. Choice sentences of the purest Latinity are selected from the writings of Cicero, to be carefully studied, learned by heart, and accurately translated. By this means the style of the author, and a familiarity with the structure and idiomatic peculiarities of the language, is gradually acquired, while valuable instruction is conveyed to the mind in the carefully selected precepts of the Roman philosopher. The increasing demand for works of this character, is a pleasing evidence of progress in classical education, and augurs well for American scholarship.

P. P. C.

To the Ladies.—In this last moment of our irksome task, we turn with pleasure to think of the approving smiles which fair readers may now and then deign to bestow upon these humble endeavors. Tradition says, that formerly they used to contribute to our pages. An "Impromptu," penned by some fair hand, accidentally found its way to our Table, a few days ago; but, since its design was to accompany a basket of fruit, we have, alas! no permission to exhibit this little gem to the public eye—

"Full many a flower," etc.

THE

YALE LITERARY MAGAZINE.

Vol. IX. JULY, 1844. No. 8.

THE RISE AND FALL OF THE SARACENS.

L'univers est un espece de livre, dont on n'a lu que la premiere page, quand on n'a vu que son pays. Le' Cosmopolite.

If the sentiment contained in the above lines be true, in connection with the material world, with that which now exists, how much more is it so in connection with the historic, with that which lives only in the records of the past. The world which lies around us, which spreads before our eyes its ample treasures of grace and beauty, and invites us to their inspection; which opens a vast museum of diversified habits and tastes, of varied climates and soils, cannot be studied by the mere perusal of one of, it may be, its least interesting pages. An acquaintance, and no slight one either, is necessary with every part, if we would arrive at a vivid as well as truthful conception of the wondrous whole. We must not limit our wanderings by a boundary which the circumstance of birth has established, and around which it will ever throw a drapery of fictitious splendor, nor confine our vision to scenes illumined by the deceitful light of domestic ties, of home associations; but we must leave these spots of "hallowed ground," and turn our steps to those where different feelings and different prejudices lend another tint to the landscape. The tree of knowledge cannot grow, if stagnant waters moisten its roots, and an unturned sod bind them; nor can enlarged ideas be formed in the mind of him who gathers every thing from the same source, who runs every thing in the same mould.

The proper study of mankind has been said to be man, and he is found in too many opposite situations, and is formed of too many conflicting ingredients, to allow the assumption of any individual, as a specimen of the class. As climate and occupation give a form to his bodily existence, so are his actions, his language, his very thoughts, all stamped with the impress of the same local influences; and the visible effects of one train of causes cannot be taken as the supposable ones of another, while these others are so widely dissimilar. If, then, an acquaintance with the world, the scene of flowing streams and waving trees, of barren rocks and boundless sands, be essential to an acquaintance with its motley denizens, we must acknowledge a greater need for opening the sacred scroll of history, if we would learn aught of those whose very dust is now annihilation. In the one case, we can but apply our glass to the few who now strut their part upon the stage, while in the other, an expanse illimitable and set thick with gems of rarest beauty, unfolds itself before us. The flowerets which nature, in her merry dance with time, has dropped from her rich tiara, are here preserved with watchful care, and their perenniel fragrance is yet unimpaired. Here, genius, and wit, and dauntless courage, with all the offspring of mental power, have each their separate niche, and though the dust and mould may have gathered about the portal of their consecrated temple, yet the freshness of their earliest birth lingers around its sculptured aisles. Youth and old age, weakness and strength, virtue and vice, here join their hands, as they offer to us the goblet of living waters; and the spirit of the PAST reassumes his discarded existence, as his lips breathe on us the breath of truth. The mist wreaths lift from before us, under the influence of an unseen sun, and as the eye pierces deeper and deeper into the regions of obscurity, and detects here and there a new truth, hid amid the masses of surrounding darkness, the soul expands and seems to hold naught beyond its powers, no, not the very source of all truth. To this pleasant retreat, then, and to one of its most grateful scenes, we would lead your steps. 'Tis true, the journey may be a tedious one, the guide incompetent, yet if you will but fasten in your minds the beautiful features of your final resting place, the ruggedness of the first will be unfelt, the presence of the last unheeded.

The portion of time with which we shall be occupied, belongs to what has been emphatically styled the dark ages, and is remarkable for being illumined by all the light, little though it were, which was then visible. Amid the almost Egyptian darkness which settled upon Europe during the middle ages, and which, first gathering in the interval between the Antonines and Diocletian, diffused itself gradually during the reign of both Merovingian and Carlovingian dynasties, and finally settled like a pall upon the Christian world, there was still a gleam of light which played upon its edges, and shone brighter for the surrounding gloom. Though ignorance, and blindness, and a deadly apathy, sat like watchers at the bedside of an expiring literature, and weakened still more its already palsied powers, with their noxious drugs, there was still a spot of surpassing loveliness, where the offspring of this dying parent strengthened his youthful limbs; and there were still guardians, by whose zealous care they were trained and improved. We look abroad at those kingdoms over which martial glory shed a fallacious brightness, and around whose name romance has entwined its artificial wreath, and we look earnestly for a poet, a historian, or even a rhymer, whose devotions to the muses, spurious though they were, might wake within our breast some kindred interest; but all in vain. The refinements which a system of chivalry necessarily engendered, do indeed meet our eyes, but they are merely bodily or social refinements, and can but poorly compensate for the want of those elegancies and that polish to which literature alone can give birth. Every thing over which the intellect presides is degenerate; the truths of science, either totally forgotten or shamefully perverted; the few ornaments which art then possessed, either disregarded or turned to unworthy objects; the relics of literature abandoned to the guardianship of monastic seclusion, and the keepers of these treasures ignorant, in most cases, of the value of the jewels, in many, of the nature of the casket entrusted to their care. The very king whose name stands first on the historic scroll of that period, never wrote that name; and the ignorance of his descendant gave impunity to a sarcasm uttered in a language but a few years before the language of the world.

But there is another and a pleasanter side to this picture. While the heart sickens and the eye turns in instinctive dislike from the rugged and illiterate hordes of northern Europe, it settles with delight upon the polished conquerors of the South. From degraded Italy, from ignorant France, it turns in ecstasy to the sunny vales of Spain, and to the refinement of a Moorish court, and a tide of sweet and thrilling emotions swell upon the soul, as it recalls the loveliness of the first, and muses over the downfall of the last. Memory flies back over the days that are gone, and asks, who are these that now cultivate the rich gardens of the Hesperides? The warlike Roman has been here, the Goth has been here, but they are gone; and whence comes he who now stands before us? Whence comes the Moor?

If we cast our eyes over the map of the Eastern hemisphere, we shall find between the tenth and thirtieth parallel of North latitude, and the thirtieth and sixtieth degree of East longitude, a large triangular plain of sand, to which geographers, since the days of Ptolemy, have assigned the name Arabia. Memorable as the scene of the Jewish wanderings, and hallowed by a thousand scriptural associations, this region of eternal sands has a still farther claim on our notice, as being the birthplace of Mahomet. Sprung from the family of Hashem, and boasting the noble blood of the Koreish, this wonderful being was born at Mecca, A. D. 572. With a mind naturally excitable, and early turned to religious objects, his youth was tinctured with the spirit of enthusiasm, which his after life so strongly developed; and we find him, while yet a boy, devoting one month of each year to religious contemplation, in a cave near his home; doubtless the birthplace of that system which was destined to carry his name over the known world. Of his youth, and indeed of his life, up to the time when he first made known to his family his divine mission, history is silent; and of the records which she affords posterior to this, we shall only glance at the most important. Whether he himself really believed in the truth of what he asserted, or whether the entire scheme owed its creation to an acute and ambitious mind, united to a conscience by no means scrupulous, I shall not stop here to discuss; the fact that he did assert "there is but one God, and Mohammed is his prophet," being sufficient, attested as it is by the consequent occurrence of a precipitate flight from his native city. Unable to convince the obstinate inhabitants of Mecca of his claims upon their hearts, he "turns to the Gentiles," and the Charegites of Medina, the germ of the future Saracens, receive from his tongue the lessons of inspiration. Elated by his popularity with the new converts, he joins the regal robe to the prophetic mantle, and weds the Koran to the sword. The beloved of God and the darling of his subjects, he appears in still another character, and the conqueror of the Koreish, the hero of fifty victories, he plants the crescent on the walls of Mecca, with a warrior's hand. Nor does he stop here. Eager to extend the religion of his heart to other shores, he looks beyond the glistening sands of his own desert home, and his death was all that saved the tottering empire of the West. With him, however, died not his religion: on the contrary, it advanced with giant strides, and but ten years from the time when, a fugitive and exile, he fled to the gates of Medina, all Arabia lifted up the voice of prayer to Allah and his prophet Abübeker ascends the vacant chair, and the "sword of God" again displays the Koran at the head of fifty thousand men. Persia is invaded, and the ruins of Cadesia are the tomb of the Sassanian dynasty. The sword, the Koran, or the tribute, are offered by the victorious Caled, and the voices of a nation of Mussulmen rise from the land which before echoed to the prayers of the followers of Ormusd. Onward still drive the hosts of the prophet, town after town yields before them, and Syria owns the religion of the desert, as its emblem waves from the walls of Ceseræa. The father-in-law of the prophet sinks to his rest, but Omar occupies his place, and the wave of conquest rolls over the ancient land of Ægypt. Othman succeeds, and the salvation of Africà adds another jewel to those which grace his brow in Paradise.

We have now glanced at the victorious Saracens in their rapid march; from India to the Atlantic the name of the prophet has been heard; and now let us look for a moment at the effects of this conquest on the religions of the vanquished nations. The religion of Persia was that of Zoroaster, and it recognized the two conflicting principles of light and darkness as its principal divinities. Somewhat similar in its principles to the fabric of Islamism, it owned no higher ground for observance than the sensual delights which that system offered, and consequently presented but few inducements for martyrdom to a people naturally luxurious and effeminate. It fell, and the mosque welcomed to her altar the trembling fugitive of the temple. In Egypt we see the same desertion of national faith, and with but a few exceptions, the Coptic, or Jacobitical, once the religion of the land, entirely disappeared. The faith of Africa was nominally Christian, and by its extinction may appear to offer a refutation of what we shall hereafter say, but it was in reality not Christian, and owed its death not to violence or persecution, but to the superior claims of a physical and sensual religion on the corrupt hearts of its followers. The very readiness with which the conquered tribes embraced the faith of the Koran, shows a want of enthusiasm and firmness in defense of their own, which history nowhere ascribes to the Christians; and their choice of apostasy, as the more agreeable alternative, when tribute was also offered, must weaken considerably their title to be called followers of Christ.

Thus, we have seen the Saracens, in their birth, a rude Arabian horde, possessing no property save their camel, and scarce a home but the trackless sands—we now find them masters of a great portion of the world. The mountains of India bounded their conquest on the East, the waves of the Atlantic washed it on the West—we must, therefore, expect a growth of ambition to correspond with the vast increase in their power, and are not surprised when we find the "eternal rock" echoing the shouts of a Moslem host on the plains of fertile Andalusia. Urged on by visions of wealth, and inflated with past success, the victorious Muza knew no limits to his arms, and the sons of the conquerors of Rome fled before the followers of the "camel driver of Mecca." The Gothic king yielded his crown with his life, and a little corner in the mountain province of Asturias was the only spot that refused to bend before the crescent of the Prophet. Onward still was the march, and France bid fair to taste the blessings of the Koran; but the field of Poictiers, and the valor of Martel, fixed the Pyrenees as the limit for the step of the Moor

Of the character and habits of the early Arabians, we know with certainty but little, since the sources of our information are, at best, but legendary collections, or the compilations of native authors not very subsequent to Mohammed himself. Still, the records which we do possess are, in most cases, worthy of belief, for our imagination can suggest but few motives for historical falsity, likely to be of any considerable weight, with the writers themselves; and, also, because in the entire mass, there are but few conflicting portions. The remarks of these authors, and, in fact, the collateral history of the times immediately following the introduction of the Koran, lead us to assign poverty and knavery as two essentials of Arabic character, from which, as sources, flowed the diverging branches of ignorance, superstition, and cruelty. Not a traveler could pass their trackless waste of sands without receiving the information that a Beduin's grandmother desired his cloak; and it required but the smallest exercise of their credulity to believe, that Mahomet's shirt sleeve was the door from which the moon departed, after entering at its collar. With the constant descent of Gabriel, however, a gradual change seems to have crept over them. Their natural ferocity and heat of passion find incentives in the pages which, from time to time, he produces; and a growing spirit of religious partisanship transforms individual fierceness into martial valor. Inflamed with a new passion, the lust of conquest, their individuality is merged in their nation's power, and vast armies spring into being, as if the work of an enchanter's wand. In their restless course, continual changes developed themselves in their character and tastes, and rendered from their very nature peculiarly susceptible, they received from every nation with whom they mingled some new impressions, both characteristic and durable. From this constant superficial change, also, some natural and fundamental transformation necessarily resulted, so that at no time so much as at the period of their highest prosperity, were the Saracens so unlike their simple original.

After the expulsion of the Goths, and the subsequent foundation of an independent Caliphate had rendered Spain a Moorish kingdom, and the divided interests of the Ommiyades, Abbassides, and Fatimites, aided by their own secluded situation, ensured peace to its shores, these changes had leisure to develop themselves. The orchards of the daughters of Hesperus once more produced their golden fruit, and in the granaries of that lovely spot were stored the seed, which now spreads its rich and waving crop over all Europe. Professing a religion avowedly sensual, the Moorish princes knew well that pleasure is tasteless, when science and art are not numbered among its handmaids, and they cherished them with a corresponding assiduity. The native fire which coursed through their veins—the beautiful scenery of their adopted home—the golden vega, smiling with its crowded vegetation—the bleak and frowning sierra—the placid and gently winding stream—all conspired to wake in their minds a love for poetry, and the language of the passions soon clothed itself in melting verse. Disregarding the style of their forefathers, which, rhymeless and unconfined, was merely an overgrown and tasteless species of recitative, the fancy of Al Raschid, in the East, and his western contemporaries reduced this "nurse of every virtue" to an art; and while it had due regard to both elegance and freedom of limb and action, still, did not disregard the decency nor the ornaments of dress. Sprung from a language pure, impassioned, and unexampled in copiousness, the verse of the poet could not but possess a fire, united with a melting tenderness, which the poetry of no other country exhibits; while, from the same causes, the more exalted flights of the art were forbidden, and, consequently, unattempted. As philosophers, the Moors of Spain stood high, though our judgment of their attainments must, it is true, be founded principally on the equivocal test of comparative excellence, rather than on any exhibitions of intrinsic merit. The peculiar philosophy which they cherished was that cultivated by the Egyptians, from whom they received it, probably through the medium of Moses, who is belived to have imparted much information to their forefathers, during his journey through Arabia. It was essentially Pythagorean; and though, from the darkness everywhere else prevalent, it shone with considerable brilliancy, was, nevertheless, in its essential elements, dregraded and superstitious, and unworthy of a name which presupposes an unbiassed search for truth. Still, though cramping rather than strengthening in its tendency, it served a most valuable purpose in keeping alive the attention, and directing the mind to study, even though this study were unworthy in itself; and even to this imperfect system may we in part ascribe the existence of those seminaries for purer and more elevated knowlege which afterwards were so numerous.

The researches of the Moorish Chemists were deep, and though their knowledge and practice were confined principally to simples, their labors evince a spirit of indefatigable perseverance, at once honorable to themselves and predictive of the final degeneracy of their science into the mysteries of alchemy. The imperfect acquaintance which they possessed with the auxiliary sciences of Mineralogy and Botany, in which last, they blindly followed the instructions of Dioscorides, a Cilician herbalist, and the belief entertained by most, that science might be rendered omnipotent, made such a result inevitable, and the secret which has puzzled another people, and a later age, was not unsought for by the Saracen. In the various departments of literature, an advance was made, not only of relative, but positive importance; and all the energies of a race of Caliphs, remarkable for their enlightened views, their wise administrations, and their munificent liberality, were directed towards the culture and improvement of letters. Colleges sprang up, professorships were instituted, and the occupants of these latter, when united with the students, amounted, in some single universities, to six thousand souls. With refinement in letters, luxury of other kinds made its appearance; and the gorgeous palaces, the sparkling fountains, the glittering gold, and costly jewels, which lent their lustre to Cordova and Seville, proclaim the magnificence, may we not add, the degeneracy of the Moor. Now was the period when every thing seemed prosperous. A bounteous nature spread before the eye a landscape of matchless beauty, and every varied shape of loveliness and grace that art could suggest, conspired to render more attractive a land unequaled on the face of the globe. A soft climate invited to that ease and inactivity which a fruitful soil justified, and not a vision of the fancy but was surpassed by the realities of this earthly Paradise. With the entire world around shrouded in the gloom of ignorance, they enjoyed a light which comparison rendered dazzling; in the midst of a rude and barbarous race of warriors, they experienced the attractions, the delights of social refinement; amid poverty, they were rich—with a religion which proclaimed limited indulgence in this world as the pass-key to eternal in another. What wonder, then, that the stream of life flowed quietly on, or that now, when all that exists of those whom its bosom then carried is an empty name, when memory reverts to scenes entwined with the bright offerings of both history and romance, we should sigh over those who are gone, or drop a tear on the grave of the Moor!

> "This was his brightest hour, too bright
> For human weal;—a glaring light,
> Like sun-beam through the rent cloud pouring,
> On the broad lake, when storms are roaring—
> Bright center of a wild and sombre scene,
> More keenly bright than summer's settled sheen."

He has gone, and the names of Ferdinand and Isabella, the stars of Christian Spain, lose some lustre when given to the betrayers of Boabdil and the exterminators of the Saracen race.

Having thus glanced at their eventful history, from the time when a poor Arab first proclaimed to his tribe the faith of the Koran, till his followers, become masters of an immense empire, left the shores of their fairest conquest a vanquished race; it would not, certainly, be unprofitable to examine briefly the causes which led to their final overthrow. In thus styling the expulsion of the Moors from Spain, we do not, of course, consider that the Saracen people then became extinct, for the followers of the Prophet and the descendants of the Moor still can be seen, but that they then perished as a race of importance and note. Of the entire line of Caliphs, the most celebrated were those of the house of Ommiyah, who formed the Cordovan branch; and, with the exception of a few names which adorn the Caliphate of Bagdat, they are the only ones under whose auspices literature, science, and art attained to any height. The forcible inroads and voluntary admission of the Turks, were gradually undermining this latter power, so that the entire glory of the Saracen name is associated with the Spanish branch, and it is from them we draw our most accurate, as well as most pleasing information. With their departure, then, ceases all our interest, and the ideas of chivalry and valor which we have linked to the name of the Moor, fade and die away. The immediate and visible causes which led to the extinction of the Saracen power in the Peninsula, are clear and easily stated, though it were a work of greater labor to discover accurately the remoter and less distinct. Of those which show themselves, even to a superficial thinker, the most obvious is the increase of dissension among themselves, which, independently of weakening them internally, gave leisure for the growth of that little band which still lived in the recesses of Asturias. The jealousy of rival Caliphs necessarily engendered divisions amongst their followers, a cause of weakness by no means small, whilst they emboldened the Christians in gradually shaking off their long-worn yoke. Little by little, these last increased in numbers and in spirit, the frontier towns fell off from their allegiance, till the conquest of Grenada again fixed a Christian prince upon the throne of Spain. Associated and auxiliary to this, was the neglect of war, and the growth of luxury, which, acting with great power on their ardent temperaments, rendered them physically incapable of resisting the hardy mountaineers. The foundation of the military orders also exerted an important influence, since these last, owing their very organization to hostility against the Moorish creed, and devoted to its destruction, formed a nucleus around which the strength of the Christians could rally and gather new power. How far their downfall can be ascribed to the necessities of time, or the discovery of a new passage to the Indies, we need not stop to consider, for their effect, if any was exercised, lies so deep below the surface as to scarce warrant the trouble of exhumation.

But though we may allow all weight to these conditions as direct operatives in the Moorish defeat, we should not still confine ourselves entirely to physical causes, however satisfactory we may deem them. If we find a tree, whose leafless boughs and withered bark proclaim its decay, and can only discover that the sap had ceased to flow, we should naturally ascribe its death to some disease of the vessels; but if we can go further, and find the worm which has gnawed at its root, we should leave this fact as incidental rather than causative, and trace the result to its primal source. The original cause of the national decline of the Arabs, then, we believe to have been the nature of their religion; and that it was so, will, we think, be proved by a few simple suggestions which must present themselves to every mind.

Of all the things which influence man's intellectual character, the two greatest are, the government under which he lives, and the religion he professes. If the former is despotic, all development of the mind is, in most instances, forbidden; and any sensuality in the latter cannot but debase his morals and enervate his intellect. It is true, the operation of these effects is dependent on many extrinsic circumstances, and is more visible at some times than at others; still, as a general thing, the results in similar cases are essentially the same. The noxious effects of both are comparatively unfelt while the arms of their subjects are producing a constant advance, but the moment that internal weakness, or satiety of conquest, renders them stationary or retrograde, these effects glare forth, and their sting is death. The acquisition of new territory and new power stimulates their minds, elates them with a sense of their own dignity, and often gives rise to high intellectual efforts, while temporal prosperity strips a corrupt religion of half its evils, by removing all necessity, and, with it, all wish for a better. But, when the course of a nation is at a stand, then the effects of both appear with increased force. Deprived of the support which excitement supplies, the mind feels the weight of an iron hand pressing it to the earth, and it turns for assistance to a religion which it then finds unequal to its support. Borne down by the combined efforts of both, its condition becomes daily worse, till sloth, superstition, and apathy have claimed it for their own. As a proof of this, the history of Rome presents itself—prosperous while a martial spirit led it onward, though possessing an imperfect government and a degraded creed, but descending with lightning speed when defeat, by removing confidence in the former, demanded consolation from the latter, itself unable to afford it. Greece, too, exhibits her eventful fate to prove our assertion. With a government a little better, but a system of religion, if any thing, worse, her onward path in arts and arms was a noble one; but a pause, and the loss of her power, and the extinction of her name, show the worthlessness of both. In both these systems, there is no regenerative, no supporting power; and though, as adjuncts, they may be harmless, yet as props, they are rotten and inefficient.

With a free government, some counteracting influences will, of course, exist; and when to this is united a spiritual code of belief, the tendencies are in the highest degree healthful and progressive. The very nature of Christianity, which is the only true spiritual religion, establishes this, from the comparative valuation which it places on the soul and body—making the former every thing, the latter nothing. It teaches man, that his pleasures, though not in themselves evil, are not good, and that every short-lived gratification of his inferior and perishable part, is injurious or destructive to the higher and immortal; and by making every self-sacrifice a source of future enjoyment, it presents a strong stimulant to present abstinence. It teaches, also, that his privations and adversities are not only not in themselves evils, but are positive blessings; that every one renders its successor less bitter, and that their only effect in any contingency must be a good one; and while it offers inducements to independent fortitude, yields, at the same time, ample aid when his powers begin to sink. It not only encourages the healthful virtues, which are essentially the sureties of a long existance, but discountenances the enervating vices, the prolific sources of decay and death. It removes to a great distance the possibility of downfall; and when defeat does come, as come it may, it is a tower of strength to which all can retire, and from whose massive walls all may draw fresh vigor and spirit.

Now, the Arabians had the fortune to possess both a government and a religion the worst which the world has ever seen; the first an implacable tyranny, the last the sensual offspring of a human mind. Still, while the sword and the Koran cut their way through the world—while commerce, wealth, leisure, and an extensive intercourse with other nations kept alive in their minds the fire of ambition, each was powerless and unfelt. But, when their conquests were arrested—when the crescent waned dim in the effulgence of the noon-day sun—when commerce chose another channel through which to roll its golden tide—and the Moorish sabre began to redden with Moorish blood, then these sleeping giants awoke, and the crash of the falling minaret, and the wreck of the sinking palace, attested their new-born powers. The sunlit shores of Spain receded from their view—the circle of their own land was narrowed down—their light grew more and more dim in the vapors of despotism and polygamy—and, without even a dying flash, sank into endless night.

Here must we take leave of this interesting people, and of their bright page of history, but we should not do so without drawing some instruction from our acquaintance with both. While memory reverts with delight to these pleasant scenes, and sports amid their varied beauties; or while, in sadder mood, she traces their gradual decline, and weeps over their final ruin, let "Instruction, sober matron," attend her steps, and give even greater depth to her impressions. Let us, while we read, remember that the course of our own favored land is now onward, but that the time may come when it can be so no longer; and let us, as a sure support in that hour of trouble, preserve her freedom unimpaired, her religion uncorrupted.

TRANSLATION FROM ANACREON.

'Twas midnight in the azure sky,
And bright Arcturus' belt on high
Was turning round Bootes' hand,
And all the busy tribes of men,
O'ercome with active labor then,
Were speechless held by Morpheus' hand;
When Love, the little urchin bright,
Presents himself in piteous plight,
And rattles loudly at my door.
"Who's there?" cried I, with peevish tone,
"Who comes at this late hour, alone?
Begone, and break my dreams no more."
To this the little rascal cried,
"Alas! I'm but a luckless child,
Who in the stormy, moonless night,
Tired, and drenched, have lost my way,
And of your kindness only pray
A shelter, which I'll well requite."
Touched by his little piteous cry,
To ope the door I straightway fly,
And seize my lamp;
He enters, and the flickering light
Reveals a little sportive wight,
Of beauty's purest stamp.
A bow was o'er his shoulder flung,
A well filled quiver by it hung,
And wings peeped out behind;
His shivering hands I warm with care,
And wring the rain drops from his hair—
How could I be so blind!
When cold at last had left his heart,
Up jumps my guest, with active start,
And grasps his bow:
"I fear," says he, "my plaything's hurt,
The string sure's spoilt, with wet and dirt,
Quick! let me try and know."
He bends—swift flies the venom'd dart—
A quivering pain shoots through my heart,
His aim had been too true;
He claps his hands and dances round,
"Oh! joy," he cries, "my bow's still sound;
Is that the case with you?"

S.

ON THE POETRY OF MORAL SENTIMENT.

Not love, not war, nor the tumultuous swell
Of civil conflict, nor the wrecks of change,
Nor duty struggling with afflictions strange—
Not these alone inspire the tuneful shell.
But where untroubled peace and concord dwell,
There, also, is the muse not loth to range. WORDSWORTH.

WHO that has wandered on some foreign shore, communing with men under the cold restrictions of custom and formality, receiving but the words of welcome where no friendship breathed, hath not felt his heart expand within him and swell with joyous tenderness, when returned to the retirement of his native land! There again his soul bursts forth in love, and holds "sweet converse" with those whose hearts are his. There again the merry laugh of early friends dispels from his brow that shade of melancholy, which the glitter and heartless splendor of the world could not chase away. *Such* is the contrast between the magnificence of fictitious poetry, and that in which we behold *nature* in her sweet simplicity, and in which the hallowed feelings of the poet call up all the sympathies of his soul. It is thus we think and feel with Cowper; his was the poetry of moral sentiment—the language of truth—the utterance of nature, revealing the springs of moral feeling in the soul. He teaches us that "nature is but a name for an effect whose cause is God," and wondering that we have never before listened to the echo of nature's voice in our own bosoms, we turn with gladness from the gilded show of the poetry of art, to the purity and freshness of natural beauties. Wordsworth, too, emphatically the poet of nature, bids us listen to the voice of that spirit that murmurs in the babbling brook, that smileth in the buttercup, and whispers in the stars of heaven.

And here, with a feeling almost approaching to reverence, let us join to the name of the greatest and best poet of the present age, that of our own Bryant. He stands in nature's temple, not, perhaps, as her high and holy priest, but as a minister of truth; and surely it can be no disparagement to the sacred office of the servants of God, to couple with it the names of the same poet—

"Whose eye
Doth glance from heaven to earth, from earth to heaven."

And if we admire the sentiment of the pagan, who, amid all the error and darkness of his times, yet, looking upon himself as set apart for the service of the virgin daughters of Jove, exclaimed—

"Me vero primum dulces ante omnia musæ
Quarum sacra fero igenti percussus amore
Accipiant"—

how much more should we regard the poets of this Christian age as an anointed priesthood, whose duty it is to diffuse purer and more exalted *truths*, than even the imagination which bound Eolus in his caves, or chained Prometheus to the horrid rocks of Caucasus, could conceive or comprehend!

Throughout the whole of Bryant's poetry there runs a stream of truth—a vein of exalted morality. It is not the result of a combining imagination—a shining edifice, reared by creative genius, yet unsubstantial as the house upon the sand—but it is a mansion in which the soul may repose with *confidence*, receiving delight and instruction from truth and nature, whose radiant forms are clearly seen through the transparent medium of a regulated imagination. Fiction, in this poetry which speaks to the *heart*, is not essential, for if the poet's breast do but swell with the emotions he wishes to excite, if his cheek is wet with those tears he wishes others to shed, he will touch a chord of sympathy in the soul, and our feelings and affections will move on harmoniously with his own; but when the imagination is to be delighted, *then* fiction becomes necessary; then it is that gnome, and sylph, and fairy sprite, flit before the eye, and that the senses are entranced by the beautiful shows of things unreal, which move before the mind, stirring not the feelings of the heart, as clouds tipped with gorgeous hues float in majestic beauty through the sky, but disturb not the quiet surface of the lake, over which their fleecy shadows pass.

There is in the soul of man a natural yearning for something more grand and more beautiful than the tangible forms of objects around us, and the poetry of moral sentiment alone gratifies this almost instinctive desire. It dispells, more fully than any other, the mist that hides from our sight the loveliness of nature, and causes us to *feel* that there is

> " A motion and a spirit that impel
> All thinking things—all objects of all thoughts,
> And roll through all things."

Yes, he who imbibes the spirit of this poetry, when straying through green fields and verdant meadows, or reclining on the flowery banks of the murmuring rivulet, or climbing the steep ascent of some rude crag, on whose tops the vaulted sky seems to rest, as if on massy walls; or when he looks abroad upon the beautiful earth, the *home* of *man*, and thence to the bright worlds above, the dwelling-places of beings unknown, will feel within him "a presence that disturbs him with the joy of devoted thought,"—a spirit mingling with his spirit, stirring the deepest feelings of the heart, and causing his soul to stand as it were on the very threshold of its prison-house, and to tremble with joyous exultation, as if about to mount from earth to heaven.

In this poetry our minds are swayed by the influence of *sanctified* genius, and are not permitted to rest satisfied with the idle reveries of a wandering imagination, nor yet with the simple emotions occasioned by new views of beautiful objects, but are led on to the contemplation of some of the noblest truths that can engage our thoughts. Do we

ON THE POETRY OF MORAL SENTIMENT.

Not love, not war, nor the tumultuous swell
Of civil conflict, nor the wrecks of change,
Nor duty struggling with afflictions strange—
Not these alone inspire the tuneful shell.
But where untroubled peace and concord dwell,
There, also, is the muse not loth to range. WORDSWORTH.

WHO that has wandered on some foreign shore, communing with men under the cold restrictions of custom and formality, receiving but the words of welcome where no friendship breathed, hath not felt his heart expand within him and swell with joyous tenderness, when returned to the retirement of his native land! There again his soul bursts forth in love, and holds "sweet converse" with those whose hearts are his. There again the merry laugh of early friends dispels from his brow that shade of melancholy, which the glitter and heartless splendor of the world could not chase away. *Such* is the contrast between the magnificence of fictitious poetry, and that in which we behold *nature* in her sweet simplicity, and in which the hallowed feelings of the poet call up all the sympathies of his soul. It is thus we think and feel with Cowper; his was the poetry of moral sentiment—the language of truth—the utterance of nature, revealing the springs of moral feeling in the soul. He teaches us that "nature is but a name for an effect whose cause is God," and wondering that we have never before listened to the echo of nature's voice in our own bosoms, we turn with gladness from the gilded show of the poetry of art, to the purity and freshness of natural beauties. Wordsworth, too, emphatically the poet of nature, bids us listen to the voice of that spirit that murmurs in the babbling brook, that smileth in the buttercup, and whispers in the stars of heaven.

And here, with a feeling almost approaching to reverence, let us join to the name of the greatest and best poet of the present age, that of our own Bryant. He stands in nature's temple, not, perhaps, as her high and holy priest, but as a minister of truth; and surely it can be no disparagement to the sacred office of the servants of God, to couple with it the names of the same poet—

"Whose eye
Doth glance from heaven to earth, from earth to heaven."

And if we admire the sentiment of the pagan, who, amid all the error and darkness of his times, yet, looking upon himself as set apart for the service of the virgin daughters of Jove, exclaimed—

"Me vero primum dulces ante omnia musæ
Quarum sacra fero igenti percussus amore
Accipiant"—

how much more should we regard the poets of this Christian age as an anointed priesthood, whose duty it is to diffuse purer and more exalted *truths*, than even the imagination which bound Eolus in his caves, or chained Prometheus to the horrid rocks of Caucasus, could conceive or comprehend!

Throughout the whole of Bryant's poetry there runs a stream of truth—a vein of exalted morality. It is not the result of a combining imagination—a shining edifice, reared by creative genius, yet unsubstantial as the house upon the sand—but it is a mansion in which the soul may repose with *confidence*, receiving delight and instruction from truth and nature, whose radiant forms are clearly seen through the transparent medium of a regulated imagination. Fiction, in this poetry which speaks to the *heart*, is not essential, for if the poet's breast do but swell with the emotions he wishes to excite, if his cheek is wet with those tears he wishes others to shed, he will touch a chord of sympathy in the soul, and our feelings and affections will move on harmoniously with his own; but when the imagination is to be delighted, *then* fiction becomes necessary; then it is that gnome, and sylph, and fairy sprite, flit before the eye, and that the senses are entranced by the beautiful shows of things unreal, which move before the mind, stirring not the feelings of the heart, as clouds tipped with gorgeous hues float in majestic beauty through the sky, but disturb not the quiet surface of the lake, over which their fleecy shadows pass.

There is in the soul of man a natural yearning for something more grand and more beautiful than the tangible forms of objects around us, and the poetry of moral sentiment alone gratifies this almost instinctive desire. It dispells, more fully than any other, the mist that hides from our sight the loveliness of nature, and causes us to *feel* that there is

> "A motion and a spirit that impel
> All thinking things—all objects of all thoughts,
> And roll through all things."

Yes, he who imbibes the spirit of this poetry, when straying through green fields and verdant meadows, or reclining on the flowery banks of the murmuring rivulet, or climbing the steep ascent of some rude crag, on whose tops the vaulted sky seems to rest, as if on massy walls; or when he looks abroad upon the beautiful earth, the *home* of *man*, and thence to the bright worlds above, the dwelling-places of beings unknown, will feel within him "a presence that disturbs him with the joy of devoted thought,"—a spirit mingling with his spirit, stirring the deepest feelings of the heart, and causing his soul to stand as it were on the very threshold of its prison-house, and to tremble with joyous exultation, as if about to mount from earth to heaven.

In this poetry our minds are swayed by the influence of *sanctified* genius, and are not permitted to rest satisfied with the idle reveries of a wandering imagination, nor yet with the simple emotions occasioned by new views of beautiful objects, but are led on to the contemplation of some of the noblest truths that can engage our thoughts. Do we

ON THE POETRY OF MORAL SENTIMENT.

Not love, not war, nor the tumultuous swell
Of civil conflict, nor the wrecks of change,
Nor duty struggling with afflictions strange—
Not these alone inspire the tuneful shell.
But where untroubled peace and concord dwell,
There, also, is the muse not loth to range. WORDSWORTH.

Who that has wandered on some foreign shore, communing with men under the cold restrictions of custom and formality, receiving but the words of welcome where no friendship breathed, hath not felt his heart expand within him and swell with joyous tenderness, when returned to the retirement of his native land! There again his soul bursts forth in love, and holds "sweet converse" with those whose hearts are his. There again the merry laugh of early friends dispels from his brow that shade of melancholy, which the glitter and heartless splendor of the world could not chase away. *Such* is the contrast between the magnificence of fictitious poetry, and that in which we behold *nature* in her sweet simplicity, and in which the hallowed feelings of the poet call up all the sympathies of his soul. It is thus we think and feel with Cowper; his was the poetry of moral sentiment—the language of truth—the utterance of nature, revealing the springs of moral feeling in the soul. He teaches us that "nature is but a name for an effect whose cause is God," and wondering that we have never before listened to the echo of nature's voice in our own bosoms, we turn with gladness from the gilded show of the poetry of art, to the purity and freshness of natural beauties. Wordsworth, too, emphatically the poet of nature, bids us listen to the voice of that spirit that murmurs in the babbling brook, that smileth in the buttercup, and whispers in the stars of heaven.

And here, with a feeling almost approaching to reverence, let us join to the name of the greatest and best poet of the present age, that of our own Bryant. He stands in nature's temple, not, perhaps, as her high and holy priest, but as a minister of truth; and surely it can be no disparagement to the sacred office of the servants of God, to couple with it the names of the same poet—

"Whose eye
Doth glance from heaven to earth, from earth to heaven."

And if we admire the sentiment of the pagan, who, amid all the error and darkness of his times, yet, looking upon himself as set apart for the service of the virgin daughters of Jove, exclaimed—

"Me vero primum dulces ante omnia musæ
Quarum sacra fero igenti percussus amore
Accipiant"—

how much more should we regard the poets of this Christian age as an anointed priesthood, whose duty it is to diffuse purer and more exalted *truths*, than even the imagination which bound Eolus in his caves, or chained Prometheus to the horrid rocks of Caucasus, could conceive or comprehend!

Throughout the whole of Bryant's poetry there runs a stream of truth—a vein of exalted morality. It is not the result of a combining imagination—a shining edifice, reared by creative genius, yet unsubstantial as the house upon the sand—but it is a mansion in which the soul may repose with *confidence*, receiving delight and instruction from truth and nature, whose radiant forms are clearly seen through the transparent medium of a regulated imagination. Fiction, in this poetry which speaks to the *heart*, is not essential, for if the poet's breast do but swell with the emotions he wishes to excite, if his cheek is wet with those tears he wishes others to shed, he will touch a chord of sympathy in the soul, and our feelings and affections will move on harmoniously with his own; but when the imagination is to be delighted, *then* fiction becomes necessary; then it is that gnome, and sylph, and fairy sprite, flit before the eye, and that the senses are entranced by the beautiful shows of things unreal, which move before the mind, stirring not the feelings of the heart, as clouds tipped with gorgeous hues float in majestic beauty through the sky, but disturb not the quiet surface of the lake, over which their fleecy shadows pass.

There is in the soul of man a natural yearning for something more grand and more beautiful than the tangible forms of objects around us, and the poetry of moral sentiment alone gratifies this almost instinctive desire. It dispells, more fully than any other, the mist that hides from our sight the loveliness of nature, and causes us to *feel* that there is

> "A motion and a spirit that impel
> All thinking things—all objects of all thoughts,
> And roll through all things."

Yes, he who imbibes the spirit of this poetry, when straying through green fields and verdant meadows, or reclining on the flowery banks of the murmuring rivulet, or climbing the steep ascent of some rude crag, on whose tops the vaulted sky seems to rest, as if on massy walls; or when he looks abroad upon the beautiful earth, the *home* of man, and thence to the bright worlds above, the dwelling-places of beings unknown, will feel within him "a presence that disturbs him with the joy of devoted thought,"—a spirit mingling with his spirit, stirring the deepest feelings of the heart, and causing his soul to stand as it were on the very threshold of its prison-house, and to tremble with joyous exultation, as if about to mount from earth to heaven.

In this poetry our minds are swayed by the influence of *sanctified* genius, and are not permitted to rest satisfied with the idle reveries of a wandering imagination, nor yet with the simple emotions occasioned by new views of beautiful objects, but are led on to the contemplation of some of the noblest truths that can engage our thoughts. Do we

stand upon the mountain's brow and look out upon a broad expanse of waters, paying the homage of our silence to the grandeur of the scene that sweeps far around us as the eye can reach? Ours is not merely a sense of swelling fullness in the bosom—of joyous expansion of the heart; but our thoughts are led directly to mingle with interests of men, or to glance quickly upwards to that Supreme Being who made the sea, and "who holdeth the waters in the hollow of his hand." Do we turn our gaze to the fruitful valleys below? The blue smoke that rises from many a cottage in the plain, either carries our thoughts downwards to the habitations of men, where love, and hope, and religion smile around the cheerful hearth, or lifts them upward far into the clear, blue heavens, until the imagination is lost in the contemplation of the Infinite—until the mind is filled with a holy awe of the Omnipotent, and the heart is melted into tenderness under the smile of love which comes from the serene heavens and sends its softening influence deep into the soul. This is moral, religious communing with nature—the most exalted exercise of the human faculties; it is "the sense sublime" of graceful beauty and majestic grandeur of external objects, unfelt by him whose moral and intellectual sensibilities wake not at the same hallowed touch. To him whose moral vision is obscured by gross sense, whose spiritual perception is clouded by dark thoughts, all this may seem unintelligible; to him, indeed, the light divine, that fills the world, pervades the universe, may be as the noonday sun to the blind man's eye. But to you who "look from nature up to nature's God," and who acknowledge an Omnipotent Spirit, and feel that what you believe is founded in reason and truth, this will not seem an idle, visionary conception, but the natural, harmonious operation of all the faculties of the soul. You will be reminded of heaven by "cliffs, fountains, seasons, times;" by all things around and above you. You will listen with rapture to the melody of waters and the music of the evening breeze. A fresh fountain of joy will gush forth in your bosoms, and a new sense of happiness be awakened within you. As ye submit yourselves to the soft influence of nature, and drink deeper and deeper at the inexhaustible fount, you will find

"Tongues in trees, books in running brooks,
Sermons in stones, and good in every thing."

The rose will wear a sweeter smile, and the breath of the hyacinth be far more grateful to your senses—

"Et quercus sudabit roscida mella."

Your minds will expand in dignity as the grandeur of the prospect opens before you, whilst your hearts will be softened and your feelings refined by that light which breaks in upon the soul from the works of creation.

But we are not confined, in this poetry, to the contemplation of *natural* perfection and beauty alone. It goes farther; it leads us to the admiration of the good and the beautiful in moral character; to

cherish those tender sensibilities, to cultivate those refined feelings, which soften the heart and purify the soul, and it urges us to a love of those amiable qualities we see in the *good*, and we insensibly strive to engraft them into our own moral being. Here we behold the reason, the imagination, and the passions, when swayed by a divine morality, moving on in harmonious unison; but when this hallowed spell is wanting, fearfully irregular, and by jarring collision, producing discord alone. Our fellow-men are here represented, *not* as marks for the shafts of ridicule or the fangs of malice, but as the objects of benevolent regard and brotherly affection. We are taught to look upward "to the primal duties which shine aloft like stars," and make them the guides of our voyage through life.

This poetry breathes a spirit of the purest love, and hence it is that tearful eyes are so often turned to heaven, whilst the soul breathes out its gratitude; hence it is that the very thoughts and emotions beam with a brighter light of benevolence, that the holiest sensations of the heart are brought into life, and that those feelings are awakened within us which unite us to humanity, and at the same time form the connecting link between us and spirits of a higher and nobler existence.

Woman, in this poetry, is not the etherealized conception of a fevered imagination, nor the object of a wild, delirious passion, but she shines with her own mild and radiant light.

> "She, like the harp, that instinctively rings,
> As the night-breathing zephyr soft sighs on its strings,
> Responds to each impulse with steady reply,
> Whether sorrow, or pleasure, her sympathy try,
> And tear-drops and smiles on her countenance play,
> Like sunshine and showers on a morning in May.
>
> She rules, by *her virtue*, the realms of the soul;
> As she glances around in the light of her smile,
> The war of the passions is hushed for awhile,
> And *Discord*, content from his fury to cease,
> Reposes, entranced, on the pillows of peace."

She is not a Sacharissa or Zelinda, to wake a Waller's muse, nor a Byron's Myrrha or Thyrsa, decked out in all the dazzling but false ornaments of a poetic imagination, but *woman*—

> "A creature not too fair or good
> For human nature's daily food,
> And yet a spirit, too, and bright,
> With something of an angel's light."

We admire her for her graceful mein, love her for the beauty of virtue, but almost adore her for the exalted moral attributes of her nature. She is that being who teaches our infant lips those accents of prayer which, however long we may wander in that "far land" of error, we can never forget. That humble supplication to "our Father who is in

heaven,"—it is the talisman of virtue; we first lisped it into a mother's ear, and as it recurs to the mind, the heart is melted into softness, and our lips unconsciously move with its words.

She is that being who assists our tottering feet in earliest infancy, who smiles upon us in the glad hours of youth, praises our good-deeds in manhood, who recalls us from the thorny way of the transgressor, who restrains us in the paths of peace, and points us the road to eternal joy.

Does any one say that this poetry is too tame?—that the spirit and fire of true poetry is wanting? Aye, that flaming fire of consuming passion, whose lurid heat sheds *no* cheerful light around, *is wanting*. No fiend ministers at this altar, kindling its fires with mean passions; but a heavenly spirit, whose wings fan a vestal flame, from which is wafted incense of gratitude and love acceptable to heaven. But, does poetry *consist* in these wild simoons of passion, which drive over the soul, deadening and uprooting the tender plants of virtue? Was it for this that "the vision and the faculty divine" were given to the poet? Was this power given to lash a Mazeppa on a wild and maddened steed, or to tell the sickening tale of Beppo? Nay, rather let us say that poetry dishonors her divine origin, unless she cherish virtue. Nay, let us turn away from this poisoned draught to "fresh fountains of pure water." Let us seek

"That serene and blessed mood,
In which the *affections* gently lead us on,
Until the breath of this corporeal frame,
And even the motion of our human blood,
Almost suspended, we are laid asleep
In body, and become a living soul.
While, with an eye made quiet by the power
Of harmony, and the deep power of joy,
We see into the life of things."

Let us cultivate this thoughtfulness—this close and intimate communion with nature. Let us turn aside from this idle pageantry—this gaudy show, which "satisfieth not," and seek, like wearied children, the neglected bosom of nature, and in the light of her smile find solace and rest.

Yes, let us leave

"The vain low strife
That makes men mad—the tug of wealth and power,
The passions and the cares that wither life,
And waste its little hour."

Let us cherish "those shadowy recollections" of our early childhood, and its days of innocence, which sometimes visit us even "in this Bank-note world;" let us seek again for *that heaven* which "lies about us in our infancy"—let us turn aside to flowing streams, to green and flowery meads, and with moistened eyes, beaming with admiration and gratitude, let us look once more upon

> "The radiant beauty shed abroad
> On all the glorious works of God;"

and as we walk in this holy communion with nature, our hearts will be softened into love, and our minds will expand with

> "That apprehensive power
> By which it is made quick to recognize
> The moral scope and aptitude of things."

Yes, those moments, in which we forget the promptings of passion and the cares of life, and, faint and disappointed, quit the noisy hum of this work-day existence, serve to bring out, to vivify, and to cherish the tender sympathies of humanity, to redeem life from its monotony, and to refresh "the human heart with dews from the urns of peace."

O! then, ye young and innocent, who tremble at the name of vice, and shudder at the thought of crime, love this poetry—hurl from your pure hands the seductive tales of poisoned and corrupted fancy, and turn to the swelling fountains of truth and love, and melancholy, dark, desponding melancholy, will never cloud with its gloomy influence the gayety of your bright thoughts. The beauties of the world in which we live, the innocent revels of God's creatures, the joys and hopes of man, can never cherish envious repinings in your bosoms; but your young hearts will learn to sympathize with the cheerfulness of nature—your minds will be stored with bright thoughts, and your imaginations enriched with beautiful images, around which will centre delightful associations to gladden the weariness of after years. And ye, who are in the evening of your days, turn once more to the gushing fountains of nature; and though she wear not for you the same glad smile as in your morning of life, a sober delight will be yours—for you will behold her bathed in the mellow light of a setting sun, and you will see that this penetrates the darkness of the grave and illumines the pathway to heaven.

K.

THE HUGUENOTS.

The improvement of man has been effected by a succession of Revolutions. Some have been mild and peaceable, the result of causes working for a long series of ages; others have burst forth on the "world's trembling multitude," sudden and powerful. Such was the Reformation of Luther. Its great principle—its noble aim—was civil and religious liberty. History records the struggles of the contest, rousing up all the energies of Europe. Foremost in this drama, stand forth the Protestants of France,—a Spartan band in the great army of Reformers. Sympathy for their sufferings, reverence for their piety, admiration of their fortitude and perseverance, and gratitude to God for the preservation of a remnant of this afflicted people, affect us when we think of the religious despotism which, for ages, warred against their souls.

The Huguenots were a people peculiar to France. Separated from their brethren of Switzerland by the vast mountain-barriers of nature, removed from intercourse with the English by a great extent of land and water, they formed a community among themselves, leagued together for the mutual defense of their country and religion. Animated by these high and noble principles, they faultered not in the hour of danger—when necessity called them to the field, they shrunk not from the sword of persecution—when the fires of Romish bigotry kindled around them, they bore their martyrdom with that unflinching constancy so characteristic of their faith, and of their cause. The love of religious liberty, arising from the conviction of duty, has, in all past time, given an undaunted spirit to its votaries. Witness the zeal of the early Christian Church! Witness the firmness of our Pilgrim fathers! Witness the persecutions of the Huguenots!

Most prominent in the history of this people, is the tragedy of Saint Bartholemew. The Protestants of that time were considered too formidable a party to be any longer tolerated. As Cato continually said in the Roman Senate, "delenda est Carthago," so did the men in power of that time unceasingly shout, "Let the Huguenots be destroyed." And, at length, their desire was well nigh accomplished. The night of St. Bartholemew gluts the all-devouring thirst of their enemies. During that terrific slaughter, the cry for mercy was drowned in the relentless shout of "Death to the Huguenots," and the light of day but added new horrors to the scene. The streets of Paris flowed with the blood of her murdered citizens; and from that city the massacre spread through all the provinces, bringing death and desolation to every part of the land. Thousands of useful and peaceable citizens were struck down by the demon of destruction, and one united cry for vengeance on such monstrous injustice arose to the throne of God, and will yet have to be silenced by the woes of coming ages. This dreadful instance of the barbarism of religious bigotry excites the indignation of the world. At that time it was *eulogized*, by many of the nations of Europe, as a glorious triumph—the cold-blooded murder of thousands, a glorious triumph—the triumph of religion!

But let us turn from such a scene, and contemplate the magnanimity of Henry, so worthily styled the Great. This Prince, ascending the throne, at a time when faction had torn his kingdom for more than a century, had exhausted its resources, and impoverished his people, who had wrongs to revenge, and crimes to punish, nobly buried them all in oblivion, and the world saw the proof of an exalted mind in the Edict of Nantes. What a contrast with the conduct of the guilty and execrated Charles, who, a century before, looked calmly on the *murder* of his subjects! This celebrated Edict placed the rights of the Huguenots on a basis, which the most flagrant violation of justice could alone overthrow; and it was to be hoped that no future Monarch of France would have the rashness to annul it. And yet, not one century had passed before its revocation filled the whole land with the blood of her slaughtered citizens. The Edict of Nantes gave to the Protestants of France a distinct and separate existence as a political body, by setting them in array against a government which recognized no such thing as religious liberty, and held to one principle alone of policy—"One God, one King, one Faith." During the reign of the Great Henry, the Huguenots exercised their rights, and liberty of conscience was secured; his death was the death of order, of peace, and of freedom.

From this time, the Huguenots, alarmed at the intrigues of the court, and the measures taken for their overthrow, were in arms; and when

"The living cloud of war"

burst upon them from the north of France, their rights, their existence as a people, were swept away. For the next half century, persecution followed persecution, until, finally, the revocation of the Edict of Nantes, by depriving the Huguenots of all securities of life and liberty—by annihilating their existence as subjects, compelled the emigration of this people. Thousands of industrious citizens left forever their native France, to seek in foreign lands the liberty denied them in their own. As their predecessors, the Pilgrims, bade their native land good-night, and lay down to rest on the shores of New England, so did the Huguenots, driven across the western ocean by persecuting fanaticism, at length find a resting-place on the shores of Carolina. The hand of welcome was held out to them—they were hailed as brothers. And noble sons of Carolina have they proved themselves! Braving the perils of savage warfare, they plunged into the wilderness; pioneers of the south, they strengthened the infant colony of Carolina by their religion and by their arms.

But to us, the settlement of the Huguenots, though not followed by consequences of such import as those succeeding the landing of the Pilgrims, was attended with the most important results. The addition of a large body of men, virtuous, industrious, inured to peril and war, but, above all, martyrs of religious liberty, would be welcomed by any people; and peculiarly fortunate was it for a small colony, pressed on every side by a savage enemy, and but poorly assisted by the mother country. Their singularly elastic and cheerful temper of mind enabled them to endure the hardships necessarily attendant on a settlement in a country, new, surrounded by enemies, and exposed to an almost tropical sun. The same spirit which made them prefer exile to slavery, sustained them in the long and arduous struggle of the Revolution. Shoulder to shoulder with their brethren in the field, they met the invading foe, and the "plains of Carolina" became the altar on which they sacrificed their blood in defense of their common country. When the "black and smoking ruins" of desolation covered the land, the same firmness which upheld their fathers in the old world, sustained their descendants in the new. The names of Horry, of Huger, and of

Marion are coupled with those of Lawrens, of Rutledge, of Pickney, and of Sumpter—names dear to every American, the watchwords of liberty. Sustained by the example of these, South Carolina proved the noble daring and heroic courage of her adopted people. Thousands of their descendants at this time hail America as the land of their birth—the land of their forefathers' adoption—the asylum of their ancestors—the land of civil and religious liberty. May its standard, reared on the solid foundation of virtue, ever wave over millions of the sons of freemen, until time shall be no more.

As we review these scenes, we cannot refrain from asking, what had the Huguenots done that they should thus be

"At the mercy of a mystery of tyranny?"

What were their crimes, that they should be deprived of all civil existence—that they should be hunted down like wild beasts—that their blood should stream under the sword? They worshiped God according to the dictates of their conscience. This was their crime—this their abomination. This doomed them to the sword, to the stake, and to exile. That they were a peaceable people, orderly, industrious, and well-disposed, is acknowledged by the Romish historians. They were aroused to revolt, when the iron yoke of oppression became too grievous to be borne—when bigotry sent forth the destroying angel—when life and liberty were crushed by oppression. Their emigration furnished many nations with numbers of useful subjects; and France now deplores the unjust policy which banished her citizens, depopulated one fourth of her kingdom, ruined her commerce, and for many years placed her under martial law. To her, the result of such policy has been disastrous in the extreme—the despotic persecutions of centuries having ended in the dreadful catastrophe of the French Revolution.

The nineteenth century has brought to the Huguenots that toleration which has permitted them to rebuild their peaceful temples, and to worship God in their own way. The conflicts of centuries have taught both parties the necessity of mutual forbearance; and the religion of reason, and the religion of authority, have learned that they can exist in the same country without continual war and fightings. The severe blow which the Romish Church received, at the time of the Revolution, in the confiscation of its property, and in the prevention of ecclesiastical interference with the affairs of State, and the wise policy of the new government, which grants religious liberty to the subject, conspire to root out from France a most fatal source of discord, destructive of the welfare of any people.

The influence of the Reformed principles has delivered the human mind from the fetters which bound it during the middle ages. To them, Science, Literature, and the Arts owe their development and progress; to them, we owe all which enables man to reach the true dignity of his nature. The mind is free from the apathy of a blind superstition. Freedom of conscience is the acknowledged right of every one. The lethargy of ages is shaken off. Shall we not honor those who conferred this great good on mankind?—shall we not revere those who periled all in the cause of religious liberty, and nobly resolved to do or die? Let us not forget that the Huguenots were the martyrs of Christianity, the sons of everlasting truth; and while we regard them with veneration, let us cherish the feelings of brothers for their descendants in the far south—let us hail them as Americans—let us hail them as members of the same great and free people.

F. M. Adams,

EDINBURG UNIVERSITY.*

It is almost unnecessary to premise, that two methods of instruction, radically the reverse of each other, have found place in the different countries of Europe, viz.: first, a partial or total dependance upon Lectures, or the so-called *German* system; and, second, the adoption of what may be termed a practical method, consisting of regular Exercises on the part of the pupil, under the inspection of tutors, constituting the *English* system. The latter calls to its aid, indeed, the assistance of Lectures, but with a different purpose, and with far less reliance upon them. This distinction has been too frequently overlooked in estimating the comparative merits of the two systems. To a neglect of ascertaining one's own purpose, and the adaptation of either method to its attainment, may be attributed the disappointment so frequently experienced by individuals, on leaving College or the University, who grieve at the consciousness of being compelled to "learn over again" that with which they have once been familiar.

The Universities of Scotland are close approximations to the "theoretical" ones of Germany. That of Edinburg consists of thirty Professorships, from which there are daily or tri-weekly Lectures. Its Academical Year commences in November. The Winter Session closes in April; and after a Vacation of several weeks, the Medical Classes in part recommence, and continue through the Summer Session until August. The Literary Classes do not assemble again until the November following. The following is a list of the Chairs:—

---

* We are indebted for the above communication, to the pen of a graduate of Edinburg, who left the Sophomore Class of Yale, some three years since, for the purpose of completing his education abroad. As it was not originally intended for the Magazine, many passages of private interest have necessarily been omitted, and some details too minute to be generally interesting; but we think that, as a comparison of the system and course of study in that University with our own, it will not be found by a student of Yale devoid of either attraction or advantage.—Ed.

I. LITERATURE AND PHILOSOPHY.

Humanity,
Greek,
Mathematics,
Logic and Metaphysics,*
Moral Philosophy, Political Economy,*
Natural Philosophy,
Rhetoric and Belles Lettres,
Practical Astronomy,
Agriculture,
†Universal History,
†Music.

II. THEOLOGY.

Divinity,
Divinity and Church History,
Hebrew, two sub-Classes.

III. LAW.

Civil Law,
Law of Scotland,
Conveyancing.

IV. MEDICINE.

Theory of Physic,
Anatomy of Physic,
Chemistry,
Practice of Physic,
Dietetics, Materia Medica, and Pharmacy,
General Pathology,
Surgery,
Military Surgery,
Midwifery,
Clinical Surgery,
Clinical Medicine,
Natural History,
Botany.

These Professorships are nearly all "Regii," in consequence of the founding of the University by James VI. of Scotland, and the vacancies are chiefly filled by the Town Council as representing her Majesty. Assembled together, the Professors form the Senatus Academicus, which is convoked on occasions of granting degrees, and for amendment of its regulations or the curriculum of study. The Senatus is divided into four Faculties of Literature, Theology, Law, and Medicine, over each of which a Professor presides, with the title of Dean of the Faculty, and before which the various topics to be introduced into the Senatus must previously be discussed—(this is the case, at least, in granting any privilege "ad eundum.")

In nearly every Class there are Examinations on the subject of the Lectures, which the student may attend or not at his option. His Certificate of attendance upon the Lectures is usually sufficient without one for the Examinations. The Examinations also embrace a certain number of works on the subject of the Lectures, in which the student is again examined at his final debut. These works are given out at the commencement of the Academical Year in the several departments, and so variable is the list, that an A. M. of one year may find himself sorely taxed to undergo, without extra preparation, the Examination of another. In order to induce attendance upon the Examinations, the honors are conferred upon such only as frequent them; thus, every Class, whose Professorship is endowed with sufficient funds, possesses a private list of honors. They consist chiefly of books—in one or two instances, they are merely nominal. There are neither Valedictory nor Salutatory Orations, nor, in fine, any honor which exceeds a prize. The most important ones, in general estimation, are

* United in one Chair.

† Nominal Chairs to which there are at present attached no Lectures.

the gold medals of the Classes of Moral and Natural Philosophy, and the first honors of the Classes of Logic and Rhetoric. In addition to these, a prize of ten guineas ($52) is annually given by the *students* to the best writer of an essay on a prescribed theme.*

II. Admission. Every person who applies for admission is received, without examination of any kind, within the pale of the University. He is supposed to know what courses are best adapted to his purpose, and whether he is sufficiently qualified to attend the Lectures in an advantageous manner. As there necessarily exists some diversity in the attainments of individuals of different ages, and from different schools, there are two or three sub-divisions in most of the Literary and Theological Classes, corresponding with the different degrees of advancement. If the student designs to attend the same Class during two or more consecutive years, he generally enters the lowest. These gradations are not in all cases voluntary—the highest sub-class in Natural Philosophy requiring an acquaintance with Fluxions, Conic Sections, Algebra, and usually some work on Mechanics. The same course of Lectures is delivered to all; but the private examinations impose the necessity of extra proficiency. On entering, the student subscribes his name in the Album, by which (as he is subsequently informed) he promises obedience to the statutes of the University; and after paying the Matriculation fee of £1, receives a ticket, which serves for an Academical year. This is conveyed to the Professor whose Lectures he designs to attend, when, after the payment of the course fee, (from £2 2s. to £4 4s.,) he receives the Professor's ticket, which entitles him to the six months' course. The Matriculation ticket, accompanied by that of a Professor, procures the student admission to the University Library, which now numbers about one hundred thousand volumes. Before receiving a book, he deposits with the Librarian a sum of money, in the proportion of £1 for two volumes, until the number of the latter reaches ten, beyond which no student is allowed to draw, without especial permission. This deposit is returned on the receipt of the books. Such a precaution is rendered in some degree necessary by the migratory character of a certain class of students. With respect to the Library, it may be remarked, that although it contains a vast number of volumes, the demands upon it, by persons who actually have little or no right to its use, as well as by the Professors, (many of whom are said to furnish their own tables from it,) are so great, that the students, to whom the "reliquia" are alone served out, fare little better than they would were its contents less and under proper regulations. Attached to the Library is a Reading-room, in which are kept a few hundred volumes for reference, where, except in case of classical works, the same difficulty prevails. It affords great conveniencies, however, for consulting and extracting from such works as are too voluminous to be conveniently conveyed to a private room.

* Here follows a long list of various prizes awarded by the *University*, which we have omitted as of little importance to a general reader.—Ed.

There are also several small collections attached to the Professorships, and also one or two belonging to societies. There is nothing, however, corresponding to the students' Libraries at Yale College.

III. COURSE OF STUDY. The peculiar facilities afforded by the German system to the students of a particular branch, allowing them to attend as many or as few courses as they please, and compelling attendance upon certain courses, only, for degrees, considerably diminishes the number of competitors for A. B. and A. M.; and out of a large number of literary students, six or eight is the average number of graduates. Another cause may be, the low estimation in which such degrees are held, while the advantages which they confer upon Medical students are so small, and a substitute is so readily afforded by private tuition of a few weeks or months immediately preceding the examinations, that a candidate for M. D. seldom commences his course with either.

There are, of course, several subjects to which the German mode cannot be so advantageously applied, and which require particular exertion on the part of the pupil. Of this nature are the Classics, and to some extent the Mathematics. In each of these branches the student submits to a daily examination in the authors, and solves a problem. In addition to these exercises, however, there is a course of Lectures delivered to the Humanity Class, on language, on the history of Literature and Science amongst the Romans, and on a variety of topics connected with the study of Latin. The Greek Professor lectures on Tragedy, Eloquence, and Lyric Poetry, with critical remarks upon the master-pieces of Grecian Literature. The requirements of the former class were, (1840)—

Virgil—The first Six Books of the Ænead.
Homer—Ody. Books i. and iii., with the principal metres; Epistles, Book i.
Cicero—Pro lege Manilia. Archia poeta.
Livy—Books xxvi. and xxvii.
Translation of an English Author into Latin prose.

For higher distinction—

Cicero—Offices, Annals of Tacitus, Books i. and ii.
Juvenal—Satires viii. and xiv.
Livy—First Four Books.

The requirements in Greek for M. A. are—

Xenophon—Memorabilia, first three Books.
Plato—Menexinus.
Aristophanes—Nubes.
Homer—Odyssea, first three Books.
Translation from some English Author into Greek prose.
Rules for Hexameter, Pentameter, Iambic and Trochaic verse.

Classical pursuits are, unfortunately, at a much lower ebb in Scotland than in any other part of the empire. So far, indeed, is this the case, that the Universities are almost the only places where Greek is properly taught, and they have, consequently, become little better than

Academies (so far as the Classics are concerned) for the several cities in which they are situated. The result is, that the instruction communicated is most elementary, and seldom exceeds that to which we have been accustomed in the better class of preparatory schools. The several authors in which the examination for the degrees takes place are not read to any considerable extent in either of the classes; and the student is not unfrequently obliged to prepare himself for this ordeal by the assistance of a private tutor. The Lectures are said to be better than could be reasonably expected from the practical portion of the courses. In the other Literary Classes there are two or three Lectures each week, the intervening days being occupied with examinations on the subjects of the Lectures, as in the Class of Logic and Metaphysics, or with such an examination in one, and an examination in the text books on the other, as in the Rhetoric Class. Several of the classes have, during part of the course, an extra Lecture or Examination on Saturday morning. All these examinations are voluntary, and the students attending them (generally more than half of the class) form the "Private Class." It is understood, however, that a student, having given his name as a member of the private class, is not at liberty to withdraw it except for urgent reasons. They are usually conducted by drawing a letter, and exhausting the names of which it is the initial. The student endeavors to give a succinct account of the Lecture, for which he is allowed sufficient time; the examination of three or four persons usually occupying the hour allotted to the purpose. In the Class of Rhetoric and Belles Lettres the answers are written, and are expected from all the members of the private class. In several classes, there are assigned topics for study during vacation, for eminence in which there are several prizes. There are also prizes for private studies on presented topics during the session—that in the Logic Class, (1841–2,) for instance, being Aristotle's observations on the Passions and Moral Characteristics, as contained in his Rhetoric.

The vacation studies in the same class for the year are, "Philosophia Græco—Romana ex fontium locis contexta," and "Philosophie de Kant." M. Cousin.

No two classes are precisely similar in their arrangements, although all differ from the same normal type. It will suffice, perhaps, to describe those of a single one—that of Rhetoric will answer our purpose. The Lectures of the Professor naturally embrace a wide range of subjects, and are capable of being rendered the most interesting in the whole Curiculum. Nearly half of the course is devoted to examining the various theories of beauty, and to the consideration of the principles of Aesthetics. This investigation consequently embraces the mutual relations of the Fine Arts, and their comparative rank as Aesthetical agents, as well as the principles of this criticism. A second portion of the Lectures is devoted to Rhetoric proper, and a third to the consideration of the Greek Classic Poets. This subject, of course, involved the much agitated Homeric question, and a comparison of the Wolfian and its antagonistic theories. It embraced, also, the history of writing in part, and a notice of the several Homeric manuscripts. The

stand upon the mountain's brow and look out upon a broad expanse of waters, paying the homage of our silence to the grandeur of the scene that sweeps far around us as the eye can reach? Ours is not merely a sense of swelling fullness in the bosom—of joyous expansion of the heart; but our thoughts are led directly to mingle with interests of men, or to glance quickly upwards to that Supreme Being who made the sea, and "who holdeth the waters in the hollow of his hand." Do we turn our gaze to the fruitful valleys below? The blue smoke that rises from many a cottage in the plain, either carries our thoughts downwards to the habitations of men, where love, and hope, and religion smile around the cheerful hearth, or lifts them upward far into the clear, blue heavens, until the imagination is lost in the contemplation of the Infinite—until the mind is filled with a holy awe of the Omnipotent, and the heart is melted into tenderness under the smile of love which comes from the serene heavens and sends its softening influence deep into the soul. This is moral, religious communing with nature—the most exalted exercise of the human faculties; it is "the sense sublime" of graceful beauty and majestic grandeur of external objects, unfelt by him whose moral and intellectual sensibilities wake not at the same hallowed touch. To him whose moral vision is obscured by gross sense, whose spiritual perception is clouded by dark thoughts, all this may seem unintelligible; to him, indeed, the light divine, that fills the world, pervades the universe, may be as the noonday sun to the blind man's eye. But to you who "look from nature up to nature's God," and who acknowledge an Omnipotent Spirit, and feel that what you believe is founded in reason and truth, this will not seem an idle, visionary conception, but the natural, harmonious operation of all the faculties of the soul. You will be reminded of heaven by "cliffs, fountains, seasons, times;" by all things around and above you. You will listen with rapture to the melody of waters and the music of the evening breeze. A fresh fountain of joy will gush forth in your bosoms, and a new sense of happiness be awakened within you. As ye submit yourselves to the soft influence of nature, and drink deeper and deeper at the inexhaustible fount, you will find

"Tongues in trees, books in running brooks,
Sermons in stones, and good in every thing."

The rose will wear a sweeter smile, and the breath of the hyacinth be far more grateful to your senses—

"Et quercus sudabit roscida mella."

Your minds will expand in dignity as the grandeur of the prospect opens before you, whilst your hearts will be softened and your feelings refined by that light which breaks in upon the soul from the works of creation.

But we are not confined, in this poetry, to the contemplation of *natural* perfection and beauty alone. It goes farther; it leads us to the admiration of the good and the beautiful in moral character; to

The statutes of the University require that the roll be called twenty-six times in each of the classes during the session. This is accomplished, either literally, or by requesting the students to leave their cards with the janitors. To obtain a certificate of *regular* attendance, necessary for a degree, the student must have been present at least twenty-four times, although qualified certificates are issued for an irregular attendance when the number of absences does not exceed four.

From the fact that the University contains no accommodation for the students, no attempt whatever is made to control their conduct while out of the lecture room. From the same cause, as well as that the hours of assembling the different classes extend from 9 A. M. to 5 P. M., there are no prayers or religious exercises of any kind. A gallery is provided in a neighboring Chapel, belonging to the Scottish Establishment, for such of the students as wish to attend Church. Members of the Church of England and Dissenters accommodate themselves in the city Churches. It will, perhaps, be desirable to afford some means of comparing the expenses attending a literary course at Edinburg with those of an American University. The various class tickets are nearly as follows :—

Latin Winter Ticket, .	£3	3s.	Logic and Metaphysics,	£3	3s.
Greek " " .	3	3	Moral Philosophy, . .	3	3
Mathematics . . .	3	3	Natural Philosophy, .	3	3
Rhetoric and Belles Lettres,	3	3			

Of these courses, several will be repeated, and, consequently, no positive allowance can be made. To this amount is to be added the matriculation ticket for four years, (£4,) then for the Diploma, (£3 3s.) and the janitor's fee.

IV. The final Examinations. The statutes require the attendance upon the classes of Greek, Logic, Moral Philosophy and Natural Philosophy in separate years. No other limit is fixed to the number or order of classes which the student may attend. The Curriculum for the degree of M. A. may be completed in the course of four years, or in a longer period, if the student choose it. For the degree of B. A. the student is examined at the close of the third year; for that of M. A. in the Classics, at the conclusion of the third, (if he prefer it;) and in Philosophy, Mathematics, and Rhetoric at the termination of the fourth, or he may be examined on all the branches at the latter time. At either period, he notifies the Dean of the Faculty of Arts of his intention to present himself for examination, and submits to his inspection the tickets of the several Professors, with those of matriculation. He is generally allowed (although this is not the case in all the branches at Edinburg) to "profess" any number of additional books on the subject of examination; and his rank in the graduation list depends almost entirely upon the voluntary portion. He is furnished with a printed scheme of examination, containing the portions of authors to be translated, and various questions arising directly or indirectly from the subject-matter of the extract—the history of the era to which it refers—

the actions of distinguished characters concerned—or from philological and critical considerations.

The Mathematical and Philosophical schemes contain problems to be solved, principles to be explained, and theories to be enumerated. Those of Moral Philosophy, Logic and Metaphysics, and Rhetoric embrace general systems, and the definition of the terms employed in each, as well as questions which arise from the more important principles.

The Examination continues three days, on each of which four hours are allowed to the subject proposed. The first day is devoted to Latin and Greek; the second to Mathematics and Natural Philosophy; and the third to Logic, Rhetoric, and Moral Philosophy. By a recent alteration, the time will, in future, be protracted to five hours per diem. If the examinations are satisfactory, the "Senatus" grant the degrees; and the names of the graduates, arranged in the order of merit displayed in the examination, are suspended in the court of the Library, and published in the city newspapers.*

THE SPIRIT'S FLIGHT.

I slept, and methought my spirit free
Soared away from its earthly home,
And mingled once more in the company
That it years ago had known.

Mid the shadowy forms of forgotten dead,
Mid the old and the young it roved,
And on airy wing it quickly sped
To the scenes that its youth had loved.

Once again, with joy, it seemingly grasped
A long lost brother's hand,
And the cherished form of a sister clasped
In its arms' encircling band.

* Lest the reader should consider this article as terminating rather abruptly, we would whisper in his ear, that there were appended thereto, in the original, several remarks of a *finishing* nature, with which it has been thought inexpedient for him to become acquainted. We have given already a *quantum suf.*—let this be a *verbum sap.*—Ed.

The reverend forms of hoary age,
That were wont its youth to guide,
Seemed to ask for the fruits of their counsels sage,
As they lingered by its side.

They passed, and a younger train appeared,
As in sadness it gazed around—
Of those who the starting post had cleared,
But the goal had never found.

The features of childhood bright were there,
And boyhood's ripening years,
And ardent youth, whose prospects fair
Had been quenched in the vale of tears.

Slowly, in silence, it saw them fade,
Like the dream of a broken slumber;
And, addressing the last, it inquiry made
Who next should swell their number.

The voiceless dead no answer gave
To my spirit's question bold:
It turned to its home, and a new-made grave,
Cried, "Look! and the tale is told."

The tale was told; and the tear-drop warm
Has gushed from many an eye,
To think that another youthful form
Has blossomed—but to die.

The tale was told: for an uncaged heart
Had flown to its rest in the sky—
From the earthly chain had been taken a part
To lengthen the one on high.

E.

PERMANENCE OF THE IMAGINATIVE PRINCIPLE.

It is the prerogative of genius to arrest those fleeting conceptions, which all men have, of the beautiful and great, and, by embodying them in language, to turn them into living realities—"thoughts that wake to perish never"—and thus, in the literal sense, to change *ideas* into *things*. He who does this—whether he works in marble or on the canvas—whether he pours forth the "winged words" of eloquence, or scatters from the pictured urn of fancy "thoughts that breathe and words that burn," is a ποιητης—a *maker*, for he adds another to those imperishable forms which are destined, gradually, to fill up the vast empire of mind.

It is an interesting inquiry, what period of society, what stage in a nation's progress, is most favorable to the exertions of this high creative power? The received theory makes it the savage state; or, at least, one but partially advanced, when society, in the language of Burke, is "still in the gristle, and not yet hardened into the bone of manhood." But is it so? Let us look at facts. Gather up the fragments which remain of early national verse, and casting aside the mist which throws enchantment around every relic of antiquity, search for the evidence of high poetic genius. Turn over the mouldy pages of English verse before the time of Chaucer, and though here and there appears a gleam of real genius, the mass is but a maze of words, betraying an uncultivated taste and poverty of conception. The same is true, in a still higher degree, of the early poetry of Spain and Portugal, and the lover of verse will look in vain in the ditties of Juan de Mena and Santillana for that delight which it is the end and aim of the poet to inspire. But there is another class, still farther back in history, and one frequently cited, the Skalds of Scandinavia and the Northmen bards. The few fragments of their ballads which tradition has preserved, possess a style of bold and broken metaphor, whose very novelty to the modern ear would conceal its numerous defects; a style, however, which is due far more to the paucity of a rude language, than to the prevalence of real genius. Quaintness of expression is too often mistaken for originality of thought, and the most pointless verses of our day, had we none better, would fall like enchanted words on the ear of the future antiquarian. The appeal, also, is often made to the age of Homer. But was Homer a savage, and his "many-colored verse" the dialect of a horde of barbarians? On the contrary, is it not evident that though he lived in an age of commotion and excitement, and threw himself back in his descriptions to a still ruder period, he lived in an age far more advanced, in every art and elegance of life, than this theory supposes? What means that picture on the shield of Achilles—its rich mosaic of silver and gold—its sculptured cities and waving harvests, with all the signs of heaven moving in solemn procession above,

"The Sun that rests not, and the Moon full orbed?"

How do his pages teem with intimations, which seem prophetic glimpses of the triumphs of modern invention, and show that there then existed immense treasures of science and art which afterwards sank into oblivion! And how could it be otherwise? When Egypt had for centuries poured forth the stores of her wisdom into the colonies of Greece, and all were turning their eyes to the Nile as the source of light and knowledge, how plain is it, that the age of Homer was one of advanced, though unequal civilization, removed much farther from a rude and barbarous period, than from the bright day of Pericles. The truth is, genius is not so much dependent on the particular *age* in which it exists, as on the *healthy action of the public mind*. Let a nation be on the ascendant scale of thought and feeling, with a heart that beats high to generous exertion, and with faith that there is opened before it a "boundless inheritance of hope," and whether it is ten or ten thousand years old, it presents the true and only field for the creative faculty in man.

We may, therefore, reject at once all these disheartening theories of the necessary decline of imaginative power. It is not so; and we shall see it is not, if we consider either the *materials* of which the poet forms his conceptions, or the *impulse* which prompts him to give them a "local habitation and a name."

The *materials* of poetic thought, of varied and beautiful combinations, are continually accumulating around us: they spread themselves out in richer profusion as we rise to loftier heights of knowledge and virtue. Think, for example, of those strong and pure emotions which burn in the bosom of a people advancing in refined and generous sentiment. Think of the thousand nice shadings of character and feeling which belong to cultivated life alone, and especially the breathings of a manly reason, and the majestic influence of a holy faith. Where, in the chaos of untaught savage mind, shall we look for those sentiments of chivalric romance and deference to the gentler sex, so beautifully inwoven with the finest strains of poetry? Where, amid the wild measures of the earlier bards, do we find those tender associations of home and kindred familiar to the civilized mind, and portrayed with such matchless grace by the gentle Cowper; or that spirit of calm philosophy which flows so richly from the nobler German poets, and from Coleridge and Wordsworth in our native tongue? Above all, in the confused fables of superstition and idolatry, what is there to arouse the genius of the poet, compared with the grand conceptions of revealed truth, which led Milton

"To pass the flaming bounds of place and time,
Where Angels tremble as they gaze?"

No! The spirit of Christianity, though moving in a higher region than Science and Philosophy, so far from obscuring the light of genius, or excluding it from its native sphere, clothes it with a new lustre, and lends it freely of a holier brightness to reflect upon mankind.

If we turn now from the materials on which genius operates, to the *impulse* it receives from the mass of intellect around, here, too, the advantage lies on the side of a cultivated age. The poet of such an age speaks not, like the early bard, to a single generation alone, nor leaves his works to be defaced by the hand of rude tradition. The fervid conceptions which he utters are impressed at once on thousands of enlightened minds, and live in a thousand imperishable forms. Time and space have no power to dim their splendor, or to check their diffusion. Borne on the ministering wings of art, they reach, with their first freshness, the utmost verge of civilization, the most distant period of time.

What an impulse is thus given to the most exalted efforts of gifted minds!

But there is a higher consideration than all this: the very *constitution of things* raises genius above all dependence upon circumstances. The great truth, that change, constant and progressive, is written on the face of nature and on the heart of man, is a sure pledge that sources of new combination shall never be wanting to imaginative minds. As the surface of the globe owes its beauty and variety to great alternating causes, to the quiet deposit of new material and the rough convulsions of a hidden power, so the cast and habit of the human intellect is constantly assuming new shapes with each succeeding age, and presenting new motives to the poet for the exercise of his power. To every generation, as it comes, the world of being is as fresh and attractive as to those which have gone before. The tide of life, which ebbs and flows unceasingly, bears back no solid treasure to oblivion, although it washes out the transient footsteps of the past. In every period of the world's history, as under every sky, childhood has anew its delightful fancies, youth its earnestness of hope and enterprise, and age its lingering regrets. And were this not true of mankind at large, it is the special birthright of genius that to *it* nothing shall be old. Beneath its inspired vision, the world, outward and visible, the hidden world of the human soul within, open fields of discovery as new and grand as if no other eye had gazed upon their wonders—for it goes forth with a pledge from its Creator, that it shall not return unto him void. With angels pinions, it ever seeks for nobler flights than those of the inferior mind, and from its loftier eminence, can take a wider and sublimer view of our common humanity.

Genius, then, as we have already said, is not dependent for its exercise and power upon the age in which it lives, but on the tone and spirit of the public mind. The great productions of the human intellect have ever sprung from among a people flushed with the excitement of intellectual progress, and ardent in their aspirations after more extended conquests. Then it is, that the strong and common impulse which animates the vast mass of popular feeling to higher ambition and achievement, urges on to a nobler emulation the nobler specimens of mind. Then it is, that the imaginative power of a whole people seems often transferred into a single soul, to be poured out in burning and immortal conceptions. Without this impulse of a nation's mind, genius can never exist in its highest excellence; and whatever shall rob a people of its heritage of generous anticipations, be it a grinding despotism, a debasing ignorance, or a conscious inferiority, must crush in the bud every exhibition of imaginative power. Of the truth of this we have a striking illustration at the present day. Why is it that American talent is triumphing over the great masters of Italy in sculpture and painting, beneath the very shadow of the Vatican and among the galleries of Florence? Why is it that the humble artist, who went forth to learn and imitate, is winning the proudest laurels from the astonished painters and statuaries of the Venitian schools? Why, but that he went forth in the spirit of his native land, full of free and exalted aspirations, among a people lying in "the region and shadow" of despotic power.

The views we have thus taken throw a cheering light on the future history of our race. The belief is universal, that a day is coming when intellectual and moral truth shall have their perfect reign on earth—when man, united in one brotherhood, shall reach the highest point of knowledge and refinement. But how gloomy the prospect, if imagination must decay as society advances, till the world sink down at last into a mere mass of intellect. Such a faith is unworthy of the nature of man—unworthy of the God of Providence. Let us rather believe, that the imaginative principle shall then have even a larger share in moulding the faculties of man—that in this rich soil shall spring up a nobler growth of mind: nobler in fervid sentiment, nobler in manly strength, nobler in the sublime attainments of creative genius—that the joys of a pure faith shall be rendered more vivid and intense by the influence of a sanctified imagination, which shall elevate all that is virtuous, and beautify all that is good.

G.

THE REIGN OF QUEEN ELIZABETH.

We have chosen this theme, not with the expectation of being able to present any thing strictly new, or even to render what we may say agreeable on account of any *air* of novelty. We are aware that the character of "the maiden Queen" has been sketched by many an able pen, that her faults and her virtues have been discussed, time and again, by writers of the highest ability, and, in short, that we could have selected no subject more hackneyed than the Elizabethan age. But, though our subject be trite and familiar, and though in its treatment we may even incur the charge of a want of originality, we have chosen it with the desire of expressing to our own satisfaction our views with regard to the institutions, events, and characters of an age the most interesting and the most important in the annals of English history.

In order fully to understand the nature of the institutions of that period, a knowledge of the public and private character of the sovereign seems indispensable; for in that lies the secret of the almost absolute dominion which Elizabeth maintained during her whole reign over her subjects. It is remarkable, that in her character there were many traits seemingly inconsistent with each other. Naturally of an amiable disposition, she was occasionally vindictive and cruel in the extreme. At times gentle and tender, when offended, she not only disregarded entirely the feelings of others, but even forgot her own dignity in acts of passionate rage. Possessing a firmness almost amounting to obstinacy, she was yet strangely fickle-minded. Though apparently open-hearted, and frank in expressing her opinions, when necessity demanded, or policy required, no one knew how better than she to exercise deceit and dissimulation. Haughty and dignified when surrounded by princes and peers, she would smile most graciously when saluted by the loud huzzas of her "*gude people.*" Frugal in the administration of her private as well as the public affairs, no King or Queen of England ever before or since delighted more in pomp and show. Gifted by nature with a capacious intellect, her mind was matured even in early life by an education the best the age afforded. Her peculiar situation in youth, tended especially to develop the powers of her intellect. Uniting the delicate wit, the quick perception, and the good taste of a woman, with the sound sense, the deep penetration, and the correct judgment of a man, she was pre-eminently well qualified for the station she occupied. Yet, as her moral character had its dark and bright sides, so also her mind had its opposite qualities.

With all her capacity, she still had her foibles. Her native good sense was often overpowered by the most whimsical fancies, while her penetration frequently failed to detect the hypocrisy of sycophants, and to prevent herself from becoming the blind dupe of flattery. Her judgment, at times, strove in vain to counteract the impulses of a foolish vanity and still more foolish envy. At one moment in secret council with Cecil respecting the most important affairs of State, the next, she would fly into a passion with a courtier, who dared to enter the presence chamber unarrayed in the appropriate habiliments. At one time communicating with Suffolk respecting the safety of the kingdom, immediately after she would listen demurely to Leicester's declarations of love. Now treating with Ambassadors from the most powerful States of Europe, and now coqueting with Raleigh—now calling into action all the powers of her mind, her energy, and her perseverance to defend her kingdom from the Spanish Armada, and now cursing her waiting maids for improperly adjusting the golden tresses of which she was so vain, her occasional weaknesses appeared in strange contrast with her general firmness of purpose. Nor did she manifest these characteristic failings only in affairs of but little importance. Even in matters of the highest moment would she allow some silly passion to gain the ascendancy over sober reason. Mary, Queen of Scots, without doubt, fell a sacrifice to the envy of her royal cousin. Though the necessity enjoined by policy has been assigned as the immediate cause of her death, yet no one, who is acquainted with the conduct of Elizabeth throughout the whole affair, can with reason deny, that as a malicious envy instigated her at first to detain her as a prisoner, so the same cause ultimately induced her to execute as a criminal her unfortunate kinswoman. The same weak tenderness, mistaken by herself for love, and which was manifested at one time by sighs and blushes, influenced her at another to appoint her favorite Essex to the Lieutenancy of Ireland, a station for which his abilities were by no means suited. Such was Elizabeth—such the strange composition of her character. We may now to better advantage enter upon the inquiry respecting the nature and operations of the English government during her reign.

There have been two apparently conflicting opinions with regard to the nature of her government, each of which has been entertained, and supported by various facts and arguments, by the most eminent historians of modern times. One opinion is that of Hume, who represents the government as an absolute monarchy, differing but little, if at all, in its operations from that of the Turkish empire. The other is the opinion of Hallam, as set forth in his Constitutional History of England, who, while he admits that the power of Elizabeth was apparently unlimited, denies that it was so in reality. Acknowledging that her subjects possessed not the forms, he asserts that they maintained the essence of liberty. While he allows that many acts of oppression were exercised against them, he yet affirms that of their substantial rights they were not deprived. Granting that the royal prerogative was regarded as more sacred than the Constitution, he yet maintains that the Sovereign dared not encroach too much upon the privileges of her subjects. But why is it that two theories (for we may properly consider these opinions as theories) so contradictory, are adopted, both of which are professedly supported by historical facts? Why is it that two writers should entertain views so different with respect to the same actions?—that from the same premises, they should deduce conclusions so widely at variance? The secret, we think, is this: Hume was a zealous advocate of the House of Stuart—Hallam equally zealous in opposition Both were seemingly actuated by party spirit, the one being a Tory, the other a Whig. The former endeavored to prove that the government was tyrannical and absolute under the dominion of the Tudors, in order to justify, in some degree, the oppression which was exercised by the Princes of the Stuart family. The latter has evidently magnified the acts of tyranny on the part of the Stuarts, in order to justify the violent opposition of the Parliaments, and the subsequent Revolution of 1688; and in his efforts to do this more effectually, he has construed differently from him the former various authoritative acts of Elizabeth, and has aimed directly to disprove the idea of her unlimited control over the kingdom. Hume argues that James the First, receiving undiminished the prerogatives of absolute power from Elizabeth, his immediate successors were constantly making concessions to the demands of unreasonable Parliaments. Hallam, asserting that the people possessed a considerable degree of freedom under the Tudors, argues that the Stuarts, attempting to deprive them of this freedom, were resisted and compelled to make the concessions they did.

It can hardly be denied, we think, that both these historians were somewhat influenced by prejudice, although Hallam is regarded, and perhaps justly, as the most impartial writor of English history. Each one was supporting a theory of his own, and it seems reasonable to suppose, that both have in their zeal unconsciously overstepped the proper limits of truth; for it seems hardly possible that either one should be so utterly mistaken, as to make the other wholly correct. Hume's comparison between Elizabeth and the Turkish Sultan, in respect to authority, is evidently erroneous. True, judging from the various exhibitions of her power, it might seem to us, who are in the enjoyment of so much liberty, under the protection of our Constitution, that her authority was confined within no very narrow limits. True, rights which we consider inalienable, were alienated. True, the royal displeasure was often followed by almost immediate death. True, the proclamations of the Sovereign, whatever their nature, however oppressive, assumed as soon as finished the force of law, and the legal statutes might be rendered null by a single exercise of the dispensatory power. True, in consequence of the jurisdiction established through the Courts of the Star Chamber, the High Commission, and the Royal Council, tribunals differing but little from the Spanish Inquisition, any person was liable at any time to be convicted upon the mere suspicion of a crime, without the slightest shadow of evidence. True, by the acts of Conformity and Supremacy, the right to worship God as conscience dictated was denied to her subjects. The press was also restricted; liberty of speech was suppressed; literary cultivation, and improvements in commerce and the arts, were prevented by unreasonable monopolies; in short, freedom, both religious and civil, seemed to be almost wholly extinct. Still, there was much to distinguish between the government of England and that of the Eastern Empire. There was a wide difference between the authority of Elizabeth and that of the Sultan of Turkey. The latter could cause the immediate death of a subject by his mandate alone, without even the mention of his crime, or the least pretence of justice or expediency; in the realm of the former, a legal process must be first instituted, the offense must be stated, and judgment given accordingly. The Englishman suffered the penalty of the *law*—the Turk received sentence at the *will* of a despot.

In England, the statutes of just and equitable Sovereigns were regarded as laws, and the decisions of impartial tribunals, previously given, but still considered as precedents, favorably influenced the administration of justice. While Elizabeth was guided by wise counselors, whom she respected, the Sultan used his Grand Vizier but as a tool to aid him in the execution of his nefarious plans, and he, upon the slightest act of disobedience, paid the penalty with his head. The former could not exercise her authority without the intervention of a Parliament and Council, in which all classes of her subjects were represented; the latter was the sole legislator, the absolute ruler of his dominions. But that which most distinguished the English from the Turkish government, was the privilege which every British subject possessed of a trial by Jury. Though this right was occasionally rendered useless, by the corruption and threatening of the jurors, still, as a general thing, it was available. The mere fact of the existence of a right, thus lying at the foundation of civil liberty, is sufficient to nullify the idea that the authority of Elizabeth was unlimited. But, on the other hand, we think there is evidence sufficient to prove satisfactorily to the unprejudiced mind, that the power of the Sovereigns of the House of Tudor was far greater than that of the Stuarts—that Elizabeth, in the exercise of her authority, greatly exceeded Charles the First. Receiving in full the prerogatives of her tyrannical father, she not only retained these, but assumed powers which Henry had not even claimed.

Of many of her oppressive acts, to which we have alluded above, Charles was not accused even by those who condemned him to death. And no one can affirm that, in any of his measures, he ever transcended the limits of Elizabeth's power. Over her Parliament she exercised almost absolute control. We know of but a single instance of a concession which she made to them—the granting a petition to abolish monopolies; and even this branch of her prerogative, after surrendering it a short time, she soon resumed—while they, not even asserting their acknowledged right to grant supplies only on condition of a redress of grievances, basely yielded on all occasions to oppressions they dared not resist. Elizabeth also claimed as hers the power to determine ecclesiastical regulations, as the supervision of the liturgy, the decision respecting doctrines of faith, and the introduction of forms and ceremonies. To this, the laity, careless of their religious liberty, and the clergy, anxious to retain possession of the revenues which the destruction of the Monasteries, under Henry, had brought to them, submitted in humble obedience. Judging, then, from such and various other exhibitions of her power, we are led to the conclusion, that the government under Elizabeth was monarchy *slightly* limited.

The question here naturally arises, what was the cause of the submission of a powerful people to the will of a single *woman?* Hallam assigns as the cause, their love of the Queen, and confidence in her generous nature. But this, we think, was not the entire cause. We are inclined toward the opinion of Hume, that their obedience was owing not only to their love, but also to their fear of the Queen. The peculiar traits of Elizabeth's character, which we have mentioned, were eminently calculated to inspire both love and fear in her subjects. The same frankness and courageous bearing which had endeared her father, cruel and vindictive as he was, to the people, influenced their feelings still more when exhibited by a woman. Her noble beauty, too, and constant, though often insincere, expressions of regard to their rights, won upon the affections of a people naturally confiding; so that whenever she appeared in public, the air was filled with the hearty acclamations of "God save good Queen Bess." The very faults of her character contributed still farther to increase their affection. The knowledge of her foibles and whims, reminding them that she, like themselves, was human, subject to like passions, increased, rather than diminished, their love. Her caprice and occasional fickle-mindedness, especially manifested in religious matters, tended much toward establishing her popularity. The recollection of her mother, Anne Boleyn, the firm friend of the Reformers, and the advocate of their doctrines, endeared her to her Protestant subjects. The same class, also, having suffered severely from the persecutions of the bloody Mary, remembered with feelings of approbation the conduct of Elizabeth, when immured, even during the period of youth, in the walls of a prison, at the command of her unnatural sister. Before her accession to the throne, she was the favorite of the Protestant party; and having shared with them in the same afflictions, having suffered for the same faith, sympathy strengthened their affections into a sincere and devoted love.

But Elizabeth, it is well known, was not a thorough Protestant. Though she rejected some of the fundamental doctrines of Romanism, she never manifested a hearty belief in the principles of the early Reformers. Her early *education* united her with the Protestants. In later life, she abhorred Romanism because it *was* Romanism, and because she had learned to do so. She despised the authority of the Pope, because it conflicted with her own. Her vanity, her self-love, rather than any religious principle, led her to profess herself favorable to the reformed doctrines. Mary, with all her cruelty, probably had more of real piety than Elizabeth. The former surrendered, voluntarily, the power she might have maintained, to the Pope; the latter refused submission to the professed head of the Church, in order that she herself might be that head—that she herself might exercise supreme authority in ecclesiastical as well as civil affairs. This was the main difference between her religion and Romanism. The forms and ceremonies, and some of the doctrines of the Romish Church, which had been unanimously rejected by the early Reformers, she warmly advocated. The pomp and show of the Catholic worship, gratifying her vanity and love of the magnificent, she introduced into the services of her own chapel. It was this apparent partiality toward the old religion that won the regard of her Catholic subjects, and rendered her a Sovereign almost as acceptable to them as to the Protestants. Indeed, many of them believed that Elizabeth was at heart one of their number. Even now, judging from her actions, it would be a question by no means easy of decision, whether she was a Protestant or Catholic. Thus, her want of firm integrity, her vanity and self-love, acted more powerfully to ensure the good will of a large portion of her subjects, than the most rigid conformity to the rules of right would have done. Such was the relation which Elizabeth bore to her people—loved and respected by both Protestants and Catholics. Doubtless, there were many among the latter class, who would gladly have seen Elizabeth at once deprived of power, even by poison or assassination. But the failure of the conspiracies in which it is supposed Philip of Spain and his emissaries were engaged, and the easy defeat of the plots with which the Queen of Scots was connected, for the deposition of Elizabeth, and the establishment of herself upon the throne, plainly prove that the Catholics, as a body, were faithful and loving subjects.

But love was not the only feeling entertained by the people toward their Queen. There was another, quite as effectual in preserving their fidelity. It was a fear of incurring a displeasure which they knew to be terrible—a kind of dread of a power the extent of which was every day exhibited. The English had not yet recovered from Henry's tyranny. They still remembered the oppression, all attempts to resist which were but vain. They had not yet forgotten the determined energy of his character, the fury of his temper, and the fierceness of his anger. They had not yet forgotten the man, by the single exercise of whose will, institutions, which for centuries had been firmly established, were at once overthrown, and a body of men the most powerful in the kingdom were humbled at his feet. But the power of Elizabeth was even greater than that of her father. From him, too, did she inherit the furious temper, the determined resolution, and the domineering will. Like him, she was vindictive and sometimes cruel. The people were well acquainted with these traits of her character. They knew, also, the powers of her mind—her wisdom in the planning, and ability in the execution of her designs. They feared, therefore, to incur her resentment, to draw forth an exhibition of her violence and her power. They preferred rather to endure oppression peaceably, until a more favorable period, under a weaker Sovereign, might present the means of an effectual resistance. Besides, Elizabeth found a powerful ally in the violence of religious feeling. The Catholics, consisting of about one third of the population, would unite in no undertaking with the main body of the Protestants. Should the latter class rise in rebellion, Elizabeth, by declaring herself of their number, (a thing which she would not hesitate a moment to do in such a crisis,) could instantly command the aid of her Catholic subjects, supported by the French and Spanish powers. Should the former class rebel, the Protestants would immediately flock to her standard, and by their assistance, she might bid defiance to all opposition. Thus, the enmity of religious sects, by giving to her the balance of power, as it were, checked the very spirit of hostility. In the latter part of her reign, when, by several unpopular acts, she had lost, in a measure, the affections of her subjects, when her appearance in public was no longer hailed with acclamations of joy, nothing but the fear of her anger, and the dread of her power, prevented the encroachments of a Parliament which had already manifested uneasiness, to say the least, under her authority. We cannot, therefore, avoid the conclusion, that fear as well as love was a cause of the general submission of her subjects.

Of the events which happened during the reign of Elizabeth, none was more important, when considered in itself, or more momentous, considered in its relations to the subsequent history of England, than the bold manifestation of the true spirit of liberty. We say this was an important event; for though historians have noticed it with but a passing remark, and have regarded it as incidental to other grander movements, it marks, in our opinion, an era in the history of liberty. We have seen the nature of the government, and the condition of the people, under the dominion of the Tudors. We have also seen that, under all their oppressions, the populace had some indistinct notions with regard to a freedom greater than that which they possessed. Indeed, with their increasing intelligence, they manifested a greater desire to maintain and secure more effectually some of their rights. Still, they had no correct ideas of liberty. Their thoughts extended but little farther than to the free enjoyment of certain privileges already established. The common people, from their early education, having imbibed the notion that in no case ought the King to be resisted, a respect, or rather awe, for their Sovereign's person and authority had instilled itself into their minds. Nor were such ideas confined to the lower classes. They prevailed among all ranks of men—among the learned as well as the ignorant, the refined as well as the rude—among philosophers and statesmen, poets and civilians. Writers upon the science of government had inculcated the sentiments, "that the King could do no wrong—that his person was sacred, his authority absolute, and directly of a divine origin." The Eutopia of Moore was considered as a series of visionary speculations, containing the principles of a government which could exist only in the imagination, representations of a freedom which could be conceived of, but never fully realized. But ideas strange and startling began to be advanced. Doubts began to arise in the minds of some, whether the opinions so generally entertained were based upon justice and reason. The doctrine began to be promulgated, novel as it was, that *the people* were endowed with certain rights which no power could justly alienate, and that from them even the King derived in part his authority. But this spirit was confined to the breasts of a few, and those, of a sect persecuted and despised on account of their religious peculiarities. It was first openly manifested by one Peter Wentworth, who, in the House of Commons, in the year 1576, fearlessly advocated the principles of civil liberty. Demanding the privilege of freedom of speech, he boldly complained of the Queen's interference with their legislative proceedings as unlawful, and denied her authority to adjourn meetings of the Parliament.

Such sentiments, as might be expected, startled and alarmed a body of men who had always yielded implicit obedience to the mandate of their Sovereign; and with a spirit of base submission, they sequestered Wentworth from the House, and committed him to prison. But their opposition was vain. He soon regained his seat in Parliament, and with the same vehemence, but with more caution, and, in consequence, greater success, advanced his liberal sentiments. But it was impossible that such principles should gain much ground while Elizabeth wielded the sceptre. It was impossible that the affections of her subjects should be at once alienated—that their fears should be allayed within the period of a few years. It was impossible that a change so vast as the advocates of liberty demanded, should be effected suddenly. Yet the main point had been gained. The *spirit* of freedom had been manifested, and all attempts toward its suppression were useless. The feeling had arisen in the minds of many, which time serves only to strengthen. The great causes were at work, the effects of which were to be visible, not immediately, but subsequently, in the increasing demands of Parliaments, in their gradual encroachments upon the royal prerogative, in the deposition of Charles the First, in the Revolution of 1688, and the final establishment of the English Constitution.

But there is still another point of view, in which the Elizabethan age is to be regarded with interest. We refer to the advancement of literature and learning. Strictly speaking, we might say that the revival of letters did not occur in England until the reign of Elizabeth. Just recovering from the bloody struggle of the two Roses, suffering, even in peace, from the avarice of the Seventh Henry, and the tyranny of the Eighth, the English people were in a condition by no means calculated to advance the progress of mind. Isolated in their situation, they were apart from the influences which were constantly operating upon the inhabitants of the Continent. The Reformation in England had not tended, as in other countries of Europe, to aid directly in the diffusion of knowledge, and a variety of other contingent causes had prevented improvements in Literature and Philosophy. Though the main body of the people were behind those of no other nations in general intelligence, still there had been wanting that attentive cultivation of letters, that intense application in scientific research, which are essential to the improvement of Literature, and the development of new truths in Philosophy. It is true, Henry Eighth, ambitious of excelling in all pursuits, having devoted considerable time in his early years to study, prided himself greatly on his literary attainments; but his information extending little farther than to a knowledge of the writings of Thomas Aquinas and the schoolmen of the middle ages, the productions of his pen were characterized by the most egregious faults and the most palpable absurdities. We are aware, that contemporary with the same Sovereign, there were a few writers of no little merit—writers who are entitled to a station above mediocrity. But if we except Chaucer, there had existed hardly another whom, at the present day, we peruse with pleasure. The style of all was rude, stiff, and uncultivated; and there were but very few who were remarkable either for the originality of their thoughts, or the sublimity of their ideas.

But the sun of Elizabeth dawned upon a different age. Never has there been a day more glorious to English Literature, than that which ushered into existence the immortal William Shakspeare. The brightest ornament of the Elizabethan age, time has served to increase and establish his fame, and he *now* maintains the highest station among poets, and receives, by almost universal consent, the enviable title of the very *first* of dramatic writers. It is needless to expatiate upon his merits. The most talented and the most learned have invariably acknowledged his superiority; and it is probable, that the future, as well as the past and present, will testify to his extraordinary merit, his inimitable excellence. Edmund Spenser, too, was another ornament of that age. The harmony of his numbers, the beauty of his expressions, the richness of his imagination, and the occasional sublimity of his conceptions, evince the highest poetical genius. His Faerie Queen, even now, is read with pleasure, and is justly ranked among the best of English literary productions. We might refer to other writers of that age, who attained to considerable eminence, and did much toward the improvement of literature, but our limits are prescribed. We cannot, however, refrain from briefly alluding to him, whom those best qualified to judge, have pronounced the greatest Philosopher the world has ever produced—Sir Francis Bacon. Gifted with a most capacious intellect, the most retentive and ready memory, the quickest perception, and the soundest judgment, the faculties of Bacon were strengthened and improved by a rigid mental cultivation. The best scholar of his day, he was master of all the learning of the ancients, besides the little the moderns had added to their stock of knowledge. A proficient in science, he by no means neglected literature. He possessed, in a remarkable degree, the rare union of a sound sense and a rich imagination. But

Philosophy was his favorite study. What Shakspeare was to Literature, that was Bacon to Philosophy. It was from his researches in that department of knowledge, that his name has acquired its great celebrity. Rejecting as absurd the systems and theories of the ancients, he scorned the idea that Philosophy should be cultivated merely for its own sake, or only to elevate the feelings and enlarge the faculties of the mind. He saw, also, at a single glance, the errors of the schoolmen, who, by uniting Philosophy with Theology, used it as an instrument to degrade the mind, and to subject it to the domination of superstition. He *himself* invented the true theory. Actuated by benevolence, and influenced by extraordinary good sense, he *himself* first conceived the idea that the great end and object of all Philosophy was the amelioration of the condition of mankind. It is *to* this conception that Science and Art have been indebted in no small measure for their rapid progress. It is *for* this conception that Bacon has ever since been regarded as the benefactor of the whole human race.

Such were the men who flourished in the reign of Elizabeth ; such the characters whose existence has contributed much toward rendering that reign the most glorious in English history. What an assembly must that have been to which Elizabeth had summoned the great scholars and authors of her day ! What a meeting that, in which the greatest poets and philosophers conversed together ! What the brilliancy of that Court, in which Elizabeth presided with royal ease and dignity, in which the sparkling wit of Shakspeare contended for the mastery with the sly humor of Johnson—in which the grave wisdom of Bacon was contrasted with the entertaining vivacity of Raleigh—and in which Sidney, the most accomplished gentleman of his age, the scholar and the soldier, distinguished alike for the graces of his person and the embellishments of his mind, rivaled each one in his own sphere, and of himself added not a little to ornament a scene which, without him, seemed almost complete.

MY CHILDHOOD'S DAYS.

I.

My childhood's days, where have ye flown?
Oh where, ye hours of bliss?
To what far, radiant realm unknown,
Free from the cares of this!
And where are ye, friends of my youth?
Have ye all falsely fled?
No! In your faithfulness and truth
Ye slumber with the dead.

II.

And where, my childhood's home, art thou?
Home of life's happy years;
Thy memory bathes my cheek, e'en now,
With sorrow's gushing tears:
For clustering round that hearth stone still,
As fondly as of yore,
We meet—Ah, no! Sad, lone and chill,
It knows us now no more.

III.

I hear no more my father's voice,
I miss my mother's smile,
That ever made *my* heart rejoice,—
Her own, how sad the while!
She taught my lips their first warm prayer,
Ere yet I learned to roam:—
Where *are* ye now? Oh! tell me where,
Are childhood's friends and home?

IV.

Be still, sad heart! though youth *has* flown,
And comes not back again;
Though friends that thou hast called thine own,
Are in Death's silent reign;—
Look thou *above! There* is thy Home
Of ever-during bliss;
And in that world of pleasures, roam
The loved ones lost from this.

CL.

EDITORS' TABLE.

We presume that by this time, dear reader, you have "marked, learnt, and inwardly digested" the mental banquet which our taste has set before you, and are now come to have a little private chat with your purveyor. Maphap you come in the character of panegyrist, mayhap of censor, or, possibly, your name swells the ranks of the "*don't-know-nor-don't-care-ists.*" Well, come as you will, you are welcome; and the more so, that it is the last chance we may have of offering you any attention, and we would not willingly be styled inhospitable. When we first undertook the Herculean task of editing your Magazine, in the simplicity of our heart, we looked upon every thing as "couleur de rose," and a smile of heavenly complacency settled on our countenance as we stole a furtive glance into futurity. Every thing appeared bright ahead; no shoals, no rocks, but a clear expanse of trackless waters, and "lots of wind" to swell the sails of our gallant craft. But, unfortunately for the correctness of human judgment, our eyes have been a little opened since the month first set in. Why, instead of a broad ocean, there's been nothing but a magnified edition of old Bunyan's slough, and if there haven't been any rocks and sandbars, whereon to go to pieces, there's been something amazingly like 'em. Verily, beloved, after a week's experience, the words of Richard seemed to strike us with unwonted force, and we felt tempted to say with him,

> "If I know how to manage these affairs,
> Thus thrust disorderly upon my hands,
> Never believe me;"

or, to cry with Bertha,

> "O for a draught of power, to steep
> The soul of agony in sleep."

But no such refreshing "drink" coming to hand, we have, in consequence, been obliged to rough it through, trusting to propitious fate, and some natural equanimity, to bear us scathless.

The imaginary vexations always *ex officio* attendant on the Editor, are by no means trifling; but the actual, positive, *five-foot-ten agonies*, that continually assail him, are unendurable. In the first place, he has just so many pages to fill, and exactly as much nothing from which to fill them. He must not only agree to furnish a modicum of nonsense himself, but he must be private tutor to the spoilt brats of everybody else's brain. He must keep his temper with the thermometer at 90°, and at the same time make progress in his vocation. Contributors must be answered with politeness, poor articles must be rejected, and the printers must have *copy*. Now, how, under heaven, can a common man reconcile these opposing necessities, and live? If, therefore, kind subscriber, (*dico pecuniam præ manu persolventibus*,) either the matter or the manner of our little offering be distasteful to thee, we must beg thee to join with us in arraigning both poor health and hot weather, and not any want of desire to please; but if thou wilt still grumble, why, we'll raise the price—we will; so take care.

Notice to Correspondents.—To this important and honorable body, we have three little specimens of advice to give, which, we hope and trust, they will follow. 1. Write your articles, if possible, so that they can be read. 2. Don't fill more than a quire. 3. In all cases, pay the postage. These are hints which we wish you one and all religiously to observe, if you regard the sanity, or even the existence of your Editors. And now we have a word for individuals.

"THOUGHTS ON ORIGINAL SIN."—This is the title of a hieroglyphicised quire of paper, bearing at the extreme end of its 24th page the cabalistic letters, APOL, whether as the commencement of the word *Apollo*, or *Apollyon*, we cannot say—most probably, however, the latter, for no mortal possessing the ordinary feelings of humanity, to say nothing of taste, could have thus tortured himself, with the expectation of torturing his readers also. Up to the reception of this article, we had thought that sin was a very common-place thing; but we must confess, that if there is any originality in it, the writer is certainly entitled to the merit of possessing it. It may gratify him to know that we have wrapped it neatly up, labelled it *highly important*, and placed it between two favorite editions of Thomas Aquinas and Jeremy Taylor—*quiescat in pace*.

THE GAMBLER'S SOLILOQUY is exceedingly graphic, and is worthy of the lips of "Deaf Dan" himself, but is still unfit for the pages of our Magazine. As moral and accountable men, we cannot consent that the intricacies of the trade should be thus unceremoniously laid open to the eyes of susceptible youth, nor can we, as champions of our mother tongue, allow such violations of its purity as are to be found in the outpourings of this bad man's heart. We hope sincerely that experience has not been the writer's master in portraiture, and that he has not felt

"The dear pleasures of the velvet plain,
The painted tablets, dealt and dealt again,"

though the skill displayed excites our liveliest fears.

"THE PROPHECY OF THE RECLUSE." "A Historical Drama, in two Acts." In the production of this dramatic prodigy, the writer has shown some powers worthy of a poet, but some, also, decidedly unworthy. The language is passable, but the construction of the plot evinces the existence of a faculty which its author would, we fear, scarcely claim. His imitative bump is certainly "large"—so large, in fact, that it becomes almost Daguerryan in its workings, in that its productions only want an appearance of life and health to counterfeit the original. Could he gratify our taste by galvanizing this anatomical specimen, and our love of truth, by affixing another name, we might possibly insert it—though we would just hint to the operator the two little lines of the Roman—

"Demens qui nimbos et non imitabile fulmen
Ære et cornipedum pulsu simularat equorum."

Of the other pieces, too numerous to mention, which have been sent us, some will be found in the present number, some, perhaps, in the next, and the remainder have "*stept out*."

Since the above was written, a communication has been presented, which the want of room compels us, very much to our sorrow, to decline. Though destitute of any specific title, it contains so much pleasant information, that our own nomenclative powers should have been exercised in its behalf, had the printer been more liberal of his space; and we would, after a slight change in its dress, have gladly adopted it. As matters stand, however, we can only give you a slight idea of its general character.

It purports to be a sort of critical notice of the Oration and Poem lately delivered by certain members of the Senior Class, though this notice is, in fact, merely an episode to the main subject. Said subject is a historical account of these *productions*, from the first years of our Collegiate Calendar, and is in substance as follows:

It appears that, as early as the foundation of our institution, it was customary for one of the Seniors, at the close of their final examination, to address the Faculty in a Latin speech, which was occasionally responded to by one of this body in English. About a century ago, Dr. Dwight (*then Tutor*) fulfilled this duty, and so much to the satisfaction of all present, that his *response* was printed, and has since been republished. After this, however, though the Latin address was continued, the answer was neglected, until the Presidency of Dr. Dwight, when Josiah Stebbins, Esq. stepped forth, and once more a response was made, applauded, and delivered to the printers. Even this noble example, however, proved ineffectual, and no man was found so hardy as, by following it, to delay for an hour the subsequent exercises, viz.: the making *and drinking* of a huge bowl of punch, a custom long since extinct, "*Et sic transit*," &c. Enraged at such neglect, our Latin widower gave up the ghost, and another creation rose, phœnix-like, from its ashes. The Seniors now procured a room in town, and appointed one of their number to deliver a *poem* to *themselves*. For some time, this plan continued, but so much personal invective, and unmanly satire, was at length employed by the *poet* of the day, that the Faculty anticipated *Councils* in voting it a *nuisance*, and changed the audience to the whole College, the exercises to a well-ordered Oration and Poem, and the scene to the Chapel. Thus far the metamorphosis rendered them like those at present listened to, but there was one difference, viz.: they were not printed. There was, 'tis true, a single exception of a Poem, printed in a number of the Christian Spectator; but, omitting this, until eleven years ago, they were none of them "introduced to the types." In 1833, both the Oration and Poem were published, with a Valedictory Hymn, in beautiful style on letter paper, and copies were given only to the graduating class. The titles are quaint, and appear on the cover in the old Black Letter. They are well worth reading, but our limits forbid their insertion. The gradual change which eleven years has wrought, both in the exterior and interior of these productions, the writer leaves to the imagination of his reader, and passes on to a critical consideration of those lately delivered. He eulogizes the "Poem by C. W. Camp," in such an unbounded manner, that the modesty of this gentleman should offer up thanks for our limited space; and bestows so much qualified censure on the "Oration by O. H. Doolittle," that love of veracity induces us to offer some more, on our own account. His criticism is a lengthy one, and one with which we personally disagree; but as our own judgment has no peculiar title to infallibility, we will deal fairly by you, and tell you to taste and judge for yourselves.

And now that this has given us a little sidelong glance at the reviewer's pen, we feel strongly tempted to handle it ourselves, and exhibit a few critical gyrations radiating round the late Anniversary of the "Yale College Bible Society." Here, as in duty bound, we should laud both speeches, speakers, and *speakees*, to say nothing of the *choir*—to which last, conscious of our small melodious bump, we should bow and say nothing. 'Twas sweet, but

"'Tis past, and all that it has left behind
Is but an echo dwelling on the ear
Of the toy taken fancy."

But out of compassion to all interested, we will tear ourselves from this attractive field, and merely wish that the cause may ever have as able advocates, and "*la belle science*" as tuneful votaries.

READER, do you ever turn over again the pages of the past for instruction, or grateful reflections? If you do, look with me once more at the golden hours which this parting month has ushered into eternity. There are many, very many, scenes of bright and unalloyed pleasure, which they will present to you again. Our social pastimes, our healthful walks or rides, our intellectual recreations, when, book in hand, we have drawn ourselves far from this bustling world; and even our innocent day-dreams, where fancy, bedecked in her Sunday suit, has tripped lightly away over hill and dale, to the melody of a warm and gushing heart; all these are the cherished spots to which memory retreats with delight. From the blended mass of good and ill which has fallen to our lot, time has distilled the base alloy, and has left the pure gold, looking even brighter in the distance. Our feelings are none too refined to look back with pleasure to the Glorious Fourth, redolent with the fumes of departed gunpowder, and to its crowd of joyous and smiling faces, and our sympathies, our affections, our kindlier feelings, all draw new vigor from its retrospect of happiness and content. But life is not all joy, and—even we—are not exempted from our share in grief. No, the cup of sorrow, too, has been tasted, and our cheeks are blanched, our voices hushed, and a wave of feeling swells upon the heart, as we remember that it has seen one more of our little band laid in his narrow bed. In the very midst of life and youth, the skeleton hand has been seen, and our tears are ineffectual to erase its writing. But a few days ago, and BURNAP was in our midst, and now the clod of the valley rests upon his youthful head. But a few days ago, and a heart warm with generous feelings, and buoyant with hope, beat in unison with our own, and now, its pulsations have ceased for ever. He whose merry laugh even yet rings in our ears, has gone to that land "where no work may be done," and the blast of the Archangel alone can wake his Lethean slumbers. The beauties of earth, its sorrows and its joys, are now to him as though they never were; and from the fresh earth of his grave comes a voice to us, saying, "Thou too art mortal."

> "Dust to its narrow house beneath,
> Soul to its place on high,"

has been uttered in our midst, and the Sophomore Class have made their first offering to "dust and the worm." We weep—'tis right that we should; but not as "those without hope." There is a place where all may look for consolation, and even we may find, with poetic Keble, that

> "'Tis sweet, as year by year we lose
> Friends out of sight, by faith to muse
> How grows in Paradise our store."

True, it is hard to look with a feeling even of resignation upon the sacrifice of one so tightly bound to us. Philosophy may exert its petrifying power upon the heart, and reason and conscience may whisper that all is for the best, but no resistance can ever quell the bubbling fountains of the soul. The effacing hand of time must be laid upon us ere the recollection will cease to retain the impressions of sorrow to which death ever gives birth, and ere the spirit of individual anxiety, and the burning thoughts which fly beyond this world to the one on high, can be laid in their quiet graves. Till then, the world may roll on in its changeless course—the accustomed voice of old acquaintanceship may strike with its wonted music on the ear—bud and blossom may load the air with their fragrance, and then fall to the earth in the unvarying round of the seasons, but a gloom will still hang over the landscape. One place will still be vacant in the hallowed circle—one voice will still be silent in its tuneful band, and the tear of affection will still be dropped at the grave of the early dead.

"Tears for the sorrowful freely be shed—
Tears for the sorrowful, tears for the dead."

We have thus brought thee, whosoever thou art that readest, almost to the termination of our number; and as it is a good, though somewhat homely maxim, which charges us not to criticise the bridge that carries us safely over, we would recommend the same silent gratitude to thee. We are acquainted with the sentence, "Whatsoever thy hand findeth to do, do it with thy might," but we nowhere recollect any such injunction as regards the tongue, and the lovers of quiet must rejoice over the omission. Read, reflect, meditate—let thy soul commune with itself in "*spirit whispers*," but let not the organ of sense intrude its unsanctified presence amid thy thoughts. Do this and it shall be well with thee; or, in language perhaps better understood, we will wish thee all prosperity in the scenes of thine approaching peril. Who can say what changes a fortnight may produce? Ah, who! Tremble, thou invalid, and shake in thy shoes, thou of absent habits, for the day of retribution is at hand. Tears and lamentations will not avail. We pity thee—we sympathize with thee—(*cease thine irreverent smile*)—we wish thee good luck; but farther than that, our power extendeth not.

One word more, and we have done—and the word is to those only whom it may concern. A week has flown by since we were promised the inspection of a little treasure which, thus far, our eyes have not seen. In the silent hours of the night, as we have tossed upon a sleepless couch, it has presented itself to our excited fancy, and has appeared in a splendor that reality could scarcely equal. We had hoped, too, that from its jewels might be gathered a few wherewith to encircle the neck of our own little bantam, and this was a prospect which we cherished with delight; but, alas, we were deceived—and the poet spoke truly when he said,

"When our sails
Are filled with happiest winds, then most we need
Some heaviness to ballast us."

Friend, knowest thou aught of any "*Red Book?*"

[illegible]

[illegible] PHILOSOPHY [illegible] ASTRONOMY

YALE COLLEGE.

Denison Olmsted

Eng.d for the Yale Literary Magazine

THE

YALE LITERARY MAGAZINE.

Vol. IX. AUGUST, 1844. No. 9.

BIOGRAPHICAL NOTICE OF PROFESSOR OLMSTED.

Denison Olmsted was born at East Hartford, June 18th, 1791. His ancestors were among the first settlers of the City of Hartford, having emigrated from the County of Essex, in England. His father was a respectable farmer, of moderate, though competent fortune, but was cut off in the meridian of life, when this his third son was only a year old.

The days of childhood were divided between the village school and the labors of the farm, to which he was very early trained. At the age of thirteen, he was placed in a country store, to be educated to the profession of a merchant; but, at his own solicitation, he was permitted, at sixteen, to exchange the life of a clerk for that of a student. He entered Yale College in 1809, and graduated in 1813. The two following years were passed in New London, in the instruction of Union School, a select Academy for boys. In 1815, he returned to College, and discharged the office of tutor the two succeeding years, pursuing at the same time the study of Theology, under the instruction of President Dwight. In 1817, he received and accepted the appointment of Professor of Chemistry in the University of North Carolina—entering upon the duties of the office near the close of the year 1818, having occupied the interval in the Laboratory of Yale College, as a private pupil of Professor Silliman.

In this situation, he spent the seven years following, during which time he commenced, under the patronage of the Legislature, a Geological Survey of North Carolina—an enterprise peculiarly worthy of note, as being the first attempt of the kind ever made in our country. He published the first scientific account of the Gold Mines of North Carolina, and made and published some original Experiments on the Illuminating Gas from cotton seed, a new and copious source of light which, it is believed, will one day come into extensive use in the manufacture of Gas Lights.

In 1825, on the decease of Professor Dutton, Mr. Olmsted was elected to the Professorship of Mathematics and Natural Philosophy in Yale College, since changed to that of Natural Philosophy and Astronomy, which station he still occupies.

Professor Olmsted's career as an author began, in 1817, with the publication, in the New Haven Religious Intelligencer, of a series of Essays, entitled, "Thoughts on the Clerical Profession." The same year, he prepared a Memoir of President Dwight for the Philadelphia "Portfolio." In 1824 and 5, he furnished the papers, above mentioned, "On the Gold Mines of N. C." and on the "Illuminating Gas," &c. for the American Journal of Science. Since that time, he has been a frequent contributor to that able and valuable Quarterly. He has also furnished for it, as well as for the Christian Spectator, the American Quarterly Register, and the New Englander, several Reviews and Biographical Sketches.

His Introduction to Natural Philosophy, 2 vols. 8vo., was published in 1831, and the Introduction to Astronomy, 1 vol. 8vo., in 1839. The substance of the latter was given to the public, in 1840, in a handsome 12mo., in the popular and attractive form of a series of Letters, addressed to a Lady. His last Work, if we except the articles in the Quarterly Register and New Englander, and a small Work, entitled, "Rudiments of Natural Philosophy and Astronomy," published during the past year, was the Life and Writings of his gifted and lamented pupil and friend, Ebenezer Porter Mason—a name which bade so fair to be one of the brightest stars in the sky of that science, which both so deeply and so passionately loved.

The accompanying Portrait of the Professor is in Mr. Hinman's best style, and is pronounced, by good judges, a most faithful and admirable likeness.

TOWNSEND PREMIUM.

A NEW era in the Literary Character of our Institution has, we confidently believe, commenced with the establishment of the Townsend Premium. In stout, manly intellect, in acute, analytic discrimination, in clear, sound judgment, in a pure, elevated taste, in energy and activity of mind, Yale has acknowledged no superior, and but one rival, in America. We are sorry we cannot say as much for purity, beauty, and classic elegance of style. The above fact inspires us with the pleasing hope, that not many College generations will pass away before this may be said with truth and with pride.

"Considerations received to my full satisfaction," as he modestly calls it—gratitude, and the warm, filial affection of a generous heart, we will say—has prompted a worthy and honored son, ISAAC H. TOWNSEND, Esq., of this city, of the Class of 1822, to institute a fund for the promotion of this important end,—"to encourage the study of our National language." We know not how he could with the same sum more substantially benefit his Alma Mater. He deserves, and will, we are sure, receive the benedictions of every true friend of our age-honored Institution, and of an American National Literature. It remains now for the members of College to do their duty in the matter. If each Class at their entrance upon the labors—or shall we say the leisure—of Senior year, when their studies are so much under their own control, would devote more time to English Composition, only a few, of course, could *receive* the honors, but all would both greatly benefit themselves, and *confer* honor upon the University, by elevating it to its true rank in the department of Rhetoric and Belles-Lettres.

We devote, as will be seen, the greater part of this number to the five Prize Essays, the first fruits of this Fund. They were read by their respective authors, in the College Chapel, before a large and intelligent audience, on Wednesday, June 5th, a day which thus henceforth becomes one of the grand gala days of College. They will speak for themselves.

By special request, for the convenience of future reference, and as a proper introduction to the Essays, we prefix a true copy of the Instrument containing the grant, with its acceptance by the College.

Whereas, ISAAC H. TOWNSEND, of the City and County of New Haven, in the State of Connecticut, has executed and delivered to the Corporation of "The President and Fellows of Yale College in New Haven," a certain instrument bearing date the 10th day of August, A. D. 1843, in the words and figures following, to wit:—

"*To all People to whom these Presents shall come*—GREETING.

"KNOW YE, That I, ISAAC H. TOWNSEND, of the City and County of New Haven, in the State of Connecticut, from my regard for Yale College, and my desire further to encourage the study of our national language in that important institution, and for the consideration of ten dollars, and other considerations, received to my full satisfaction of the Corporation of 'The President and Fellows of Yale College in

New Haven,' do hereby give, grant, transfer, and deliver, to the said Corporation, one thousand dollars ($1,000) in money.

"To have and to hold the premises, with all appurtenances, unto the said Corporation and its successors and assigns for ever, for the objects and purposes following, that is to say:

"*First.* The said Corporation shall make loans of the said money in such sums and on such terms as it shall deem expedient; each loan to be evidenced by a note or bond in favor of the said Corporation, and every note and bond to be secured by a mortgage of unincumbered real estate in the State of Connecticut, of double the value of the amount of the note or bond secured thereon:—with liberty to vary, transpose, and exchange loans from time to time, at the discretion of the said Corporation or its agents, for other loans, of the description and security aforesaid; and with power to receive and collect, from time to time, the interests and profits of all the loans aforesaid.

"*Second.* The said Corporation shall annually pay out the interests and profits of the loans aforesaid, in five (5) premiums, of twelve dollars ($12) each, to the authors in the Senior Class of the best original compositions in the English language. The subjects for the said compositions shall be proposed, from time to time, soon after the beginning of each academical year; and all the members of the Senior Class in the said College, for the time being, shall have liberty to write for the premiums. The subjects shall be selected by the Faculty of the College, unless, in any year or years, the Faculty shall consider it expedient to refer to each student the selection of his own subject. The premiums shall be awarded by the Faculty, or by a committee designated by the Faculty for the purpose. No discrimination shall be made among the compositions to which premiums shall be awarded. All compositions receiving premiums shall be read in public, at a meeting of the members of the College, and, as far as practicable, by their respective authors; and shall then be preserved among the papers of the College.

"*Third.* The said Corporation shall be responsible for the safe keeping and correct management of the fund aforesaid, and shall make good each and every deficiency or loss that it may sustain, either of principal or income; so that there shall be a full and permanent principal of one thousand dollars, and so that the sum of sixty dollars shall be regularly applied each year as aforesaid, under all circumstances whatever.

"In witness whereof, I have hereunto placed my hand and seal, at the city of New Haven, this 10th day of August, A. D. 1843.

ISAAC H. TOWNSEND." [L. S.]

And whereas the said Isaac H. Townsend, in connection with the delivery of the instrument aforesaid, has paid to the corporation aforesaid the said sum of one thousand dollars mentioned in the said instrument, upon and for the objects and purposes in the said instrument fully and at large expressed:

Now THEREFORE KNOW ALL MEN BY THESE PRESENTS, That we, "The President and Fellows of Yale College in New Haven," the Corporation named in the instrument aforesaid, have accepted and received, and hereby do accept and receive the said instrument, and the said sum of money therein mentioned:—and we do hereby covenant and agree with the said Isaac H. Townsend, and his heirs, executors and administrators, that we and our successors shall and will, at all times and forever, fully and faithfully keep, observe and perform all the terms and provisions of the instrument aforesaid, by us or our successors to be kept, observed or performed, according to the true intent and meaning of the said instrument.

And we hereby direct that this instrument, when executed, be recorded upon the records of this Corporation, and then delivered to the said Isaac H. Townsend.

In witness whereof, we, the said Corporation, at the City of New Haven, on this 17th day of August, A. D. 1843, have hereunto placed our corporate seal and the signature of our President.

[Seal of Yale College.] JEREMIAH DAY, *President.*

New Haven, August 17th, 1843.

TOWNSEND PRIZE ESSAYS.

THE TRUE AIMS OF LIFE.

BY EZEKIEL P. BELDEN, NEW HAVEN.

One of the most obvious and curious errors of life, and especially of American life, is the inadequate value attached to the present—the immoderate outlay for results several years hence—and the narrow use made of *to-day*. The causes of this error are several. The utter vanity of the passing hour, except for repentance, is one of the themes overpreached, if it may be said without irreverence, from the pulpit. The hollowness of present pleasure, and aspirations after something unattained, are the diseased iteration and burthen of poetry. The paramount importance of forecast, accumulation, and exclusive devotion to present care, for future leisure and ease, is the engrossing drift of all maxims of business. To these causes may be added, the necessity weighing upon a man of making position for himself, in a country where there is no inheritance but of money or land, where a father's consequence and honors are of little value to the son, and the urgent habit engendered by this of expending the whole strength, mental and physical, on worldly prosperity. If we may illustrate it by an humble figure, the vehicle which an American builds to conduct him to fortune is complete when the wheels are put together. Rather than wait for the building of the carriage body, he drives through life standing uncomfortably on the axle.

Reference is not had, in these remarks, to personal comforts abandoned, or to pleasures or luxuries set aside for business. The value, even of these, might be worth ascertaining, and a passing estimate is, probably, put on them by all who forego them. We speak of the neglects of character. We speak of sands which run through the glass of the present hour and are never turned back. A book written hastily, may be revised and improved. A picture sketched in outline, may be retouched and colored to the fancy. A strange land traveled through in haste, may be returned to at leisure and studied with better profit. But the steps of life, the opportunities of each successive hour, are fatally irrevocable; and our present object is partly to show what those opportunities are, and, if thus lost, how irreparable.

It is extraordinary how, in following out trains of thought on all moral subjects, we find the best precepts in Scripture; and in the parable of "*the talents*," it seems to us, lies the true instruction on this subject. Talents of gold and silver are among the least valuable of the dowries which God has provided for his children in this world. Whatever gives one human being influence over another, whatever is of the nature of power, is a trust which he that gathers us into families, puts into the hands of individuals for the common good.

Some minds are originally constituted of such strength as to be able to sway others; and this command over the judgments and persuasions of mankind is of all talents the most important, and, according to the manner in which it is employed, most productive of good or evil. Hence, common usage has nearly confined the use of the word *talents* to this one species of power. A *mastery in language* is another gift, by which some men are enabled to lead others, and that, oftentimes, without any distinguished mental powers. Nay, so formed are mankind *to be influenced* where they *cannot influence*, to take the impression of other minds where they cannot communicate the image of their own, that the sweet and graceful utterance of even common and borrowed thoughts, carries men's convictions and feelings along with it more successfully than the strongest intellect and the best language, unaided by the charms of the voice.

The relations in which we stand to each other in society open other sources of influence by which we are reciprocally affected and moved. The *master's superiority* causes his example and advice to come with weight to a servant. The *parent* has for many years an absolute control over his child. A *family name* is sometimes of power in a community; and *certain professions* command public respect. But, not to enlarge upon particulars, powers of one kind or other are distributed over the whole face of society; and he that has a friend to whom he is dear, a neighbor to whom he is useful, or a fellow creature whose condition he may render better or worse by looks, speeches, or actions, has a talent which he may either improve, or neglect, or abuse, and upon the use of which depend his true character and future condition.

Fluctuating as all the individual component parts of society are, it is a manifest proof of a superintending Providence, that the variety and relative fitness of its members are uniformly preserved. We could not fix upon any individual child as fit for this or that station, or profession, or calling; but we should be warranted by experience in pronouncing that, in the present generation of children, there will be found every power, and all the skill that society needs, or has ever called into exercise. *No known talent has wholly failed.* Some powers, as in poetry, painting, and sculpture, are wholly individual—they cannot be communicated from one to another—they grow and die with the possessors; yet, in civilized and highly cultivated society, there is never an extreme dearth of these powers—they appear to be generally adequate to the necessity which there is for them. Like some of the most beautiful and fragrant flowers, they cannot be raised from their own seed, but may be safely reckoned upon here and there amongst more common plants.

Such is the care of the great Arbiter of human life, that, while there is a sufficient uniformity in human nature to give the race a kindred feeling for each other, there shall be a sufficient diversity to distinguish individuals, to make them mutually serviceable, and to strengthen the common sympathy of nature by a sense of self-interest. And yet, there are those who would war against the very principle of creation, and, while our Maker displays his perfection in the regular variety, the boundless but proportionate differences in his creatures, would bend the puny force of human laws to compel a uniformity of faith, a uniformity of mind. Vain and senseless bigotry! which would strike out of nature all but one form, one color!—which would extinguish the eye in the body, and have all head or all arm!—which would amputate all of the mind but one common, one low branch of thought!

The talents of various kinds which Providence allots to mankind, are so many capacities of virtue. It might, indeed, as well be said, that they are means of individual improvement and happiness; but we state it thus, because it may be proved that, as society is constituted, no individual can improve himself who does not contribute to the advancement of society, and that no one can be truly and permanently happy who is not, according to his measure, doing good to his fellow creatures. The converse of the latter proposition is equally clear, namely, that no one can entirely want happiness whose life is beneficial to mankind. And the reason of both propositions will be found to be, that virtue, however defined or explained, is nothing else than that course of conduct which is, upon the whole, most for the advantage of the agent, considered in connection with other beings.

Every talent may be reckoned a capacity of virtue, because, in the suitable exercise of it, social good is the sure result. No one is born with a talent for mischief. Any power may be perverted to evil; but as we judge of the use and design of a machine, not from its irregularities and accidental miscarriages, but from its general operation and tendency, so we must estimate the action of that busy creature man, from its more ordinary, which is its more easy and natural course. A talent ill-employed may seem, on a superficial glance, sometimes advantageous to its possessor; but no one can doubt whether it would not be better for him, on the whole, and always better for him as a social being, that it should be employed well. Providence has decided the question by ordaining that the human powers should wear best and longest in a train of virtuous exercise; an evil affection may act for the moment as a powerful stimulant, but in proportion as it quickens, it corrodes and enfeebles the faculties.

It is not necessary, to constitute a virtuous action, that he who performs it should, at the moment, weigh all its tendencies, and perceive clearly its moral qualities. It is sufficient that he is obeying a habit formed and continued under a general sense of its rectitude. The most common deeds of our lives may, therefore, be among the most virtuous, as they are certainly those which affect most intimately the peace and comfort of our families and neighborhood. He that uses the lowest talent invariably for the good of society, is so far a virtuous man; and the daily laborer, who can scarcely tell what virtue means, may, in the tenor of his humble life, be heaping up, by his industry, a treasure of virtue against that day when every man shall be rewarded according to his deeds.

In nothing are the wisdom and goodness of Providence more apparent, than in the *variety of talents* allotted to mankind, and in the stin lants to *every man's cultivation of his own*, as his true aims of life. S ciety is a beautiful body, but its beauty is not in the perfection of eye or the hand only, but in every limb, nerve, and feature, every ma peculiar talent, whatever it be, brought to its fullest perfection. A to our mind, the *discovery of what we are capable of*, and the *developm of these capabilities*, are the *true aims of our present existence!*

THE NEW ENGLAND CHARACTER.

BY ORRIS S. FERRY, BETHEL, CONN.

New England, in point of political importance, occupies an emin station among the great divisions of this country.

Its invigorating climate, its variety of soil and production, its ma fold facilities for internal communication, and its extensive line of s coast, present the most powerful incitements to industry and the m abundant sources of wealth.

Neither have these natural advantages remained unimproved. T thriving villages and busy cities, the wide-spread commerce, the hap governments, and general prosperity of the six Eastern States, affo at once, the simplest explanation of their influence, and the highest comium upon the character of their people.

Yet, by some strange perversity of feeling or judgment, unfavora notions respecting the men, the habits, and the customs existing he are extremely prevalent in other portions of this Union. Prejudic engendered by sectional jealousy, and nourished by limited inte gence or observation, have been fostered by the skill of the mounteba and the wit of the author, till they have grown to formidable dimensio and acquired almost invincible strength. To oppose these sentime with a citation of facts, or an array of argument, would be a hopel task—for against such prepossessions, the testimony of the senses a the dictates of reason are equally unavailing. It is not our intenti therefore, to discuss opinions or combat misconceptions, but, as clea as possible, to express what we conceive to be the truth.

We have said that the present condition of the Eastern States affo the highest encomium upon the character of their inhabitants. W make this assertion, because we believe that no country, or section country, can attain and preserve a station of exalted prosperity, unl its people possess great moral and intellectual qualities. To exhibit development of these qualities in the New England character, a their happy influence upon the community, is the object of the pres essay.

The leading trait in this character is religious principle. Not a mere ceremonial morality, but a genuine Christian influence breathes throughout all the land. We do not affirm that vice has no existence here—human nature is incapable of perfection; but we are not aware of any species of crime which is *popular* in New England.

The sympathies of society are on the side of truth and rectitude; public opinion is based on the Word of God, and he that would despise the one must defy the other. The religious principle of these States is not mere bigotry, or blind sectarianism. The spirit is alike in all denominations. Its kindly influence extends to the fallen and degraded, wherever they may be found, under whatever banner they may have enlisted. While it condemns and avoids guilt, it pities the offender. It is a merciful as well as an upright judge. Active at home, it also looks abroad for fields of labor. It sends the Missionary to the remote isles of the sea, and widens at the same time the domains of Christianity and civilization. It is neither cold formality or rigid austerity. It heightens the innocent pleasures of youth, and alleviates the toils of manhood—renders yet holier the sweet ties of domestic life—gives to old age tranquillity, and makes the grave but the portal to another and a better world. Friendship, love, all the gentler and purer affections of our nature are strengthened and ennobled by its influence. In the fierceness of party conflict, it is not forgotten; and political excitement hath never taught the people of New England to neglect to meet in a common temple, to bow before a common altar, and to worship a common God. It is no new thing under the sun; it was transmitted to us from the first civilized men who trod these shores. Time has proved its value. Neither is it destined speedily to pass away. Its bonds are soft as silk, but strong as iron. It is hallowed by reminiscences of bygone days—by the recollections of childhood, and the cherished sentiments of maturer years. In the family circle, and by the family altar, it hath fixed its abode; and so long as men look back with loving remembrance and fond regret to their early life, its power will not diminish. Its symbols are the ministers and the house of God; and its voice is heard in the sound of Church bells, which each seventh day echo from every mountain and ring through every valley in the land. It speaks, also, from the very soil which our fathers tilled, and from the pleasant places where they first planted the ensign of civilization. It is engraven on the hearts of the people.

Wherever the true spirit of Christianity prevails, men speedily become well informed. Knowledge is the handmaid of religion. Hence, arises the general intelligence which prevails throughout New England. The early settlers of these States loved education, because they loved the Bible. That their posterity should retain their faith inviolate, both in principle and action, was the wish nearest to their hearts; secondary, and subservient to this, was their earnest desire for the diffusion of knowledge.

They labored alike to promote both these objects. "Side by side they erected the school-house and the house of God." Their example has survived them, and its power has not ceased to be felt among their descendants. In the forests of Maine, among the mountains of New Hampshire and Vermont, along the pleasant valley of the Connecticut, everywhere, the fountains of wisdom are opened, and all who thirst may drink thereat. Hundreds yearly go forth from our colleges, thousands from our academies, and tens of thousands from our village schools. The poorest receive instruction as well as the richest; the farmer is not doomed to toil in ignorance, and the mechanic is often as well informed as the professional man.

The people of New England are frequently charged with undue inquisitiveness, but we are not satisfied as to the grounds of the accusation. That they love knowledge, and are not backward in seeking it, we freely grant. Truth will not reveal herself without application and inquiry. Save us from the man who asks no questions! He must remain stationary, while his neighbors advance, and before manhood has passed, he is a generation behind the age. He does little for himself—nothing for the world. His existence is a blank. A nation of such men could never rise in the scale of civilization. Science could have no attractions for them, art no allurements, literature no charms. Beauty could excite no admiration in their bosoms, sublimity no awe, power no reverence; the sum of their attainments would be to live, to eat, to sleep, and at last to die, unimproving and unimproved. It would be as if they alighted on the earth, looked at it for a moment with a gaze of stupid wonder, and then vanished into "Hades and thick night." Such, we are grateful, is *not* the condition of the New England people. Possessing much information, they have learned its value, and desire its increase. They are not ashamed to ask for it—they are not unwilling to impart it freely to others.

Knowledge is not considered as a treasure, to be hoarded up and enjoyed by a few privileged individuals, but as the common property of all. The law of the land hath provided that there shall be no monopoly in this commodity—hath given to all men an equal share in its benefits. Instruction is obtained by many different methods: from the seminaries of learning, from the public lecturer, and through the common medium of books. Reading is a universal habit. By it, the youthful imagination is excited, the cares of riper years are alleviated, and the listlessness of old age dissipated. We have seen a New England farmer, after his daily toil was ended, sit down by his fireside to peruse the histories of Robertson or Gibbon; we have seen a New England mechanic return from the workshop, and, for a while, forget his labors in contemplation of the great creations of Shakspeare or Milton.

As the inhabitants of the Eastern States are a religious and intelligent people, we should expect to find among them a spirit of free obedience to the just authority of law. Men possessed of the two great characteristics which we have described, are neither calculated to endure the caprice of arbitrary power, or to rush into the mad vortex of anarchy and civil confusion. They would be likely to be, at the same time, independent and well governed. Independent, because they would know their rights, and consider it a sacred duty to themselves and their posterity to maintain them; well governed, because they could appreciate the value of social order, and understood that to labor for its preservation, is in conformity with the will of God. And such we find to be the condition of things in New England. There is no country on earth where people are more jealous of their liberties—none where the proper restrictions of a free government meet with a more ready or cheerful submission. To the honest and upright, the bonds of the law are almost invisible. The husbandman views his meadows and grain fields, assured that the rewards of his labor are secured to him, but forgetting that he owes that security to the strong arm of the law. The scholar in his study, or the merchant at his desk, fears no violence, no injury of life or limb, but they seldom remember that it is the law which provides for the safety of their property and themselves. The greatest blessings are often the least observed. The restraints of law, which to the well-meaning are thus invisible as threads of gossamer, become to the guilty fetters of triple steel, curbing their evil passions, and frustrating their iniquitous schemes. Hence, for this latter class of men, New England affords no refuge; they are glad to flee beyond its limits, beyond the reach of its institutions—while the former possess its territories in peace, and enjoy its kindly protection.

The Eastern States have long been distinguished, above other portions of this Union, for the industry and enterprise of their inhabitants. We need not dwell at length upon these traits of character. Their effects are seen in a land rescued from barbarism, and, in the short space of two centuries, raised to an equality with the most enlightened nations of the earth; in barren wastes converted into fertile plains; in pleasant villages springing up and attaining to wealth and influence within the memory of a single generation; in the hum of busy cities, rising toward heaven from places where, a little while ago, no sound disturbed the silence of the primeval forest; in a commerce which visits the remotest lands, and explores every sea; in the cultivation of our western wilds, and in the diffusion of civilization and Christianity among the savage and idolatrous nations of the globe; at home and abroad—in the happiness of the family circle, in the peace of the community, in the prosperity of our country. It is natural that industry should prevail here—religion, intelligence, the welfare of society, all demand it; and if we have correctly ascribed these latter traits to the New England character, we do not well see how the former could be wanting. Enterprise serves as its pioneer—seeking out those places where its power can be most effectually applied—guiding navigation across unknown waters, and sustaining the hardy emigrant through a life of danger and privation.

Frugality is a necessary attendant to successful industry, and, hence, a prominent characteristic of New England. This last trait has been made the ground of a charge of penuriousness, as we think, most unjustly. If it be liberality to waste the products of labor in luxury or extravagance—to squander money upon wild and fanciful schemes—to lavish treasures indiscriminately upon every object, good, bad, or indifferent—then, we confess, the inhabitants of the Eastern States may not boast of it. But if, on the contrary, it be evidence of really enlarged views, to appropriate princely revenues for the support of education—to build houses of refuge for the sick, the speechless, the blind, for the unfortunate and afflicted of every description—to send the herald of the Cross to every part of the earth—then may New England be justly proud of what she has done, and is now doing. There is such a thing as mistaken generosity, which entangles its unhappy possessor in the mazes of popular applause, and consigns him, at last, to beggary and an unhonored grave. We desire no such attribute—we prefer that frugality which is the offspring of industry, and the parent of true munificence.

No class of men could possess the qualities which we have enumerated and, at the same time, be devoid of honesty. Fair dealing is essential to a long course of successful enterprise. Individuals soon learn upon whom they can rely, and they will trust no other. Hence, we consider the prosperity of the people of these States as additional evidence of their integrity. Let those who would accuse us of unjust exaction, or unrighteous bargaining, ask themselves where is the proof of this. They will await an answer in vain. It is a charge originated and promulgated by persons of the same stamp as a distinguished individual who lately visited this portion of our country, and after being received with the most unbounded hospitality, departed to assure the world that our ancient laws, in his estimation, had neither given us more enlarged views, or rendered us more upright in our dealings. The old adage, "Honesty is the best policy," is well understood here; and we know of no country where the transactions of life are regulated more in conformity with its spirit.

We might enlarge upon the traits of New England character—its cool, calculating sagacity—its fervent patriotism—its unwavering courage and indomitable energy; but our limited space forbids the undertaking. We think that we have already written enough to show the absurdity of many common prejudices, to remove some hasty misconceptions, and to give, at least, a partial insight into the nature of our subject. That the qualities which we have enumerated *are* such as would naturally lead to exalted prosperity, all, we believe, will readily grant. That they are rightly ascribed to the people of these Eastern States, daily experience will abundantly testify. We may have spoken somewhat too favorably, for we were born upon the soil of New England, and bred beneath its skies; and we have learned to honor its customs, to admire its institutions, and to love even its rugged exterior. But it needs no friend to write its praises. By its own merits, it well can afford to stand or fall. Its sons have done much for the cause of virtue and knowledge—much for themselves—much for our whole country—much for the world; and the gratitude which is felt toward them has become a cherished sentiment, which posterity "will not willingly let die."

THE PERMANENCY OF MODERN SOCIETY.

BY EDWARD A. RAYMOND, CANANDAIGUA, N. Y.

ALTHOUGH no one may reasonably doubt the continuance of the present state of society, or see any causes for its retrogression, yet, from the very nature of the case, we cannot *assert* its permanency. Change and progress have been, and still are, its watchwords. But the history of the past exhibits impediments, interruptions, and even cessations with which it has met, and we know not but that causes, arising in some way out of its now existing constitution, *may* produce revolution and overthrow. By reviewing some parts of its past progress, and noticing some of the principal causes which have entered into its fluctuations, we shall be the better able to judge of its present foundations, and of their stability; and in doing so, we will take the case of those two States that appear in the best light of any of antiquity.

The first is the Grecian, which presents many of those great characteristics that distinguish enlightened society. To whatever causes it may be owing, we revert to this as the chosen field, upon which learning, eloquence, and the elevated and generous sentiments of human nature first displayed themselves. It has been hallowed by the mightiest and noblest exertions of intellect and imagination, and by the perfect creations of genius and art. In all *these*, it has proved itself the *Alma Mater* of the world. But, while the national character of her sons thus constituted Greece the radiating point of intellectual and political superiority, there were elementary defects in her social organization, for which there was no remedy but their entire removal, and which arose as the offspring of a false religion and false philosophy. To us who, in this day, are indebted for our knowledge on this subject to *revealed realities*, it may be a matter of surprise, that a nation preeminent for mental vigor and penetration, should have been thus trammeled, and that a tissue of fabrications, originating in the base superstition of their predecessors, or in the creative imaginations of their own poets, should have received popular credence for so long a time. But such was the fact, and the great attempt to change it, resulted in the death of the reformer; and is the expediency or necessity of having moral principle the basis of society a problem for us to solve now? The varied experience of the world leaves this no longer a bare theory. But a brief inquiry as to what society is, and the reason of its formation, may not be here inappropriate. Evidently it grew out of the fundamental constitution of human nature, and is an association of individuals, relinquishing their natural rights as *individuals*, and henceforth possessing interests and rights to a certain extent common and equal. And it was *politically* organized to meet the necessities arising out of its own corruptions. Hence, its organization, having this object in view, must be formed upon moral principles—in no other way can the need be supplied by counteracting influences. But such being the express and sole design of all the various forms in which society has ever existed, to have incorporated into them no system of morality at all, or a false system, is just so far thwarting that design. "No other proof than the numerous, full, and explicit declarations of the ancients themselves is needed, to show a frightful extent of moral corruption among the Greeks," and that this arose from the spirit of their religion, and from peculiar Hellenic institutions. With all this was intimately associated most of their philosophy. Its advocates, with a few worthy exceptions, were involved in the same errors as the people at large. In the words of another, "Instead of observation and experiments, they satisfied themselves with constructing *theories;* and these wanting fact for their basis, have only served to perplex the understanding, and to retard equally the advancement of sound morality and the progress of useful knowledge." Such a union of false religion and philosophy could not produce other effects than it did; and society, in its individual and collective capacity, deeply *felt* them. Here was a radical defect, for which nothing else could compensate; and however much we may admire the many excellencies with which the Grecian character shone forth, we cannot but acknowledge, that it here lacked that dignity of elevated principle which belongs to the soul in its *most* exalted nature.

Inseparably connected with its social constitution, was its political; and although peculiar in its details to each respective state, one spirit animated all. Yet, it was only in times of common emergency that it most fully and grandly developed itself. Intestine dissensions, and hostile emulations, gradually and permanently overthrew what otherwise would have been the fairest fabric of antiquity. Experience, philosophy, and patriotism, taught no precept which a misdirected ambition did not annul. In fine, that was, like other barbarous and unenlightened ages, the scene of conquest and continued strife for power—when international law and friendship were unknown—when the evils and corruptions of idolatry, to the nation and the individual, were not to be counteracted by the most refined taste for the beautiful and sublime in the works of genius and art. The absence of correct princples, which proved so lamentable a deficiency to society in the abstract, pervaded all its institutions; and it is needless, for our present purpose, to inquire into the particular imperfections in the construction and consequent irregularity in the operation of her political machinery, when the broad foundations upon which all governments must rest were so utterly misconceived. Society and government, originating from the weakness and dependence of man, simultaneously and inseparably, are equally exposed to corruption and decay; and so indissoluble is their union, that when the purity and stability of the one is affected, the final ruin of the other is inevitable.

There must be some *vital principle,* deeply settled in the internal constitution of society, to enable it to meet and withstand the shocks to which it is ever liable—to impart to it a health and vigor which shall be a sufficient safeguard against contaminations from within and without. The passions and desires of the human heart, unrestrained by any sense of obligation, are ever ready to burst forth upon it with irresistible violence, or insidiously enfeeble its energies. The rise, progress, and decline of the Grecian character furnishes a mournful demonstration of this truth. It shows how weak a defense is made against such powerful foes, by human philosophy and legislation unaided.

If we now turn to Rome, the same great, preserving, strengthening principles were wanting in the structure of her social and political systems. Let the particular characteristics in each have been as they may, here is the ground of the *important* deficiency. Before the might of the Roman arm, the whole earth quailed ; and yet, within herself were elements of dissolution and decay, against which was provided no protection. These finally developed themselves, like an overwhelming flood, bearing away on its bosom the wreck of former power and grandeur. There was, indeed, intellectual greatness to admire in individuals ; but the *nation* was far from being enlightened, either in the mind or heart. *Here*, rather than in physical strength, is the security of its independence—nay, of its *existence*. Should we, therefore, wonder at the result in either case ? Was it not the *direct*, *legitimate* consequence of a sufficient cause ?

We have thus noticed the character and short duration of the basis upon which society then stood, in the two most interesting and liberal States of antiquity.

Let us now consider principles wholly opposed to the former, and upon which modern society is founded.

The political movements that had been making during the middle ages, were, in truth, only preparing the way for the ameliorating influences of Christianity on Western Europe. The Feudal system, the most prominent social institution of the times, however oppressive and unjust in its immediate operations, was, in fact, the chief preservative against consolidated monarchies, whose existing character would have guarantied no protection to their subjects but slavery. By the existence of independent Barons, whose united forces could at any moment successfully encounter the attempts of government, it was rendered unable to effect this, and, moreover, was compelled to yield continually to their demands. There are two distinct forms in which *central* power resides—one, where an *individual* will is superior to all others—the other, where the public will, " the result of mutual concurrence," is supreme. Neither of these do we find at this period ; and the system of which we are speaking, tended directly to crush all efforts to establish either. Hence, a scheme, which the private interests of individuals led them to devise, became a balance wheel to check the otherwise too great condensation of power, on the one hand, and the premature ascendancy of democratic principles on the other. The combined operation of moral and political causes was silently revolutionizing society, and moulding its chaotic elements gradually into a new and glorious constitution, that was to possess a character, and rest upon a foundation, different from any that had preceded. It was a slow and unceasing process, yet one *fully* commensurate with the mighty result to be effected—a process which was to continue from age to age, working out the progressive developments of that result, and leaving them enstamped upon each. Here was the germ of future civilization; and thus, the soil in which it was to be planted was prepared to receive the light and warmth of the sun of Christianity. Here we see the *new* principle, that had, as it were, sprung up a second time in the sixteenth century, beginning to be incorporated into our social and political systems, forming the *grand distinction* between this and preceding times—a distinction, too, so important as cannot fail to arrest our attention to its nature and effects. Whatever faults there may have been in the government and legislation of those ancient Republics, their overthrow can be easily traced back to the want of all true moral principle in the people, and, especially, were deleterious influences from such a source *felt* in a *popular* government. But, as the individual needs the dictates of enlightened conscience to restrain the power of passion in the soul, and to impart a strength which shall make it impregnable to all the assaults of vice, so society, upon this same basis, may encounter all *its* enemies. This is the position of modern society—its great *conservative* principle is an acknowledged obligation to *revealed duty*.

The law that Christianity has introduced, is that of peace and brotherhood between man and his fellow. It has brought with it happiness, the great end of all human concerns to the individual and the nation, and that, not unsatisfying and temporary, but coming up from a pure, exhaustless fountain. It quenches the energy of consuming passion in the soul, and leads it on to successive elevations, until it clothes it with its own inherent majesty; and while thus conquering and purifying the *heart*, it quickens into vigorous action all the mental faculties, and prepares the way for the march of improvement and discovery in every branch of knowledge. Its aim and end, in all respects, is to exalt human nature—to invest it with the dignity and sublimity that belong to its own Infinite Author. To what other cause *can* we attribute the contrast between the present and the past? Not simply to the idea that each successive age *must* be in advance of its predecessor, in time and character equally, and that thus the goal of the one becomes the starting point of the other; or that there is a *natural law* of progress in society, resulting necessarily from its constitution, "which in the upheaving from age to age of principles and events, and the advance of civilization," is disconnected with extraneous influences instilled into it by the spirit of Christianity—this the unity and philosophy of history does not substantiate. It cannot but produce, then, upon society effects that are consonant with its high character; and thus its own *renovating, conservatory* spirit has been infused into it—a spirit too mighty, too great, to yield supremacy to any opponent. Here rests the law. Springing up *certainly* and only from such a source, ought we to wonder at its *sustaining, defending* power? It stands forth as the *living, acting* personation of these moral principles; and hence, as their representative, it is the safeguard of the health and existence of society; but take away these, and their influence on the conduct of men, and abstract law is a dead letter. Thus, that deficiency in having some preservative against the corruptions, dissensions, and consequent decay which we have seen in the *best*, morally and politically, regulated States of antiquity, is in our day fully supplied; and the causes from which they fell, are now counteracted by principles that are engrafted into our social and civil organizations, which we know cannot be *permanently* subdued. Hence, we have no reason to fear a relapse into primitive darkness, mental and moral. Revolutions are to be expected, but those only that will usher in a still brighter day; and while change is impressed upon society, it is its *glory* that unceasing progress is likewise. As time and improvement are thus continually bearing us onward and upward, each successive step places us on a surer foundation—this is the *stability* of *change*.

If, from the elevation we have now attained, we look back upon the past, human weakness is the great lesson taught in the varied scenes and actors which rise before us—that when man relies on his own unaided powers, he must fall; yet, we see, for our instruction, in that final issue, the evident operations of distinct causes.

As man advances morally and intellectually, so does government. These three great constituent elements of society must be inseperable, for the permanence of either; and it was reserved for us, in *this* day, to witness the realization of the most ardent hopes of the philanthropic statesman—the union of government and freedom. However defective our system may be, it *has* a foundation like none other; and let it be the glory of *our* age, that we have advanced even thus far, and that *future* ages may revert to it as *the memorable* epoch in their history, while they succeed each other in that progress which has no goal.

POETRY, ORIGINALLY A SACRED PRINCIPLE, AS INDICATED BY ITS EARLY HISTORY.

BY HOLLIS RUSSELL, BINGHAM, MAINE.

If we may regard as real the representations of the inspired poet, man's first awakening into existence was hailed with the hymn of the "morning stars," as they "sang together" the praises of the great Creator. There was heard the *adoration* of religion and the *melody* of *song*. These falling, as we may say, thus in unison upon his opening spirit at its birth, left in it the tinge of their commingled influence, to become thenceforth connubial elements of the human soul; or, in whatever manner these two principles were communicated, certain it is, man, in his nature, is no less truly a poetic than a religious being. In all time, wherever he has been found, however groveling and degenerate, still have religion and poetry unequivocally manifested their co-existence within him. The one, with sovereign attitude, commanding the soul's obedience to some Supreme Power, imminent to punish and destroy, as well as to bless and save; the other, in gentler mood, wooing the heart to love and adoration, and, accompanying man through all the scenes of life, seeking to cheer him in sorrow, to prolong and repeat his joys, and to gild even his fears with the iris-hues of hope; and when, by the light of truth, the path of virtue has been revealed, strewing the asperities of the way with flowers, and calling up visions of beauty to beckon the pilgrim onward.

That such is the dignity and office of poetry, is often overlooked. Some, even of high repute in literature, have gravely doubted whether the dreams of superstition and the fables of mythology be not more congenial with the spirit of poesy than the truths and glories of the Christian religion.

Without confining our attention particularly to that inquiry, it will be the purpose of this attempt to consider, in a general manner, the chief aspects in the moral history of poetry, down to the commencement of the Christian era, noting such indications as may appear of the original sacredness and design of the poetic principle.

Especially important to our subject is the history of that peculiar people the Hebrews. Deriving their lineage immediately from the first pair, and acknowledging even no civil statutes, other than the revelation of the Creator, among such a people, we may confidently look to find the inherent principles of the soul most truly and distinctly developed. And in this original community, poetry, the learned assure us, was employed, even before the Mosaic age, as the language of adoration and religious truth.

Their proverbs, and "sayings of the wise," extant, from the remotest period of time, were, in their kind, poems, conveying moral precepts and decrees of divine law, in such form as should best recommend them to the memory. In poetry were rehearsed the works and attributes of Jehovah. It was, too, the remembrancer of solemn transactions, and the prophetess of future events; and over the bleeding sacrifice, it was the priestess of truth, to kindle and feed the flame of devotion. Thus were worship and singing observed in unison at our earliest notice of human society.

And pursuing our subject through the subsequent vicissitudes in the history of this people, we may say, first, amid the general apostasy of Israel, poetry continued true to its mission. It would not utter the harsh notes of murmuring and complaint, and but feebly, at best, would it ever chant the praises of strange gods. At such times, it fled to the bosoms of the Prophets, and there abode to mourn over the ingratitude of Israel, entreating to repentance, and denouncing the fearful vengeance of Jehovah. To the last, we hear its voice, deprecating the approaching evil, and chiding the perfidy of "a foolish people and unwise," who "desert the God that made them, and despise the rock of their salvation"—now weeping in secret places, and, replete with holy indignation, calling upon the heavens and the earth, and pleading its cause before the mountains and the hills—and now awakening "the sublime of desolation," while it proclaims to the rebellious city its impending doom—when Jehovah shall "stretch over it the line of devastation and the plummet of emptiness,* wiping Jerusalem, and turning it upside down."

But the solemn warnings of prophecy were unheeded, and the impending vengeance fell. Jerusalem was ravished by the Gentile, and Israel became a bond-slave to his enemies. Then the proud spirit of the Jew was at length humbled, and in tears of penitence and grief, he consecrates anew his vows of eternal devotion to Zion; and poetry, silent during the period of his rebellion, now wells up freely from his deep heart. By the rivers of Babylon they sat them down and wept, and the burden of their plaintive song was ever, "If I forget thee, O Jerusalem!—If I prefer thee not above my chief joy." And throughout the term of their humiliation, whether the afflicted people breathed forth their supplications to the God of Zion, that he would "return and visit his vine;" or the captive prophet consoled them with the assurance of his care, whose benevolence was more tender and constant than the yearnings of maternal affection; or turned him to denounce the vengeance of heaven upon their proud oppressors; or kindled into rapture at the bright visions of glory in the future, when the days of their mourning should cease, and Jehovah be their everlasting guide—in these, and in all instances, wherever the sacred spirit of religion breathed, there still was heard the melodious voice of poesy.

Thus was it during the days of their captivity; and when these were accomplished, and the bonds of the oppressor were loosed, this "faculty divine" was none the less called into sacred requisition. As their fathers, on the banks of the sea, whose waters had parted to cleave them a passage, had raised their triumphal song to Him whose wrath had "consumed their enemies like stubble," who "did blow with his breath, and they were covered in the sea," so they, arrived once more at Zion, hymn anew the praises of the God of Jacob, who "heard their cry in trouble, and saved them out of their distresses," "breaking the gates of brass, and cutting the bars of iron in sunder." And when the tyrant of Babylon was smitten, and his "glory brought down to the dust," the sacred Muse took up the theme, and in the sublimity of her strain the hills and the cedars of Lebanon rejoice at his fate—hell from beneath is stirred at his coming—the ghosts of departed kings rise up to insult him—and Jehovah himself exults over his destruction.

Reinstated in their native land, religion is again enlarged into perfect liberty, and endowed with ample means of exercise. Poetry abounds. The sacred Muse, ever venerated in the hearts of the holy, is now invested with royal dignity, and the King of Israel is the prince of song.† No less than four thousand singers are appointed, whose life-long vocation it is to officiate in the temple and perform the sacred hymns. And on all the occasions of life—the array of battle, the anointing of a king, the nuptial feast, and the funereal train, whatever religion acknowledged and hallowed, over it poetry lingered and sang.

* Variations from the common translation are from Bishop Lowth.

† The writer here had his mind upon *philosophical* rather than *chronological* truth.

It was the vehicle of the words of wisdom. The son of Abraham was blest with its influence in all his private conditions. It had a triumphal ode for his joy, a consoling lay for his grief. It moaned over his couch in the hour of affliction, and sang an hymn of praise at his recovery. In war, it allured him to hide his fears beneath the pavilion of the God of Sabaoth, and when peace came, lifted his heart in thankfulness to Salem's King.

All that is terrific and sublime in the scene of a drowning world, in the flames of Sodom, and in the thunders of Sinai—and all that is gentle and fair in the sweetest smiles of nature, and in the holy faithfulness of love, were alike the themes of its hallowed discourse. For Israel's Muse partook of the nature of Israel's God, who, while "he rides on the wings of the wind," and "maketh the mountains to tremble at his voice," heedeth the ravens when they cry, and adorns the lilies of the vale.

Thus, among this primitive and chosen people, was poetry the consort of religion—languishing away in the apostate heart, and awakening to life and sublimity only when that heart returned to allegiance and holiness; and ever, in the days of Zion's prosperity, cherished as a sacred principle meet to be enshrined in the sanctuary of God.

If we turn, next, to the Gentile nations, we shall there also perceive intimations of the original sacredness of poetry. From them, all light of revelation was removed. Still, of the truth of their high original some record, whose purport they could not clearly decipher, was written indelibly within them. Like the Maid of the Enchanted Isle, who retained ever the dim remembrance of brighter scenes in some forgotten period of the past, so did the inmost spirit of the bewildered Gentile unceasingly testify of a primeval idea of purity and truth, even long after it had lost the wisdom to account whence that notion was derived. To this idea his better nature eagerly turned, and sought to love and adore. He built it shrines, and named for it gods. Unto it he paid his vows and offered sacrifice. These were the promptings of religion. Then, that purity and truth he labored to express in words of befitting beauty and sublimity, and that was the effort of poetry; or rather, perhaps, we should say, these darkling ceremonies of worship, combined with song, had been delivered to them through successive generations, even from Eden and Mount Ararat, and their continuance forever secured by the immortality of the religious and poetic principles.

Accordingly, at our earliest knowledge of these nations, poetry was employed only for sacred purposes. The true religion was lost from among them, and the Muse, forlorn of her proper spouse, wandered singing hymns and chanting vain orisons about the fanes and temples, wherein was said to be enshrined a deity. She was found at sacrificial altars, and in the sepulchral procession, and wherever the name of religion was invoked, participating in the fabulous oblations, and straining bewildered notes over unhallowed incense.

Eternal truth, the prototype of their ever inward idea of the pure and perfect, was hidden to them behind an impenetrable veil. Only its consort poetry was discovered; and so divine were her lineaments, so celestial her voice, her mien so like a deity, at first they only gazed, listened, and venerated; but by degrees, through long exile from her conjugal spirit, her pristine glory began to wane away. Familiarity was dissipating the awe that invested her; even worship was swallowed up in admiration, till at last they forgot the divinity of her nature in the ravishment of her song. No longer, now, was she a daughter of Zion, striking her harp to the high praises of Jehovah; but rather Melpomene, with her buskins and dagger, or a Proserpine, gathering flowers in the hapless plains of Enna.

Still was she beautiful. For unholy hands had arrayed her, as it were, in Tyrean purple, and decked her bosom with pearls; and, practiced in the school of the Graces, the music of her motion was complete. Intoxicated with delight, the idolatrous multitude abused her charms, to ennoble ever unhallowed scene of terrestrial passion. She must frequent the banquets of Venus, and debase her song to the gross and prurient ears of lust. She must grace the revels of the Wine-God, and mingle her delicate voice with the howlings of the infuriate bacchanal. And when the sound of battle was heard, they espoused her to steel-clad Mars, and Amazon poetry, stiff with the panoply of war, must sound a martial note, and forth to

"The tumult and the rage of fight."

Yet was she often noble, even in slavery. At times, as if revolting from her masters, would she mount heaven-ward and sing of "the wandering planets," and "the rolling spheres," and of "the serene omnipotent Father," in strains worthy her divine original. Sometimes, too, she would choose a tender lay, and discoursing to the better feelings of the human heart, evoke thence emotions of such azure purity as would not stain an angel's bosom; and always she seemed most content, and her song was sweetest and loftiest, when the theme was nearest to truth and virtue, and the majesty of God.

Thus, both with the Jew and the Gentile, was poetry, in the beginning, eminently religious; and thus, through all the various conditions of these ancient people, as if evincing the peculiar congeniality of the two principles, has poetry most freely and fully developed its power when in intimate alliance with religion.

Meanwhile, over the Gentile world, particularly with the erudite Greek and proud Roman, art and study had exhausted their cunning to humanize the divine nature of poetry, and transmute her intrinsic sanctity into the more familiar graces of a choral nymph; and, cultivated by long effort, this violent perversion had even grown into stability, till now scarce a trace of her original sanctity could be descried. Israel, too, had again relapsed into the sluggishness and delusion of sin. The Prophets had passed away; and the religion of the Temple, though refulgent with gold, and inscribed to the true God, was but a rigid cadaverous form. The quickening spirit had departed, and with it, poetry had expired. Only her name and her songs were preserved in the record of the past. With all else pertaining to the human soul, it lay, groveling and debased, beneath the desolating blight of sin.

Then came the era of Redemption. And lo! again religion and poetry, united as in the beginning, return to heal and sanctify the human race. At his creation, the Angels had seized their harps, and taught the notes of poetry to man. Those Angel-tones had languished away, and, buried amid the discords of passion, were long since lost from the earth. And now, upon the advent of the Great Restorer of mankind, again the heavenly choir descend, and renewing that primal strain, open the Christian era with a song.

In the privacy of midnight, when all profaner noises were hushed, over the solitary plains of Bethlehem they hovered, and again, as at first, "sang together for joy," adding now most of all, "*Peace on earth, for unto you is born a Saviour.*" This, would they teach, should be the theme, this the inspiration of all future songs. Already had its prelude been chanted from the inspired lips of Elizabeth and Mary, when, premonished by the Angel-visit, they mused over the approaching advent of Elias and the Christ; and anon aged Simeon clasped the Messiah in his arms, and poured forth his soul in the same exulting strains.

Nor was the world now left to the precepts of holy men, or the ensample of Angels alone, to learn the divine dignity of poetry. That truth the Great Teacher himself, in his prophetic monitions, and lessons of filial confidence, often vindicated; and as his mission was introduced with teaching his disciples to pray, so, at its close, he blended his voice with theirs, and "sang an hymn." And, allying the exercise to that sacrament ordained to perpetuate the remembrance of man's redemption, he forever consecrated poetry with the new baptism of Christianity, and appointed it his mission, to sing the truths and blessings of the Gospel. Accordingly, during those early days of the purity and grandeur of the Christian religion, amid the working of miracles, the gift of tongues, and the solemn voice of prayer, the Disciples failed not to commune together with "psalms and hymns, and spiritual songs."

Thus, was poetry in the human soul at the first connate, and ever after intimately linked with the religious principle. And although most artfully embellished among the nations ignorant of the true God, perhaps for the very reason that they knew nought else so divine and true on which the heart might indulge its worship; still, despite of all the ornaments and graces of art, it has ever fallen beneath the perfection of its power, save when hallowed and sustained by the religion of Jehovah. And thus has the spirit that sanctifies approved itself no less efficacious to refine the affections, and elevate the soul, to the lofty mood of poetry. For it is the holy heart, inditing sentiments of eternal truth, that has reached at once the tenderest lays and the sublimest heights of song.

And, we may add, in later times, under the Christian dispensation, in Italy, in Spain, or in England, even to our day, the proudest, the most god-like efforts of the Muse, have been when the theme was religious and the poet a Christian. And when time is no more, heaven above would want its richest joy, its highest glory, without the song of "Moses and the Lamb."

THE CONNECTION OF COMMON SENSE WITH LITERARY EXCELLENCE.

BY JONATHAN WHITE, RANDOLPH, MASS.

With many discordant opinions respecting the precise signification and office of common sense, philosophers usually concur in assigning it a very subordinate rank in the mind, or altogether denying its existence as a distinct innate faculty. In general acceptation, however, it has a definite and comprehensive meaning. It may be considered as the ordinary judgment of mankind in reference to matters of expediency, implying such a practical knowledge of the world, and such a quick sense of propriety in the regulation of the conduct, as can result only from an habitual estimation of things and events as they are.

The importance of this faculty in the common transactions of life, none are disposed to call in question. Its agency may be traced in the multiplied instances of prompt and decisive action which determine the success of every enterprise, while they necessarily exclude any conscious process of reasoning; and notwithstanding its operations, from their frequency and certainty, come to be almost as unnoticed as the beatings of the heart, the stigma which invariably rests upon any violation of its dictates clearly evinces the conviction of mankind in regard to its connection with the welfare both of individuals and of society at large. But when we turn to the higher vocations of literature, the case seems quite reversed. The works of great, inventive minds are claimed to be things of another order, in the production and judgment of which, little occasion can be afforded for the exercise of a faculty inherent as well in the lowliest as the most exalted intellects. Men eminent in letters even, have not been unwilling to arrogate to themselves the distinction implied in this notion, and have contributed not a little to confirm and perpetuate it. Genius, receiving from the same source direction and character, has often been seduced to an utter alienation from society, while society in turn, not without compassion for its lot, has left it to move about in a world of its own creation, unreal and unrealized; indeed, so eloquently have critics pleaded in extenuation of its errors, its exemption from all laws which obtain among ordinary minds, that eccentricity, nay, utter recklessness of the first principles of prudence, have come to be very commonly regarded as not merely a casual evidence of it, but an essential element. It may not be unprofitable to consider briefly whether these opinions have foundation in the nature of things.

Literature, it would seem to be scarcely necessary to observe, is worthy of attention only so far as it exerts a practical influence upon human life. To regard it as a mere repository of thought, or an embodiment of passive principles, destitute of any power to move the reason or the passions of men, is to degrade it infinitely below its rightful position in respect of dignity and importance. Most pernicious are the consequences of such a mistaken idea, to both literature and people; its whole tendency is destructive of that fashioning influence which should be exerted by each upon the other. For while men of letters display their brilliant conceits as pictures to be gazed at, and truth itself is an idle trophy, won by hard conflict with ignorance and error, it is not wonderful that the rest of mankind look upon their boasted achievements as upon the "rattling twigs and sprays of winter, which afford neither food nor shelter." Not so; thoughts are properly instruments of action, and are valuable only as they manifest themselves in the accomplishment of specific results; truth is earnestly and consistently sought by the greatest minds, because it is felt to be a living, energizing principle, which, once brought to light, will live on and act for ever. An action, therefore, is as truly the ultimate end of intellectual exertion, as of physical. Between the external forms, indeed, under which it is manifested, and the immediate purposes for which it is put forth in the two cases, there may be no comparison, yet its essence is the same in both; it is an action still exerted, directly or remotely, upon human nature as its subject. Hence in the very qualities, by reason of which the common affairs of life demand a steady and rational view of the end proposed to be accomplished, a ready perception of the best means, and a skillful adjustment of these to varying circumstances; in a word, the full and legitimate exercise of common sense, in precisely these qualities we discover a close analogy between the operations of active life and the operations of the mind; and nothing can be more irrational than to endeavor to secure efficiency in one by spurning those powers and faculties which, above all others, are acknowledged to be needful to ensure it in the other.

In the conduct of literary attainments, however, the importance of common sense is not to be estimated solely or chiefly by the results of its direct and independent operations. It acquires peculiar prominence and value from the relations which it sustains to the higher intellectual faculties; for, by rendering available the stores of learning, by giving stability to the achievements of reason, and restraining the excesses of imagination, it vastly promotes the success of efforts which it is incompetent to produce. And when we reflect how often the noblest endowments bestowed upon man are, for all purposes of usefulness, utterly subverted by a single wrong direction, it would seem impossible to conceive the genuine influence of common sense to be superseded by the presence of other the most brilliant and vigorous powers. Indispensable, therefore, is its agency to the formation of a sound literary character. The keen sensibility, the ardent enthusiasm, the habit of solitary meditation, and the intense devotedness to an individual pursuit, which constitute the perfection of such a character, are but too justly reproached with a tendency to extravagance and error, when unaccompanied by an ordinary judgment. The very fullness of power of a creative mind is its peril. The vividness of its own conceptions too often serves to exclude those rational views of their relations to the realities of the outer world, and that sympathy with the feelings and opinions on which they are to act, which form the proper stimulus of the mind, without which it loses its healthy tone of action and becomes the mere creature of impulse and caprice.

The man of genius, who has shaken off the trammels of sense and custom and become a law unto himself, may, indeed, produce works valuable for their incidental and subordinate excellences, but there remains no security that the object of his labors will not wholly fail of accomplishment. The imbecility of ill balanced intellect is betrayed in all its productions; incompleteness and incongruity are the indubitable traces of their origin. We need only refer, for familiar examples, to the virtuous corsairs of a Byron and the grossly material spiritualities of a Shelly. It matters very little, moreover, that the world be assured, again and again, that such impossible abstractions are no violations of good taste, and are replete with individual conceptions of transcendent beauty; not careful to answer in these matters, it still asserts the prerogative of judging by its own standard of common sense; a very reasonable standard, surely; for, what intuitive truths are in philosophy, such are the dictates of common sense in literature. They are first principles, and necessarily lie beyond the decisions of taste, at the foundation of all enduring excellence. To its own sufficient cost, therefore, does self-sufficing genius, arrogating to itself special immunities, set these principles at naught. If, disdaining to stand in the old ways, and see which is the right and good way and walk therein, it recklessly pursue a devious course, arraying against the authority of ages the fancies of a day, and trampling in its scorn on the world and the world's precepts, it must reap the bitter reward, the world's contempt. Nor is this unjust. For what do they, but trifle with the understanding and grossly insult the self-love of mankind, who, in their works, dwell avowedly and exclusively on the possession of mysterious powers, by reason of which they bless themselves from all alliance with their race!

In addition to the utility of common sense in securing reasonableness to the aims and certainty to the efforts of men of letters, we observe, also, that in respect of practical knowledge, it affords high vantage ground which cannot well be abandoned. Presenting ever the realities of things in their natural and obvious relations, it leads to a ready perception of general principles, which are otherwise attainable, if at all, by much painful experience. Especially to that deep insight into the nature of man, as well as that sagacious mode of observing the great objects of his thoughts and absorbing interests of his life, so essential to the purposes of literature, no qualification is of more avail than the lively sympathy which common sense establishes between man and his fellow-men. To what absurd and difficult means does not the author frequently resort, in order to arrive at those simple truths respecting human nature, which are perfectly within the grasp of common judgment, or lie open to observation, so that he who runs may read! Turning his mind inward upon itself, he labors with the earnestness and enthusiasm of a solitary artist, to determine, by mere efforts of intelligence, all possible modes of existence, and subject them to the arbitrary canons of an ideal system. The objects of sense, all that is grand and lovely in the external world or in the actions of men, are dimly seen through the distorting medium of his visions, which are fashioned not after the eternanl patterns of nature, but according to the traits of his own individuality. Now if there is an element which should preëminently characterize the views and principles, we do not say of the historian, the critic and philosopher, but of the orator and the poet, whose object is to strike those chords which shall vibrate throughout the universe of rational being, it is the element of universality; and this, both reason and experience teach us, is not to be attained where intellectual labor is resolved into one all-engrossing effort of consciousness. It does not result from the attempts of an individual mind to fathom itself, nor from the anatomy of a single human heart, even though such anatomy bring to light the whole range of passions disembodied. It can result only from an habitual common sense observation and common sense interpretation of human nature; without these, impassioned eloquence and the "vision and faculty divine" are idle gifts. We are far from meaning, by this, to aver that poets and orators are to seek inspiration by mingling with the world and its affairs; that they must not often retire from the "garish light of day," to meditate profoundly within the solitude of their own minds. But to attempt, by the aid of introspection alone, to portray just expressions of the emotions and passions of men, as they are developed in social life—as well might the painter task himself to depict the clouds in their ever changing forms and hues, by a rigid application of the laws which govern light and vapor!

The mind, it is true, is said to create; but it creates of materials already existing. The world, with its innumerable objects of beauty and grandeur, awakening kindred emotions in all; real life, with its joys and sorrows, its hopes and fears, experienced alike by all, these furnish the substance, imagination only the varying form. Surely, then, it were the part of wisdom, that men of even the loftiest intellect, since they can hope to influence universal mind only through the medium of 'things that do appear,' should seek to contemplate these in some measure as their less gifted fellow-beings contemplate them; should cherish those feelings and faculties which most nearly assimilate them to their race. It was not by endeavoring to compel universal suffrage to ideal and conventional forms, that the sculptors of ancient Greece gave to the world perennial models in their art. The spontaneous thoughts and emotions of men, no less than the manifold aspects of nature, were made their study, till the sublime creations of their genius were but the bodying forth of the condensed judgment of mankind. Such is the condition of immortality in works of art, works which overwhelm the mind at a single glance and command assent; how important is it, then, that the productions of literature which, to be appreciated at all, must be understood, should give language to the unwritten thoughts and boundless aspirations which exist in every the most unlettered mind; in other words, that they be founded on the deep-seated, unchangeable principles of common sense. Is it objected that in this way literature becomes imitative and superficial? We answer, it is when common sense breaks over the bounds which an artificial taste would prescribe, when it exposes narrow views and transient modes of thought, when it imparts dignity and meaning and vigor to the workings of the mind, it is then only that originality can characterize the productions of intellect. Real existences, emotions, and passions, whose variety is profound as it is endless, afford ample scope for the highest powers of creative genius. The orator may exalt and expand and vivify, with Promethean heat, the profoundest elements of the soul; the poet may clothe in sublimest imagery all that is tender and terrible in our being, or, as nature's high priest, may explore the inmost recesses of her temple, fearlessly enter its holy of holies, and with its own sacred fire light up the dread mysteries of creation. Nay, more; it is the glory of genius that it bids defiance to arbitrary forms and is wild above rules of art, that it bursts the bars and ties of an earth-born prudence and soars to its native element beyond this "visible diurnal sphere;" yet, in its loftiest moods, there are laws which bind it to all of mortal mould, and which it may not transgress with impunity.

Of the direct influence of the faculty of common sense upon the mind itself, why speak? None can be insensible to its vast importance as a regulator of all the intellectual powers, preserving their just balance and harmonious development, their free and manifold exercise. Wherever it is wanting, the noblest energies and the finest sensibilities, however they may dazzle and amaze for a time, either languish and decay, or, by the very intensity of their action, become the quick ministers of their own destruction. *Health* of mind is subverted, without which there can be neither greatness nor happiness. Indeed to the simple dereliction of this faculty, we doubt not, may be justly attributed far the greater portion of what are supposed to be the peculiar infirmities and misfortunes of genius. It is sad to behold a Shelly, in the pride of intellect, binding life to a splendid error, whose end is blasted hope, mortification, and hate; sad, to witness a Byron, striving hard and successfully to convert the precious gifts of Providence into sources of unmingled misery; most sad, to hear the endless wailings of a Rosseau over imaginary wrongs and self-inflicted sufferings; yet we have abundant examples to warrant us in the presumption that irritability constitutes no part of a great and healthy mind. Such a mind, though alive to every impulse from without, is still master of its sensibility; it is tranquil in the consciousness of underived, indestructible energies. Nor does it ever, scorpion-like, turn these into instruments of self-torture, when hemmed in by the fires of real persecution, but then, most of all, exults in the opportunity of teaching the world a sublime lesson of endurance.

The history of literature, did our limits allow us to adduce its testimony, would most fully substantiate the justness of the views which have been taken of our subject. Those great productions which have endured through all the vicissitudes of ages, making a deep impression on the hearts of men, and conducting their powers to higher and still higher modes of action, have been the utterance of minds which have lived and thought under the constant direction of a strong ordinary judgment. Where this has been the prominent characteristic, even without possessing the highest order of talents, men have attained great eminence in letters and enjoyed a permanent fame; while innumerable sons of genius, who have been endowed with exquisite sensibilities, high imagination, and godlike reason, but who have scorned to share a blessing with the body of mankind, aspiring to be "stars and dwell apart," have only drawn contempt upon themselves and their pursuits. Literature, as well as science, has had its ages of Alchemy; and nothing can be more humiliating than to reflect upon the amount of learning, industry, and talents, which have been worse than wasted during these long and dark periods of divorce from common sense. Nor, indeed, can we fail to notice, in works of the present day, painful instances of departure from that spirit of reality and practicability which so generally commends them to the warm interest of community. A proneness to deify intellectual power and clothe it with the highest attributes of virtue, as if it were an end to be sought for itself alone, too often leads, through a sickly self-consciousness, to downright infidelity; an infidelity which affects not the heart merely, corrupting the springs of action, and resting, with a "weight heavy as frost," upon nobler aspirations, but which sets the mind on the pinnacle of the great intellectual temple, reared and adorned by contributions of all past ages, and from this lofty station bids it gaze on the monuments of thought and industry as all its own; bids it glory, not in what it has accomplished, or purposes to accomplish, but in its connection with the infinitude of mind, and there rest satisfied.

It has been our purpose simply to present, in vindication of common sense, the more prominent claims which, though obvious to all upon reflection, are too often overlooked, and, general as our remarks have necessarily been, we trust they have shown that there subsists an intimate relation between this faculty and extensive, permanent influence in literature; that however humble the position which it occupies among the intellectual powers, it yields to none in importance; for though it does not constitute greatness, we do not speak lightly when we affirm that there can be no greatness without it.

THE THREE GOBLETS.

Yes! I have drained full many a cup
  Which seemed of festal sweetness:
When Pleasure's bubbles sparkled up,
  I drank, but cursed their fleetness.
I drained now wine, now love, until
  The dregs lay darkly there:
I tasted deep, for then, as still,
  I scorned the thought of care.
Maddened, I drank my very soul,
But left no joy within the bowl.

And I have drained Ambition's cup,
  When flowing to the full,
And Glory's draught in blood I quaff'd
  From my vanquish'd foeman's skull.
Again the tempting cup was seen,
  Filled with a nation's tears;
I took it, though I saw within
  Remorse and damning fears.
'Twas to the bottom—and I fell;
Then woke to feel an earthly hell.

One cup remains—why halting stand
  And fear that endless sleep?
'Tis offered by a ghastly hand,
  Which beckons to drink deep.
This draught, proud soul, will rest impart;
  Thou wilt not thirst again.
'Twill drown thy sorrows, swelling heart,
  And still the pulse of pain.
I'll revel with my latest breath:
Give me, give me, the cup of Death!

ACTION IN ORATORY.

"Demosthenem ferunt ei, qui quaesivesset, quid primum esset in dicendo, actionem; quid secundum, idem, et idem tertium respondisse." Cicero Brut. 38.

Few have ever denied, and still fewer withstood, the power of action in the orator. The above opinion of the sovereign of orators which Cicero has given us, he himself approves, and elsewhere calls it "id, in quo oratoris vis illa divina." Yet, even with such testimony, there are writers and teachers, and we will add, eloquent speakers, of the present day, who, if they do not wholly deny, have but very little faith in its efficacy. They say it is all artificial; there is no soul in action—it is nothing but pantomime. There is, undoubtedly, much that is plausible in this, and there are many facts that appear to sustain such an opinion. There are, however, at least, as many facts and reasons to sustain the former. Neither, therefore, can be the truth, yet both are true. He who wielded at will the fierce democracy of Athens, and, without phalanx or javelin, made the usurper of the Macedonian throne tremble, could not have been mistaken as to what constituted his power. The almost motionless figure of Edwards, on the other hand, causing his audience involuntarily to rise from their seats, and cry out in despair, indicates, surely, no ordinary power. Can these, now, be reconciled? Where are the points of difference between the advocates of the two opinions, and what the common characteristics of both classes of speakers?

We regard the difference to consist in the meaning attached to the word Action. Most of the advocates for it regard it as an art to be acquired in its perfection by adherence to a system of rules. Accordingly, in our High Schools and Academies, in our "Eloquent Extracts," and selections for declamation, we have specific directions given for the position of the feet, the inclination of the body, the angle which the wrist must make with the shoulder, and the peculiar curve of the palm. We have, too, the precise elevation to which the hands must be raised in a burst of surprise, how close they must clasp, and how many wrinkles the brow must contain in a passage of agony, and with what violence the forehead must be struck when the speaker is overwhelmed with despair. It is no wonder, therefore—it is perfectly proper, that such principles should meet with opposition and ridicule. But it is neither fair nor, much less, ridiculous to object to all action because, forsooth, a particular mode of teaching or aquiring it is contemptible. We might just as well object to riding on horseback, because children sometimes ride hobby-horses. The astonishing power it wields, when properly used, renders the question, what constitutes true oratorical action, one of special interest to all who expect to become public speakers.

Who that has ever heard Webster in one of his loftiest and sublimest strains, when the unbreathing stillness of every heart, as it kindled with indignation, dissolved with pity, or dilated with glorious pride, told the full triumph of the orator, remembers what was his position, and what his gesture. Of the thousands that were swayed by the mighty power of Demosthenes, on that day when, having vanquished Aeschines, he descended from the Bema to be and to remain without a rival in the world, how many could tell their children what was the elevation of his hand, and what the fire of his large bright eye, while uttering that impassionate and thrilling oath, "No, my countrymen! no! by those generous souls," etc? Few, very few, indeed, we fear. "Quid si ipsum audissetis" was all that even his crushed opponent could tell his pupils at Rhodes about it. Yet both, we know, made use of action; both owed to it much of the magic influence of their success. The spirit-stirring harangues of leaders, too, at the hour of battle, and of the wild men of our own forests at their council fires, have been full of action; but without the recollection of a single gesture, their hearers have gone forth to fight, to achieve, perhaps to die.

Now, every weaned child knows, that the illustrious Grecian made action his special and constant study, and he knows, too, that the Indian's school-house is the pathless forest, and his books the leaves of the trees and the stars of heaven. Wherein, then, consists the identity of the action in both cases? We answer, *in being of the spirit, not of the body.* The communion, the sympathy, and the intercourse of spirits is by action. The influence of a body over spirits, or a spirit, be it never so bright and burning, over bodies, has been, and can be, nothing whatever. They must be brought into communion before the slightest feeling can be awakened, or any other effect produced than that of Galvanism upon some stiffened old subject of the Pharaohs. Here, then, and here only, is the common and real point of agreement between what are improperly called the natural and the artificial orator. Recognizing, or instinctively realizing this, both are alike capable of successfully accomplishing their common end—the persuasion of men.

There is one idea involved in this definition which requires to be distinctly understood, in order fully to comprehend its precision. We have said that true oratorical action is the action of the Spirit. Now, as the motions of the body are not caused or controlled by chance, much less are the actions of the nobler and more perfect part of our nature. It is awakened into life, and roused to high efforts, by causes, and according to laws, coeval and coexistent with its being. Its grand motive power is truth. Truth, *in its minutiæ and naked force*—not shaded or adorned—not festooned with flowers, nor imbedded in gems. The highest style of oratorical action, then, we define to be THE ACTION OF THE SPIRIT, *under the direct influence of truth,* DEVELOPED THROUGH THE ORGANS OF THE BODY. This alone embraces and reconciles the facts already given, which have occasioned the diversity of theory and practice on the subject. This elevates it to that exalted position which justly entitles it to be called the "oratoris vis divina," and secures it from the unhallowed claim of cold and heartless mimics of sacred and secular eloquence.

Of what advantage, therefore, we shall be asked, is its study? We answer, much every way. The body is the panoply of the spirit. Through it, the spirit exerts its power and fights its battles. Through its various changes alone, we become acquainted with the amazing energies, the glorious creations, the steady, ardent faith, the holy aspirations, and the deep, abiding love of its celestial habitant. Is it meet that such armor be rusted and soiled? If the sword of the spirit will do its work in either case, is it not better that its point and double edge be burnished and keen, that it may cut and pierce to the dividing asunder of the joints and marrow, rather than tear and hack its way thither.

Expression of countenance, gesture, attitude, and utterance are the principal modes of Action. The first named, and in our opinion, first in importance, is common to both classes of orators, and, with the exception of the eye, can be improved but very little by culture. This being the most delicate and beautiful organ, the spirit seems to have selected as the purest medium for the manifestation of its passions and emotions. Its sparkling, fiery glow—its fixed, riving gaze—its mellow loveliness—its fascinating side glance—and its innocent, sympathetic tear, have meanings which cannot be spoken nor painted. Yet how wofully has it been neglected. Some men, while speaking, look nowhere; others, and they are not fools, allow their eyes to wander and straggle everywhere; in a third class, the eyelids seem to be playing what the boys call "tag;" while that most abominable fashion, for in nine cases out of ten it is nothing more, in most modern speakers, of wearing glasses, completely deprives them of the whole power of this voiceless, but all-important coadjutor—a loss, for which no possible compensation can be made. We could, absolutely, almost wish that men, if they must be public speakers, would literally obey the Scriptures in this thing—if their eyes do offend, to pluck them out and cast them away. The remaining three, gesture, attitude, and elocution, are governed chiefly by the prevailing taste, or rather, we should say, are becoming more conformed to the laws of aesthetics. No one will surely question the essential importance to the orator of an acquaintance with the laws and operations of mind, for a thorough intimacy with them will ensure the highest conformity to their requirements, and, of course, the highest success; and that, we maintain, is the sole object of the study.

With such knowledge and cultivation, what a power does he possess! Look at Demosthenes. The State that had bred Miltiades, Cimon, and Thrasybulus, won the battles of Marathon and Salamis, and gloried in being the residence and the favorite of the gods, had, by the enervating effects of luxury and its concomitant indolence, sunk to the borders of slavery. The great heart of one young patriot, notwithstanding all, burned for the salvation of his country, and almost instantaneously it burst forth in that lofty and withering phillippic against her destroyer. A most exact and minute acquaintance with her previous history and existing condition completed his qualification for the superhuman task. Had human power been capable of rescuing and redeeming it, the fourteen years incessant efforts of this fearless spirit could not fail of success. Her gods could not do it. The Pantheon their tower, as it rose like a crown of glory from the Acropolis, awed not the heart, curbed not the ambition of her invader, and Grecian freedom was no more. Yet did not Demosthenes relax his labors in the great work. The power which a deep conviction of the justice of his cause, a thorough knowledge of it in all its bearings, and years of cultivation, had given him over men, made him through life a terror to tyrants—so that an acknowledgment of it was extorted even from Philip, when he declared that he was more afraid of *that man* than he was of all the fleets and armies of the Athenians.

Look at Mirabeau. What a spirit's was his! Where, but in some of those bold creations of Milton, do we see any thing like it! His life, if not itself a tragedy, may be called one ACT in that terrible tragedy of the

French Revolution. We scarcely ever hear of him thinking—it is all ACTION, ACTION, ACTION! His speeches, in the National Assembly, are not speeches, as men commonly understand the word, but passionate outbursts of what a distinguished divine of our country, of very similar genius,* calls "logic on fire." The spirit that, during those wild convulsions, agitated the nation, had infused itself into his being; and the instinctive rapidity with which he could analyze the most complicated questions, and deduce principles from apparently isolated facts, made him best fitted of all those daring men to control, and guide to some grand issue, such raging, lawless elements. He was an orator of the first rank.

Look at Henry. The disregard and contempt with which the petitions of the Colonies for redress of grievances had been treated by the parent State, had banished from his mind the thought of compromise, and left, in its stead, the boiling indignation and revenge of a naturally choleric temperament. Few, probably none, of the leading men of the day, dreamed of resistance. While an assembly of his native State, which had met to deliberate upon public business, were awaiting some action, he rose and offered two resolutions; first, that a well regulated Militia was the natural strength of the State, and, secondly, that this force be immediately organized. He took his seat. This was a virtual declaration of war. A number of the most prominent members were on the floor in an instant, not only not to discuss, but even to denounce them as suicidal, and the mover as almost a parricide. They ended, and he arose. His exordium was mild, direct, and short. "But as he entered upon his subject, his eye gathered fire; his form grew erect; every nerve was strung, and his whole soul seemed to be in a blaze." The curled lip forgot its sneer, the scowl forsook the angry brow, the brazen wall of prejudice was razed to its foundation, and the triumphant orator held the breathless multitude under complete sway, and bore them along upon the mighty and irresistible torrent of his eloquence. "I know not what course others may take, but as for me," cried he, with both arms extended aloft, his brow knit, every feature marked with the resolute purpose of his soul, and his voice swelled to its boldest note of exclamation, "give me Liberty, or give me death." The rest we have known long and well.

Numerous are the instances where similar power has been exerted, and with equal success; all, whatever may have been their motives, their profession, or their birth-place, combining to illustrate the truth, that the foundation of true Oratorical Action lies deep in the inward, not the outward, man. On the other hand, they as truly declare the essential importance of study and cultivation to the formation of the full stature of a perfect orator.

---

* Who that has ever heard the illustrious Beecher, the apostle of Christianity in the Great West, will not concur in this opinion? The comparison, of course, extends no farther, and we are gratified that it does not; while we cannot help mourning that powers so commanding, so transcendent, as those of the ambitious Frenchman, have done no more to bless the world.

The Pulpit, the Senate, and the Bar, demand of all who intend to be actors in them, that they labor to be noblemen in their profession. The nature of the subject, as we have defined and exemplified it, assures them that they cannot be such by mere gymnastic or vocal exercises. Hypocrisy (ὑπο κρίσις, stage playing, under acting) may, just as hypocrisy in every station of life may, answer well enough for a while, and in certain regions, but the constitution of human nature cannot long be disregarded. By its refusal to yield, in the slightest degree, it indignantly declares its detestation of all such soulless mockery. How sincere and honest is NATURE, in all her works! No hypocrisy, no falsehood, does she ever assume to the candid inquirer. She never has betrayed, and never will "betray the heart that loves her." MAN, too, will always open his heart to a sincere brother; he cannot help it; while all that DEITY himself asks is, that we should not insult Him, but that all who worship Him, do so in SPIRIT and in TRUTH. Action has a language of its own—it is itself language—it is the language of dumb men and dumb beasts; but when aided by the living voice, prompted by the warm, beating heart, uttering its voice through the glistening eye, the open, manly forehead, and glowing cheek, it becomes the combined eloquence of the reason and the heart, and no power on earth or in hell can stay its effect.

MYSTERY.

A FRAGMENT.

AND his awed soul its untaught homage paid
To mystery. And is it not a God—
That viewless, omnipresent mystery?

E'en in the lowest depths of hell resteth
Her foot, and towering thence, above the earth,
Above the skies, and upward still, beyond
The seventh heavens lifting her shadowy head,
She bears it far above th' eternal throne
In unknown chambers of immensity.
Enchanting wonder, like a magic robe,
Hangs heavily, investing her vast form;
And in its ample folds, do Sorcery
And Superstition lurk, and kennel there,
And breed their brood of lies; and Ignorance—
That proudly, purblind monster of the dark—
With heavy tread anticipates her path.

And when in majesty she moveth by,
Old men and maidens, kings and mendicants,
The wise and fool, the virtuous and the vile—
All bow their heads, and the awed soul lies still,
As in the presence of a Deity.
For none can sink beneath her deep descent,
And none can rise above her upward reach,
And none are valiant to withstand her power.
And yet she hath her dwelling everywhere.
She lives in every little flower that blooms;
She comes and breathes on us in every breeze
That stirs: beneath the covert of the dark
She stalks about; and when those streaming rays
At eve illume the pole, there too her seat
She hath, in radiance unapproachable.
In the loud bursting of the thunderbolt,
She speaks to us—and in the earthquake's groan.
And from old Ocean's caves comes up her voice,
In sadly solemn tones. Oft is she found
Careering in the hurricane, and in
The tempest raging; and when the fury
Of the storm is laid, and from the azure
Sky the glad sun looks forth anew to greet
The dewy earth, there too is mystery,
In every pouring beam of light. In glens
And caverns of the earth she has a home;
And all along the paths of science she
Hath reared her frequent shrines, where the wond'ring
Pilgrim must pause and do her reverence.
And she hath put her mark in all the books
Of men, and in the Book of God. And oft
She shows herself in new and nameless freaks,
Till even sage philosophy, able
No longer to be wise, wrinkling her brow,
Sits dumb with wonder.
Aye, all the wide world,
And we ourselves, are full of mystery.
Mystery lives with us in life; in death
Lies by our side, sleeps with us in the grave,
Shall waken with us at the Angel's trump,
And dwell with us throughout eternity.

A MUSE-ING EXCURSION.

How many, how pleasing, how almost sacred, are the associations connected with the land of Homer and of Grecian song! A few days' sail across the Ægean, by Rhodes and Cyprus, will bring us to scenes connected with associations as many, as pleasing, and altogether sacred. Yet now we choose not such a trip. In our present mood, we prefer to remain and ramble over the grounds where Thespis and Æschylus used to delight the simple-hearted rustics with the first rude representations of the histronic art: where Leonidas, with his brave Spartan company, marched

> "In perfect phalanx, to the Dorian mood
> Of flutes and soft recorders;"

where they stood and where they sleep. We like to stroll along under the shade of the plane trees, on the banks of the Ilyssus, or upon the beach of Phalerum, where Demosthenes used to bark and bellow, to cure his stammering; then follow the crowd to the Pnyx, where this same stammerer, with a forest of Athenians around him, the home of the gods above him, Salamis on his right hand and the Acropolis on his left, made heaven and earth respond to his reasoning and his appeals. Here, too, are the Lyceum and the Academy, the cradles of Sophistry and Philosophy. We cannot go a step, we cannot cross a hillock, a meadow, or a rill, where we may not see or feel impressions of some of those old Greeks, of whom we have heard, read, or dreamed. Here it is good for man to be alone. Here he will choose to be still, and listen: there are "sermons in these stones, books in her running brooks, tongues in her trees," music in her mountain breezes, and eloquent teachings in all. But we must not tarry even here. We pass along by Platea and Leuctra. How the heart will not stop its throbbings, nor Grecian patriotism cease to force itself upon the thoughts. In the little plain between the two cities, the hopes and the hosts of Persia were forever crushed; and beneath yonder Tumulus—next in glorious recollection to that at Marathon—not forgotten and not unsung, lie a thousand Spartans. Aristides and Epaminondas fought here.

We are now approaching the main object of our excursion—the place which so many have visited, and so many more have longed to visit, which neither the scornful step of the Moslem nor the heartless pillaging of the Antiquarian can unhallow—Mount Helicon. All thanks to the gods and goddesses of fountains, here is the sacred Aganippe, furnishing to the way-wearied pilgrim its waters to allay his thirst, its history and poetry to regale his fancy, and the rich, mellow landscape, that waves smilingly all around, to please the eye and delight the taste. Southward, in the distance, is the noble Gulf of Corinth, its coast so skirted with mountains, and its shores so tastefully fringed with shrubbery, that it seems as though his Oceanic Majesty had destined it as a summer retreat from the boisterous commotions of his royal home. Just behind is the clear and romantic Permessus, gaily flowing onward, as if proud of the air it cooled and the soil it was fertilizing. On its banks are the laurels and tamarisks that have wept for Gallus—

"Gallum etiam lauri, etiam flevêre myricae"—

and in its many shady recesses are the play-grounds and the haunts of the lovely Naiades.

The mountain side, in every direction, is clothed in the tasteful and elegant attire of Nature. The pine tree and the plane, the olive and the myrtle, the bay, the oleander, and the hazel, shade and adorn almost every rood. Shrubbery, such as the classic muse has delighted to paint, bloom in every dell and about every crag. Rich and pleasing as would be the plentiful carpet of green spread under all, it is rendered gay and gorgeous by the abundance of flowers that dot and ornament it, scenting the air with their mingling fragrance; the amaranth and the pink, the blushing violet, the pansy, and the pale jessamine, with a thousand other

"Flowers of more mingled hue,
Than the purpled scarf can shew."

This singular combination, so unlike and so superior to the scenery anywhere else, is accounted for by the residence here of Orpheus, the enchanting tones of whose lyre charmed hither all that was beautiful and lovely in animate or inanimate nature.

Refreshed by my rest, I rose to ascend the mountain. My attention was arrested by the snow-turbaned summit of Parnassus, rising in the distance like the swelling dome of some old mosque. Whilst gazing upon it, and thinking of its sweet Castalian fountain and its Pythia, of Delphi and "the woods that wave o'er Delphi's steep," I could not but appropriate the rapturous language of Byron:

"Oh, thou Parnassus! whom I now survey,
Not in the phrenzy of a dreamer's eye,
Not in the fabled landscape of a lay,
But soaring snow-clad through thy native sky,
In the wild pomp of mountain majesty."

It is difficult to say how much longer I would have soliloquized, had not my eyes and thoughts been diverted by a far different and more interesting sight. On my right, at a short distance from where I had been sitting, approached a company of gorgeously yet elegantly dressed females. Grace was conspicuous in every motion, and life and joy shone on every countenance. They were the "Sacred Nine." Now on ordinary occasions, we (that is, the writer) do not profess to be conscious of any peculiar aversion to the company of the fair—nay, we can even conceive a possibility of enjoying it, provided they make no inquiries as to our private feelings—we are delicate on that point. But, on the present occasion, here we were, all alone: no parent near to protect or counsel; no magistrate's office within several miles; with too much pride to run, and not courage enough to stand. Some sympathyzing friend would probably suggest to us the sixth verse of the seventeenth chapter of Ishmael: "Of two evils, choose the least." But here were almost a dozen; now which, we would like to be informed, was the "least." It simply amounted to this: which was most desirable for a man, all things considered, to hang himself, commit suicide, or put an end to his existence? We had pretty nearly decided the question in the affirmative, when we found ourselves essentially circumvallated and mum. "Oh!" cried we, in utter diminution of soul, "Oh, for a lodge"—but we could perceive of no chink or perforation where we should not have "rooms to let." In this condition, while just about being kicked by an ant, with whom we had had a short discussion on personal identity, one of the daughters of Jupiter spoke. My heart bounded, and the blood tingled through every vein and artery. The mild tone and delicate form of the fair speaker inspired me with confidence.

"You are doubtless a stranger here, sir," half-inquiringly asked Calliope. Her dark, beautiful eye, and bewitching smile, entirely overcame me. Behind her stood Thalia and Erato, richly indulging themselves in laughter and sport at my expense, though apparently admiring the long golden tresses of their favorite sister. While on her left stood in order, Clio, Euterpe, Melpomene, Terpsichore, Urania, and Polyhymnia, evidently surveying every attitude and expression of the stranger.

"Yes," I answered, "I am, indeed, a stranger; yet I have not come with the associations which urge and entice so many to these consecrated groves and hallowed fountains. I have come as a pilgrim, hoping to see the soil so celebrated in story and in song, to breathe its air, to taste its waters, and faintly expecting, though secretly wishing, to obtain a glimpse of the lovely spirits that dwelt and sported and sang in its sacred haunts." At this last remark, several of the sisters smiled, and Melpomene, stepping back, under a pretence of picking some violets, began to hum a most charming air; and in a few moments, as if forgetting herself, she broke forth into notes so enrapturing,

"That Orpheus' self might heave his head
From golden slumber on a bed
Of heaped Elysian flowers, and hear
Such strains as would have won the ear
Of Pluto, to have quite set free
His half regained Eurydice."

I observed Erato cast a roguish glance at Clio, calling her attention to the stranger, who, in his ecstasy, had so far forgotten his relative position as to have lost all control of his lower jaw, which by this time had experienced a most serious downfall. A slight titter from Thalia restored my equilibrium. What added to the ludicrousness of the affair was, that Polyhymnia had made several ineffectual attempts to address me. Then, with that delicacy which always characterizes true refinement, as if answering my remarks, she observed—

"Many, indeed, sir, are the visitors to these scenes. At one time may be seen a being of majestic countenance, large, clear eye, and lofty brow, in form and expression resembling more an incarnate angel than a man; at another, one of bent form, mild face, quiet, meditative look, sitting alone, and entering in solemn silence into his soul, as into some vast Cathedral, whether the full swelling peals of the heart summon the thoughts, like bright worshipers, to communion with each other and with God. Then comes the young buoyant spirit, bounding over these knolls, and through these copses—a soul of passion sparkling in his eye, bathing himself in our mountain winds, and sporting with its storms and lightnings as with playmates. By and by, we are pleased, and sometimes amused, by the visit of some pensive, heart-broken youth. His step is irregular; the falling of a grape or an olive startles him; and if he meets with a little pink or daisy, which a lambkin or some of my sisters may have trampled upon in their gambols, he will stop and try to revive it, while his tears, like a parent's, or like dew, are falling on its petals."

"Thus, you observe," continued she, "how"—"present company excepted, I suppose, sister," interrupted Thalia, who longed to call forth some remarks upon the last visitor, (a prompt blush saved him)—"you observe, sir, how singularly diverse, also, are the characters of our lovers. Out of these, however," she added, "there are but few whom we shall always remember, and fewer still whom we love to remember, (present company excepted? whispered I, aside to Thalia.) Every nation has had its representatives. Some of them are buried in the great sea of the past, and some yet shine, like stars, in the firmament. Italy, Spain, Germany, and France have the names of sons and daughters in our Album."

"But," said I, surprised at their omission, "has sea-girt England and the young and gallant America no leaf in it?" "Why," she smilingly answered, "I supposed they were so well known, that even an allusion to them was unnecessary. For the same reason I have made no mention of our own bards, as familiar to us as our Naiades and Dryades. Yonder is the wreathed tomb of Orpheus; those willows have voluntarily gathered around to protect, and to lament him. His very dust has infused into the soil, and the surrounding air musical breathing, which, rising at morning and evening twilight among the mourning branches, murmur his requiem. The grave of Linus too is here. Linus, slain by one, who, as being the ablest, ought to have been the first to defend, the last to harm him.* His favorite lyre wails melancholy music at the mention of his name."

Maternal hearts had been touched by this recital. Calliope and Urania began to sob and weep at the recollection of the short and happy life, but sad death of their children. Wishing to divert a current of

* Hercules.

thought and feeling so undesirable at this time, to one more pleasing, I asked Polyhymnia, who had partaken largely of the sympathy, whether she would not give me some account of those to whom she had referred, the "Poets and Poetry" of England and America—the mother and daughter. "O mater pulchra, filia pulchrior," said Clio, in a low tone, but sufficiently distinct to be heard by me.

"It would afford me much pleasure," she replied, "to gratify you, but the declining sun reminds us that our evening sacrifice will demand our presence and attention soon." "Sister," said Clio, looking at a dial that stood just above the fountain, "it is yet more than an hour before Apollo requires our services at the grove; can you not entertain the stranger during that time? we will stay with you." The affectionate and wishful glance that accompanied this request, could not be resisted. Of the effect upon the stranger's feelings we will say nothing. We were almost sorry we had not proposed a walk: (did you ever take a walk, dear reader?)

"I can therefore," continued Polyhymnia, "speak of very few of them, and that briefly.

"Of him whom a brother has called the 'Sweet Swan of Avon,' what shall I say? So much was he among us, so dignified and thoughtful, yet so familiar and kind, that we regarded him more as a father than a visitor. At the recital of a story by Euterpe, he would sit with eyes like fixed stars, bright and motionless, as if he would penetrate into the dim future, or were revolving, within the depths of his soul, thoughts of life, of truth, and of man, too great for an angel. Again he might be seen reclining at the base of some portly old oak, listening in transports and unobserved to a story of Melpomene, while the Hamadryades from above were in tiny convulsions of laughter at his efforts to elude observation. Now and then he would close his eyes in reverie or in very ecstasy, and the little mischievous creatures would creep down and destroy his thoughts and his temper, by plucking his moustaches, and tickling his chin with a humming-bird's feather. Often too, has he joined with us in our afternoon sports upon the banks of yonder stream, along the mountain side, or in some of our excursions to Parnassus and Castalia. He is gone. We have not his remains among us, but our hearts and our home will ever be a sacred cenotaph, to preserve his name in unfading remembrance.

"'Milton! who can speak of Milton! Had he not been a habitant of earth, he doubtless would have been a seraph, or one of Heaven's fairest, brightest spirits.' 'Urania, however,' she delicately observed, 'having been his favorite, can speak of him better than any one else, if she will.'" All eyes were now turned to the noble, angelic form of Urania, whose cheek modesty had tinged with a light vermillion glow.

"Gladly would I speak," said she, "of one I so much loved, so nearly worshiped. He was indeed among us, but could hardly be said to have been with us. His thoughts were in, and of heaven; and it seemed as if he only came hither, expecting that from this lofty summit he could see further, and more distinctly over its spangled battlements, through the vista of its golden streets, onward and upward towards the throne radiant with glory and with Deity. Though he ceased not, in his own words,

> ———' to wander where the muses haunt,
> Clear spring or shady grove or sunny hill,
> Smit with the love of sacred song,'

yet to this his 'Aonian Mount,' he preferred Sion hill; to Castalia, Hippocrene, and Aganippe, 'Siloa's brook that flowed fast by the oracle of God,' to the muses of earth, the muse and the music of heaven."

Erato observing that the hour was fast gliding away, whispered to me that Thalia wished very much to speak of Byron.

"Byron also," said I, addressing no one particularly, "has often doubtless visited you." At the mention of his name a smile began to play upon every countenance. No one spoke. The unusual silence would soon have become ludicrous or embarrassing, had not Polyhymnia (Thalia had turned away overcome with laughter) relieved it by saying: "his Lordship's manners, sir, were exceedingly fascinating. His conversation so attracted most of the sisters as to interfere with their services at the Museum. At length our sire was compelled to interdict them the pleasure of his company, except at stated hours for the reception of visitors. He too is with the dead. Short and eventful was his life and mournful its close. The seeds he planted have sprung up. A few blossomed and died. Many from the peculiar nature of the soil in which they are sown, brought forth much fruit; but when the soil was changed, or they transplanted, finding there no nutriment, they starved, withered and fell. A few bloom on, ever green and ever fruitful, and will bloom on for ever; no winds will blanch, no frosts chill them; the unchangeable in humanity is their soil, their rain and their sunshine."

Silvery notes, like the whispers of a spirit, were now heard from the distance, calling the sacred sisters to their home. They joined hands to prepare for returning. A glance here, a smile there, a young tear peeping out yonder, with a few other expressions (which are nobody's business but our own) closed the delightful entertainment. Away they tripped, keeping time to the music of Melpomone's voice, and soon were recounting to the Old Lyrist the adventures and sports of another day. The "stranger" is convalescent. O.

TOWN OF SOMNIA, LAND OF NOD, April 1st, 0001.

STANZAS FOR MUSIC.

DEDICATED TO L——.

If in the garden of the heart
  Thou see'st sweet blossom spring;—
Or hear'st the heaven-tuned soul impart
  Such tones as seraphs sing;—
Or in affection's genial bower
  Dost taste its fruits of bliss;—
Or feelest Love with wizard power
  Thrill thee with loveliness;—
Let Joy's fair fountains gush awhile,
And crown thy beauty with a smile.

But if those heart-flowers thou should'st see
  To wither, droop, and die;—
Or hear'st that angel harp to be
  Despoiled of harmony;—
Or tastest naught but dust within
  Affection's fruit so fair;—
Or feel'st a pang where Love has been,
  Who, flying, left it there;—
Weep—till the parching scene appears
Wet, as from heaven, with dews of tears.

But if thou see'st those flowers spring
  In amaranthine bloom;—
And hear'st those heavenly echoes ring
  To worlds beyond the tomb;—
And should the fruit which cheer'd thy taste,
  Immortal sweetness prove;—
And should thy heart of love find rest
  In an eternal love;—
Smile not!—too holy is the bliss:
Weep not!—when dawns thy happiness.

EDITORS' TABLE.

WITH this number, kind readers, kinder subscribers, and most kind payers, we close Volume IX. of our valuable Magazine. It needs and asks no commendation; yet we are confident it will receive a warm and spontaneous one from every living son of Yale. We have endeavored to increase its value and its attractions, and the approving smiles, and more substantial support, of many whom we respect and honor, incline us to believe that we have not wholly failed.

We design to spare no thought and no labor, consistent with our duties here, to render our next Volume more interesting and permanently valuable to every member and friend of College. Our present number will give some idea (we hope a faint one) of our plan. In one word, we wish to make it more exclusively OUR OWN, a YALE Magazine. There are Magazines enough for the "million" and for the "people." This shall be ours—ours not alone in its strictly Literary department, but in its Historical, Biographical, Statistical, and Miscellaneous departments; and ours once, it will always be ours, for

"Dum meus grata manet," &c. &c.

The tenth Volume will also contain one, and in all probability two, Engravings. Every thing, however, we need hardly say, must depend upon the generous and united support of the members of the University. We have claims upon them, and we have a right to expect they will be met.

NOTICES TO OUR CORRESPONDENTS and of NEW BOOKS, we are reluctantly compelled, for want of time, to defer. Publishers will please hand in their books immediately.

We have been favored with the following very brief notice of the OLDEST LIVING GRADUATE OF YALE COLLEGE, which, we doubt not, will be interesting to all. This is the Rev. ELISHA S. WILLIAMS, a Baptist Clergyman, residing in Beverly, Mass., who graduated in 1775, and is now in his eighty-seventh year. He is, therefore, including the present graduating Class, at the head of the 2,774 living Alumni:—

Rev. Elisha Scott Williams, son of Rev. Eliphalet Williams, D. D., of East Hartford, and grandson, by his mother, of Rector Elisha Williams, was born October 7, 1757. He was a school-mate of Col. John Trumbull, under Master Tisdale, at Lebanon, and entered Yale College in 1771.

Dr. Dwight was his tutor, for whom he retains a great admiration. Mr. W. was his Freshman, as the phrase then was, which brought him into some familiarity with his instructor.

There was no public Commencement at his graduation, on account of the war. He was in the battle of Trenton; afterwards, going to sea, was in an action with the British ship Levant, of 32 guns, in which the Captain of the American ship was killed.

He was ordained as a Baptist Minister in 1794, preached three or four years at Brunswick, Me., and was pastor of a Baptist congregation at Beverly, Mass., from

1803 to 1815. He has preached quite statedly till within three or four years, and now preaches occasionally.

Though not free from the infirmities of age, he retains much muscular vigor, is animated in conversation, and strongly attached to the religious principles which he has imbibed.

He has been twice married, and has six children now living. His second wife died in 1842.

COLLEGIANA.—In a few days, amici et sodales, after this our little butterfly shall have come forth from her ugly chrysalis of yellow proofs, daubed manuscripts, &c. &c. arrayed in the beautiful and elegant robes of a new life, the widely and well known Commencement of our venerable University will have returned.

What an assemblage of associations, grave, gay, joyous, and merry, cluster around this occasion! Reverend sires, crowned with years, with wisdom, and with honors, return to bestow their smiles and benedictions upon those who are soon to succeed them, and upon their common foster-mother—elder brothers, who have come back from campaigns of five, ten, and twenty years, to look once more upon the scenes and friends of their boyhood—fathers and mothers who have waited with trembling hopes for the event that is this day to gladden their hearts and all but complete their happiness. This last remark is eminently true, though in a different and peculiar sense, of others in that assembly. We do not insinuate, of course; by no means; we might subject ourselves to the *lex talionis* one year hence, if we should.

Bright-eyed and rosy-cheeked cousins of every degree, from the first to the thirty-second inclusive, will spangle in the collection, neither few nor far between. Belles and beaux, lovers and loved ones, will compose no small part of the remainder; all making use of the exercises as a text to discourse of the past and the future, of the budding and growth of first love, of undying affection, solemn vows, and "partings, such as press the life from out young hearts," and——but our feelings will not allow us to proceed.

On Tuesday evening, the "Concio ad Clerum" will be delivered by Rev. ABEL MCEWEN, of New London, Conn.

On Wednesday morning, Rev. WILLIAM T. DWIGHT, of Portland, Me., will deliver the address before the Alumni.

In the afternoon the exercises of the Theological Department will be held in the Centre Church. The Triennial Catalogue of this Department has just been published, showing the number in former classes to be 431

" " present classes, ... 64

Making a total of 495

The ORDER OF EXERCISES is as follows:

1. SACRED MUSIC.

2. PRAYER.

3. "Lights and Shades of the Pastor's Life," by JOHN P. GULLIVER, *Boston, Mass.*

4. "The Material World as subservient to the Intellectual and Moral," by LUCIUS Q. CURTIS, *Torringford, Conn.*

5. "Intermixture of Philosophy with Early Christianity," by BIRDSEY G. NORTHROP, *Kent, Conn.*

6. "Consequence of Erroneous Views of the Design of Penalty," by CHARLES FABRIQUE, *Oxford, Conn.*

7. SACRED MUSIC.

8. "The Saxon Race as 'The Peculiar People' of Modern Times," by AZARIAH ELDREDGE, *Yarmouthport, Mass.*

9. "The Power of the Christian Ministry," by A. HUNTINGTON CLAPP, *Boston, Mass.*

10. "John Robinson," by WILLIAM T. EUSTIS, *Boston, Mass.*

11. SACRED MUSIC.

12. "Personal Responsibility of the Christian Minister," by SAMUEL W. BARNUM, *Stamford, Conn.*

13. "Progress in Theology," by EDGAR PERKINS, *Clinton, Conn.*

14. "Attempts to Disparage the Memory of our Puritan Ancestors," by SAMUEL J. M. MERWIN, *New Haven, Conn.*

GRADUATING CLASS.

SAMUEL W. BARNUM,	HENRY COOLEY,	ERASTUS DAY,
WILLIAM DICK,	JOHN C. DOWNER,	GUSTAVUS L. FOSTER,
CHARLES HAMMOND,	CHARLES JEROME,	JOHN H. KEDZIE,
SAMUEL J. M. MERWIN,	EDGAR PERKINS,	ROSWELL R. SNOW,
INCREASE N. TARBOX,	ISAIAH C. THACHER,	JOHN S. WHITTLESEY.

On Wednesday evening, the Oration before the Phi Beta Kappa Society will be pronounced by Hon. WILLIS HALL, of New York, and the Poem by GEORGE H. COLTON, Esq., author of "Tecumseh."

Thursday, the 15th, will be *the* day of the year. The graduating class numbers one hundred and four, the largest class that has ever graduated from this Institution, and we believe from any other in the country.

We feel very much like offering a few words of counsel to those young men as they are now going out into the world to meet its trials, &c. &c. &c., but we fear we might be anticipating the Valedictory, or the advice of some other friend who feels equally interested with ourselves in their welfare, and who will probably have more time than we can spare at present. The Order of Exercises is as follows:—

ORDER OF EXERCISES, &c.

FORENOON.

1. SACRED MUSIC.

2. PRAYER by the President.

3. Salutatory Oration in Latin, by EDWARD WARREN ROOT, *Conway, Mass.*

4. Oration, "On the Immutability of Principle," by ARTHUR WARD, *Belleville, N. J.*

5. Dissertation, "On the Dependence of Man on Man as developed by Political Economy," by CHRISTOPHER CUSHING, *South Scituate, Mass.*

6. Oration, "The Christian Statesman," by DELOS WHITE BEADLE, *St. Catherine's, Canada.*

7. INSTRUMENTAL MUSIC.

8. Dissertation, "Change," by JOHN ADAMS DANA, *Princeton, Mass.*

9. Oration, "The Schoolmaster," by CHARLES LITTLE, *Columbia, Ct.*

10. Dissertation, "On the Relations of Society to Government," by SAMUEL MINOR, *Woodbury, Ct.*

11. Dissertation, "Nature," by MARTIN KELLOGG WHITTLESEY, *Newington, Ct.*

12. INSTRUMENTAL MUSIC.

13. Colloquy, "The Impostor," by EZEKIEL PORTER BELDEN, *New Haven. Ct.*
J. A. DANA, *Princeton, Mass.*
E. P. BELDEN, *New Haven, Ct.*
C. P. WILLCOX, *New Haven, Ct.*
E. W. ROOT, *Conway, Mass.*

14. INSTRUMENTAL MUSIC.

15. Oration, "Washington's Administration," by THOMAS MERRITT THOMPSON, *Roxbury, Mass.*

16. Dissertation, "The Language of Silence," by JOHN WESLEY SHEPHERD, *Huntsville, Ala.*

17. Dissertation, "Moral Courage," by GEORGE SLOCUM FOLGER SAVAGE, *Middletown, Ct.*

18. Poem, "Nathan Hale," by JAMES AUSTIN SHELDON, *Rupert, Vt.*

19. INSTRUMENTAL MUSIC.

20. Oration, "Posthumous Honor," by CHARLES ROLLIN LYNDE, *Brooklyn, N. Y.*

21. Dissertation, "Obstinacy," by WILLIAM SMITH, *Manlius, N. Y.*

22. Oration, "The well-balanced Mind," by ALEXANDER FISHER OLMSTED, *New Haven, Ct.*

23. Dissertation, "Liberty and Law," by CYPRIAN PORTER WILLCOX, *New Haven, Ct.*

24. Dissertation, "The Licentiousness of the Age in Philosophy and Religion," by JAMES ELLISON VAN BOKKELEN,* *Newbern, N. C.*

25. INSTRUMENTAL MUSIC.

26. Oration, "On the maxim, 'Vox Populi, Vox Dei,'" by HENRY WADHAMS BUEL, *Litchfield, Ct.*

27. Dissertation, "Characteristics of the Historian," by EDWARD DAVID SELDEN, *New Haven, Ct.*

28. Oration, "Unity of Purpose," by JOHN WELSH DULLES, *Philadelphia, Pa.*

29. Oration, "Our Politicians not Statesmen," by WILLIAM SMITH, *Onondaga Co., N. Y.*

30. INSTRUMENTAL MUSIC.

31. Colloquy, "Phreno-Mnemotechny," by HOLLIS RUSSELL, *Bingham, Me.*
H. RUSSELL, *Bingham, Me.*
J. W. WATERMAN, *Binghampton, N. Y.*
N. C. CHAPIN, *Hartford, Ct.*

32. VOCAL MUSIC.

AFTERNOON.

1. SACRED MUSIC.

2. Dissertation, "The Destiny of the English Race," by EDWARD ARTEMAS RAYMOND, *Canandaigua, N. Y.*

---

* Excused from speaking on account of ill health.

3. Oration, "Great Men," by MARSHALL BULLARD ANGIER, *Southborough, Mass.*

4. Oration, "On the Study of American History," by JOHN WETHERELL, *Oxford, Mass.*

5. Dissertation, "On the Poetry of Heathen Mythology," by HUGH BRADY WILKINS, *Pittsburg, Pa.*

6. INSTRUMENTAL MUSIC.

7. Dissertation, "American System of Female Education," by JOSHUA WHITNEY WATERMAN, *Binghamton, N. Y.*

8. Dissertation, "On the Origin of Knighthood," by EZEKIEL PORTER BELDEN, *New Haven, Ct.*

9. Dissertation, "Science, the Interpreter of Nature," by MYRON BARRETT, *North East, N. Y.*

10. Oration, "National Portraits," by CHARLES WHITTLESEY CAMP, *New Preston, Ct.*

11. VOCAL MUSIC.

12. Poem, "Palmyra," by EDWIN ADOLPHUS BULKLEY, *New York City.*

13. Oration, "The Limits of Knowledge still Distant," by DENISON OLMSTED, Jr., *New Haven, Ct.*

14. Oration, "Russia and Europe," by JAMES LINTON CUNNINGHAM, *Chambers Co., Ala.*

15. Oration, "On the Intellectual Character of the Age," by SAMUEL TOWNER ROGERS,* *New Fairfield, Ct.*

16. Dissertation, "Anthropography," by HOLLIS RUSSELL, *Bingham, Me.*

17. INSTRUMENTAL MUSIC.

18. Oration, "A pure National Morality, necessary to the perpetuation of our Free Institutions," by WILLIAM HORACE ELLIOT, *New Haven, Ct.*

19. Oration, "The Philosophical Interrogatory—Why?" by NATHAN COLTON CHAPIN, *Hartford, Ct.*

20. Oration, "Theology, the Mother of Science," by CHARLES AUGUSTUS MAISON, *Poughkeepsie, N. Y.*

21. Oration, "On the grounds of the Reverence claimed for Antiquity," by THERON GAYLORD COLTON, *New Haven, Ct.*

22. INSTRUMENTAL MUSIC.

23. Philosophical Oration, "On the Progress of American Society," by JONATHAN WHITE, *Randolph, Mass.*

24. Oration, "Young Men, their Field of Action," with the Valedictory Address, by EDWIN WRIGHT, *Lebanon, Ct.*

25. DEGREES CONFERRED.

26. PRAYER by the President.

27. SACRED MUSIC.

The music will be unusually fine—the Boston Brigade Band, aided by the "Beethoven Society." In the evening, the Society will give a Concert, aided by the Band; this, we have no doubt, will be a splendid affair. Gentlemen of the Press admitted free, of course—hem!

---

* Necessarily absent and excused from speaking.

The Triennial Catalogue of the College has been published in its usual neat style. The three hundred that have been added since the last, have sensibly increased its size.

We have just received the second No. of the "William's Monthly Miscellany." The young gentlemen who conduct it, we will admit, are *raw*-ther inexperienced, but they must persevere, and study some of the productions of "Great Masters." (Inquire within.) They must be careful, too, in their next number, not to publish the "Table of Contents," and forget the contents themselves; that would be unpleasant.

730

Lightning Source UK Ltd.
Milton Keynes UK
UKHW012244110219
337137UK00006B/979/P